Managing Customer Experience and Relationships

Managing Customer Experience and Relationships

A Strategic Framework

Third Edition

DON PEPPERS
MARTHA ROGERS

WILEY

Library of Congress Cataloging-in-Publication Data:

Names: Peppers, Don, author. | Rogers, Martha, 1952– author.
Title: Managing customer experience and relationships : a strategic framework
    / Don Peppers, Martha Rogers.
Description: 3rd edition. | Hoboken, New Jersey : John Wiley & Sons, Inc.,
    [2017] | Series: Wiley corporate F&A series | Includes index.
Identifiers: LCCN 2016023735 (print) | LCCN 2016036342 (ebook) | ISBN
    978-1-119-23625-2 (cloth) | ISBN 978-1-119-23982-6 (pdf) | ISBN 978-1-119-23981-9
    (epub) | 978-1-119-23983-3 (obook)
Subjects: LCSH: Customer relations—Management. | Consumers' preferences. |
    Relationship marketing. | Information storage and retrieval
    systems—Marketing.
Classification: LCC HF5415.5 .P458 2017 (print) | LCC HF5415.5 (ebook) | DDC
    658.8/12—dc23
LC record available at https://lccn.loc.gov/2016023735

Printed in the United States of America

10 9 8 7 6 5 4 3 2 1

Contents

Foreword

When I first started writing about marketing 45 years ago, the Industrial Age was in its prime. Manufacturers churned out products on massive assembly lines and stored them in huge warehouses, where they patiently waited for retailers to order and shelve boxes and bottles so that customers could buy them. Market leaders enjoyed great market shares from their carefully crafted mass-production, mass-distribution, and mass-advertising campaigns.

What the Industrial Age taught us is that if an enterprise wanted to make money, it needed to be efficient at large-scale manufacturing and distribution. The enterprise needed to manufacture millions of standard products and distribute them in the same way to all of their customers. Mass producers relied on numerous intermediaries to finance, distribute, stock, and sell the goods to ever-expanding geographical markets. However, in the process, producers grew increasingly removed from any direct contact with end users.

Producers tried to make up for what they didn't know about end users by using a barrage of marketing research methods, primarily customer panels, focus groups, and large-scale customer surveys. The aim was not to learn about individual customers but about large customer segments, such as "women ages 30 to 55." The exception occurred in business-to-business marketing, where each salesperson knew each customer and prospect as an individual. Well-trained salespeople were cognizant of each customer's buying habits, preferences, and peculiarities. Even here, however, much of this information was never codified. When a salesperson retired or quit, the company lost a great deal of specific customer information. Only more recently, with sales automation software and loyalty-building programs, have business-to-business enterprises begun capturing detailed information about each customer on the company's mainframe computer.

As for the consumer market, interest in knowing consumers as individuals lagged behind the business-to-business marketplace. The exception occurred with direct mailers and catalog marketers who collected and analyzed data on individual customers. Direct marketers purchased mailing lists and kept records of their transactions with individual customers. The individual customer's stream of transactions provided clues as to other items that might interest that customer. For example, in the case of consumer appliances, the company could at least know when a customer might be ready to replace an older appliance with a new one if the price was right.

Getting Better at Consumer Marketing

With the passage of time, direct marketers became increasingly sophisticated. They supplemented mail contact with the adroit use of the telephone and telemarketing. The growing use of credit cards and customers' willingness to give their credit card numbers to merchants greatly stimulated direct marketing. The emergence of fax machines further facilitated the exchange of information and the placing of orders. Soon the Internet and e-mail provided the ultimate facilitation of direct marketing. Customers could view products visually and verbally order them easily, receive confirmation, and know when the goods would arrive. Now that experience is enhanced by the way customers speak to one another. Even companies that don't really understand social networking realize they have to get on board. If 33 million people are in a room, you have to visit that room.[1]

But whether a company was ready for *customer relationship management* depended on more than conducting numerous transactions with individual customers. Companies needed to build comprehensive *customer databases*. Companies had been maintaining product databases, sales force databases, and dealer databases. Now they needed to build, maintain, mine, and manage a customer database that could be used by company personnel in sales, marketing, credit, accounting, and other company functions.

As customer database marketing grew, several different names came to describe it, including individualized marketing, customer intimacy, technology-enabled marketing, dialogue marketing, interactive marketing, permission marketing, and one-to-one marketing.

Modern technology makes it possible for enterprises to learn more about individual customers, remember those needs, and shape the company's offerings, services, messages, and interactions to each valued customer. The new technologies make mass customization (otherwise an oxymoron) possible.

At the same time, technology is only a partial factor in helping companies do genuine one-to-one marketing. The following quotes about customer relationship marketing (CRM) make this point vividly:

> *CRM is not a software package. It's not a database. It's not a call center or a Web site. It's not a loyalty program, a customer service program, a customer acquisition program, or a win-back program. CRM is an entire philosophy.*

—Steve Silver

---

[1] Juliette Powell, *33 Million People in the Room* (Upper Saddle River, NJ: Financial Times Press, 2009), pp. 8–9.

A CRM program is typically 45 percent dependent on the right executive leadership, 40 percent on project management implementation, and 15 percent on technology.

—Edmund Thompson, Gartner Group

Whereas in the Industrial Age, companies focused on winning market share and new customers, more of today's companies are focusing on share of customer, namely, increasing their business with each existing customer. These companies are focusing on customer retention, customer loyalty, and customer satisfaction as the important marketing tasks, and customer experience management and increasing customer value as key management objectives.

CRM and its kindred customer-focused efforts are more than just an outgrowth of direct marketing and the advent of new technology. This approach requires new skills, systems, processes, and employee mind-sets. As the Interactive Age progresses, mass marketing must give way to new principles for targeting, attracting, winning, serving, and satisfying markets. As advertising costs have risen and mass media has lost some effectiveness, mass marketing is now more costly and more wasteful. Companies are better prepared to identify meaningful segments and niches and address the individual customers within the targeted groups. They are becoming aware, however, that many customers are uncomfortable about their loss of privacy and the increase in solicitations by mail, phone, and e-mail. Ultimately, companies will have to move from an "invasive" approach to prospects and customers to a "permissions" approach. On the flip side, customers—now in contact with millions of other customers—have never been more informed or empowered.

The full potential of CRM is only beginning to be realized. Of course, every company must offer great products and services. But now, rather than pursue all types of customers at great expense only to lose many of them, the objective is to focus only on those particular customers with current and long-term potential in order to preserve and increase their value to the company.

Philip Kotler
S. C. Johnson Distinguished Professor of International Marketing,
Kellogg School of Management, Northwestern University

Philip Kotler is widely known as the father of modern marketing. His textbook *Marketing Management,* coauthored with Kevin Keller, has become the foundational text for marketing courses around the globe. First published in 1976 by Prentice Hall, it is now in its 15th edition.

Preface

In 1993 we published our first book, *The One to One Future: Building Relationships One Customer at a Time* (New York: Currency/Doubleday). We had no way of knowing how or when ubiquitous, cost-efficient interactivity would arrive, but the march of technology was inevitable, and we felt strongly that genuinely interactive media channels would become widely available sooner or later, in one form or another. And when interactivity did arrive, we suggested, the nature of marketing would have to change forever. At the time, marketing consisted primarily of crafting outbound messages creative or noticeable enough to break through the clutter of other one-way messages. These messages promoted standardized, mass-produced products with unique selling propositions that appealed to the most commonly held interests among the widest possible markets of consumers.

In sharp contrast to this model of marketing, we maintained that interactive technologies would compel businesses to try to build relationships with individual customers, one customer at a time. To our minds, this new type of marketing—which we dubbed "one-to-one marketing" or "1to1 marketing"—represented literally a different dimension of competition. We predicted that in the one-to-one future, the battle for market share would be supplemented by a battle for "share of customer"; product management organizations would have to be altered to accommodate managing individual customer relationships as well; and the decreasing returns of production economics would be supplanted by *increasing* returns of relationship economics.

We did not know it at the time, but also in 1993, the first genuinely useful Web browser, Mosaic, was introduced, and by the end of 1994, the World Wide Web had begun making major inroads into business and academia. This meant that interactivity arrived even sooner than we had suspected it would, via a more robust, vibrant technology than we anticipated. Over the next 10 years, our predictions about the nature of marketing in an interactive world proved uncannily accurate, and we were gratified at the popularity our little book enjoyed among the many marketers and information technology professionals wrestling with the question of how, exactly, to use this new capability for interacting with their customers on the Web. The term *one-to-one marketing* was often used interchangeably with the easier-to-say computer-industry acronym *CRM*, standing for "customer relationship management." Some think of CRM as a reference only to the software, but from our standpoint, the 1to1 rose smells as sweet by any other jargon.

By the time the first edition of *Managing Customer Relationships* was written, 10 years later, many other academics, business consultants, and authorities had become involved in analyzing, understanding, and profiting from the CRM revolution. Our goal with the first edition was to provide a comprehensive overview of the background, methodology, and particulars of managing customer relationships for competitive advantage. Although we significantly updated the material in the second edition, and now again in this third edition, we believe the original approach has in fact been confirmed. So we will begin with background and history, outline the *Identify-Differentiate-Interact-Customize* (IDIC) framework, and then address metrics, data management, customer management, and company organization.

Since our first edition of that first book came out, the steady march of technology has continued to change the business environment, bringing us two particularly important developments, each of which requires some treatment in this new edition. One has to do with the increasing influence of social media—including everything from blogging and microblogging to sharing and collaboration Web sites such as Facebook, Twitter, LinkedIn, YouTube, Amazon, Instagram, and eBay. The other has to do with the increasing proliferation of mobile devices and interactive services for them, including not just broadband Wi-Fi at places like business hotels, Starbucks, and McDonald's, but smartphones that can surf the Web, keep your calendar, deliver movies, and track your location, as well.

Over the past few years, there has also been a major change in the way businesses think about the process of value creation itself, given their new technological capabilities to track and interact with customers, one at a time. Increasingly, companies are coming face-to-face with the question of how to optimize their businesses around individual customers. When you think about it, this is the very central issue when configuring a Web site, or when trying to design the work processes or scripting for a call center, or when outlining new procedures for sales reps or point-of-sale operations. Each of these tasks involves optimizing around a customer, and none of them can be completed adequately without answering the question, "What is the right communication or offer for *this* customer, at *this* time?"

But a business can answer this kind of question accurately only by disregarding its existing, product-based metrics and using customer-based metrics instead. This is because the fundamental issue at stake is how to maximize the value a particular customer creates for the enterprise, a task that contrasts sharply with the financial objective of the old form of marketing (mass marketing), which was maximizing the value that a particular product or brand created for the enterprise. So we have considerably upgraded the financial issues we consider in the metrics discussion in this edition of *Managing Customer Experience and Relationships*.

Among other things, we will suggest that a metric, Return on Customer^{SM}, is sometimes more appropriate for gauging the degree to which a particular customer or group of customers is generating value for a business. Return on investment (ROI) measures the efficiency with which a business employs its capital to create value, and Return on Customer (ROC) is designed to measure the efficiency with which it employs its customers to create value. The ROC metric is simple to understand, in principle, but it requires a sophisticated approach to comprehending and analyzing customer lifetime values and customer equity. With the computer analytics available today, however, this is no longer an insurmountable or even a particularly expensive or difficult task. And this kind of customer-based financial metric will ensure that a company properly uses customer value as the basis for executive decisions.[1]

In the years since the second edition of this book was released, we have continued to teach seminars and workshops at universities and in for-profit and nonprofit organizations, and we have collaborated in depth with our own firm's working consultants in various Peppers & Rogers Group offices around the world, from São Paulo to Dubai, and from London to Johannesburg. We have wrestled with the serious, real-world business problems of taking a customer-centric approach to business in different business categories, from telecom, financial services, and retailing, to packaged goods, pharmaceuticals, and business to business. Over the years, our experience in all these categories has reinforced our belief that the basic IDIC model (identify, differentiate, interact, customize) for thinking about customer relationships is valid, practical, and useful, and that financial metrics based on customer value make the most sense. And we have continued documenting these issues, coauthoring a total of eight business trade books, in addition to this textbook.

The biggest change in this third edition, reflected in the title itself, is the additional consideration of the importance of the creation of better and more personalized customer experiences. CX (customer experience) plays an increasingly greater strategic role, and we've devoted much discussion to it, as well as to the idea of CX journey mapping.

While we obviously know more about our own work than anyone else's, and this book draws heavily on our fairly extensive direct experience in the work environment, we also continue to believe that a textbook like this should reflect some of the excellent work done by others, which is substantial. So, as with the first two editions, you will find much in this edition that is excerpted from others' works or written by others specifically for this textbook.

When it first appeared in 2004, *Managing Customer Relationships* was the first book designed specifically to help the pedagogy of customer relationship management, with an emphasis on customer strategies and building customer value. It is because of the wonderful feedback we have had over the years with respect to its usefulness for professors and students that we have undertaken this third edition. And while we hope this revised work will continue to guide and teach our readers, we also encourage our readers to continue to teach us. Our goal is not just to build the most useful learning tool available on the subject but to continue improving it as well. To that end, you may always contact us directly with suggestions, comments, critiques, and ideas. Simply e-mail us at mr@mrogersphd.com.

---

[1] Return on Customer^{SM} and ROC^{SM} are trademarks of Peppers & Rogers Group.

How to Use This Book

Each chapter begins with an overview and closes with a summary (which is also an explanation of how the chapter ties into the next chapter), Food for Thought (a series of discussion questions), and a glossary. In addition, chapters include these elements:

- Glossary terms are printed in boldface the first time they appear in a chapter, and their definitions are located at the end of that chapter. All of the glossary terms are included in the index, for a broader reference of usage in the book.
- Sidebars provide supplemental discussions and real-world examples of chapter concepts and ideas. These are italicized in the Contents.
- Contributed material is indicated by a shaded background, with contributor names and affiliations appearing at the beginning of each contribution.

We anticipate that this book will be used in one of two ways: Some readers will start at the beginning and read it through to the end. Others will keep it on hand and use it as a reference book. For both readers, we have tried to make sure the index is useful for searching by names of people and companies as well as terms, acronyms, and concepts.

If you have suggestions about how readers can use this book, please share those at mr@mrogersphd.com.

Acknowledgments

We started the research and planning for the first edition of this book in 2001. Our goal was to provide a handbook/textbook for students of the customer-centric movement to focus companies on customers and to build the value of an enterprise by building the value of the customer base. We have made many friends along the way and have had some interesting debates. We can only begin to scratch the surface in naming those who have touched the current revision of this book and helped to shape it into a tool we hope our readers will find useful.

We are honored to have contributed the royalties and proceeds from the sale of this book to Duke University, where Martha has served as an adjunct professor.

Thanks to Dr. Julie Edell Britton, who team-taught the Managing Customer Value course at Duke with Martha for many years, and to Rick Staelin, who has always supported the work toward this textbook and the development of this field. Additional thanks to all of the marketing faculty members at Duke, especially Christine Moorman, Wagner Kamakura, Carl Mela, and Dan Ariely, and all those who have used and promoted the book and its topics.

The voices of the many contributors who have shared their viewpoints have helped to make this book what it is; and you will see their names listed on the contents pages and throughout the text. We thank each of you for taking the time to participate in this project and to share your views and insights with students, professors, and other users of this book. And, as big as this book is, it is not big enough to include formally all the great thinking and contributions of the many academicians and practitioners who wrestle with deeper understanding of how to make companies more successful by serving customers better. We thank all of you, too, as well as all those at dozens of universities who have used the first or second edition of the book to teach courses, and all those who have used the book as a reference work to try to make the world a better marketplace. Please keep us posted on your work!

This work has been greatly strengthened by the critiques from some of the most knowledgeable minds in this field, who have taken the time to review the book and share their insights and suggestions with us. This is an enormous undertaking and a huge professional favor, and we owe great thanks to Becky Carroll, Jeff Gilleland, Mary Jo Bitner, James Ward, Ray Burke, Anthony Davidson, Susan Geib, Rashi Glazer, Jim Karrh, Neil Lichtman at NYU, Charlotte Mason, Janis McFaul, Ralph Oliva, Phil Pfeifer, Marian Moore, David Reibstein, and Jag Sheth. Thanks to John

Deighton, Jon Anton, Devavrat Purohit, and Preyas Desai for additional contributions, and we also appreciate the support and input from Mary Gros and Corinna Gilbert. And thanks to Maureen Morrin and to Eric Greenberg at Rutgers, and to John Westman, executive vice president of Novellus, Inc., and adjunct professor of the Boston College Carroll School of Management.

Much of this work has been based on the experiences and learning we have gleaned from our clients and the audiences we have been privileged to encounter in our work with Peppers & Rogers Group. Dozens and dozens of the talented folks who have been PRGers over the past years have contributed to our thinking—many more than the ones whose citations appear within this book, and more than we are able to list here. Our clients, our consulting partners and consultants, and our analysts are the ones who demonstrate every day that building a customer-centric company is difficult but doable and worthwhile financially. Special thanks go to Hamit Hamutcu, Orkun Oguz, Caglar Gogus, Mounir Ariss, Ozan Bayulgen, Amine Jabali, and Onder Oguzhan for their thinking and support. We also thank Tulay Idil, Bengu Gun, and Aysegul Kuyumcu for research. And to Thomas Schmalzl, Annette Webb, Mila D'Antonio, Elizabeth Glagowski, and Mike Dandrea of the 1to1 Media team, our gratitude for a million things and for putting up with us generally. We also appreciate the work Tom Lacki has done toward this book and our thinking, as well as the work of Valerie Peck, Alan Pennington, and Deanna Lawrence. Special additional thanks for ideas in the original edition that have survived to this version to Elizabeth Stewart, Tom Shimko, Tom Niehaus, Abby Wheeler, Lisa Hayford-Goodmaster, Lisa Regelman, and many other Peppers & Rogers Group alumni as well as winners of the 1to1 Impact Awards and PRG/1to1 Customer Champions, who are best in class at customer value building.

Plain and simple, we could not have gotten this book done without the leadership and project management of Marji Chimes, the talented and intrepid leader for years of 1to1 Media and an integral part of the success of Peppers & Rogers Group, now a unit of Teletech, or the dedicated day-to-day help from Susan Tocco and Lisa Troland. And the real secret sauce to finishing the many details has been Amanda Rooker—a truly resourceful researcher and relentlessly encouraging and gifted content editor, who has patiently and capably assisted in winding us through the morass of secondary research and minutiae generated by a project of this scope.

Our editor at John Wiley & Sons, Sheck Cho, has been an enthusiastic supporter of and guide for the project since day one. As always, thanks to our literary agent, Rafe Sagalyn, for his insight and patience.

We thank the many professors and instructors who are teaching the first Customer Strategy or CRM course at their schools and who have shared their course syllabi. By so doing, they have helped us shape what we hope will be a useful book for them, their students, and all our readers who need a ready reference as we all continue the journey toward building stronger, more profitable, and more successful organizations by focusing on growing the value of every customer.

About the Authors

Don Peppers and Martha Rogers, Ph.D., are the founders of Peppers & Rogers Group, a leading customer-centric management consulting firm with offices and clients worldwide, and now a unit of TeleTech Holdings (TTEC). They have developed many of the principles of the customer relationship management field. They have been ranked by Satmetrix as the world's #1 most influential authorities on customer experience management. Peppers and Rogers were inducted into the Direct Marketing Association Hall of Fame in 2013, and have received many other accolades and awards.

Together, Peppers and Rogers have coauthored a legacy of international best-sellers that have collectively sold well over a million copies in 18 languages. Peppers and Rogers's newest book, their ninth, is *Extreme Trust: Turning Proactive Honesty and Flawless Execution into Long-Term Profits*, which debuted in a revised and updated paperback in 2016. It suggests that social networks and rapidly increasing transparency have combined to raise customer expectations regarding the trustworthiness of the companies and organizations they deal with. *Rules to Break & Laws to Follow*, published in 2008, was named as the inaugural title to Microsoft's "Executive Leadership Series." Among the other best-sellers authored by Peppers and Rogers, their first—*The One to One Future* (1993)—was called "one of the two or three most important business books ever written," while *BusinessWeek* called it the "bible of the customer strategy revolution," and Tom Peters named it his choice for "book of the year" in 1993. *Enterprise One to One* (1997) received a 5-star rating from the *Wall Street Journal*. *One to One B2B* made the *New York Times* business best-seller list within a month of its publication in 2001. Their 2005 book *Return on Customer* was named one of the 15 "most important reads" of 2005 by *Fast Company*, and was cited again in 2007 on its list of the 25 "Best Books" in business.

Prior to founding Peppers & Rogers Group, Don Peppers served as the CEO of a top-20 direct marketing agency, and his book *Life's a Pitch: Then You Buy* (1995) chronicles his exploits as a celebrated new-business rainmaker in the advertising industry. He holds degrees in astronautical engineering from the Air Force Academy and in public affairs from Princeton University's Woodrow Wilson School. Peppers also has a popular voice in the business media and is a top "INfluencer" on LinkedIn, with well over a quarter million followers for his regular blog posts on innovation, technology, trust, corporate culture, and customer experience.

Martha Rogers is the founder of Trustability Metrix, a firm designed to help companies understand how to measure and improve their levels of trust by customers, employees, and business partners. After a career in advertising copywriting and management, Rogers has taught at several universities, most recently as an adjunct professor at the Fuqua School of Business at Duke University, where she co-directed the Teradata Center for Customer Strategy. Rogers has been widely published in academic and trade journals, including *Harvard Business Review, Journal of Advertising Research, Journal of Public Policy and Marketing*, and *Journal of Applied Psychology*. She has been named International Sales and Marketing Executives' Educator of the Year. Rogers earned her Ph.D. at the University of Tennessee as a Bickel fellow.

PART I

Principles of Managing Customer Experience and Relationships

The *Learning Relationship* works like this: If you're my customer and I get you to talk to me, and I remember what you tell me, then I get smarter and smarter about you. I know something about you my competitors don't know. So I can do things for you my competitors can't do, because they don't know you as well as I do. Before long, you can get something from me you can't get anywhere else, for any price. At the very least, you'd have to start all over somewhere else, but starting over is more costly than staying with me, so long as you like me and trust me to look out for your best interests.

CHAPTER 1

Evolution of Relationships with Customers and Strategic Customer Experiences

No company can succeed without customers. If you don't have customers, you don't have a business. You have a hobby.

—Don Peppers and Martha Rogers

Think about it: By definition, customers are every company's source of revenue. No company will ever realize income from any other entity except the customers it has now and the customers it will have in the future. Brands don't pay money. Products don't. Sales regions don't. Thus, in many ways, a firm's most valuable financial asset is its customer base, and, given our new and unfolding technological capabilities to *recognize,* measure, and manage relationships with each of those customers individually, and to create and improve their experiences with our companies, a forward-thinking firm must focus on deliberately preserving and increasing the value of that customer base. **Customer strategy** is not a fleeting assignment for the marketing department; rather, it is an ongoing business imperative that requires the involvement of the entire enterprise. Organizations manage their customer experiences and relationships effectively in order to remain competitive. Technological advancements have enabled firms to manage customer relationships more efficiently and to create better **customer experience,** but technology has also empowered customers to inform themselves and one another and to demand much more from the companies they do business with. The goal of this book is not just to acquaint the reader with the techniques of managing customer experiences and relationships. The more ambitious goal of this book is to help the reader understand the essence of customer strategy and how to apply it to the task of managing a successful enterprise in the twenty-first century.

The dynamics of the customer-enterprise relationship have changed dramatically over time. Customers have always been at the heart of an enterprise's long-term growth strategies, marketing and sales efforts, product development, labor and resource allocation, and overall profitability directives. Historically, enterprises have encouraged the active participation of a sampling of customers in the research and development of their products and services. But until recently, enterprises have been structured and managed around the products and services they create and sell. Driven by assembly-line technology, mass media, and mass distribution, which appeared at the beginning of the twentieth century, the Industrial Age was dominated by businesses that sought to mass-produce products and to gain a competitive advantage by manufacturing a product that was perceived by most customers as better than its closest competitor. Product innovation, therefore, was the important key to business success. To increase its overall market share, the twentieth-century enterprise would use mass marketing and mass advertising to reach the greatest number of potential customers.

As a result, most twentieth-century products and services eventually became highly commoditized. Branding emerged to offset this perception of being like all the other competitors; in fact, branding from its beginning was, in a way, an expensive substitute for relationships companies could not have with their newly blossomed masses of customers. Facilitated by lots and lots of mass-media advertising, brands have helped add value through familiarity, image, and trust. Historically, brands have played a critical role in helping customers distinguish what they deem to be the best products and services. A primary enterprise goal has been to improve brand awareness of products and services and to increase brand preference and brand loyalty among consumers. For many consumers, a brand name has traditionally testified to the trustworthiness or quality of a product or service. Today, though, more and more, customers say they value brands, but their opinions are based on their "relationship with the brand"—so brand reputation is actually becoming *one and the same* with customers' experience with the brand, product, or company (including relationships).[1] Indeed, consumers are often content as long as they can buy one brand of a consumer-packaged good that they know and respect.

---

[1] Christof Binder and Dominique M. Hanssens, "Why Strong Customer Relationships Trump Powerful Brands," *Harvard Business Review*, April 14, 2015, available at https://hbr.org/2015/04/why-strong-customer-relationships-trump-powerful-brands, reports research on brand valuation of a company at the time of merger or acquisition. They discovered that over a 10-year period from 2003 to 2013, "brand valuations declined by nearly half (from 18 percent to 10 percent [of total company value]) while customer relationship values doubled (climbing from 9 percent to 18 percent). Acquirers have decisively moved from investing into businesses with strong *brands* to businesses with strong *customer relationships*." See also Anita Chang Beattie, "Catching the Eye of the Chinese Shopper," *Advertising Age* 83, no. 44 (2012), p. 20; and Masaaki Kotabe's chapter, "Emerging Markets," in *Marketing in the 21st Century: New World Marketing*, ed. Bruce David Keillor (Westport, CT: Praeger, 2007).

> For many years, enterprises depended on gaining the competitive advantage from the best brands. Brands have been untouchable, immutable, and inflexible parts of the twentieth-century mass-marketing era. But in the interactive era of the twenty-first century, enterprises are instead strategizing how to gain sustainable competitive advantage from "brands" that create the best customer experience, based on the information they gather about customers.

For many years, enterprises depended on gaining the competitive advantage from the best brands. Brands have been untouchable, immutable, and inflexible parts of the twentieth-century mass-marketing era. But in the **interactive era** of the twenty-first century, firms are instead strategizing how to gain sustainable competitive advantage from the *information* they gather about customers. As a result, enterprises are creating a *two-way brand,* one that thrives on customer information and interaction. The two-way brand, or *branded relationship,* transforms itself based on the ongoing dialogue between the enterprise and the customer. The branded relationship is "aware" of the customer (giving new meaning to the term *brand awareness*) and constantly changes to suit the needs of that particular individual. In current discussions, the focus is on ways to redefine the "brand reputation" as more customer oriented, using phrases such as "brand engagement with customer," "brand relationship with customer," and the customer's "brand experience." Add to this the transparency for brands and rampant ratings for products initiated by social media, and it's clear why companies are realizing that what customers say about them is more important than what the companies say about themselves.

Roots of Customer Relationships and Experience

Once you strip away all the activities that keep everybody busy every day, the goal of every enterprise is simply to get, keep, and grow customers. This is true for non-profits (where the "customers" may be donors or volunteers) as well as for-profits, for small businesses as well as large, for public as well as private enterprises. It is true for hospitals, governments, universities, and other institutions as well. What does it mean for an enterprise to focus on its customers as the key to competitive advantage? Obviously, it does *not* mean giving up whatever product edge or operational efficiencies might have provided an advantage in the past. It does mean using new strategies, nearly always requiring new technologies, to focus on growing the value of the company by deliberately and strategically growing the **value of the customer base.**

> What does it mean for an enterprise to focus on its customers as the key to competitive advantage? It means creating new shareholder value by deliberately preserving and growing the value of the customer base.

To some executives, **customer relationship management (CRM)** is a technology or software solution that helps track data and information about customers to enable better **customer service**. Others think of CRM, or one-to-one, as an elaborate marketing or customer service discipline. We even recently heard CRM described as "personalized e-mail."

To us, "managing customer experience and relationships" is what companies do to optimize the value of each customer, and "managing customer experiences" is what companies do because they understand the customer's perspective and what it is—and should be—like to be our customer. This book is about much more than setting up a business Web site or redirecting some of the mass-media budget into the call-center database or cloud analytics or **social networking.** It's about increasing the value of the company through specific customer strategies (see Exhibit 1.1).

Companies determined to build successful and profitable customer relationships understand that the process of becoming an enterprise focused on building its value by building customer value doesn't begin with installing technology, but instead begins with:

- A strategy or an ongoing process that helps transform the enterprise from a focus on traditional selling or manufacturing to a **customer focus** while increasing revenues and profits in the current period and the long term.
- The leadership and commitment necessary to cascade throughout the organization the thinking and decision-making capability that puts customer value and relationships first as the direct path to increasing shareholder value.

The reality is that becoming a **customer-strategy enterprise** is about using information to gain a competitive advantage and deliver growth and profit. In its

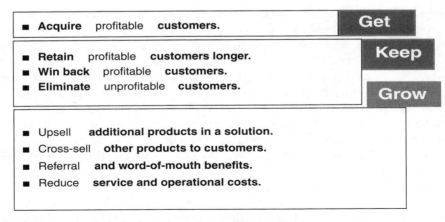

EXHIBIT 1.1   Increasing the Value of the Customer Base

most generalized form, CRM can be thought of as a set of business practices designed, simply, to put an enterprise into closer and closer touch with its customers, in order to learn more about each one and to deliver greater and greater value to each one, with the overall goal of making each one more valuable to the firm to increase the value of the enterprise. It is an enterprise-wide approach to understanding and influencing customer behavior through meaningful analysis and communications to improve customer acquisition, customer retention, and customer profitability.[2] **Customer centricity** is distinguishable from product centricity and from technology centricity. These differences will be discussed more in Exhibit 1.3 later in this chapter.

Defined more precisely, what makes customer centricity into a truly different model for doing business and competing in the marketplace, is this: It is an enterprise-wide business strategy for achieving customer-specific objectives by taking customer-specific actions. It is

> Enterprises determined to build successful, profitable customer relationships understand that the process of becoming an enterprise focused on building its value by building customer value doesn't begin with installing technology but rather begins with:
>
> - A strategy or an ongoing process that helps transform the enterprise from a focus on traditional selling or manufacturing to a customer focus while increasing revenues and profits in the current period and the long term.
> - The leadership and commitment necessary to cascade throughout the organization the thinking and decision-making capability that put customer value and relationships first as the direct path to increasing shareholder value.

---

[2]Peter Fader, *Customer Centricity: Focus on the Right Customers for Strategic Advantage,* Wharton Executive Essentials, 2nd ed., 2012 (1st ed., 2011); Ju-Yeon Lee, Shrihari Sridhar, Conor Henderson, and Robert W. Palmatier, *Effect of Customer-Centric Structure on Firm Performance,* Marketing Science Institute Working Paper Series, Report No. 12–111, available at http://www.lehigh.edu/~incbeug/Attachments/Lee%20et%20al%202012%20MSI_Report.pdf, accessed February 3, 2016; Erik M. van Raaij, "The Strategic Value of Customer Profitability Analysis," *Marketing Intelligence & Planning* 23, no. 4/5 (2005): 372–381, accessed January 28, 2010, available at ABI/INFORM Global (document ID: 908236781); Sunil Gupta and Donald R. Lehmann, *Managing Customers as Investments* (Philadelphia: Wharton School Publishing, 2005); Robert S. Kaplan, "A Balanced Scorecard Approach to Measure Customer Profitability," Harvard Business School's Working Knowledge Web site, August 8, 2005, available at: http://hbswk.hbs.edu/item/4938.html, accessed January 28, 2010; Phillip E. Pfeifer, Mark E. Haskins, and Robert M. Conroy, "Customer Lifetime Value, Customer Profitability, and the Treatment of Acquisition Spending," *Journal of Managerial Issues* 17, no. 1 (Spring 2005): 11–25; George S. Day, *Market-Driven Strategy: Processes for Creating Value* (New York: Free Press, 1999); Don Peppers and Martha Rogers, *The One to One Future* (New York: Doubleday Books, 1993); Ronald S. Swift, *Accelerating Customer Relationships: Using CRM and Relationship Technologies* (Upper Saddle River, NJ: Prentice Hall, 2001); Fred Reichheld, *The Loyalty Effect* (Boston: Harvard Business School Press, 1996); and Fred Reichheld and Rob Markey, *The Ultimate Question 2.0: How Net Promoter Companies Thrive in a Customer Driven World* (Cambridge, MA: Harvard Business Review Press, 2011).

enterprise-wide because it can't merely be assigned to marketing if it is to have any hope of success. Its objectives are customer-specific because the goal is to increase the value of each customer. Therefore, the firm will take customer-specific actions for each customer, often made possible by new technologies.

In essence, building the value of the customer base requires a business to *treat different customers differently*. Today, there is a customer-focus revolution under way among businesses. It represents an inevitable—literally, irresistible—movement. All businesses will be embracing customer strategies sooner or later, with varying degrees of enthusiasm and success, for two primary reasons:

> An enterprise-wide business strategy for customer centricity achieves customer-specific objectives by taking customer-specific actions.

1. All customers, in all walks of life, in all industries, all over the world, want to be individually and personally served.
2. It is simply a more efficient way of doing business.

We find examples of customer-specific behavior, and business initiatives driven by customer-specific insights, all around us today[3]:

- An airline offers a passenger in the airport waiting for his flight to arrive an upgrade offer to business class through a phone app he has used to check his flight status, as an apology for a 45-minute departure delay.
- A woman receives an e-mail before her eight-month obstetrics appointment that gives information about what to expect at the appointment and her baby's stage of growth. A month later, the same woman receives a notification of her baby's immunization appointment that is triggered when she leaves the hospital with her newborn.
- A retail clothes company sends a message to a customer it knows is standing outside one of their stores to come in and use a 15 percent discount, sometimes with a sweetener such as free shipping. Or the items appear as a reminder next to the newspaper articles the shopper reads next morning.
- A business sees that a customer has left their Web site, abandoning a cart with selected products before checkout, and sends an e-mail with more detailed information about those specific products to the customer the next day.
- An outdoor gear company sees that their tents are being discussed on a social channel and sends a free tent as a trial sample to a consistent product supporter.
- A group of three friends open the Web page of the same kitchenware company that they all have ordered from in the past. Each friend views a different offer featured on the company home page on her device.

---

[3] Thanks to the SalesForce Marketing Cloud Web site for inspiring many of these examples; available at http://www.salesforce.com/marketing-cloud/overview/, accessed December 4, 2015.

- A customer service representative sees a complaint a customer has made on a social channel and is able to view at the same time his purchasing history and order status. The service rep uses that information to reply to the complaint via the same social channel.
- Instead of mailing out the same offer to everyone, a company waits for specific trigger behavior from a customer and increases response rates 25-fold.
- An insurance company not only handles a claim for property damage but also connects the insured party with a contractor in her area who can bypass the purchasing department and do the repairs directly.
- A supervisor orders more computer components by going to a Web page that displays his firm's contract terms, his own spending to date, and his departmental authorizations.
- Sitting in the call center, a service rep sees a "smart dialogue" suggestion pop onto a monitor during a call with a customer, suggesting a question the company wants to ask that customer (not the same question being asked of all customers who call this week).

Taking customer-specific action, treating different customers differently, improving each customer's experience with the company or product, building the value of the customer base, creating and managing relationships with individual customers that go on through time to get better and deeper—that's what this book is about. In the chapters that follow, we will look at lots of examples. The overall business goal of this strategy is to make the enterprise as profitable as possible over time by taking steps to increase the value of the customer base. The enterprise makes itself, its products, and/or its services so satisfying, convenient, or valuable to the customer that she becomes more willing to devote her time and money to this enterprise than to any competitor. Building the value of customers increases the value of the **demand chain,** the stream of business that flows from the customer down through the retailer all the way to the manufacturer. A customer-strategy enterprise interacts directly with an individual customer. The customer tells the enterprise about how he would like to be served. Based on this interaction, the enterprise, in turn, modifies its behavior with respect to this particular customer. In essence, the concept implies a specific, one-customer-to-one-enterprise relationship, as is the case when the customer's input drives the enterprise's output for that particular customer.[4]

A suite of buzzwords have come to surround this endeavor: customer relationship management (CRM), **one-to-one marketing, customer experience management,**

---

[4] Ranjay Gulati, "From Inside-Out to Outside-In Thinking," *Economic Times*, May 10, 2013, available at http://ranjaygulati.com/rg/images/the-economic-times_from-inside-out-to-inside-in-thinking.pdf, accessed on February 3, 2016. Also see Ranjay Gulati, "The Quest for Customer Focus," *Harvard Business Review* 83, no. 4 (April 2005): 92–101. Also see Don Peppers and Martha Rogers, Ph.D., *One to One B2B* (New York: Doubleday Broadway Books, 2001).

customer value management, customer focus, **customer orientation,** customer centricity, **customer experience journey mapping,** and more. You can see it in the titles on the business cards: Chief Marketing Officer, of course, but also a host of others, including "Chief Relationship Officer," "**Customer Care** Leader," "Customer Value Management Director," and even "Customer Revolutionary" at one firm. Like all new initiatives, this customer approach (different from the strictly financial approach or product-profitability approach of the previous century) suffers when it is poorly understood, improperly applied, and incorrectly measured and managed. But by any name, strategies designed to build the value of the customer base by building relationships with one customer at a time, or with well-defined groups of identifiable customers, are by no means ephemeral trends or fads any more than computers or connectivity are.

A good example of a business offering that benefits from individual customer relationships can be seen in online banking services, in which a consumer spends several hours, usually spread over several sessions, setting up an online account and inputting payee addresses and account numbers, in order to be able to pay bills electronically each month. If a competitor opens a branch in town offering slightly lower checking fees or higher savings rates, this consumer is unlikely to switch banks. He has invested time and energy in a relationship with the first bank, and it is simply more convenient to remain loyal to the first bank than to teach the second bank how to serve him in the same way. In this example, it should also be noted that the bank now has increased the value of the customer to the bank and has simultaneously reduced the cost of serving the customer, as it costs the bank less to serve a customer online than at the teller window or by phone.

Clearly, "customer strategy" involves much more than marketing, and it cannot deliver optimum return on investment of money or customers without integrating individual customer information into every corporate function, from customer service to production, logistics, and channel management. A formal change in the organizational structure usually is necessary to become an enterprise focused on growing customer value. As this book shows, customer strategy is both an operational and an analytical process. **Operational CRM** focuses on the software installations and the changes in process affecting the day-to-day operations of a firm—operations that will produce and deliver different treatments to different customers. **Analytical CRM** focuses on the strategic planning needed to build customer value as well as the cultural, measurement, and organizational changes required to implement that strategy successfully.

Focusing on Customers Is New to Business Strategy

The move to a customer-strategy **business model** has come of age at a critical juncture in business history, when managers are deeply concerned about declining customer loyalty as a result of greater transparency and universal access to information, declining trust in many large institutions and most businesses, and increasing choices for customers. As customer loyalty decreases, profit margins decline, too, because the most frequently used customer acquisition tactic is price cutting. Enterprises are facing a radically different competitive landscape as the information about their customers is becoming more plentiful and as the customers themselves are demanding more interactions with companies and creating more connections with each other. Thus, a coordinated effort to get, keep, and grow valuable customers has taken on a greater and far more relevant role in forging a successful long-term, profitable business strategy.

If the last quarter of the twentieth century heralded the dawn of a new competitive arena, in which commoditized products and services have become less reliable as the source for business profitability and success, it is the new computer technologies and applications that have arisen that assist companies in managing their interactions with customers. These technologies have spawned enterprise-wide information systems that help to harness information about customers, analyze the information, and use the data to serve customers better. Technologies such as **enterprise resource planning (ERP)** systems, supply chain management (SCM) software, enterprise application integration (EAI) software, **data warehousing, sales force automation (SFA),** marketing resource management (MRM), and a host of other enterprise software applications have helped companies to mass-customize their products and services, literally delivering individually configured communications, products, or services to unique customers in response to their individual feedback and specifications.

The accessibility of the new technologies is motivating enterprises to reconsider how they develop and manage customer relationships and map the customer experience journey. More and more chief executive officers (CEOs) of leading enterprises have made the shift to a customer-strategy business model a top business priority for the twenty-first century. Technology is making it possible for enterprises to conduct business at an intimate, individual customer level. Indeed, technology is driving the shift. Computers can enable enterprises to remember individual customer needs and estimate the future potential revenue the customer will bring to the enterprise. What's clear is that technology is the enabler; it's the *tail*, and the one-to-one customer relationship is the *dog*.

Traditional Marketing Redux

Historically, traditional marketing efforts have centered on the "four Ps"—product, price, promotional activity, and place—popularized by marketing experts E. Jerome McCarthy[a] and Philip Kotler. These efforts have been enhanced by our greater (and deeper) understanding of consumer behavior, organizational behavior, market research, segmentation, and targeting. In other

(continued)

(Continued)

words, using traditional sampling and aggregate data, a broad understanding of the market has preceded the application of the four Ps, which enterprises have deployed in their marketing strategy to bring uniform products and services to the mass market for decades.[b] In essence, the four Ps are all about the "get" part of "get, keep, and grow customers." These terms have been the focal point for building market share and driving sales of products and services to consumers. The customer needed to believe that the enterprise's offerings would be superior in delivering the "four Cs": customer value, lower costs, better convenience, and better communication.[c] Marketing strategies have revolved around targeting broadly defined market segments through heavy doses of advertising and promotion.

This approach first began to take shape in the 1950s. Fast-growing living standards and equally fast-rising consumer demand made organizations aware of the effectiveness of a supply-driven marketing strategy. By approaching the market on the strength of the organization's specific abilities, and creating a product supply in accordance with those abilities, it was possible for the firm to control and guide the sales process. Central to the strategic choices taken in the area of marketing were the—now traditional—marketing instruments of product, price, place, and promotion—the same instruments that served as the foundation for Philip Kotler's theory and the same instruments that still assume an important role in marketing and customer relations today.

The four Ps all, of course, relate to the aggregate market rather than to individual customers. The market being considered could be a large mass market or a smaller niche market, but the four Ps have helped define how an enterprise should behave toward all the customers within the aggregate market:

1. *Product* is defined in terms of the average customer—what *most* members of the aggregate market want or need. This is the product brought to market, and it is delivered the same way for every customer in the market. The definition of *product* extends to standard variations in size, color, style, and units of sale as well as customer service and aftermarket service capabilities.

2. *Place* is a distribution system or sales channel. How and where is the product sold? Is it sold in stores? By dealers? Through franchisees? At a single location or through widely dispersed outlets, such as fast-food stores and ATMs? Can it be delivered directly to the purchaser?

3. *Price* refers not only to the ultimate retail price a product brings but also to intermediate prices, beginning with wholesale; and it takes account of the availability of credit to a customer and the prevailing interest rate. The price is set at a level designed to "clear the market," assuming that everyone will pay the *same* price—which is only fair because everyone will get the same

product. And even though different customers within a market actually have different levels of desire for the same product, the market price will generally be the same for everybody.

4. *Promotion* has also worked traditionally in a fundamentally nonaddressable, noninteractive way. The various customers in a mass market are all passive recipients of the promotional message, whether it is delivered through mass media or interpersonally, through salespeople. Marketers have traditionally recognized the trade-off between the cost of delivering a message and the benefit of personalizing it to a recipient. A sales call can cost between $300 and $500 (a 2012 Center for Exhibition Industry Research study put the average cost of a business-to-business [B2B] sales call at $596),[d] but at least it allows for the personalization of the promotion process. The CPM or cost per thousand to reach an audience through mass media is far lower but requires that the same message be sent to everyone. Ultimately, the way a product is promoted is designed to differentiate it from all the other, competitive products. Except for different messages aimed at different segments of the market, promotion doesn't change by *customer* but by *product*.

Initial Assessment: Where Is a Firm on the Customer Strategy Map?

Recognizing that two families of technology have mandated the competitive approach of building customer value by building customer relationships, we can map any organization—large or small, public or private, profit or nonprofit—by the level of its capabilities in the arenas of *interacting* with customers and *tailoring* for them. A company would be rated high on the interactivity dimension if it knows the names of its individual customers and if it can send different messages to different customers and can remember the feedback from each one. A low rating would go to a company that doesn't know its customers' identities or does but continues to send the same message the same way to everybody. On the tailoring dimension, a firm would rate highly if it mass-customizes in lot sizes of one; it would rate low if it sells the same thing pretty much the same way to everybody. Based on its rating in these two dimensions, a company can be pinpointed on the Enterprise Strategy Map (see Exhibit 1.2).

> *Quadrant I: Traditional Mass Marketing.* Companies that compete primarily on cost efficiencies based on economies of scale and low price. Companies in this quadrant are doomed to **commoditization** and price competition.
>
> *Quadrant II: Niche Marketing.* Companies that focus on target markets, or niches, and produce goods and services designed for those defined

(continued)

(Continued)

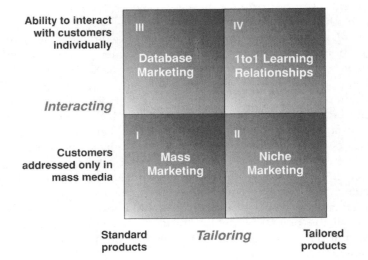

EXHIBIT 1.2   Enterprise Strategy Map
Source: Don Peppers and Martha Rogers, Ph.D., *Enterprise One to One* (New York: Doubleday/Currency, 1997).

    customer groups. This more strategic and targeted method of mass marketing still offers the same thing the same way to everyone, but for a small, relatively homogeneous group.

Quadrant III: Database Marketing. Companies utilize database management to get better, more efficient use of their mailing lists and other customer information. Generally focused primarily on continuation of traditional strategies but at lower costs to serve.

Quadrant IV: Learning Relationships based on individual analytics. Companies use data about customers to predict what each one needs next and then are able to treat different customers differently and increase mutual value with customers.

    In Quadrants I through III, the focus is still primarily on the product to be sold, with an eye to finding customers for that product. In Quadrant IV, the direction of the strategy changes; the Quadrant IV company focuses on a customer and finds products for that customer.

    To realize the highest possible return on the customer base, the goal of an enterprise will be to move up and to the right on the Enterprise Strategy Map.

- To move up on the Enterprise Strategy Map, an enterprise has to be able to recognize individual customers' names and addresses, to send different messages to different customers, and to remember the responses of each.
- To move to the right on the Enterprise Strategy Map, an enterprise has to be able to increase its production and logistics flexibility. The most flexible production would entail customizing and delivering individual products for individual customers. The least flexible would be mass-producing a standardized product or service for a large market. (We talk more about customization in Chapter 10.)

[a] E. Jerome McCarthy, *Basic Marketing: A Managerial Approach* (Homewood, IL: Irwin, 1958).
[b] Philip Kotler, *Marketing Management: Analysis, Planning, Implementation, and Control*, 9th ed. (Upper Saddle River, NJ: Prentice Hall, 1997), pp. 92–93.
[c] Philip Kotler, *Kotler on Marketing* (New York: Free Press, 1999), pp. 116–120.
[d] Bloomberg Business, "Sales Moves Beyond Face-to-Face Deals onto the Web," January 10, 2013, available at: http://www.bloomberg.com/bw/articles/2013--01--10/sales-moves-beyond-face-to-face-deals-onto-the-web; "The Cost of a Sales Call," 4D Sales, accessed February 3, 2016, available at: http://4dsales.com/the-cost-of-a-sales-call/, accessed February 3, 2016.

Managing Customer Relationships and Experience Is a Different Dimension of Competition

The story goes that in 1996, the executives at Barnes & Noble bookstores invited Jeff Bezos, the founder of a startup named Amazon.com, to lunch, with a proposition. Amazon.com had not yet made any profit (and would not, for its first 28 quarters in a row), so the nice guys at the well-established bookstore offered, as a favor to Jeff, to buy him out—before they launched barnesandnoble.com, the online version of the bookstore chain. They argued that Jeff's relatively unknown brand would not stand up to their highly popular name and that he should make some money on his software and systems. He declined.

How did that turn out? Twenty years after that lunch meeting, in 2016, Barnes & Noble had a market cap of US$667 million and Amazon.com had a market cap of US$323 billion.[5] So whether the lunch ever really took place or not, the story still serves to illustrate the fundamental difference between a very well run *product-oriented* company (Barnes & Noble, which has stores to populate with products and tries to find customers for those products) and a fairly well run *customer-oriented* company (Amazon.com, which got us all as customers to buy books and DVDs, and now wants to sell each of us everything). *Note:* One of the authors, who lives in New York City, found the best selection and service from Amazon.com for a refrigerator bought for and installed in an Upper West Side apartment.

[5] NYSE BKS, NASDAQ AMZN, accessed January 2, 2016.

A lot can be understood about how traditional, market-driven competition is different from today's customer-driven competition by examining Exhibit 1.3. The direction of success for a traditional aggregate-market enterprise (i.e., a traditional company that sees its customers in markets of aggregate groups) is to acquire more customers (widen the horizontal bar), whereas the direction of success for the customer-driven enterprise is to keep customers longer and grow them bigger (lengthen the vertical bar). The width of the horizontal bar can be thought of as an enterprise's market share—the proportion of total customers who have their needs satisfied by a particular enterprise, or the percentage of total products in an industry sold by this particular firm. But the customer-value enterprise focuses on share of customer—the percentage of this customer's business that a particular firm gets—represented by the height of the vertical bar. Think of it this way: Kellogg's can either sell as many boxes of Corn Flakes as possible to whomever will buy them, even though sometimes Corn Flakes will cannibalize Raisin Bran sales, or Kellogg's can concentrate on making sure its products are on Mrs. Smith's breakfast table every day for the rest of her life, and thus represent a steady or growing percentage of that breakfast table's offerings. Toyota can try to sell as many Camrys as possible, for any price, to anyone who will buy; or it can, by knowing Mrs. Smith better, make sure all the cars in Mrs. Smith's garage are Toyota brands, including the used car she buys for her teenage son, and that Mrs. Smith uses Toyota financing, and gets her service, maintenance, and repairs at Toyota dealerships throughout her driving lifetime.

Although the tasks for growing market share are different from those for building share of customer, the two strategies are not antithetical. A company can simultaneously focus on getting new customers and growing the value of and keeping

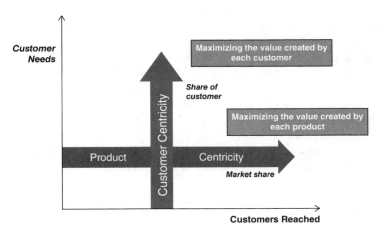

EXHIBIT 1.3   Objective of Customer Centricity

the customers it already has.[6] Customer-strategy enterprises are required to interact with a customer and use that customer's feedback from this interaction to deliver a customized product or service. Market-driven efforts can be strategically effective and even more efficient at meeting individual customer needs when a customer-specific philosophy is conducted on top of them. The customer-driven process is time-dependent and evolutionary, as the product or service is continuously fine-tuned and the customer is increasingly differentiated from other customers.

The principles of a customer-focused business model differ in many ways from mass marketing. Specifically:

The aggregate-market enterprise competes by differentiating products, whereas the customer-driven enterprise competes by differentiating customers.

The traditional, aggregate-market enterprise attempts to establish an actual product differentiation (by launching new products or modifying or extending established product lines) or a perceived one (with advertising and public relations). The customer-driven enterprise caters to one customer at a time and relies on differentiating each customer from all the others.

The traditional marketing company, no matter how friendly, ultimately sees customers as adversaries, and vice versa. The company and the customer play a zero-sum game: If the customer gets a discount, the company loses profit margin. Their interests have traditionally been at odds: The customer wants to buy as much product as possible for the lowest price, while the company wants to sell the least product possible for the highest price. If an enterprise and a customer have no relationship prior to a purchase, and they have no relationship following it, then their entire interaction is centered on a single, solitary transaction and the profitability of that transaction. Thus, in a transaction-based, product-centric business model, buyer and seller are adversaries, no matter how much the seller may try not to act the part. In this business model, practically the only assurance a customer has that he can trust the product and service being sold to him is the general reputation of the brand itself.[7]

By contrast, the customer-based enterprise aligns customer collaboration with profitability. Compare the behaviors that result from both sides if each transaction occurs in the context of a longer-term relationship. For starters, a one-to-one enterprise would likely be willing to fix a problem raised by a single transaction at a loss if the relationship with the customer were profitable long term (see Exhibit 1.4).

---

[6] Srividya Sridharan, "Evolve Your Approach to Acquisition and Retention," Forrester Research, Inc., December 12, 2012, available at www.forrester.com. Also see George S. Day, *Market-Driven Strategy: Processes for Creating Value* (New York: Free Press, 1999), for a useful discussion of the difference between "market-driven" and "market-driving" strategies.

[7] Marco Bertini and John T. Gourville, "Pricing to Create Shared Value," *Harvard Business Review*, June 2012, available at https://hbr.org/2012/06/pricing-to-create-shared-value, accessed February 3, 2016; Don Peppers and Martha Rogers, Ph.D., *The One to One Manager* (New York: Doubleday, 1999).

EXHIBIT 1.4   Comparison of Market-Share and Share-of-Customer Strategies

Market-Share Strategy	Share-of-Customer Strategy
Company sees products and brands as the source of all company value.	Company sees customers as—by definition—the only source of revenue.
Product (or brand) managers sell one product at a time to as many customers as possible.	Customer manager sells as many products as possible to one customer at a time.
Differentiate products from competitors.	Differentiate customers from each other.
Sell *to* customers.	Collaborate *with* customers.
Find a constant stream of new customers.	Find a constant stream of new business from established customers.
Company makes sure each product, and likely each transaction, is profitable, even at the cost of a customer's confidence.	Company makes sure each customer is profitable, even if that means losing money on an occasional product or transaction.
Use mass media to build brand and announce products.	Use interactive communication to determine individual needs and communicate with each individual.

The central purpose of managing customer relationships and experiences is for the enterprise to focus on increasing the overall value of its customer base—and customer retention is critical to its success. Increasing the value of the customer base, whether through *cross-selling* (getting customers to buy other products and services), *upselling* (getting customers to buy more expensive offerings), or customer referrals, will lead to a more profitable enterprise. The enterprise can also reduce the cost of serving its best customers by making it more convenient for them to buy from the enterprise (e.g., by using Amazon's one-click ordering process or online banking rather than a bank teller).

> The central purpose of managing customer relationships and experiences is for the enterprise to focus on increasing the overall value of its customer base—and customer retention is critical to its success.

Technology Accelerates—It Is Not the Same as—Building Customer Value

The interactive era has accelerated the adoption and facilitation of this highly interactive collaboration between the customer and the company. In addition, technological advancements have contributed to an enterprise's capability to capture the feedback of its customer, then customize some aspect of its products or services to suit each customer's individual needs. Enterprises require a highly sophisticated level of integrated activity to enable this customization and personalized customer interaction to occur. To effectuate customer-focused business relationships, an enterprise must integrate the disparate information systems, databases, business units, customer touchpoints—everywhere the company touches the customer and vice versa—and many other facets of its business to ensure that all employees who interact with customers have real-time access to current customer information. The objective is to optimize each customer interaction and ensure that the dialogue is seamless—that each conversation picks up from where the last one ended. And to participate in a transparent and helpful way in conversations customers have with each other online.

> Technology has made possible the mass customization of products and services, enabling businesses to treat different customers differently, in a cost-efficient way.

Many software companies have developed enterprise point solutions and suites of software applications that, when deployed, elevate an enterprise's capabilities to transform itself to a customer-driven model. And as we said earlier, while one-to-one customer relationships are enabled by technology, executives at firms with strong customer relationships and burgeoning **customer equity (CE)** believe that the enabling technology should be viewed as the means to an end, not the end itself. Managing customer experiences and relationships is an ongoing business process, not merely a technology. But technology has provided the catalyst for CRM to manifest itself within the enterprise. Computer databases help companies remember and keep track of individual interactions with their customers. Within seconds, customer service representatives can retrieve entire histories of customer transactions and make adjustments to customer records. Technology has made possible the mass customization of products and services, enabling businesses to treat different customers differently, in a cost-efficient way. (You'll find more about mass customization in Chapter 10.) Technology empowers enterprises and their customer contact personnel, marketing and sales functions, and managers by equipping them with substantially more intelligence about their customers.

> The foundation for an enterprise focused on building its value by building the value of the customer base is unique: Establish relationships with customers on an individual basis, then use the information gathered to treat different customers differently and increase the value of each one to the firm.

Implementing an effective customer strategy can be challenging and costly because of the sophisticated technology and skill set needed by relationship managers to execute the customer-driven business model. A business model focused on building customer value often requires the coordinated delivery of products and services aligned with enterprise financial objectives that meet customer value requirements. While enterprises are experimenting with a wide array of technology and software solutions from different vendors to satisfy their customer-driven needs, they are learning that they cannot depend on technology alone to do the job. Before it can be implemented successfully, managing customer relationships individually requires committed leadership from the upper management of the enterprise and wholehearted participation throughout the organization as well. Although customer strategies are driven by new technological capabilities, the technology alone does not make a company customer-centric. The payoff can be great, but the need to build the strategy to get, keep, and grow customers is even more important than the technology required to implement that strategy.

> The firms that are best at building customer value are not the ones that ask, "How can we use new technologies to get our customers to buy more?" Instead they are the companies that ask, *"How can we use new technologies to deliver more value to our customers?"*

The foundation for an enterprise focused on building its value by building the value of the customer base is unique: Establish trustable relationships with customers on an individual basis, then use the information gathered to treat different customers differently and increase the value of each one to the firm. The overarching theme of such an enterprise is that the customer is the most valuable asset the company has; that's why the primary goals are to get, keep, and grow profitable customers. Use technology to take the customer's point of view, and act on that as a competitive advantage.

What Is a Relationship? Is That Different from Customer Experience?

What does it mean for an enterprise and a customer to have a *relationship* with each other? Do customers have relationships with enterprises that do not know them? Can the enterprise be said to have a relationship with a customer it does not know? Is a relationship possible if the company knows the customer and tailors offers and communications, remembers things for the customer, and deliberately builds customer experience—even if the customer is not aware of a "relationship"? Is it possible for a customer to have a relationship with a brand? Perhaps what is thought to be a customer's relationship with a brand is more accurately described as the customer's attitude or predisposition toward the brand. This attitude is a combination of impressions from actual experiences with that brand, as well as what one has heard about the brand from ads (company-originated communication), from news, and from others (comments from friends and ratings by strangers). Experts have studied the nature of relationships in business for many years, and there are many different perspectives on the fundamental purpose of relationships in business strategies.

This book is about managing customer relationships and experiences more effectively in the twenty-first century, which is governed by a more individualized approach. The critical business objective can no longer be limited to acquiring the most customers and gaining the greatest market share for a product or service. Instead, to be successful going forward, now that it's possible to deal individually with separate customers, the business objective must include establishing meaningful and profitable relationships with, at the least, the most valuable customers and making the overall customer base more valuable. Technological advances during the last quarter of the twentieth century have mandated this shift in philosophy.

In short, the enterprise strives to get a customer, keep that customer for a lifetime, and grow the value of the customer to the enterprise. Relationships are the crux of the customer-strategy enterprise. Relationships between customers and enterprises provide the framework for everything else connected to the customer-value business model, even if the customer is not aware of the "relationship." After all, the customer is aware of what she experiences with the company. In fact, we could say that *managing the customer relationship is all about what the company does, and customer experience is what the customer feels like as a result*. The exchange between a customer and the enterprise becomes mutually beneficial, as customers give information in return for personalized service that meets their individual needs. This interaction forms the basis of the *Learning Relationship,* based on a collaborative dialogue between the enterprise and the customer that grows smarter and smarter with each successive interaction.[8]

> Managing the customer relationship is all about what the company does, and customer experience is what the customer feels like as a result.

Who Is the Customer?

Throughout this book, we refer to *customers* in a generic way. To some, the term will conjure up the mental image of shoppers. To others, those shoppers are *end users* or *consumers,* and the customers are upstream businesses in the distribution chain—the companies that buy from producers and either sell directly to end users or manufacture their own product. In this book, *customer* refers to the constituents of an organization, whether it's a business-to-business customer (which could mean the purchasing agent or user at the customer company, or the entire customer company) or an end-user consumer (an individual or a family/household)—or, for that matter, a hotel patron, a hospital patient, a charitable contributor, a voter, a university student or alum, a blood donor, a theme-park guest, and so on. That means the *competition* is anything a customer might choose that would preclude choosing the organization that is trying to build a relationship with that customer. The word *customer* includes both current and prospective buyers and users.

---

[8] B. Joseph Pine II, Don Peppers, and Martha Rogers, Ph.D., "Do You Want to Keep Your Customers Forever?" *Harvard Business Review* 73, no. 2 (March–April 1995): 103–114.

How to Think about Customer Experience

In our view, any useful definition of *customer experience* should be based on straightforward language, while at the same time clearly differentiating the term from all the other marketing terms and buzzwords, such as *customer service, brand preference, customer satisfaction, CRM,* or *customer loyalty.*

Customer experience is the sum total of a customer's individual interactions with a product or company, over time.

- *Individual* means that we are talking about each different customer's own individual perception or impression of the experience. What you intend to provide a customer is not nearly as important as how the customer perceives what you provide.
- *Interactions* occur in addressable or reciprocal channels, that is, non–mass media. Marketing campaigns, taglines, and brand messages may be important, but they aren't interactions, so they lie outside the "customer experience" domain. On the other hand, improving your mobile app by, for instance, embedding voice or chat connections into it would definitely improve your customer experience. When a company makes it easier for a prospect to find information about its product, for instance, that company is improving the "customer experience" even though the prospect may never actually become a customer.
- When we talk about "customer experience," we are only including direct contact. The interactions a customer has in person or online with other people or companies about a brand or product or company are not really a part of it, although, of course, how your company actually *engages* with customers and prospects within various social channels is, because it is a direct interaction.
- *Customer experience applies to all of a company's marketing, selling, and servicing entities.* In addition to your own company, it includes dealers and distributors, marketing and advertising agencies, any retailers that sell your product, and any service firms that install or repair your company's product or that handle customer inquiries or interactions of any kind. For each of these interactions, you can contract out the task but not the responsibility—at least not as far as the customer is concerned.
- *Each customer's experience is not an isolated event,* but accumulates through time. A company improves its customer experience, for instance, when it makes it easier for a repeat customer to get back to his or her preferred configuration, or when a call-center agent already knows what a prospect was recently trying to find out on the Web site.
- A company cannot improve customer experience without considering all of these issues, including how each one impacts the others. Integrating all interaction channels is one of the first, and possibly the most important, steps a company can take to improve customer experience.

Learning Relationships: The Crux of Managing Customer Relationships

The basic strategy behind Learning Relationships is that the enterpri
tomer the opportunity to teach it what he wants, remember it, give it Dac.
and keep his business. The more the customer teaches the company, the better
the company can provide exactly what the customer wants and the more the customer has invested in the relationship. Ergo, the customer will more likely choose
to continue dealing with the enterprise rather than spend the extra time and effort
required to establish a similar relationship elsewhere.[9]

The Learning Relationship works like this: If you're my customer and I get you to
talk to me, and I remember what you tell me, then I get smarter and smarter about you.
I know something about you that my competitors don't know. So I can do things for
you my competitors can't do, because they don't know you as well as I do. Before long,
you can get something from me you can't get anywhere else, for any price. At the very
least, you'd have to start all over somewhere else, but starting over is more costly than
staying with me, so long as you like me and trust me to look out for your best interests.

This happens every time a customer buys groceries by updating her online grocery list[10] or adds a favorite movie to her "My List" online. Even if a competitor were
to establish exactly the same capabilities, a customer already involved in a Learning
Relationship with an enterprise would have to spend time and energy—sometimes
a lot of time and energy—teaching the competitor what the current enterprise
already knows. This creates a significant **switching cost** for the customer, as the
value of what the enterprise is providing continues to increase, partly as the result
of the customer's own time and effort. The result is that the customer becomes more
loyal to the enterprise because it is simply in the customer's own interest to do so.
It is more worthwhile for the customer to remain loyal than to switch. As the relationship progresses, the customer's convenience increases, and the enterprise
becomes more valuable to the customer, allowing the enterprise to protect its profit
margin with the customer, often while reducing the cost of serving that customer.

Learning Relationships provide the basis for a completely different arena of competition, separate and distinct from traditional, product-based competition. An enterprise cannot prevent its competitor from offering a product or service that is perceived
to be as good as its own offering. Once a competitor offers a similar product or service, the enterprise's own offering is reduced to commodity status. But enterprises
that engage in collaborative Learning Relationships with individual customers gain a
distinct competitive advantage because they know something about one customer
that a competitor does not know. In a Learning Relationship, the enterprise learns
about an individual customer through his transactions and interactions during the
process of doing business. The customer, in turn, learns about the enterprise through
his successive purchase experiences and other interactions. Thus, in addition to an
increase in customer loyalty, two other benefits come from Learning Relationships:

---

[9] B. Joseph Pine II, Don Peppers, and Martha Rogers, Ph.D., "Do You Want to Keep Your
Customers Forever?"

[10] Adele Berndt and Annekie Brink, *Customer Relationship Management and Customer Service*
(Lansdowne, South Africa: Juta, 2004), p. 25.

1. *The customer learns more about his own preferences from each experience and from the firm's feedback,* and is therefore able to shop, purchase, and handle some aspect of his life more efficiently and effectively than was possible prior to this relationship.

2. *The enterprise learns more about its own strengths and weaknesses from each interaction and from the customer's feedback,* and is therefore able to market, communicate, and handle some aspects of its own tactics or strategy more efficiently and effectively than was possible prior to the relationship.[11]

Cultivating Learning Relationships depends on an enterprise's capability to elicit and manage useful information about customers. Customers, whether they are consumers or other enterprises, do not want more choices. Customers simply want exactly what they want—when, where, and how they want it. And technology is now making it more and more possible for companies to give it to them, allowing enterprises to collect large amounts of data on individual customers' needs and then use that data to customize products and services for each customer—that is, to treat different customers differently.[12] This ability to use customer information to offer a customer the most relevant product at the right price, at the right moment, is at the heart of the kind of customer experience that builds share of customer and loyalty.

> Customers, whether they are consumers or other enterprises, do not want more choice. Customers simply want *what they want* when, where, and how they want it.

One of the implications of this shift is an imperative to consider and manage the two ways customers create value for an enterprise. We've already said that a product focus tends to make companies think more about the value of a current transaction than the long-term value of the customer who is the company's partner in that transaction. But building Learning Relationships has value only to a company that links its own growth and future success to its ability to keep and grow customers, and therefore commits to building long-term relationships with customers. This means we find stronger commitments to customer trust, employee trust, meeting community responsibilities, and otherwise thinking about long-term, sustainable strategies.

---

[11] Steve Blank, "Why the Lean Startup Changes Everything," *Harvard Business Review,* May 2013, available at https://hbr.org/2013/05/why-the-lean-start-up-changes-everything, accessed February 3, 2016; Katherine Lemon, Don Peppers, and Martha Rogers, Ph.D., "Managing the Customer Lifetime Value: The Role of Learning Relationships," working paper.

[12] David C. Edelman and Marc Singer, "Competing on Customer Journeys," *Harvard Business Review* 93, no. 11 (November 2015): 88–100; Joe Stanhope, "Behavioral Targeting Powers Customized Content and Increased Conversion," Forrester Research, Inc., June 13, 2012, available at www.forrester.com; Jeff Bertolucci, "Big Data: Matching Personalities in the Call Center," *Information Week,* February 17, 2015, available at http://www.informationweek.com/big-data/big-data-analytics/big-data-matching-personalities-in-the-call-center/d/d-id/1319108, accessed February 3, 2016. Also see B. Joseph Pine II, Don Peppers, and Martha Rogers, Ph.D., "Do You Want to Keep Your Customers Forever?" in *Markets of One: Creating Customer-Unique Value through Mass Customization,* eds. James H. Gilmore and B. Joseph Pine II (Boston: Harvard Business School Publishing, 2000).

Companies that are in the business of building the value of the customer base are companies that understand the importance of balancing short-term and long-term success. We talk more about that in Chapters 5 and 11.

Return on Customer: Measuring the Efficiency with Which Customers Create Value

Most business executives would agree, intellectually, that *customers* represent the surest route to business growth—getting more customers, keeping them longer, and making them more profitable. Most understand that the customer base itself is a revenue-producing asset for their company—and that the value it throws off ultimately drives the company's economic worth. Nevertheless, when companies measure their financial results, they rarely if ever take into account any changes in the value of this underlying asset, with the result that they are blind—*and financial analysts are blind*—to one of the most significant factors driving business success.

Think about your personal investments. Imagine you asked your broker to calculate your return on investment for your portfolio of stocks and bonds. She would tally the dividend and interest payments you received during the year, and then note the increases or decreases in the value of the various stocks and bonds in the portfolio. Current income plus underlying value changes. The result, when compared to the amount you began the year with, would give you this year's ROI (return on investment). But suppose she chose to ignore any changes in the underlying value of your securities, limiting her analysis solely to dividends and interest. Would you accept this as a legitimate picture of your financial results? No.

Well, this is exactly the way nearly all of today's investors assess the financial performance of the companies they invest in, because this is the only way companies report their results. They count the "dividends" from their customers and ignore any increase (or decrease) in the value of the underlying assets. But just as a portfolio of securities is made up of individual stocks and bonds that not only produce dividends and interest but also go up and down in value during the course of the year, a company is, at its roots, a portfolio of customers, who not only buy things from the firm in the current period but also go up and down in value.

Return on investment quantifies how well a firm creates value from a given investment. But what quantifies how well a company creates value from its *customers?* For this you need the metric of Return on Customer℠ (ROC℠). The ROC equation has the same form as an ROI equation. ROC equals a firm's current-period cash flow from its customers plus any changes in the underlying customer equity, divided by the total customer equity at the beginning of the period.

Source: Excerpted from Don Peppers and Martha Rogers, Ph.D., *Return on Customer* (New York: Currency/Doubleday, 2008), pp. 6–7. Return on Customer will be discussed in more detail in Chapter 11.

When it comes to customers, businesses are shifting their focus from product sales transactions to **relationship equity.** Most soon recognize that they simply do not know the full extent of their profitability by customer.[13] Not all customers are equal. Some are not worth the time or financial investment of establishing Learning Relationships, nor are all customers willing to devote the effort required to sustain such a relationship. Enterprises need to decide early on which customers they want to have relationships with, which they do not, and what type of relationships to nurture. (See Chapter 5 on customer value differentiation.) But the advantages to the enterprise of growing Learning Relationships with valuable and potentially valuable customers are immense. Because much of what is sold to the customer may be customized to his precise needs, the enterprise can, for example, potentially charge a premium (as the customer may be less price sensitive to customized products and services) and increase its profit margin.[14] The product or service is worth more to the customer because he has helped shape and mold it to his own specifications. The product or service, in essence, has become *decommoditized* and is now uniquely valuable to this particular customer.

Managing customer relationships effectively is a practice not limited to products and services. When establishing interactive Learning Relationships with valuable customers, customer-strategy enterprises remember a customer's specific needs for the basic product but also the goods, services, and communications that surround the product, such as how the customer would prefer to be invoiced or how the product should be packaged. Even an enterprise that sells a commodity-like product or service can think of it as a bundle of ancillary services, delivery times, invoicing schedules, personalized reminders and updates, and other features that are rarely commodities. The key is for the enterprise to focus on customizing to each individual customer's needs. A teenager in California had gotten a text from her wireless phone service suggesting her parents could save money if she texted "4040" in an offer to switch her to a cell phone plan that was a better fit for her and the way she actually uses the service. She was so impressed she made a point of telling us about it. And of course, she told all her friends at school—and on Twitter and Facebook. The coverage, the hardware, the central customer service, and the "brand" all remained the same. But the customer experience, based on actual usage interaction with the customer—information not available to competitors—improved the customer relationship, increased loyalty and lifetime value of the customer, and positively influenced other customers as well.

---

[13] Peter O'Neill, "Differentiate with the Five C's of Community Marketing," Forrester Research, Inc., March 24, 2011, available at www.forrester.com; Carrie Johnson and Elizabeth Davis, with Kate van Geldern, "Beyond Sales: Driving eBusiness with Engagement," May 15, 2009, Forrester Research, Inc., www.forrester.com, accessed September 1, 2010; Jeff Sands, "Account-Based Marketing," *B to B* 91, no. 6 (2006): 11.

[14] J. P. Gownder, "Mass Customization Is (Finally) the Future of Products," Forrester Research, Inc., April 15, 2011, available at www.forrester.com. Also see Pine, Peppers, and Rogers, "Do You Want to Keep Your Customers Forever?"

When a customer teaches an enterprise what he wants or how he wants it, the customer and the enterprise are, in essence, *collaborating* on the sale of the product. The more the customer teaches the enterprise, the less likely the customer will want to leave. The key is to design products, services, and communications that customers *value,* and on which a customer and a marketer will have to collaborate for the customer to receive the product, service, or benefit.

Enterprises that build Learning Relationships clear a wider path to customer profitability than companies that focus on price-driven transactions. They move from a make-to-forecast business model to a make-to-order model, as Dell Computer did when it

> Enterprises that build Learning Relationships clear a wider path to customer profitability than companies that focus on price-driven transactions.

created a company that reduced inventory levels by building each computer after it was paid for. By focusing on gathering information about individual customers and using that information to customize communications, products, and services, enterprises can more accurately predict inventory and production levels. Fewer orders may be lost because mass customization can build the products on demand and thus make available to a given customer products that cannot be stocked ad infinitum. (Again, we will discuss customization further in Chapter 10.) Inventoryless distribution from a made-to-order business model can prevent shortages caused in distribution channels as well as reduce inventory carrying costs. The result is fewer "opportunity" losses. Furthermore, efficient mass-customization operations can ship built-to-order custom products faster than competitors that have to customize products from scratch.[15]

Learning Relationships have less to do with creating a fondness on the part of a customer for a particular product or brand and more to do with a company's capability to remember and deliver based on prior interactions with a customer. An enterprise that engages in a Learning Relationship creates a *bond of value* for the customer, a reason for an individual customer or small groups of customers with similar needs to lose interest in dealing with a competitor, provided that the enterprise continues to

> Learning Relationships have less to do with creating a fondness on the part of a customer for a particular product or brand and more to do with a company's capability to remember and deliver based on prior interactions with a customer.

deliver a product and service quality at a fair price and to remember to act on the customer's preferences and tastes.[16] Learning Relationships may also be based on an

---

[15] Hyun-Hwa Lee and Eunyoug Chang, "Consumer Attitudes toward Online Mass Customization: An Application of Extended Technology Acceptance Model," *Journal of Computer-Mediated Communication* 16, no. 2 (January 2011): 171–200; Fabrizio Salvador, Pablo Martin de Holan, and Frank T. Pillar, "Cracking the Code of Mass Customization," *MIT Sloan Management Review* 50, no. 3 (Spring 2009): 71–78.

[16] Pedro S. Coelho and Jörg Henseler, "Creating Customer Loyalty through Service Customization," *European Journal of Marketing* 46, no. 3/4 (2012): 332–356; Pine, Peppers, and Rogers, "Do You Want to Keep Your Customers Forever?" pp. 103–104.

inherent trust between a customer and an enterprise. For example, a customer might divulge his credit card number to an organization, which records it and remembers it for future transactions. The customer trusts that the enterprise will keep his credit card number confidential. The enterprise makes it easier and faster for him to buy because he no longer has to repeat his credit card number each time he makes a purchase. (In the next chapter, we'll learn more about the link between attitude and behavior in relationships.)

The Technology Revolution and the Customer Revolution

During the past century, as enterprises sought to acquire as many customers as they possibly could, the local proprietor's influence over customer purchases decreased. Store owners or managers became little more than order takers, stocking their shelves with the goods that consumers would see advertised in the local newspaper or on television and radio. Mass-media advertising became a more effective way to publicize a product and generate transactions for a wide audience. But now technology has made it possible, and therefore competitively necessary, for enterprises to behave, once again, like small-town proprietors and deal with their customers individually, one customer at a time.

At the same time, technology has generated a business model that we will refer to as the **trust platform**.[17] Becoming prominent since the last edition of this book, trust platforms are epitomized by companies such as Uber, Airbnb, and TaskRabbit. This kind of business depends on using interactive technology to connect willing buyers with willing sellers, while relying on crowd-sourced feedback to ensure mutual trust. Rather than a "sharing" economy, trust platforms facilitate an "initiative" economy, based on the entrepreneurial initiatives of thousands of individuals, all seamlessly connected to the larger network.

We must note that social interactions are not as manageable as a company's marketing and other functions are. The social interactions a company has with customers and other people can't be directed the same way advertising campaigns or cost-cutting initiatives can. Instead, in the e–social world, what companies are likely to find is that top-down, command-and-control organizations are not trustable, while self-organized collections of employees and partners motivated by a common purpose and socially empowered to take action are more trustable.

---

[17] Thomas L. Friedman, "And Now for a Bit of Good News . . . ," Sunday Review, *New York Times*, July 19, 2014, available at http://www.nytimes.com/2014/07/20/opinion/sunday/thomas-l-friedman-and-now-for-a-bit-of-good-news.html?_r=0, accessed February 4, 2016.

Customers Have Changed, Too

The technological revolution has spawned another revolution, one led by the customers themselves, who now demand products just the way they want them and flawless customer service. Enterprises are realizing that they really know little or nothing about their individual customers and so are mobilizing to capture a clearer understanding of each customer's needs. Customers, meanwhile, want to be treated less like numbers and more like the individuals they are, with distinct, individual requirements and preferences. They are actively communicating these demands back to the enterprise (and, through social media and mobile apps, with each other!). Where they would once bargain with a business, they now tell managers of brand retail chains what they are prepared to pay and specify how they want products designed, styled, assembled, delivered, and maintained. When it comes to ordering, consumers want to be treated with respect. The capability of an enterprise to remember customers and their logistical information not only makes ordering easier for customers but also lets them know that they are important. Computer applications that enable options such as "one-click," or express, ordering on the Web are creating the expectation that good online providers take the time to get to know customers as individuals so they can provide this higher level of service.[18]

The customer revolution is part of the reason enterprises are committing themselves to keep and grow their most valuable customers. Today's consumers and businesses have become more sophisticated about shopping for their needs across multiple channels; more and more CMOs refer to this **multiple channel marketing** as **omnichannel marketing**, but what it really means is that customers will come at companies in various ways, in ways that suit those customers, and companies must be ready to present a logical, coherent response to each customer—not just messages sent through media channels—and to remember what is learned through each interaction and apply that learning to all channels. The idea here is not just to make sure that we prepare and send a message, but to make sure each customer receives one. The online channel, in particular, enables shoppers to locate the goods and services they desire quickly and at a price they are willing to pay, which forces enterprises to compete on value propositions other than lowest price.

Customer Retention and Enterprise Profitability

Enterprises strive to increase profitability without losing high-margin customers by increasing their customer retention rates or the percentage of customers who have met a specified number of repurchases over a finite period of time. A retained customer, however, is not necessarily a loyal customer. The customer may give business to a competing enterprise for many different reasons.

---

[18] See Dave Frankland, "The Intelligent Approach to Customer Intelligence" (October 16, 2009), Forrester Research, Inc., available at www.forrester.com.

Royal Bank of Canada's 16 Million Loyal Customers

Organizations have accelerated their customer-focused strategies during the last few years, but managing customer relationships has been a business discipline for many years. Before the Industrial Revolution, and before mass production was born, merchants established their businesses around *keeping* customers.

Small towns typically had a general store, a local bank, and a barbershop. Each proprietor met and knew each one of his customers individually. The bank teller, for example, knew that Mr. Johnson cashed his paycheck each Friday afternoon. When Mr. Johnson came into the bank, the bank teller already had his cash ready for him in twenties and tens, just as he liked it. If Mr. Johnson unexpectedly stopped cashing his paycheck at the bank, the teller would wonder what had happened to him. In short, the bank depended on the relationship with the individual customer and how much the people who worked for the bank knew about that customer. The teller's memory in this example is akin to today's data warehouses, which can store millions of data points, transaction histories, and characteristics about customers. Personal memory enabled the teller to fulfill each customer's individual banking needs and, ultimately, to build a profitable relationship with each one. The more the teller knew about a customer, the more convenient he could make banking for that customer—and the more likely the customer would continue to use the bank.

But here's the important question 100 years later: Can an international financial services enterprise with 18 million customers[a] ever hope to deliver the same intimate customer service as a small-town bank? The attitude at Royal Bank of Canada (RBC), according to several of its executives, is "Absolutely."

According to McKinsey's EMEA Banking Practice,

> *Royal Bank of Canada (RBC) pursues this kind of a niche strategy with great success. After identifying attractive customer groups via micro-segmentation, RBC tailors products for each group. Their approach comprises three layers of segmentation. First, "basic segmentation" defines five customer groups using demographic criteria. Next, "strategic segmentation" cuts the customer base into a multitude of subsegments by factors such as profitability, risk profile, or customer lifetime value. Finally, "tactical segmentation" focuses primarily on product sales, drawing on parameters such as probability of purchase, risk of cancellation, or frequency with which products are used.*

> *This micro-segmentation helped RBC detect a previously neglected customer segment: senior citizens spending the winter in Florida. The bank developed a "VIP Banking" account for this segment that includes a senior rebate for eligible clients above 60, travel discounts, easy access to Canadian funds, a*

consolidated account review online, ability to leverage a Canadian credit history for mortgages in the US, and a toll-free number for cross-border banking questions. As a result, over the last five years sales per customer have more than doubled, the attrition rate has dropped by nearly 50 percent, and net income has grown by 75 percent. Other examples are the Swiss Bank Coop's financial advice for women, the Dutch Rabobank's package for the divorced, or Wells Fargo's offer for soldiers. Managing all these opportunities systematically will create a sustainable development agenda.[b]

As far back as the 1990s, RBC developed superior computing and database power, along with sophisticated statistical programs, to analyze customer information and test specific actions it should take with specific customers. Only then could the bank's frontline personnel deliver more effective personal contact and attention to individual customers.

To learn the most about its customers, RBC has undertaken an intense, ongoing statistical analysis of them. It is developing and refining the prototype for an algorithm to model the long-term lifetime values of its individual customers. Part of this effort includes a "client potential" model that measures how "growable" certain kinds of customers are to the bank. The bank also analyzes a customer's vulnerability to attrition and tries to flag the most vulnerable before they defect, in order to take preventive action in a focused, effective way.

To expand share of customer, Royal Bank also tries to predict statistically which additional services a customer might want to buy, and when. Royal Bank not only makes different offers to different customers, it also equips its sales and service people with detailed customer profiles. Thus, rather than providing a one-size-fits-all service, the bank's customer-contact people spend their time and energy making on-the-spot decisions based on each customer's individual situation and value. Note that this type of business practice not only benefits from individual customer interactions, it *requires* individual interactions to achieve the greatest success. As an RBC executive told the authors of this book, the bank discovered it "could lift contributions and penetration rates by up to 10 percent by virtue of the contact alone." (We look at Royal Bank's customer-profitability strategies more in Part III.)

[a] According to Royal Bank of Canada Web site's corporate profile, RBC "currently serves more than 16 million personal, business, public sector, and institutional clients through offices in Canada, the U.S. and 38 other countries." Available at http://www.rbc.com/aboutus/index.html, accessed February 4, 2016.
[b] McKinsey & Company, EMEA Banking Practice, "Banking on Customer Centricity: Transforming Banks into Customer-Centric Organizations," April 2012, available at http://www.mckinsey.com/search.aspx?q=banking+on+customer+centricity, accessed February 4, 2016.

In 1990, Fred Reichheld and W. Earl Sasser analyzed the profit per customer in different service areas, categorized by the number of years that a customer had been with a particular enterprise.[19] In this groundbreaking study, they discovered that the longer a customer remains with an enterprise, the more profitable she becomes. Average profit from a first-year customer for the credit card industry was $30; for the industrial laundry industry, $144; for the industrial distribution industry, $45; and for the automobile servicing industry, $25.

Four factors contributed to the underlying profit growth:

1. *Profit derived from increased purchases.* Customers grow larger over time and need to purchase in greater quantities.
2. *Profit from reduced operating costs.* As customers become more experienced, they make fewer demands on the supplier and fewer mistakes when involved in the operational processes, thus contributing to greater productivity for the seller and for themselves.
3. *Profit from referrals to other customers.* Less needs to be spent on advertising and promotion due to word-of-mouth recommendations from satisfied customers.
4. *Profit from price premium.* New customers can benefit from introductory promotional discounts, while long-term customers are more likely to pay regular prices.

No matter what the industry, the longer an enterprise keeps a customer, the more value that customer can generate for shareholders.[20] Reichheld and Sasser found in a classic study that for one auto service company, the expected profit from a fourth-year customer is more than triple the profit that same customer generates in the first year. Other industries studied showed similar positive results (see Exhibit 1.5).

---

[19] Frederick F. Reichheld and W. Earl Sasser Jr., "Zero Defections: Quality Comes to Services," *Harvard Business Review* 73 (September–October 1990): 59–75. Fred Reichheld is the father of the Net Promoter Score (NPS), which is a measure of the quality of a company's customer relationships and indicator of profitability. The score is based on what Reichheld calls the ultimate question: "Would you recommend us to a friend?" Customers can be sorted into detractors or promoters based on their answers, and percentages of each category give the Net Promoter score. Reichheld lays out the Net Promoter System and gives many examples of standout companies that have high profitability and high Net Promoter ratings in his book *The Ultimate Question 2.0: How Net Promoter Companies Thrive in a Customer-Driven World* (Boston: Harvard Business Review Press, 2011), written with Rob Markey.

[20] *Authors' note:* This point is not without controversy. Some research has shown that in some instances—especially those where a business is very dependent on one or a very few customers, such as automotive parts makers—a long-term customer has the power to extract so many concessions that the company's margins are squeezed sometimes to the breaking point. But generally, academic research and real-world experience have demonstrated that if a company acquires the right customers, the longer those customers continue to do business, the more profitable they become—for many reasons, especially reduction in churn replacement costs, increasing value to the customer of the relationship, and positive word of mouth and social networking by a contented or delighted customer.

EXHIBIT 1.5   Profit One Customer Generates over Time

Industry	Year 1	Year 2	Year 3	Year 4	Year 5
Credit Card	$30	$42	$44	$49	$55
Industrial Laundry	$144	$166	$192	$222	$256
Industrial Distribution	$45	$99	$123	$144	$168
Auto Servicing	$25	$35	$70	$88	$88

Source: Frederick F. Reichheld and W. Earl Sasser Jr., "Zero Defections: Quality Comes to Services," *Harvard Business Review* 68:5 (September–October 1990): 106.

> No matter what the industry, the longer an enterprise keeps a customer, the more value that customer can generate for shareholders.

Enterprises that build stronger individual customer relationships enhance customer loyalty, as they are providing each customer with what he needs.[21] Loyalty building requires the enterprise to emphasize the value of its products or services and to show that it is interested in building a relationship with the customer.[22] The enterprise realizes that it must build a stable customer base rather than concentrate on single sales.[23]

---

[21] *Authors' note:* Which comes first, loyalty or satisfaction? In a 2008 article, Mark Johnson, Eugene Sivadas, and Ellen Garbarino questioned the directionality of the link between satisfaction and loyalty, suggesting there is more evidence to indicate that loyalty leads to customer satisfaction rather than satisfaction (customer relationships) leading to loyalty; see "Customer Satisfaction, Perceived Risk, and Affective Commitment," *Journal of Services Marketing* 22, no. 4/5 (2008): 353–362. Also see an earlier article, which originally questioned some of our assertions here: Ellen Garbarino and Mark Johnson, "The Different Roles of Satisfaction, Trust, and Commitment in Customer Relationships," *Journal of Marketing* 63 (April 1999): 70–87. More recent articles by Flint, Blocker, and Boutin (2011) and Chen (2012), among others, squarely support the link between satisfaction and loyalty. See Daniel J. Flint, Christopher P. Blocker, and Philip J. Boutin Jr., "Customer Value Anticipation, Customer Satisfaction and Loyalty: An Empirical Examination," *Industrial Marketing Management* 40, no. 2 (February 2011): 219–230; and Shu-Ching Chen, "The Customer Satisfaction–Loyalty Relation in an Interactive E-Service Setting: The Mediators," *Journal of Retailing and Consumer Services* 19, no. 2 (March 2012): 202–210.

[22] Jill Griffin, *Customer Loyalty: How to Earn It, How to Keep It* (San Francisco: Jossey-Bass, 1997).

[23] For a different view of the value of loyalty, see Werner Reinartz and Mark Eisenbeiss, "Managing Customer Loyalty to Maximize Customer Equity," in *Handbook of Research on Customer Equity in Marketing*, eds. V. Kumar and Denish Shah (Northampton, MA: Edward Elgar, 2015), pp. 139–159; and Werner Reinartz and V. Kumar, "The Mismanagement of Customer Loyalty," *Harvard Business Review* (July 2002): 86–94. Reinartz and Kumar's work shows that more loyal customers are not necessarily more profitable as a class, especially using their methodology of one moment in time; but we should also point out that in the case of an individual customer, the more loyalty and the greater share of customer achieved from one customer over time, the more valuable by definition that individual customer will become.

A customer-strategy firm will want to reduce customer defections because they result in the loss of investments the firm has made in creating and developing customer relationships. Customers are the lifeblood of any business. They are, literally, the only source of its revenue.[24] Loyal customers are more profitable because they likely buy more over time if they are satisfied. It costs less for the enterprise to serve retained customers over time because transactions with repeat customers become more routine. Loyal customers tend to refer other new customers to the enterprise, thereby creating new sources of revenue.[25] It stands to reason that if the central goal of a customer-strategy company is to increase the overall value of its customer base, then continuing its relationships with its most profitable customers will be high on its list of priorities.

On average, U.S. corporations tend to lose half their customers in five years, half their employees in four, and half their investors in less than one.[26] In his classic study on the subject, Fred Reichheld described a possible future in which the only business relationships will be onetime, opportunistic transactions between virtual strangers.[27] However, he found that disloyalty could stunt corporate performance by 25 to 50 percent, sometimes more. In contrast, enterprises that concentrate on finding and keeping good customers, productive employees, and supportive investors continue to generate superior results. For this reason, the primary responsibility for customer retention or defection lies in the chief executive's office.

The ROI of Building Customer Relationships in Financial Services

Managing individual customer relationships has a profound effect on enhancing long-term customer loyalty, thereby increasing the enterprise's long-term profitability. Relationship strategies, for example, have a substantial effect on customer retention in the financial services sector. A study conducted by Peppers & Rogers Group (with Roper Starch Worldwide) found that—looking at a group of "satisfied customers"—only 1 percent of consumers who rate their financial services

---

[24] *Authors' note:* Some may question the statement: "Customers are a company's only source of revenue." By definition, however, this is literally true. If a company sells products, for example, then the revenue does not come from the products; it comes from the customers who buy them. And if that same company also runs some ancillary businesses—say, renting out unused real estate space or spare capital—then those who make lease payments or interest payments are also customers.

[25] Philip Kotler and Milton Kotler, *Market Your Way to Grow: Eight Ways to Win* (Hoboken, NJ: John Wiley & Sons, 2013); Phillip Kotler, *Kotler on Marketing* (New York: Free Press, 1999).

[26] Fred Reichheld, "Learning from Customer Defections," *Harvard Business Review* 74:2 (March–April 1996): 87–88.

[27] Reichheld, *The Loyalty Effect.*

provider high on relationship management say they are likely to switch away products. One-fourth of consumers (26 percent) who rate their primary financial services provider as low on relationship management attributes say they are likely to switch away one or more products during the next 12 months. The financial implications of these findings are staggering (see Exhibit 1.6). Using a conservative average annual profitability per household for U.S. retail banks of $100, a reduction in attrition of 9 percent represents over $700 million in incremental profits for all U.S. households with accounts. If an individual financial institution with 20,000 customers can reduce attrition by 9 percentage points by providing excellent customer relationship management (e.g., recognizing returning customers, anticipating their needs, etc.), that institution can increase profits by $180,000. For a similar-size financial institution with an average household profitability of $500, the increase in profitability climbs to $900,000.

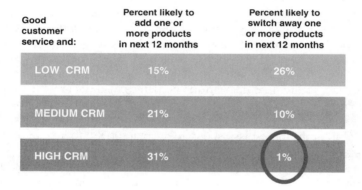

EXHIBIT 1.6   Benefits of CRM in Financial Services
Source: Peppers & Rogers Group, Roper Starch Worldwide survey, September 2000.

Customer loyalty is closely associated with customer relationships and may, in certain cases, be directly related to the level of each customer's satisfaction over time.[28] According to James Barnes, satisfaction is tied to what the customer gets from

---

[28] *Authors' note:* It is generally a challenge to agree on what we all mean by "customer satisfaction." See Richard L. Oliver, *Satisfaction: A Behavioral Perspective on the Consumer* (New York: Routledge, 2015). Additionally, Dave Power III has defined customer satisfaction as measuring the difference between what the customer expects to get and what he perceives he gets. More and more we are becoming capable of measuring what Pine and Gilmore call "customer sacrifice," which is the difference between what the customer wants exactly and what the customer settles for. B. Joseph Pine and James Gilmore, "Satisfaction, Sacrifice, Surprise: Three Small Steps Create One Giant Leap into the Experience Economy," *Strategy and Leadership* 28, no. 1 (January–February 2000): 18.

dealing with a company as compared with what he has to commit to those dealings or interactions.[29] For now, it's enough to know that the customer satisfaction issue is controversial—maybe even problematic. There are issues of relativity (are laptop users just harder to satisfy than desktop users, or are they really less satisfied?) and skew (is the satisfaction score the result of a bunch of people who are more or less satisfied, or a bimodal group whose members either love or hate the product?). Barnes believes that by increasing the value that the customer perceives in each interaction with the company, enterprises are more likely to increase customer satisfaction levels, leading to higher customer retention rates. When customers are retained because they enjoy the service they are receiving, they are more likely to become loyal customers. This loyalty leads to repeat buying and increased share of customer. (We will discuss more about the differences between attitudinal loyalty and behavioral loyalty, as well as ways to measure loyalty and retention, in the next chapter.)

Retaining customers is more beneficial to the enterprise for another reason: Acquiring new customers is costly. Consider the banking industry. Averaging across channels, banks can spend at least $200 to replace each customer who defects. So if a bank has a clientele of 50,000 customers and loses 5 percent of those customers each year, it would need to spend $500,000 or more each year simply to maintain its customer base.[30] Many Internet startup companies, without any brand-name recognition, faced an early demise during the 2000–2001 dot-com bubble bust, largely because they could not recoup the costs associated with acquiring new customers. The typical Internet "pure-play" spent an average of $82 to acquire one customer in 1999, a 95 percent increase over the $42 spent on average in 1998.[31] Much of that increase can be attributed to the dot-com companies' struggle to build brand awareness during 1999, which caused Web-based firms to increase offline advertising spending by an astounding 518 percent. Based on marketing costs related to their online business, in 1999, offline-based companies spent an average of $12 to acquire a new customer, down from $22 the previous year. Online firms spent an unsustainable 119 percent of their revenues on marketing in 1999. Even with the advantages of established brands, offline companies spent a still-high 36 percent.

> The problem is simple arithmetic. Given the high cost of customer acquisition, a company can never realize any potential profit from most customers, especially if a customer leaves the franchise.

---

[29] James G. Barnes, *Secrets of Customer Relationship Management* (New York: McGraw-Hill, 2001).

[30] Banks' customer acquisition costs can vary wildly, between $150 and $3,600, depending on the source, the product, and the channel, so $200 is a more-than-conservative figure.

[31] Boston Consulting Group and Shop.org, "The State of Online Retailing" (April 2000), available at www.shop.org/web/guest/research/store.

EXHIBIT 1.7   Customer Acquisition Costs (2015)

Branch/store	$154
Phone	$145
Web	$92
Mobile	$88

Source: Martin Gill with Zia Daniell Wigder, Rachel Roizen, and Alexander Causey, "Use Customer-Centric Metrics to Benchmark Your Digital Success," Forrester Research, Inc., February 5, 2015.

The problem is simple arithmetic. Given the high cost of customer acquisition, a company can never realize any potential profit from most customers, especially if a customer leaves the franchise (see Exhibit 1.7). High levels of customer churn trouble all types of enterprises, not just those in the online and wireless industries. The problem partly results from the way companies reward sales representatives: with scalable commissions and bonuses for acquiring the most customers. Fact is, many reps have little, if any, incentive for keeping and growing an established customer. In some cases, if a customer leaves, the sales representative can even be rewarded for bringing the same customer back again!

Although it's always somebody's designated mission to get new customers, too many companies still don't have anybody responsible for making sure this or that particular customer sticks around or becomes profitable. Often, a service company with high levels of churn needs to rethink not only how its reps engage in customer relationships but also how they are rewarded (or not) for nurturing those relationships and for increasing the long-term value to the enterprise of particular customers. Throughout this book, we will see that becoming a customer-value enterprise is difficult. It is a strategy that can never be handled by one particular department within the enterprise. Managing customer relationships and experiences is an ongoing process—one that requires the support and involvement of every functional area in the organization, from the upper echelons of management through production and finance, to each sales representative or contact-center operator. Indeed, customer-driven competition requires enterprises to integrate five principal business functions into their overall customer strategy:

1. *Financial custodianship of the customer base.* The customer-strategy enterprise treats the customer base as its primary *asset* and carefully manages the investment it makes in this asset, moving toward balancing the value of this asset to the long-term as well as the short-term success of the company.
2. *Production, logistics, and service delivery.* Enterprises must be capable of customizing their offerings to the needs and preferences of each individual customer. The Learning Relationship with a customer is useful only to the extent that interaction from the customer is actually incorporated in the way the enterprise behaves toward that customer.

3. *Marketing communications, customer service, and interaction.* Marketing communications and all forms of customer interaction and connectivity need to be combined into a unified function to ensure seamless individual customer dialogue.

4. *Sales distribution and channel management.* A difficult challenge is to transform a distribution system that was created to disseminate standardized products at uniform prices into one that delivers customized products at individualized prices. **Disintermediation** of the distribution network by leaping over the "middleman" is sometimes one solution to selling to individual customers.

5. *Organizational management strategy.* Enterprises must organize themselves internally by placing managers in charge of customers and customer relationships rather than of just products and programs.[32]

A customer-strategy enterprise seeks to create one centralized view of each customer across all business units. Every employee who interacts with a customer has to have real-time access to current information about that individual customer so that it is possible to pick up each conversation from where the last one left off. The goal is instant interactivity with the customer. This process can be achieved only through the complete and seamless integration of every enterprise business unit and process.

Summary

A customer-strategy enterprise seeks to identify what creates value for each customer and then to deliver that value to him. As other chapters in this book will demonstrate, a customer-value business strategy is a highly measurable process that can increase enterprise profitability and shareholder value. We also show that the foundation for growing a profitable customer-strategy enterprise lies in establishing stronger relationships with individual customers. Enterprises that foster relationships with individual customers pave a path to profitability. The challenge is to understand how to establish these critical relationships and how to optimize them for profits. Learning Relationships provide the framework for understanding how to build customer value.

Increasing the value of the customer base by focusing on customers individually and treating different customers differently will benefit the enterprise in many ways. But before we can delve into the intricacies of the business strategies behind this objective, and before we can review the CRM analytical tools and techniques required to carry out this strategy, we need to establish a foundation of knowledge with respect to how enterprises have developed relationships with customers over the years. That is our goal for the next chapter.

---

[32] Don Peppers and Martha Rogers, Ph.D., *Rules to Break and Laws to Follow: How Your Business Can Beat the Crisis of Short-Termism* (Hoboken, NJ: John Wiley & Sons, 2008).

Food for Thought

1. Understanding customers is not a new idea. Mass marketers have done it for years. But because they see everyone in a market as being alike—or at least everyone in a niche or a segment as being alike—they "understand" Customer A by asking 1,200 (or so) total strangers in a sample group from A's segment a few questions, then extrapolating the average results to the rest of the segment, including A. This is logical if all customers in a group are viewed as homogeneous. What will a company likely do differently in terms of understanding customers if it is able to see one customer at a time, remember what each customer tells the company, and treat different customers differently?

2. If retention is so much more profitable than acquisition, why have companies persisted for so long in spending more on getting new customers than keeping the ones they have? What would persuade them to change course?

3. How can we account for the upheaval in orientation from focusing on product profitability to focusing on customer profitability? If it's such a good idea, why didn't companies operate from the perspective of building customer value 50 years ago?

4. In the age of information (and connectivity), what will be happening to the four Ps, traditional advertising, and branding? What happens next?

5. "The new interactive technologies are not enough to cement a relationship, because companies need to change their *behavior* toward a customer and not just their *communication*." Explain what this statement means. Do you agree or disagree?

Glossary

Analytical CRM (*see also* Operational CRM)   The software installations, data requirements, and day-to-day procedural changes required at a firm to understand and anticipate individual customer needs, in order to be able to manage relationships better. In the four-step IDIC process, analytical CRM involves the first two steps, identifying and differentiating customers.

Business model   How a company builds economic value.

Commoditization   The steady erosion in unique selling propositions and unduplicated product features that comes about inevitably, as competitors seek to improve their offerings and end up imitating the more successful features and benefits.

Customer care   *See* Customer service.

Customer centricity   A "specific approach to doing business that focuses on the customer. Customer/client centric businesses ensure that the customer is at the center of a business philosophy, operations or ideas. These businesses believe that their customers/clients are the only reason they exist and use every means at their disposal to keep the customer/client happy and satisfied."[33] At the core of customer centricity is the understanding that customer profitability is at least as important as product profitability.

Customer equity (CE)   The value to the firm of building a relationship with a customer, or the sum of the value of all current and future relationships with current and potential customers. This term can be applied to individual customers or groups of customers, or the entire customer base of a company. See also the definition of customer equity in Chapter 11.

Customer experience   The totality of a customer's individual interactions with a brand, over time.

Customer experience journey mapping   *See* Customer journey mapping.

Customer experience management   The processes, tools, and procedures required to affect individual customer experiences at an enterprise.

Customer focus   *See* Customer orientation.

Customer journey mapping   A process of diagramming all the steps a customer takes when engaging with a company to buy, use, or service its product or offering. Also called "customer experience journey mapping." See the section on this subject in Chapter 13.

Customer orientation   An attitude or mind-set that attempts to take the customer's perspective when making business decisions or implementing policies. Also called *customer focus*.

Customer relationship management (CRM)   As a term, *CRM* can refer either to the activities and processes a company must engage in to manage individual relationships with its customers (as explored extensively in this textbook), or to the suite of software, data, and analytics tools required to carry out those activities and processes more cost efficiently.

Customer service   Customer service involves helping a customer gain the full use and advantage of whatever product or service was bought. When something goes wrong with a product, or when a customer has some kind of problem with it, the process of helping the customer overcome this problem is often referred to as "customer care."

Customer strategy   An organization's plan for managing its customer experiences and relationships effectively in order to remain competitive. At its heart, customer strategy is increasing the value of the company by increasing the value of the customer base.

Customer-strategy enterprise   An organization that builds its business model around increasing the value of the customer base. This term applies to companies that may be product oriented, operations focused, or customer intimate.

---

[33] "Client Centric," Investopedia, available at http://www.investopedia.com/terms/c/client-centric.asp, accessed February 15, 2016.

Customer value management Managing a business's strategies and tactics (including sales, marketing, production, and distribution) in a manner designed to increase the value of its customer base.

Data warehousing A process that captures, stores, and analyzes a single view of enterprise data to gain business insight for improved decision making.

Demand chain As contrasted with the supply chain, "demand chain" refers to the chain of demand from customers, through retailers, distributors, and other intermediaries, all the way back to the manufacturer.

Disintermediation Going directly to customers by skipping a usual distribution channel; for example, a manufacturer selling directly to consumers without a retailer.

Enterprise resource planning (ERP) The automation of a company's back-office management.

Interactive era The current period in business and technological history, characterized by a dominance of interactive media rather than the one-way mass media more typical from 1910 to 1995. Also refers to a growing trend for businesses to encourage feedback from individual customers rather than relying solely on one-way messages directed at customers, and to participate with their customers in social networking.

Multiple channel marketing An organization's capability of selling through more than one distribution channel (e.g., a Web site, a toll-free number, mail-order catalog). Can also refer to the approach of interacting with customers through more than one channel of communication (e.g., a Web site form, online chat, social media, text, e-mail, fax, direct mail, phone).

Omnichannel marketing A marketing buzzword referring to the capability of interacting and transacting with customers in any or all channels, in order to ensure that every interaction takes place in the channel of the customer's own choice.

One-to-one marketing The process of treating different customers differently and building ongoing relationships with individual customers, by using customer databases, interactivity, and mass-customization technologies. "One to one marketing" was originally espoused in the 1993 book *The One to One Future: Building Relationships One Customer at a Time*, by Don Peppers and Martha Rogers, Ph.D. As more technologies were developed to execute this kind of business strategy, the term *customer relationship management* came to be more frequently used.

Operational CRM (*see also* **Analytical CRM**) The software installations, data requirements, and day-to-day procedural changes required at a firm to manage interactions and transactions with individual customers on an ongoing basis. In the four-step IDIC process, operational CRM involves the last two steps, interacting with and customizing for customers.

Relationship equity *See* Customer equity.

Sales force automation (SFA) Connecting the sales force to headquarters and to each other through computer portability, contact management, ordering software, and other mechanisms.

Share of customer (SOC)   For a customer-focused enterprise, share of customer is a conceptual metric designed to show what proportion of a customer's overall need is being met by the enterprise. It is not the same as "share of wallet," which refers to the specific share of a customer's spending in a particular product or service category. If, for instance, a family owns two cars, and one of them is your car company's brand, then you have a 50 percent share of wallet with this customer, in the car category. But by offering maintenance and repairs, insurance, financing, and perhaps even driver training or trip planning, you can substantially increase your "share of customer."

Social networking   The ability of individuals to connect instantly with each other often and easily online in groups. For business, it's about using technology to initiate and develop relationships into connected groups (networks), usually forming around a specific goal or interest.

Switching cost   The cost, in time, effort, emotion, or money, to a business customer or end-user consumer of switching to a firm's competitor.

Trust platform   A business that uses interactive technology to connect willing buyers with willing sellers, while relying on crowd-sourced feedback to ensure mutual trust. Uber and Airbnb are examples of trust platforms.

Value of the customer base   *See* Customer equity.

CHAPTER 2

The Thinking behind Customer Relationships That Leads to Good Experiences

Things have never been more like they are today in history.

—Dwight D. Eisenhower

So far, our discussion of customer relationships, **customer experience**, and customer value has shown how businesses are undergoing a vast cultural shift—transforming from the mass marketing, product-siloed thinking of the Industrial Age to the customer-empowered culture of the **Information Age** and the **Age of Transparency**, where the primary goal is building relationships with individual customers who become measurably more valuable to the enterprise. In this new business era, managing individual customer relationships means an organization will use the knowledge gained from these relationships to improve the quality of the overall customer experience. Consequently, it is incumbent on the enterprise to understand what constitutes a relationship, how relationships are formed, and how they can be strengthened or weakened. Many different perspectives have been developed about what comprises customer relationships and how businesses can profit from them. So before we can move forward with our discussion of becoming a customer-focused enterprise, we need to explore a couple of views besides our own about relationships.

By the early 2000s, many companies acknowledged the importance of building "relationships" with customers—of improving customer experience, taking the customer's point of view, and taking steps to measure and manage customer value. In many cases, companies that had been product-oriented changed their philosophy, their culture, their metrics, and even their organizational structure to put customers at the forefront.

Why Do Companies Work at Being "Customer-Centric"?

Becoming customer-centric has not been easy, and not without controversy. Some believed that employees matter more than customers, since without great, engaged employees, an enterprise will have a hard time building strong customer relationships and building **customer equity.** Others continued to focus on cash flow and on making sure that strong product managers were held responsible for product promotion, distribution, and profitability. Ad agencies continued to tend "brand promise." But while all of these are important to a successful business, a growing number of firms have recognized that three things are true about a company's customers. Because of these truths, a company stands its best chance of success when it focuses on increasing customer value through outstanding customer experiences and relationships.

1. *Customers are scarce.* There are successful organizations that do not have "products," but there is no such thing as a successful firm that doesn't have "customers." And despite the fact that the world has billions of people, only so many of them will ever want a particular company's offering. That company's ability to find them, win them, get as much business from them as possible, and keep them for a long time will be the determining factor in how much it can ever grow the size of its business. There are only so many hungry people, right now, within reach of a neighborhood pizzeria, and each of those people can cook for themselves, or go to a competitor, or start a diet today and not eat at all. Customers are scarcer than products, services, new ideas, or channels. For all but those companies in real financial trouble, customers are even scarcer than capital itself. There is no secondary market for customers. They can't be borrowed at the bank and paid back with interest. Once a company's leaders realize this fact, they may make decisions differently, as we will see in Part III.

2. *Customers are the sole source of all a company's revenue.* Products don't pay a company any money, ever. Neither do brands or services, or employees, or marketing programs, or stores, or factories. Only customers generate revenue for a business—the customers the business has today and the customers it will have in the future. All the other stuff is important to a business only to the extent that it contributes to generating more revenue from customers. Thus, the goal will not just be to create value from each product or channel or even the greatest return on the investment of money, but instead to make sure the company creates the greatest value from each of its customers.

3. *Customers create value in two ways.* Today, they are generating profit this quarter (or not), and—also today—the experience they are having with a particular company's product, its brand, its contact center, or any of the rest of what it is selling is also causing them to become more (or less) likely to do more business with the company in the future, to become more (or less) likely to recommend it to friends, to think kindly of it (or not) when they need something else in its category. It's interesting that nearly every company is very, very good

at measuring and managing one way that customers create value: Companies know how much they spent making money from customers this quarter and what their revenue was from customers this quarter—since that's the total of the cost and revenue on the quarterly books. But many companies are content not to know the second part of this equation: They don't know, don't measure, and don't manage what is happening to underlying customer equity while the current numbers are falling into place. That means understanding a company's Return on Customer (ROC) is as important as understanding the return on investment (ROI).[1] We talk a lot more about ROC in Chapter 11.[2]

ROI answers the question: How much value does your company create for the money it uses?

ROC answers the question: How much value does your company create for the customers it has?

If customers are scarce, if they create all the revenue for a company, and if the value they do create is measurable and manageable in the short term and the long term, as of today, then it's natural for companies to want to understand and remember what customers need and to meet those needs better than a competitor that doesn't know the same things about the customers. Customer information provides a very powerful competitive advantage. Companies want to use this information to provide a positive experience for customers and possibly to engage customers in a "relationship" that enables the company to provide better and better service.[3]

---

[1] John Drummond, "Long-Term Marketing a New Paradigm Shift," *Guardian*, November 16, 2012, available at http://www.theguardian.com/sustainable-business/blog/marketing-long-term-paradigm-new-markets, accessed February 4, 2016. Also see Dominic Barton, "Capitalism for the Long Term," *Harvard Business Review*, March 2011. Accessed 10/13/2015 at https://hbr.org/2011/03/capitalism-for-the-long-term/ar/1. Also, Janamitra Devan, Anna Kristina Millan, and Pranav Shirke published a research finding in "Balancing Short- and Long-Term Performance," *McKinsey Quarterly*, no. 1 (2005): 31–33. They examined 266 companies and grouped them into four groups of High versus Low Short-Term versus Long-Term performance over a 20-year period. They discovered that those companies that balanced strong long- and short-term performance had higher Total Shareholder Return, lasted longer than their more mediocre competitors, enjoyed three years longer incumbency from chief executives on average, and had less volatility in stock prices. Companies with strong short-term performance but weak long-term performance enjoyed less volatile stock prices but came out poorly on other measures. The most successful companies were seen to have "instilled a long-term mind-set."

[2] Don Peppers and Martha Rogers, Ph.D., *Rules to Break and Laws to Follow: How Your Business Can Beat the Crisis of Short-Termism* (Hoboken, NJ: John Wiley & Sons, 2008). Also see Don Peppers and Martha Rogers, Ph.D., *Return on Customer: Creating Maximum Value from Your Scarcest Resource* (New York: Currency/Doubleday, 2005).

[3] Drummond, "Long-Term Marketing a New Paradigm Shift"; and Peppers and Rogers, *Rules to Break and Laws to Follow: How Your Business Can Beat the Crisis of Short-Termism.*

What Characterizes a Relationship?

Merriam-Webster defines *relationship* as "the state of being related or interrelated."[4] Because we are talking specifically about relationships between businesses and their customers, it is important that we agree on a few of the elements that make up a genuine relationship. And while dictionary definitions are not bad as starting points, the most important issue for us to consider is how well our own definition of *relationship* helps companies succeed in the "customer dimension" of competition. So, rather than settle for a few words from a dictionary, let's list some of the distinct qualities that should characterize a relationship between an enterprise and a customer.

First, a relationship implies **mutuality.** In order for any "state of affairs" to be considered a relationship, both parties have to participate in and be aware of the existence of the relationship. This means that relationships must inherently be two-way in nature. This might seem like common sense. You can't have a relationship with another person if she doesn't have a relationship with you, right? But it's a very important distinction for parsing out what does and doesn't constitute relationship-building activities with customers. Can a person have a genuine relationship with a brand? Well, it doesn't happen just because the customer herself likes the brand and buys it repeatedly. A customer can have a great deal of affection for a brand all by herself but, by our definition, a relationship between the customer and the brand can be said to exist only if the brand (i.e., the enterprise behind the brand) is also aware of the individual customer's existence, creating a neodefinition with an interesting new twist for the term *brand awareness.*

Second, relationships are driven by *interaction.* When two parties interact, they exchange information, and this information exchange is a central engine for building on the relationship. Information exchange, of course, also implies mutuality. But interactions don't have to take place by phone or in person or on the Web. An interaction takes place when a customer buys a product from the company that sells it. Every interaction adds to the total information content possible in the relationship.

Continuing Roles for Mass Media and Branding

- Communicate to nonusers who have not yet raised their hands.
- Build image and brand identity.
- Establish a brand position with nonusers to help users make a statement about their own image.

---

[4] Relationship: Merriam Webster Online Dictionary, www.merriam-webster.com/dictionary/relationship, accessed February 4, 2016.

This point leads to the third characteristic of a relationship: It is **iterative** in nature. That is, since both parties are interacting mutually, the interactions themselves build up a history over time—a context. This context gives a relationship's future interactions greater and greater efficiency, because every successive interaction represents an iteration on all the previous ones that have gone before it. The more you communicate with any one person, the less you need to say the next time around to get your point across. One practical implication of the iterative nature of a customer relationship is that it generates a convenience benefit to the customer for continuing the relationship. Amazon.com remembers your book preferences, your address, and your credit card number, based on your previous interactions with it. To purchase your next book from Amazon.com, you need only find the book and click on it. If you've bought enough books already at Amazon.com, you might not even need to find the next one—the company can do a pretty good job of finding it for you. The richer the context of any customer relationship, the more difficult it will be for the customer to re-create it elsewhere, and so the more loyal the customer is likely to be. (We find that Amazon.com recommends to each of us all of the new books we write—not surprising, since they're all very relevant!)

Another characteristic of a customer relationship is that it will be driven by an *ongoing benefit* to both parties. Convenience is one type of benefit for customers, but not the only one. Participating in a relationship will involve a cost in money, time, or effort, and no customer will engage for long in any relationship if there is not enough continuing benefit to offset this cost. However, precisely because of the context of the relationship and its continuing benefit to both parties, each party in a relationship has an incentive to recover from mistakes. This is because the future value that each party expects from the continued relationship can easily outweigh the current cost of remedying an error or problem.

Characteristics of a Genuine Business Relationship

- Mutual
- Interactive
- Iterative
- Provides ongoing benefit to both parties
- Requires a change in behavior for both parties
- Unique
- Requires—and produces—trust

Relationships also require a *change in behavior* on the part of both parties—the enterprise as well as the customer—in order to continue. After all, what drives the ongoing benefit of a relationship is not only its context—its history of interactions, developed over time—but also the fact that each party's current and future actions appropriately reflect that historical context. This is an important characteristic to note separately, because companies sometimes mistakenly believe that interactions with customers need only involve routine, outbound communications, delivered the same way to every customer. But unless the enterprise's actions toward a particular customer are somehow tailored to reflect that customer's own input, there will be no ongoing benefit for the customer, and as a result the customer might not elect to continue the relationship.

Yet another characteristic of a relationship, so obvious it might not seem worth mentioning, is *uniqueness*. Every relationship is different. Relationships are constituted with individuals, not with populations. As a result, an enterprise that seeks to engage its customers in relationships must be prepared to participate in different interactions, remember different histories, and engage in different behaviors toward different customers.

Finally, the ultimate requirement and product of a successful, continuing relationship is *trust*. Trust is a quality worth a book all by itself,[5] but fundamentally what we are talking about is the commonsense proposition that if customers develop a relationship with an enterprise, they tend more and more to trust the enterprise to act in their own interest. Trust and affection and satisfaction are all related feelings on the part of a customer toward a company with which he has a relationship. They constitute the more emotional elements of a relationship; but for an enterprise to acknowledge and use these elements profitably, it must be able to reconcile its own culture and behavior with the requirement of generating and sustaining the trust of a customer. (For more on this issue, see Chapters 3 and 9.)

Over 20 years ago, business professors Jag Sheth and Atul Parvatiyar predicted that companies are "likely to undertake efforts to institutionalize the relationship with consumers—that is, to create a corporate bonding instead of a bonding between a frontline salesperson and consumer alone."[6]

Customer orientation is powerful in theory but, some say, troubled in practice. In some industries, customer satisfaction rates in the United States fall while complaints, boycotts, and other consumer discontent rise, fueled in size and velocity by social media. Some say there has been a decline in the fundamentals of relationship building among enterprise executives who are more concerned with increasing quarterly profits for their own sake than establishing closer ties to profitable customers.

---

[5] See Don Peppers and Martha Rogers, Ph.D., *Extreme Trust: Turning Proactive Honesty and Flawless Execution into Long-Term Profits* (New York: Portfolio/Penguin, 2016); Stephen M. R. Covey and Greg Link with Rebecca R. Merrill, *Smart Trust: The Defining Skill That Transforms Managers into Leaders* (New York: Free Press, 2012); Chris Brogan and Julien Smith, *Trust Agents: Using the Web to Build Influence, Improve Reputation, and Earn Trust* (Hoboken, NJ: John Wiley & Sons, 2009); and Charles H. Green, *Trust-Based Selling: Using Customer Focus and Collaboration to Build Long-Term Relationships* (New York: McGraw-Hill, 2006).

[6] Jagdish N. Sheth and Atul Parvatiyar, "Relationship Marketing in Consumer Markets: Antecedents and Consequences," *Journal of the Academy of Marketing Science* 23, no. 4 (1995): 265. See also Atul Parvatiyar and Jagdish N. Sheth, eds., *Handbook of Relationship Marketing* (Thousand Oaks, CA: Sage, 1999).

Every aspect of customer relationship management and managing customer relationships and experiences is affected by the firm's understanding of relationships. Enterprises must examine and fully comprehend the basic foundations of relationships in general, and the basic principles of the Learning Relationship in particular, before embarking on a customer relationship or customer experience initiative.

Views on relationships and their role in business vary, but all provide a relevant perspective to building a framework for relationships. Jim Barnes says that relationships between enterprises and their customers can exist at four different levels[7]:

1. *Intimate* relationships are characterized as personal and friendly and generally involve the disclosure of personal information. Such relationships may involve physical touch, as in the relationship between doctors and patients or hairstylists and clients.
2. *Face-to-face* customer relationships may or may not require the customer to reveal personal information. Such relationships often occur in a retail store.
3. *Distant* relationships involve less frequent interactions and might occur over the telephone, online, or through videoconferencing.
4. *No-contact* relationships rarely or never require a customer to interact with an enterprise directly. Customers typically interact with a distributor or agent, as in the case of buying a favorite brand of soda at a supermarket.

We should also acknowledge that a company may build a "relationship" with a customer that the customer has no emotional interest in. By learning from a customer, or a small group of customers with similar needs and behaviors, the company may be able to offer the right product at the right time and provide convenience to a customer who may not be emotionally attached to the product or company but does more and more business with it because it's easier to continue with the current provider than to switch. In many other cases, of course, the "relationship" is specifically enjoyed by the customer—at the extreme by the Harley-Davidson customer who tattoos the company's brand on his bicep.

We have discussed the foundation of relationship theory and the benefits of getting, keeping, and growing customers, and, so far, the discussion has included concepts that foster an often-emotional involvement between the customer and the enterprise. The Learning Relationship is a highly personal experience for the customer that ensures that it is always in the customer's self-interest to remain with the enterprise with which he first developed the relationship. We believe this may go beyond emotional attachment and beyond a customer's favoritism for any enterprise. It may or may not be derived from some sense of obligation or duty. Instead, many scholars believe that by establishing a Learning Relationship, the customer-focused enterprise increases customer retention by making loyalty more beneficial for the customer than non-loyalty.

---

[7] James G. Barnes, *Secrets of Customer Relationship Management* (New York: McGraw-Hill, 2001).

Here, we present a different view of customer relationships: Although many disagree, Jim Barnes believes relationships work only when the customer acknowledges that we are having one.

Building Genuine Customer Connections: A Framework for Understanding Customer Relationships

James G. Barnes
Professor Emeritus, Memorial University of Newfoundland, and Chief Customer Strategist, BMAI-Strategy

The establishment of relationships is a fundamental part of human life. Most people have many different relationships, some of which have lasted for many years, and some of which are closer or more intimate than others. When people think about "relationships," most often they think of personal relationships that are most important to them, namely, those with family, friends, neighbors, classmates, or the people with whom they work. Some close relationships are very important to us, and we would feel a tremendous sense of loss if the people involved were no longer around. We trust them, we rely on them, and they play a central role in our lives.

What is really interesting is that people often use very similar language when they talk about businesses with which they deal or brands that they buy regularly. Can customers establish a long-lasting relationship with a brand of ketchup, a coffee shop, or a hotel chain? I suspect the folks at Heinz, Starbucks, and Marriott would unanimously agree that they can and do. We can all think of brands that we and our families have been using for years or even for generations. We all have favorite restaurants, a regular pub or sports bar, a deli where Julie behind the counter knows exactly how thick to slice our pastrami, and a stylist who has been cutting our hair just right for years.

They Are People, After All

At the end of the day, customers are people and they bring to the role of customer the same set of needs and emotions that they exhibit in other facets of their daily lives. If a business is interested in establishing genuine (as opposed to synthetic or artificial) relationships with its customers, relationships that will last for many years, then it must understand the psychology that underlies the establishment of relationships in general.

Customers do not deliberately set out to establish relationships with other people or with brands of shampoo, cologne, or beer. Relationships evolve over time, and some evolve to the point where there is an extremely strong connection with the company or brand. Relationships must be nurtured and, once they are established, customers feel a genuine, long-lasting sense of loyalty to the company. Most customers want to deal with businesses and use brands that they can trust and rely on; organizations with which they feel comfortable and that treat them fairly and honestly. Unless business executives understand how customers develop such relationships and what customers get from them, they will not begin to understand how to build a solid customer connection.

Many businesses focus their attention on the development of customer relationships and acknowledge that customers do indeed develop strong emotional connections to certain companies and brands. Most understand the potential long-term value of a loyal customer. It is clearly more productive for a business to encourage its customers to come back and do business with it over and over again rather than having to deal with **customer churn,** where new customers must be recruited in a constant struggle to replace those who are leaving. One of the objectives, therefore, in building customer relationships is to reduce customer turnover by increasing retention.

Retention Is Not a Relationship

But customer retention is not the same as a customer relationship. Retention, meaning that customers continue to buy from a company over time—they have been retained—is essentially a behavioral concept. There are many ways in which businesses succeed in encouraging customers to return—including so-called loyalty programs—none of which leads to the establishment of genuine customer relationships. Retention is behavioral loyalty; relationships imply the existence of **emotional loyalty.**

A relationship in its simplest form and as understood by customers is based on feelings and emotions. It is not behavioral, although there are behavioral outcomes of customers developing solid relationships with firms; customers go back again and again, they spend more money there, they buy more items at full price, rather than waiting for the sales, and they speak glowingly about the company or brand to their friends and associates. But such behavior is the *result* of the relationship and not the relationship itself.

There is, however, a tendency in some businesses to mistake behavior for loyalty. Just because customers buy a large percentage of their items in a particular product or service category from a certain company or visit on a regular basis does not mean that they are loyal or that a relationship exists. It is possible for a company to develop a high level of "behavioral loyalty" among its customers, while having relatively little emotional loyalty. For example, many customers will buy a large percentage of their groceries from a supermarket that is close

(continued)

(Continued)

to their home. They shop there every week and they have been doing so for years. When asked why they are "loyal," customers will point to factors such as convenience of location, 24-hour opening, large parking lots, speedy checkouts, one-stop shopping, and so on. All of these reasons relate to functional factors that drive repeat buying. These customers may be described as "functionally loyal" because the factors that drive their behavior are largely functional or operational.

Among the functionally loyal, there is often a notable absence of a sense of attachment to the company—little or no emotional connection. If these behaviorally loyal regular shoppers were to move across town or to a new city, they would likely seek out an equally convenient supermarket for most of their grocery shopping. This form of loyalty, therefore, is extremely vulnerable; there is no relationship from the customers' perspective. As soon as they see a better deal or more convenience elsewhere, they're gone.

Contrast this with other customers who shop regularly at the same supermarket, often driving past two or three competing supermarkets to get there. When asked why they shop where they do, they will say that they are known there, employees recognize them, they feel comfortable shopping there, they have come to know the cashiers and engage in conversation with them, or they go there with friends for coffee. There is among this group of customers evidence of *emotional* loyalty, a connection between the company and its customers, a lasting bond that is grounded not in functional factors, but in genuine emotions. When these customers move to a new location, they seek out a branch of *their* supermarket.

Who Decides It's a Relationship?

Customer relationships develop over time, just as do interpersonal relationships. No company or brand can simply decide that it will establish a relationship with a particular group of customers and then go out and do it, because it is the customers themselves who will decide whether a relationship can develop. Relationships are, by definition, two-sided in nature; they must be mutually felt. We all know what happens to relationships where only one of the parties is getting any benefit. Therefore, in order to attract customers to the point where a relationship might be said to exist, a company must genuinely care about its customers. For a customer relationship strategy to work, a company must establish a focus on the customer, a commitment to a genuine understanding of the customer, and a culture in which every employee believes that the customer comes first. In short, the company needs to have a **customer strategy,** one focused on ensuring that everything the company does is oriented toward building solid customer relationships.[a]

Think for a moment about those businesses and brands to which you and your family return again and again. You probably wouldn't do so unless you were receiving some unique form of value that you simply can't get anywhere else. You feel special when you walk through the door. The employees know you there and treat you like a friend. They engage in conversation with you and go out of their way to help you find the things you need. You trust their advice. You can rely on them to deliver on time, and offer you quality products at a reasonable price.

Actually, you may even admit that you may be paying a slightly higher price than you could get from a competing business, but it is worth it to you because of the other, less tangible things that you derive from the relationship. Such companies create value beyond price. In fact, they are able to *earn* the prices they charge precisely because of the additional emotional value they provide.

By thinking about the relationships that you, your friends, and family have already established with businesses, we begin to reveal some of the essential characteristics of genuine customer relationships. You don't go back to your favorite businesses only because they have the lowest price in town or because they have a frequent-shopper program. You go back primarily because of how you are treated, the quality of service provided, the people with whom you deal, and ultimately how you are made to feel.

I make what I believe is an important distinction between *genuine* customer relationships and those that are artificial or synthetic. Some companies, through the use of marketing tools such as frequent-shopper or frequent-flyer programs, have succeeded in creating high levels of behavioral loyalty, driven largely by the rewards that customers obtain by giving a company a large share of their business. Will such programs succeed in driving an increased share of wallet and repeat buying? Yes, in many cases they will. But such attempts to build customer relationships are not based on a strategy to create an emotional connection, but rather see relationships from the perspective of the company and the benefits that it will derive from increased frequency of purchase.

At the end of the day, it is the customer who understands what a customer relationship involves. One of the difficulties that some businesses have in establishing long-lasting customer relationships stems from the fact that many simply don't understand their customers.

The Need for Insight

One of the fundamental needs that underlie the establishment of successful customer relationships is for companies to obtain the kind of insight needed to understand what is actually a very complex concept. They must understand customers and they must understand the nature of the genuine relationship. If

(continued)

(Continued)

we are to truly understand the emotional connection between customers and brands, then we need to understand how customers live their daily lives and where various companies and brands fit in. What role do they play? What does Heinz ketchup or Starbucks coffee or Chanel No. 5 really enable a customer to do? What does The Home Depot, or State Farm, or Wells Fargo help customers accomplish?

To obtain customer insight, we must understand customers as people. We need a more *humanistic* view of customers and of marketing.[b] We need to understand what they need to get done in their daily lives, what their goals and ambitions are, and how they define success. By knowing such things, a business can understand how it can play a role in allowing customers to accomplish the things that they want to get done and to achieve success. On the other hand, insight gathering also involves understanding the things that customers wish to avoid or that they dread happening. Understanding those things that customers do not want to happen allows a business to intervene and help the customer in preventing them. Understanding the complexities of consumer behavior and how customers develop lasting relationships requires deep thinking on the part of marketing practitioners and involves the application of principles from psychology and other human sciences.[c]

Companies that are successful in building genuine relationships with customers are rewarded well into the future. Not only do they experience lower rates of customer turnover, but their customers stay with them longer, give them a higher share of spend, buy more items at full price, reduce their tendency to shop around, and recommend the company or brand to their friends and family members. Think again about those companies and brands that you couldn't do without and how you deal with them. That's how genuinely loyal customers treat their favorite stores and brands.

A Framework for Understanding: The 5 E's of Customer Relationships

The following represents a framework that I have developed that helps me think more deeply about the concept of customer relationships and the factors that are important in allowing companies and brands to connect more closely with their customers. I've labeled it the 5 E's of Customer Relationships.

CUSTOMER ENVIRONMENT　　If a company is to be successful in establishing genuine relationships with a large number of its customers, it must first have a deep understanding of the *environment* in which the customer operates. We are dealing here with the notion of **customer context;** everything that customers do happens within a wider context. Every day, customers have things they must get done; they face challenges and opportunities. There are things that they are looking forward to and things that they dread. Companies, if they are to understand how to build relationships, must first understand what is going on in the lives of their customers. What are their goals; what are they trying to accomplish; what are they looking forward to? Only by knowing such things can a company play the role of partner or facilitator in helping its customers get those things done.

Many years ago, Harvard professor Theodore Levitt famously observed that no customer ever went out to buy a quarter-inch drill. What the customer needed, of course, was a quarter-inch hole. This was Levitt's insightful way of saying that all products and services are bought, not for their own inherent features, but for what they enable their purchasers to do; people need solutions to what they are facing. More recently, Christensen et al. (2007) have written about the job that we hire products to do, suggesting that the customer at the supermarket this afternoon doesn't really want or need those raspberries he is buying; what he really wants is an attractive dessert to serve his guests at dinner.[d] Every product and service a customer buys represents a means to an end. What the customer really wants to accomplish is often three or four steps ahead and well out of the sight of the business.

Some authors have written of "conceptual consumption," arguing that not only do customers buy products and services for the outcomes they provide, but even more for the feelings or emotions those products enable them to enjoy or avoid.[e] Therefore, we buy a Canon DSLR camera, not only to enable us to have photographs to show friends or to post on Facebook, but more important to enshrine memories and to facilitate sharing. Similarly, we don't buy paint merely to obtain a fresh new look in the living room, but to hear the "oohs" and "aahs" of friends and neighbors.

To be able to facilitate success by enabling customers to achieve the things they need to get done, to receive the accolades of friends, or to look good in the eyes of people who are important to them, companies must understand the context in which customers are operating. Companies that succeed in helping customers achieve the praises of guests for a dessert well-made or the favorable comments of visiting parents-in-law when they enter the recently decorated living room will be well on their way to establishing genuine customer relationships.

CUSTOMER EXPECTATIONS It probably goes without saying that, in order to be successful in impressing customers, companies should set out to at least meet customer *expectations*. The company that falls short of meeting expectations can be confident that customers are already moving on to deal with one of its competitors. Meeting customer expectations is obviously important, but is not sufficient to move customers toward the establishment of genuine relationships.

(continued)

(Continued)

Research has shown that customers have considerable difficulty verbalizing what they expect from the companies with which they deal.[f] My experience is that customer expectations are, for the most part, largely predictable and bounded by the customer's experience in dealing with similar companies or brands. For example, if we were to ask a customer who is planning a business trip to Chicago what she expects of the airline that will be taking her there, she is likely to tell us that she expects to be able to buy her ticket online, to check in from her office, to be able to check her suitcase efficiently, to have her flight depart and arrive on time, and to find her suitcase intact on the luggage carousel when she arrives.

In short, the customer expects the airline to do exactly what well-run airlines are expected to do, nothing more. Her expectations extend primarily to operational components of the travel experience. The customer will be satisfied if the airline delivers on those things that she expects of it, and will likely give it a 9 or even a 10 in a postflight customer satisfaction survey if they get all of these things right. *But, satisfaction does not make a relationship.* Satisfaction is a short-term state driven mainly by predictable, operational aspects of the company's value proposition. Other research indicates that even the most satisfied customers remain receptive to competitive offers and are prone to defect.[g] A customer relationship that has achieved only satisfaction is a vulnerable one.[h]

What our airline customer is *not* expecting may be just as important as what she expects of the airline. She is clearly not expecting a flight attendant to retrieve the iPhone that she has left in the seat pocket and to bring it to her as she stands at the baggage carousel. These are the kind of events that customers don't think of when they are asked to state their expectations. Yet, by delivering her iPhone, the flight attendant has exceeded subconscious expectations and created a state of customer delight. That episode then becomes the basis for storytelling; you know, the ones that always begin, "You'll never believe what happened to me yesterday. . . ."

From the company's perspective, it is as important to understand what customers are not expecting as it is to know what they are expecting. Ultimately, *customers are not expecting to be surprised.* Creating customer surprise by doing the unexpected is an important part of building genuine, emotion-based customer relationships. As Lehrer (2009) observed, "nothing focuses the mind like surprise."[i] Companies should plan to surprise and delight their customers more often; to deliver *story-worthy* customer experiences.

CUSTOMER EMOTIONS Relationships are essentially *emotional constructs*. When asked about their most important relationships, most people will make mention of other people with whom they are close: family members, friends, neighbors, workmates, their Saturday morning foursome, the girls on the bowling team.

In other words, people generally use the word *relationships* when discussing interpersonal connections. But customers also build emotional connections with companies and brands—ultimately reaching a stage where they would miss them if they were no longer available.

In attempting to build genuine customer relationships, companies must, therefore, set out to reduce negative emotions and strengthen positive ones.[j] It is useful, in this regard, to think about a hierarchy of emotions, ranging from relatively weak emotions to particularly strong ones. On the negative side, some fairly mild emotions are merely irritants. For example, a customer may experience confusion, annoyance, or frustration in dealing with a certain business. These feelings may not lead the customer to decide never to deal with the company again, but, if left unaddressed, may lead to a situation where the customer simply walks away, or at least "tweets" negatively. If a company continues to frustrate, disappoint, let down, or ignore its customers, ultimately more strongly felt negative emotions such as anger, hatred, and disgust will emerge and any hope of developing a long-term relationship will be lost.

However, positive customer relationships that last for years or even decades begin with some relatively weak positive emotions such as comfort level, friendliness, and affection. Ultimately, the strongest and longest-lasting customer relationships are characterized by deep positive emotions that are regularly referred to by loyal customers, including love, pride, and respect. In research projects that I have conducted with a major telecom company and an international grocery chain we found more than 70 percent of customers agreed with the statement, "I am proud to be a _____ customer." We regularly hear shoppers comment, "I just love shopping there."

CUSTOMER EXPERIENCE   There has been a lot of attention paid in recent years to the customer *experience,* and it represents an important contribution to an expanded view of how relationships develop.[k] Simply put, a succession of positive experiences is likely over time to develop into a genuine relationship. On the other hand, inconsistency in the delivery of the customer experience—or, worse, a series of negative experiences—will lead to little hope of solid relationships being developed. Unfortunately, many businesses seem to take a narrow view of what customer experience entails, often seeing it simply as the *in-store* experience or the *online* experience. As a result, they fail to realize the potential that exists to create long-lasting customer relationships through delivering impressive customer experiences.

Some writers on the subject suggest that the customer experience is something that can be orchestrated or that must involve some form of entertainment.[l] But *every* interaction with a company or brand is an experience, whether it involves face-to-face contact with employees, telephone interaction with a call

(continued)

(Continued)

center, online buying, visits to the Web site or Facebook page, or actual use of the product. My research suggests that companies need to think about customer experiences at four levels.

First, and this is the view of customer experience that is most often discussed in business, companies must be *easy to do business with*. This assumes that customer experience is all about access and convenience; how easy do we make it for customers to order from us, to get served in our stores, to speak with someone on the telephone? Being "easy to deal with" means returning their calls, delivering when we said we would, and generally not putting barriers in the way of good service.

Second, I believe that an important part of the customer experience involves *interaction with employees*. Many customer experiences involve meeting or talking with employees or others who represent the company or brand. This interpersonal interaction is central to the development of a positive customer relationship. Indeed, many customer relationships are based on the customer's relationship with individual employees—think travel agents, mechanics, and hair stylists. This view that the customer experience is delivered or cocreated by employees suggests implications for human resources and is one of the main reasons why HR must be an active partner in the development of a customer relationship strategy.

Third, we must realize that the customer experience does not end when the customer makes the purchase—there is *post-sale experience*. Many services, for example, are continuously delivered, and the customer experiences the service on an ongoing basis, often without giving it a lot of thought. The customer, therefore, has an ongoing relationship with banks, cable and telecom companies, Internet service providers, and others. In the case of tangible products, many are used for months if not years. The satisfaction and enjoyment that the customer obtains from "product in use" is important in determining whether a long-term relationship will develop. So an important part of the customer experience involves delivery, helping set up the product, helping the customer obtain maximum value from it, fixing it if it breaks, and offering advice on how to use it properly. Often, this seems to be forgotten by businesses. For example, I hear from customers of auto dealers who do not receive any communication for the entire length of the four-year lease. Customers feel let down, disappointed, or abandoned as a result. Companies need to have a "keep in touch" strategy, making occasional meaningful contact with customers as they use their products and services. Not doing so represents a missed opportunity to strengthen the relationship.

Finally, businesses need to think about the customer *experiences that they can create or enhance*. This represents a proactive side of customer experience delivery. Think about the kinds of experiences that companies create by organizing workshops, inviting customers to seminars, or providing them with meaningful, relevant, and, therefore, valuable information. Think, for example, how The Home Depot helps the "all-thumbs" father build that tree house for his son. Think also about how Avis might make my long weekend in the Napa Valley truly memorable. Think how Canon might help me get a "You took that!!??!!" reaction when my friends see the framed black-and-white photo in my living room.

CUSTOMER ENGAGEMENT   Customer relationship strategists have increasingly focused on the creation of *customer engagement.*[m] This concept builds on the notion that, by involving customers more in the production and delivery of products and services, we can create a higher level of commitment. How, for example, can we get customers to become partners, to become involved in the cocreation of products and services, to become actively engaged in the delivery of desired solutions and outcomes? This is, I believe, an important part of the success that IKEA has enjoyed around the world. Not only does this much-admired company offer reasonably priced furniture of reasonable quality, but the customer puts part of himself into every item through his involvement in its assembly.

Dell allows its customers to build their own laptop computers. Customers go to The Home Depot to learn how to lay ceramic tile or to build shelves in the kids' closet. Committed customers of the Running Room train together with other novice runners for their first 10K race. In all cases, the customer puts something of himself or herself into the creation of the value proposition by partnering with the business to get something done, to achieve success. An engaged and involved customer is more likely to spread positive word of mouth, to create communities for the business, leading to a codependency that eventually becomes a solid, genuine relationship.

Customer engagement is now seen as a logical extension of and a result of ongoing positive customer experiences. Over time, as a result of being closely involved with a firm—through various forms of interaction—a sense of connection develops that goes well beyond being merely satisfied with the effective delivery of transactions.[n] Truly engaged customers become advocates and provide genuine endorsements and referrals, leading to customer-led growth for the firm.

Overview

The most successful customer relationships are those grounded in an emotional attachment. Companies must accept the fact that, if they hope to see customers coming back again and again, and singing their praises to friends and family members, they must pay attention to how they make their customers feel. To

(continued)

(*Continued*)

really impress their customers, they will also have to invest in customer insight so they can truly understand what those customers need to get done and how they need companies and brands to help them. Customer relationship building should not be seen as the sole or even the principal responsibility of the marketing department[o]; in fact, building customer loyalty must be accepted as the responsibility of every employee. Lasting customer relationships and, ultimately, high levels of customer engagement result from the consistently effective delivery of customer experiences, the responsibility for which rests largely with the employees with whom customers interact.

[a] J. G. Barnes, *Build Your Customer Strategy: A Guide to Creating Profitable Customer Relationships* (Hoboken, NJ: John Wiley & Sons, 2006).

[b] Rowena Heal, "Seven Ways to Humanise Your Brand," downloaded from mycustomer .com, November 6, 2015.

[c] Christian Madsbjerg and Mikkel B. Rasmussen, *The Moment of Clarity: Using the Human Sciences to Solve Your Biggest Business Problems* (Boston: Harvard Business School Press, 2014); Gerald Zaltman and Lindsay Zaltman, *Marketing Metaphoria: What Deep Metaphors Reveal about the Minds of Consumers* (Boston: Harvard Business School Press, 2008).

[d] Clayton M. Christensen, S. D. Anthony, G. Berstell, and D. Nitterhouse, "Finding the Right Job for Your Product," *MIT Sloan Management Review* 48, no. 3 (2007): 38–47.

[e] D. Ariely and M. I. Norton, "Conceptual Consumption," *Annual Review of Psychology* 60 (2009): 475–499.

[f] V. A. Zeithaml, L. L. Berry, and A. Parasuraman, "The Nature and Determinants of Customer Expectations of Service," *Journal of the Academy of Marketing Science* 21, no. 1 (1993): 1–12.

[g] R. L. Oliver, *Satisfaction: A Behavioral Perspective on the Customer*, 2nd ed. (Armonk, NY: M. E. Sharpe, 2009).

[h] Scott Magids, Alan Zorfas, and Daniel Leemon, "What Separates the Best Customers from the Merely Satisfied," downloaded from hbr.org, December 3, 2015.

[i] Jonah Lehrer, *How We Decide* (Boston: Houghton Mifflin Harcourt, 2009).

[j] Scott Magids, Alan Zorfas, and Daniel Leemon, "The New Science of Customer Emotions," *Harvard Business Review* 93, no. 11 (November 2015): 66–76.

[k] Christopher Meyer and Andre Schwager, "Understanding Customer Experience," *Harvard Business Review* 85, no. 2 (February 2007): 117–126.

[l] B. Joseph Pine II and James H. Gilmore, *The Experience Economy: Work Is Theatre and Every Business a Stage* (Boston: Harvard Business School Press, 1999).

[m] Peter C. Verhoef, Werner J. Reinhartz, and Manfred Krafft, "Customer Engagement as a New Perspective in Customer Management," *Journal of Service Research* 13, no. 3 (2010): 247–252.

[n] Jennifer D. Chandler and Robert F. Lusch, "Service Systems: A Broadened Framework and Research Agenda on Value Propositions, Engagement, and Service Experience," *Journal of Service Research* 18, no. 1 (February 2015).

[o] Alexander Jutkowitz, "Marketing Is Dead, and Loyalty Killed It," downloaded from hbr.org, February 18, 2015.

Customer Loyalty: Is It an Attitude? Or a Behavior?

Definitions of customer loyalty usually take one of two different directions: attitudinal or behavioral. Although each of these directions is valid, when used separately, they have different implications and lead to very different prescriptions for businesses. The most helpful way for businesses to approach the issue of improving customer loyalty is to rely on both these definitions simultaneously.

Attitudinal loyalty implies that the loyalty of a customer is in the customer's state of mind. By this definition, a customer is "loyal" to a brand or a company if the customer has a positive, preferential attitude toward it. He likes the company, its products, its services, or its brands, and he therefore prefers to buy from it, rather than from the company's competitors. In purely economic terms, the attitudinal definition of customer loyalty would mean that someone who is willing to pay a premium for Brand A over Brand B, even when the products they represent are virtually equivalent, should be considered "loyal" to Brand A. But the emphasis is on "willingness" rather than on actual behavior per se. In terms of attitudes, then, increasing a customer's loyalty is virtually equivalent to increasing the customer's preference for the brand. It is closely tied to customer satisfaction, and any company wanting to increase loyalty, in attitudinal terms, will concentrate on improving its product, its image, its service, or other elements of the customer experience, relative to its competitors.

Behavioral loyalty, however, relies on a customer's actual conduct, regardless of the attitudes or preferences that underlie that conduct. By this definition, a customer should be considered "loyal" to a company simply because she buys from it and then continues to buy from it. Behavioral loyalty is concerned with repurchase activity, rather than attitudes or preferences. Thus, it is theoretically possible for a customer to be "loyal" to a brand even if they don't really like it, provided there are other reasons for repeat purchase. A discount airline with poor service standards, for instance, might have customers who are behaviorally loyal but not attitudinally loyal, if its prices are significantly lower than those of other airlines. (Some Londoners lamented that they hated RyanAir every weekend they took it to Barcelona!) And a business-to-business firm selling complex services may rely on long-term contracts in order to ensure it is adequately compensated for high setup costs. (We once participated in a meeting with high-tech executives at their headquarters in which one of the executives joked that their primary customer loyalty tactic was probably the lawsuit.) In its most raw form, behavioral loyalty is similar to what can be described as **functional loyalty,** in that there is no emotional content or sense of attachment to the company on the customer's part.

In the behavioral definition, customer loyalty is not the *cause* of brand preference but simply one *result* of it, and brand preference is not the only thing that might lead to behavioral loyalty. A company wanting to increase behavioral customer loyalty will focus on whatever tactics will in fact increase the amount of repurchase. These tactics can easily include improving brand preference, product quality, or customer satisfaction, but they may also include long-term legal contracts or prices so low that service is almost nonexistent.

Behavioral customer loyalty is easier to measure because it can be objectively observed, while assessing attitudinal loyalty requires more expensive and subjective polling and surveying techniques. But positive attitudes do tend to drive positive behaviors. Even if a firm observes *loyal* behavior, if the customer has no genuine *attitude* of loyalty, then the relationship will be highly vulnerable to competition. If a competitor enters the market at a comparable price, for instance, the customer once loyal to your discount product can easily disappear.[8] The truth is, if an enterprise wants a clear and unambiguous guide to action, it needs to pay attention to both definitions of customer loyalty. Attitudinal loyalty without behavioral loyalty has no financial benefit for a firm, but behavioral loyalty without attitudinal loyalty is unsustainable. Defining loyalty purely as an attitude is not very useful, because that attitude can exist completely apart from any continuing relationship on the part of a customer, and this simply flies in the face of the common English definition of the word *loyalty*. Customer A and Customer B might have an equally loyal *attitude* toward a particular product, but what if Customer A has never even consumed that product before, while Customer B has consumed it regularly in the past? Moreover, attitudinal loyalty and brand preference seem to be redundant, so why introduce a separate term at all? However, defining loyalty in purely behavioral terms is equally unsatisfactory; monopolies have behaviorally loyal customers.

A better insight into what customer loyalty really means can be gained by examining the policies companies introduce to improve it. A credit card company or mobile phone carrier, for instance, often concerns itself with reducing its "customer churn" rates. *Churn* is a colloquial term meaning "defection." These companies often can count the customers who voluntarily elect to leave their franchises every month, and it is a legitimate and time-honored business practice to try to reduce this churn rate. A company usually tackles the churn problem with both reactive and proactive tactics. Reactive tactics can include predictive modeling to identify those customers who are most likely to try to leave the franchise in the near future and then trying to intercede in advance; or actively trying to persuade churning customers not to leave at the point they announce they want to defect; or perhaps attempting to win defectors back immediately with offers of special pricing or improved services. Proactive tactics, however, can include identifying as many of the service and pricing problems

> Attitudinal loyalty without behavioral loyalty has no financial benefit for a firm, but behavioral loyalty without attitudinal loyalty is unsustainable.

---

[8] Thanks to Doug Pruden (http://customerexperiencepartners.com), Esteban Kolsky (www.estebankolsky.com), Wim Rampen (http://contactcenterintelligence.wordpress.com), and Mark Ratekin (www.walkerinfo.com) for their insights provided in comments on our Strategy Speaks blog post: http://www.peppersandrogersgroup.com/blog/2009/10/customer-loyalty-is-it-an-atti.html#more.

that cause customers to want to leave in the first place, and trying to fix them; or perhaps designing new, customized products and services that do a better job of locking customers in for convenience reasons; or improving service friendliness and competence to increase customer affection for the brand.

A company trying to reduce its customer churn—and thereby increase its customer loyalty—shouldn't think of customer churn as a disease but as the symptom of a disease, somewhat like a fever. If a fever is severe enough, the doctor will want to treat it immediately and directly, but she also knows that the only long-term solution to reducing a fever is to cure the underlying disease causing it. If we pursue this analogy, we could visualize a lack of behavioral loyalty in our customer base as a fever that is affecting our company while the actual disease causing this fever is a lack of attitudinal loyalty.[9]

When dealing with the issue of customer loyalty, a firm should try to forge as direct a connection as possible to loyalty's actual financial results. That is, we ought to be able to "connect the dots" between whatever strategies and tactics we employ to increase our customers' loyalty and the actual economic outcomes of those actions. The **customer-strategy enterprise** will want to quantify the benefit of a customer's increasing loyalty, and the most direct and unambiguous metric to deploy for this task is the customer's *lifetime value,* as described in Chapter 5.

Loyalty Programs

A "loyalty program" is a promotion that awards points, miles, or other benefits to a customer in exchange for the customer's doing business with the program's sponsoring company. Also known as a frequent-shopper or frequent-flyer program, loyalty programs are sometimes referred to as *frequency marketing.* The distinction between behavioral and attitudinal loyalty, however, suggests an important criterion for evaluating the benefits and effects of whatever loyalty program a company implements.

Probably the most commonly found type of program is one that simply awards prizes to customers and ends right there, with little effort put into transforming the company's subsequent behavior or "treatment" of individual customers to reflect the needs or preferences revealed by the customer's own transactions. The problem is that while awards and prizes will in fact generate behavioral loyalty, by themselves they amount to little more than bribes for customer transactions—really just a sophisticated form of price competition. The faux loyalty generated will have little impact on customer attitudes or intentions,

(continued)

---

[9] Thanks to former Peppers & Rogers Group consultant Ozan Bayulgen for this very useful "fever" analogy.

(Continued)

as evidenced by the fact that most consumers are members of several different loyalty programs for competitive firms simultaneously.

A more effective kind of loyalty program is one that uses the information provided by a customer's rewarded behavior to fashion more relevant, personalized, or satisfying services or offers for that individual customer, thereby earning more and more of the customer's attitudinal loyalty as well. In this kind of program the discounts and prizes given to customers are, in effect, incentives to ensure that the company can accurately track customer transactions and interactions over time, allowing it to compile a useful profile of customer needs and to tailor future offers and experiences for that customer.

Tesco, the largest grocery retailer in the United Kingdom, was the first major company to use a combination of technology and relationship strategy to execute a true loyalty program. Beginning in 1994, the Tesco Clubcard program used the information generated by its Clubcard membership to tailor each of its mailing pieces to each of its millions of Clubcard member households individually, through mass-customized printing capabilities.[a] Each mailing piece included personally relevant offers for its addressee and represented incremental income for Tesco, based on an estimated 25 percent response rate. (In Chapter 4, we will talk more about how Tesco's capability to identify individual customers contributed to its success.)

Loyalty programs have become ubiquitous marketing tools in a variety of industries, from grocery stores and airlines to credit-card and packaged-goods retailers, restaurant chains, and others. They are even used as a tool for managing and engaging employees and for encouraging healthy lifestyle habits. Starbucks became the first major retailer in the United States to offer its own mobile payment technology tied to a popular loyalty program and generates over three million mobile transactions a week in the United States alone.[b] As these kinds of programs have proliferated, however, a few important "best practices" have emerged, exemplified by successful programs from Sainsbury and Starwood Hotels and Resorts, among others,[c] which we can summarize in this way:[d]

- *Never waste an opportunity to gain insight about a customer.* An effective loyalty program will offer a choice of services or treatments that reveal something about a customer's personal preferences. For example, if customers can identify their own prize in advance, the company can gain additional insight into what motivates particular customers. Loyalty programs in financial services, for instance, take advantage of the insights gained by identifying someone who chooses an award for lifetime achievement compared to one who chooses the largest prize for short-term behaviors. Providing points in return for completing surveys or responding to inquiries can also generate insight.

- *An effective program offers modularity, enabling participants to mix and match aspects to their own preferences.* Modular offerings are a practical way to allow for customer-driven personalization of a program without going to the extreme of full customization. Key aspects of the program, such as member qualification, can be developed with several alternatives, and customers can be offered a set of guided choices to select from. A sophisticated marketing approach would offer different sets of choices for different groups of customers based on their value—so everybody wouldn't be choosing from the same set. For example, a lower-value customer might choose from rewards alternatives that include a service upgrade, while high-value customers might have choices that include additional redemptions or alternative merchandise. In addition, modularity will allow a program to incorporate partners and cosponsors more easily.

- *Consumers value openness. They want a service or program that works with other programs.* The more open a loyalty program is, the more beneficial and attractive it will be to customers. Transferable points and rewards offer the customer the greatest flexibility in using program earnings. As a program gains confidence and customer insight, it can mature to a more and more open proposition without endangering customer loyalty, because the barrier to a customer's switching will no longer be pure economics (i.e., the value of the points earned) but convenience (having to "teach" another program about individual desires and preferences). Openness is inevitable in loyalty marketing programs, and companies must choose whether to lead the charge or to react to it.

- *A loyalty program should be managed around customers, not products.* The customer-strategy firm will align the organization of a loyalty program around certain identified sets of customers and then measure people by the positive impact they have on customer behaviors within these different groups. The marketing effort should be organized so that the customers whose behaviors are intended to be affected are the responsibility of managers whose evaluations are based on improving the numbers. This is the most direct way to make progress in each customer segment and to improve the loyalty (and lifetime values) of the individual customers in each segment.

- *Above all else: simplicity.* A program with fewer rules and restrictions is more engaging to the customer. It's better for a company to narrow its offers to those that can be delivered dependably rather than to include elements that can't be relied on. Airline programs frequently suffer, for instance, when they offer high-value redemptions that are not very readily available. Such offers often do more harm than good, by unnecessarily raising customer expectations and then not delivering. If a company can't deliver reliably on what it promises in its loyalty program, it risks undermining trust in the brand.

(continued)

(*Continued*)

---

[a] "Tesco Clubcard Signs Up One Million Customers since Relaunch," *Marketing Magazine*, October 5, 2009, available at www.marketingmagazine.co.uk/news/943397/Tesco-Clubcard-signs-one-million-customers-relaunch/, accessed September 1, 2010.
[b] Marie-Claude Nideau and Marc Singer, "The Secret to Creating Loyalty Programs That Actually Work," *Business Insider*, March 21, 2014, available at http://www.businessinsider.com/effective-loyalty-programs-2014--3, accessed February 4, 2016; Bruce Horovitz, "Earn Starbucks Loyalty Points beyond Cafes," *USA Today,* March 20, 2013, available at http://www.usatoday.com/story/money/business/2013/03/20/starbucks-loyalty-program/2003583/, accessed February 4, 2016; Jim Tierney, "Loyalty Program Triggers Starbucks' Record Q2," *Loyalty360 Daily News*, April 26, 2013, available at http://loyalty360.org/resources/article/loyalty-program-triggers-starbucks-record-q2, accessed February 4, 2016. See also Starbucks's privacy policy at http://www.starbucks.com/about-us/company-information/online-policies/privacy-policy.
[c] Nideau and Singer, "The Secret to Creating Loyalty Programs That Actually Work"; *Hotel Management* editorial staff, "Starwood Targets Meeting Planners with SPG Pro Loyalty Program," *Hotel Management,* October 13, 2014, available at http://www.hotelmanage-ment.net/sales-marketing/starwood-targets-meeting-planners-travel-agents-with-spg-pro-loyalty-program-29151, accessed February 4, 2016; Mark R. Vodrasek, "Redefining Service Innovation at Starwood," *McKinsey Quarterly*, February 2015.
[d] Although most studies, including corporate and industry research reports, find that successful loyalty programs improve company financial performance, not everyone is convinced; Nideau and Singer do not tout the connection: Nideau and Singer, "The Secret to Creating Loyalty Programs That Actually Work."

The important thing to remember about loyalty programs is that most are just a "me, too" way of reducing profit margin. Once all the major players in a space offer one, it's just a bribe for doing business with a particular restaurant, store, airline, or product consumable. In contrast, the best-practice loyalty programs are the ones that offer a reward in exchange for ongoing customer information (shopping basket data, or preferred services and routes, for example) and then *use that information* to serve a customer better than a company that does not have the information.

Summary

Our goal for this chapter has been to give the reader a grounded perspective of how Learning Relationships enable enterprises to develop more personalized and collaborative interactions with individual customers. Our next step is to begin to understand "the business sense" of building a customer-strategy enterprise. Learning Relationships, after all, result in many pragmatic and financial benefits, not only for the customer but also for the enterprise that engages in them. The objective of increasing the overall **value of the customer base** by getting, keeping, and growing one customer, and then another and another, is achieved through these highly interactive relationships.

The enterprise determined to increase the value of the customer base will start with a commitment to increase customer value and then move to implement the strategic levels of the Learning Relationship. The tasks needed to make this happen are: identifying their customers individually, ranking them by their value to the company, differentiating them by their needs, interacting with each of them, and customizing some aspect of the business for each. From the enterprise's perspective, these tasks are by no means chronological or finite. We will examine each of them more carefully in the next chapters.

Food for Thought

1. Based on what we now know about the essence of relationships, is it possible for a customer to have a relationship with a commercial (or other) firm? Is it possible for a customer to have a relationship with a brand? Is it possible for a firm to have a relationship with a customer—especially a customer who is one of millions of customers? If you said no to any of these questions, what conditions would have to be met before a relationship *would* be possible?

2. James Barnes says an important ingredient to a good relationship is an emotional connection, but customer relationships have elsewhere been referred to as a *bond of value* or a *bond of convenience*. What do you think? Do customers have to love a product or company in order to have a "relationship" with that enterprise? Or is a perceived benefit—especially one that grows from a vested interest—enough? How would you approach a debate on this controversy?

3. Pick a brand that you will always buy. What happened specifically to create this loyalty from you? Is there anything that could dissolve your loyalty or make it even stronger?[10]

Glossary

Age of Transparency   The era of human history characterized by increasing levels of transparency in all human affairs, as a result of the pervasive interconnectedness of people, using social media and other ubiquitously available communications technology.

---

[10] This question was suggested by reviewer John Westman.

ıal loyalty *or* emotional loyalty (*see also* Behavioral loyalty) Atti- ˌcustomer loyalty, also called *emotional loyalty,* is manifest by a customer's good wishes or affection toward a product or brand. When a customer "likes" a brand, as measured in surveys of customer opinions or attitudes, the customer can be said to be attitudinally loyal.

Behavioral loyalty *or* functional loyalty (*see also* Attitudinal loyalty) Behavioral customer loyalty, also called *functional loyalty,* is evidenced by a customer's repeated patronage, as measured by the customer's actual buying behavior.

Customer churn The rate at which customers leave and enter the franchise. High churn indicates a simultaneously high number of defecting customers and high number of new customers. Usually a symptom of low customer loyalty. Also called *churn rate.*

Customer context The environment in which the customer operates.

Customer equity (CE) The value to the firm of building a relationship with a customer, or the sum of the value of all current and future relationships with current and potential customers. This term can be applied to individual customers or groups of customers, or the entire customer base of a company. See also the definition of *customer equity* in chapter 11, especially as it relates to customer *lifetime value.*

Customer experience The totality of a customer's individual interactions with a brand over time.

Customer orientation An attitude or mind-set that attempts to take the customer's perspective when making business decisions or implementing policies.

Customer strategy An organization's plan for managing its customer experiences and relationships effectively in order to remain competitive. Customer strategy is building the value of the company by building the value of the customer base.

Customer-strategy enterprise An organization that builds its business model around increasing the value of the customer base. This term applies to companies that may be product oriented, operations focused, or customer intimate.

Emotional loyalty *See* Attitudinal loyalty.

Functional loyalty *See* Behavioral loyalty.

Information Age "A period in human history characterized by the shift from traditional industry that the Industrial Revolution brought through industrialization, to an economy based on information computerization." [Wikipedia]

Iterative Building on itself. Conversations are iterative when they pick up where they left off. A customer relationship can be "iterative" if both the enterprise and the customer remember their previous interactions with each other, so that with future interactions they do not need to start all over again from the beginning. In effect, an iterative relationship is one that gets smarter and smarter over time, as an enterprise conforms its behavior (for this particular customer) with the customer's previously expressed needs and preferences.

Mutuality   Refers to the two-way nature of a relationship.

Procedural fairness   Based on the perception that procedures and processes are fair and are focused on behaviors, regardless of outcome.

Relational (collaborative) versus discrete (transactional) customer strategies   Relational customer strategies take into account the lifetime costs and payoffs of the total of all projectable interactions and transactions with a customer, while discrete or transactional strategies are based primarily on the directly measurable financial value of the current transaction. This distinction is important because the cost of maintaining a customer relationship is often incurred in the current period, while the value achieved by the relationship might not be realized until later, in future (non-current) transactions. For example, a company following a relational customer strategy will likely be willing to resolve a customer's complaint about a single transaction by taking a loss on the current transaction, while a company following a transactional strategy will not.

Value of the customer base   *See* Customer equity.

PART II

IDIC Implementation Process: A Model for Managing Customer Relationships and Improving Customer Experiences

In order for a firm to build customer value through managed relationships and best-practice customer experiences, the company must identify customers, differentiate them, interact with them, and customize some aspect of its behavior toward them.

CHAPTER 3

Customer Relationships: Basic Building Blocks of IDIC and Trust

The purest treasure mortal times can afford is a spotless reputation.

—William Shakespeare

Building good customer experiences may look easy. But in order for a firm to build customer value through managed relationships, the company must engage in a four-step process we call **IDIC** (*identifying* customers, *differentiating* them, *interacting* with them, and *customizing* for them). These steps represent the mechanics of any genuine relationship, which by definition will involve **mutuality** and customer-specific action. But while the IDIC process represents the *mechanics* of a relationship, generating a customer's trust should be the most important *objective* of that process. Relationships simply cannot happen except in the context of customer trust. In succeeding chapters, we take a more detailed look at each of the IDIC tasks as well as at the subject of trust itself, but for now, what's important is to get an overview of both the mechanics and the objective of relationship building.

We've seen that the customer relationship idea has many nuances. For instance, there likely will be an emotional component to most successful customer relationships (at least in consumer marketing), but it's important to recognize that the reverse of this statement is not necessarily true: The fact that you have an emotional attachment to a company does not mean you have a relationship with that company.

We can't afford to dismiss entirely the notion that nonemotional relationships between an enterprise and its customer do, in fact, exist. For instance, you probably have no actual emotional connection with one or more banks whose credit cards you carry in your wallet. But, everyone keeps asking, does that mean you have no *relationship* with such a company, even though it communicates with you monthly, tracks your purchases, and (at least in the best cases) proactively offers you a new card configuration based on your own personal usage pattern? Yes, there might be an element of emotion involved in this relationship, but must that always be the case?

Conversely, you might have a highly emotional attachment to an enterprise, but if the enterprise itself isn't even "aware" that you exist, does this constitute anything we can call a relationship? The simple truth is that, in most cases, your relationship with a brand is analogous to your relationship with a movie star. You might love his movies, you might follow his activities avidly via social media, but will he even know who you are? It can be said to be a relationship only if the movie star some-how also acknowledges it—through personally responding to your posts or inviting you to events, for example. This is because, as we said in Chapter 2, the most basic, core feature of any *relationship* is mutuality. Mutual awareness of another party is a prerequisite to establishing a relationship between two parties, whether we are talking about movie star and fan or enterprise and customer. People who are emo-tionally involved with a brand, not unlike the most avid fans of a rock music group, are usually engaged in one-way affection. There's nothing wrong with this at all. One-way affection for a brand has sold a lot of merchandise. But this kind of affec-tion will be only part of a relationship if the brand is mutually involved; and in the overwhelming majority of cases, it is not.

So let's return to the basic, definitional characteristics of a relationship, as outlined at the beginning of Chapter 2, and try to derive from this list of charac-teristics a set of actions that an enterprise ought to take if it wants to establish relationships with its customers through deeper insights that lead to better expe-riences. A relationship is mutual, interactive, and **iterative** in nature, develop-ing its own richer and richer context over time. A relationship must provide an ongoing benefit to each party; it must change each party's behavior toward the other party; and it will therefore be uniquely different from one set of relation-ship participants to the next. Finally, a successful relationship will lead each party to trust the other. In fact, the more effective and successful the relationship is, from a business-building standpoint, the more it will be characterized by a high level of trust.

Trust and Relationships Happen in Unison

We've been looking at relationship characteristics that are part of analytic descrip-tions of the nature of a relationship while the last characteristic—trust—is a much richer term that could serve as a proxy for all the affection and favorable emotion that most of us associate with a successful relationship. In any case, what should be apparent from the outset is that we are talking about an enterprise engaging in customer-specific behaviors. That is, because relationships involve mutuality and uniqueness, an enterprise can easily have a wonderful relationship with one customer but no relationship at all with another. It can have a deep, very profitable relationship with one customer but a troubled, highly unprofitable relationship with another. An enterprise cannot have the same relationship with both Mary and Shirley any more than Mary can have the same relationship with both her banker and her yoga instructor.

A business strategy based on managing customer relationships, then, necessarily involves treating different customers differently. A firm must be able to identify and recognize different, individual customers, and it must know what makes one customer different from another. It must be able to interact individually with any customer on the other end of a relationship, and it must somehow change its behavior to meet the specific needs of that customer, as it discovers those needs. And to build trust, it must act in the customer's best interest as well as its own.

In short, in order for an enterprise to engage in the practice of treating different customers differently, it must integrate the customer into the company and adapt its products and services to the customer's own, individual needs. But as a company begins to understand the customer, interact with him, learn from him, and provide feedback based on that learning, the customer's view of what he is buying from the company will probably also begin to change. For instance, a person may shop at L.L. Bean initially to buy a sweater. But over time, he may browse the L.L. Bean Web site or flip through the catalog to match other clothes to the sweater, or look for Christmas gift ideas, or research camping equipment. Now L.L. Bean has become more than just a place to buy sweaters; it is a source of valuable information about future purchases. Ultimately, this is likely to increase the importance of trust as an element in the relationship. So will the no-questions-asked return policy as well as the fast, reasonably priced shipping. The more the customer trusts L.L. Bean, the more likely he will be to accept its offers and recommendations (which in turn are based on his own clicks and purchasing history).[1]

It is customer information that gives an enterprise the capability to differentiate its customers one from another. Customer information is an economic asset, just

---

[1] See Linn Viktoria Rampl, Tim Eberhardt, Reinhard Schütte, and Peter Kenning, "Consumer Trust in Food Retailers: Conceptual Framework and Empirical Evidence," *International Journal of Retail & Distribution Management* 40, no. 4 (2012): 254–272; Michele Gorgoglione, Umberto Panniello, and Alexander Tuzhilin, "The Effect of Context-Aware Recommendations on Customer Purchasing Behavior and Trust," in *Proceedings of the Fifth ACM Conference on Recommender Systems* (New York: ACM, 2011), 85–92; Peter Kenning, "The Influence of General Trust and Specific Trust on Buying Behaviour," *International Journal of Retail & Distribution Management* 36 (2008): 461; and Ellen Garbarino and Mark Johnson, "The Different Roles of Satisfaction, Trust, and Commitment in Customer Relationships," *Journal of Marketing* 63 (April 1999): 70–87.

like a piece of equipment, a factory, or a patent. It has the capability to improve an enterprise's productivity and reduce its unit costs. Individual customer information, if used properly, can yield a return for many years. And because customer information is based on an individual, not a group, it is more useful for its scope rather than its scale. When two enterprises are competing for the same individual customer's business, the company with the greatest scope of information about that customer and the ability to use it will probably be the more effective competitor. And because technology now makes it possible for businesses of nearly any size to keep track of individual relationships with individual customers, the scale of a company's operations may become less important as a competitive advantage. Cultivating a profitable customer relationship with any one customer will depend primarily on having information about that specific customer and using it wisely. It will matter more than who has the biggest pile of customers.

Once a company begins to take a customer-specific view of its business, it will begin to think of its customers as assets that must be managed carefully, in the same way any other corporate asset should be managed. From a strictly financial perspective, this kind of strategy will tend to focus more corporate resources on satisfying the needs of those customers offering higher long-term value to the firm while limiting or reducing the resources allocated to lower-value customers. But, operationally, increasing the long-term value of a particular customer will necessitate addressing that customer's own individual needs, even to the point of tailoring—or at least mass-customizing—individual products and services for individual customers.

> Cultivating a profitable customer relationship depends primarily on having information about a specific customer and using it wisely. It matters more than who has the biggest pile of customers.

The technologies that allow a company to track individual customers and treat them differently have made it possible to create what is, in effect, an individual *feedback loop* for each customer. This loop ensures that a successful relationship continues to get better and better, one customer at a time. When such a relationship exists between a customer and an enterprise, many traditional marketing principles, formerly held sacred, will simply be irrelevant, at least insofar as that particular customer is concerned. No longer must the enterprise rely on surveys of current or potential customers to determine which action is appropriate for this customer; nor is it necessary to plot the reach and frequency with which its advertising message is getting out, in order to determine its effectiveness with *this* customer. Instead, the customer and the enterprise are mutually engaged in a continuously improving relationship: "I know you. You tell me what makes this work for you. I do it. You tell me if I did it right. I remember that, and I do it even better for you next time."

However you look at it, trust is probably the single most important ingredient in any personal interaction or relationship. After all, if what you learn from someone else can't be trusted, then it's not worth learning, right? And if you want to have any kind of influence with others, then what you communicate to them has to be seen as being trustworthy. Short of threat of job loss or brute force, in fact, being trustworthy is the only way your own perspectives, suggestions, persuasive appeals, or demands can have any impact on others at all. Whether you're telling or selling, cajoling or consoling, what matters most is the level of trust others have in you.[2]

Most businesses and other organizations think that they're already customer-centric and that they are basically trustworthy, even though their customers might disagree. How is the **customer service** at your organization? Seventy-five percent of CEOs think they "provide above-average customer service," but 59 percent of consumers say they are somewhat or extremely upset with these same companies' service. In one infamous study reported by Bill Price and David Jaffe, 80 percent of executives thought their companies provided superior customer service, but only 8 percent of the customers of those companies thought they received it.[3]

Even though no company can ever be certain what's in any particular customer's mind, companies today do have much more capable technologies for analyzing their customers' needs and protecting their interests. Sometimes, all that's required for a superior experience that leads to a valuable relationship is for a company to use its own processes to help a customer avoid a costly and preventable mistake. Peapod, the online grocery service, for instance, has software that will check with you about a likely typo before you buy something highly unusual ("Do you really want to buy 120 lemons?").[4]

And the best companies are also using their greatly improved information technology (IT) capabilities to do a better job of remembering their customers' individual needs and preferences, and then becoming smarter and more insightful over time, and using this insight to create a better customer experience. Imagine how a company might use its own database of past customer transactions for the customer's benefit. If you order a book from Amazon that you already bought from the company, you will be reminded before your order is processed. Same with iTunes. These are examples of genuinely trustable behavior. In each case, the company's database gives it a memory that can sometimes be superior to the customer's memory. It would not be cheating for Amazon or iTunes simply to accept your money, thank you very much.

And note that "doing the right thing," at least in this case, is mutually beneficial. Even as Amazon offers you the chance to opt out of a purchase you've

---

[2] See Ed Keller and Brad Fay, *The Face-to-Face Book: Why Real Relationships Rule in a Digital Marketplace* (New York: Free Press, 2012).

[3] Bill Price and David Jaffe did some pretty interesting research for their book, *The Best Service Is No Service* (San Francisco: Jossey-Bass, 2008), including looking at the discrepancies between how good companies think their service is and how lousy the customers think it is.

[4] The Peapod example comes from Ian Ayres, *Super Crunchers: Why Thinking-by-Numbers Is the New Way to Be Smart* (New York: Bantam, 2007), p. 170.

already made, they also reduce the likelihood that you'll receive the book, realize you already have it, and return it. And when iTunes warns you that you're about to duplicate a song you already own, they are making it less likely they'll have to execute a labor-intensive and costly refund process, or that you'll think badly of them aloud on Twitter. This is exactly how "reciprocity" is supposed to work—as a win-win.

In addition to the company–customer feedback loop involving clickthroughs and purchasing history, customer satisfaction surveys, questionnaires, and even customer complaints across devices, a company may also gain insight about customer wants, needs, or expectations by monitoring customers' social media communications with other customers (see Chapter 8). A company has the opportunity to learn from conversations taking place in online social networks. This is highly important for companies trying to build relationships with their customers for three main reasons:

1. Social networks have high impact on the flow and quality of information. As opposed to a belief in impersonal and generic sources, customers prefer to rely on peers and their perspectives.
2. Information within networks disseminates quickly across devices and impacts word-of-mouth referrals and recommendations.
3. Social networks of customers also carry the implication of trust as the information becomes more personalized with experience and familiarity of the members of the social network.[5]
4. Even beyond known members of a network, the total strangers, who are viewed as peers, who rate products and services on Web sites, are also trusted as references and recommenders for or against products, making Amazon.com one of the largest social networking sites in the world.

The secret to keeping and growing a single customer forever is this feedback loop. Creating it requires the customer's own participation and effort along with his trust in the company that's getting his information. It is the effort on the part of the customer that results in a better product or service than the customer can get anywhere else from any company that is not so far up a particular customer's learning curve. The successive interactions that characterize such a Learning Relationship ultimately result in the enterprise's capability to make its products and services highly valuable to an individual customer; indeed, the Learning Relationship, because it is unique to that customer, and because it has been formed in large part from the customer's own participation, can become *irreplaceably* valuable to that customer, ensuring the customer's long-term loyalty and value to the enterprise.

---

[5] See Mark Granovetter, "The Impact of Social Structure on Economic Outcomes," *Journal of Economic Perspectives* 19, no. 1 (Winter 2005): 33–50; and Clara Shih, *The Facebook Era* (Boston: Pearson Education, 2009), pp. 29ff.

IDIC: Four Implementation Tasks for Creating and Managing Customer Experiences and Relationships

Setting up and managing individual customer relationships can be broken up into four interrelated implementation tasks. These implementation tasks are based on the unique, customer-specific, and iterative character of such relationships. We list them roughly in the sequence in which they will likely be accomplished, although, as we see later in this book, there is a great deal of overlap among these implementation tasks (e.g., an enterprise might use its Web presence primarily to attract the most valuable customers and identify them individually rather than as a customer interaction platform), and there may be good reason for accomplishing them in a different order:

> An enterprise must be able to recognize a customer when he comes back, in person, by phone, online, or wherever.

1. ***Identify*** *customers.* Relationships are possible only with individuals, not with markets, segments, or populations. Therefore, the first task in setting up a relationship is to identify, individually, the party at the other end of the relationship.

Many companies don't really know the identities of many of their customers, so for them this first step is difficult but absolutely crucial. For all companies, the "identify" task also entails organizing the enterprise's various information resources so that the company can take a customer-specific view of its business. It means ensuring that the company has a mechanism for tagging individual customers not just with a product code that identifies what's been sold but also with a customer code that identifies the party that the enterprise is doing business with—the party at the other end of the mutual relationship. An enterprise must be able to *recognize* a customer when he comes back, in person, by phone, online, by mobile app, or wherever. Moreover, enterprises need to "know" and remember each customer in as much detail as possible—including the habits, preferences, and other characteristics that make each customer unique. When you log in to Cabela's online account, the company knows about your last order, because you've been identified.

> Customers represent different levels of value to the enterprise, and they have different needs from the enterprise. The customer's needs drive his behavior, and his behavior is what the enterprise observes in order to estimate his value.

2. ***Differentiate*** *customers.* Knowing how customers are different allows a company (a) to focus its resources on those customers who will bring in the most value for the enterprise, and (b) to devise and implement customer-specific strategies designed to satisfy individually different

customer needs and improve each customer's experience. Customers represent different levels of value to the enterprise, and they have different needs from the enterprise. The customer's needs drive his behavior, and his behavior is what the enterprise observes in order to estimate his value. Although not a new concept, *customer grouping*—the process by which customers are clustered into categories based on a specified variable—is a critical step in understanding and profitably serving customers. Specifically, the "customer differentiation" task involves an enterprise in categorizing its customers by both their value to the firm and by what needs they have. Some call centers constantly change the order to serve based on the different values of those customers who are waiting on hold. Although it would be ideal to answer every call on the second ring, when that's not possible, it would be better to vault the customers keeping you in business ahead of the customers of lower value. In most contact centers, this reshuffling is not at all apparent to customers.

3. ***Interact*** *with customers.* Enterprises must improve the effectiveness of their interactions with customers. Each successive interaction with a customer should take place in the context of all previous interactions with that customer. A bank

> A conversation with a customer should pick up where the last one left off. And a company should never ask the same question twice.

may ask one question in each month's electronic statement, and next month's question may depend on last month's answer. A conversation with a customer should pick up where the last one left off. Effective customer interactions provide better insight into a customer's needs and don't waste a customer's time by asking the same question more than once, even in different parts of the organization.

4. ***Customize*** *treatment.* The enterprise should tailor the customer's experience, based on that individual's needs and value, to make it more relevant to the customer, to make the customer's life a little easier and better. To engage a cus-

> The enterprise should adapt some aspect of its behavior toward a customer, based on that individual's needs and value.

tomer in an ongoing Learning Relationship, an enterprise needs to adapt its behavior to satisfy the customer's expressed needs. Doing this might entail mass-customizing a product or tailoring some aspect of its service.[6] This customization could involve the format or timing of an invoice or how a product is packaged.

This IDIC process implementation model can also be broken into two broad categories of activities: *insight* and *action* (see Exhibit 3.1). The enterprise conducts

---

[6] Marisa Peacock, "Demand for Tailored Customer Experiences Put Brand Loyalty at Risk," CMSWire, March 20, 2013, http://www.cmswire.com/cms/customer-experience/demand-for-tailored-customer-experiences-put-brand-loyalty-at-risk-020137.php, accessed February 11, 2016; and Don Peppers, Martha Rogers, Ph.D., and Bob Dorf, *The One to One Fieldbook: The Complete Toolkit for Implementing a 1to1 Marketing Program* (New York: Doubleday, 1999).

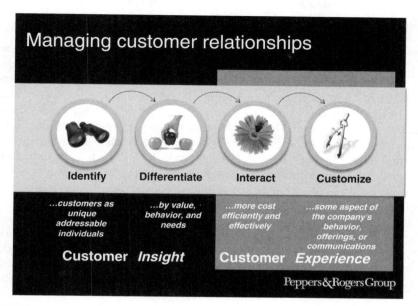

EXHIBIT 3.1   IDIC: Analysis and Action

the first two tasks, identify and differentiate, behind the scenes and out of the customer's sight; they constitute *insight*. The latter two tasks, interact and customize, are customer-facing steps that require participation on the part of the individual customer. Visible to the customer, they constitute *action*. You'll recall from Chapter 1 that "interacting" and "customizing" are the two capabilities an enterprise must have in order to engage customers in relationships and that the degree to which a firm uses each of these capabilities is an easy way to categorize the type of **customer strategy** it is pursuing—mass, niche, database, or one-to-one Learning Relationship. We can also think of the identify and differentiate steps as the tasks that make up "analytical customer relationship and experience management" or "customer insight," while interact and customize are the tasks involved in "operational customer relationship and experience management" or "customer experience."

Throughout the rest of this book, we refer back to this set of four implementation tasks as the *IDIC methodology*. As a model for relationship management processes, this methodology can be applied in any number of situations. For instance, it could help a company understand the steps it must take to make better use of its call center for initiating and strengthening customer relationships. Applied to a sales force, it could be used to understand the strengths and weaknesses of a new contact management application or to improve a sales compensation policy. We devote specific chapters in the book to examining all the activities and processes, as well as the pitfalls and problems, associated with each of these four tasks.

How Does Trust Characterize a Learning Relationship?

Before we begin this journey, we will spend the rest of this chapter discussing in greater detail just what it means to say that trust is a quality that will characterize a good customer relationship. In an enterprise focused on customer-specific activities, any single customer's purchase transactions will take place within the context of that customer's previous transactions as well as future ones. The buyer and seller collaborate, with the buyer interacting to specify the product, and the seller responding with some change in behavior appropriate for that buyer. In other words, the buyer and seller, in a relationship, must be willing to trust each other *far beyond the general reputation of the brand*. By extension, we can easily see that the more "relationship-like" any series of purchase transactions is, the more that trust will become a central element in it.

When a company is focused on building **customer equity**, earning customer trust becomes an inherent goal of its decision making. It's not possible to balance the creation of long- and short-term value, to build Return on Customer, or to focus resources on getting customers to share information that helps us build superior customer experiences unless the company understands that the lifetime values of customers are just as important as current sales and profits.

A relationship of trust is one in which both parties feel "comfortable" continuing to interact and deal with each other, whether during a purchase, an interaction, or a service transaction. Trust rarely happens instantaneously. Even if the trusted source has been recommended by another, a customer must "feel" the trust from within before he will begin to divulge personal information about himself.

The Speed of Trust

Stephen M. R. Covey
Cofounder and CEO, CoveyLink Worldwide

Simply put, trust means confidence. The opposite of trust—distrust—is suspicion. When you trust people, you have confidence in them—in their integrity and in their abilities. When you distrust people, you are suspicious of them—of their integrity, their agenda, their capabilities, or their track record. It's that simple. We have all had experiences that validate the difference between relationships that are built on trust and those that are not. These experiences clearly tell us the difference is not small; it is dramatic.

■ ■ ■

Trust is a function of two things: *character* and *competence*. Character includes your integrity, your motive, your intent with people. Competence includes your capabilities, your skills, your results, your track record. And both are vital.

With the increasing focus on ethics in our society, the character side of trust is fast becoming the price of entry in the new global economy. However, the differentiating and often ignored side of trust—competence—is equally essential. You might think a person is sincere, even honest, but you won't trust that person fully if he or she doesn't get great results. And the opposite is true. A person might have great skills and talents and a good track record, but if he or she is not honest, you're not going to trust that person either. For example, I might trust someone's character implicitly, even enough to leave him in charge of my children when I'm out of town. But I might not trust that same person in a business situation because he doesn't have the competence to handle it. On the other hand, I might trust someone in a business deal whom I would never leave with my children; not necessarily because he wasn't honest or capable, but because he wasn't the kind of caring person I would want for my children.

While it may come more naturally for us to think of trust in terms of character, it's equally important for us to think in terms of competence. Think about it: People trust people who make things happen. They give the new curriculum to their most competent instructors. They give the promising projects or sales leads to those who have delivered in the past. Recognizing the role of competence helps us identify and give language to underlying trust issues we otherwise can't put a finger on. From a line leader's perspective, the competence dimension rounds out and helps give trust its harder, more pragmatic edge.

Here's another way to look at it: The increasing concern about ethics has been good for our society. Ethics (which is part of character) is foundational to trust, but by itself is insufficient. You can have ethics without trust but you can't have trust without ethics. Trust, which encompasses ethics, is the bigger idea.

Excerpt from Stephen M. R. Covey and Rebecca R. Merrill, *The Speed of Trust: The One Thing That Changes Everything* (New York: Free Press, 2006), pp. 5, 30.

According to Covey and Merrill, "the true transformation starts with building credibility at the personal level." The best leaders are those who have made trust an explicit objective, being aware of the quantifiable costs associated with the lack of it in a company or a relationship. One of the simplest ways to look at the quantifiable costs of a so-called soft factor, such as trust, is to think about a simple transaction taking place between two parties. When the two parties in business trust each other, they can act more quickly and minimize the frictional costs of the transaction, such as spending on lawyers, contracts, or due diligence. With the increase in trust in a given relationship, not only are costs lower, but the time required to complete the transaction also goes down significantly. Covey points out that when Warren

Buffett's Berkshire Hathaway acquired McLane Distribution from Wal-Mart, the $23 billion acquisition was sealed over a handshake and completed in less than a month because both parties knew and trusted each other completely. Normally, a deal like this would have required six months or more to execute and perhaps several million dollars of legal and accounting fees.[7]

The element of trust is an indispensable component of a healthy, growing relationship between a company and its customer, but it may not be an absolute requirement for every relationship. A customer may remain in a relationship with a company either because he desires the relationship or simply because he perceives no suitable alternative. It should be obvious, however, which relationship will be the stronger, from the standpoint of increasing the customer's long-term value to the enterprise and encouraging her to be impervious to competitive offers. The customer's own level of commitment to his relationship with a company will depend on the extent to which the relationship derives from dedication, rather than from constraint. Trust-based relationships foster dedication.[8] In one study, researchers determined that "trust, as a higher-order construct," plays "a central role in the relationship customers have with their financial institutions" and in fact, that "trust can have an immediate effect on the decision that customers must make, either to pursue or to end their relationship with a firm."[9]

Enterprises create trust-based customer relationships through the actions of their employees and partners and through company strategies and policies. There are sound ways to think about the trust-building process and the policies necessary to generate trust. In the next section, Charles Green shares his views on trust between customer and supplier by discussing what he calls the "myths" of trust.

---

[7] Stephen M. R. Covey and Rebecca R. Merrill, *The Speed of Trust: The One Thing That Changes Everything* (New York: Free Press, 2006), pp. 13–15. See also Stephen M. R. Covey and Greg Link, with Rebecca R. Merrill, *Smart Trust: The Defining Skill That Transforms Managers into Leaders* (New York: Free Press, 2013).

[8] Younghee Song, Won-Moo Hur, and Minsung Kim, "Brand Trust and Affect in the Luxury Brand–Customer Relationship," *Social Behavior and Personality: An International Journal* 40, no. 2 (2012): 331–338; Nha Nguyen, André Leclerc, and Gaston LeBlanc, "The Mediating Role of Customer Trust on Customer Loyalty," *Journal of Service Science and Management* 6, no. 1 (2013): 96–109; Kuo-Ming Chu, "The Construction Model of Customer Trust, Perceived Value and Customer Loyalty," *Journal of American Academy of Business* 14, no. 2 (March 2009): 98–103; Nelson N. H. Liao and Tsui-chih Wu, "The Pivotal Role of Trust in Customer Loyalty: Empirical Research on the System Integration Market in Taiwan," *Business Review* 12, no. 2 (Summer 2009): 277–283; Gregory S. Black, "Trust and Commitment: Reciprocal and Multidimensional Concepts in Distribution Relationships," *S.A.M. Advanced Management Journal* 73, no. 1 (Winter 2008): 46–55; and Leonard L. Berry, *Discovering the Soul of Service* (New York: Free Press, 1999).

[9] Nguyen, Leclerc, and LeBlanc, "The Mediating Role of Customer Trust on Customer Loyalty," 96–109.

The Trust Equation: Generating Customer Trust

Charles H. Green
CEO, Trusted Advisor Associates

It's no secret: There's a link between strong customer relationships, customer loyalty, and profitability. The economics of customer retention are well understood at this point.

But the role of trust in the economic equation—despite being intuitively related to "loyalty"—is still questioned. High levels of customer satisfaction don't guarantee loyalty (though high levels of dissatisfaction clearly lead to disloyalty). It is only when *extremely* high levels of customer satisfaction are encountered that we find a major upswing in customer loyalty, and hence in customer profitability.

There are some data to suggest that extremely high levels of customer satisfaction and loyalty are also examples of extremely high trust.[a] One study shows that trustworthy publicly traded companies have outperformed market averages as measured by stock prices over a multiyear period.[b]

This suggests the presence or absence of trust is a significant driver of economic profit.

But trust is a deceptively simple concept; the steps required to generate a customer's trust aren't always obvious. Some aspects of trust can appear downright paradoxical—for example, the statement "I don't know" in a sales context is actually more credible than a fumbling attempt at demonstrating competence.

Many discussions of trust fail to clarify whether they are talking about personal or institutional trust. I may trust a company to deliver goods on time, but I only trust people to empathize with the loss of my pet.

A common source of confusion is a failure to distinguish between trustors and trustees. A trust relationship requires an interaction of both—one to do the risk-taking of trusting (the trustor), and the other (the trustee) to prove trustworthy (or not).

But the most helpful clarification may lie in simply better defining "trustworthiness." To do this, consider the Trust Equation. (See Exhibit 3.2 and Exhibit 3.3.)

The first two of these components—credibility and reliability—operate mainly in the rational realm. The second two—intimacy and **self-orientation**—are largely nonrational (*not* the same as irrational).[c]

Since 2007, the Trust Equation has been converted into an online self-assessment called the Trust Quotient, and over 60,000 responses have been collected. The data reveal some findings about trustworthiness, and allow us to counteract some frequent myths.

(continued)

(Continued)

EXHIBIT 3.2   The Trust Equation
Source: Trusted Advisor Associates LLC. © 2010 Trusted Advisor Associates LLC. All rights reserved.

Words	Actions	Safety	Focus
Credibility	Reliability	Intimacy	Orientation
Truthfulness Credentials	Dependability Predictability	Discretion Empathy	Motives Attention
I can trust what she says about…	*I can trust him to…*	*I can trust her with…*	*I can trust that he cares about…*

Trust and Influence

EXHIBIT 3.3   Components of Trustworthiness
Source: Trusted Advisor Associates LLC. © 2010 Trusted Advisor Associates LLC. All rights reserved.

Finding 1: Women are more trustworthy than men.

Trustworthiness has a clear gender bias: women score significantly higher than men, almost entirely due to higher scores on the intimacy component. This statistical result is backed up in our workshops, where only one out of several hundreds of groups around the world, asked on an unprompted basis, felt that men are more trustworthy than women.

This is further backed up by surveys like Gallup's,[d] ranking the trustworthiness of differing occupations. Since 1999, in the United States, nursing has been the number one most trusted occupation. (Least trusted professions typically include politicians, car and insurance salesmen, and lawyers.) It's no accident that nursing is predominantly a female profession.

Finding 2: The most powerful trustworthiness factor is intimacy.

High intimacy scores are more frequently correlated with high overall trust quotient scores than any of the other factors. The least effective component is credibility—a finding that runs counter to strongly held beliefs in many so-called expertise-based businesses.

This emphatically does not mean that credibility or reliability are unimportant. Rather, they are used as gating factors for decisions to buy or to take advice, with the final decision being swayed more by intimacy and low self-orientation. They are also most likely to be cited as reasons for rejection (or acceptance), as in, "People buy with the heart and rationalize it with the brain."

The Trust Equation also allows us to pinpoint several Trust Myths.

Myth 1: Intimate customer relationships require time and proximity.

Fact: Intimacy can be gained instantaneously; it can be conveyed by a tone of voice, by attentive listening, or by a sense of being understood. It isn't dependent on proximity or prior relationships; consider interactions by way of various social media, and conversations between seatmates on transcontinental plane flights.

Myth 2: Trust takes time.

Fact: Only one component of trustworthiness requires the repetition of experiences, not time per se; that component is reliability. And, increasingly, experiences can be accumulated more quickly in a today's connected world.

Myth 3: More customized contact is better.

Fact: If I am passed from one customer service agent to another and the second agent knows my name and transaction history, I find it pleasing. If a cold-call direct marketer knows my name and transaction history, I find it creepy. Context and intent are everything.

Myth 4: People trust companies.

Fact: Reliability and some forms of credibility are the only trust components people associate with enterprises, though, of course, people can have those qualities, too. However, intimacy and self-orientation are traits associated with people alone. Trust in organizations is of a "shallower" type than personal trust, and given to more rapid shifts.

(continued)

(Continued)

Myth 5: People like to be asked their opinion.

Fact: People like to be *listened to,* but that's not the same thing as merely being asked. When was the last time you filled out an anonymous in-room hotel service questionnaire?

The Trust Equation shows us how mindless application of technologies, even with the best of intent, can backfire and reduce trust. For example:

False accuracy. Errors in detailed information, such as street names, reduce credibility.

Presumed intimacy. Using precise information as a lever, as in "Now that you bought green house paint, you'll probably be wanting XYZ," can feel like Big Brother is watching, which not only reduces intimacy but greatly increases perceived self-orientation.

Inconsistent application of CRM. If an automated answering system asks a customer to key in an ID, don't ask her to repeat it verbally later in the call; doing so reduces perceived reliability.

Treating all kinds of trust as fungible. "I trust my dog with my life—but not with my ham sandwich." To be meaningful, we have to ask: Trust to do what? To say what? To behave how?

It is one thing to trust a company to give us good information about benefits of a $10 product; it is another to trust the same company with our private finances. A system that doesn't distinguish between the contexts of trust is a tone-deaf system.

Today's more powerful access to AI [Artificial Intelligence] and Big Data increase the risk of a particular personal foible: giving the "answer" before the customer feels they've been heard. Sales experts like Neil Rackham (and therapists, and counselors, and wise friends) have long pointed out the single biggest error in sales and advice giving is to offer up a solution before the receiver feels their situation has been heard and understood.

To generate trust, the enterprise must address all four components of it in the customer's mind—credibility, reliability, intimacy, and self-orientation (i.e., the self-orientation of the seller).

Credibility Enhancers

Online information is an excellent vehicle for increasing a customer's sense of credibility of the seller. This is partly because the buyer can browse at her own pace and depth. But it is also because the online buyer is free to assess credibility without any of the social interactions necessary to judge intimacy or self-orientation. You don't have to be polite when reading a Web site; nor does the site (usually) tell you to hurry up or slow down.

Reliability Enhancers

Reliability can be enhanced in several ways. The most obvious is to be religious about delivering on promises made: don't ask the customer to input an ID number if you're going to ask him to repeat it later in the call; don't mislead customers regarding availability; and so forth. Another is to create a number of implied promises and then deliver on them. Such promises might include a call back within X minutes, a successful handoff on a service call, or a revision made to a database. Yet another is to improve familiarity; customers perceive as reliable a company that can adapt its ways to their own habits, whether in the form of mildly customized Web sites, adoption of personal terms on a phone call, or matching the formality of language to the other.

Intimacy Enhancers

Customer relationships offer big chances to either increase or destroy intimacy. Intimacy is all about security, comfort, integrity, confidentiality, and a sense of safety. Someone with detailed information about me can make me feel very good or very bad, entirely depending on how they handle that information. If they hide their knowledge of me or pretend it doesn't exist, then they run the risk of appearing like Big Brother. If, however, the information is openly acknowledged, then it can become a useful tool.

Similarly, if a company flaunts customer-specific data with no apparent purpose in mind, it will appear cavalier and untrustworthy. But if it brings specific information to bear on the problem at hand ("Do you want to use the same MasterCard number you used last time?"), then it becomes highly useful.

Consider two different ways a customer service rep (CSR) might use customer-specific information in an interaction with the customer:

Version A
Customer: I'm calling because my computer start button won't engage; it's ticket number LFX897A.

CSR: OK, this is your fourth call on the "won't start" problem. Are you sure you did what we suggested last time?

Version B
Customer: I'm calling because my computer start button won't engage; it's ticket number LFX897A.

CSR: Hmm, my records say this is your fourth call on that ticket number; is that right? You must be getting a little frustrated by now; tell me about the problem.

(continued)

(Continued)

Trust isn't about just having the right technologies or information available. It's about how that information is deployed, how proficiently the customer-contact people operate with it, and, above all, whether the business is prepared to acknowledge that meeting genuine customer needs is the most important overall goal—seen this way, profits are by-products, not goals.

Orientation Enhancers

CRM can increase or decrease trust, and trust can drive firm profitability. But there is a catch-22: You can't use trust to drive profitability if you focus solely on your own bottom line. If anything, the application of CRM raises the already-high stakes on the self-orientation part of the Trust Equation.

Customer focus is widely considered a "good." But there are two kinds of customer focus. One is focus on the customer for the sake of the enterprise. The other is focus directly on the customer's interests, with the belief that if those needs are addressed, the enterprise will also be well served.[e]

Customers know the difference. If the research implications are right—that trusted relationships are profitable relationships—then the fastest way to kill trust is to demonstrate that you are only in it for the money, for yourself. If your customers trust you, you'll be very profitable; but if you try to become profitable by using trust as a self-serving tactic, it won't work.

There is nothing wrong, of course, with strategic customer management, and customer profitability studies, and technological tools. But an enterprise's focus is critical to establishing relationships of trust with its customers. People don't trust enterprises that act clearly, consistently, and only in their own self-interests.

The question is not whether CRM should be used as a profit management tool—of course it should. The larger question is whether profit is best maximized by acting directly on profit levers or by focusing on identifying and meeting customer needs. An enterprise with purely mercenary aims such as "increase share of wallet" or "eliminate unprofitable customers" has a mind-set that is fundamentally self-oriented at the outset. The implementation runs the risk of never getting to the larger, win-win implications of CRM: to find out truly what customers need, and then to make informed decisions on the basis of that knowledge—including customer focus, deselection, and so forth.[f]

---

[a] See Don Peppers and Martha Rogers, Ph.D., *Extreme Trust: Turning Proactive Honesty and Flawless Execution into Long-Term Profits* (New York: Portfolio/Penguin, 2016); and William T. Brooks and Tom Travisano, *You're Working Too Hard to Make the Sale!: More Than 100 Insider Tools to Sell Faster and Easier,* rev. 2nd ed. (Burr Ridge, IL: Irwin Professional Publishing, 2005).

[b] Barbara Brooks Kimmel, "'Return on Trust': The Business Case," *Trust Across America,* Spring 2015, available at http://trustacrossamerica.com/documents/index/Return-Methodology.pdf, accessed February 10, 2016.

[c] *Note from authors:* Charles Green's use of the terms *rational* and *nonrational* closely parallels the more widely accepted terms *cognitive,* which refers to thinking, and *affective,* which refers to feeling. These terms may also be seen as reflecting the current controversy about rational versus "emotional" processes.

[d] "Why Nurses Again Top Gallup's List of 'Most Trusted' Professionals," *Daily Briefing,* Advisory Board Company, January 5, 2015, available at https://www.advisory.com/daily-briefing/2015/01/05/why-nurses-again-top-gallups-list-of-most-trusted-professionals, accessed February 10, 2016.

[e] *Note from authors:* We might say that a vulture is highly customer-centric and customer-focused. It's just that the purpose of the focus has nothing to do with what's good for the "customer"—and everything to do with the vulture itself.

[f] See Trusted Advisor Associates' various articles on the Trust Quotient, an online self-assessment built on the Trust Equation, including Charles H. Green, "Think Expertise Will Make You More Trusted? Think Again" (2015), available at http://trustedadvisor.com/public/files/pdf/TA_White_Paper.pdf, accessed February 10, 2016; and Charles H. Green, "Trust in Business: The Core Concepts" (2007), available at http://trustedadvisor.com/cgreen.articles/38/Trust-in-Business-The-Core-Concepts# equation, accessed February 10, 2016.

> People do not tend to trust enterprises that act clearly, consistently, and only in the company's own self-interest.

Green's outline here of the types of policies and practices necessary to create a trust-building environment for customers is very helpful. One of the most important aspects of his essay is the concept he introduces regarding an enterprise's self-orientation. It is closely akin to what we call the **trusted agent**[10] concept.

---

[10] Don Peppers and Martha Rogers, Ph.D., *Extreme Trust: Turning Proactive Honesty and Flawless Execution into Long-Term Profits* (Portfolio/Penguin, 2016); Edelman, "Executive Summary," Trust Barometer: 2015 Annual Global Study, available at http://www.edelman.com/insights/intellectual-property/2015-edelman-trust-barometer/trust-and-innovation-edelman-trust-barometer/executive-summary/, accessed February 11, 2016; Andrew Winston, "What VW Didn't Understand About Trust," *Harvard Business Review,* September 23, 2015, available at https://hbr.org/2015/09/what-vw-didnt-understand-about-trust, accessed February 11, 2016; David H. Maister, Charles H. Green, and Robert M. Galford, *The Trusted Advisor* (New York: Touchstone, 2000); Charles H. Green, *Trust-Based Selling* (New York: McGraw-Hill, 2006); and Covey and Merrill, *Speed of Trust.*

Becoming More and More Trustable to Customers

Green's formula places the enterprise's perceived level of self-interest in the denominator of the Trust Equation because he believes that the degree to which a customer is likely to trust any company is inversely proportional to the amount of "me-first" attitude shown by the company. The more it appears to a customer that the enterprise is acting in its own interest, the less willing the customer will be to trust the enterprise's suggestions and recommendations. And we know that the more a customer does trust an enterprise, the more the customer is likely to want to continue a relationship with it, increase the scope of the relationship, and recommend the company or product to others.

It follows that the most secure, most influential, most profitable type of relationship between an enterprise and a customer is one in which the customer actually trusts the enterprise to act in his own interest. In such a relationship, the customer perceives the enterprise to be his trusted agent, making recommendations and giving advice that furthers the customer's interest, even when it occasionally conflicts with the enterprise's self-interest, at least in the short term.

With technology reducing barriers between customers and a choice of companies, a seller's reputation is now a distinguishing asset—and one that is continuously available for inspection by the buyer on a variety of online review sites. Trustworthiness has become more transparent, and as a result even distant strangers can confidently conduct business when integrity has been demonstrated and documented. Trust and fairness make the wheels of commerce turn.[11]

Edelman's Trust Barometer underscores the importance to customers of companies that seek to serve customer interests as well as their own. "The trust-building opportunity for business, therefore, lies squarely in the area of integrity and engagement. These areas encompass actions such as having ethical business practices, taking responsibility to address issues or crises, having transparent and open business practices, listening to customer needs and feedback, treating employees well, placing customers ahead of profit and communicating frequently on the state of the business."[12]

In a later section on how to manage the company to be more customer-centric and make customers more valuable, we'll talk more about even higher levels of trust both supported and mandated by emerging technologies and levels of transparency.

---

[11] Maggie McGrath, "Why Consumer Reports Says You Can't Trust Angie's List," *Forbes*, September 18, 2013, available at http://www.forbes.com/sites/maggiemcgrath/2013/09/18/why-consumer-reports-says-you-cant-trust-angies-list, accessed February 10, 2016; Geoff Beattie, "The Number One Thing Consumers Want from Brands? Honesty," FastCompany, November 14, 2014, available at http://www.fastcompany.com/3038488/the-number-one-thing-consumers-want-from-brands-honesty, accessed February 11, 2016; Peppers and Rogers, *Extreme Trust*, and Don Peppers and Martha Rogers, Ph.D., *Rules to Break & Laws to Follow: How Your Business Can Beat the Crisis of Short-Termism* (Hoboken, NJ: John Wiley & Sons, 2008).

[12] Edelman, "Executive Summary," Trust Barometer: 2015 Annual Global Study, available at http://www.edelman.com/insights/intellectual-property/2015-edelman-trust-barometer/trust-and-innovation-edelman-trust-barometer/executive-summary/, accessed February 11, 2016.

For now, let's just look at the basics:

Everybody's talking about "trust" these days, and many use the term as a synonym for what we might call "reputation," or "regard," or "popularity," or "familiarity." Brand equity like this is valuable and worth pursuing, but it's not the same as "trustworthiness," any more than fresh paint and a freshly mown lawn can reveal whether or not a house has a solid foundation.

Some of the best books on business and personal relationships have been written on the broader subject of trust. These books—even just the really good ones—are too numerous to mention here, but we do want to acknowledge the works of Stephen M. R. Covey, Charles H. Green, and a host of others, and we suspect you've read at least some of them. We also acknowledge the work done by the Edelman Trust Barometer[13] and Bruce Temkin. What we need to understand is why transparency means that simple trustworthiness is no longer sufficient, and why a more extreme form of trust—or "trustability"—will soon be the new standard by which consumers measure the businesses and brands they buy from.[14]

---

[13] The principle behind the annual Edelman Trust Barometer is this: Unlike reputation, which is based on an aggregate of past experiences with a company or brand, *trust* is a forward-facing metric of stakeholder expectation. The Edelman Trust Barometer, available at http://www.edelman .com/trust (accessed February 11, 2016), has been surveying the attitudes of the educated toward institutions in twenty-three countries for more than a decade, and it's a crucial source for understanding global and national trends in public trust of institutional sectors such as business, government, nongovernmental organizations, and the media. In 2015, trust in all institutions dropped.

Also see Richard Edelman's Key Findings address, 2011 Trust Barometer Findings: Global & Country Insights, available at http://www.edelman.com/trust/2011/, accessed September 8, 2011.

The Temkin Trust Ratings uses feedback from 10,000 U.S. consumers to rate 268 organizations across 19 industries. Not surprisingly, the bottom of the ratings in 2014 were dominated by TV service providers and Internet service providers.

[14] Stephen M. R. Covey and Rebecca R. Merrill's extremely well-written book *The Speed of Trust: The One Thing That Changes Everything* (New York: Free Press, 2006) is based on this formula: "When trust goes up, speed will also go up and cost will go down. . . . When trust goes down, speed will go down and cost will go up." In their taxonomy, trust is built (and can be rebuilt) on two things: competence and character. (Fundamentally, Covey and Merrill's idea of "character" is parallel to our concept of "good intentions.") They talk about five waves of trust: self-trust (credibility), relationship trust (trust-building behaviors), organizational trust (measuring low-trust "taxes" and high-trust dividends), market trust (reputation), and societal trust (contribution). See also Stephen M. R. Covey and Greg Link, *Smart Trust: The Defining Skill That Transforms Managers into Leaders* (New York: Free Press, 2012). David Hutchens and Barry Rellaford wrote a short fable that succinctly illustrates the power of trust, based on the principles of Covey and Merrill's book: *A Slice of Trust* (Layton, UT: Gibbs Smith, 2011).

Also see David Maister, Charles H. Green, and Robert Galford, *The Trusted Advisor* (Touchstone, 2000); Charles H. Green, *Trust-Based Selling* (McGraw-Hill, 2006); and Charles H. Green and Andrea P. Howe, *The Trusted Advisor Fieldbook: A Comprehensive Toolkit for Leading with Trust* (Hoboken, NJ: John Wiley & Sons, 2011). Green and his colleagues are highly respected for their work in helping companies build trusted relationships with their customers over the years—mostly in B2B settings. Their Trust Equation is based on the idea that self-orientation

For the most part, the business authors who've written about trust in the past have developed their own taxonomies to catalog the various elements that make up trustworthiness, ranging from dependability and reliability to honesty and authenticity. The most direct way to think about trust is in terms of a combination of *good*

---

is the most influential component in building trust—and it's negative. Even if you have all the other components of trust, self-interest can neutralize them all. And to put it all into perspective, see Geoffrey Hosking, *Trust: A History* (Oxford: Oxford University Press, 2014).

$$Trust = \frac{Credibility + Reliability + Intimacy}{Self\text{-}Orientation}$$

More recently, David K. Williams wrote *The 7 Non-Negotiables of Winning* (Hoboken, NJ: John Wiley & Sons, 2013) and emphasized the role of trust in his Forbes.com article, "The Most Valuable Business Commodity: Trust," June 20, 2013, available at http://www.forbes.com/sites/davidkwilliams/2013/06/20/the-most-valuable-business-commodity-trust/#2715e4857a0b7e78cc721c06, accessed February 11, 2016.

Amazon.com's description of Joel Peterson's *The 10 Laws of Trust: Building the Bonds That Make a Business Great* (New York: AMACOM, 2016) describes how JetBlue chairman Joel Peterson explores how a culture of trust gives companies an edge. Consider this: What does it feel like to work for a firm where leaders and colleagues trust one another? Freed from micromanagement and rivalry, every employee contributes his or her best. Risk taking and innovation become the norm. And, as Peterson notes, "When a company has a reputation for fair dealing, its costs drop: Trust cuts the time spent second-guessing and lawyering."

The Compass and The Nail: How the Patagonia Model of Loyalty Can Save Your Business, and Might Just Save the Planet by Craig Wilson (Los Angeles: Rare Bird Books, 2015) examines how companies create rabid loyalty through the company with possibly the most rabid fans, Patagonia.

You may also want to note that in Chris Brogan and Julien Smith's book *Trust Agents: Using the Web to Build Influence, Improve Reputation, and Earn Trust*, 2nd ed. (Hoboken, NJ: John Wiley & Sons, 2010), the authors emphasize that the Web should be treated as one big cocktail party, and your goal should be to humanize and not monetize the Web. The way to be a "trust agent" is to share ideas, facts, and insights freely—knowing that investing in relationships always brings a return eventually, even if you're not focusing on that return in the moment. The goal is to simply be a helpful person—generous and other-focused. This is what builds trust. They advise us never to be "that guy"—who's always trying to turn the conversation back to himself or his business, who makes you want to run when you see him coming.

In *The Economics of Integrity: From Dairy Farmers to Toyota, How Wealth Is Built on Trust and What That Means for Our Future* (New York: HarperStudio, 2010), financial journalist Anna Bernasek profiles nine businesses whose success has been built on trust, and in our new "age of responsibility," argues that businesses must start with a "DNA of integrity," whose nucleus includes disclosure, norms, and accountability (p. 147).

Kathy Bloomgarden points out in *Trust: The Secret Weapon of Effective Business Leaders* (London: St. Martin's Press, 2007) that recent corporate scandals have decimated public trust in global companies and in the office of the CEO in particular. Bloomgarden emphasizes that CEOs must actively earn the trust of a company's stakeholders if they want to keep their jobs in this highly skeptical environment.

Also see Peter Firestein, *Crisis of Character: Building Corporate Reputation in the Age of Skepticism* (New York: Sterling, 2009). Firestein, a corporate reputation risk consultant,

intentions and *competence*. In other words, being *trustworthy* requires doing the right thing—and doing things right.[15]

---

presents a variety of case studies from some of the best-known brands in the world, illustrating how companies with behind-closed-doors strategies end up doing lasting harm to their reputations and thus their existence. Alternatively, he presents the Seven Strategies of Reputation Leadership to help corporations build a trustable reputation right into the core of their decision-making structures.

Joe Healey is a consultant and banking executive who has been speaking on the importance of trust in business leadership for 20 years. In *Radical Trust: How Today's Great Leaders Convert People to Partners* (Hoboken, NJ: John Wiley & Sons, 2007), Healey uses four case studies to show how trust is no longer merely a moral choice but a requirement for competitive advantage. According to Healey, trust requires four competencies: execution, character, communication, and loyalty.

Also see Geoffrey A. Hosking, *Trust: Money, Markets, and Society* (London: Seagull Books, 2010). Hosking argues that the stability of a global economy depends on trust, which includes a robust understanding of exactly how trust is developed, how it's maintained, how it's broken, and how it's repaired. Key to this is understanding where to place trust, as he cites misplaced trust in financial sectors and state welfare systems as precursors to the global economic crisis in 2007.

John Kador, *Effective Apology: Mending Fences, Building Bridges, and Restoring Trust* (San Francisco: Berrett-Koehler, 2009), explains why, as transparency grows and everyone seems to be apologizing for something, we don't necessarily need more apologies, just more effective ones. And if trust is a renewable asset that needs to be developed consciously, broken, and then rebuilt, an effective apology becomes a vital skill to master.

Roderick M. Kramer, a social psychologist and Stanford professor, argues that despite overwhelming evidence of corporate deceit, and despite the many books and articles that promote trust as if it's a hard sell, we still tend to trust too readily. He examines common human trust activators, such as physical similarities and the presence of touch, and after showing how easily we're fooled, he argues for "tempered trust." See "Rethinking Trust," *Harvard Business Review* 87 (June 2009): 68–77. Kramer also authored *Organizational Trust* (Oxford: Oxford University Press, 2006), and *Trust and Distrust in Organizations* (New York: Russell Sage Foundation, 2004) with Karen Cook.

[15] Consider Robert Solomon and Fernando Flores, *Building Trust: In Business, Politics, Relationships, and Life* (Oxford University Press, 2003). Solomon and Flores argue that although trust is an important precursor to any interaction, it should be neither a static quality nor a knee-jerk reaction. Trust is a skill to be developed, and the authors explain how to go from simple or naive trust to authentic, fully conscious trust in a number of contexts, including business. Nevertheless, the book is still out on "privacy." Many of the senior executives at Facebook have come to believe in what is often called *radical transparency*. Everything will be known, because the world is inevitably evolving into a social system in which everything can be seen by everyone else. But while this might spell the end of what passed for privacy during the twentieth century, proponents of radical transparency maintain it's not at all a bad future. On the contrary, it's something we should welcome. More transparency leads to more honesty. It's exactly what your grandmother used to tell you: If you don't want people to find out you did it, don't do it. Some Facebook users suggest that the existence of Facebook makes it more difficult to cheat on your girlfriend or boyfriend, for instance. See David Kirkpatrick, *The Facebook Effect* (New York: Simon & Schuster, 2011), p. 210.

Earning the customer's trust is one of the earliest goals in any enterprise's effort to build a long-term relationship. Only in a relationship of trust can information pass back and forth freely between buyer and seller. Moreover, in a world of increasingly commodity-like products and services, a relationship founded on trust can provide a genuinely sustainable competitive edge. Trust is the currency of all commerce.

The Age of Transparency

Dov Seidman
CEO, LRN, and author of HOW

In the olden days (before about 1995), when people wanted to buy, say, a toaster, they would pick a local store known for its good selection or good pricing of small appliances and buy the one that seemed best for their needs. If they were particularly industrious, thrifty, or enamored of the process, they might call or visit two or three stores before making their purchase, dig out back issues of consumers' testing magazines, or consult a catalog or two to compare price and features. As more businesses went online, people suddenly had the ability to shop not only within their local area, but almost anywhere. Large and trusted online retailers were added to the shopping mix, giving consumers a few more options if they wished to pursue them. Between June 2004 and March 2005, however, as e-commerce began exploding worldwide, people who bought online suddenly became more prone to visiting 10 or more Web sites before returning to a favored location hours or days later to make a purchase. As of 2014, almost one-fifth of all online sales had actually moved to mobile devices like tablets and smartphones,[a] and in the same year 84 percent of shoppers used smartphones to compare prices and research, even while in a physical store.[b]

It has been said that information is like a toddler: it goes everywhere, gets into everything, and you can't always control it.[c] Someone should have told that to David Edmondson, former CEO of RadioShack. For consumers, easy access to information about vendors has become an advantage; for those like Edmondson, who had something to hide, it has meant devastation. When he joined RadioShack in 1994, Edmondson invented a couple of lines for his resume in the form of college degrees in theology and psychology from Pacific Coast Baptist College in California that he never earned. In February 2006, after just eight months at the top of his profession, he was forced to resign. Though the school had relocated to Oklahoma and renamed itself, a reporter from the *Fort Worth Star-Telegram* tracked it down and uncovered the discrepancies. Edmondson's career, built on the foundation of these lies, lay in pieces at his feet.[d]

He's not alone, of course. The news is full of examples of the mighty who have taken the fall. Kenneth Lonchar, former CFO and Executive Vice President of Silicon Valley software storage firm Veritas (the Latin word for truth), got caught in 2002 claiming a false Stanford MBA.[e] University of Notre Dame head football coach George O'Leary resigned when it was revealed that he had not only lied on his resume about playing football at his alma mater, but he had also falsely claimed a master's degree.[f] Even Jeff Taylor, founder of online job-search company Monster.com, posted on his own web site an executive biography touting a phony Harvard MBA.[g] Increased scrutiny of the behavior of individuals is not limited to the executive suite or even behavior within the walls of an organization. In 2015, video emerged of Benjamin Golden, a mobile commerce executive at Taco Bell, drunkenly assaulting his Uber driver on a ride home on Halloween night. Within 24 hours of the video going viral on YouTube, Golden had been fired, and he issued an apology through his lawyers.[h]

We live in the **Age of Transparency**. In 1994, it might have been easy to get away with such shenanigans, but with the massive shift of personal records and personal profiles to databases easily accessed over the Internet, virtually everything about you can be discovered quite easily. The fact that the *New Oxford American Dictionary* lists "Google" as a verb makes this perfectly clear, as does the sample sentence it uses to illuminate its meaning: "You meet someone, swap numbers, fix a date, and then Google them through 1,346,966,000 Web pages."[i] In short, we are not only more interconnected than ever before, our interconnectedness has rendered us morally interdependent. Our actions affect more people than ever, in ways they never have before.

In July 2015, within 24 hours of the first reports coming out that a lion named Cecil had been shot just outside the grounds of a nature preserve in Zimbabwe, his killer had already been identified as Walter Palmer, a part-time big-game hunter and full-time dentist from Minnesota. That same day, thousands of negative and occasionally threatening reviews flooded his practice's Yelp page, and someone spray painted the words *Lion Killer* on his Florida vacation home.[j] Within a week, a Change.org petition with over 200,000 signatures successfully pressured Delta Airlines to change its policies about transporting game trophies, and within two months 40 more airlines followed suit.[k] Despite the fact that Palmer had committed no crime and possessed the appropriate permits to hunt lions in Zimbabwe and Delta had not actually been his carrier on his flight to or from Africa, technology-assisted transparency created a wave of outrage that demanded—and received—change.

Before transparency allowed them to peer through the tall trees, outside observers could discern the outline of a forest but thought little about what was growing beneath. Companies, for instance, could form a joint venture to protect themselves from the ramifications of a dubious enterprise, believing that if the

(continued)

(Continued)

unit got into trouble it would not hurt the reputation of the parent company. In a transparent world, however, when your joint venture transgresses, everybody knows who owns it. In the past, training its managers in proper conduct was sufficient to protect a company's reputation because line employees had little contact with the outside world and rarely got a company into trouble. Now any employee can say something about a company on social media and the next day it might appear in the *New York Times*. As the front-page profile of Amazon's "inhumane" working culture from the summer of 2015 shows, it has never been easier to find dissatisfied employees and bring their opinions together to form a public and unfavorable narrative.[l] The new transparency doesn't allow you to hide in the dark underbrush, to have a joint venture here, or hire an agent there. Observers can easily tell the trees from the forest.

An information society also breeds a surveillance society. People are more curious, and they *look* a lot more. They *look* because it is suddenly easy to do so; looking costs little, requires even less effort, and pays off with everything from the best prices for goods and services to revelations of the unsavory. Around the world, viewers are glued to their television sets by "reality TV," programming that purports to give true glimpses of private lives (the United States now has a whole network dedicated to it, and the British version of *Celebrity Big Brother* touched off an international incident[m]). We've always been interested in what was happening next door, but now we can actually see it. It's like examining a drop of water under a microscope. When you first place the drop on the slide, it looks clear and pristine. But the microscope's lens reveals a hidden world. With each adjustment of the magnification you see organisms and objects that before you could only have imagined; what first appeared clear and unpolluted suddenly appears messy and complex. Microscope technology changes the way you look at water, and with your curiosity thus piqued, you can't help but wonder what worlds might exist within other familiar objects.

People look more often because the looking is easier and there has been more to find. Imagine the gratification of Heather Landy, the *Fort Worth Star-Telegram* staff writer who uncovered David Edmondson's embellished RadioShack resume. She began her investigation "into Edmondson's credentials after learning that the executive, who started two churches before making the transition to a full-time business career, [was] scheduled to go to court . . . to fight his third drunken-driving charge."[n] Corporate scandals, celebrity breakups, political corruption: each day's news—delivered instantly via television, social media, video stream, RSS feed, and smartphone—exposes the transgressions of the icons of the age. Whether the media are addicted to it because they have so much bandwidth/airtime/column space to fill or we're hooked by our newfound access, in the **Information Age**, once we've gotten a taste of scandal, we can't seem to get enough.

Source: Partial reprint with permission of John Wiley & Sons from Dov Seidman, *HOW: Why How We Do Anything Means Everything* (Hoboken, NJ: John Wiley & Sons, 2011).

[a] "E-Commerce Pulse Quarterly Report, Q1 2014," Custora, April 2014.

[b] "The New Digital Divide: Digital's Influence on In Store Sales," Deloitte, April 2014.

[c] Lev Grossman and Hannah Beech, "Google under the Gun," *Time*, February 5, 2006.

[d] Heather Landy, "RadioShack CEO Admits 'Misstatements,'" *Fort Worth Star-Telegram*, February 16, 2006.

[e] "Veritas CFO Resigns over Falsified Resume," TheStreet.com, www.thestreet.com/markets/marketfeatures/l0045724.html.

[f] "Academic, Athletic Irregularities Force Resignation," ESPN, December 14, 2001.

[g] Rob Wright, "A Monster.com of a Problem," *VARBusiness*, February 13, 2003.

[h] Dan Mangan, "Ousted Taco Bell Exec Sorry for Uber Car Fracas: Attorney," CNBC.com, November 3, 2015.

[i] *The New Oxford American Dictionary*, 2nd ed., s.v. "Google."

[j] Dale Lately, "One Star Human Being," Slate.com, August 21, 2015.

[k] "More than 40 Airlines Adopt Wildlife Trophy Bans after Cecil the Lion's Death," Humane Society of the United States, August 26, 2015.

[l] Jodi Kantor and David Streitfeld, "Inside Amazon: Wrestling Big Ideas in a Bruising Workplace," *New York Times*, August 16, 2015.

[m] "Anger over Big Brother 'Racism,'" BBC News, January 16, 2007.

[n] Landy, "RadioShack CEO."

One of the hallmarks of any free-market economic system is that price and quality information are conveniently available to all customers.[16] Until recently, however, information about a company's service reputation, or about the overall customer experience at a firm, was not as conveniently available. Social media and mobile technology have revolutionized this, allowing customers quick and easy access, 24/7,

---

[16] A Forrester report has shown that 67 percent of U.S. adults surveyed online trust brand or product recommendations from family and friends, 21 percent trust e-mails from companies or brands, 19 percent trust social media posts from companies or brands, and 14 percent trust text ads and Web site ads, respectively (Fatemeh Khatibloo with Eric G. Brown, Christopher McClean, Shar VanBoskirk, Kristopher Arcand, Alexander Spiliotes, and Tyler Thurston, "The Mechanics of Trust," Forrester Research, Inc., April 26, 2016, available at www.forrester.com, accessed June 16, 2016).But although most of us remember the Edelman Trust Barometer's famous 2006 finding that "a person like me" was the most trusted source of information (http://www.edelman.com/news/showone.asp?id=102), more recently the Trust Barometer has shown that people now trust academic and technical experts slightly more than peers (2016 Edelman Trust Barometer: Executive Summary, p. 8, available at http://www.edelman.com/insights/intellectual-property/2016-edelman-trust-barometer/executive-summary/, accessed June 16, 2016). How can both be true? The key may be in the difference between online and offline. Most of us recognize that offline friends are more influential than online friends, yet many studies don't make this distinction. See Charles Green's comment at http://trustedadvisor.com/trustmatters/can-you-trust-the-data-on-trust, accessed February 11, 2016, about how Edelman measures trust. And thanks to Amanda Rooker for these ideas.

to what other customers are saying about a brand or a business.[17] Other customers' opinions on all aspects of their relationship with a company are widely available online, and growing even more available at the speed of Moore's law (see below).[18] And one key part of any company's overall service reputation has to do with whether it can be expected to act in the customer's interest. Is the firm really trustable?

Whatever a company does, good or bad, will be spread at Internet speed:

- Everywhere ("online" is ubiquitous)
- Immediately (news travels fast)
- Permanently (not enough lawyers on the planet to take stuff off the Net)

Transparency will increase because of technological progress, and progress is inevitable. It cannot be avoided, averted, or slowed down. But what makes this particular aspect of technology so different is the degree to which it will heighten and magnify people's interconnectedness. We are all social by nature. We like being with others, telling stories, whispering rumors, playing games, laughing, entertaining, and being entertained. We like to share ideas, get feedback, discuss nuances, and sharpen our own thinking with other people's perspectives. We even look to others in order to know what our own true feelings should be. Being social is an essential ingredient of human nature. The term *antisocial* is an indictment, implying that someone is unfriendly, cold, or misanthropic. If you're antisocial, something's wrong with you.

As important as our social nature is, however, social media and other interactive technologies have injected it with steroids. Before our very eyes, we are being transformed into a dynamic and robust network of electronically interconnected people in a worldwide, 24/7 bazaar of creating and sharing, collaborating, publishing, critiquing, helping, learning, entertaining, competing, and having fun. The volume and speed of our interactions with others grow in lockstep with Moore's law,[19] which specifies that computers will get about a thousand times more powerful every 15 to 20 years. But this also means that every 15 to 20 years we will interact a thousand times as much with others—by voice, phone, text, e-mail, status update, and other means we don't even know about yet.[20] The steady march of technological prog-

---

[17] John R. Patterson and Chip R. Bell, *Wired and Dangerous: How Your Customers Have Changed and What to Do About It* (San Francisco: Berrett-Koehler, 2011), p. 50. The average post is read by 45 people, and 62 percent of customers who hear about a bad experience on social media stop doing business with, or avoid doing business with, the offending company.
[18] Kirkpatrick, *The Facebook Effect*, p. 275. "And in mid-2008 the word *Facebook* passed *sex* in frequency as a search term on Google worldwide."
[19] Moore's law is named after Gordon Moore, a cofounder of Intel, who pointed out in 1965 that the number of transistors that could be fit onto a square inch of silicon doubled roughly every two years.
[20] As Professor Robert Wolcott says, "Today is the slowest pace we will experience the rest of our lives." Quoted at the World Marketing Summit, Tokyo, October 13, 2015.

ress brings us steadily better devices, better online tools and platforms, and better mechanisms for managing. What it adds up to is *more* interactions that are faster, cheaper, and more convenient. At this rate we are destined to interact everywhere, all the time, with anyone anywhere.[21, 22]

Basic Principles of Twenty-First-Century Trustability

If a business wants to be trustable, and to succeed in a more transparent, hyper-interactive world, then the company needs to live by these three basic principles:

Do things right. Be competent. Manage the functions, processes, and details right in order to make it easy for customers to do business with you. And pay attention to the customer's experience, not just the company's financial performance.

Do the right thing. Ensure that the way your organization makes money aligns with the needs and best interests of your customers. You can't be trustable if you're entirely focused on the short term. Customer relationships link short-term actions to long-term value.

Be proactive. Knowing that a customer's interest is not being well served but not doing anything about it is untrustable. Not knowing is incompetent.

Source: Adapted from Don Peppers and Martha Rogers, Ph.D., *Extreme Trust: Turning Proactive Honesty and Flawless Execution into Long-Term Profits* (New York: Portfolio/ Penguin, 2016).

Think of this new form of higher-level trust as "trustability." What is meant by trustability is very simple: "proactive trustworthiness." Honesty, transparency, empathy—all the qualities anyone would associate with a true friend, a business will also need to demonstrate, just to stay in business.

---

[21] Mark Zuckerberg, founder of Facebook, has asserted that every 15 to 20 years we will interact a thousand times as much with others. This is sometimes referred to as "Zuckerberg's law."
[22] Periscope—just what it sounds like—a place to go that will peek up and see what's going on in the world—has grown faster than anyone imagined except Twitter, which bought the site for "a substantial eight-figure sum" two months before it launched, and attracted a million users in its first ten days. J. J. McCorvey interviewing Periscope CEO Kayvon Beykpour, *Fast Company*, September 2015, p. 38.

Do Things Right and Do the Right Thing

On the surface the two primary components of trust—good intentions and competence—would seem to be two completely different and independent qualities. Intention is a state of mind, and since nobody can read minds, the only way to get any indication of someone else's intent is by inferring it from their words and actions. We judge their intent by what we would intend ourselves, if we were to speak or act in a similar way.[23]

"Competence," on the other hand, is not a state of mind at all but a demonstrable talent or capability. A competent firm executes well, has reliable and disciplined people carrying out its policies, and doesn't make stupid mistakes. Proficiency and competence are directly observable. And they are an important part of the "customer experience"—how it feels to be a company's customer. Delivering a better, more frictionless customer experience is the reason you connect your siloed databases in the first place. It's why you send your people to seminars on mobile best practices, and increase your company's efficiency so you can save your customers time and help them find and get what they need without any roadblocks, at a fair price. While competence may seem to be more visible than good intentions, it is still a quality that has to be deliberately built over time. Companies don't just spring into existence fully capable of good service, high-quality production, and customer insight. One of the biggest learnings for many companies, when they begin a "listening" program to monitor problems involving their brand on Twitter, Facebook, and other social media platforms, is that just trying to identify who within a large corporation has actual responsibility for a problem can often be mind-numbingly difficult.

To become competent requires some amount of deliberation and intent on the company's part. Without good intentions, it's doubtful that a firm would actually go to the trouble to build up enough competence to treat customers fairly, or "do things right."[24] Or, turning the issue around, suppose you buy from a company that promises it will always respect your interest, but when dealing with their customer service representatives you find that they don't understand your problem, they can't answer the phone in less than five minutes, their right hand doesn't know what the left is doing, they can't remember your specifications from last time, or they treat every customer, including you, exactly the same. They screw up a lot, and even

---

[23] See Christopher Meyer and Andre Schwager, "Understanding Customer Experience," *Harvard Business Review* (February 2007):117–126.

[24] Some companies that have every intention of treating customers fairly still create hassles and waste a customer's time. First, they make a mistake. Then they make you wait on hold when you call, or wait days after you contact them. When they finally answer you, they make it *your* responsibility to set things up so they can fix the problem they caused. (This is usually where we say, "You want me to bring it in? That will take me about an hour. Since I'm not on your payroll, who will pay my hourly fee to do that work?" Why do companies think their customers' time is worth nothing?)

though they act nice and *mean* well, it's just too difficult to do business with them. There's so much friction in their customer experience that you can't rely on them. In this situation, you'd have to find yourself asking just how good their intentions could actually be, right? If they *really* intended to protect your interests, wouldn't they have made a little more effort?[25]

Be Proactive

Has something like this happened to you? A friend's Internet and television signal was on the fritz one evening, and when he called the cable company he got a recorded message saying there had been a disruption in his area but that service would likely be restored sometime after midnight. The next day he called the cable provider to be sure his bill that month reflected a credit for the previous day, when the service was out. The service rep confirmed that the service had indeed been out in his area, and that his account would be credited, no problem. Out of curiosity, however, the customer asked the rep whether his company had already planned to give him the credit, since they knew he was one of the hundreds of households that experienced the outage. His answer: "No, we only give refunds to those who call in to ask for them."

This cable company—not unlike most other cable companies and subscription-based businesses—is minimizing the cost of issuing refunds, not by denying them to people who are entitled, but simply by requiring people to request them first.

But this method for handling refunds is less and less satisfactory to customers, who are used to having their needs met and their problems addressed in a more automated, easier, frictionless fashion. This is exactly what Amazon has begun doing. In a letter to shareholders,[26] CEO Jeff Bezos explained that Amazon no longer waits for a customer to contact the company with a complaint. When Amazon's computer system detects that a video ordered from the company doesn't stream

---

[25] Here's a great idea: "Becoming human-centric also creates new knowledge flows for the company that may not have existed in the past. For instance, if everyone at your company began receiving daily reports on the top social media opinions expressed about your company, its brands, and its executives, instead of just monthly market share or sales data, wouldn't this transparency profoundly affect decision making across various groups? Wouldn't it provide customer support with insights into how that function could be improved? Wouldn't such knowledge improve the planning, pricing, and promotion of your next product? Wouldn't it give your salespeople new ideas on new segments (think 'tribes') that they should be targeting?" For more on this, see Francois Gossieaux and Ed Moran, *The Hyper-Social Organization: Eclipse Your Competition by Leveraging Social Media* (New York: McGraw-Hill, 2010), Kindle edition, Loc. 1272–1276.

[26] You'll find the 2013 letter from Jeff Bezos to Amazon's stakeholders at http://www.sec.gov/Archives/edgar/data/1018724/000119312513151836/d511111dex991.htm, accessed February 11, 2016.

well, for instance, or that a purchased product became available at a lower price, the company simply e-mails the customer a credit without even waiting for the customer to detect the problem or call in about it.

Proactive refunds are likely to become ever more common, as companies try to provide ever more easy and frictionless customer experiences, and as customers themselves continue to share these more and more frictionless customer experiences with their friends and colleagues.

Ironic, isn't it, that some banks use their customer databases and analytics tools to craft highly sophisticated pictures of their customers' and prospects' value, profitability, and credit risk and then bombard them with two billion credit card solicitations every year.[27] Why don't more of them do what Royal Bank of Canada (RBC) has done? RBC has used its superior insight to extend automatic overdraft protection (with no fee!) to low-risk customers (that is, *most* customers). That way, the customer gets a break—and so does the bank; instead of having to pay a service rep to handle a call from a reliable customer who demands the fee be rescinded, the bank chooses instead to send a note explaining "this one's on us" and how to avoid this in the future, reducing their own costs in the process. Rather than incurring costs and resentment, and then netting no fee anyway, the bank saves the costs, builds goodwill, and *then* nets no fee. During the first 10 years after instituting this approach, RBC increased per-customer profitability by 13 percent.[28]

Many professional relationships are based on the concept of the trusted agent. Doctors, lawyers, psychologists, and financial planners must learn a lot about a customer before they can make their individualized recommendations; and their sense of professionalism compels them to make these recommendations in the best interests of their customers. This is, in fact, one of the hallmarks of any profession—that the client's interest will be paramount. The truth is, it's in a doctor's interest to keep her patients ill, so she can continue treating and billing them. But true professionals don't act in their own self-interest; they act in the client's interest, as trusted agents.

Trust isn't just "nice": it's a necessity for all companies wishing to enhance the value of their business. In Chapter 11, we'll look more closely at the cost of distrust and the financial returns of trust. For now, it's enough to know that when a customer decides not to buy, more than 50 percent of the time the primary factor is a lack

---

[27] According to Synovate Mail Monitor, the world's consumers received 2.73 billion credit card solicitations in 2010. See Mark Huffman, "Credit Card Offers on the Increase," ConsumerAffairs .com, January 27, 2011, at http://www.consumeraffairs.com/news04/2011/01/credit-card-offers-on-the-increase.html, accessed February 11, 2016. Also see Becky Yerak, "Credit Card Offers and Incentives Expected to Pick Up in 2011," *Los Angeles Times* online, January 1, 2011, available at http://articles.latimes.com/2011/jan/01/business/la-fi-credit-cards-20110101, accessed February 11, 2016.

[28] Peppers and Rogers, *Extreme Trust*.

of trust.[29] Additionally, the strength of a customer's relationship to the company—strongly influenced by trust—has a direct impact on a customer's intention to purchase more products/services, to recommend the company to family and friends, and to remain a customer.[30] In total, these business outcomes that are contingent on trust can either enhance or diminish a company's value.

For example, consider the case of First Direct, a division of HSBC Bank. The company was named the United Kingdom's most trusted mortgage provider and most trusted current account provider.[31] First Direct has also been profitable every year since 1995, and, among its new customers, more than one in four come because of a referral.[32]

When General Robert McDermott took the helm at the USAA insurance company in 1968, he turned this stodgy, bureaucratic company into what was to become a virtual icon of great customer service and customer trust. To do so he instituted a large amount of reorganization, retraining, computer technology, and reengineering. In addition, he implemented a single, overriding company policy with respect to customer service, which he called his "Golden Rule of Customer Service." McDermott's policy, to be adhered to by all USAA employees, was: "Treat the customer the way you would want to be treated if you were the customer." And, today, the trusted agent mentality at USAA has earned it one of the most loyal and valuable customer bases in the financial services industry, now in its third generation.

Conditions exist today that make it even more competitively important for enterprises to take on a role as trusted agent for their customers. In particular:

---

[29] Edelman, "Executive Summary," *Trust Barometer: 2015 Annual Global Study*, available at http://www.edelman.com/insights/intellectual-property/2015-edelman-trust-barometer/trust-and-innovation-edelman-trust-barometer/executive-summary/, accessed February 11, 2016; Blake Landau, "Winning True Customer Loyalty and Trust in a Recession: A Conversation with Expert Shaun Smith" (March 23, 2009), available at http://www.customermanagementiq.com/podcenter.cfm?externalID=71, accessed July 23, 2009.

[30] Edelman, "Executive Summary"; Luc Bondar and Thomas Lacki, Ph.D., "Connecting with Wireless Customers: The Relationship Opportunity" (2009), available at http://loyalty.carlsonmarketing.com, accessed July 23, 2009.

[31] Mark King, "Revealed: The UK's Most Trusted Financial Providers," *Moneywise*, July 6, 2015, available at http://www.moneywise.co.uk/banking-saving/savings-accounts-isas/revealed-the-uks-most-trusted-financial-providers, accessed February 11, 2016; Nathalie de Marcellis-Warin and Serban Teodoresco, *Corporate Reputation: Is Your Most Strategic Asset at Risk?* Cirano Center for Interuniversity Research and Analysis on Organizations, Burgundy Report, 2012, available at http://www.cirano.qc.ca/files/publications/2012RB-01.pdf, accessed February 11, 2016.

[32] From First Direct company Web site, http://www.newsroom.firstdirect.com/press/about-first-direct, accessed February 11, 2016.

- *Commoditization.* Traditional marketers have always viewed customers through the lens of "Which product are we trying to sell?" Accordingly, in the old economy, a key driver of value was the "rent" producers of products could extract—derived from restricted information flows, brand "uniqueness," and other high-friction elements. Today, the Internet and computer technology have dramatically reduced the friction that used to characterize the exchange of information. As a result, products are becoming more and more like interchangeable commodities, which thereby puts the squeeze on rents.
- *Needs, not products.* More relevant—more rent producing than specific products—are the surrounding services. Customers are not looking for products as much as they are searching for experiences or solutions to problems. Consequently, value propositions are shifting. Value will increasingly be produced based on what companies know about "that customer" and what they do to provide customized product/service bundles to meet that customer's needs or to solve that customer's problem.

To foster a trusted relationship, a customer-based enterprise ensures that it always has a customer's interest in mind. It would not hesitate, for instance, to sell a customer a competitor's product rather than send the customer away empty-handed to look for help at the competitor's door. The focus of every twentieth-century business was its product and inventory. In the twenty-first century, a company's products are, of course, important, but *a company can still exist without any products at all.* Now the company *must* have customers to thrive. A trusted agent is one that can be relied on to make the customer's interest paramount, to speak on the customer's behalf in all its dealings.

> The focus of every twentieth-century business was its product and inventory. In the twenty-first century, a company's products are, of course, important, but a company can still exist without any products at all. Now the company must have customers to thrive.

The Man with the Folding Chair

A sales manager at Siemens AG often carried a folding chair into internal meetings with sales representatives. At first, the other participants in the meeting were puzzled. "Who are you expecting to join us?" someone asked. "Shouldn't we just get some more chairs brought in here?" others suggested.

"No," the manager replied, "This is my customer's chair. I brought it into the meeting so my customer can sit right here and listen to our discussion." The simple presence of the folding chair always changed the character of the meeting. It reminded everyone of the importance of the customers and caused everyone to ask, "What would our customer say?" and "How would our customer react?" It changed the very language and focus of the conversation.

The sales manager eventually became known as "Der Mann mit dem Klapp-stuhl," or "the man with the folding chair." The lesson he taught was powerful: Never fail to consider the customer's perspective in every decision.

Source: Adapted from Don Peppers & Martha Rogers, Ph.D., *Rules to Break & Laws to Follow: How Your Business Can Beat the Crisis of Short-Termism* (Hoboken, NJ: John Wiley & Sons, 2008), pp. 61–62.

A trusted agent's role is to improve the customer's ability to make choices, to manage his life or business. If that means using the agent's own products or services, so much the better. But in any given situation, it might well mean not using the agent's products. An online bookstore, for example, might warn a customer that the book she just ordered does not fit her Web profile and that other people who have read and enjoyed books similar to the ones she has bought from the bookstore in the past have not liked this particular book. As of this writing, Amazon.com has a policy somewhat (but not exactly) like this in place. Click on a book, and using a one-to-five-star system, Amazon will predict your rating of it, based on your previous purchases and ratings of other books, and incorporating all the other book buyers who have tastes and preferences somewhat similar to yours. While the company displays higher ratings prominently, it doesn't show any ratings on some books—perhaps the ones you might not score so highly.

The trusted agent is confident that, in the long term, its knowledge of a customer's individual needs and preferences can be *monetized* at a higher value and with greater dependability than can a product or service differentiation. The trusted agent is betting that customer relationships will give it a refuge from the assault of product and service commoditization. Instead of focusing on the profitability of a single transaction, the trusted agent focuses on the profitability of the long-term relationship with the customer. Wall Street calls it *loyalty equity,* a concept that is virtually synonymous with *customer equity* and **relationship equity** (see Chapters 1, 5, 11, and 13).

How, exactly, can a trusted agent actually go about monetizing a relationship if it doesn't push its own products in a preferential way? Many possible trusted agent **business models** exist. The easiest to imagine is the financial counselor who recommends a variety of products and services to a customer, even though some of these might be offered by competitors. The counselor will likely get a disproportionate share of the customer's business simply because the customer trusts his judgment. Trusted agency is almost certainly the future of relationship management. A trusted agent will recommend product-service combinations based on a customer's individual needs, irrespective of the level of profit that will be made on any particular transaction and nearly irrespective of the companies that might participate in the product-service delivery. Trusted agency is a compelling, perhaps irresistible, response against the increasing commoditization of products and services.

Relationships, to be effective, must be built on trust, but the problem is that most enterprises view their businesses and their enabling technologies through the "wrong end of the telescope." If an enterprise starts by asking how it can use interactivity, databases, social networking, innovation, and personalization to sell its customers more

> The right question to ask is "How can the enterprise use interactivity, databases, social networking, innovation, and personalization technologies to add value for its customers, by saving them time or money or by creating a better fitting or more appropriate offering?"

products, then failure is almost inevitable. This view of the issue is highly self-oriented and simply cannot build a significant level of customer trust. Without trust, customer relationships will not take root, and the company, in the end, will find it impossible to achieve its business goals. The right question to ask, instead, is how can the enterprise use interactivity, databases, social networking, innovation, and personalization technologies to add value for its customers, by saving them time or money or by creating a better fitting or more appropriate offering?

Again, what we've been talking about here is basic, old-fashioned trust—absolutely necessary for successful and sustainable relationships built on positive experiences. Now we must examine trust at a more modern and higher level, required by emerging technologies, social media and interconnectivity, and the resulting transparency. This new, higher level of trust—what we call Extreme Trust, or *Trustability*—means that companies increase financial value because they

- Do things right, and
- Do the right thing,
- Proactively.

Relationships Require Information, but Information Comes Only with Trust

Customers will ultimately have to decide how much information they are willing to share about themselves with an enterprise. Those who are freer with their information may be able to receive more customized and personal service but will sacrifice a level of privacy. The future of a customer-strategy business world depends on gaining the customer's trust; relationships don't exist without it, partly and specifically because the relationship and the experiences that generate it depend on acting toward a customer in a way that is most relevant and valuable to *that* customer, which depends on the information from *that* specific customer. Furthermore, a customer who is willing to "collaborate" may have a higher value to a company, but "willingness to collaborate" will be possible only when a customer trusts a company to use his information fairly. Without trust, customers will not give an enterprise the information it needs in order to serve that customer better. Lose customer trust and everything is lost. If a customer wasn't sure that his insurance company was not sharing his vital information with other companies, would he even think about filling out all those forms? If a customer does not trust her bank, would she give it every single iota of financial information about her business to qualify for a loan? (Businesses give their patronage to more than one bank so they won't be unduly dependent on any single institution, but some consumers give their business to more than one bank so that no single financial institution will have complete knowledge of their finances.)

Previously, we spoke about **trust platforms** such as Uber and Airbnb. One of the things that makes these companies, as well as eBay and others, work so well is a two-way rating system. After each Uber ride, the customer has an easy way to rate the driver, but the driver also rates the customer who just left the car. Smart customers know they shouldn't ride with drivers with low ratings, and they also try to keep their own ratings high by showing up at the meeting point on time, keeping the car clean, and being polite. That way, future drivers caught in high-demand situations will be far more likely to pick up better customers rather than the rude, late ones!

In handling customer information, mistakes sometimes do happen. In these cases, it is critical for the company to take prompt action to minimize the consequence of the error and to maximize the restoration of customer trust. An apology goes a long way in rebuilding the relationship, especially one that has three characteristics:

1. It must be truly sincere, must forthrightly acknowledge the wrongdoing, and must reiterate the importance that the company places on its trustworthiness.
2. It must accept responsibility for the mistake rather than attempting to shift the blame to another party (e.g., the company's database management vendor).
3. It must articulate what the company has learned through the incident and how it is improving its processes and procedures to ensure that the mishap is not repeated.

When these steps are taken, most customers are willing to forgive temporary bouts of incompetence, provided that goodwill is demonstrated.

The late marketing guru Fred Newell wrote that as marketers develop more and more information about the lives and lifestyles of customers, the privacy issue heats up around the world.

> *Privacy issues will have to be examined from fresh perspectives if we are to continue the delicate balance between the marketer's need for information and the consumer's desire to control that information. The marketing community, so anxious for a continuing flow of customer information, must work to keep the balance by sharing more positive stories of customer benefits, to balance the media focus on Big-Brotherism, and the legislators' zeal to "protect us" from ourselves.*[33]

---

[33] Frederick Newell, *The New Rules of Marketing* (New York: McGraw-Hill Professional Book Group, 1997).

Once customers feel assured that their data are safe with the company, the next logical step is to make it comfortable for them to share more and more information. It is better to build a customer relationship gradually, one piece at a time, than to flood the relationship with massive doses of data. At every step of the collaboration, enterprises

> P rivacy issues will have to be examined from fresh perspectives if we are to continue the delicate balance between the marketer's need for information and the consumer's desire to control that information.
> —Fred Newell

need to concentrate on gathering the information useful to them. To build the necessary trust for customers to share that information, enterprises often need to offer their customers something of value in return. Many offer direct, cash-oriented benefits such as discounts, coupons, or promotions. Not surprisingly, some of the most successful companies working on this kind of "information exchange" take steps to individualize the offer so that it has greater value to a particular customer.

Customers are also becoming comfortable using automatic personalization tools on the Web. Although these tools are fine for customizing Web sites, they often fall short for nurturing enterprise/customer relationships. The enterprise must work harder truly to get to know the customer. A customer is more likely to stay loyal if she has taken the time to personalize a Web site herself *and the enterprise acts on the information given*. One of the primary goals of the enterprise focused on building customer value is to use the information it gathers about a customer to customize some aspect of its product or service to suit the customer's needs. The enterprise should begin to offer the customer things relevant to him, things that the customer could never find anywhere else, not from any generic offering that doesn't have information to use about him to meet his needs better. As a result, the customer will trust the company more. Once the flow of information begins between the customer and the enterprise, it is imperative for the enterprise to enable the customer to feel she controls her information. The enterprise should enable the customer to use the information to save her time and money and deliver value. All of this will fulfill the customer's expectations of trust and earn her lifetime loyalty. Using a customer's information to her advantage might involve reminding her when she is going to run out of a product she uses regularly or developing a related product or service she could use.

The irony of the ongoing privacy debate is that, provided the customer is doing business with a legitimate enterprise committed to responsible privacy protection, if the information flow to the enterprise is severed, the ultimate loser will be the consumer himself. Precise product targeting can dramatically lower marketing costs and subsequently product prices. Although some consumers have said that they want customized offerings and the advantages enterprises can give them by tracking their personal data, it is essential to guarantee that the customized benefits provided will not jeopardize their privacy. Customers need to know that the company will use that data in a limited way for services agreed on in advance. Without such trust, customization is not a benefit.

Scenario: Governments Develop Learning Relationships with "Citizen-Customers"

As people have become accustomed to the highly interactive, instantaneous, and personalized digital services from businesses, they're beginning to expect a similar level of service from their governments.[a] As a result, governments are beginning to see their citizens as customers and are thus becoming more "citizen-centric."

For example, at www.recreation.gov, the federal government provides citizens easy access to recreation information from the Army Corps of Engineers, the U.S. Forest Service, the National Park Service, the Bureau of Land Management, the Bureau of Reclamation, the Fish and Wildlife Service, and the National Archives. You can make reservations online at 2,500 federal areas across the country, and (if you register and provide some personal information), the site can help you tailor a planned trip with locations, activities, and tours.[b] In some states, motor vehicle departments provide customized and personalized online services such as renewing your driver's license, renewing your vehicle registration, changing your address, ordering new license plates, and even buying car insurance (after checking the most recent state insurance requirements). Municipalities allow residents to pay parking tickets and municipal bills online.

Municipalities, for instance, that develop Learning Relationships with their individual citizens can benefit primarily by being able to spend taxpayer money more productively and fairly. Suppose the parks department of a small city were to distribute bar-coded cards that could be swiped each time a citizen uses a parks service, permitting easy identification, record keeping, and tracking of individual interactions. By identifying who is using the city's swimming pools, playing fields, summer camps, or senior citizens' programs, the agency can see which services are in higher demand on the part of particular citizens or types of citizens. It might then be able to save money by customizing the seasonal fliers and catalogs it mails. For those citizens who have shown an interest in park concerts, e-mail messages could notify them of upcoming events. Perhaps the department's services could even be tailored to reflect the more specific needs of the town's most interested and active citizens.

Sometimes, private Learning Relationships lead to better government services. When New York City's taxi business faced strangling competition by the much more user-friendly Uber, the taxi system, in desperation, adopted a program called Arro, which approximated the most popular features of Uber and other car service apps.[c]

One thing that is very clear is that building a Learning Relationship between a citizen and a government will require just as much trust as does building a commercial relationship. But can a government really build this kind of trust?

(continued)

(*Continued*)

And would the answer to this question be different in different countries? If a government were indeed capable of providing a great deal more convenience to you, would you trust it with the information required to do so?

E-ZPass, an automated toll-collection technology designed to reduce traffic volume in several states, including New York City's bridge and tunnel tollbooths, provides a tool for the government to use individual information to improve itself and the efficiency of its public service: the roads, bridges, and tunnels. The electronic pass automatically identifies the vehicle as it passes through the tollbooth and automatically charges the toll to the owner's credit or debit card. This both permits faster movement through the tolls and enables database tracking of an individual's whereabouts (and presumably the speed with which the car gets from one checkpoint to the next!). The New York Transit Authority has maintained that the owner's information will be protected. Becoming a genuine, citizen-focused government agency, therefore, requires much more thought and effort than a few programs such as E-ZPass. As businesses everywhere are discovering, what really ensures a customer's goodwill and loyalty is not just putting up a Web site but creating a Learning Relationship with her.

Some cities have already begun monitoring traffic intersections with video surveillance to nab vehicles that run through red lights. But what if the city decided to keep track of your vehicle's location as it passed video cameras around town? Or what if it kept records of photos of you and your passengers without your knowledge?

In the context of a government developing individual relationships with its citizen-customers, a give-and-take scenario emerges with respect to the right to privacy and the demand for personalization (see Chapter 9 for a detailed discussion on privacy). In this scenario, the citizen-customers would want a government that could personalize their experience of living and working in the city; at the same time they would want to be able to trust the government enough to protect and respect any personal information that it gathered about them. The government, in contrast, would want to collect as much information as possible about each citizen-customer to create a more personalized living experience.

It must be noted, however, that, with respect to privacy, there is a big difference between a government and an enterprise. An enterprise that collects personal information about a customer would hold it in confidence from other enterprises because its proprietary nature provides a competitive advantage. The more it knows about an individual customer that its competitor does not know, the better an enterprise can personalize its relationship with that customer and grow its share of that customer's business. The customer would be less likely to defect to a competitor. A government, however, would like to know all it could about its citizens and might find advantages in sharing information with other government agencies. One government agency, for example, might like the capability to cross-check a criminal's driver's license number with his Social Security number and all of his prior aliases. Although this would make it harder to commit a crime under such a jurisdiction, many citizen-customers would likely object to such an invasion of privacy. Indeed, a number of influential citizens objected to allowing intelligence agencies and criminal investigation agencies to share information about specific suspects in an effort to prevent future terrorist attacks—a government activity that was made legal by the Patriot Act passed post–September 11, 2001.

---

[a] Jared Serbu, "Treating Citizens as Customers," Federal News Radio, August 7, 2015, available at http://federalnewsradio.com/federal-drive/2015/08/jared-serbu-treating-citizens-as-customers/, accessed February 11, 2016; and Partnership for Public Service, *Serving Citizens: Strategies for Customer-Centered Government in the Digital Age*, September 2014, available at http://ourpublicservice.org/publications/viewcontentdetails .php?id=246, accessed February 11, 2016.

[b] Serbu, "Treating Citizens as Customers."

[c] David Alba, "NYC's Taxis Finally Launch an App to Compete with Uber," *Wired*, August 28, 2015, available at http://www.wired.com/2015/08/arrow-ny-taxis-app/, accessed January 4, 2016.

What would it really mean for a business to be proactively trustworthy, rather than merely "trustworthy"? And to build Learning Relationships based on trust, and to develop customer value by improving customer experiences?

It isn't overly difficult to imagine how trustability would operate in any given business category. We only need to put ourselves in the customer's shoes. To drive it home for real, let's drill down to what it would mean for a particular business. Let's explore what trustability would mean for a mobile telephone carrier.

How Mobile Phone Companies Operate Today

The typical mobile carrier today is not very proactive about protecting the interests of its customers. Verizon Wireless, for instance, used to sell many of its smartphones with buttons that could easily result in connecting to the Internet unintentionally, generating a per-usage data charge of as much as $2 at a time. After an FCC investigation, the company installed a "landing page" for users accessing the Internet—so if you do push a button by mistake you can cancel the transaction before incurring a fee. Even with this change, however, many users continued to find mysterious data charges on their phone bills. If someone "never" uses the Internet from their mobile phone because of the cost, for instance, then why would they have incurred these charges, except by mistake?

According to the *New York Times*, the company seemed to be charging customers for their mistakes intentionally, in full knowledge that the charges were erroneous.

This, at least, was the allegation leveled by one of Verizon's own customer service reps, in a communication with one of the newspaper's reporters. Verizon's phones had a feature that allowed users to block accidental Internet access altogether, but according to this employee, the company had instructed its reps *not* to inform customers about this feature unless they specifically asked about it! And the company went to some effort to ensure that refunds were only grudgingly given, if at all, covering a maximum of a single month of erroneous charges.

Now think about this for a bit, because the truth of the matter is, even if all these allegations are 100 percent true, Verizon did nothing illegal or even technically "untrustworthy." It isn't cheating a customer to charge them what you say you're going to charge them when they themselves use their very own fingers to press a button that makes it happen. It isn't technically a violation of trust simply to refrain from telling a customer how to avoid making mistakes with your product. So why was this employee so upset? Because *even though the company wasn't proactively deceiving customers, it wasn't proactively protecting their interests either.* Verizon was trustworthy, in the old-fashioned sense, but not *trustable*, the way companies have to be in the Age of Transparency. No high-level Trustability. No proactive honesty and competence.[34] There's much to admire about Verizon's approach to building customer value. There are a lot of executives at Verizon working hard to exhibit goodwill and competence. So this story about making money on customer mistakes is disappointing.

How a Trustable Mobile Phone Company Would Operate

Within an environment of smartphones and increasingly capable wireless services, the charges a mobile carrier assesses can be complex, and complexity presents a tempting opportunity to take advantage of customers. It might involve allowing customers to incur unintended data charges, or it might be failing to put a customer on

---

[34] See David Pogue, "Is Verizon Wireless Making It Harder to Avoid Charges?" *New York Times*, June 17, 2010, available at http://www.nytimes.com/2010/06/17/technology/personaltech/17pogue-email.html?_r=1, accessed February 11, 2016. Here's more on the story: David Pogue wrote an earlier blog about how you could call Verizon to block all data charges, and you could go online and change your own settings (very possible to do, although not intuitive—one forum shows you how at http://www.dslreports.com/forum/r23507198-How-to-block-Verizon-Wirelesss-data-services, accessed February 11, 2016). But although any user was able to block data services online, Verizon still charged you $1.99 each time you accidentally accessed the Internet, because even to get the message "you don't have this service" it still took 0.06 MB of data, and they still charged a minimum of $1.99 for 1 MB. So even blocking it officially and legitimately did not stop the charges. See David Pogue, "Verizon: How Much Do You Charge Now?" blog post, *New York Times*, November 12, 2009, available at http://www.nytimes.com/2009/11/12/technology/personaltech/12pogue-email.html, accessed February 11, 2016.

the most beneficial or cost-efficient calling plan for their usage patterns. Or it could result from simple neglect (categorized as incompetence): If a customer is due to get a new phone at the end of his two-year contract, for instance, but doesn't notice when a period of two years elapses, a trustable mobile phone company would proactively remind him and invite him to come in to choose a new one. However, most mobile operators do not, preferring to "let sleeping dogs lie," and continue to collect on a fully paid-up contract while waiting for the customer to request an upgrade for some other reason.

A genuinely trustable telecom operator would proactively assign customers to the most economical calling plans automatically, based on their calling, texting, and data usage. Already, mobile companies in crowded retail markets around the world do this, as they are trying to position themselves as more trustable in order to gain a competitive advantage.

Vodafone Turkey launched a "Customer Bill of Rights" program designed to do exactly that. The company assures its customers that it will always act in their interest, whether that involves proactively assigning a customer to the right calling plan or counseling a customer on how to spend less for messaging and roaming.

Other mobile companies (and some other subscription-based businesses) have started sending e-mails or making outbound calls to customers at bill-paying time to remind them of the upcoming payment deadline. AT&T calls at least some of its customers before the due date by which a late fee would be assessed. A friend of ours reports having received one of these proactive service calls, and said: "Experiencing this was pretty nice. I personally feel that AT&T is looking out for me by doing this. They're building customer trust." So at least in this arena, AT&T is not one of those me-first companies, always trying to fool customers out of their money.

And since genuine trustability requires being completely transparent, if a customer is about to subscribe from a home or business address prone to poor network coverage or slow broadband connectivity, a trustable telecom company would advise him or her in advance of this weakness in its offering, perhaps providing a discount or other benefit until such time as service in the customer's home area is improved. After all, with today's online tools it won't take a new customer any time at all to have the flaws in a company's system pointed out by other customers, so the best strategy for a mobile carrier with a weakness in its offering is simply to communicate frankly about flaws and weaknesses in advance, as a way to inspire customers that they can have confidence in the company's suggestions and recommendations. Higher trust, stronger relationship, better customer experience.

Mere trustworthiness, fine until now, will no longer be enough to compete with companies that have figured out how to be genuinely trustable. In Chapter 11, we'll take this discussion a step further: *How much more would a customer be willing to pay to do business with a mobile carrier he considers to be trustable?*

Summary

Trust is the currency of all commerce. The single most powerful position in any customer's mind is a position of trust. For that reason, earning the customer's trust almost

> Trust is the currency of all commerce.

always becomes one of the earliest goals in any effort to build a long-term relationship with a customer and to build shareholder value by growing customer equity. Business expert Tom Peters points out: "In our world gone mad, trust is, paradoxically, more important than ever."[35] Let's face it: In a world of increasingly commodity-like products and services, a relationship founded on trust is the only genuinely sustainable competitive edge. Without trust, you're back to square one: *price competition*. The alternative is to build trusted Learning Relationships with customers, one customer at a time, and the way to build a Learning Relationship is IDIC: Identify, Differentiate, Interact, Customize.

In Chapter 4, we talk in more detail about the first implementation task in the IDIC methodology: identifying customers.

Food for Thought

1. Think about the companies you do business with as a customer. Name an example of a company that identified and recognized you, one that differentiated you by need or value, one that has made interaction easy and fun, and one that has changed something about the way it does business with you now, based on what it knows about you.

2. Do you agree or disagree that a relationship must always be characterized by some level of emotional involvement? Why?

3. Now that you've read Green's essay on trust, can you think of examples of companies that have little or no self-orientation? What are the signs that a company has too much self-orientation? (Check the company's stock performance for the past 15 years.)

4. In the past few years we have seen many examples of the breakdown between company governance and stakeholder interests. Do you think these corporate scandals might have played out differently if the corporations involved had built their businesses on the basis of becoming trusted agents for their customers? Is it really possible for companies to be trusted? What about governments? Political candidates and officeholders? Nonprofit organizations? What is the difference between the ones that are untrustable and those that are trustable?

---

[35] Tom Peters, at www.tompeters.com.

Glossary

Age of Transparency   The era of human history characterized by increasing levels of transparency in all human affairs, as a result of the pervasive interconnectedness of people, using social media and other ubiquitously available communications technology.

Business model   How a company builds economic value.

Customer equity (CE)   The value to the firm of building a relationship with a customer, or the sum of the value of all current and future relationships with current and potential customers. Term can be applied to individual customers or groups of customers, or the entire customer base of a company. See also the definition of customer equity in Chapter 11.

Customer focus   An attitude or mind-set that attempts to take the customer's perspective when making business decisions or implementing policies. Also called *customer orientation.*

Customer service   Customer service involves helping a customer gain the full use and advantage of whatever product or service was bought. When something goes wrong with a product, or when a customer has some kind of problem with it, the process of helping the customer overcome this problem is often referred to as *customer care.*

Customer strategy   An organization's plan for managing its customer experiences and relationships effectively in order to remain competitive. Customer strategy is building the value of the company by building the value of the customer base.

Customize   Become relevant by doing something for a customer that no competition can do that doesn't have all the information about that customer that you do.

Differentiate   Prioritize by value; understand different needs. Identify, recognize, link, remember.

Identify   Recognize and remember each customer regardless of the channel by or geographic area in which the customer leaves information about himself. Be able to link information about each customer to generate a complete picture of each customer.

IDIC   Stands for Identify-Differentiate-Interact-Customize.

Information Age   "A period in human history characterized by the shift from traditional industry that the Industrial Revolution brought through industrialization, to an economy based on information computerization." [Wikipedia]

Interact   Generate and remember feedback.

Iterative   Building on itself. Conversations are iterative when they pick up where they left off. A customer relationship can be "iterative" if both the enterprise and the customer remember their previous interactions with each other, so that with future interactions they do not need to start all over again from the beginning. In effect, an iterative relationship is one that gets smarter and smarter over time, as an enterprise conforms its behavior (for this particular customer) with the customer's previously expressed needs and preferences.

Mutuality   Refers to the two-way nature of a relationship.

Relationship equity   *See* Customer equity.

Self-orientation   Self-interest. A company that focuses on building customer value is obviously interested in its own bottom line but believes the bottom line is best served by focusing on the needs of customers.

Trust platform   A business that uses interactive technology to connect willing buyers with willing sellers, while relying on crowd-sourced feedback to ensure mutual trust. Uber and Airbnb are examples of trust platforms.

Trusted agent   A person or organization that makes recommendations and gives advice to a customer that furthers the customer's own interest, even when it occasionally conflicts with the enterprise's own self-interest, at least in the short term.

CHAPTER 4

Identifying Customers

It wasn't raining when Noah built the Ark.

—Howard Ruff

Before any relationship can start, both parties have to know each other's identities and be able to build a comprehensive view of the other. The goal of identifying customers refers not so much to figuring out which customers we want (that comes later) but to *recognizing* each customer *as that customer* each time we come in contact with her and then linking those different data points to develop a full picture of each particular customer. This chapter addresses the issue of "**identify**" for consumers as well as for business customers and defines the different elements of this "identify" task. We also address frequency marketing in the context of customer identification.

A ll enterprises use information about their customers to make smarter decisions. But for most traditional marketing decisions and actions, information is really needed only at the aggregate, or market, level. That is, any marketer needs to know the *average* demand for a particular product feature within a population of prospective customers, or the range of prices that this market population will find attractive. The enterprise then uses this information to plan its production and distribution as well as its marketing and sales activities.

But building relationships with customers necessarily involves making decisions and taking actions at the level of the *individual* customer, using customer-specific information in addition to information about the aggregate characteristics of the market population. This is because a "relationship" inherently implies some type of mutual interaction between two individual parties. We cannot have a "relationship" with a population or group but only with another individual. So the competitor trying to win with superior customer relationship strategies needs first to know the individual *identities* of the customers who make up the traditional marketer's aggregate market population. Then the enterprise will make different marketing, sales, distribution, and production decisions, and take different actions, with respect to different customers, to create better experiences and increase customer value, even within the same market or niche population.

We can see this in action. Husband asks wife if she saw the additional stories about gun control suggested on the *New York Times* Web site they each read that morning on their own computers. Wife answers with a laugh that those were the extra stories offered to *him;* she had seen suggestions for stories about stock market prospects in China. The items advertised were different, too, of course.

Individual Information Requires Customer Recognition

The essence of managing customer relationships is *treating different customers differently;* therefore, the first requirement for any enterprise to engage in this type of competition is simply to "know" one customer from another. However, identifying individual customers is not an easy process, and too often not a perfect one. It was not that many years ago when a British utility launched a December promotion to acknowledge its very best customers by mailing each of them a holiday greeting card. To the astonishment of its management, nearly 25 percent of these cards were returned to the company unopened in January. Apparently, many of the firm's "most valuable customers" were actually *lampposts.* Until that time, this company's management had equated electric meters with customers, comfortable in the knowledge that because they tracked meters, they also tracked customers. But lampposts don't read mail or make decisions.

Most enterprises will find it difficult simply to compile a complete and accurate list of all the uniquely individual customers they serve, though some businesses and industries are more naturally able to identify their customers than others. Consider the differences among these businesses, and consider the advantage that would accrue to a company that's able to identify individual customers and **recognize** each one at every contact:

- *Telecommunications companies* sell many of their services directly to end-user consumers. After all, to bill a customer for her calls in any given sales period, a phone company's computers must track that customer's calling activities— numbers connected to, time spent in each connection, day of week, and time of day. But even a cell phone company will likely make some sales to prepaid customers whose identities it can't actually learn, because they buy their top-up cards in convenience stores or through distributors, and often prepaid customers want to maintain their anonymity. Such a firm may also serve a number of corporate clients whose end users are not specifically identified. And some service providers offer friends and family deals that mean one name stands for half a dozen human customers.

- *Retail banks* must know individual customer identities to keep track of each customer's banking activities and balances. Historically, banks have been organized along lines of business, with credit cards, checking accounts, and home equity loans processed in completely different divisions. As a result, information about whether a branch banking customer is also a credit card customer often has not always been readily available to either separate division. More and more banks are recognizing the need to coordinate and integrate information across product divisions, to produce a complete relationship profile of the customer accessible to all divisions in real time.[1] Westpac New Zealand Bank is using Bluetooth beacon connections and biometrics such as fingerprints along with traditional account numbers, ATM cards, and caller ID to identify customers in a way that delivers the most complete real-time picture of customer interaction with the bank. In addition, all banking products used by the customer (such as mortgages, retirement, checking accounts, investments, etc.) are tracked in one customer profile. While this capability is available at more and more financial services institutions, the goal for Westpac goes a step further; they want employees to use that data to anticipate individual customer needs.[2]

- *Consumer packaged goods* companies sell their grocery and personal care products in supermarkets, drugstores, and other retail outlets. Although their true end customers are those who walk into the stores and buy these products, there is no technically simple way for the packaged goods companies to find out who these retail consumers are or to link their individual identities with their buying histories, except in some cases by using a "loyalty card" or other information-collection program. However, EdgeVerve offers a suite of services called Consumer Connect, a sensor-based way for retailers and consumer packaged goods

[1] Bernhard Warner, "How One Retail Bank Is Using Digital Tools and Real-Time Data to Strengthen Customer Relationships [Photos]," *Forbes*, September 24, 2015, available at http://www.forbes.com/sites/ibm/2015/09/24/how-one-retail-bank-is-using-digital-tools-and-real-time-data-to-strengthen-customer-relationships-photos/, accessed February 4, 2016; Tibco Software, Inc., "Achieving Customer Centricity in Retail Banking," 2006, available at www.tibco.com/multimedia/solution-brief-achieving-customer-centricity-in-retail-banking_tcm8–2434.pdf, accessed September 1, 2010.

[2] Warner, "How One Retail Bank Is Using Digital Tools and Real-Time Data to Strengthen Customer Relationships [Photos]"; IBM.com/wild ducks podcast with Bernhard Warner and Westpac New Zealand's Simon Pomeroy, "Digital Tools and Real-Time Data Are Turning Banking Upside Down in New Zealand," September 22, 2015, available at https://soundcloud.com/ibmwildducks/09-how-one-retail-bank-is-using-digital-tools-and-real-time-data-to-strengthen-customer-relationships, accessed February 4, 2016; and Tony Danova, "Beacons: What They Are, How They Work and Why Apple's iBeacon Technology Is Ahead of the Pack," *Business Insider*, October 23, 2014, available at http://www.businessinsider.com/beacons-and-ibeacons-create-a-new-market-2013–12, accessed February 4, 2016.

companies all to monitor and share information about customer movement and what is bought off store display shelves by whom, in real time, if customers have given their individual permission.[3] SK Telecom has also recently released Smart Shopper, an **omnichannel marketing** platform that allows "cartless shopping." Upon entering the store, customers can use a special barcode scanner to add items to their virtual shopping cart. To check out, they confirm and pay for their purchases at a self-checkout counter, and the items will be delivered to their homes at a designated date and time.[4]

- *Insurance companies* can nearly always tell you how many policies they have written, but many still cannot tell you how many customers they have or even how many households or businesses they serve. This is changing, of course, as more and more insurance companies recognize the need to base the organization and the reward structure for policy sales on customers.[5]

- *A computer equipment company* selling systems to other companies in a business-to-business environment may be able to identify the businesses it is selling to, but it is much more difficult for the firm to identify the *individual* players who actually participate in each organization's decision to buy, and then to repurchase. Yet within any business customer it is these players—decision makers, influencers, specifiers, approvers, contract authorities, purchasing agents, reviewers, end users—with whom the selling company should be developing relationships. Thus, some Web-based selling and contact-management tools are now able to help keep this information in a way that's useful to the selling company.[6]

---

[3]For more about Consumer Connect and its TradeEdge technology, see EdgeVerve's company Web site at https://www.edgeverve.com/tradeedge/offerings/pages/merchandising-audit-tools.aspx, accessed February 4, 2016. Consumer Connect was originally released by Infosys as Shopping 360: see Infosys press release, "Infosys Technologies Launches Breakthrough Services for Retailers and Consumer Packaged Goods Companies," Bangalore, India (July 31, 2008), available at: www.infosys.com/newsroom/press-releases/Pages/launches-breakthrough-services-retailers.aspx, accessed September 1, 2010.

[4]"SK Telecom Unveils the Future of Shopping at Mobile World Congress 2015," press release, February 25, 2015, available at http://www.sktelecom.com/en/press/detail.do?idx=1103, accessed February 4, 2016.

[5]"Playing for Keeps: How Insurers Can Win Customers One at a Time," PricewaterhouseCoopers, *FS Viewpoint*, July 2014, available at https://www.pwc.com/us/en/financial-services/publications/viewpoints/assets/fs-viewpoint-insurance-customer-service.pdf, accessed February 4, 2016; "Reimagining Customer Relationships: Key Findings from the EY Global Consumer Insurance Survey 2014," Ernst and Young Global Limited, available at http://www.ey.com/Publication/vwLUAssets/ey-2014-global-customer-insurance-survey/$FILE/ey-global-customer-insurance-survey.pdf, accessed February 4, 2016; and Nadine Gatzert, Ines Holzmuller, and Hato Schmeiser, "Creating Customer Value in Participating Life Insurance," working papers on Risk Management and Insurance, no. 64, Institute of Insurance Economics, University of St. Gallen (January 2009).

[6]Marco Nink and John H. Fleming, "B2B Companies: Do You Know Who Your Customer Is?" online *Gallup Business Journal*, November 22, 2014, available at http://www.gallup.com/businessjournal/179309/b2b-companies-know-customer.aspx, accessed February 4, 2016.

- *Carmakers*, as well as state and local governments, have for decades recorded the current owner of each registered automobile by the vehicle identification number (VIN), visible through the front window of any car. However, even though the owner of each car can be determined this way, the cars belonging to each owner cannot. More recently, carmakers have created smartphone apps that allow customers to digitally access their owner's manual, dealership service options, and appointment reminders, and control remotely certain aspects of their car, in exchange for their contact information, car make and model, and permission to collect data from their device.[7]
- *Cable and media entertainment companies* often have unknown customer prospects use their website. How does the company actively reengage a customer after she leaves the site if it doesn't know who she is? Some companies are implementing customer data technology to identify that Web site visitor, determine whether she is a hot prospect, and send a follow-up e-mail specific to the interest of that individual customer.[8]

Identifying customers, therefore, is not usually very easy, and the degree of difficulty any company faces in identifying its own customers is largely a function of its **business model** and its channel structure. But to engage any of its customers in relationships, an enterprise needs to know these customers' identities. Thus, it must first understand the limitations, make choices, and set priorities with respect to its need to identify individual customers. How many end-customer identities are actually known to the enterprise today? How accurate are these identities? How much duplication and overlap is there in the data? What proportion of all customer identities is known? Are there ways the enterprise could uncover a larger number of customer identities? If so, which customer identities does the enterprise want to access first?

---

[7]Examples include the MyChevrolet app, Nissan Leaf app, and the BMW i Remote app. See Eric Holtzclaw, "How to Collect Personal Data without Angering Your Customers," *Inc.*, August 22, 2013, available at http://www.inc.com/eric-v-holtzclaw/how-to-collect-personal-data-without-angering-your-customers.html, accessed February 4, 2016; "BMW ConnectedDrive and BMW i Remote App World Premiere: Apple Watch Controls Functions of BMW i Models," April 24, 2014, available at https://www.press.bmwgroup.com/global/pressDetail.html?title=bmw-connecteddrive-and-bmw-i-remote-app-world-premiere-apple-watch-controls-functions-of-bmw-i-models&outputChannelId=6&id=T0214583EN&left_menu_item=node_5238, accessed April 22, 2016; Farzad Henareh, "What Can Car Manufacturers Learn from Retailers?" MyCustomer Blog post, December 15, 2014, available at http://www.mycustomer.com/blogs-post/what-can-vehicle-manufacturers-learn-retailers/168766, accessed February 4, 2016; and Richard Barrington, "Hard Lessons from CRM Experience: Six Mistakes to Avoid," VendorGuru white paper; available at www.vendorguru.com, p. 4, accessed February 2, 2010.
[8]Martha Rogers, Ph.D., Rashmi Vittal, and Tom Hoffman, "Omnichannel Identities: Connecting Marketers with Real People," webinar by 1to1 Media and Neustar, September 24, 2015, available at https://www.neustar.biz/blog/webinar-omnichannel-identities-connecting-marketers-with-real-people, accessed February 4, 2016.

With the explosion in customer touch points, slight variations in a customer's profile can easily result in fragmented data about that customer. Furthermore, the data is constantly in flux. According to Neustar, each year,

- 75 million Americans change phone carriers.
- 45 million change phone numbers.
- 40 million relocate.
- 2.1 million legally change their names.

Meanwhile, with rising privacy rules, publicly available information on individuals is declining, and therefore it's harder to use public data to create and maintain a customer's information file.[9]

Step 1: How Much Customer Identification Does a Company Already Have?

To assess more accurately how much customer-identifying information it already has, an enterprise should:

- *Take an inventory of all of the customer data already available in any kind of electronic format.* Customer identification information might be stored in several electronic places, such as the Web server, the contact center database, or the cloud storage of the mobile app program.
- *Find customer-identifying information that is "on file" but not electronically compiled.* Data about customers that has been written down but not electronically recorded should be transferred to a computer database, if it is valuable, so that it will be accessible internally and protected from loss or unnecessary duplication.

Only after it assesses its current inventory of customer-identifying information should a company launch its own programs for gathering more. Programs designed to collect customer-identifying information might include, for instance, the purchase of the data, if it is available, from various third-party database companies; the scheduling of an event to be attended by customers; or a contest, a frequency marketing program, or some other promotion that encourages customers to "raise their hands."

The Real Objective of Loyalty Programs and Frequency Marketing Plans

Frequency marketing is a tactic by which an enterprise rewards its customers with points, discounts, merchandise, or other incentives, in return for the customer patronizing the enterprise on a repeated basis. Often called loyalty programs (see Chapter 2), frequency marketing programs can provide indispensable tools enabling companies to identify and track customers, one customer at

---

[9]Rogers, Vittal, and Hoffman, "Omnichannel Identities."

a time, across different operating units or divisions, through different channels, and over long periods of time. By providing the customer with an incentive for purchasing that is linked to the customer's previous purchases, the enterprise ensures that she has an interest in identifying herself to the company and "raising her hand" whenever she deals with the company. The customer wants the incentive, and in order to get it, she must engage in activity that allows the enterprise to identify her and track her transactions, over time.

It is not absolutely necessary for a frequency marketing program to be linked to a customer ID system. Top Value stamps and S&H Green Stamps programs were very popular in the 1950s and 1960s. As a consumer, you might choose to shop at grocery stores or gas stations that gave away Green Stamps. You'd pay your bill and get a receipt and your stamps in exchange. Then you would go home and paste the stamps into the right places on the pages of the little paperback book you had been given. Six books would get you a toaster; 4,300 books would buy a fishing boat. These giveaways were not used to identify customers; they involved no central customer database and maintained no records of individual purchase transactions. Although a trading stamps program is technically a frequency marketing program, because customers are indeed rewarded for the frequency and volume of their purchases, such an "unlinked" program with no computer database of transaction information is practically useless when it comes to aiding a company in its effort to build customer relationships or improving customer experience, beyond the giveaway.

The primary objective of a modern-day frequency marketing program should be to accumulate customer information by encouraging purchasers to identify themselves. For some companies—particularly those firms that find it difficult to identify and track customers who nevertheless engage in frequent or repeated transactions—frequency marketing programs can perform a vital part of the "identify" task, allowing a firm to link the interactions and transactions of a single customer from one event to the next. Frequent-shopper programs launched by grocery chains and other retail operators are excellent examples of this kind of frequency marketing.

There is an important implication here with respect to how a program creates value for the enterprise. If goods and services are simply discounted with points or prizes, and that's the entire program, then it is a *parity strategy;* once competitors match the points or the rewards, the only thing the sponsoring company will end up with is reduced profit margins. But if, say, the points are given in exchange for shopping basket data or other information about a customer that can be used to deepen the relationship, then the information derived is an investment that can generate profits as the company uses the data to build a more loyal relationship with a customer.

(continued)

(*Continued*)

As a matter of practice, many companies implement such programs with the sole intention of rewarding customers for giving them more of their patronage. The risk to the enterprise of doing this is that if the frequency program is a success, competitors will eventually offer customers the same or similar rewards structures for buying from them. Over time, the program will be reduced to nothing more than a sophisticated form of price competition, as in fact did happen to the S&H Green Stamps program when other stamp programs were introduced and consumers simply kept various stamps at home in separate cigar boxes.

To a customer, the incentive itself (e.g., free miles, free goods, prizes, discounts, upgrades, etc.) will often be the most immediate motive for participating. Then it is up to the enterprise to use the information to treat the customer differently. Airline frequent-flyer programs tier their customers into different levels—platinum, gold, silver, and so forth—and then provide special benefits to the highest tiers, from priority check-in lines to occasional upgrades. It is the information about an individual customer's ongoing purchases and needs that enables the enterprise to tailor its behavior or **customize** its product or service for that particular customer. The greater the level of customization, the more loyal customers can become.

It is not always so easy to figure out how to treat different customers differently, however, even when they can be individually identified and tracked. A grocery store's frequency marketing program can return a rich detail of information about the individual shopping habits of the store's customers, but what should the store then do with this information? Literally, of course, the store can't rearrange the merchandise to meet the needs of any particular customer entering the store. Nevertheless, it should be possible to use the information about the mix of products consumed by a single customer in such a way as to make highly customized offers to that customer, when those offers are communicated either by postal mail or through interactive technologies. Tesco, a United Kingdom–based supermarket chain,[a] was one of the first to create a highly successful frequency marketing program that illustrates exactly what it means to make different offers to different customers (see Chapters 2 and 10).

In May 2009, Tesco's Clubcard loyalty program boasted 16 million active card holders in the United Kingdom,[b] and its members' purchases accounted for about 80 percent of all Tesco's in-store transactions at the relaunch.

After implementing Clubcard, in-store product turnover increased more than 51 percent behind a mere 15 percent increase in floor space. The company credited its success with the fact that it was engaged in "rifle-shot" marketing to its customer base rather than the more traditional scatter-shot approach of the mass merchant. The Clubcard program allowed Tesco to link product information with each individual customer's past purchases. So, for example, based on its individual customer data, Tesco could send a Clubcard member a personalized letter with coupons aimed squarely at that particular customer's own shopping needs. This program generated an astonishingly *high* redemption rate of some 90 percent! Tesco **differentiated** more than 5,000 different "needs segments" among its customers and used that insight to send out highly customized offers. All members also received a mass-customized quarterly magazine.

Tesco originally defined eight primary "life state" customer groups, with each edition's editorial content specifically written for its target group. Counting the multiplicity of third-party advertisements, Tesco's magazines were printed and distributed in literally hundreds of thousands of combinations.

Now of course, Web-based grocery delivery services such as Fresh Direct and Peapod make it easier and easier for a regular customer to reorder online.[c] And the latest trend among Millennials is ordering pre-prepared ingredients from food services, which allows the easiest possible home preparation of meals.[d] In every individual case, the company remembers much of what works for the customer and is able to tailor suggestions to one customer at a time, going far beyond points rewards programs. Many enterprises have continued to develop this type of loyalty program with great success. A more recent approach is to enmesh the loyalty program in an improved customer experience, as Starbucks has done. In 2011, Starbucks was the first national retailer to incorporate mobile payment technology into its loyalty program—and in 2013 the program generated over 3 million transactions per week just in the United States.[e] (See Chapter 2.)

Starbucks then combined its loyalty program with a mobile app that allows ordering and payment from a mobile phone and pickup without waiting in line. Each purchase is automatically recorded in their loyalty program. The customer benefits from time saved, ease of purchase, and rewards points (toward a free item), and Starbucks benefits from information, including data about customer's device and its usage, and customer's physical location. The company also, with customers' permission, gathers information about customers from other sources like social media. The company can then get a fuller picture of each customer's complete Starbucks experience and improve it in a way that works for both the company and the customer.[f]

Starbucks also added to their loyalty program rewards for purchase of Starbucks products in other retail stores, like grocery stores. It is not as easy to report these purchases—customers must type in a code from the product package themselves after purchase—but the move to count purchases outside the company's own stores and Web site has been considered revolutionary.[g] Because the cost of the technology that manages loyalty programs and frequency marketing has continued to decline, smaller and smaller companies are able to build deep relationships with customers, profitably, even if it's only a few customers and

(continued)

(*Continued*)

not millions. Zane's Cycles, based in Branford, Connecticut, began building relationships with customers by offering free annual basic bicycle maintenance in exchange for contact and user-preference information, which owner Chris Zane used to win a greater share of each cyclist's business.

Some enterprises charge customers a membership fee to belong to a frequency marketing program. Car rental companies, for example, have in the past had programs that charge customers a separate membership fee to guarantee preferential treatment at airports; these programs tracked the customer's individual transactions as well. Customers who are willing to invest money in a continuing Learning Relationship with an enterprise become committed to the collaborative solution of a problem. And any enterprise that collaborates with its customers is more likely to be able to ask the types of questions needed to achieve a higher share of a customer's business. It is easier for the enterprise to ask questions of a customer who has agreed to enter a relationship.

The bottom line is this: Don't skip a step. If your frequency program is only a card with points for shopping, that doesn't give you a chance to become a customer's preferred choice. Instead, make the program the basis of an incentive to partner with a customer for her own benefit to learn more about what she needs and wants. Use that information to do things for her that no one else who doesn't have that information can do. That can create the customer experience that creates customer loyalty.

---

[a] See http://www.tescoplc.com/ for updated corporate information; accessed February 4, 2016.

[b] "Tesco Clubcard Signs Up One Million Customers Since Relaunch," *Marketing Magazine,* May 10, 2009, available at www.marketingmagazine.co.uk/news/943397/Tesco-Clubcard-signs-one-million-customers-relaunch/, accessed February 4, 2016.

[c] Tanya Dua, "Lit or Thirsty? FreshDirect's New Food App Speaks Fluent Millennial," Digiday, February 2, 2016, available at https://digiday.com/brands/yasss/, accessed February 4, 2016; Marina Mayer, "How Retailers' Food Delivery Service Changes the Consumer Shopping Experience," *Refrigerated and Frozen Foods* 25, no. 11 (November 2015): 6.

[d] Elizabeth Segran, "The $5 Billion Battle for the American Dinner Plate," *Fast Company,* October 2015, available at http://www.fastcompany.com/3046685/most-creative-people/the-5-billion-battle-for-the-american-dinner-plate, accessed February 4, 2016.

[e] Jim Tierney, "Loyalty Program Triggers Starbucks' Record Q2," Loyalty360 Daily News, April 26, 2013, http://loyalty360.org/resources/article/loyalty-program-triggers-starbucks-record-q2, accessed February 4, 2016.

[f] See Starbucks' privacy policy for loyalty program at http://www.starbucks.com/about-us/company-information/online-policies/privacy-policy, accessed February 4, 2016.

[g] Bruce Horovitz, "Earn Starbucks Loyalty Points Beyond Cafes," *USA Today,* March 20, 2013, available at http://www.usatoday.com/story/money/business/2013/03/20/starbucks-loyalty-program/2003583/, accessed February 4, 2016.

Step 2: Get Customers to Identify Themselves, Making Sure to Accurately Identify Customers on Any Channel

Sales contests and sponsored events are often designed for the specific purpose of gathering potential and established customer names and addresses. But to engage a customer in a genuine relationship, a company must also be able to link the customer to her own specific purchase and service transaction behavior. Analyzing past behavior is probably the single most useful method for modeling a customer's future value, as we'll see in Chapter 5, on customer differentiation, and Chapter 12, on analytics. So although a onetime contest or promotion might help a company identify customers it did not previously "know," linking the customer's identity to her actual transactions is also important.

Frequency marketing programs, when they are executed strategically, suit both purposes, providing not only a mechanism to identify customers, but also a means to link customers, over time, with the specific transactions they undertake. Such programs have been used for years to strengthen relationships with individual customers, but it's important to recognize that a frequency marketing program is a tactic, not a strategy. It is an important enabling step for a broader relationship strategy because a frequency marketing program provides a company with a mechanism for identifying and tracking customers individually, but this will lead to a genuine relationship-management strategy only when the company actually uses the information it gets in this way to design different treatments for different customers.

What Does *Identify* Mean?

Given that the purpose of identifying individual customers is to facilitate the development of relationships with them individually, we are using the word *identify* in its broadest possible form. What we are really saying is that an enterprise must undertake all of these identification activities:

Identification Activities

- *Define.* Decide what information will comprise the actual customer's identity: Is it name and address? Mobile phone number? E-mail address? Home phone number? Account number? Householding information?
- *Find.* Our customers are out there—if we can see them properly, we can see a lot that helps us serve them better. An omnichannel approach, which includes information from every possible channel, such as call centers, Web sites, interactive voice response (IVR) systems, instant messaging, social, and in-store interactions, is crucial.[10]
- *Collect.* Arrange to collect these customer identities. Collection mechanisms could include frequent-shopper bar codes; credit card data; paper applications;

---

[10]Rogers, Vittal, and Hoffman, "Omnichannel Identities."

Web-based interactions via Web site, e-mail, blog comments, Facebook, Instagram, or Twitter; radio frequency identification (RFID) microchips (such as E-ZPass and Exxon-Mobil's Speedpass); or any number of other vehicles.

- *Link*. Once a customer's identity is fixed, it must be linked to all transactions and interactions with that customer, at all points of contact, and within all the enterprise's different operating units and divisions. It is one thing, for instance, to identify the consumer who goes into a grocery store, but a frequent-shopper program is usually the primary mechanism to link that shopper's activities together, so that the enterprise knows it is the same shopper, every time he comes into the store or makes an online purchase.[11] Also, if a customer shops online for a product but then contacts the company's call center to order it, the relationship-oriented enterprise wants to be able to link that customer's online interactions with her call-in order. The goal is to see each customer as one complete customer, and not as a series of independent events, people, or contacts.

- *Integrate*. The customer's identity must not only be linked to all interactions and transactions; it must also be integrated into the information systems the enterprise uses to run its business. Frequent-flyer identities need to be integrated into the flight reservations data system. Household banking identities need to be integrated into the small business records maintained by the bank.

- *Recognize*. The customer who returns to a different part of the organization needs to be recognized as the same customer, not a different one. In other words, the customer who visits the Web site today, goes into the store or the bank branch tomorrow, and calls the toll-free number next week needs to be recognized as the same customer, not three separate events or visitors.

- *Store*. Identifying information about individual customers must be linked, stored, and maintained in one or several electronic databases.

- *Update*. All customer data, including customer-identifying data, is subject to change and must be regularly verified, updated, improved, or revised.

- *Analyze*. Customer identities must serve as the key inputs for analyzing individual customer differences (see Chapter 12).

- *Make available*. The data on customer identities maintained in an enterprise's databases must be made available to the people and functions within the enterprise that need access to it. Especially in a service organization, making individual customer-identifying information available to frontline service personnel is important. Computers help enterprises codify, aggregate, filter, and sort customer information for their own and their customers' benefit. Storing customer identification information in an accessible format is critical to the success of a customer-centered enterprise.

---

[11]Other information collection tools, such as the wireless, sensor-based tracking systems mentioned earlier, could supplement or replace a frequent-shopper program. See EdgeVerve company Web site at https://www.edgeverve.com/tradeedge/offerings/pages/merchandising-audit-tools.aspx, accessed February 4, 2016.

- *Secure and protect.* Because individual customer identities are both competitively sensitive and threatening to individual customer privacy, it is critical to secure this information to prevent its unauthorized use.

Technology is enabling enterprises to identify customers in ways never before imagined. Many businesspeople still hand out business cards, but computer contact databases and sophisticated customer information cloud-based **data warehousing** are far more important than physical cards for the same reason that public libraries long ago abandoned their card catalog systems: because card catalog systems cost much more than their electronic counterparts and are available for search only in the physical library building. Sophisticated electronic data systems allow library patrons to search a library's holdings from anywhere and help the library cut its own costs at the same time.

Integrated computer databases don't just reduce costs. More important, they also help identify patterns that aren't visible when the data is kept in filing systems or in separate data silos. The more the company integrates data from all corners of the enterprise, even including the extended enterprise, the richer in value the customer information becomes in planning and executing customer-focused strategies.

The end customer of an enterprise is the one who consumes the product or service it provides. That said, sometimes it is more of an indirect relationship, which makes it more difficult to tag the customer and link information to her. Sometimes, a product or service might be purchased by one customer and used by another member of the household or by the recipient of a gift. And as we discuss later, sometimes an end user will be an employee of a company while it is the company's purchasing department that actually buys the product. Regardless of these intermediary relationships, however, it is the end user who is at the top of the food chain and the end user whose relationship with the enterprise is most important, because this is the person whose needs will or won't be met by the product.

Customer Identification in a B2B Setting

A business-to-business (B2B) enterprise still must identify customers, and many of the issues are the same, but there are some important differences that merit additional consideration. For instance, when selling to business customers, the B2B enterprise must consider who will be on the other side of the relationship. Will it be the purchasing manager or the executive who signs the purchase order? Will it be the financial vice president who approved the contract? Or will it be the production supervisor or line engineer who actually uses the product? The correct way for an enterprise to approach a B2B scenario is to think of each of these individuals as a part of the customer base. Each is important in his or her own way, and each one should be identified and tracked. The greatest challenge for many businesses that sell to other businesses is identifying the product's end users. Discovering who, within the corporate customer's organization, puts a product to work (i.e., who depends on the product to do her job) is often quite difficult. Some methods for identifying end users include[12]:

- If the product consumes any replenishable supplies (e.g., inks, drill bits, recording paper, chemicals), providing a convenient method for reordering these supplies is an obvious service for end users.
- If the product is complicated to use, requiring a detailed online instruction manual or perhaps different sets of application notes or even training, one way to secure end-user identities is to offer such instructions in a simplified format, tailored to all devices.
- If the product needs periodic maintenance or calibration or regular service for any reason, the enterprise can use these occasions to identify end users.

B2B firms use many strategies to get to know the various role players within the corporations they are selling to, from end users to chief financial officers—setting up personal meetings, participating at trade shows, swapping business cards, sponsoring seminars and other events, inviting people to work-related entertainment occasions, and so forth. But the single most important method for identifying the "relationships within relationships" at an **enterprise customer** is to provide a service or a benefit for the customer that can really be fully realized only when the players themselves reveal their identities and participate actively in the relationship. Thus, even though relationship marketing has always been a standard tool in the B2B space, today's new technologies are making it possible more than ever before to manage the actual mechanics of these individual relationships from the enterprise level. In so doing, the enterprise ensures that the relationship itself adheres to the enterprise, not just to the sales representative or other employee conducting the activity.

Customer Identification in a B2C Setting: Unify Omnichannel Marketing Programs

Can we identify—and recognize again and again—*millions* of customers? In the business-to-consumer (B2C) space, the technology-driven **customer relationship management (CRM)** movement has only recently made it possible even to conceive of the possibility of managing individual consumer relationships. But while managing relationships within the B2C space might be a relatively new idea, mass marketers have always understood that customer information is critical and that the possible ways of identifying customers are nearly limitless.

Certain technologies have made it possible to identify customers without their active involvement. ExxonMobil, the gasoline retailer, dispenses RFID microchips that can be carried around on the keychain of a customer who participates in its

---

[12]Nink and Fleming, "B2B Companies"; Don Peppers, Martha Rogers, Ph.D., and Bob Dorf, *The One to One Fieldbook: The Complete Toolkit for Implementing a 1to1 Marketing Program* (New York: Doubleday, 1999).

Speedpass campaign. When the customer drives up to a gas pump, the microchip device automatically identifies the customer and charges the customer's credit card for the transaction. The customer is rewarded with a speedier exit from the gas pump (although she still must pump her own gas). The company, in turn, can identify each customer every time she buys gas at any ExxonMobil station and link that identification with every transaction.

Of course, few would deny that the Internet gave the biggest push to the customer relationship movement in the B2C arena. Not only did the World Wide Web provide tools to existing firms with which they could interact more effectively with their customers and identify an increasing number of them individually, but it also led to the creation of many new, Internet-based businesses with extremely streamlined business models based on direct, one-to-one relationships with individual customers, online.

Writer Stewart Alsop described the way Amazon.com led the way at the turn of the new century:

> *What Amazon.com has done [in 2001] is invent and implement a model for interacting with millions of customers, one at a time. Old-line companies can't do that—I like Nordstrom, Eddie Bauer, Starbucks, and Shell, but they have to reach out to me with mass advertising and marketing. Amazon's technology gives me exactly what I want, in an extraordinarily responsive way. The underlying technology, in fact, is revolutionizing the way companies do business on the Web.*[13]

Customer Data Revolution

> The computer has brought about "three awesome powers": the power to *record*, the power to *find*, and the power to *compare*.
>
> —Stan Rapp

Clearly, in the **Information Age**, an enterprise can reach and communicate with individual customers one at a time, it can observe as customers talk to each other about the company, and it can follow strategies for its customer interactions that are based on relevant, customer-specific information stored in a customer database. The computer can now store millions of customer records—not just names and addresses, but age, gender, marital status and family configuration, buying habits, history, devices, and demographic and psychographic profiles. Individuals can be selected from this database by one, two, three, or more of their identifying characteristics. CRM expert

---

[13]Back in 2001, *Fortune* columnist Stewart Alsop rightly pegged Amazon.com not only as a technology company when most relegated it to the more mundane role of e-tailer but as one of the few companies that had "mastered the use of technology in serving individual customers." Stewart Alsop, "I'm Betting on Amazon," *Fortune,* April 30, 2001, 48.

Stan Rapp has said that the computer has brought about "three awesome powers": the power to *record*, the power to *find*, and the *power* to compare.[14]

- *The computer's power to record.* In precomputer days, there would have been no point in recording by typewriter dozens of bits of information about each customer or prospect on thousands of index cards. Without the computer, there would have been no practical way to make use of such information. As computer data storage rapidly became more economical, however, it became possible and desirable to build up and use a prospect or customer record with great detail.
- *The computer's power to find.* Selections can be made from the prospect or customer file by any field definitions or combination of field definitions.
- *The computer's power to compare.* Information on customers with one set of characteristics can be compared to customer information using a different set of characteristics. For instance, the computer can compare a list of *older people* and a list of *golfers*.

For all its power, however, the truth is that when it comes to customer-oriented activities, the computer is an underutilized technology at most businesses—not because companies don't want to use it but because most customer data are simply not fit for use in an analytical database. The development of a database of customer information requires a data model—the tool required to bring data complexities under control. The *data model* defines the structure of the database and lays out a map for how information about customers will be organized and deployed.

What Data Do We Need When We Identify a Customer?

After it has mined its existing customer databases and developed a plan to gather new customer information, the enterprise then decides how to tag its customers' individual identities. Names are not always a sufficient customer identifier. More than one customer might have the same name, or a customer might use several different varieties of the same name—middle initial, nickname, maiden name, and so forth. To use a customer database effectively, therefore, it is usually necessary to assign unique and reliable customer numbers or identifiers to each individual customer record. It could be the customer's e-mail address, phone number, a "user name" selected by the customer, or an internally generated identifier.

---

[14]Stan Rapp, *The Great Marketing Turnaround* (Upper Saddle River, NJ: Prentice Hall, 1990). And see his book, co-authored with Sebastian Jespersen, *Entangling Brand and Consumer* (forthcoming); excerpt published as Stan Rapp and Sebastian Jespersen, "Entangling Brand and Consumer: Go Beyond Mere Engagement to Forge Enduring Ties with Customers," *Advertising Age*, October 12, 2015, available at http://adage.coverleaf.com/advertisingage/20 151012/?pm=2&u1=friend&pg=32#pg32, accessed February 4, 2016.

In addition to transaction details, other types of data generated from internal operations can make significant contributions. Information relating to billing and account status, **customer service** interactions, back orders, product shipment, product returns, claims history, and internal operating costs all can significantly affect an enterprise's understanding of its customers. Directly supplied data consists of data obtained directly from customers, prospects, or suspects. It is generally captured from lead-generation questionnaires, customer surveys, warranty registrations, customer service interactions, Web site responses, or other direct interactions with individuals.

Directly supplied data consists of three obvious types:

1. ***Behavioral data***, such as purchase and buying habits, clickstream data gleaned from the way a firm's Web site visitor clicks through the firm's Web site, interactions with the company, communication channels chosen, language used, product consumption, and company share of wallet.
2. ***Attitudinal data***, reflecting attitudes about products, such as satisfaction levels, perceived competitive positioning, desired features, and unmet needs as well as lifestyles, brand preferences, social and personal values, opinions, and the like.
3. ***Demographic*** (i.e., "descriptive") ***data***, such as age, income, education level, marital status, household composition, gender, home ownership, and so on.

In categorizing data contained in a customer database, it's important to recognize that some data—*stable data,* such as birth date or gender—will need to be gathered only once. Once verified for accuracy, these data can survive in a database over long periods and many programs. Updates of stable data should be undertaken to correct errors, but, except for errors, stable data won't need much alteration. In contrast, there are other data—*adaptive data,* such as a person's intended purchases or even her feelings about a particular political candidate—that will need constant updating and cleansing. This is not a binary classification, of course. In reality, some data are *relatively* more stable or adaptive than other data. And part of the challenge comes from the fact that customers relate at different times to different parts of the organization: Web site (online marketing), bill paying (accounting), in-house (e.g., store management).

Why Is Identification Important?

Ultimately, of course, the central purpose of collecting customer information is to enable the development of closer, more profitable relationships with individual customers by creating consistently better experiences for each of them. In many cases, these relationships will be facilitated by the availability to the enterprise of information that will make the customer's next transaction simpler, faster, or cheaper. Remembering a customer's logistical information, for instance, will make reordering easier for her, and therefore more likely. Remembering this type of information will also lead the customer to believe she is important to the company and that her patronage is valued.

Additionally, it's important to "identify" customers to reduce the waste in serving them. For example, one data cleansing company helped a Fortune 500 consumer electronics firm match unidentified callers in real time with existing customer data, including additional data that could be appended to the current interaction, enabling 54 percent of unidentified callers to be identified in real time, saving $13.8 million in additional data work, and increasing customer satisfaction through better experiences.[15] Some companies are also now able to identify callers in the first few seconds of a call through voice or speech recognition.[16]

In order to make any of this work, however, it is essential for the enterprise to establish a trusting relationship with the customer, so she feels free to share information. A vocal privacy-protection movement—perhaps more active in Europe than in North America—has been energized by the increasing role that individual information plays in ordinary commerce and the perceived threat to individual privacy that this poses. However, both practical experience and a number of academic studies have shown that the vast majority of consumers are not at all reluctant to share their individual information when there is a clear value proposition for doing so and when they trust the company. Therefore, if a company can demonstrate to the customer that individual information will be used to deliver tangible benefits (and provided the customer trusts the enterprise to hold the information reasonably confidential beyond that), then the customer is usually more than willing to allow use of the information. Trusting relationships or not, protecting customer privacy and ensuring the safety and security of customer-specific information are critical issues in the implementation of customer strategies and will be discussed in greater detail in Chapter 9.

Integrating Data to Identify Customers

The process of identifying customers in order to engage them in relationships requires that customer-identifying information be integrated into many different aspects of an enterprise's business activities. It used to be that customer data could be collected over a period of time, and the customer database would be updated with revised profile and analytic information in batches. On weekends, perhaps, or late at night, information collected since the last update would be used to update the customer database. Increasingly, however, companies rely on Web sites and call centers to interact with customers, and this places a much greater emphasis on ensuring real-time access to customer-identifying information.

Enterprises must be able to capture customer information and organize it, aggregate it, integrate it, and disseminate it to any individual or group, throughout the enterprise, in real time. Technology is enabling enterprises to accelerate the flow of customer information at the most strategically timed moment. Enterprises strive for

---

[15] Rogers, Vittal, and Hoffman, "Omnichannel Identities."
[16] One example is "Real-Time Authentication" by NICE Systems, a bio-based software tool that identifies (authenticates) a caller, once she has given her name, through highly accurate individual voice recognition.

zero latency—that is, no lag time required—for the flow of information from customer to database to decision maker (or to a rules-based decision-making "engine"). The computer-driven processes of data mining, collaborative filtering, and predictive modeling will increasingly alter the process of forecasting how consumers behave and what they want,[17] and, as more and more real-time interactivity continues to permeate all aspects of our lives, we can expect customers to demand more and more real-time service, which means enterprises will need real-time access to customer data.

In any service context, it is critical that an enterprise's customer-facing people have ready access to customer-identifying data as well as to the records attached to particular customer identities. Making valuable customer information available to front-line, customer-facing employees, whether they work on board a passenger airliner, behind the counter at a retail bank branch, or at the call center for an automobile manufacturer, is an increasingly important task at all B2C enterprises.

Westpac New Zealand Bank, for example, uses a device-neutral platform to provide real-time data from all channels to both customers and employees. To assemble that customer profile, Westpac must identify customers at all digital and physical branches, and over all departments and 120 services. Earlier in the chapter, we described how the bank uses both traditional methods, such as account numbers, caller ID, ATM cards, as well as cutting-edge ID technologies, such as beacons that identify through smartphones and biometrics that can identify with a fingerprint. Because employees have real-time access to all customer interactions in every category and real-time financial analytics, they can pick up the "conversation" with an individual customer wherever it last left off and anticipate needs—to be proactive in relationships with customers rather than just reactive.

Chief Digital Officer Simon Pomeroy says automating the high-volume, low-value transactions through digital banking, combined with the real-time customer information and analytics, has allowed his employees to spend time on learning about customers and establishing relationships. Statistics bear this out. Interactions with customers are up from having conversations with 40 percent of customers in 2012, most of which were reactive, to interacting with 92 percent of customers in 2014, many of which were proactive.[18]

---

[17]Dolores Romero Morales and Jingbo Wang, "Forecasting Cancellation Rates for Services Booking Revenue Management Using Data Mining," *European Journal of Operational Research* 202, no. 2 (April 2010): 554–562; Heung-Nam Kim et al., "Collaborative Filtering Based on Collaborative Tagging for Enhancing the Quality of Customer Recommendation," *Electronic Commerce Research and Applications* 9, no. 1 (January–February 2010): 73–83; Rodolfo Ledesma, "Predictive Modeling of Enrollment Yield for a Small Private College," *Atlantic Economic Journal* 37, no. 3 (September 2009): 323.

[18]IBM.com/wild ducks podcast with Bernhard Warner and Westpac New Zealand's Simon Pomeroy, "Digital Tools and Real-Time Data Are Turning Banking Upside Down in New Zealand," September 22, 2015, available at https://soundcloud.com/ibmwildducks/09-how-one-retail-bank-is-using-digital-tools-and-real-time-data-to-strengthen-customer-relationships, accessed February 4, 2016.

The Role of the "Internet of Things" and Smart Products in Managing Relationships with Customers

Professor Rashi Glazer clarifies the implications of an enterprise-wide view of the customer—what several authorities have called "one view of the truth" and others have called the "360-degree view of the customer." Professor Glazer has pointed out that "perhaps the most important implication of the Information Age for business is the emergence of information-intensive or *smart* markets—that is, markets defined by frequent turnovers in the general stock of knowledge or information embodied in products and services and possessed by firms and consumers. In contrast to traditional "dumb" markets—which are static, fixed, and basically information-poor—smart markets are dynamic, turbulent, and information-rich.

He continues: "Smart markets are based on smart products, those product and service offerings that have intelligence or computational capability built into them and therefore can adapt or respond to changes in the environment as they interact with customers. Smart markets are also characterized by smart consumers, consumers who, from the standpoint of the firm, are continually 'speaking' (i.e., they are not mute, or 'dumb') and, in so doing, educate or teach the firm about who they are and what they want. In such an environment, competition is less about who has the best products and more about which firm can spend the most time interacting with—and therefore learning from—its customers.

"A major implication of information-intensive, or smart, markets is the widespread breaking down of boundaries where there once were well-defined roles or discrete categories:

- Boundaries between products are breaking down (in particular, the boundary between products and services).
- Within the firm, boundaries between departments are breaking down, as no department or area has all the information necessary (and the flow of information between departments is not fast enough) to respond to customer requests before the competition does.
- Most significantly, the boundaries between the firm and the external world are breaking down: between the firm and its competitors, as firms realize they need to partner in order to put in place the infrastructure issues necessary for the sale of their own products; and, of course, between the firm and its customers, as customers participate or collaborate in the design and delivery of their own products, and as communications become more interactive and two-way—never mind the increase in interconnectivity among customers.

> The organizing 'tool,' or asset, on which the full range of information-intensive strategies is based is the customer information file (CIF), a single virtual database that captures all relevant information about a firm's customers. The database is described as 'virtual' because, while operating as if it were an integrated single source housed in one location, it may in reality comprise several isolated databases stored in separate places throughout an organization."[19]

Summary

The first task to accomplish in building relationships with a customer is to *recognize* each one at every point of contact, across all products purchased or locations contacted, through every communication channel, over time, and link the information so that one view of each customer is established. Doing this requires knowing the identity of each customer at every contact point in the organization.

Food for Thought

1. Describe and name two companies you have done business with as a customer.
2. One of them treats you as if you are a new customer every time you show up, or at least any time you show up anywhere you haven't done business with the company before. At the other company, you are recognized as you, every time you have any dealings with the company. What's the effect on you of these disparate approaches? How would you guess each company manages its data, given their different approaches to customers?
3. How can a company identify customers when those customers don't talk to its representatives very often, if at all—at least not individually? (Consider a pet food manufacturer that sells to retailers, not directly to consumers. Or a convenience store that operates on a cash basis. Or a fast-food chain. Or a business-to-business company that doesn't have a human sales force.)

   What will encourage customers to "raise their hands" and agree to be identified and recognized?

---

[19] Rashi Glazer is retired professor and codirector of the Management of Technology Program, Walter A. Hass School of Business, University of California at Berkeley. From Rashi Glazer, "Role of Smart Markets in Managing Relationships with Customers," in Don Peppers and Martha Rogers, Ph.D., *Managing Customer Relationships: A Strategic Framework*, 2nd ed. (Hoboken, NJ: John Wiley & Sons, 2011). See also Rashi Glazer's "Meta-Technologies and Innovation Leadership: Why There May Be Nothing New Under the Sun," *California Management Review* 50 (Fall 2007): 120–143; and "Winning in Smart Markets," *Sloan Management Review* 40 (Summer 1999): 59–69.

Glossary

Attitudinal data   Directly supplied data that reflect attitudes about products, such as satisfaction levels, perceived competitive positioning, desired features, and unmet needs as well as lifestyles, brand preferences, social and personal values, and opinions.

Behavioral data   Directly supplied data that include purchase and buying habits, clickstream data, interactions with the company, communication channels chosen, language used, product consumption, company share of wallet, and so on.

Business model   How a company builds economic value.

Customer relationship management (CRM)   As a term, *CRM* can refer either to the activities and processes a company must engage in to manage individual relationships with its customers (as explored extensively in this textbook), or to the suite of software, data, and analytics tools required to carry out those activities and processes more cost efficiently.

Customer service   Customer service involves helping a customer gain the full use and advantage of whatever product or service was bought. When something goes wrong with a product, or when a customer has some kind of problem with it, the process of helping the customer overcome this problem is often referred to as "customer care."

Customize   Become relevant by doing something for a customer that no competition can do that doesn't have all the information about that customer that you do.

Data warehousing   A process that captures, stores, and analyzes a single view of enterprise data to gain business insight for improved decision making.

Demographic data   Directly supplied data that include age, income, education level, marital status, household composition, gender, home ownership, and so on.

Differentiate   Prioritize by value; understand different needs. Identify, recognize, link, remember.

Enterprise customer   A business that buys goods and services from a business-to-business (B2B) vendor, characterized by complex "relationships within relationships" often involving specifiers, approvers, reviewers, and other individuals within the customer organization who all have varying roles and degrees of influence over the purchasing decision.

Identify (*see also* Recognize)   Recognize and remember each customer regardless of the channel by or geographic area in which the customer leaves information about himself. Be able to link information about each customer to generate a complete picture of each customer.

Information Age   "A period in human history characterized by the shift from traditional industry that the Industrial Revolution brought through industrialization, to an economy based on information computerization." [Wikipedia]

Internet of Things (IoT) A term describing the network of products and other objects that have intelligence or computational capability built into them, along with interconnectedness to the Web, via Wi-Fi or other technology. As defined by the ITU, a UN agency, the IoT is "a global infrastructure for the information society, enabling advanced services by interconnecting (physical and virtual) things based on existing and evolving interoperable information and communication technologies" (http://www.itu.int/en/ITU-T/gsi/iot/Pages/default.aspx, accessed April 6, 2016).

Omnichannel marketing A marketing buzzword referring to the capability of interacting and transacting with customers in any or all channels, in order to ensure that every interaction takes place in the channel of the customer's own choice.

Recognize (*see also* Identify) The ability to identify an individual customer as that customer through any shopping or buying channel, within any product purchase category, across locations or geographies, and over time. These individual data points are linked for a universally recognized, or identified, customer.

Zero latency No lag time required for the flow of information from customer, to database, to decision maker (or to a rules-based decision-making engine).

CHAPTER 5

Differentiating Customers: Some Customers Are Worth More Than Others

The result of long-term relationships is better and better quality, and lower and lower costs.

—W. Edwards Deming

All value created by a business comes from customers. Without a customer or client, at some level, no business can create any shareholder value at all, and this simple fact is inherent in the very nature of a business. By definition, a business exists to create and serve customers and, in so doing, to generate economic value for its stakeholders. But some customers will create more value for a business than others will, and understanding the differences among customers, in terms of the value they each will or could create, is critical to managing individual customer relationships. In this chapter, we explore the most fundamental ideas about the value that customers represent for an enterprise, including both a customer's "actual" value and "potential" value. We show how a firm can use insights about customer value to better allocate resources and prioritize sales, marketing, and service efforts. We consider whether and under what conditions a firm should consider "firing" very low-value or even negative-value customers.

Identifying each customer individually and linking the information about that customer to various business functions prepares the **customer-strategy enterprise** to engage each customer in a mutual collaboration that will grow stronger over time. The first step is to identify and recognize each customer at every touch point. As we saw in Chapter 4, when the "identify" task is properly executed, information about individual customers should allow a company to see each customer completely, as one customer, throughout the organization. And seeing customers individually will enable the company to compare them—to ***differentiate*** customers, one from another. By understanding that one customer is different from another, the enterprise reaches an important step in the development of an interactive, customer-centric Learning Relationship with each customer.

The inability to see customers as being different does not mean the customers are the same in needs or value, only that the firm sees them that way. Understanding, analyzing, and profiting from individual customer differences are tasks that go to the very heart of what it means to be a customer-strategy or customer-centric enterprise—an enterprise that engages in customer-specific behaviors, in order to increase the overall value of its customer base.

> The inability to see customers as being different does not mean the customers are the same in needs or value or behaviors, only that the firm sees them that way.

Customers are different in two principal ways: Different customers have different *values to* the enterprise, and different customers have different *needs from* the enterprise. The entire value proposition between an enterprise and a customer can be captured in terms of the value the customer provides for the firm and the value the firm provides for the customer (i.e., what needs the firm can meet for the customer). All other customer differences, from demographics and psychographics, to behaviors, transactional histories, and attitudes, represent the tools and concepts marketers must use simply to get at these two most fundamental differences. Behaviors are in some instances the most observable, and thus the ability of a company to track differences in customer behaviors allows deeper understanding, and for that reason, we talk about differentiating customers by the value they have *to* the company, the needs they have *from* the company, and the behaviors they manifest that help us understand value and needs, as illustrated in Exhibit 5.1.

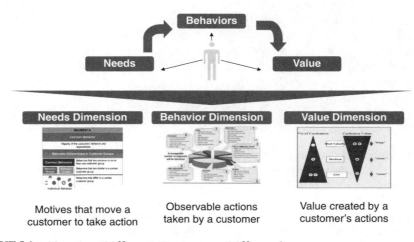

EXHIBIT 5.1   Treating Different Customers Differently

Knowing which customers are most valuable and least valuable to the enterprise will enable a company to prioritize its competitive efforts, allocating relatively more time, effort, and resources to those customers likely to yield higher returns. In effect, an enterprise's financial objectives with respect to any single customer will be defined by the value the customer is currently creating for the enterprise (her **actual value**) as well as the **potential value** the customer *could* create for the enterprise, if the firm could present the exact right offerings at the right time as needed by the customer and thus change the customer's behavior in a way that works for both the customer and the enterprise. Of course, changing a customer's behavior (which is the basic objective of all marketing activity) can be accomplished only by appealing to the customer's own personal motives, or needs. So while understanding a customer's value profile will determine a firm's financial objectives for that customer, the strategies and tactics required to achieve those objectives require an understanding of that customer's needs. It should be noted that a customer has value to the enterprise in two ways that matter to shareholders and decision makers: A customer has current value (revenue minus cost to serve) as well as long-term value *in the present* that goes up or down based on experience with the company or brand, influence from the outside, and changes in his own needs.

In this chapter, we discuss the concept of customer *valuation*, including various ways a company might rank its customers by their individual values to the enterprise. In Chapter 6, we address the issue of customer needs. Importantly, we return again and again throughout the book to these two issues: the different valuations and needs of different individual customers.

Customer Value Is a Future-Oriented Variable

Mail-order firms, credit card companies, telecommunications firms, and other marketers with direct connections to their consumer customers often try to understand their marketing universe by doing a simple form of prioritization called *decile analysis*—ranking their customers in order of their value to the company and then dividing this top-to-bottom list of customers into 10 equal portions, or deciles, with each decile comprising 10 percent of the customers. In this way, the marketer can begin to analyze the differences between those customers who populate the most valuable one or two deciles and those who populate the less valuable deciles. A credit card company may find, for instance, that 65 percent of top-decile customers are married and have two cards on the same account while only 30 percent of other, less valuable customers have these characteristics. Or a Web-based retailer may find that a majority of customers in the bottom three or four deciles have never before bought anything by direct mail or Internet or from a mobile device while 85 percent of those in the top two deciles have.

It would not be unusual for a decile analysis to reveal that 50 percent, or even 95 percent, of a company's profit comes from the top one or two deciles of customers. Mail-order houses and other direct marketers are more likely than other marketers to have used decile analysis in the past, largely as a means for evaluating the productivity of their mailing campaigns, but this kind of customer ranking analysis will become increasingly important as more companies begin to adopt a **customer focus**.[1]

But just how does a company rank-order its customers by their value in the first place? What data would the credit card company use to analyze its customers individually and then array them from top to bottom in terms of their value? And what variables would go into the Internet retailer's customer rankings? What do we mean when we talk about the value of a customer, anyway?

For our purposes, the value a customer represents to an enterprise should be thought of as the same type of value any other financial asset would represent. To say that some customers have more value for the enterprise than others is merely to acknowledge that some customers are more valuable, as assets, than others are. The primary objective of a customer-strategy enterprise should be to increase the value of its customer base, for the simple reason that customers are the source of all short-term revenue and all long-term value creation, by definition. In other words, a company should strive to increase the sum total of all the individual financial assets known as customers.

But this is not as simple as it might sound, because in the same way any other financial asset should be valued, a customer's value to the enterprise is a function of the profit the customer will generate *in the future* for the enterprise.

Let's take a specific example. Suppose a company has two business customers. Customer A generated $1,000 per month in profit for the enterprise over the past two years, while Customer B generated $500 in monthly profit during the same period. Which customer is worth more to the enterprise?

Knowing only what we've been told so far, we can say it's *probable* that Customer A is worth more than Customer B, but this is not a certainty. If Customer A were to generate $1,000 in profit per month in all future months, while Customer B were to generate $500 per month in all future months, then certainly A is worth twice as much to the enterprise as B. But what if we know that Customer A plans to merge its operations into another firm in three months and switch to a different supplier altogether, while Customer B plans to continue doing its regular volume with the company for the foreseeable future? In that case, our ranking of these two

---

[1] Harsha Aeron, Ashwani Kumar, and Janakiraman Moorthy, "Data Mining Framework for Customer Lifetime Value-Based Segmentation," *Journal of Database Marketing & Customer Strategy Management* 19, no. 1 (March, 2012): 17–30; Álvaro Julio Cuadros and Victoria Eugenia Domínguez, "Customer Segmentation Model Based on Value Generation for Marketing Strategies Formulation," *Estudios Gerenciales: Journal of Management and Economics for Iberoamerica* 30, no. 130 (January–March 2014): 25–30. Also see Don Peppers and Martha Rogers, Ph.D., *Return on Customer: Creating Maximum Value from Your Scarcest Resource* (New York: Currency/Doubleday, 2005); and Don Peppers and Martha Rogers, Ph.D., *The One to One Future* (New York: Doubleday, 1993).

customers would be reversed, and we would consider B to be worth more than A. However, if what actually happened was that a competitor derailed A's merger while B went bankrupt and ceased all operations the following month, then our assessment would still be wrong.

By definition, a customer's value to an enterprise, as a financial asset, is a future-oriented variable. Therefore, it is a quantity that can truly be ascertained only from the customer's actual behavior *in the future*. We mortals can analyze data points from past behavior, we can interview a customer to try to understand the customer's future opportunities and intent, and we can even conclude contractual agreements with customers to guarantee performance for the contract period, but the plain truth is that, without clairvoyant powers, we can't *know* what a customer's true value is until the future actually happens, even though we have better and better analytical tools to *predict* what will happen. (Despite the improvements in quantitative analysis available, one study discovered that less than half of all firms are able to measure customer lifetime value, thereby essentially closing off the ability to make optimum strategic decisions.)[2]

However, until that future does happen, we can affect its outcome—at least partially—by our own actions. Suppose we were to find a revenue stream for Customer B that allowed it to continue in business rather than going bankrupt. By our own deliberate action, in this case, we would have changed B's value to our firm as a financial asset.

To think about customer valuation, therefore, we need to use two different but related concepts:

1. *Actual value* is the customer's value, given what we currently know or predict about the customer's future behavior.
2. *Potential value* is what the customer's value as an asset to the enterprise *could* represent if, through some conscious strategy on our part, we could change the customer's future behavior in some way.

Customer Lifetime Value

The "actual value" of a customer, as we defined it, is equivalent to a quantity frequently termed customer **lifetime value (LTV).** Defined precisely, a customer's LTV is the net present value of the expected future stream of financial contributions from the customer.[3] Every customer of an enterprise today will be responsible for some

---

[2] Graham Charlton, "Just 42% of Companies Are Able to Measure Customer Lifetime Value," *Econsultancy* blog, April 8, 2014, https://econsultancy.com/blog/64659-just-42-of-companies-are-able-to-measure-customer-lifetime-value/, accessed February 4, 2016.

[3] It should be noted that a vigorous body of research and literature is emerging in this important field and the notes in this book should be supplemented with a review of the latest findings. Also see Peppers and Rogers, *Return on Customer,* as well as the next resources:

specific series of events in the future, each of which will have a financial impact on the enterprise—the purchase of a product, a blog post about the company, payment for a service, remittance of a subscription fee, a product rating on a Web retailing site, a product exchange or upgrade, a warranty claim, a help-line telephone call, the referral of another customer, and so forth. Each such event will take place at a particular time in the future and will have a financial impact that has a particular value at that time. The net present value **(NPV)**, today, of each of these future value-creating events can be derived by applying a discount rate to it to factor in the time value of money as well as the likelihood of the event. LTV is, in essence, the sum of the NPVs of all such future events attributed to a particular customer's actions.

Andrews, Katherine Zoe. "Optimizing Customer Value and Resource Allocation," *Insights from MSI* (Winter 2003–2004): 1, 2. Offers a straightforward value analysis with attendant prioritization and treatment strategies.

Berger, Paul D. "Connected Lifetime Value: The Impact of Social Media," *Journal of Direct, Data and Digital Marketing Practice* 12 (2011): 328–344. doi: 10.1057/dddmp.2011.2. Introduces CCLV (Connected Customer Lifetime Value), which encompasses not only the present net value of a customer based on purchase prediction but also the predicted value of influence associated with a customer's social network connections.

Berger, Paul, Naras Echambadi, Morris George, Donald R. Lehmann, Ross Rizley, and Rajkumar Venkatesan. "From Customer Lifetime Value to Shareholder Value: Theory, Empirical Evidence, and Issues for Future Research," *Journal of Service Research* 9, no. 2 (November 2006): 156–167.

Blattberg, Robert, Gary Getz, and Jacquelyn S. Thomas. *Customer Equity: Building and Managing Relationships as Valuable Assets.* Boston: Harvard Business School Press, 2001. Classic view focuses on measuring so that marketers can allocate resources wisely between acquisition and retention efforts.

Bolton, Ruth N., Katherine N. Lemon, and Peter C. Verhoef. "The Theoretical Underpinnings of Customer Asset Management: A Framework and Propositions for Future Research," *Journal of the Academy of Marketing Science* 32, no. 3 (2004): 271–292. Proposes CUSAMS—customer asset management of services—and claims that CUSAMS enable service organizations to make a comprehensive assessment of the value of their customers, and to understand the influence of marketing instruments on them. Examines leading indicators of key customer behaviors reflecting the length, depth, and breadth of customer/service-organization relationship: duration, usage, and cross-buying.

Braun, Michael, David A. Schweidel, and Eli Stein. "Transaction Attributes and Customer Valuation," *Journal of Marketing Research* 52, no. 6 (2015): 848–864. Using a B2B service provider, study estimates revenue lost by service provider when it fails to deliver requested level of service, and shows that loss is greater than gain of exceeding customer's requested level of service. Value measure based on past purchase activity (recency and frequency).

Charlton, Graham. "Just 42% of Companies Are Able to Measure Customer Lifetime Value," *Econsultancy* blog, April 8, 2014, https://econsultancy.com/blog/64659-just-42-of-companies-are-able-to-measure-customer-lifetime-value/, accessed February 4, 2016.

Farris, Paul W., Dominique Hanssens, James D. Lenskold, and David J. Reibstein. "Marketing Return on Investment: Seeking Clarity for Concept and Measurement," *Applied Marketing Analytics* 1, no. 3 (Summer 2015): 267–282.

One useful way to think about the different types of events and activities that different customers will be involved in is to visualize each customer as having a **trajectory** that carries the customer through time in a financial relationship with the enterprise. For example, a customer could begin his relationship at a particular starting point and at a particular spending level. At some point, he increases his spending, taking another product line from the company; later he also begins paying more for some added service. Still later he has a complaint, and it costs the company some expense to resolve it. He refers another customer to the company, and that customer then begins her own trajectory, creating a whole additional value stream. Eventually, perhaps several years or decades later, the original customer "leaves the

Gross, Neil. "Commentary: Valuing 'Intangibles' Is a Tough Job, but It Has to Be Done," *BusinessWeek,* August 6, 2001, pp. 54–55. If companies can account for intangibles on a balance sheet when there's a merger or acquisition, why not all the time? Worries that FASB (Financial Accounting Standards Board) will never buy it because any whiff of subjectivity leads to a label of "voodoo accounting."

Gupta, Sunil. "What Is a Free Customer Worth?" *Harvard Business Review* 86, no. 11 (November 2008): 102–109.

Gupta, Sunil, and Donald R. Lehmann. "Customer Lifetime Value and Firm Valuation," *Journal of Relationship Marketing* 5, nos. 2/3 (2006): 87–110.

Gupta, Sunil, and Donald R. Lehmann. *Managing Customers as Investments: The Strategic Value of Customers in the Long Run.* Philadelphia: Wharton School Publishing, 2005. Although its focus is still primarily on investment choices surrounding marketing decisions, it is the best discussion we've seen yet of ROMI or "return on marketing investment."

Gupta, Sunil, Donald R. Lehmann, and Jennifer Ames Stuart. "Valuing Customers," *Journal of Marketing Research* (February 2004): 7–18. Makes the case that much of the financial value of the firm depends on assets not listed on the balance sheet—for example, brands, customers, employees, and knowledge. Demonstrates how valuing customers makes it feasible to value firms, including high-growth firms with negative earnings. Study examines Capital One, Ameritrade, E*TRADE, Amazon.com, and eBay.

Holm, Morten, V. Kumar, and Carsten Rohde. "Measuring Customer Profitability in Complex Environments: An Interdisciplinary Contingency Framework," *Journal of the Academy of Marketing Science* 40, no. 3 (May 2012): 387–401.

Joo, Young-Hyuck, Yunsik Kim, and Suk-Joon Yang. "Valuing Customers for Social Network Services," *Journal of Business Research* 64, no. 11 (November 2011): 1239–1244.

Keiningham, Timothy, Sunil Gupta, Lerzan Aksoy, and Alexander Buoye. "The High Price of Customer Satisfaction." *MIT Sloan Management Review* 55, no. 3 (Spring 2014). Small excerpt available at http://sloanreview.mit.edu/article/the-high-price-of-customer-satisfaction/, accessed February 5, 2016.

Koosha, Hamidreza, and Amir Albadvi. "Customer Lifetime Valuation Using Real Options Analysis," *Journal of Marketing Analytics* 3 (2015): 122–134.

Kordupleski, Ray, *Mastering Customer Value Management: The Art and Science of Creating Competitive Advantage.* Cincinnati: Pinnaflex Educational Resources, 2003.

Kotler, Philip, Marian Dingena, and Waldemar Pfoertsch. "Driving Change with Strategic Customers," in *Transformational Sales: Making a Difference with Strategic Customers* (Cham, Switzerland: Springer International, 2016).

franchise," because his children grow up, or he decides to switch to another product altogether, or he gets divorced, or retires, or dies. At this point, his relationship with the enterprise comes to an end. (We could describe a business customer's trajectory in the same way. Although a "business" may have an indefinite future potential as a customer, each of the individual potential end users, purchasing agents, influencers, and so forth eventually will quit, get promoted or transferred or fired, retire, or die.)

Different customers will have different trajectories. In a way, the lifetime value of each customer amounts to the NPV of the financial contribution represented by that customer's trajectory through the customer base. From a customer's stream of positive contributions, including product and service purchases, an enterprise must deduct the expenses associated with that customer, including the cost of

Kumar, V. *Profitable Customer Engagement: Concept, Metrics, and Strategies* (New Delhi: Sage, 2013).

Kumar, V., and Anita Pansari. "Aggregate and Individual Level Customer Lifetime Value," in *Handbook of Research on Customer Equity in Marketing*, eds. V. Kumar and Denish Shah, 44–75 (Cheltenham, UK: Elgar, 2015).

Kumar, V., and Werner Reinartz. "Customer Analytics Part I" and "Customer Analytics Part II" in *Customer Relationship Management: Concept, Strategy, and Tools*, 89–141 (Heidelberg: Springer, 2012). Summaries of each chapter provided at http://link.springer.com/book/10.1007/978--3--642--20110--3, accessed February 5, 2016.

Larivière, Bart, T. Keiningham, B. Cooil, Lerzan Aksoy, and Edward C. Malthouse. "A Longitudinal Examination of the Three-Component Model of Customer Commitment and Loyalty: The Importance of Identifying Customer Segments and Using Panel Survey Data," *Journal of Service Management,* 2015.

Malthouse, Edward C. *Segmentation and Lifetime Value Models: Using SAS* (Cary, NC: SAS Institute, 2013).

Mark, Tanya, Rakesh Niraj, and Niraj Dawar. "Uncovering Customer Profitability Segments for Business Customers," *Journal of Business-to-Business Marketing* 19, no. 1 (2012): 1–32. Analysis yields six different value-based groups.

Mathias, Peter F., and Noel Capon. "Managing Strategic Customer Relationships as Assets: Developing Customer Relationship Capital," White paper, Columbia University, 2003. Refers to customer equity as CRC (customer relationship capital), discusses six steps for creating and acquiring the future customer wallet (using only business-to-business applications).

Niraj, Rakesh, Mahendra Gupta, and Chakravarthi Narasimhan. "Customer Profitability in a Supply Chain," *Journal of Marketing* 65, no. 3 (July 2001): 1–16. Emphasizes the need for individual customer profitability calculations if customer lifetime values are to be determined.

Persson, Andreas, and Lynette Ryals. "Making Customer Relationship Decisions: Analytics v Rules of Thumb," *Journal of Business Research* 67, no. 8 (August, 2014): 1725–1732.

Rust, Roland T., V. Kumar, and Rajkumar Venkatesan. "Will the Frog Change into a Prince? Predicting Future Customer Profitability," *International Journal of Research in Marketing* 28, no. 4 (December 2011): 281–294. Explores the limitations of using historic profitability to predict future profitability of customers. Offers new model that could help identify customers who, with the right marketing effort, could increase the most in value.

maintaining a relationship. For instance, relationships usually require some amount of individual communication, via phone, mail, e-mail, or face-to-face meetings. These costs, along with any others that apply to a specific individual customer, will reduce the customer's LTV. It sometimes happens that the costs associated with a customer actually outweigh the customer's positive contributions altogether, in which case the customer's LTV is **below zero (BZ).**

Rust, Roland T., Katherine N. Lemon, and Valarie A. Zeithaml. "Return on Marketing: Using Customer Equity to Focus Marketing Strategy," *Journal of Marketing* 68, no. 1 (Winter 2004): 109–127. Presents a strategic framework that enables competing marketing strategy options to be weighed on the basis of projected financial return. Defines *customer equity* as the total discounted lifetime values summed over all of the firm's current and potential customers.

Rust, Roland T., Christine Moorman, and Gaurav Bhalla. "Rethinking Marketing," *Harvard Business Review* 88, no. 1 (January–February 2010): 94–101.

Ryals, Lynette. *Managing Customers Profitably.* Hoboken, NJ: John Wiley & Sons, 2008.

Schulze, Christian, Bernd Skiera, and Thorsten Wiesel. "Linking Customer and Financial Metrics to Shareholder Value: The Leverage Effect in Customer-Based Valuation," *Journal of Marketing* 76, no. 2 (March 2012): 17–32.

David A. Schweidel, Young-Hoon Park, and Zainab Jamal. "A Multiactivity Latent Attrition Model for Customer Base Analysis," *Marketing Science* 33, no. 2 (January 2014): 273–286.

Stahl, Heinz K., Kurt Matzler, and Hans H. Hinterhuber. "Linking Customer Lifetime Value with Shareholder Value," *Industrial Marketing Management* 32, no. 4 (2003): 267–279. Emphasizes increasing importance of ability to evaluate market strategies against ability to deliver shareholder value; therefore, acquisition and maintenance of customers must result in improved cash flows and shareholder value. Argues that customers are assets and shareholder value increases by accelerating and enhancing cash flows, reducing cash flow volatility and vulnerability, and increasing residual value of the firm.

Tarasi, Crina O., Ruth N. Bolton, Anders Gustafsson, and Beth A. Walker. "Relationship Characteristics and Cash Flow Variability: Implications for Satisfaction, Loyalty, and Customer Portfolio Management." *Journal of Service Research* 16, no. 2 (2013): 121–137.

Tarasi, Crina O., Ruth N. Bolton, Michael D. Hutt, and Beth A. Walker. "Balancing Risk and Return in a Customer Portfolio," *Journal of Marketing* 75 (May 2011): 1–17.

Thomas, Jacquelyn S., Werner Reinartz, and V. Kumar. "Getting the Most out of All Your Customers," *Harvard Business Review* 82, nos. 7–8 (July–August 2004): 116–123. Builds on the Return on Marketing Investment literature by asserting that profitability of customers matters more than their raw numbers or their loyalty.

Woodall, Tony. "Conceptualising 'Value for the Customer': An Attributional, Structural, and Dispositional Analysis," *Academy of Marketing Science Review*, no. 12 (2003): 1–42.

Woodruff, Robert B. "Customer Value: The Next Source of Competitive Advantage," *Journal of the Academy of Marketing* Science 25, no. 2 (1997): 139–153.

This sampling cannot serve as an exhaustive review of this important body of literature, since it is developing faster than a textbook or reference book can keep up with. Rather, this list serves as an introduction and basis for understanding and evaluating the ongoing work by others.

We are using the term *contribution*, as opposed to *profit*, deliberately, because the value of a particular customer is equivalent to the marginal contribution of that customer, when he is added to the business in which the enterprise is already engaged. Suppose we add up all the positive and negative cash flows an enterprise will generate over the next few years, and the total is $X. But then Customer A's trajectory of financial transactions is removed from the enterprise, and the positive and negative cash flows will only amount to a lesser total of $Y. The customer's marginal contribution is equal to X − Y. The NPV of those various contributions by Customer A is the customer's LTV. There are additional "contributions" a customer can make, not all of them monetary. Aside from the obvious **word of mouth (WOM)** given by a customer, a nonprofit organization looks to volunteer work or other participation.

In practice, of course, it is not possible for an enterprise to know what any particular customer's future contributions will actually be, and if we want to be able to make current decisions based on this future-oriented number, then we will have to estimate it in some way. Traditionally, the most reliable predictor of a customer's future behavior has been thought to be that customer's past behavior. We are usually quite justified in making the commonsense assumption that a customer who has generated $1,000 of profit each month for the last two years will continue to generate that profit level for some period of time in the future, even though we simultaneously acknowledge that any number of forces can appear that will change this simplistic trend at any moment. (That's why so many of the researchers listed in footnote 3, and others, are hard at work looking for alternative and more accurate ways to predict a customer's future value.) Various computational techniques can be used to model the probable trajectories of particular types of customers more precisely and to project these expected trajectories into the future. Some companies have customer databases that allow highly sophisticated modeling and analysis. Such analysis can sometimes be used to give an enterprise advance warning when a credit card customer, or a cell phone customer, or a Web site subscriber, is about to defect to a competitor. A whole class of statistical analysis tools, frequently termed ***predictive analytics***, is designed to help businesses sift through the historic records of certain types of customers, in order to model the likely behaviors of other, similar customers in the future.

According to the late CRM consultant Frederick Newell, LTV models have a number of uses. They can help an enterprise determine how much it can afford to spend to acquire a new customer or perhaps a certain type of new customer. They can help a firm decide just how much it would be worth to retain an existing customer. With a model that predicts higher values for certain types of customers, an enterprise can target its customer acquisition efforts in order to concentrate on attracting higher-value customers. And, of course, the LTV measurement represents a more economically correct way to evaluate marketing investments compared to simply counting immediate sales.[4]

---

[4] See footnote 3 for a current overview of the topic.

Although sophisticated modeling methods help to quantify LTV, many variables cannot be easily quantified, such as the assistance a customer might give an enterprise in designing a new product, or the value derived from the customer's referral of another customer, or the customer's willingness to advocate for the product or company on a social networking Web site. Any model that attempts to calculate individual customer LTVs should employ some or all of these data, quantified and weighted appropriately:

- Repeat customer purchases.
- Greater profit and/or lower cost (per sale) from repeat customers than from initial customers (converting prospects).
- Indirect benefits from customers, such as referrals. (Imagine that you are a book author and Oprah Winfrey bought and likes your book!)
- Willingness to collaborate—the customer's level of comfort and trust with the company and participation in data exchange that results in the opportunity for better customer experience (sometimes called relationship strength).
- Willingness to refer—word of mouth—as well as social media sharing and rating
- Customers' stated willingness to do business in the future rather than switch suppliers.
- Customer records.
- Transaction records (summary and detail).
- Products and product costs.
- Cost to serve/support.
- Marketing and transaction costs (including acquisition costs).
- Response rates to marketing/advertising efforts.
- Company- or industry-specific information.

The objective of LTV modeling is to use these and other data points to create a historically quantifiable representation of the customer and to compare that customer's history with other customers. Based on this analysis, the enterprise forecasts the customer's future trajectory with the enterprise, including how much he or she will spend, and over what period.

For our purposes, it is sufficient to know that:

- The actual value of a customer is the value of the customer as a financial asset, which is equivalent to the customer's lifetime value—the NPV of future cash flows associated with that customer. (This is the current value, assuming business as usual.)
- LTV is a quantity that no enterprise can ever calculate precisely, no matter how sophisticated its predictive analytics programs and statistical models are.
- Nevertheless, even though—like many of the widely accepted "numbers" calculated to report business performance—it can never be precisely known, LTV is a real financial number, and every enterprise has an interest in understanding

it as accurately as possible and positively affecting its customers' LTVs to the extent possible, and—as we shall see in Chapter 13—to hold members of the organization responsible for exactly that.

As difficult as LTV and actual value may be to model, *potential* value is an even more elusive quantity, involving not just guesses regarding a customer's most likely future behavior but guesses regarding the customer's options for future behavior.

Still, potential value isn't impossible to estimate, especially if the analysis begins with a set of customers who have already been assigned actual values or LTVs. Probably the most straightforward way to estimate a customer's potential value is to look at the range of LTVs for similar customers and then to make the arbitrary assumption that in an ideal world it should at least be possible to turn lower-LTV customers into higher-LTV customers. In the consumer business, this means examining the LTVs for customers who are perhaps at the same income level, or have the same family size, or live in the same neighborhoods. For business-to-business (B2B) customers, it would mean comparing the LTVs of corporate customers in the same vertical industries, with the same sales levels, or profit, or employment levels, and so forth.

The problem at many companies is that a customer's "value to the firm" is confused with the customer's current profitability. Often, measuring customer profitability at all, even in the short term, is an achievement for a firm. But when a customer's LTV is taken into account, the results will be more revealing, and estimating potential values will yield still more insight.

Recognizing the Hidden Potential Value in Customers

It is understandable that a firm's marketing analysts may be reluctant to forecast future behaviors for a customer when they haven't already observed and modeled those behaviors in the customer's transactional history. But consider the idea that today's customer might actually increase his or her patronage with a firm considerably, based solely on the fact that, as time goes on, the customer matures into an older and more productive person. Royal Bank of Canada (RBC)[5] was one of the first banks to look carefully and analytically at the youth segment as a promising group of retail banking customers when most banks were overlooking this segment due to their low current (actual) value. RBC recognized the high potential value of young college students, many of whom would become highly paid professionals in the future. The bank gained a competitive advantage by reaching out to and building loyalty in this segment early on, even though their current value was low. In a similar way, certain groups of customers who are in a temporary financial slump,

---

[5] V. G. Narayanan and Lisa Brem, "Case Study: Customer Profitability and Customer Relationship Management at RBC Financial Group (abridged)," *Journal of Interactive Marketing* 16, no. 3 (Summer 2002): 76.

or even in bankruptcy, could have the potential to be promising and high-value customers in the future. A bank that identifies such customers (differentiating them from other customers who are bankrupt now and likely to remain in financial distress for the long term) and reaches out to them at this difficult stage in their lives is certain to win these customers' loyalty and trust.

In telecommunications, some companies find hidden word-of-mouth power in the ranks of their currently low-value "public-sector employees" segment. For example, when Sprint once offered attractive rates and group discounts to this public-sector group, the word-of-mouth impact resulted in increased new customer acquisitions, increasing the company's profitability and market share.[6] A close look at the needs of the customers was of course an enabling step in this strategy, where the telecommunications company was able to find the rate, payment, or discount benefits that best suited the needs and payment behavior of this customer group. The benefits could easily have been missed, however, had this company looked solely at these customers' historically based actual values.

Taking into account the "customer influence" factor in modeling lifetime value is even more critical in some industries where a small number of customers exert a disproportionate share of influence on others' buying decisions, such as in the pharmaceuticals industry. The primary customers here, at least in most countries, are physicians, and some physicians almost always stand out for the amount of influence they have on the medical practices of other physicians. Identifying and trying to quantify the value of such "key opinion leaders" (KOLs) is a high priority for pharmaceutical companies, such as Abbott Labs, Bristol-Myers Squibb, and Biogen Idec.[7] KOLs usually are viewed by their peers as experts in specific therapeutic areas, and as such they exert immense influence over other doctors when it comes to the types of medications to be prescribed and the kinds of medical treatments to be administered in these therapeutic areas. Even though some KOLs may have low actual values themselves, in terms of the prescriptions they write in their own medical practice, their influence is disproportionately valuable. Some pharmaceutical companies (e.g., Roche[8]) even try to identify rising KOL stars, who are for the most part relatively less well-known professionals who show signs of future success

---

[6] Advisory Opinion No. 05–1, "Conditions under Which a State Employee May Accept a Discount on Goods or Services"; Sprint PCS ("Sprint") provides wireless telephone services for OTDA and other state agencies through a contract approved by the State Office of General Services (2004), available at: www.nyintegrity.org/advisory/ethc/05- 01.htm, accessed September 1, 2010. As of January 2016, Sprint continued to offer a discount on personal Sprint services for government employees and members of Group Purchasing Organizations: https://business.sprint.com/industry/government/.

[7] Rachel Farrow, "Forging Key Opinion Leader Relationships: Developing the Next Generation," *TVF Communications* (July 2008), available at www.tvfcommunications.com/publications .aspx, accessed September 1, 2010.

[8] Farrow, "Forging Key Opinion Leader Relationships: Developing the Next Generation."

and influence. The companies then invite these rising stars to participate in medical education and other activities, hoping to build long-lasting relationships.

One industry in which potential value can be an important differentiator is the airline business. Because of their widely used frequent-flyer programs, airlines usually have a fairly good handle on the transactional histories of their most frequent travelers who are, for the most part, business flyers. But even if a business traveler flies 75,000 miles a year on an airline, the airline has no way of knowing, from its own transactional records, whether that traveler is flying another 150,000 miles on competitive carriers, and thus has a large potential value. So, in trying to estimate the potential value of an airline customer, it is critical to look at external data sources (and, in some cases, simply to *ask* a customer in order to get share-of-customer information) when such sources are available and perhaps to tap into the data available from distributor partners, such as travel websites or credit card firms. Lifestyle changes can also create shifts in the potential value of a customer and should be taken into account. Southwest Airlines, for example, identified and sent relevant offers to some currently low-value customers who moved to another country as expatriates, and these customers proved to have high potential value as evidenced by their future travels on holidays to their home country.

In addition to overlooking customers with high potential value, some companies make wrong and unprofitable investments in customers who seem to be high in value now but in fact have a low or sometimes negative potential value. In the retailer category, companies like Best Buy, Victoria's Secret, and Home Depot[9] have begun tracking customer returns for potential denial of repeat returners, preventing losses from this group who prove to be below zero customers over the long term.

Another company that avoided unnecessary investment in low-potential-value customers is Capital One Bank, which recognized its low-potential-value customers and adjusted its reactive retention strategy to deemphasize them. (After all, why should the company go out of its way to retain a low-value customer?) One variable that can reduce the potential value of a financial services customer is financial risk. Understanding the likelihood that a customer will need to be charged off in the future is an important function for any credit-granting institution. Capital One, while giving incentives and positive offers to its high-value customers who want to close their accounts in order to save them, encouraged the high-risk customers (i.e., low-potential-value customers) to close their accounts with the bank. This policy helps to minimize future financial losses to the bank, improving overall profitability and also making sure that the bank's **most valuable customers (MVCs)** are not subsidizing its lowest-value customers, which is more trustworthy behavior than

---

[9] Jennifer C. Kerr, Associated Press, "Retailers Tracking What Customers Return," *USA Today*, August 12, 2013, http://www.usatoday.com/story/money/business/2013/08/12/retailers-tracking-customers-returns/2642607/, accessed February 4, 2016; and Rajiv Lal, Carin-Isabel Knoop, and Irina Tarsis, "Best Buy Co., Inc.: Customer-Centricity," *Harvard Business School Cases*, April 1, 2006, p. 1.

expecting good customers to pay more than they might to cover the losses caused by bad customers.

Assessing customer value as a combination of current and potential value is no longer a choice if a firm wants to remain truly competitive. Estimating a customer's potential value is certainly more complex than simply trying to forecast actual value, or LTV, and requires a deeper look into factors such as needs, lifestyle phases, and behavioral trends. But making a genuine attempt to do so will likely prove quite beneficial.[10]

Growing Share of Customer

With respect to its relationship with a customer, the goal of any customer-strategy enterprise should be to positively alter the customer's financial trajectory, increasing the customer's overall value to the enterprise. The challenge, however, is to know how much the enterprise really can alter that trajectory—how much increase in the customer's value an enterprise can actually generate. (A new baby will go through 7,000 diapers between birth and toilet training. If your company sells disposable diapers, your goal will, of course, be to get as many of the diapers used to be your brand. But there's likely not anything you can do to get Mom and Dad to have a second infant!)

Unrealized potential value is a term used to denote the amount by which the enterprise could increase the value of a particular customer if it applied a strategy for doing so. It's a very straightforward concept, really, because the unrealized potential of a customer is simply the difference between the customer's potential value and actual value. It represents the potential *additional* business a customer is capable of doing with the enterprise, much of which may never materialize. As an enterprise realizes more and more of a customer's *potential* value, however, it can be said to have a greater and greater share of that customer's business. (Indeed, if we divide a customer's actual value by the customer's potential value, the quotient should give us "**share of customer**.")

Increasing share of customer[11] is an important goal for a customer-strategy enterprise and can be accomplished by increasing the amount of business a customer does, over and above what was otherwise expected (i.e., by applying a strategy to favorably affect the customer's trajectory). This is often referred to as "share of wallet."

---

[10] Thanks to former Peppers & Rogers consultant Pelin Turunc for her contribution to this section.

[11] *Share of customer* (SOC) refers to the percentage of total business conducted by a customer with a particular enterprise, in the product and service arena offered by that enterprise. For example, if a voter contributes a total of $1,000 in the 2024 presidential primaries to several candidates, the candidate who gets a $400 contribution would have a 40 percent SOC with that voter. If a Christmas shopper buys most of his presents at Toys "R" Us, generating December purchases there of $800, as compared to a combined total of all other shopping of $400, then Toys "R" Us would have an SOC of $800 of a total $1,200 in holiday shopping, or SOC = 67 percent. See Chapter 1 for a complete discussion of share of customer.

For example, a bank might have a relationship with a customer who has a checking account, an auto loan, and a certificate of deposit. The customer provides a regular profit to the bank each month, generated by transaction fees and the investment spread between the bank's own investment and borrowing rates, compared to the lending and savings rates it offers the customer. The net present value of this income stream over the customer's likely future tenure is the customer's LTV. This LTV amount is equivalent to the present value of the financial benefits the bank would lose in the future, if the customer were to defect to another financial services organization today.

But suppose that, in addition to the accounts the customer now maintains at the bank, he also has a home mortgage at a competitive institution. This loan represents unrealized potential value for the bank, while it represents actual value to the bank's competitor. The expected profit from that loan is one aspect of the customer's potential value to the bank, which may devise a strategy to win the customer's mortgage loan business away from its competitor.

Or suppose this customer owns a home computer and modem but doesn't participate in the bank's online banking service. If he were to do more of his banking online, however, the cost of handling his transactions would decline, his likelihood of defection would decline, and his value to the bank would increase. Thus, the increased profit the bank could realize if the customer banked online represents another aspect of the customer's potential value to the bank.

Or perhaps the customer is a night student attempting to qualify for a more financially rewarding career. If the bank could help him achieve this objective, he would earn more money and do more banking, and his value to the bank would increase. All these possibilities represent real opportunities for a bank to capture some of a customer's unrealized potential value.

Assessing a Customer's Potential Value

In trying to assess a particular customer's potential value, some of the questions you want to answer include:

- How much of the customer's business currently goes to your competition, but might be pried away with the right approach or relationship?
- How much more of a customer's business could you capture if you modify your treatment of him? If you improve his experience with you?
- How many more product lines might the customer buy from you? What other services or products could you sell the customer if you had the products available?
- What additional value would you capture if you could prevent the customer's defection?
- The customer has needs you know about. How can you identify the needs you don't yet know about?

- How much could you reduce the cost of serving this customer, while maintaining his satisfaction?
- How much could this customer be worth in terms of referrals, social sharing, and other nonmonetary contributions?
- How does this customer treat people in her social networks—and how much *positive* social influence does she have as a result? (Mere numbers don't necessarily indicate positive influence.) How might this translate into profitable word of mouth?

Your opportunity for organic growth is directly related to the unrealized potential values of your current and future customers. But that is just your perspective. From the customer's perspective, potential value has to do with [the customer's] *need*. This is important:

The outside limit of any customer's value is defined by the customer's need, not by your current product or service offering.

See also Don Peppers and Martha Rogers, Ph.D., *Return on Customer* (New York: Currency/Doubleday, 2005).

Different Customers Have Different Values

Increasing a customer's value encompasses the central mission of an enterprise: to *get, keep,* and *grow* its customers. When it understands the value of individual customers relative to other customers, an enterprise can allocate its resources more effectively, because it is quite likely that a small proportion of its most valuable customers will account for a large proportion of the enterprise's profitability. This is an important principle of customer differentiation, and at its core is what is known as the Pareto principle, which asserts that 80 percent of any enterprise's business comes from just 20 percent of its customers.[12] The Pareto principle implies

> The outside limit of any customer's value is defined by the customer's need, not by your current product or service offering.

[12] Philip Kotler and Milton Kotler, *Winning Global Markets: How Businesses Invest and Prosper in the World's High-Growth Cities* (Hoboken, NJ: John Wiley & Sons, 2014); Tarun Kushwaha and Venkatesh Shankar, "Are Multichannel Customers Really More Valuable? The Moderating Role of Product Category Characteristics," *Journal of Marketing* 77, no. 4 (July 2013): 67–85; Rajkumar Venkatesan, "Customer-Lifetime-Value-Based Resource Allocation," in *Handbook of Research on Customer Equity in Marketing*, eds. V. Kumar and Denish Shah (Cheltenham, UK: Elgar, 2015), pp. 283–305; and Fadly Hamka, Harry Bouwman, Mark de Reuver, and Maarten Kroesen, "Mobile Customer Segmentation Based on Smartphone Measurement," *Telematics and Informatics* 31, no. 2 (May 2014): 220–227. For application in attributing value to different customer segments, see V. Kumar and Denish Shah, "Expanding the Role of Marketing: From Customer Equity to Market Capitalization," *Journal of Marketing* 73 (November 2009): 121.

that an Internet retailer ranking its customers into deciles by value is likely to find that the top two deciles of customers account for 80 percent of the business the company is doing. Obviously, the percentages can vary widely among different businesses, and one company might find that the top 20 percent of its customers do 95 percent of its business while another company finds that the top 20 percent of its customers do only 40 percent of its business. But in virtually every business, some customers are worth more than others. When the distribution of customer values is highly concentrated within just a small portion of the customer base, we say that the **value skew** of the customer base is steep.

Pareto Principle and Power-Law Distributions

When it comes to analyzing how customer values are distributed, the 80–20 Pareto principle does not result in a "normal" distribution, like a bell curve. (See Exhibit 5.2.) The Pareto principle is a special case of what mathematicians call a power-law distribution, or a log-normal distribution. The key to understanding how a power law differs from a bell curve is to recognize that power laws go on and on with the same kind of distribution. (For this reason, we say that power-law distributions are "scale-free.")

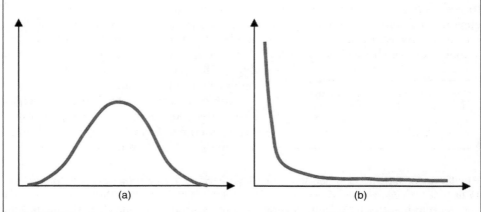

EXHIBIT 5.2   (a) Bell Curve or Normal Distribution and (b) Power-Law or Log-Normal Distribution

For instance, if customer lifetime values are distributed according to the 80–20 Pareto principle, so that the top 20 percent of customers account for

80 percent of the total value, then the 20 percent of *that* top 20 percent of customers will account for 80 percent of *that* 80 percent of value. In other words, just 4 percent of customers (20 percent of 20 percent) will account for 64 percent of a company's total lifetime values (80 percent of 80 percent). Multiply it again and you'll find that fewer than 1 percent of customers will account for more than 50 percent of all customer lifetime value, and so forth.

It's important to remember that all such distributions are still inherently random, and no random distribution of discrete quantities (e.g., individual customer lifetime values) will ever conform precisely to a particular mathematical formula. But it's easy to be confused by the Pareto principle, because it represents a power law, while many of the natural phenomena we observe in everyday life are distributed according to the more intuitively understandable bell curve. Human height, for instance, is distributed according to a bell curve, while wealth is distributed according to a power law. If you walk down a crowded city street and catalog the different heights of the people you encounter, chances are you'll see an occasional 6 foot 6 person or maybe even someone who is nearly 7 feet tall, but the odds of finding someone much taller than 7 feet 6 inches are vanishingly small. (You'll also see one or two adults who are under 5 feet tall and maybe even an occasional person less than 4 feet 6 inches.)

Wealth, however, has no natural upper limit and is distributed according to a power law. Let's suppose human height were distributed the same way personal wealth is distributed, with the average "height" of wealth being about 6 feet. If that were the case, then when you walked down the street you'd run into a few people in the 5- to 7-foot range, but most of the people you meet would actually be shorter than 3 feet tall, and the vast majority of *them* would be only a few inches high! Every block or so, however, you'd encounter a couple of people 20 feet tall, and you'd likely see a 100-foot-tall person or even a 500-foot-tall person once in a great while. The longer you walk, the more likely you'll see someone even taller than the last giant you encountered. If you happened to run into the two tallest people in the United States, Bill Gates and Warren Buffett, they would each tower over the city, their heads more than a mile in the sky. Now, that would be a power-law distribution.

Power-law distributions characterize many kinds of measurable quantities that are based on networks, including the increasing proliferation of Internet-enabled social networks. As technology improves and continues to connect customers more and more closely together, power-law distributions can be expected to characterize things like the number of comments accumulated by different blogs, or the number of viewers of different YouTube videos, or the number of Twitter followers acquired by various users. As we will read in Chapter 8, this is an important and more or less universal characteristic of social networks.

While LTV is the variable an enterprise wants to know, often a financial or statistical model is too difficult or costly to create. Instead, the enterprise may find some proxy variable to be nearly as useful. A *proxy variable* is a number, other than LTV, that can be used to rank customers in rough order of LTV, or as close to that order as possible, given the information and analytics available. A proxy variable should be easy to measure, but it obviously will not provide the same degree of accuracy when it comes to quantifying a customer's actual value or ranking customers relative to each other.

For instance, many direct marketers use a proxy variable called RFM, for *recency, frequency,* and *monetary value,* to rank-order their customers in terms of their value. The RFM model is based on individual customer purchase histories and incorporates three separate but quantified components:

1. *Recency.* Date of this customer's most recent transaction.
2. *Frequency.* How often this customer has bought in the past.
3. *Monetary value.* How much this customer has spent in the most recent specified period.

An airline, by contrast, might use a customer's frequent-flyer mileage as a proxy variable to differentiate one customer's value from another's. The mileage total for the past year, or the past two years, or some other period, will be a good indicator of the customer's value, but it won't be entirely accurate. For instance, it won't tell the airline whether the customer usually flies in first class or in coach, and it won't tell whether the customer always purchases the least expensive seat, frequently chooses to stay over on Saturdays, and takes advantage of various other pricing complexities and loopholes in order to guarantee always obtaining the lowest fare. And, as we noted before, it doesn't reveal anything about potential value based on share of customer.

A proxy variable is, in effect, a representation of a customer's value to the enterprise rather than a quantification of it. Nevertheless, proxy variables can be efficient tools for helping an enterprise rank its customers based on value, and with this ranking the company still can apply different strategies to different customers, based on their relative worth. Although more feasible all the time, sophisticated LTV models can be expensive and time consuming to create. If an enterprise is to explore and benefit from customer valuation principles, proxy variables that allow initial rank-ordering of customers by value are a good starting point.

The goal of value differentiation is not a *historical* understanding but a *predictive* plan of action. RFM and other, similar, proxy-variable methods show that while differentiating among customers can be mathematically complex, it is still fundamentally a simple principle.

> The goal of value differentiation is not a *historical* understanding, but a *predictive* plan of action.

Customer Value Categories

Every customer has an actual value and a potential value. By visualizing the customer base in terms of how customers are distributed across actual and potential values, marketing managers can categorize customers into different value profiles, based on the type of financial goal the enterprise wants to achieve with each customer. For instance, one of a company's goals for a customer with a high unrealized potential value would be to grow its share of customer (in order to realize some of this value), while one of the goals for a customer with low actual value and low potential value would be to minimize servicing costs. By thinking of individual customers in terms of both each one's actual value (i.e., current LTV) and its unrealized potential values (i.e., growth potential), a company could array its customers roughly as shown in Exhibit 5.3. (We will talk more about managing experiences and values for these customers in Chapter 14.)

Five different categories of customers are shown on this diagram, and an enterprise should have different strategic goals for each one:

1. *Most valuable customers (MVCs).* In the lower right quadrant of Exhibit 5.3, MVCs are the customers who have the highest actual value to the enterprise. This could be for any or all of a number of different reasons: they do the highest volume of business, yield the highest margins, stay more loyal, cost less to serve, and/or have the highest referral value. MVCs are also customers with whom the company probably has the greatest share of customer. These may or may not be the traditional "heavy users" of a product; the MVC may, for example, fly a lot less often but always pays full fare for first-class tickets. The primary financial objective an enterprise will have for its MVCs is retention, because these are the customers likely giving the company the bulk of its profitability to begin

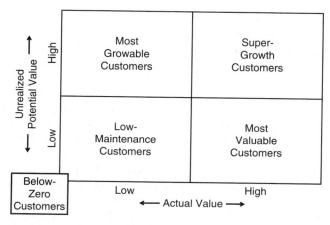

EXHIBIT 5.3   Customer Value Matrix

with. In the airline business, these are the "platinum flyers" in the frequent-flyer program. In order to retain these customers' patronage, an airline will give out bonus miles, offer special check-in lines, provide club benefits, and so forth. For a pharmaceutical company marketing prescription drugs to physicians, however, the most valuable customers may be those particular physicians who have the most influence over other physicians. (See "Customer Referral Value.")

2. ***Most growable customers (MGCs).*** *In the upper left* quadrant of Exhibit 5.3, MGCs are customers who have little actual value to the enterprise today but significant growth potential. Here, of course, the enterprise's financial objective is to realize some of that potential value. As a practical matter, these customers are often large-volume or high-profit customers who simply patronize a different company. MGCs are often, in fact, the MVCs of the enterprise's competitors. So the company's objective will be to change the dynamics in some way so as to achieve a higher share of each of these customers' business. (Don't forget, however, that the reverse is also true: Your own MVCs are your competitors' MGCs.)

3. ***Low-maintenance customers.*** In the lower left quadrant are customers who have little current value to the enterprise and little growth potential. But they are still worth something (i.e., they are still profitable, at some level), and there may indeed be a whole lot of them. The enterprise's financial objective for low-maintenance customers should be to streamline the services provided to them and to drive more and more interactions into more cost-efficient, automated channels. For a retail bank, for instance, these are the vast bulk of middle-market customers whose value will increase substantially if they can be convinced to use the bank's online services rather than taking the time and attention of tellers at the branch.

4. ***Super-growth customers.*** In the upper right quadrant of Exhibit 5.3, many enterprises will have just a few customers who have substantial actual value *and also* a significant amount of untapped growth potential. This is more likely to be true for B2B firms than for consumer-marketing companies. If a company sells to corporate customers, it will likely have a few very large firms in its customer base that are giant, immense firms that already give the company a substantial amount of business. That is, they are likely already high-value customers, but they are so immense that they could still give the enterprise much more business. No matter what size B2B firm an enterprise is, if it sells to Microsoft, or Intel, or Toyota, or GE, or other corporate customers with similarly large financial profiles, chances are these customers are super-growth customers. The business objective here is not just to retain the business already achieved but to mine the account for more. There is one caveat, however: Sometimes super-growth customers, who obviously know that they represent immense opportunity for the companies they buy from, use their customer relationships to drive very hard bargains, squeezing margins down as they push volumes up. They can be merciless, because they know they are highly valuable to the firms they choose to buy from. (See "Dealing with Tough Customers.")

5. ***Below zeros (BZs).*** With very low or negative actual and potential values, BZs are customers who, no matter what effort a company makes, are still likely to generate less revenue than they cost to serve. No matter what the firm does, no matter what strategy it follows, a BZ customer is highly unlikely ever to show a positive net value to the enterprise. Nearly every company has at least a few of these customers. For a telecommunications company, a BZ might be a customer who moves often and leaves the last month or two unpaid at each address. For a retail bank, a BZ might be a customer who has little on deposit with the bank, but tends to use the teller window often. (Some banks in the United States estimate that as many as 40 to 50 percent of their retail customers are, in fact, BZs.) For a B2B firm, there can be a razor-thin difference between a super-growth customer and a BZ, because some giant business clients can threaten to drive margins down so low that they no longer cover the cost of servicing the account. The enterprise's strategy for a BZ should be to create incentives either to convert the customer's trajectory into a breakeven or profitable one (e.g., by imposing service charges for services previously given away for free) or to encourage the BZ—very politely—to become someone else's unprofitable customer.

This categorization of customers by their value profiles is fairly arbitrary, because it presumes customers can be split into just a few tight groups, based on actual and potential value. But whether the enterprise uses the MVC-MGC-BZ typology or not, what should be clear is that the enterprise should have different financial objectives for, and invest different resources in, different customers, based on its assessment of the kind of value each customer is or is not creating for it already and what kind of value is possible.

Customer Referral Value

Obviously, some customers will refer new customers to an enterprise more frequently than others will, and this represents real value "created" by the referring customers. In most situations, a customer who comes into the enterprise's franchise because of another customer's referral is likely to be more satisfied with the service he or she receives, more loyal, and often significantly more valuable to the business than a customer who comes in through normal marketing or sales channels. This is only logical, because a friend's recommendation is a highly trusted vote of confidence. With social media and ratings systems, this referral value is now on steroids.

An enterprise should try to track customer referrals by individual customer, of course. For one thing, the enterprise needs to consider the fact of a referral in a customer's transactional records, because referred customers as well as

(continued)

(Continued)

referring customers may tend to have different patterns of behavior and trajectories. In addition, the enterprise probably should thank the referring customer or provide other positive feedback that encourages additional referrals (although explicit monetary rewards are tricky here, as we will discuss soon).

The **Net Promoter Score (NPS),** outlined by Fred Reichheld and owned by Satmetrix, is a compact metric designed to quantify the strength of a company's word-of-mouth reputation among existing customers.[a] Leading Bain consultant Reichheld suggests a business survey of its customers to ask how willing they would be to recommend the business or product to a friend or colleague, on a scale of 1 to 10. The NPS is then calculated by subtracting the percentage of "detractors," who rate the likelihood anywhere from 1 to 6, from the percentage of "promoters," who rate it 9 or 10. With research from Bain and Satmetrix, Reichheld claims that the resulting metric is positively correlated not only with customer loyalty but with a company's growth prospects and its general financial performance. Reichheld also argues strongly that if a customer is willing to refer another customer, then he must be relatively more satisfied (and therefore more likely to remain loyal and valuable) himself as well.[b] As a very simple number based on a single question, NPS doesn't offer a lot of diagnostic benefit—that is, by itself, it isn't likely to say much about why a customer is or is not willing to recommend, but it has to be admired for its simplicity and practicality as well as its intuitive logic. More recently, NPS has been expanded by its adopters to a transformative system for businesses rather than just a metric.[c]

Significantly, calculating NPS requires subtracting detractors from promoters, which is an excellent idea, because customer dissatisfaction has been found to be a much better predictor of defection than customer satisfaction is of loyalty. Despite this fact, most companies that do track their customer satisfaction scores don't bother trying to track dissatisfaction scores. This is a big mistake, because when customers talk about a company with other customers, it isn't always positive. And negative word of mouth can be an insidious, destructive force all by itself, with a real effect on the financial value of the firm. (More about this in Chapter 8, when we discuss social media.)

At least one study suggests that a customer's actual referral value—that is, the true financial value of a customer's referrals to an enterprise—is not well correlated with the value created by the customer's own spending. In other words, although a customer may refer others to a business, this doesn't necessarily mean that the customer herself spends much more than other customers. In a *Harvard Business Review* article, "How Valuable Is Word of Mouth?" the authors developed a comprehensive model for calculating the value of referrals, taking into account the likelihood that a referred customer might have become a customer anyway, even without the referral. They then applied their model to a sample set of customers taken from two different actual firms—one telecom company and one financial services firm. What they found was that the value created by customer referrals is a very significant component of overall customer lifetime values. A decile analysis of customer spending values (CSVs) and customer referral values (CRVs) for the telecom company's customers would look like Exhibit 5.4. A very high-value social influencer is called a *buzz agent*, and many companies now solicit them.[d]

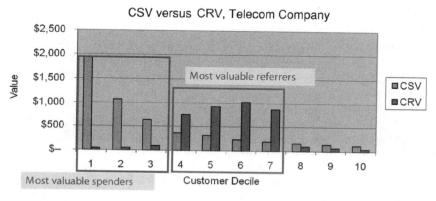

EXHIBIT 5.4   Decile Analysis of Customer Spending Values (CSVs) and Customer Referral Values (CRVs)

Rewarding customers with monetary incentives for referring other customers can be helpful sometimes in encouraging more referrals. This is the basis for the classic direct marketing strategy colloquially known as member-get-a-member and is a common feature even today of many airline frequent-flyer programs. Then there was the classic "Friends and Family" program launched by MCI, which was a remarkable success in the long-distance business in the 1990s. Name 10 friends or family members you make long-distance calls to, and if they become MCI customers, then everyone in your "circle" of friends and family will get a 10 percent discount off their calls to one another. More recently, Sprint PCS has made it a practice to give any customer who refers another customer a service credit of $20, while Scottrade, the online brokerage firm, provides a few free stock trades to both referring and referred customers.[e] But the very best and likely most valuable referrals will come without requiring any monetary incentive. If a customer is very happy with a company's product or service, then she is much more likely to see referring her friend to the company as doing the friend a favor. If, however, a financial incentive is offered, then (the customer might think) how confident can the company be in the quality of its product?

(continued)

(*Continued*)

A highly successful online banking service in the United Kingdom, for instance, had a reputation for extremely good **customer service.** By its own analysis, this bank had customer satisfaction levels and "willingness to recommend" levels far above its nearest bricks-and-mortar banking competitors. Moreover, the bank had grown substantially in the past through customer recommendations. Citing Market & Opinion Research International, the firm's own Web site claimed it was "the UK's most recommended bank."[f]

However, after a few years in business, it had apparently begun to wear out its welcome among many of its most loyal customers. One customer, for instance, reported to the authors that while he used to recommend the bank to his friends regularly, he had stopped doing so. Why? Because lately the bank had been sending him repeated, irrelevant solicitations by mail. A 12-year customer of the bank, he "never borrows," but he and his wife now get about one solicitation a week for mortgages or loans. "I still bank there. It's a good bank," he says. "But I used to recommend [this bank] all the time to friends and others. I just thought I was doing a good turn for my friends by recommending it to them. But now they're more like all the other banks out there—just trying to hustle me for more business. So I haven't recommended them recently to anyone. Also, I know several other customers who feel the same way."[g] And this may be one reason why this bank now pays its customers £25 for each new customer recommended to it. Put another way: The bank's current lower customer experience levels required it to pay a fee for recommendations it formerly got for free.

---

[a] Fred Reichheld with Rob Markey, *The Ultimate Question 2.0: How Net Promoter Companies Thrive in a Customer-Driven World* (Boston: Harvard Business Review Press, 2011).
[b] Reichheld with Markey, *The Ultimate Question 2.0*; Danny Pimentel Claro and Adriana Bruscato Bortoluzzo, "Profiling the Buzz Agent: Product Referral and the Study of Social Community and Brand Attachment," *BAR* (*Brazilian Administration Review*) 12, no. 2 (April/June 2015), available at http://www.scielo.br/scielo.php?pid=S1807--76922015000200209&script=sci_arttext, accessed February 4, 2016.
[c] In *The Ultimate Question 2.0*, Reichheld lays out the Net Promoter *System*, claiming that the Net Promoter *Score*, which he explains thoroughly in *2.0*, has been expanded by its adopters to a transformative system for businesses rather than just a metric. He gives many examples of standout companies that have high profitability and high Net Promoter ratings.
[d] The authors defined customer lifetime values in terms of spending only, but we will call this "customer spending value," while in our definition of "lifetime value" customer referrals are already included.

[e] V. Kumar, "How Valuable Is Word of Mouth?" *Harvard Business Review* 85, no. 10 (October 2007): 139–146; Claro and Bortoluzzo, "Profiling the Buzz Agent"; Xevelonakis Evangelos, "Social Influence and Customer Referral Value," in AITNER's (Athens Institute for Education and Research) Conference Paper Series MKT2015–1605, available at http://www.atiner.gr/papers/MKT2015--1605.pdf, accessed February 4, 2016.
[f] Customer interview, November 12, 2003.
[g] Customer interview, November 12, 2003.

One large B2B company performed a value analysis of its customer base and arrayed its customers by actual value and unrealized potential value, creating the scattergram shown in Exhibit 5.5. Each of the dots in the exhibit represents a different business customer. The customers in this graph who occupy the long spike out to the right represent this company's MVCs. Clearly, these are the customers giving the company the most business, and few of them have much unrealized potential value, because the company is getting the bulk of each one's patronage in its category. Down in the lower left of the graph we can find a few customers who have less than zero actual value; these (of course) are this company's BZ customers.

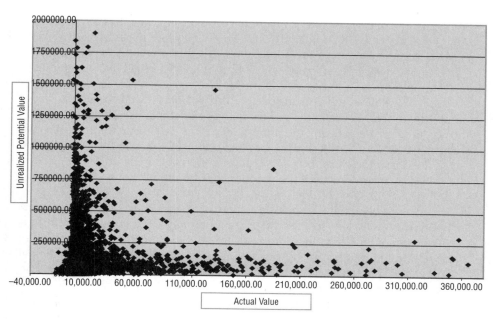

EXHIBIT 5.5   **National Accounts' Actual versus Unrealized Potential Value**

The tall spike up the left-hand side of the scattergram represents this company's MGCs. These are the customers who don't give the firm much of their business right now but clearly have a great deal of business to give it, if they could be convinced to do so. You might note that the horizontal-vertical scales on this scattergram are not the same—that is, the vertical spike, if drawn to the same scale as the horizontal one, would soar up the page much farther than the illustration allows. And most of the customers in this vertical spike are the company's *competitor's* MVCs.

Is It Fair to "Fire" Unprofitable Customers?

As a company gets better at predicting actual and strategic value, it will become clear that just as 20 percent or so of its customers will likely account for the lion's share of the firm's profitability, another relatively small group of customers is likely to account for the lion's share of service costs and transaction losses. It is not uncommon for a retail bank, for instance, to do a customer valuation analysis and learn that 110 percent of its profit comes from just the top 30 percent or so of its customers while the vast bulk of customers are either breakeven or unprofitable for the bank, when considered individually. Other businesses have similar problems, although retail banking is probably one of the most extreme examples.

Because of traditional marketing's heavy emphasis on customer acquisition, for many companies, it would be anathema even to suggest it, but the plain truth is that, in many cases, a company would simply be more profitable if it were to *get rid* of some customers—provided, of course, that the customers it rids itself of are the ones who create losses without profit and who will likely continue to do so in the future.

Before leaping to the conclusion that this is unfair to customers, consider that it is the profitable customers—a company's best, most valuable customers—who are, in effect, subsidizing the unprofitable ones. So "firing" unprofitable customers is not at all a hostile activity but one designed to make the overall value proposition fairer for everybody. Nevertheless, there are some important ground rules to follow when reducing the number of BZ customers at a company:

- However a company defines the value of a customer, the analysis must apply the same way to everyone. The company engaging in careful customer value differentiation does not care about skin color, gender, religion, or political views. It cares only about each customer's actual and potential value, and it acts accordingly. This may disadvantage some customers who have long ago abandoned loyalty in favor of coupon clipping or other price shopping but will appropriately reward the customers who are keeping the business in business.

- Some companies, such as utilities or telecommunications firms (or banks, in some countries), have enjoyed monopoly or near-monopoly status in the past through regulatory directive. Even if they are no longer government-sanctioned monopolies, as the established incumbents these firms are likely to continue to have universal service mandates that require them to serve any and all customers. Such firms still may choose to define value or customer profitability in a more sophisticated way than simple revenue minus cost of service. The telephone company that provides basic service to Aunt Matilda in a rural area cannot hope to make a "profit" on her, in the strictest financial sense, but rather than classifying her as a BZ customer, it might consider her part of the company's mission to serve the community. Moreover, accomplishing this mission probably will be related to the company's regulatory situation, and foreswearing such a customer might violate a legal requirement. For such a company, the real BZ customers would be those who move every few months and leave the final bill unpaid, requiring extra collection efforts; or who often cause mishaps with neighborhood lines; or who frequently change carriers or otherwise create excessive paperwork. These customers can be omitted from promotional mailing lists and other spending efforts. It's okay to stop spending money trying to get a customer to generate a greater loss for the firm.
- Most important: Nothing about customer differentiation means treating anybody badly, ever. The enterprise that treats different customers differently will be required to maintain a consistently high "floor" of service that is the result of a fundamental recognition that customers are a twenty-first-century firm's most valuable asset, and—by definition—the firm's only source of revenue.

> Nothing about customer differentiation means treating anybody badly. Ever.

Dealing with Tough Customers

Sometimes, because of the structure of an enterprise's own industry or its distribution network, or simply because of the type of market it has to deal with, it will have to cope with very powerful customers—customers who have a great deal of negotiating leverage in their relationship with the vendors they buy from. Customers like these, while they may represent super-growth customers when considered in one light, are large enough that they can also demand and

(continued)

(*Continued*)

get highly favorable terms, in the form of lower prices, better service, priority delivery, and so forth. Occasionally, such customers are so powerful that they may all but require an enterprise to lose money just to serve them. But extremely large customers also have prestigious names and are difficult for any company to resist.

In retailing, the giant megastores and category killers, such as Wal-Mart or some of the fast-food chains, are very tough customers.[a] In the high-tech field, companies that manufacture components in mature markets, such as microchips, must sell to tough customers like Lenovo and Hewlett-Packard. In the automotive category, almost all of the manufacturers are large, difficult to deal with, and obsessively concerned with price.

It's important for a company to keep its perspective when serving "oppressive but necessary customers."[b] In the first place, a firm can make rational decisions with respect to such relationships only if it understands its customers' actual and potential values across the entire enterprise. But in addition, management at the enterprise should keep in mind that it really is a power struggle, so their firm must somehow develop more power for itself in the relationship. (Ironically, given all our discussion about "trust," a tough customer will very likely trust the enterprise, but it's the enterprise that will need to step carefully when dealing with this customer.) The goal, however, is to serve the customer's best interests, and the enterprise won't be able to do this if it has to give up on the relationship entirely because it has become too one-sided.

One former senior executive at Company X, a Fortune 100 technology firm, says that "[Company X] was always looked upon as the must-win account for every supplier—and we knew that well. So we routinely adopted very tough positions and made stringent demands." According to this executive, the company's "typical behavior" with respect to suppliers was to "work closely with that company, study them, and try to extract as much of the process and knowledge as possible, then fire the supplier and do it ourselves. Overall, being self-sufficient was always a key objective. A few companies managed to avoid this ultimate fate by continually innovating faster than we [at Company X] could absorb; so they maintained the ability to deliver new value each year."

This is the policy that many large and powerful buyers follow, especially in highly competitive environments or during periods of rapid and potentially **disruptive innovation.** The problem, when selling to such a customer, is that it will be very difficult to increase profitability or even to maintain it. It will be nearly impossible to establish any kind of loyalty or to protect margins—but that is, in fact, the purpose behind the customer's behavior in the first place. When dealing with suppliers, this kind of customer wants to use its power to hammer its costs down; and powerful firms have powerful hammers.

Sometimes an enterprise can maintain loyalty and protect its margins with tough customers by perpetually innovating new products or services, staying ahead of the customers themselves. Magna International sells automobile parts to all the world's giant auto companies. Automotive companies are renowned for their tight-fistedness, their tough price negotiations, and their buying power. This is a brutal environment for a seller, but Magna is an innovative firm. With 285 manufacturing operations and 83 product-development, engineering, and sales centers employing 125,525 people around the world,[c] Magna is a large company—but it is still at a disadvantage when it comes to selling to most of its gigantic customers.

Magna set up its Magna Steyr operation specifically to cater to the most important unmet needs of these auto giants.[d] As the auto business has matured, it has seen increased fluctuations in demand for particular models. The car companies themselves are often unable to cope with these demands, and a "hot" model might be sold out for months at a time. Rather than selling auto parts at arm's length, the Magna Steyr division brings together all the capabilities required to manufacture cars, from parts to engineering, design, and production. For example, when demand for the new Mercedes M-Class SUV exceeded the capabilities of Mercedes's Tuscaloosa assembly line in late 1998, Magna Steyr was producing additional M-Class vehicles for Daimler-Chrysler on its own assembly line in Graz, Austria, within just nine months. Recently, Magna Steyr made a similar deal with Jaguar Land Rover.[e] This kind of service can help a firm protect its margins even with the toughest customers. And as a strategic asset, Magna Steyr's capabilities provide the company with a sustainable competitive advantage over its own competitors.

Sometimes an enterprise can deal effectively with tough customers by devising some service or offering that is **customized** to each customer's own needs, or that is available only because of the enterprise's own, larger breadth of experience or knowledge of the marketplace. In the commercial explosives business, Orica is a global company serving a large number of mining companies and quarry operators.[f] Quarry operators want their blasts to break rocks up into pieces of optimal size. An ineffective blast might leave the rock in chunks too large to be processed in an economically viable way. But as many as 20 different variables have to be considered when calibrating an explosive blast, and each quarry's ability to experiment with these parameters is limited. Because of its size, and the many different mines and quarries Orica deals with, the company can collect a great deal of information from around the world, cataloging input parameters and blast results for a wide variety of situations. As a result, Orica has developed a sound understanding of blasting techniques and now offers

(continued)

(*Continued*)

to take charge of the entire blasting process for a customer, selling a service contract for broken rocks of a specific size. This service has two advantages for Orica's customers:

1. They minimize the risk of poorly executed blasts. With an Orica contract, a customer, together with Orica, basically establishes a "floor price" for correctly broken-up rock.
2. Many of a customer's fixed costs, such as equipment for drilling and employees to manage the process, now become variable costs, which makes it that much easier for the company to manage each separate blasting project for its own customers. What makes this service useful to customers is the fact that Orica is uniquely positioned to compile information on blast techniques and parameters in a wide variety of situations. Any single one of its customers would have a great deal of difficulty duplicating this expertise.

Four principal tactics can be used to improve and maintain the value of even the toughest customers, and each of these tactics involves increasing the enterprise's relative power, uniqueness, or indispensability in the relationship:

1. *Customization of services or products.* An enterprise can build high-end, customized services around the more commodity-like products or services it sells, which creates **switching costs** that increase a customer's willingness to remain loyal, rather than bidding out the contract at every opportunity. Ideally, the enterprise will lock the customer into a Learning Relationship, but most tough customers will be wary of allowing such relationships to develop. The trick here is for the company to ensure that whatever high-end services are developed can be duplicated only by its competitors with great effort, even if they are instructed in advance (and they almost certainly will be by this tough customer!). This was Orica's strategy in offering "broken rock of a certain size" to customers rather than simply selling them explosives.
2. *Perpetual, cost-efficient innovation.* To the extent that an enterprise can stay ahead of its tough customer with innovative product or service ideas, it will always have something to sell. The organizational mission must center on being nimbler, more creative, and cost efficient—all at the same time. But the value such a firm is really bringing to the customer here is innovation, not the products themselves. Many tough customers will do their best to absorb a seller's innovation in order to do it themselves or perhaps even to disseminate it to the seller's own competitors, in order to maintain vigorous competition and low prices. In either case, the customers' motive is to regain their negotiating power in dealing with the seller. So perpetual innovation

is just that—perpetual. If a company can keep the wheels spinning fast enough, and provided that it doesn't lose control of costs, it can safely deal with very tough buyers. This is the strategy behind Magna Steyr's relationship with auto company customers.

3. *Personal relationships* within the customer organization. In the end, businesses have no brains, and they make no decisions. Only the people within a business make decisions, and people are both rational and emotional by nature. Therefore, the individuals within the enterprise need to have personal relationships with the individuals within the customer's organization. In the high-tech or automotive arena, this might mean developing relationships with the engineers within a customer's organization who are responsible for designing the company's components into the final product. In the retailing business, it could mean developing relationships with the regional merchandising managers who get promoted based on the success of the programs the enterprise helps organize for them.

4. *Appeals directly to end users.* A highly desirable brand or a completely unique product in heavy demand by the customer's own customers will pull a seller's products through the customer's own organization more easily. The "Intel Inside" advertising campaign is designed to create pull-through for Intel. When Mattel offers Toys "R" Us an exclusive arrangement for particular configurations, or products with brand names such as "Barbie" or "Transformers" or "Harry Potter," it is making itself indispensable to this very tough customer. Similarly, any sort of information system or added service that saves time or effort for the end user can also be expected to put pressure on a tough customer. Dell's Web pages for enterprise customers not only save money for the customers but also give Dell a direct, one-to-one relationship with the executives who actually have the Dell computers on their desks.

Management should never forget, however, that selling to a tough customer is a deliberate decision, and it's possible sometimes that this decision will be made for the wrong reason. There are almost always choices to be made when thinking about the types of customers to serve, but often companies focus on the very large, most visible and "strategic" customers (i.e., tough customers), in the erroneous belief that simply because of their size they will be the most profitable. But, according to the former technology executive from Company X:

> *Overall, I don't think that we at [Company X] are all that different from most category-dominant companies. These guys know they're good and can get away with demanding just about anything. What many suppliers discover*

(continued)

(Continued)

> *sooner or later is that despite the outward allure of serving a company like ours, once you actually win the business, the long-term payoff can be too painful to harvest. It was not unusual for a supplier to "fire" us as a customer by politely declining to bid on the next program.*

[a] Nathan Layne, "Wal-Mart Puts the Squeeze on Suppliers to Share Its Pain as Earnings Sag," *Reuters Business News,* October 19, 2015, available at http://www.reuters.com/article/2015/10/19/us-wal-mart-suppliers-insight-idUSKCN0SD0CZ20151019#uReCgVdXTL4i2Sgw.97, accessed February 4, 2016.

[b] Thanks to Bob Langer, Tom Spitale, Vernon Tirey, Steve Skinner, and Lorenz Esguerra for their perspectives on the issues in this section on "tough customers." The term *oppressive-but-necessary customers* is from Tom Spitale.

[c] Available at http://www.magna.com/media/magna-facts-figures/facts-figures, accessed February 4, 2016.

[d] For more about Magna, see http://www.magna.com/capabilities/vehicle-engineering-contract-manufacturing/product-services/contract-manufacturing, accessed February 4, 2016.

[e] "Jaguar Land Rover Signs Contract Manufacturing Deal with Magna Steyr," Jaguar Land Rover press release, July 1, 2015, available at http://newsroom.jaguarlandrover.com/en-us/jlr-corp/news/2015/7/jlr_manufacturing_magnasteyr/, accessed February 4, 2016.

[f] See www.oricaminingservices.com, accessed February 4, 2016. See also Jill Jusko, "How to Build a Better Supplier Partnership," *IndustryWeek*, May 12, 2011, available at http://www.industryweek.com/global-economy/how-build-better-supplier-partnership, accessed February 4, 2016; and the Executive Office of the President and the U.S. Department of Commerce, *Supply Chain Innovation: Strengthening America's Small Manufacturers*, a White House report (March 2015), available at https://www.whitehouse.gov/sites/default/files/docs/supply_chain_innovation_report.pdf, accessed February 4, 2016.

Managing the Mix of Customers

One way to think about the process of managing customer relationships is that the enterprise is attempting to improve its situation not just by adding as many new customers as possible to the customer base but also by managing the mix of customers it deals with. It wants to add to the number of MVCs, create more profitability from its MGCs, and minimize its BZs. An enterprise in this situation could choose either to emphasize adding new customers to its customer base or (instead or in addition) to increase the values of the customers in its customer base. So imagine if an enterprise

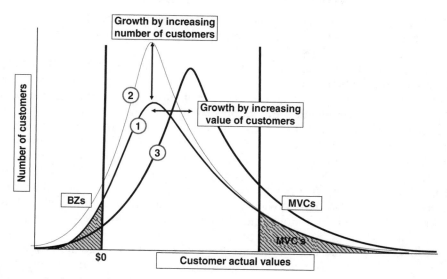

EXHIBIT 5.6   Managing the Mix of Customers

were to plot the distribution of its customer values on a chart, as in Exhibit 5.6, with actual values of customers shown across the bottom axis and the number of customers shown up the vertical axis.

Curve 1 on Exhibit 5.6 shows the enterprise's current mix of customers, with just a few BZs and MVCs and the bulk of customers lying in between these two extremes. By applying a customer-acquisition marketing strategy the enterprise will end up acquiring more and more customers, but these customers are likely to show the same mix of valuations as in its current customer base, as shown by Curve 2. Market share will likely improve, but the mix of customers will almost certainly remain the same. In fact, a customer acquisition strategy often results in a degraded **mix of customer values,** when an enterprise focuses on the number of customers acquired (as happens at many companies) without respect to their values. Almost by definition, low-value customers are easier to acquire than high-value customers. If the only variable being measured by the firm's management is the *number* of customers acquired, then average customer values will almost certainly decline rather than remain the same.

If, however, the enterprise employs a customer-centric strategy, it will not be trying to acquire just *any* customers; instead, it will be focusing its customer acquisition efforts on acquiring higher-value customers. Moreover, it will focus a lot of its effort on improving the value of its existing customers, and moving them up in value individually. The result of such a strategy is shown as Curve 3 in Exhibit 5.6. An enterprise that launches a successful CRM effort will end up shifting the customer mix itself, moving the entire customer base into a higher set of values.

Creating a valuable customer base requires understanding the distribution of customer relationship values and investing in acquisition, development, and retention accordingly.[13] Think of this as **customer value management.** By taking the time to understand the value profile of a customer relative to other customers, enterprises can begin to allocate resources intentionally to ensure that the most valuable customers remain loyal. The future of an enterprise, therefore, depends on how effectively it acquires profitable new customers, develops the profitability of existing customers, and retains existing profitable relationships.[14] Customers will want to spend money with a business that serves them well, and that is nearly always a company that knows them well and uses that knowledge to build relationships in which customers perceive great value and benefit.[15]

Certainly one of the most important benefits of ranking customers by value is that the enterprise can more rationally allocate its resources and marketing efforts, focusing more on high-value and high-growth customers and less on low-value customers. Moreover, the enterprise will likely find it less attractive, as a marketing tactic, to acquire strangers as "customers"—some of whom will never be worth anything to the company.

Janet LeBlanc, named a 1to1 Customer Champion by 1to1 Media, tells the story about how Canada Post differentiated its customers by value and, in the process, increased top-line revenue and cut costs to serve as well.

---

[13] Peter C. Verhoef and Katherine N. Lemon, "Successful Customer Value Management: Key Lessons and Emerging Trends," *European Management Journal* 31, no. 1 (February 2013): 1–15; Michael Lewis, "Customer Acquisitions Promotions and Customer Asset Value," *Journal of Marketing Research* 43 (May 2006): 195–203; and Roland T. Rust, Katherine N. Lemon, and Valarie Zeithaml, "Return on Marketing: Using Customer Equity to Focus Marketing Strategy," *Journal of Marketing* 68 (January 2004): 109–127.

[14] Peter Fader, *Customer Centricity: Focus on the Right Customers for Strategic Advantage*, 2nd ed. (Philadelphia: Wharton Digital Press, 2012); and Yichen Lin Jr., Jung Lyu, Hwan-Yann Su, and Yulan Hsing, "A Feasibility Study of the Customer Relationship Management Application on Small and Medium Enterprises," *Journal of Scientific and Technological Studies* 41, no. 1 (2007): 54.

[15] *Building Trusted Relationships through Analytics and Experience,* a Forbes Insight Report (Ernst and Young, 2015), available at http://www.ey.com/Publication/vwLUAssets/EY-building-trusted-relationships-through-analytics-and-experience/$FILE/EY-building-trusted-relationships-through-analytics-and-experience.pdf, accessed February 5, 2016; and Jeff Durr, "Building Successful Business to Business Relationships," *Gallup Business Journal,* November 13, 2014, online at http://www.gallup.com/businessjournal/179378/building-exceptional-business-business-relationships.aspx, accessed February 5, 2016.

Canada Post Customer Value Management Program: Using Value to Differentiate Customer Relationships

Janet LeBlanc
Principal, Janet LeBlanc & Associates; Former Director, Customer Value Management, Canada Post

Canada Post is a major contributor to the Canadian economy, generating almost $5.5 billion in gross domestic product and $9 billion in labor income. With a 150-year history of serving Canadian consumers and businesses, Canada Post is the country's leading delivery organization, serving 32 million consumers through 6,700 post offices across the country. Every day, it delivers 40 million messages to over 14 million addresses as of 2010—a number that increases by 240,000 annually. A key driver of the Canadian economy, Canada Post's size and scale make it a formidable presence on the Canadian landscape, recognized as one of Canada's top 10 brands—one that Canadians trust.

Canada Post is in the business of connecting Canadians. Its 72,000 employees work around the clock to process 11 billion pieces of mail, parcels, and messages each year to every corner of our vast country. Focusing on these daily operational requirements had at one point led Canada Post to be inward looking—cultivating an "inside-out" culture where the needs of the company were put before the customer experience. Furthermore, Canada Post had traditionally and successfully operated in an environment with very little competition. However, with emerging communication technologies and multinational courier companies, the world has become much smaller and competition for business more fierce.

Canada Post faces intense competition in all its lines of business. The exclusive privilege of collecting and delivering the mail is becoming irrelevant as businesses, which generate 90 percent of Canada Post revenues, see in electronic communications a means to significantly reduce their costs of reaching customers. The erosion of transaction mail (bills, invoices, notices, statements) is a phenomenon that Canada Post and all postal administrations around the world have been coping with.

To meet these challenges, Canada Post embarked on a major transformational change with the vision to become a more modern postal service. Over the last decade, these changes have included the implementation of an **enterprise resource planning (ERP)** system, improved process performance, development of new technologies, and, most recently, the investment in new plants and equipment. These upgrades have and will continue to positively impact its ability to serve and create value for customers.

(continued)

(*Continued*)

Company executives realized that if it was to be successful in the future, it needed to turn its focus outward, building customer relationships and making customer growth a priority by building flexibility into its business and responding more quickly to evolving needs.

Canada Post embarked on a journey to bring customers to the forefront of its business. In a little more than three years, Canada Post defined what customers value most, measured and tracked weekly performance in the marketplace, and identified customer-value metrics and competitive benchmarks to maximize customer value and drive cultural change across the organization. Today, its award-winning Customer Value Management program guides business strategy, helps focus redesign efforts, and shapes employee incentives and rewards.

Canada Post wanted its Customer Value Management program to be more than just research. It needed it to be a data-driven functional model used across all lines of business to help the organization prioritize its efforts and focus resources on those customers who yield the highest value. The company needed to shift its view from market development to customer development with the goal of revenue protection and growth.

But how do you focus on individual customer development when you are mandated to provide universal service to all Canadians? And what tools can you use to rank customers according to their true value to the organization and their potential value?

The Customer Value Management program became an important tool to understand a customer's current strength and to influence a customer's future behavior in order to impact unrealized potential.

Canada Post surveys more than 25,000 customers each year to measure the end-to-end customer experience, including its products' features and benefits; how the product was delivered; and the service customers received from any one of its seven channels, including contact with a telephone service agent or its Web site, through face-to-face interaction with a sales representative, or interaction with a letter carrier or delivery person. Each customer is asked to evaluate the overall experience based on his perception of quality, the overall perceived value received, and the likelihood of recommending Canada Post to a friend or colleague. These three questions comprise its Customer Value Index. Those customers who rated Canada Post a top two box rating of 9 or 10 on a 10-point scale for all three questions were viewed as loyal to the organization and were calculated as part of its Customer Value Index.

This Customer Value Index is used as a proxy variable to assess the strength of the relationship customers have with Canada Post and the potential value they could bring to the organization. Using the Customer Value Index rating, Canada Post classifies customers into a loyalty classification (see Exhibit 5.1). Those customers who rated Canada Post a 9 or 10 on all three Customer Value Index questions are ranked as loyal; conversely, customers who rated Canada Post a 6 or below are considered "at risk." Customers with variable ratings are classified as either positive or hesitant.

EXHIBIT 5.7   Managing Customer Value: Canada Post's Customer Value Index and Loyalty Classification

Loyalty Classification	Range	Rating	Description
Loyal	Top Two Box	9–10	Customers rated Canada Post a 9 or 10 on all three questions.
Positive	Top Four Box Mixed Answer	7–10	Customers rated Canada Post a 7 to 10 on all three questions. Does not include loyalty group.
Hesitant	Mixed Answer	1–10	Customers gave a mix of ratings on the questions ranging from 1 to 10.
At Risk	Bottom Six Box	1–6	Customers rated Canada Post a 1 to 6 on all three questions.

Detailed linkage analysis revealed a strong link, making it clear that loyal and positive customers contributed more revenue to Canada Post than those who were classified as hesitant or at risk. This finding was an important discovery as it helped to direct the resources and activities of the organization's sales, marketing, and operations teams toward areas of opportunity and growth or potential risk.

Canada Post used this value and loyalty classification plan to guide the account development strategies of its sales and marketing teams. Sales strategies for customers classified as loyal and positive were focused on cross-sell and up-sell opportunities. Customer retention plans were put in place to meet the needs of customers identified as hesitant or at risk.

A closed-loop process was also created to feed sales representatives with the Customer Value Index rating and overall evaluation of the experience for each of their customers who completed a survey. Sales representatives were alerted to a new Customer Value Index rating from their customers when received, indicating those areas of opportunity and potential risk. Sales managers and sale representatives were trained to review the findings and initiate a business review with their customers to understand the required action plans and initiatives. The business objective was to strengthen the relationship to grow and protect the business.

As difficult as relationships are to strengthen, they are remarkably easy to lose. Customers who identified themselves as "at risk" by rating Canada Post a

(continued)

(Continued)

6 or below on its three Customer Value Index questions were highly likely to defect or erode their business. A detailed analysis revealed that customers who were identified as "at risk" defected within a year and took not only one line of business revenue with them but all of their Canada Post revenue. In fact, for one line of business, more than 50 percent of customers who identified themselves as "at risk" or "hesitant" defected.

All customers were grouped into one of four categories based on current Canada Post revenue: "growth," "lost," "eroding," or "new." By using the Customer Value Index as its proxy variable, Canada Post could validate whether customers who classified themselves as loyal or positive were in fact spending more with Canada Post and had growing revenue. The results showed that for one line of business, almost 75 percent of customers who were classified in the category of "growth" were rated as loyal or positive to Canada Post. This finding was important for Canada Post because it validated the measurement proxy within its Customer Value Management program as a significant indicator of the strength of the relationship that customers had with the company.

This structured approach to managing the customer relationship has been extremely valuable to Canada Post. Many companies use loyalty data to monitor relationship health, but few consistently act on the data in order to solve identified customer problems to ensure retention. By integrating the process of using customer data to pinpoint strengths and opportunities throughout the company, Canada Post instituted an ongoing customer management strategy focused on revenue growth and retention.

When Canada Post launched its Customer Value Management program in 2003, it wanted customer value to influence strategic planning and to incorporate customer data into the annual business planning process and the identification of process improvement initiatives. The Customer Value Management program identifies the critical elements essential to making progress from the customers' perspective, directs scarce resources, and creates alignment across the organization for those areas that matter most to customers. Its successful implementation is a major achievement, moving Canada Post closer to its goal of becoming a world-class provider of physical and electronic delivery services.

Summary

For an enterprise to engage its customers in relationships, it must be prepared to treat different customers differently. Before designing its relationship-building strategy, the firm must understand the nature of its customers' differences, one from another. From Chapter 5, we know that the value of a customer is a function of the future business the customer does with the enterprise, and that different customers have different values. Knowing which customers are more valuable allows an enterprise to allocate its relationship-building efforts to concentrate first on those customers who will yield the best financial return. However, because the future patronage of any customer is not something that can actually be known in the present, making decisions with respect to customer valuation necessarily involves approximation and subjectivity. Companies with large numbers of customers whose transactions are electronically tracked in a detailed way might be able to use advanced statistical modeling techniques to make reasonably accurate forecasts of the future business that particular types of customers will likely do with the firm, but for the vast majority of enterprises, no such scientific models may be readily available. Instead, companies that rank their customers by value usually do so by using a mix of judgment and proxy variables—at least at first.

As this chapter has shown, the enterprise that defines, quantifies, and ranks the value of its individual customers takes great strides toward becoming a business truly based on growing customer value. By relying on a taxonomy of customer types based on their value profile—including not just actual values but unrealized potential values as well—the enterprise can create a useful model for how it would like to alter the trajectories of individual customers. Not only can it devote a greater portion of its internal resources to serving its most valuable customers, but it also can set more rational financial objectives for each customer, based on that customer's value profile.

Setting financial objectives is only a part of the job, however. To achieve those objectives for each customer, no matter what they are, the enterprise will have to alter the customer's trajectory. It will have to help change the customer's behavior in a way that benefits the customer; that is, it will need to get a customer to do something (or not do something) that he or she was not otherwise going to do. To do this in the most efficient way possible, the enterprise needs to be able to appeal directly to the customer's motivations. It must communicate to the customer in a way that the customer is going to understand. It must, in a word, understand the customer's own perspective and needs.

In Chapter 6, we will explore how the enterprise can differentiate its customers based not just on their value profiles, but on their individual needs as well.

Food for Thought

1. Why is it not enough to consider average customer value?
2. How often should actual value be calculated? Potential value? Why?
3. Search the Web for a company that has successfully "fired" customers in the past. If you were facing a detractor—someone who said that it's wrong to treat different customers differently—how would you defend "firing" customers in this reported or even a hypothetical instance?
4. What policies are successful, and what policies are likely to create mistrust? What are likely to be the best measures of actual and potential value for each

of the listed customer bases? How would you confirm that your answer is right? Would the company likely be best served by proxy or statistical/financial value analysis?

- Customers for a B2B electronics components distributor
- Customers for a dry cleaner
- Customers for an automobile manufacturer; for an automobile dealer
- Customers for a chemical supply company
- Customers for a discount department store
- Customers for a large regional supermarket chain
- Customers for a long-haul trucking company
- Customers for Disney World; for Six Flags; for Club Med
- Customers for CNN; for HBO (Caution: They're different. CNN sells viewers to advertisers while HBO sells programming to viewers.)
- "Customers" for a political campaign; for the American Cancer Society; for NPR (formerly National Public Radio); for Habitat for Humanity

5. For each of the companies listed in number 4, what's the next step? How does a company use the information about customer value to make managerial decisions?

Glossary

Actual value   The net present value of the future financial contributions attributable to a customer, behaving as we expect her to behave—knowing what we know now, and with no different actions on our part.

Below zero (BZ)   The below-zero customer will, no matter what strategy or effort is applied toward him, always cost the company and its best customers more than he contributes.

Customer focus   An attitude or mind-set that attempts to take the customer's perspective when making business decisions or implementing policies. Also called *customer orientation*.

Customer service   Customer service involves helping a customer gain the full use and advantage of whatever product or service was bought. When something goes wrong with a product, or when a customer has some kind of problem with it, the process of helping the customer overcome this problem is often referred to as "customer care."

Customer-strategy enterprise   An organization that builds its business model around increasing the value of the customer base. This term applies to companies that may be product oriented, operations focused, or customer intimate.

Customer value management   Managing a business's strategies and tactics (including sales, marketing, production, and distribution) in a manner designed to increase the value of its customer base.

Customize   Become relevant by doing something for a customer that no competition can do that doesn't have all the information about that customer that you do.

Differentiate   Prioritize by value; understand different needs. Identify, recognize, link, remember.

Disruptive innovation   Innovation likely to upset an established business model that governs how a number of competitors operate. Uber, for instance, is an innovation that disrupts how most established taxi and limousine services operate.

Enterprise resource planning (ERP)   The automation of a company's back-office management.

Identify   Recognize and remember each customer regardless of the channel by or geographic area in which the customer leaves information about himself. Be able to link information about each customer to generate a complete picture of each customer.

Lifetime value (LTV)   Synonymous with "actual value." The net present value of the future financial contributions attributable to a customer, behaving as we expect her to behave—knowing what we know now, and with no different actions on our part.

Low-maintenance customers   Customers with low actual values and low unrealized potential values. They are not very profitable for the enterprise individually, nor do they have much growth potential individually. But there are probably a lot of them.

Mix of customer values   For a particular company, the mix refers to the percentage of most valuable customers versus most growable customers versus below-zero customers.

Most growable customers (MGCs)   Customers with high unrealized potential values. These are the customers who have the most growth potential: growth that can be realized through cross-selling, through keeping customers for a longer period, or perhaps by changing their behavior and getting them to operate in a way that costs the enterprise less money.

Most valuable customers (MVCs)   Customers with high actual values but not a lot of unrealized growth potential. These are the customers who do the most business, yield the highest margins, are most willing to collaborate, and tend to be the most loyal.

NPV   Net present value.

Net Promoter Score (NPS)   A compact metric owned by Satmetrix and designed initially by Bain's Fred Reichheld to quantify the strength of a company's word-of-mouth reputation among existing customers, and widely used as a proxy for customer satisfaction. See www.satmetrix.com.

Potential value   The net present value of the future financial contributions that *could* be attributed to a customer, if through conscious action we succeed in changing the customer's behavior.

Predictive analytics   A wide class of statistical analysis tools designed to help businesses sift through customer records and other data in order to model the likely future behaviors of other, similar customers.

Share of customer   For a customer-focused enterprise, share of customer is a conceptual metric designed to show what proportion of a customer's overall need is being met by the enterprise. It is not the same as "share of wallet," which refers to the specific share of a customer's spending in a particular product or service category. If, for instance, a family owns two cars, and one of them is your car company's brand, then you have a 50 percent share of wallet with this customer, in the car category. But by offering maintenance and repairs, insurance, financing, and perhaps even driver training or trip planning, you can substantially increase your "share of customer."

Super-growth customers   Customers with high actual value and high unrealized potential value as well.

Switching cost   The cost, in time, effort, emotion, or money, to a business customer or end-user consumer of switching to a firm's competitor.

Trajectory   The path of the customer's financial relationship through time with the enterprise.

Unrealized potential value   The difference between a customer's potential value and a customer's actual value (i.e., the customer's lifetime value).

Value skew   The distribution of lifetime values by customer ranges from high to low. For some companies, this distribution shows that it takes a fairly large percentage of customers to account for the bulk of the company's total worth. Such a company would have a shallow value skew. Another company, at which a tiny percentage of customers' accounts for a very large part of the company's total value, can be described as having a steep value skew.

Word of mouth (WOM)   A customer's willingness to refer a product or service to others. This referral value may be as small as an oral mention to one friend, or a robust announcement on social media, or may be as powerful as going "viral."

CHAPTER **6**

Differentiating Customers
by Their Needs

Strive not to be a success, but rather to be of value.

—Albert Einstein

All value for a business is created by customers, but the reason any single customer creates value for a business is to meet that particular customer's own individual **needs.** While it's important to recognize that different customers will create different amounts of value for the enterprise (i.e., some customers are worth more than other customers, a subject we explored in Chapter 5), it's even more important to understand how customers differ in terms of their individual needs, and this is the topic we will tackle in this chapter. Individual customer valuation methods are fairly well established as an important stepping-stone for managing the **customer-strategy enterprise.** Academics and business professionals alike spend much time and energy testing the effectiveness of alternative methods and models. But differentiating customers based on their needs is still a relatively new idea, not so widely practiced by companies in a formal way—not even by those professing to take a customer-centric approach to business. At its heart, needs differentiation of customers involves using feedback from an identifiable, individual customer to predict that customer's needs better than any competitor can who doesn't have that feedback. In addition to categorizing customers by their value profiles (see Chapter 5), it is vital to categorize customers based on their individually expressed needs, when they are similar. This is the only practical way to set up criteria for treating different customers differently.

Having a good knowledge of customers' value is certainly important, but to use customer-centric tools and customer strategies to increase a customer's value, the business must be able to see things from the customer's perspective, with the realization that there are many different types of customers whose perspective must be individually understood. Value differentiation by itself will not give a company this perspective. Think about it: Except for very frequent flyers, customers don't usually know or care what their value is to a business. Customers simply want to have their problem solved, and every customer has his own slightly different twist on how the process should be handled, even if more than one customer wants a problem solved a particular way. The key to building a customer's value is under-standing how *this* customer wants it solved. So one key to building profitable rela-tionships is developing an understanding of how customers are different in terms of their needs and how such needs-based differences relate to different customer values, both actual and potential. What behavior changes on the customer's part can be accomplished by meeting those needs? What are the triggers that will allow the firm to actualize some of that **unrealized potential value?**

In this chapter, we consider the different needs of different customers and the role that customer needs to play in an enterprise's relationship-building effort. In most situations, it makes sense to **differentiate** customers first by their value and then by their needs.[1] In this way, the relationship-building process, which can be expensive, will begin with the company's higher-value customers, for whom the investment is more likely to be worthwhile. (An important exception to this general rule, however, applies to treating different customers differently on the Internet through mobile and other devices. On the Web, the incremental costs of automated interaction are near zero, so it makes little difference whether an enterprise differ-entiates just its top customers by their needs or all its customers.)

Definitions

Before going too much further, let's pause to define the important terms relevant to this discussion.

Needs

When we refer to customer needs, we are using the term in its most generic sense. That is, what a customer needs from an enterprise is, by our definition, what she wants, what she prefers, or what she would like. In this sense, we do not distinguish a customer's needs from her wants. For that matter, we do not distinguish needs from preferences, wishes, desires, or whims. Each of these terms might imply some nuance of need—perhaps the intensity of the need or the permanence of it—but to simplify our discussion, we will refer to them all as "needs."

---

[1] In the view of some, differentiating by value first, then needs, may appear to focus first on the company's needs, then those of the customers; but another way to look at this order of strate-gic imperatives is to think about how a company that used to treat every customer's needs as equally important will now focus more on the needs of those customers who contribute the most to the success of the firm and therefore will put the needs of some customers ahead of the needs of other customers, thus allocating resources best for the most valuable customers.

It is what a customer needs from an enterprise that is the driving force behind the customer's behavior. Needs represent the "why" (and often, the "how") behind a customer's actions. How customers want to buy may be as important as why they want to buy. The presumption has been that frequent purchasers use the product differently from irregular purchasers, but it may be that they alternatively or additionally like the available channel better. For that matter, it may be that they like the communications channel better. The point is that needs are not just about product usage but about an ***expanded need set*** (which we discuss fully in Chapter 10) or the combination of product, cross-buy product and services opportunities, delivery channels, communication style and channels, invoicing methods, and so on.

In a relationship, what the enterprise most wants is to influence customer behavior in a way that is financially beneficial to the enterprise; therefore, understanding the customer's basic need is critical. It could be said that while the amount the customer pays the enterprise is a component of the customer's value to the enterprise,

> It could be said that while the amount the customer pays the enterprise is a component of the customer's value to the enterprise, the need that the enterprise satisfies represents the enterprise's value to the customer.

the need that the enterprise satisfies represents the enterprise's value to the customer. Needs and value are, essentially, both sides of the value proposition between enterprise and customer—what the customer can do for the enterprise and what the enterprise can do for the customer.

Customers

Now that we have defined both customer value and customer needs, we should pause for a reminder of the definition of *customer* before continuing with our discussion. In Chapter 1, we defined what we mean by customer. On the surface, the definition should be obvious. A customer is one who "gives his custom" to a store or business; someone who patronizes a business is the business's *customer.* However, the overwhelming majority of enterprises serve multiple types of customers, and these different types of customers have different characteristics in terms of their value and their individual needs.

A brand-name clothing manufacturer, for instance, has two sets of customers: the end-user consumers who wear the clothes and the retailers that buy the clothes from the manufacturer and sell them to consumers. As a customer base, clothing consumers do not have as steep a **value skew** as, say, a hotel's customer base, even though some consumers might buy new clothes every week. (In other words, the discrepancy in value between the most valuable consumers and the average will generally be smaller for a particular clothing merchant.) But all consumers of the clothing manufacturer do want different combinations of sizes, colors, and styles. So even though clothing consumers may not be highly differentiated in terms of their value, they are highly differentiated in terms of their needs. Retailer customers also have very different needs: Some need more help with marketing, or with advertising co-op dollars, or with displays. Different retailers will have very different requirements for invoice format and timing or for shipping and delivery. They may need different palletization or precoded price tags. Interestingly, retailers will also vary widely in their values to the clothing manufacturer—with much more value skew than consumers will show. Some large department store chains will sell far more stock than can a local mom-and-pop clothing shop. And some growing online retailers have stocking and timing issues that are quite different from retailers who sell mostly through in-store displays. Thus, retailer customers display high levels of differentiation in terms of both their needs and their value.

For the clothing manufacturer, if the enterprise expresses an interest in improving its relationships with its customers, the question to answer is: which customers? And this is, in fact, the type of structure in which most enterprises operate. They won't all sell products to retailers, but the vast majority of businesses do have distribution partners of some kind—online and bricks-and-mortar retailers, dealers, brokers, representatives, value-added resellers, and so forth. Moreover, a business that sells to other businesses, whether these business customers are a part of a distribution chain or not, really is selling to the *people* within those businesses, people of varying levels of influence and authority. Putting in place a relationship program involving business customers will necessarily entail dealing with purchasing agents, approvers, influencers, decision makers, and possibly end users within the business customer's organization, and each of these people will have quite different motivations in choosing to buy.

The logical first step for any enterprise embarking on a relationship-building program, therefore, is to decide which sets of customers to focus on. A relationship-building strategy aimed at end-user consumers can (and, in most cases, should) involve some or all of the intermediaries in the value chain in some way. However, it is a perfectly legitimate goal to seek stronger and deeper relationships with a particular set of intermediaries. The basic objective of relationship building with any set of customers is to increase the value of the customer base; thus, it's important to understand from the beginning exactly which customer base is going to be measured and evaluated. Then, when focusing on that customer base, the enterprise must be able to map out its customers in terms of their different values and needs.

It is easy to confuse a customer's needs with a product's **benefits.** Companies create products and services with benefits that are specifically designed to satisfy customer needs, *but the benefits themselves are not equivalent to needs.* In traditional marketing discipline, a product's benefits are the advantages that customers get from using the product, based on its features and **attributes.** But features, attributes, and benefits are all based on the product rather than on the customer. Needs, in contrast, are based on the customer, not the product. Two different customers might use the same product, based on the same features and attributes, to satisfy very different needs.

> Companies create products and services with benefits that are specifically designed to satisfy customer needs, *but the benefits themselves are not equivalent to needs.*

When it focuses on the customer's need, the enterprise will find it easier to increase its **share of customer,** because ultimately it will seek to solve a greater and greater portion of the customer's problem—that is, to meet a larger and larger share of the customer's need. And because the customer's need is not directly related to the product, meeting the need might, in fact, lead an enterprise to develop or procure other products and services for the customer that are totally unrelated to the original product but closely related to the customer's need. That's why focusing on customer needs rather than on product features often will reveal that different customers purchase the same product in order to satisfy very different individual needs.[2]

Demographics Do Not Reveal Needs

Forty years ago, a groundbreaking marketing article asked: "Are Grace Slick and Tricia Nixon Cox the same person?" Grace Slick, lead singer for the rock group Jefferson Starship, and Tricia Nixon Cox, the preppy daughter of Richard Nixon who married Dwight Eisenhower's grandson, were demographically indistinguishable. They were both urban, working women, college graduates, age 25 to 35, at similar income levels, household of three, including one child.

What made this question startling in the early 1970s was that it undermined the validity of the traditional demographic tools that marketers had been using for decades to segment consumers into distinct, identifiable groups. With demographic statistics, mass marketers thought they could distinguish a quiz show's audience from, say, a news program's. Then marketers could compare these audiences with the demographics of soap buyers, tire purchasers, or beer drinkers. The more effectively a marketer could define her own customers and target prospects, differentiating this group from all the other consumers who were not her target, the more efficiently she could get her message across in a world of limited television channels, radio stations, magazines, and newspapers. She could buy media that would reach a higher proportion of her own target audience.

But demographics could not explain the distinctly nondemographic differences between Grace Slick and Tricia Nixon Cox. So as computer capabilities and speeds grew, marketers began to collect additional information to distinguish consumers, not by their age and gender, but by their attitudes toward themselves, their families and society, their beliefs, their values, their behaviors, and their lifestyles.

Source: Excerpted from Don Peppers and Martha Rogers, Ph.D., *The One to One Future* (1993), in reference to John O'Toole, "Are Grace Slick and Tricia Nixon Cox the Same Person?" *Journal of Advertising* 2 (1973): 32–34.

---

[2]A large body of academic research, as well as trade articles and professional work, has been published on the topics of benefits, attributes, and needs as well as the findings about the different reasons two customers with the same transaction history are motivated to buy the same products.

Differentiating Customers by Need: An Illustration

Consider a company that manufactures interlocking toy blocks for children, such as Lego® or Mega Bloks, and suppose this firm goes to market with a set of blocks suitable for constructing a spaceship. Three 7-year-old children playing with this set of blocks might all have different needs for it. One child might use the blocks to play a make-believe role, perhaps assembling a spaceship and then pretending to be an astronaut on a mission to Mars. Another child might enjoy simply following the directions, meticulously assembling the same spaceship in exact detail, according to the instructions. Once the ship is built, however, the child would be less interested in it. A third child might use the block set meant to construct a spaceship to build something entirely different, drawn from his own vivid imagination. This child simply wouldn't enjoy putting together a toy according to someone else's diagram.

Each of these three children may enjoy playing with the same set of blocks, but each is doing so to satisfy a different set of needs. Moreover, it is the child's need that, *if known to the marketer,* provides the key to increasing the child's value as a customer. If the toy manufacturer actually knew each child's individual needs, and if it had the capability to deal with each child individually, by treating each one differently, it could easily increase its share of each child's toy-and-entertainment consumption. For example, for the "actors," it might offer costumes and other props, along with storybooks and videos or DVDs, to assist the children in their imaginative role-playing activities. For the "engineers," it might offer blueprints for additional toys to be assembled using the spaceship set; or it might offer more complex diagrams for multiset connections if the company knew all the sets owned by this child. And for the more creative types, the "artists," the company might provide pieces in unusual colors or shapes, or perhaps supplemental sets of parts that have not been planned into any diagrams at all.

We can use this example to compare and contrast the different roles of product attributes and benefits versus customer needs. Exhibit 6.1 shows that each product attribute yields a particular benefit that consumers of the product can enjoy.

It should be easy to see that each product attribute can be easily linked to a particular type of benefit. And the benefits will appeal differently to different customers, but each benefit springs directly from each attribute. If, instead, we were to map out the *types of customers* who buy this product, based on the needs of these end users as just outlined, we could then list the additional products and services that each type of customer might want, based on what that customer needs from this and other products. If we just looked at our actor, artist, or engineer end-user customers to see which needs they wanted to address, then our table would look like Exhibit 6.2.

EXHIBIT 6.1   **Product Attributes versus Benefits**

Product Attribute	Product Benefit
Toys in fantasy configurations	Recognizable make-believe situations
Colorful, unusual shapes that easily interlock	Large variety of interesting combinations
Meticulously preplanned, logically detailed instructions	Complex directions that are nevertheless easy to follow

EXHIBIT 6.2   **Beyond Benefits: Customer Needs**

Customer Need	Additional Products and Services
Actor: Role-playing, pretending, fantasizing	Costumes, videos, storybook, toys
Artist: Creating, making stuff up, doing things differently	Colors and paints, unique add-ons, nonsequitur parts
Engineer: Solving problems, completing puzzles	More diagrams, problems, logical extensions

This is only a hypothetical example, of course, and we could easily come up with several additional types of customers, based on the needs they are satisfying with these construction blocks. For instance, there might be some girls who want the spaceship set of blocks because they are really interested in rockets, outer space, and other things astronautical. Or there might be some boys who want the set because they are collectors of these kinds of building-block toys, and they want to add this to a large set of other, similar toys. Or there might be others who like to use this kind of toy to invite friends over to work together on the assembly. Any single child might, in fact, have any combination of these needs that she wishes to satisfy, either at different times or in combination.

The point is, by *taking the customer's own perspective, the customer's point of view*—by concentrating on understanding each different customer's needs—the enterprise will more easily be able to influence customer behavior by meeting his needs better, and changing the future behavior of a customer by becoming more valuable to him is the key to realizing additional value from that customer.

Scenario: Financial Services

A large business-to-business (B2B) financial services organization faced both increasing competition and product **commoditization.**[a] The customers of this firm are channel members—the brokers and financial advisers (FAs) who sell stocks and bonds and other financial instruments to consumer clients from their own business. The enterprise sought to increase loyalty and reduce the effects of

(continued)

(*Continued*)

cost cutting among these channel-member customers by meeting their individual needs, one customer at a time. Research, based on interviews with the enterprise's sales staff and customers, uncovered several key customer needs.

Five needs-based portfolios were identified and given nicknames—High-Potential Newbies, Marketing Machines, Active Growers, Transitional Players, and Cruise Controls—in a research project that combined customer needs information with customer valuation. As a result, the enterprise determined its customers' needs while at the same time uncovering which high-value customers posed the greatest defection risk. This led to the development of a defection reduction strategy to retain those customers. For customers not at risk of defection, the organization developed interaction strategies to begin meeting their needs immediately.

As it builds relationships with these customers over time, the financial services enterprise will seek to increase customer knowledge and to act on the individual needs of its customers. In the process, both the enterprise and its customers will benefit. For the enterprise, an interaction strategy for each FA, based on the individual FA's needs and value, will provide clear direction and focus for the sales force. As more needs are uncovered, the firm will be able to offer more products and services. Ultimately, defection will be reduced, which should substantially reduce marketing and sales costs.

For the customers themselves, the relationship-building program should improve the relevance and usefulness of incoming information from the enterprise. This will enable individual FAs to run their own businesses faster, more efficiently, and in a way that is likely to please their own clients more.

[a] Thanks to Jennifer Monahan, Nichole Clark, Laura Cococcia, Bill Pink, Valerie Popeck, and Sophie Vlessing for the ideas here.

Understanding Customer Behaviors and Needs

Understanding the differences in customer behaviors, and the needs underlying these behaviors, is critical for all stages in a company: from product development to financial consolidation, from production planning to strategic planning or marketing budgeting. All decisions and activities made by customers in order to evaluate, purchase, use, and dispose of any goods or services offered by a company are subject to being captured in the transactional record and are subject to behavioral analysis.

A customer's need is what she wants, prefers, or wishes while her behavior is what she does or how she acts in order to satisfy this need. In other words, "needs" are the "why" of a customer's actions, and "behaviors" are the "what." Behaviors can be observed directly, and from behaviors an enterprise can often infer things about a customer's needs. This hierarchy or logical ordering in these two notions, that customer needs drive customer behaviors, is a critical pillar for the relationship-marketing practitioner.

All companies want to understand why and how customers make their buying decisions. Factors that affect this process are analytically assessed and examined, then reexamined. Clearly segmenting customers by their needs and behaviors will allow an enterprise to **identify** and describe different categories of customers and ensure that its marketing efforts are effective for each of these groups.

Characterizing Customers by Their Needs and Behaviors

Companies now have comprehensive systems and processes to capture and store customer data covering almost every aspect of a customer's relationship with a firm. Descriptive characteristics like gender, age, and income, along with transactional data such as interactions, purchases, and payments, and usage-related measures such as service requests—all this information can be captured and stored by the enterprise. The information companies store on individual customers is usually referred to as customer profiles.

Let's consider a customer database in a bank environment where there has been a significant information technology (IT) investment. The department in charge of business intelligence can describe the same customer in two different ways, providing two different profiles:

1. Customer is married, is European, has two children, lives in an upscale neighborhood, and is a member of a frequent-flyer program.
2. Customer visited the online banking site once a week over the past six months, always visiting the site at least once in the first three days of each month; has a tenure of more than two years; uses investment tools; checks her statement and balance regularly; pays her credit debts promptly and has a clear credit history; and has increased her assets under management by 5 percent in the past three months.

The first profile is demographic. It is a set of characteristics that are less dynamic compared to the second profile. These data probably are stored by other companies doing business with this customer as well, and perhaps even by the bank's own competitors. The second profile is behavior-based, and involves a record derived from what the customer is actually doing or has done in the past with this bank. Details of her behavior are dynamic and only available inside the bank's database, thus providing the bank with an opportunity for competitive advantage—if the bank uses the information to serve this customer better than other firms that do not have the specific customer information.

Both profiles are important in their own ways. For someone preparing an advertising campaign, creating a marketing strategy, or deciding on content for a piece of marketing communication, the first profile is very useful, because it defines the customer (or the market) at a macro level and provides clues to editorial direction. If someone in the bank's marketing department just wanted to describe this customer to someone else, this is the profile they would probably use. The second type of profile, however, is about needs, action, and behavior and is certainly more relevant than the demographic profile for any executive at the bank who really wants to know what customers are doing. Will this customer visit again? Will she buy again? What is the risk she will default on her credit or cost the bank money? These are the questions an executive tries to answer by looking at behavioral records.

But let's now assume that the business intelligence department can produce a third profile on this customer as well:

3. The customer manages the future of her family and her children very carefully, and this is her primary motivation while using the bank's products and services. She is comfortable with technology and enjoys engaging with the bank online rather than having to visit branches, because she is always pressed for time.

This new profile actually defines *why* this particular customer uses the banking services she uses. It shows why she prefers online services and why she has accumulated an investment account. Moreover, while different customers will have different needs, many of these needs will be shared by others. Needs describe the root causes behind a customer's actions, whether those actions include choosing to work with another bank or staying loyal to this bank and subscribing to a new service.

It's important to get the sequence right. Needs are not based on a customer's value or behavior. Rather, a customer's needs drive her behavior, and her behavior is what generates her value to the business. The needs just described are not generic, true-for-everybody statements, such as "I want to have cheaper products with higher quality." They are very specific needs, valid only for some portion of the bank's customers.

> Behaviors are the customers' footprints on a company.

Behaviors are the customers' footprints on a company. They represent the evidence of customers trying to meet their needs, and this evidence is likely to be accumulated in different company systems over different periods of time.[3]

Needs May Not Be Rational, but Everybody Has Them

In his classic book, *Predictably Irrational*,[a] Dan Ariely makes the case that humans are irrational in what they want and what they do but—oddly enough—in completely predictable ways. Some of the research he cites draws from lab work on rats and other animals. In one of the most telling studies, mice were offered a food pellet instantly if they pressed a green button. If, instead, they pressed a purple button, they could get *10* pellets, but they had to wait 10 whole seconds, which must seem like forever in mouse time. If they pressed the purple

---

[3] Thanks to former Peppers & Rogers Group manager Kerem Can Ozkısacık, Ph.D., for his contribution to this section.

button, and—while they were waiting for the big reward—had a chance to press the green button, they could not stop themselves and just had to press the green button—even after they figured out that pressing the green button stopped the delivery of the 10 pellets from the purple button. They learned that if they could not (and therefore did not) press the green button, but they had already pressed the purple button, they did in fact get their 10 pellets after a delay.

What did they do about this situation? Enter the red button, which, as it turns out, makes it impossible to press the green button. So the mice learned to press the purple button, then immediately press the red button, then press the green button all they wanted, but since pressing the red button had turned off the green button, the mice still got to collect the big win of 10 pellets.[b]

And this is just lab mice, managing to balance their own short- and long-term goals. Can companies do as well? And can we understand that the same customer wrestles with multiple kinds of needs at the same time?

This customer needs thing: It's complicated.

---

[a] Dan Ariely, *Predictably Irrational: The Hidden Forces That Shape Our Decisions* (New York: HarperCollins, 2008).

[b] Paraphrased from a story told by Dan Ariely in a keynote address to the Duke University Fuqua School of Business Marketing Club annual conference, January 27, 2010.

Why Doesn't Every Company Already Differentiate Its Customers by Needs?

It is reasonable to ask, if the logic outlined is so compelling, why toy manufacturers and other firms aren't already attempting to differentiate customers by needs. Many firms that have traditionally sold through retailers still believe that the hurdles to doing so are sizable. For example, most toy manufacturers sell their products through retailers and have little or no direct contact with the end users of their products. In order to make contact with consumers, a manufacturer would have to either launch a program in cooperation with its retailing partners or figure out how to go around those retailers altogether—a course of action likely to arouse considerable resentment among the retailers themselves. So the majority of a manufacturer's end-user consumers are destined to remain unknown to the enterprise. Moreover, even if it had its customers' identities, the manufacturer still would have to find some means of interacting with the customers individually and of processing their feedback, in order to learn their genuine needs. Then it would have to be able to translate those needs into different actions, requiring a mechanism for actually offering and delivering different products and services to different consumers. Nevertheless, some companies, such as Lego, still sell through storefront and online retailers, but also sell directly to consumers through a Web site. Lego, for instance, offers free shipping every day at http://shop.lego.com/en-US/. Its Web site is highly interactive, keeping track of what a particular kid likes to do there by use of login and password, and a (free) subscription magazine, thereby logging an address, all in addition to their store site, which offers some exclusive parts and sets you can't get elsewhere.

Doing all this sets up a direct competitive relationship with the very retailers that the manufacturers still depend on for a large percentage of sales. And real resources are required to take these steps to build direct relationships. These obstacles make it very difficult for toy manufacturers simply to leap into a relationship-building program with toy consumers at the very end of the value chain. That said, the manufacturer does not have to launch such a program for all consumers at once. Rather, it could start by identifying its most avid fans, its highest-volume, most valuable consumer customers. Perhaps it could devise a strategy for treating each of those highly valuable customers to individually different products and services, in a way that wouldn't undermine retailer relationships. A Web site designed to attract and entertain such consumers could play this kind of role, and the toymaker could take advantage of **social networking** connectivity as well. Although the toy manufacturer still would encourage other shoppers to buy its products in stores, perhaps it could begin to offer more specialized sets and pieces directly to catalog and Web purchasers. If it had a system for doing this, launching a program designed to make different types of offers to different types of end-user consumers—based on their individual needs—would be much simpler and would, for practical reasons, start that process with customers of high value.

Indeed, the primary reason so many firms are now attempting to engage their customers in relationships is that the new tools of information technology—not just the Internet in general and social networking sites in particular, through an increasing number of devices, but customer databases, **sales force automation,** marketing and customer analytics applications, and the like—are making this type of activity ever more cost efficient and practical.[4] But for an enterprise engaged in relationship building, the "hot button," in terms of generating increased patronage from the customer, is the customer's need.

Categorizing Customers by Their Needs

In the end, behavior change on the part of the customer is what customer-based strategies are all about. To capture any part of a customer's unrealized potential value requires us to induce a change in the customer's behavior; we want the customer to buy from an additional product line, or take the financing package as well as the product, or interact on the less expensive Web site rather than through the call center, and so forth. This is why understanding customer needs is so critical to success. The customer is master of his own behavior, and that behavior will change only if our strategy and offer can appeal persuasively to his very own needs—not what we want his needs to be or some average of needs for a bunch of different

---

[4] Martin Lindstrom, *Small Data: The Tiny Clues That Uncover Huge Trends* (London: St. Martin's Press, 2016).

customers. Being able to see the situation from the *customer's point of view* is key to any successful customer-based strategy.

But in order to take action, at some point, different customers must be categorized into different groups, based on their needs. Clearly, it would be too costly for most firms to treat every single customer with a custom-designed set of product features or services. Instead, using information technology, the customer-focused enterprise categorizes customers into finer and finer groups, based on what is known about each customer, and then matches each group with an appropriately mass-customized product-and-service offering. (More about **mass customization** and the actual mechanics of the process in Chapter 10.)

One big problem is the complexity of describing and categorizing customers by their needs. There are as many dimensions and nuances to customer needs as there are analysts to imagine them. For consumers, there are deeply held beliefs, psychological predispositions, life stages, moods, ambitions, and the like. For business customers, there are business strategy differences, financial reporting horizons, collegial or hierarchical decision-making styles, and other corporate differences— not to mention the individual motivations of the players within the customer organizations, including decision makers, approvers, specifiers, reviewers, and others involved in shaping the company's behavior.

Marketing has always relied on appealing to different customers in different ways. Market segmentation is a highly developed, sophisticated discipline, but it is based primarily on products and the appeal of product benefits rather than on customers and their broader set of needs considered in a holistic fashion for each individual customer. To address customers as *different types of customers,* rather than as recipients of a product's different benefits, the customer-based enterprise must think beyond market segmentation per se. Rather than grouping customers into *segments* based on the product's appeal, the customer-based enterprise places customers into *portfolios* based primarily on type of need.

A **market segment** is made up of customers with a similar attribute. A **customer portfolio** is made up of customers with similar needs. The market segmentation approach is based on appealing to the segment's attribute, while the customer portfolio approach is based on meeting each customer's broader need, based on the customer's own worldview. If segments and portfolios were made up of toys, then red fire trucks might be in a *segment* of toys that included red checkers sets, red dolly makeup lipsticks, and red blocks. But red fire trucks would be in a *portfolio* of toys that included ambulances, fireboats, police cars, and maybe medical helicopters, along with fire hats and axes, stuffed Dalmatians, and ladders. A market segment might be composed of women, over age 45, with household incomes in excess of $50,000. A portfolio of customers might be made up of women who value friendships and like to entertain.

In Chapter 13, we will discuss customer management, including the grouping of customers into portfolios. There is a continuing role for traditional market segmentation, even in a highly evolved customer-strategy enterprise, because understanding how a product's benefits match up with the attributes of different customers continues to be an important marketing activity. But as the enterprise gains greater and greater insight into the actual motivations of particular categories of customers, it will find that managing relationships cannot be accomplished in segment categories, because any single customer can easily be found in more than one segment. Instead, when they take the customer's perspective, the managers at a customer-strategy enterprise will learn that they must meet the complex, *multiple needs* of each customer, as an individual. And doing this will require categorizing customers according to their own, broader needs rather than according to how they react to the product's individually considered attributes and benefits. Each customer can appear in only one portfolio.

> A single customer can be found in more than one customer "segment" but in only one customer "portfolio."

Understanding Needs

Understanding different customers' different needs is critical to any serious relationship-building program. Some of the characteristics of customer needs should be given careful consideration:

- *Customer needs can be situational in nature.* Not only will two different consumers often buy the same product to satisfy different needs, but a customer's needs might change from event to event, and it's important to recognize when this occurs. An airline might think it has two customer types—business travelers and leisure travelers—but in reality this typology refers to events, not customers. Even the most frequent business traveler will occasionally be traveling for leisure, perhaps with a spouse or family instead of the usual solo travel, and in that event she will need different services from the airline than she needs when she travels on business.
- *Customer needs are dynamic and can change over time as well.* People are changeable creatures; our lives evolve from one stage to another, we move from place to place, we change our minds. Moreover, certain types of people change their minds more often than others, tending to be less predictable. That said, the fact that a certain type of customer is not predictable is a customer characteristic itself, which can be used to help guide an enterprise's treatment of that customer. Marriage, new babies, and retirement typically lead to profound changes in needs for most people.
- *Customers have different intensities of needs and different need profiles.* Even when two customers have a similar need, one customer will have that need intensely while the other may feel the need but less intensely and perhaps in a different profile, combined with other needs. One homemaker is committed to running a very "green" kitchen, while another wants to take care of the environment where it makes sense but also has the need to save time as much as possible and may use paper plates so she doesn't have to spend so much time washing dishes.
- *Customer needs often correlate with customer value.* Although it is not always true, more often than not a high-value customer is likely to have certain types of needs

in common with other high-value customers. Similarly, a below-zero customer's needs are more likely than not to be similar to other below-zero customers' needs. A business that can correlate customer value with customer needs is generally in a good situation, because by satisfying certain types of needs, it can do a more efficient job of winning the long-term loyalty of higher-value customers.

- *The most fundamental human needs are psychological.* When dealing with human beings as customers (as opposed to companies or organizations), understanding the psychological differences among people can provide useful guidance for treating different customers differently.

- *Some needs are shared by other customers while some needs are uniquely individual.* When an online bookstore makes an automated book recommendation to an individual customer, this recommendation is based on the fact that other customers who have bought similar books as this customer has bought in the past have also bought the book being recommended now. There are hundreds of thousands of books a person could buy at an online bookstore, but people who buy similar books do so because they share similar needs. A retailer with a good database of past customer purchases can use **community knowledge**, purchases, and traits found in common among disparate customers, to infer which products the members of a particular community of customers might find more appealing. Software for sorting through groups of customers to find commonalities is called **collaborative filtering** (more about these concepts later in this chapter). However, if a florist remembers a customer's wedding anniversary or a relative's birthday and sends the customer a reminder, the florist is very likely to get a great deal more business, simply by remembering these unique dates for each customer. But any single customer's wedding anniversary has very little to do with any other customer's anniversary date. In both the bookstore's and the florist's case, individual customer needs are being met, but some needs are unique and personal while some are tastes or preferences that are shared by other customers, as well (see Exhibit 6.3).

- *There is no single best way to differentiate customers by their needs.* As difficult as it is to predict and quantify a customer's value to the enterprise, at least the final result will be measured in economic terms. Value ranking, in other words, is done in one dimension: the financial dimension.[5] But when an enterprise sets out to differentiate its customers by their needs, it is embarking on a creative

---

[5] And the financial dimension is not limited to for-profits: For nonprofit organizations, the financial dimension might include maximizing funds from outside sources or maintaining fiscal stability. See April Burbank, "Nonprofits Have Customers Too," *Forbes,* June 28, 2012, available at http://www.forbes.com/sites/ashoka/2012/06/28/nonprofits-have-customers-too-2/, accessed February 5, 2016; Steve Rothschild, *The Non Nonprofit: For-Profit Thinking for Nonprofit Success* (San Francisco: Jossey-Bass, 2012); and Michael Martello, John G. Watson, and Michael J. Fischer, "Implementing a Balanced Scorecard in a Not-for-Profit Organization," *Journal of Business and Economics Research* 6, no. 9 (September 2008): 68. For nonprofits, "customer" or member, or donor, or volunteer value may include proxies for financial value such as willingness to participate, compliance rates, voting record, donations of time and volunteerism, and so forth.

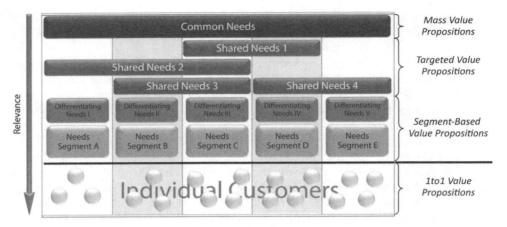

EXHIBIT 6.3   Common and Shared Needs of Customers

expedition, with no fixed dimension of reference. There are as many ways to differentiate customers by their needs as there are creative ways to understand the deepest human motivations. The value of any particular type of needs-based differentiation is to be found solely in its usefulness for affecting the different behaviors of different customers.

■ *Even in B2B settings, a firm's customers are not really another "company," with a clearly defined, homogeneous set of needs.* Instead, customers are a combination of purchasing agents, who need low prices; end users, who need benefits and attributes; the managers of the end users, who need those end users to be productive; and so on.

Community Knowledge

In the competition for a customer, the successful enterprise is the one with the most knowledge about an individual customer's needs. In a successful Learning Relationship, the enterprise acts in the customer's own individual interest as a result of taking the customer's point of view. What if the customer were to maintain her own list of specifications and purchases? If the record of a customer's consumption of groceries were maintained on her own computer rather than on a supermarket's computer, this would undercut the competitive advantage that **customization** gives to an enterprise. Each week a whole cadre of supermarkets could simply "bid" on the customer's list of grocery needs, reducing the level of competition once again to the lowest price. The customer-strategy enterprise can avoid this vulnerability, as it has devised a way to treat an individual customer based on the knowledge of that customer's transactions as well as on the transactions of many other customers who have similarities to her. This is known as *community knowledge.*

Community knowledge comes from the accumulation of information about a whole community of customer tastes and preferences. It is the body of knowledge that an enterprise acquires with respect to customers who have similar tastes and needs, enabling the firm actually to *anticipate* what an individual customer needs, even before the customer knows he needs it. The *collaborative filtering* software that sorts through customers for similarities is essentially a matching engine, allowing a company to serve up products or services to a particular customer based on what other customers with similar tastes or preferences have preferred in this particular product or service.

Technology has accelerated the rate at which enterprises can apply community knowledge to better understand individual customers. This tool can help not just the individual consumers of a company like an online bookstore, but also B2B customers. The idea of community knowledge has a direct lineage from one of the most important values any B2B business can bring its own business customers: education about what other customers with similar needs are doing—in the aggregate, of course, never individually. Firms know that they must teach their customers as well as be taught by them. An enterprise brings insight to a customer based on its dealings with a large number of that customer's own competitors. Community knowledge can yield immense benefits to many businesses, but especially to those businesses that have:

- *Cost-efficient, interactive connections with customers as a matter of routine,* such as online businesses, banks and financial institutions, retail stores, and B2B marketers, all of which communicate and interact with their customers directly and on a regular basis.
- *Customers who are highly differentiated by their needs,* including businesses that sell news and information, movies and other entertainment, books, fashion, automobiles, computers, groceries, hotel stays, and health care, among other things.

Marketing expert Fred Wiersema[6] has said that there are three characteristics of market leadership: bringing out the product's full benefits, improving the customer's usage process, and breaking completely new ground with the customer. Any one of these types of customer education can come from the knowledge an enterprise acquires by serving other customers. An enterprise with a large number of customers can use community knowledge to lead a customer to a product or service that the enterprise knows the customer is likely to need, even though the customer may be totally unaware of this need. It might be as simple as choosing a hotel in a city the customer has never visited, but it could also apply to pursuing an appropriate investment and savings strategy, even though the customer may not have thought of it yet.

---

[6] Fred Wiersema, *Customer Intimacy: Pick Your Partners, Shape Your Culture, Win Together* (Middleboro, MA: Country Press, 1996). Also see Wiersema's *What's Your Customer's Problem?* (New Word City, 2011), electronic book.

Pharmaceutical Industry Example

Consider, for example, the pharmaceutical category. Traditionally, "pharma" companies didn't engage in much relationship building with end-user consumers (i.e., the patients for whom their drugs are prescribed). Rather, they always considered their primary customers to be the prescribing physicians and other health care providers, along with pharmacies, employers, medical insurance organizations, and the government bodies charged with overseeing the health care industry. Although pharma companies operate differently in different countries, depending on convention and regulatory regime, around the world they are now trying to become more patient-centered with their business strategies and processes. In the United States, this change has been facilitated by the Affordable Care Act ("Obamacare"), which permits consumers to have a bit more say in the kinds of medical coverage they choose, but on a global basis the move toward patient-centered thinking is being driven by the simple fact that technology now gives patients access to more information and control than ever before.

Taking a more patient-centered approach to the business, of course, has moral overtones as well. Who wouldn't want to work for a company whose mission is to improve everyone's health, rather than simply making as much money as possible from their patented drugs? According to Gitte Aabo, CEO of Leo Pharma, a Denmark-based company, "We strongly believe that when we focus on people, the business will follow. And that means for us as a company that there are cases where we know that we can actually meet an unmet need for the patients, but we are unable to make the business case. . . . If we are able to meet the unmet need even though we can't make the business case, we will do it anyway."[7] But as difficult as it may be to make a strong business case for patient-centered policies, declaring patient health itself to be the company's mission is likely to dramatically improve Leo's ability to hire and retain highly motivated employees. Kimberly Stoddart, Vice President of Human Resources and Communications at Leo Pharma Canada, suggests, "When we are looking to hire new people, we show the video to candidates. We can tell immediately whether the concept motivates them, and to what extent, which we then explore. If it doesn't, they're not for us."[8]

Putting patient-centric policies into practice, of course, requires the same sort of disciplines and processes that customer-centric policies require in any other industry, including needs-based differentiation of patients, whenever that will improve each patient's experience.

One U.S. pharma company sells medicines for diabetes, which can be kept in check through constant vigilance, but as is the case with many such diseases,

---

[7] Eyeforpharma, "Overcoming Barriers to Patient Centricity at LEO Pharma," YouTube video, January 5, 2016, available at https://www.youtube.com/watch?v=Psa6q2obH-U, accessed February 5, 2016.

[8] Eyeforpharma, "Patient-Centred Culture by Design," white paper, January 7, 2016, p. 14, available at http://www.janssen.com/emea/sites/www_janssen_com_emea/files/2792_07jan16_pccultures_whitepaper_v13.pdf, accessed February 5, 2016.

compliance is a constant problem. Patients often simply fail to keep up the medical treatment or they fail to monitor their own condition properly. The company knows that patients want help in understanding and dealing with the disease, so its Web site is designed to serve as a resource for patient information and support, as well as for physicians and other providers. The benefits for the pharmaceutical company and for the patient are straightforward: A better-informed and-supported patient is likely to exhibit better compliance, which will both keep the patient healthier and sell more of the pharmaceutical company's drugs—a better, more successful patient experience, in other words, and a more profitable business as well.

Knowing that different patients will need different types of support and assistance, this pharma enterprise undertook to design a more patient-centered Web site by first conducting a research survey of patients, which revealed that a patient's attitude toward keeping the disease in check will tend to drive her individual needs from the Web site. Newly diagnosed patients for the most part simply want any and all information related to their condition, in order to select content they feel is most relevant to their own problems. However, as patients come to grips with their sickness, their attitudes evolve, and the pharma company's research led it to group them into three different categories:

1. *Individualists.* This type of patient relies on herself to make educated decisions on how to manage her disease. The Web site will steer individualists toward online clinical support. They can opt in to **customized** electronic newsletters or take advantage of a number of online health-tracking tools and apps.
2. *Abdicators.* This patient's attitude toward the disease is more one of resignation and detachment. An abdicator has basically decided that she will "just have to live with the conditions of her disease," so she ends up depending on the help given by a significant other—perhaps a spouse, a parent, or an adult child. So the site will direct abdicators to various caregiver resources, and provide planning information related to nutrition and meals.
3. *Connectors.* This type of patient welcomes as much information and support as she can get from others to help her make educated decisions about how to manage her disease. She values the opinions of other patients with similar conditions, so the site directs connectors to online chat rooms and electronic bulletin boards, where they can meet and converse with other patients. There is an "e-buddy" feature that pairs a patient up with someone similar to herself, not just for information but for support and consolation.

For the pharmaceutical company to design a Web site that is truly customer focused, it should try to figure out, for each returning visitor, what the particular mind-set of that visitor is, and then serve up the best features and benefits for that particular type of patient. The easier the enterprise can make it for different patients to find the support and assistance they need, individually, the more valuable those patients will become for the enterprise, and vice versa.

At this juncture, however, it is important once again to separate our thinking about the features and benefits of the Web site (i.e., the product, in this case) from the actual psychological needs and predispositions of the Web site visitors themselves. Any one of the visitors might in fact use any of the Web site's many features on any particular visit. That means each of the Web site's benefits will probably overlap several different types of customers, with different types of needs. But the customers themselves do not overlap—they are unique individuals with their own unique psychology and motivation. It is only our categorization of these unique and different customers into needs-based groups that might give us the illusion that they are the same. They may be similar in their needs, but at a deeper level, they are still uniquely individual, and this will be true no matter how many additional categories, or portfolios, we create. We simply categorize customers in order to better comprehend their differences by making generalizations about them.

Gary Adamson, who served as past president of Medimetrix/Unison Marketing in Denver, Colorado, said the power of health care integration lies in creating the ability to do things differently for each customer, not to do more of the same for all customers.[9] One of Medimetrix's clients, Community Hospitals in Indianapolis, Indiana, for example, implemented "Patient-Focused Medicine," a **customer relationship management (CRM)** initiative aimed at four constituent groups: patients, physicians, employees, and payers. The hospital has found that most medical practitioners customize the "care *for* you" component of health care by individually diagnosing and treating medical disorders. But Community also individualizes the "care *about* you" component—the part that makes most patients at most hospitals feel like one in a herd of cattle.

The real opportunity lies in building a Learning Relationship between the health care provider and the customer. A drugstore, for example, might know a customer buys the same over-the-counter remedy every month. But if the same drugstore detects that the customer is suddenly buying the product every week, it could personalize its service by asking her whether she is having a health problem and how it could assist her with personal information or other types of medication. Already, the pharmacy is the last resort for many patients to help spot possible drug interactions for prescription and over-the-counter drugs prescribed and recommended by a variety of different physicians. Using information to serve the customer better helps the drugstore create a long-lasting bond with this customer.

Using Needs Differentiation to Build Customer Value

The scenarios of the toy manufacturer and the pharmaceutical company show how each had to be aware of its respective individual customer's needs so it could act on them. Once a particular customer's needs are known, the company is better

---

[9] Don Peppers, Martha Rogers, Ph.D., and Bob Dorf, *The One to One Fieldbook* (New York: Doubleday, 1999).

able to put itself in the place of the customer and can offer the treatment that is best for that customer. Each company gets the information about customer needs primarily by interacting. Therefore, an open dialogue between the customer and the enterprise is critical for needs differentiation. Moreover, customer needs are complex and intricate enough that the more a customer interacts with an enterprise, the more learning an enterprise will gain about the particular preferences, desires, wants, and whims of that customer. Provided that the enterprise has the capability required to act on this more and more detailed customer insight, by treating the customer differently, it will be able to create a rich and enduring Learning Relationship.

A successful Learning Relationship with a customer is founded on changes in the enterprise's behavior toward the customer based on the use of more in-depth knowledge about that particular customer. Knowing the individual customer's needs is essential to nurturing the Learning Relationship. As the firm learns more about a customer, it compiles a gold mine of data that should, within the bounds of privacy protection, be made available to all those at the enterprise who interact with the customer. Kraft, for example, empowers its salespeople with the data they need to make intelligent recommendations to a retailer. (The retailer is Kraft's most direct customer, and the retailer sells Kraft products to end-user consumers, who can also be considered Kraft's customers.) Kraft has assembled a centralized information system that integrates data from three internal database sources. One database contains information about the individual stores that track purchases of consumers by category and price. Another database contains consumer demographics and buying-habit information at food stores nationwide. A third database, purchased from an outside vendor, has geodemographic data aligned by zip code.

> Information is the raw material that is transformed into knowledge through its organization, analysis, and understanding. This knowledge then must be applied and managed in ways that best support investment decisions and resource deployment.

But truly to get to know a consumer through interactions directly with her, enterprises must do more than gather and analyze aggregated quantitative information. Accumulating information is only a first step in creating the knowledge needed to pursue a customer-centered strategy successfully. Information is the raw material that is transformed into knowledge through its organization, analysis, and understanding. This knowledge then must be applied and managed in ways that best support investment decisions and resource deployment.

Customer knowledge management is the effective leverage of information and experience in the acquisition, development, and retention of a profitable customer.

Gathering superior customer knowledge without codifying and leveraging it across the enterprise results in missed opportunities.[10]

Scenario: Universities Differentiate Students' Needs

If you are reading this section of this chapter of this book, the chances are good that you aren't just using this book as a professional reference in your daily job, but instead are using it as a textbook for a course or class on marketing, or on business strategy, or how business reacts strategically to technology. The newspaper you read online today probably discussed some new industry that has been profoundly changed by technology and financial realities. It's not just health care, real estate sales, and taxis that have been "Uberized."

Colleges and universities, too, whether they are Ivy League, state schools, small liberal arts enclaves, city junior colleges, or online offerings, are dramatically changing the nature of "higher education." Redefining the roles and meaning of "student" and "professor" is just part of it.

According to *The Economist*:

Fees in private non-profit universities in America rose by 28% in real terms in the decade to 2012, and have continued to edge up. Public universities increased their fees by 27% in the five years to 2012. Their average fees are now almost $8,400 for students studying in-state, and more than $19,000 for the rest. At private colleges average tuition is more than $30,000 (two-thirds of students benefit from bursaries of one sort or another). American student debt adds up to $1.2 trillion, with more than 7m people in default.

For a long time the debt seemed worth it. For most students the "graduate premium" of better-paid jobs still repays the cost of getting a degree. But not all courses pay for themselves, and flatter graduate salaries mean it takes students longer to start earning good money. Student enrollments in America, which rose from 15.2m in 1999 to 20.4m in 2011, have slowed, falling by 2% a year later.

[10] Soumit Sain and Silvio Wilde, *Customer Knowledge Management: Leveraging Soft Skills to Improve Customer Focus* (Cham, Switzerland: Springer, 2014); Silvio Wilde, *Customer Knowledge Management: Improving Customer Relationships through Knowledge Application* (Berlin and Heidelberg: Springer-Verlag, 2011); and Stavros Sindakis, Audrey Depeige, and Eleni Anoyrkati, "Customer-Centered Knowledge Management: Challenges and Implications for Knowledge-Based Innovation in the Public Transport Sector," *Journal of Knowledge Management* 19, no. 3 (2015): 559–578.

Small private colleges are now struggling to balance their books. Susan Fitzgerald of Moody's, a credit-rating agency, foresees a "death spiral" of closures. William Bowen, a former president of Princeton University, talks of a "cost disease," in which universities are investing extravagantly in shiny graduate centres, libraries and accommodation to attract traditional students.[a]

But the growth opportunity is in retooling students over age 35 who are losing jobs to outsourcing and automation; their numbers have tripled since the 1990s.[b] Online universities have not yet been successful in figuring out the right combination to ensure their own success.[c]

But we are starting to see some universities succeeding by building Learning Relationships with individual students as well as with the corporate concerns and alumni that are already providing much of the funding for tuition and research, and by focusing on meeting the *needs* of the most valuable (nontraditional) students, mimicking the strategies of a growing number of for-profit companies in a variety of industries around the world.

For example, Franklin University, an accredited, not-for-profit organization that has both physical campuses and a large online offering, is radically student-focused in both. One of the authors of this book (Rogers) served on the board for Franklin in the 1990s, when then-president Paul Otte initiated the role of Student Services Associates (SSAs), who would shepherd a student from application to graduation, with every interaction captured in a database to help that student customer over time.

For Franklin, customer-focused strategies—led originally by past university president Paul Otte and now by current president Dr. David R. Decker—have translated directly into revenue increases and greater share of student. In the mid-1990s, 60 percent of students were freshmen and sophomores; now 60 percent are juniors and seniors, another 10 to 12 percent are continuing on to graduate school, and surveys indicate higher levels of student satisfaction.[d] Franklin offers "structure and support that helps balance [student] education with work, family, and other life priorities."[e]

Contrast this with EdX, which offers MOOCs, or mass open online courses (usually in the form of professors lecturing on video). Anyone can take the classes or courses for free and pay only a modest price to get verification that he/she completed the course (under $100). (It should be noted that the failure rate of MOOC courses is high, and they are challenging to complete for students without traditional college experience; to date, they often serve as supplemental study materials and free tutoring for students taking more traditional coursework. There hasn't been any effort to learn about the needs or value of any current or past attendees.) Working with

(continued)

(Continued)

established institutions, such as Arizona State University, may improve the odds, but the jury is still out.[f]

We will see additional efforts to upend the traditional educational process. Minerva is a four-year college that was founded like an entrepreneurial startup. It is for-profit (but so are traditional universities, Minerva's founders assert), and it will cost $28,000 a year, which covers tuition and room and board, to go live in a dorm and take courses online. The first cohort starts in San Francisco, with expansion planned to other international cities, seven in four years.

Minerva is using a technology platform to deliver online classes that do not resemble lectures in any way (unlike traditional university online courses or popular MOOCs) but offer provoking seminar-style engagement with a real-time teacher. Classes are capped at 19 students. The traditional lecture is described as a good way for universities to teach (cost saving) but not a good way for students to learn. Student learning needs and experience are the focus of research-driven teaching methods and immersion in different cultures. Minerva has attracted superstars of higher education to be deans and teachers and motivated students from around the world.

"The Minerva boast is that it will strip the university experience down to the aspects that are shown to contribute directly to student learning. Lectures, gone. Tenure, gone. Gothic architecture, football, ivy crawling up the walls—gone, gone, gone."[g]

Higher education has a variety of different customers. Students, parents, employers, government, states, and donors are just some examples. Instead of measuring the success of a university by the number of students it enrolls, or even the cutoff point for admission, a customer-focused university gauges its success by the projected increase or decrease in a particular student's expected future value. The university no longer focuses just on acquiring more students but on retaining existing learners and growing the business each gives the institution in continuing education and alumni contributions, for life.

As more universities consider their options for achieving those goals without leaving graduates in crippling debt, attention often turns to alumni as the answer. Institutions of higher learning have understood that prolonging relationships with alumni can improve the accuracy of the fundraising list, which in turn improves fundraising response rates and donor **lifetime value.** The number of schools that are implementing strategies for those purposes is increasing.

Because it is now possible to keep track of relationships with individual students, the size of a university is becoming a less potent competitive advantage. A university of any size has the opportunity to use information about each student to secure more of that individual's participation. Notwithstanding the "brand" or status value of a handful of high-status Ivy League and top-ranked higher education institutions, securing and keeping the participation of more students will likely depend on who has and uses the most information about a specific student, not on who has the most students.

To compete, the customer-focused university has to integrate its entire range of business functions around satisfying the individual needs of each individual student. The school's organizational structure itself will have to be altered, and it must embrace significant change, affecting virtually every department, division, administrator, and employee. Once it has migrated to a customer-strategy model, the university will be able to generate unprecedented levels of participant loyalty by offering an unprecedented level of customization and relationship building.

Student-customer valuation will require measures of success based on individual student results, not just product or program measures. Rather than seeing whether enough students enrolled in a particular course to justify its existence, for instance, the institution will also predict whether a particular student is valuable enough to justify a certain level of expenditure.

The customer-focused university will be able to calculate share of student on an individual, participant-by-participant basis, with the goal of capturing a greater share of dollars, time, and other investment in learning. The customer-focused university builds a Learning Relationship with each student by interacting over time and continuing to increase its level of relevance to each student by understanding her motivation. Although participation in the university should be motivation enough, the customer-focused university will understand whether a student is, for example, taking a course because of interest in the material, admiration for the professor, a need to be respected, a desire to make business contacts, as part of a degree program, career participation, or some other reason. Remembering what each student wants and finding ways to make the collaboration effort valuable to the participant leads to mass-customizing the offering, the response, the dialogue process, the level of **recognition**, the opportunity for active participation, and so on.

To draw alumni in and keep the relationships going, academic institutions are building peer-to-peer communities on their Web sites that foster involvement and camaraderie. Free services include a lifelong university-branded e-mail address, searchable alumni directories, and customizable Web pages. For some institutions, the central focus of their Web community is the alumni database; others take a portal approach, using diverse content as the core property. Most universities hope that alumni will set the school's Web portal as their default Web browser home page.

Here's the point: More and more, the "university" will be recognizable not by its physical location or traditional delivery methods, but by the combination of expertise, research, and content offered by professors coupled with the value and needs of individual students and alums.

---

[a] "The Digital Degree: The Future of Universities," *Economist*, June 28, 2014, available at http://www.economist.com/news/briefing/21605899-staid-higher-education-business-about-experience-welcome-earthquake-digital, accessed February 5, 2016.
[b] "The Digital Degree: The Future of Universities."

(continued)

(*Continued*)

[c] Valerie Strauss, "Largest For-Profit University in U.S. Loses Hundreds of Thousands of Students," *Washington Post*, March 26, 2015, available at https://www.washington-post.com/news/answer-sheet/wp/2015/03/26/largest-for-profit-university-in-u-s-loses-hundreds-of-thousands-of-students/, accessed February 5, 2016. See, for example, information about the University of Florida's distance learning program at http://www.distance.ufl.edu/, as well as Penn State's at http://www.worldcampus.psu.edu/how-online-learning-works/how-it-works-faqs.

[d] For more on how Franklin University is differentiating its offerings according to students' needs, see http://www.franklin.edu/about-franklin/mission-philosophy/four-cornerstones-of-educational-philosophy/providing-access-to-educational-opportunities.

[e] Source: http://www.franklin.edu/public-administration-bachelors-degree-program-why-franklin.

[f] Source: https://www.edx.org/gfa.

[g] Minerva Graeme Wood, "The Future of College?" *Atlantic Monthly*, September 2014, available at http://www.theatlantic.com/magazine/archive/2014/09/the-future-of-college/375071/, accessed February 5, 2016. Also see https://www.minerva.kgi.edu/.

Summary

We have now discussed the necessity of knowing who the customer is (identifying) and knowing how the customer is different individually (valuation and needs, often indicated by behavior). Getting this information implies that the enterprise will need to interact with each customer to understand each one better. Once the enterprise has ranked customers by their value to the enterprise and differentiated them based on their needs, it conducts an ongoing, collaborative dialogue with each customer. This interaction helps the enterprise to learn more about the customer, as the customer provides feedback about her needs. The enterprise can then use the customer's feedback to modify its service and products to meet her needs (i.e., to "customize" some aspect of the customer's treatment to the needs of that particular customer).

The "identify" and "differentiate" steps in the Identify-Differentiate-Interact-Customize (IDIC) taxonomy for developing and managing customer relationships can be accomplished by an enterprise largely with no actual participation by the customer. That is, a customer won't necessarily have to know or involve herself in the process that the enterprise uses to identify her, as a customer, or to rank her by value, or even to evaluate her needs, as a customer. These first two steps—"identify" and "differentiate"—can be thought of as the "customer insight" phase of relationship management. However, the third step—"interact"—requires the customer's participation. Interaction and customization can only really take place with the customer's direct involvement. These latter two steps could be thought of as managing the "customer experience," based on the insight developed.

Interacting with customers, the third step in the IDIC taxonomy, is o
point of discussion.

Food for Thought

1. Why has more progress been made on customer value differentiation than on customer needs differentiation?
2. If it could only do one, is it more likely that a customer-oriented company would rank all of its customers differentiated by value or differentiate all of its customers by need?
3. Is it possible to meet individual needs? Is it feasible? Describe three examples where doing this has been profitable.
4. For each of the listed product categories, name a branded example, then hypothesize about how you might categorize customers by their different needs, in the same way our sample toy company and pharmaceutical company did. Unless noted for you, you can choose whether the brand is business to consumer (B2C) or B2B:
   - Automobiles (consumer)
   - Automobiles (B2B, i.e., fleet usage)
   - Air transportation
   - Cosmetics
   - Computer software (B2B)
   - Pet food
   - Refrigerators
   - Pneumatic valves
   - Hotel rooms

Glossary

Attributes   Physical features of the product.

Benefits   Advantages that customers get from using the product. Not to be confused with needs, as different customers will get different advantages from the same product.

Collaborative filtering   Software designed to sort through groups of customers to find commonalities among different customers.

Commoditization   The steady erosion in unique selling propositions and unduplicated product features that comes about inevitably, as competitors seek to improve their offerings and end up imitating the more successful features and benefits.

Community knowledge   The body of customer data that shows what different customers have in common among themselves, including purchases, behaviors, and traits. Collaborative filtering is software for mining this community knowledge.

Customer portfolio   A group of similar customers. The customer-focused enterprise will design different treatments for different portfolios of customers.

Customer relationship management (CRM)   As a term, CRM can refer either to the activities and processes a company must engage in to manage individual relationships with its customers (as explored extensively in this textbook), or to the suite of software, data, and analytics tools required to carry out those activities and processes more cost efficiently.

Customer-strategy enterprise   An organization that builds its business model around increasing the value of the customer base. This term applies to companies that may be product oriented, operations focused, or customer intimate.

Customization   Most often, customization and mass customization refer to the modularized building of an offering to a customer based on that customer's individual feedback, thus serving as the basis of a Learning Relationship. Note the distinction from personalization, which generally simply means putting someone's name on the product.

Customize   Become relevant by doing something for a customer that no competition can do that doesn't have all the information about that customer that you do.

Differentiate   Prioritize by value; understand different needs. Identify, recognize, link, remember.

Expanded need set   The capability of a company to think of a product it sells as a suite of product plus service plus communication as well as the next product and service the need for the original product implies. The sale of a faucet implies the need for the installation of that faucet, and maybe an entire bathroom upgrade and strong nesting instinct.

Identify   Recognize and remember each customer regardless of the channel by or geographic area in which the customer leaves information about himself. To be able to link information about each customer to generate a complete picture of each customer.

Lifetime value (LTV)   Synonymous with "actual value." The net present value of the future financial contributions attributable to a customer, behaving as we expect her to behave—knowing what we know now, and with no different actions on our part.

Market segment   A group of customers who share a common attribute. Product benefits are targeted to the market segments thought most likely to desire the benefit.

Mass customization   *See* Customization.

Needs   What a customer needs from an enterprise is, by our definition, synonymous with what she wants, prefers, or would like. In this sense, we do not distinguish a customer's needs from her wants. For that matter, we do not distinguish needs from preferences, wishes, desires, or whims. Each of these terms might imply some nuance of need—perhaps the intensity of the need or the permanence of it—but in each case we are still talking, generically, about the customer's needs.

Recognition   *See also* Identify.

Sales force automation (SFA)   Connecting the sales force to headquarters and to each other through computer portability, contact management, ordering software, and other mechanisms.

Share of customer   For a customer-focused enterprise, share of customer is a conceptual metric designed to show what proportion of a customer's overall need is being met by the enterprise. It is not the same as "share of wallet," which refers to the specific share of a customer's spending in a particular product or service category. If, for instance, a family owns two cars, and one of them is your car company's brand, then you have a 50 percent share of wallet with this customer, in the car category. But by offering maintenance and repairs, insurance, financing, and perhaps even driver training or trip planning, you can substantially increase your share of customer.

Social networking   The ability of individuals to connect instantly with each other often and easily online in groups. For business, it's about using technology to initiate and develop relationships into connected groups (networks), usually forming around a specific goal or interest.

Unrealized potential value   The difference between a customer's potential value and a customer's actual value (i.e., the customer's lifetime value).

Value skew   The distribution of lifetime values by customer ranges from high to low. For some companies, this distribution shows that it takes a fairly large percentage of customers to account for the bulk of the company's total worth. Such a company would have a shallow value skew. Another company, at which a tiny percentage of customers' accounts for a very large part of the company's total value, can be described as having a steep value skew.

CHAPTER 7

Interacting with Customers: Customer Collaboration Strategy

Most conversations are simply monologues delivered in the presence of witnesses.

—Margaret Millar

So far, we have discussed the ways an enterprise can **identify** and **differentiate** customers. Both of these efforts help the enterprise prepare to treat different customers differently. But, essentially, both "identify" and "differentiate" are analytical tasks. They are at the heart of the efforts, working behind the scenes to gather information about a customer, to rank him by his value to the company and to differentiate his **needs** accordingly. These tasks aren't really visible to a customer. In this chapter, we introduce a part of the Identify-Differentiate-Interact-Customize (**IDIC**) implementation methodology that gets the customer directly involved: interaction. We will see different viewpoints on the broad and growing emphasis on *interaction* with customers. But even as the discussion touches on the general and the particular, the main reason for interaction remains the same: to get more information directly from a customer in order to serve him in a way no competitor can who doesn't have the information.

Managing customer experiences and individual customer relationships is a difficult, ongoing process that evolves as the customer and the enterprise deepen their awareness of and involvement with each other. To reach this new plateau of intimacy, the enterprise must get as close to the customer as it can. It must be able to understand the customer in ways that no competitor does. The only viable method of getting to know an individual, to understand him, and to get information about him is to **interact** with him—one to one.

In Chapter 2, we began to define customer experience and a relationship. We listed several important characteristics in our definition of the term *relationship;* but one of the most fundamental of these characteristics is interaction. A relationship, by its very definition, is characterized by two-way communication between the two parties to the relationship (and often, in an increasingly interconnected age, among all parties).

Interacting with customers acquires a new importance for a **customer-strategy enterprise**—an enterprise aimed at creating and cultivating relationships with individual customers. The enterprise is no longer merely talking to a customer during a transaction and then waiting (or hoping) the customer will return again to buy. For the customer-strategy enterprise, interacting *with* individual customers becomes a mutually beneficial experience. The enterprise learns about the customer so it can understand his value to the enterprise and his individual needs. But in a relationship the customer learns, too—about becoming a more proficient consumer or purchasing agent for a business. The interaction, in essence, is now a *collaboration* in which the enterprise and the customer work together to make this transaction, and each successive one, more beneficial for both. The focus shifts from a one-way message or a onetime sale to a continuous, iterative process, which de facto moves both customer and enterprise from a transactional approach to a relationship approach. The goal of the process is to be more and more satisfying for the customer, as the enterprise's Learning Relationship with that customer improves. The result of this collaboration, if it is to be successful, is that both the customer and the enterprise will benefit and want to continue to work together. This is no longer about generating messages about your organization. This is about *generating feedback,* creating a collaborative feedback loop with each customer by treating her in a way that the customer herself has specified during the interaction, whether it's face to face, via text, online, through **social media**, or all of the above.

Interacting with an individual customer enables an enterprise to become both an expert on its business and an expert on each of its customers. It comes to know more and more about a customer so that eventually it can predict what the customer will need next and where and how he will want it. Like a good servant of a previous century, the enterprise becomes indispensable.

Customer-strategy enterprises ensure that each customer gets exactly what he needs, no matter what, and this priority should extend from the front line all the way to upper management. Years ago, South-

> Successful communication is no longer about generating messages. It's about *generating feedback.*

west Airlines created a high-level position to coordinate all proactive customer communications—from the information sent to frontline representatives when flights are delayed, to personally sending letters and vouchers to customers thus inconvenienced. All the while, when the inevitable delay does occur, Southwest flight attendants and even pilots walk the aisles to update passengers and answer questions, conveying genuine concern in the moment. For a company to be truly customer-centric, interaction must happen at all levels, so as many employees as possible know what it feels like to be a customer.[1]

More and more, this learning and feedback includes participation in the social media where your customers hang out—new media that are developing so fast that a listing here would be outdated by the time this book hits print.

In this chapter, we show how a customer-strategy enterprise interacts with its customers in order to generate and use individual feedback from each customer to strengthen and deepen its relationship with that customer. This two-way communication can best be referred to as a dialogue, which serves to inform the relationship.

Dialogue Requirements

An enterprise should meet six criteria before it can be considered engaged in a genuine dialogue with an individual customer:

1. *Parties at both ends have been clearly identified.* The enterprise knows who the customer is, if he has shopped there before, what he has bought, and other characteristics about him. The customer, too, knows which enterprise he's doing business with.

2. *All parties in the dialogue must be able to participate in it.* Each party should have the means to communicate with the other. Until the arrival of cost-efficient interactive technologies, and especially the Internet, social media, and mobile, most marketing-oriented interactions with individual customers were prohibitively costly, and it was very difficult for a customer to make herself heard.

3. *All parties to a dialogue must want to participate in it.* The subject of a dialogue must be of interest to the customer as well as to the enterprise.

4. *Dialogues can be controlled by anyone in the exchange.* A dialogue involves **mutuality**, and as a mutual exchange of information and points of view, it might go in any direction that either party chooses for it. This is in contrast to, say, advertising, which is under the complete control of the advertiser. Companies that engage their customers in dialogues, in other words, must be prepared for many different outcomes.

5. *A dialogue with an individual customer will change an enterprise's behavior toward that individual and change that individual's behavior toward the enterprise.* An enterprise should begin to engage in a dialogue with a customer only if it can alter its future course of action in some way as a result of the dialogue.

---

[1] Meredith Estep, "Why Southwest Is Ranked 'Excellent' in Customer Service," *Examiner*, April 4, 2013, available at http://www.examiner.com/article/why-southwest-is-ranked-excellent-customer-service, accessed February 6, 2016. Southwest ranked a close second after JetBlue in customer experience in 2015. See Temkin ratings, available at http://temkinratings.com/temkin-ratings/temkin-customer-service-ratings-2015/, accessed February 6, 2016.

6. *A dialogue should pick up where it last left off.* This is what gives a relationship its "context" and what can cement the customer's loyalty. If prior communication between the enterprise and the customer has occurred, it should continue seamlessly, as if it had never ended.[2]

Implicit and Explicit Bargains

Conducting a dialogue with a customer is having an exchange of thoughts; it's a form of mental collaboration. It might mean handling a customer inquiry or gathering background information on the customer. But that is only the beginning. Many customers are simply not willing to converse with enterprises. And rare is the customer who admits that she enjoys receiving an unsolicited sales pitch or telemarketing phone call. For an enterprise to engage a customer in a productive, mutually beneficial dialogue, it must conduct interesting conversations with an individual customer, on his terms, learning a little at a time, instead of trying to sell more products every time it converses with him.

If the customer-strategy enterprise is to remain a dependable collaborator with its customers, then it must not adopt a *self-oriented attitude* (see Chapter 2, which emphasizes the importance to the enterprise of *not* being self-oriented in its approach to customer relationships). Instead of sales-oriented commercials and interruptive, product-oriented marketing messages, the customer-strategy enterprise will use interactive technologies to provide something of value to the customer. By providing this value, the enterprise is inviting the customer to begin and sustain a dialogue. The resulting feedback increases the scope of the customer relationship, which is critical to increasing the enterprise's share of that customer's business.

For example, think about television. When advertisers sponsor a television program, they are in effect making an implicit bargain with viewers: "Watch our ad and see the show for free." During television's early decades, these **implicit bargains** made a lot of sense, because viewers had only a few other channels to choose from and no remote control to make it easy to change the channel. In the early days, everybody watched commercials. But as choices of content proliferated, the problem for marketers was that, because the traditional broadcast television medium has been **nonaddressable**,[3] there has been no real way to tie the particular consumer who watches the television show back to the ad or to know whether she saw it in the first place. There is also no real incentive, usually, for the consumer even to watch the ad, since with DVR or TiVo, she can just avoid it.

---

[2] Don Peppers and Martha Rogers, Ph.D., *Enterprise One to One* (New York: Doubleday, 1997).
[3] Customers who are individually addressable can be sent individually different messages. Mass media are characterized by nonaddressability, since mass media send the same message to everyone simultaneously.

But today's television viewer lives in a vastly different environment. Not only are there hundreds of channels from which to choose, but people are also watching television more selectively, with instant—and constant—control. Audiences have the power to tune out commercials at their will or even to block out the advertisements altogether. And video delivered via Internet connections is beginning to replace the traditional broadcast model, as more and more consumers are downloading full-length movies and television programs and wirelessly pushing them to their large-screen television monitors for viewing. Interactive TV has arrived and it's on a variety of devices. Only two decades ago, more households in the United States had a TV than had a refrigerator, but now, 5 million homes in America, and the number is growing fast, are "zero TV" households—that is, they have given up cable and satellite connections in favor of streaming content. Tens of millions more combine traditional and streaming, and may eventually cut the cable cord. In streaming households and many cable and satellite households, directing interactive personalized ads to a particular viewer is a real capability.[4] These technological trends are driven not just by innovation but by intense consumer demand for choice and immediacy.

However, interactive communications technologies are two-way and individually **addressable**. Because of these attributes, interactive media equip marketers with the tools to make "explicit" bargains rather than "implicit" ones with their consumers. They can interact, one to one, directly with their individual media customers. An **explicit bargain** is, in effect, a "deal" that an enterprise makes with an individual to secure the individual's time, attention, or feedback. Dialogue and interaction have such important roles to play, in terms of improving and enhancing a relationship, that often it is useful for an enterprise actually to "compensate" customers, in the form of discounts, rebates, or free services, in exchange for the customer participating in a dialogue.

The interactive world is chock full of examples of explicit bargains. Hundreds of Web site operators around the globe, from Facebook to Google, offer free digital services to customers who are agreeable to receiving advertising messages or facilitating the delivery of ad messages to others. Some of the ads are highly targeted, and even based on the content of the e-mail messages themselves. For example, if a Gmail user writes a personal message to a friend discussing, say, a trip to the Bahamas, Google will likely show banner ads on the e-mail page that promote air travel, vacation packages, or hotels. Marketers routinely buy "keywords" from Internet search engines, so that when a consumer searches for, say, "flat-screen televisions," the marketer's own ad will appear prominently within the search results. It is standard practice for a Web site operator to require a visitor to register, providing personal identifying data and preferences, in return for gaining access to the site's more detailed information or automated tools.

---

[4] "Guess What, Marketers? Interactive TV Is Actually Here," *Forbes*, May 20, 2013, http://www.forbes.com/sites/onmarketing/2013/05/20/guess-what-marketers-interactive-tv-is-actually-here/, accessed January 8, 2016.

Do Consumers Really Want One-to-One Marketing?

Imagine a study that asks customers whether they like the idea of tailored ads and personalized news. The problems with such a survey should be obvious: First, people really don't like advertising and marketing messages in general. (Is that a surprise to anyone?) Of course, they don't want tailored advertising, but they don't want untailored advertising either.[5] Imagine if a study asked this question instead:

> *Please tell me whether you would prefer the Web sites you visit to show you ads tailored to your interests or, instead, to charge you a small fee for viewing the Web sites.*

And, of course, we all know what the answer to that question would be. You don't need a survey to demonstrate it, because the history of the Web already makes it very clear that free, ad-supported content will triumph over paid content at least 90 percent of the time.

But, second, any rookie market researcher can tell you that consumers who are asked generalized questions like this often have difficulty visualizing the actual situation. The right way to have asked this question would have been to demonstrate it to the consumer directly. For instance, prior to asking these questions, what if the interviewer had first asked:

> *Please tell me whether you prefer diet drinks or nondiet drinks.*

And then they could ask:

> *Please tell me whether you would prefer the Web sites you visit to show you ads for diet drinks or for nondiet drinks? (Pick one.)*

There is still, however, a very important lesson to be drawn from this discussion: the fact that consumers don't see any benefit to tailoring is an indictment of most of us marketers, because we have done such a lame job of tailoring our messages and making them genuinely relevant to our customers. It is not surprising that ordinary consumers would have difficulty visualizing personalized advertising messages, because even today, with all the computer power and interactive technologies available to marketers, most consumers have very rarely witnessed personalized ads that are genuinely relevant!

---

[5] A study much like the first one mentioned above was conducted by Stephanie Clifford, "Two-Thirds of Americans Object to Online Tracking," *New York Times,* September 29, 2009, available at http://www.nytimes.com/2009/09/30/business/media/30adco.html, accessed January 8, 2016. But in a blog post by Don Peppers, "Do Consumers Really Want One-to-One Marketing?" October 21, 2009, available at www.1to1media.com/weblog/2009/ 10/do consumers really want one-t.html#more, accessed September 1, 2010, we can envision whether customers may want to rethink this swap of content for pitches, if they are asked the right way.

Explicit bargains with consumers are certainly not confined to the Web either. One international survey discovered that online customers are not very aware of how and how much data about them is collected, but once they learn about it, they expect something in return. One example is product enhancement, such as when the Samsung Galaxy phone uses your calling information to populate your "Favorites" list automatically. Disney uses MagicBands in its parks as a way to swipe for room access, food payment, and preferred attraction access. Google's virtual assistant can read the time in your calendar that you have an appointment and remind you to leave in time to make it.[6]

In an interactive medium, an advertiser can secure a consumer's actual permission and agreement, individually. By making personal preference information a part of this bargain, the service can also ensure that the ads or promotions delivered to a particular subscriber are more personally relevant, in effect increasing the value of the interaction to the marketer by increasing its relevance to the consumer. Explicit bargains like this are good examples of what author Seth Godin calls "permission marketing" (a concept we discuss in more detail in Chapter 9), in which a customer has agreed, or given permission, to receive personalized messages.

Two-Way, Addressable Media: A Sampling

In contrast to the one-way media that characterized mass marketing, the future of customer relationships will be interactive. Not "I talk, you listen" but "You talk, I listen," and vice versa, and "We all talk, and everybody can listen in." Likewise, more and more media are "addressable." That means I can send a particular message to a particular individual at a known "address," whether that address is a geographic address on a street, or an e-mail address, or Facebook account, or telephone number, or mobile phone, or a combination of these and other new interactive, addressable media available every day.

- *The Internet.* The Internet has become one of the most effective media to engage a customer in an individual interaction. An enterprise's Web site is a highly customizable platform for collaborating with customers and learning about their individual needs effectively and inexpensively. Many websites offer live chat now too. (We talk more about the Internet as a venue for customization in Chapter 10.)

(continued)

---

[6] Timothy Morey, Theodore "Theo" Forbath, and Allison Schoop, "Customer Data: Designing for Transparency and Trust," *Harvard Business Review*, May 2015, available at https://hbr .org/2015/05/customer-data-designing-for-transparency-and-trust, accessed January 8, 2016.

(*Continued*)

- *Social media.* While technically just one aspect of the Internet, the Web sites and online services that have been constructed to allow people simply to create content for other people and to share conversations and comments with others who have similar or intersecting interests—sites such as Twitter, YouTube, Instagram, Pinterest, Facebook, Tumblr, and LinkedIn—represent a major change in how consumers acquire information and interact with their environments. The social media phenomenon is complex and rich enough all by itself to require a customer-strategy enterprise to plan deliberate strategies for dealing with social media, in an effort to build and strengthen its customer relationships.
- *Wireless.* The increasing proliferation of wireless technology is promising to "unhook" people from the network of cables and wires that used to connect them to the ground, freeing them not just to surf the Web using their iPhones, Android devices, and other smartphones but also to connect their devices wirelessly to the Internet in coffee shops, hamburger outlets, universities, airliners, and even many major cities, where ubiquitous Wi-Fi technology has been installed for everybody. It is becoming clear that in the twenty-first century, not just in developed countries but across the whole world, people are going to be connected to the network and able to interact electronically with companies and other people more often than they will be offline, using in-app messaging, push app messaging, Web site push messaging,[a] and more. (Indeed, the very term *online* has now been rendered an archaic usage, much like "dialing" a phone number, or even leaving "voicemail," which many companies and many individuals just don't use anymore. These terms will mystify our grandchildren as much as the word *typewriter* will.)
- *E-mail.* Enterprises are using e-mail to write personalized messages to customers about their latest product offerings, sales promotions, customer inquiries, and many other important topics (we discuss more about e-mail later in this chapter).
- *Texting (SMS—Short Message Service) and instant messaging (IM).* Texting from a mobile phone and using the instant messaging feature of various e-mail and online services is another mechanism for quick, highly efficient interactions. Although it's a more common business practice outside the United States, marketers can incorporate text-back codes to encourage customers to interact with them wherever they are, at any time—because everyone always has their mobile phone with them. Always.
- *Fax.* Fax machines are a highly interactive medium. The customer can fax an order to the enterprise. Or the enterprise can use a fax-on-demand service to enable customers to request product or service information via their fax machines. The enterprise also can fax customized catalogs, product

information sheets, newsletters, and other documents to the customer on request. Fax also makes it easy to reach those who do not have online capability. But fax is itself on the way out, being replaced by digital scanning in most nonlegal settings.

■ *Beacons.* Can identify and reach individual customers in settings where the Wi-Fi signal is weak.[b]

■ *Digital video recorders.* The digital recording device, such as TiVo and others like it, has revolutionized television by enabling audiences to create highly personalized TV-viewing and streaming experiences. **Digital video recorders (DVRs)** are also changing television advertising. Instead of bombarding viewers with commercials that are not relevant, advertisers now have the opportunity to personalize their messages. Knowing the viewers' demographics and viewing preferences, advertisers will be better able to match their ads to the right people.

■ *Interactive voice response.* Now a feature at most call centers, **interactive voice response (IVR)** software provides instructions for callers to "push one to check your current balance, push two to transfer funds," and so forth. One frequent problem with IVRs is that companies tend to use them more to reduce their costs than to improve their service, with the result that customers often are frustrated if the choice they want is not offered or if it becomes difficult to contact a "live" human. (We have often wondered why customers are not offered the opportunity to "press 1 for wait music that is country-western, press 2 for hip-hop, press 3 for Broadway musicals," and so on.)

■ *Wearable technology.* It doesn't matter that Google Glass has not been successful or that the Apple Watch has had limited success. What does matter is that customers are bound to be wearing their technology 24/7 sooner or later, and marketers will have to adapt.[c]

■ *The **Internet of Things**.* When your customer's doorbell rings her smartphone and allows her to see who's at her door so she can answer as if she were home, and her FitBit compares how many flights of stairs she climbed today versus last year or her best friend, then the amount of data about her that helps you serve her better is expanding exponentially.[d]

■ *More new media every week.* No print listing can keep up with the myriad of ways popular and esoteric that people of different generations and technical expertise will use and adapt to connect with each other and the companies they do business with.

---

[a] Tim Simonite, "Alert! Websites Will Soon Start Pushing App-Style Notifications," *MIT Technology Review*, October 28, 2014, available at http://www.technologyreview.com/news/531971/alert-websites-will-soon-start-pushing-app-style-notifications/, accessed February 6, 2016. For more about individualized messaging from Web sites, see Roost at https://goroost.com/.

(continued)

(*Continued*)

[b] Tony Danova, "Beacons: What They Are, How They Work and Why Apple's iBeacon Technology Is Ahead of the Pack," *Business Insider*, October 23, 2014, available at http://www.businessinsider.com/beacons-and-ibeacons-create-a-new-market-2013-12, accessed February 6, 2016.

[c] For what wearable technology might mean for marketing of the future, see Marcus Taylor, "19 Implications of Google Glass and Wearable Tech on Marketing," 2014, Venture Harbour Web page, https://www.ventureharbour.com/19-implications-google-glass-wearable-tech-marketing/, accessed February 7, 2016; Garrett Sloane, "Brands and Agencies Are Starting to Experiment with Google Glass," *Adweek*, March 2, 2014, available at http://www.adweek.com/news/advertising-branding/brands-and-agencies-are-starting-experiment-google-glass-156040, accessed February 7, 2016; and Thomas Husson, "Why Marketers Should Care about the Apple Watch," *Advertising, Age*, June 26, 2015, available at http://adage.com/article/digitalnext/marketers-care-apple-watch/299219/, accessed February 7, 2016.

[d] Graham Charlton, "What Are the Opportunities for Digital Marketing and the Internet of Things?" *Econsultancy* blog, June 8, 2015, https://econsultancy.com/blog/66544-what-are-the-opportunities-for-digital-marketing-and-the-internet-of-things/, accessed February 7, 2016.

Technology of Interaction Requires Integrating across the Entire Enterprise

Most business-to-business (B2B) companies already have active sales forces engaged in some form of relationship building with the accounts they serve, but new technologies allow them to automate a sales force to better ensure that customer interactions are coordinated among different players within an account and that the records of these interactions are captured electronically. For a business-to-consumer (B2C) company, however, interactive technologies enable it to create a consumer-accessible Web site, and to coordinate the interactions that take place on this Web site with the interactions that take place at the call center and at the point of sale and at any other point of contact with the customer. The universal question for such an enterprise, wrestling with how to use these technologies, is: What is the right communication or offer for *this* particular customer, choosing to interact with us at this time to use this technology?

The point is that the arrival of cost-efficient interactive technologies has pretty much forced companies in all industries, all over the world, to take a step back and reconsider their business processes entirely. To deal with interactivity, they must create new processes that are oriented around the coordination of all these newly possible customer interactions. And they must ensure that the interactions themselves not only run efficiently but are effective at building more solid, profitable relationships with customers.

Don Schultz, Stanley Tannenbaum, and Robert Lauterborn's classic book, *The New Marketing Paradigm: Integrated Marketing Communications,*[7] documented the problems that occur whenever a single customer ends up seeing a mishmash of uncoordinated advertising commercials, direct-mail campaigns, invoices, and policy documents, and made the case for consistent marketing communications across the entire enterprise. Today, sophisticated interactive technologies enable enterprises to ensure that their customer-contact personnel can remember an individual customer and his preferences. And so we have seen the field of customer communications evolve from "integrated" to "multichannel" to "**omnichannel**." A company can use software that creates an "ecosystem" of data about its customers and cull information from all of the touch points where it interacts with customers—call centers, Web sites, social media, e-mail, and other places. If the enterprise can better understand its customers, it can better serve them by providing individually tailored offers or promotions and more insightful **customer service**.[8] The result is that integrating the enterprise's marketing communications is no longer a cutting-edge strategy but a must-have standard. In fact, it's not preposterous to assume that going forward, the default marketing strategies will be digital and individualized, with a secondary effort in more traditional media.[9]

The enterprise has to integrate all of its customer-directed communication channels so that it can accurately identify each customer no matter how an individual customer or a customer company contacts the enterprise. If a customer called two weeks ago to order a product and then sent an e-mail yesterday to inquire about his order status, and then tweeted that he didn't hear back from the company fast enough, the enterprise should be able to provide an accurate response for the customer quickly and efficiently. The company should remember more about the customer with each successive interaction. More important, as we said before, it should never have to ask a customer the same question more than once, because it has a 360-degree view of the customer, and "remembers" the customer's feedback across the organization. The more the enterprise remembers about a customer, the more unrewarding it becomes

---

[7] Don E. Schultz, Stanley I. Tannenbaum, and Robert F. Lauterborn, *The New Marketing Paradigm: Integrated Marketing* Communications (New York: McGraw-Hill, 1996). Also see Steve Olenski, "Integrated Marketing Communication: Then and Now," *Forbes*, May 31, 2012, available at http://www.forbes.com/sites/marketshare/2012/05/31/integrated-marketing-communications-then-now/, accessed February 7, 2016.

[8] Markus Stahlberg and Ville Maila, *Multichannel Marketing Ecosystems: Creating Connected Customer Experiences* (London: Kogan Page, 2013); and Jim Ericson, "25 Top Information Managers: 2010; Movers, Shakers, and Game Changers Who Are Making Information Work for Business," *Information Management* 20, no. 2 (April 2010): 10.

[9] Dave Nash, Doug Armstrong, and Michael Robertson, "Customer Experience 2.0: How Data, Technology, and Advanced Analytics Are Taking an Integrated, Seamless Customer Experience to the Next Frontier," *Journal of Integrated Marketing Communications* (2013): 32–39.

to the customer to defect. The customer-strategy enterprise ensures that its interactive, broadcast, and print messages are not just *laterally* coordinated across various media, such as television, print, sales promotion, e-mail, and direct mail, but that its communications with every customer are *longitudinally* coordinated, over the life of that individual customer's relationship with the firm.

Providing any kind of dialogue tool to customers enables the enterprise to secure deeper, more profitable, and less competitively vulnerable relationships with each of them. The deeper each relationship becomes, and the more it is based on dialogue, the less regimented that relationship will be. The customer may want to expand the dialogue on his own volition because he knows that each time he speaks to the enterprise, it will listen. Today, what most enterprises fail at is not the mechanics of interacting but the *strategy* of it—the substance and direction of customer interaction itself.

> Today, what most enterprises fail at is not the mechanics of interacting but the *strategy* of it—the substance and direction of customer interaction itself.

Companies that employ such integration of customer data and coordination of customer interaction develop reputations as highly competent, service-oriented firms with excellent customer loyalty. Dell Computer has used direct mail, e-mail, personal contact by sales representatives, and special access to what amounts to intranet Web sites for large Dell accounts to stay connected with those customers.[10] JetBlue's reputation for service[11] has been burnished by its extremely good online interaction efficiency and the seamless connections that customers experience among the airline's reservations, ticketing, baggage tracking, and flight operations systems. Walgreens pharmacy has merged traditional and new media by offering newsprint and online clippable coupons, pharmacists in-store, as well as a 24/7 chat line to a pharmacist over a mobile app. Additionally, customers can refill a prescription in-store or

---

[10] John Wheeler and Mark Krueger, "Electrifying Customer Relationships," *Customer Relationship Management* [online], September 1999, available at: www.destinationcrm.com/Articles/Older-Articles/The-Edge/E-Lectrifying-Customer-Relationships-48441.aspx, accessed September 1, 2010.

[11] David Gianatasio, "JetBlue Knows How to Communicate with Customers in Social and When to Shut Up," *AdWeek*, September 9, 2013, http://www.adweek.com/news/advertising-branding/jetblue-knows-how-communicate-customers-social-and-when-shut-152246, accessed January 8, 2016. JetBlue provides an excellent example of how day-in and day-out investment in long-term customer equity and trust pays off on a bad day. After apologizing for stranding passengers on planes for hours, JetBlue still faced blogosphere resentment. Their own best customers came to the rescue, encouraging everyone else to come back to the airline.

scan the prescription label with a mobile app.[12] *Fast Company* credited Walgreens' omnichannel presence as one of the reasons the company was named one of the Top Ten health care companies for 2013.[13]

Over time, a customer who interacts with a competent customer-strategy enterprise will come to feel that he is "known" by the enterprise. When he makes contact with the enterprise, that part of the organization—whether it is a call rep or a service counter or any other part of the firm—should have immediate access to his customer information, such as previous shipment dates, status of returns or credits, payment information, and details about the last discussion. A customer does not necessarily want to receive more information from the enterprise; rather he wants to receive better, more focused information—information that is relevant to him, individually.

Integrating the interactions with a customer across an entire enterprise requires the enterprise to develop a solid understanding of all the points at which a customer "touches" the firm. Stated another way, the customer-strategy enterprise needs to be able to see itself through the eyes of its customers, recognizing that those customers will be experiencing the enterprise in a variety of different situations, through different media, dealing with different systems, and using different technologies. Mapping out these touch points is one of the first tasks many customer-strategy enterprises choose to undertake, and one comprehensive process for accomplishing the task is outlined in the next section by Mounir Ariss, a former managing partner at Peppers & Rogers Group.

Managing Customer Experiences by Taking the Customer's Perspective

Mounir Ariss

Over the past few years, more organizations around the world have started increasing their focus on establishing Customer Experience as a strategic differentiator. Creating more convenience to the customers and reducing friction from their experiences have become an essential component of acquiring, serving, retaining, and growing customers.

(continued)

---

[12] "Walgreen Expands Telehealth Platform to Offer Virtual Doctor Visits through MDLIVE via Walgreen's Mobile App," Press release, December 8, 2014, available at http://news.walgreens .com/press-releases/walgreens-expands-telehealth-platform-to-offer-virtual-doctor-visits-through-mdlive-via-walgreens-mobile-app.htm, accessed February 7, 2016. For more about Walgreens' digital services, see http://www.walgreens.com/.

[13] Michael Johnson, "Fast Company Places Walgreens on Its 'Top 10' List of Most Innovative Healthcare Companies," *Drug Store News*, February 11, 2013, available at http://www .drugstorenews.com/article/fast-company-places-walgreens-its-top-10-list-most-innovative-healthcare-companies, accessed February 7, 2016.

(*Continued*)

The proliferation and advancement of digital technologies has supported these trends. Furthermore, the different success stories of digital disruptors have increased the sense of urgency for traditional businesses to invest more in omnichannel customer experiences.

A customer's experience with a brand or an enterprise can be thought of as occurring in three different dimensions:

- *Physical.* Pertaining to the design of click-and-mortar presence, including physical locations such as stores, sales and service offices, bank branches, Web site, app, and so forth. The physical dimension includes not just the location itself but factors such as the availability of parking space, pedestrian accessibility, interior design, even the smoothness of flow of customers within the premises as well as the ease of use for the Web site or app.
- *Emotional.* Harder to pin down, but highly important to the customer experience, the emotional dimension is related to the culture of the customer-facing employees and their behaviors when interacting with a customer. Sometimes companies must go through a comprehensive **business process reengineering (BPR)** when it comes to dealing with their customers due to a culture that is just not customer oriented. Culture-change programs, while challenging, can achieve results. The key is to create awareness and desire for change while enabling employees, measuring them, and providing constant feedback. A culture-change program could start with managing basic behavioral changes such as training contact center employees on the 10 things never to say to a customer or on how to deal with difficult customers. If continuously reinforced, over time, those basic behaviors turn into habits and the habits become part of the culture.
- *Logical.* The "logical" issues at a company include the firm's business processes, information flows, and technology components. This is often the first dimension of the customer experience addressed by enterprises trying to become more customer-centric. Understanding (and then modifying) its business processes is an important step any company must take in order to begin managing customer relationships in a more directed, beneficial way.

Within the IDIC framework, "identify" and "differentiate" are purely internal steps to a company. They could be done without the customer knowing about them. However, "interact" and "**customize**," as the names indicate, are external steps where a company is actually managing the customer's experience. Several tools are now available document the customer experience, diagnose gaps, and redesign it.

The key steps in transforming the customer experience closely follow the IDIC framework. Starting with *identifying* customers and *differentiating* them based on their needs and behaviors, we need to clearly understand the following:

1. *Benefits:* What benefits is the customer looking to achieve from interacting with us and buying our product? By understanding this, we gain insight into decision making drivers for our customers and could event detect some latent needs.
2. *Effort:* What effort does the customer have to go through to receive our product or service? By understanding this, we would gain perspective into what impressions we are creating with our customers and how are we simplifying/complicating their lives.
3. *Frictions:* What are the difficulties that the customer may face to achieve their goal?

Once the above is defined, we go into the *interact* and *customize* components of IDIC:

1. *Benefits:* How can we design our interactions and customize them in order to help the customers meet more of their goals in every interaction?
2. *Effort:* How can we simplify those interactions to reduce the effort a customer has to take?
3. *Frictions:* How can we use digital technologies to take away some of those frictions?

Example: In 2015, Amazon introduced the Amazon Dash button as a way to increase the shopping convenience for high-frequency household goods (coffee, soap, detergent, etc.) of their Prime customers. Customer order Dash buttons from Amazon for a small fee, install the Dash buttons in convenient locations in their home, and can order the related items from Amazon by pressing the button. The small fee is then discounted from the first order.

Let's take a look at the above three dimensions:

1. *Benefits:* Customers are shopping from Amazon for convenience (save time, one-click ordering, receive suggestions based on shopping history, not having to provide address and payment information over and over again, etc.).
2. *Effort:* Shopping from Amazon is usually a low-effort task. The highest amount of effort could come from having to search for items.
3. *Frictions:* The frictions are usually few. The key frictions could come from having to switch on a laptop to go into the website, navigate the shopping experience on the small screen of a cell phone, or from having to remember to order an item that a customer is running out of.

(continued)

(Continued)

With the Dash buttons, Amazon has actually found a way to further reduce the friction in the interactions of their highest value customers.

The key to succeeding in such efforts is to take an outside-in view of customer interactions instead of the traditional inside-out view typically taken in BPR work. This approach is usually an eye-opener for organizations, and very often it is one of the rare times the customer perspective is actually brought to the attention of senior executives and explicitly considered in designing some interactions. One way to obtain senior management buy-in to transforming the customer experience is to have members of the senior management team of an organization to go through that experience themselves: for example, asking the executives of a financial services institution to go through the process of opening an account and then applying for a credit card at the enterprise where they themselves are employed. This can be thought of as a **Customer Interaction and Experience Touchmap,** which is used in various approaches to understand what it's like to be the customer of a particular company. Usually, such an experience could be eye-opening since many of those executives would find just how frustrating completing the application forms can be; some will be surprised at how their customer-facing employees lack the information needed and even at the interpersonal skills required to deal with customers. Sources of frustration include not just the sheer volume of information being requested in an application form but also the fact that much of the requested information is already stored in the bank's own systems, even though it is demanded from the customer anew, multiple times, in different application forms.

In addition to looking at customer interactions from the customer's own perspective, a company needs to link those interactions with the enterprise's internal processes, systems, and high-level information flows. This allows a company to easily identify organizational silos and broken processes, insufficient or nonexistent information sharing, poor system integration, and the general lack of cooperation among departments found at many companies. In our experience, most firms are already aware of many of the issues highlighted but they have rarely been able to see all the ways they link to customer issues and how seriously they inhibit a good customer experience.

Customer Journey Mapping

To put the above into action we need to ask ourselves a few questions:

- How do we identify the benefits, efforts, and frictions for customers?
- How do we differentiate them based on the different customer segments that we have?

Fortunately, over the past few years several tools have become available to support mapping customer journeys and designing customer experiences. The following list includes a number of functions enabled by such tools:

- *Recognition of the different customer personas.* Taking the customer's point of view necessarily involves recognizing that different customers will have very different perspectives. The basic premise of managing customer relationships is "treating different customers differently." When designing journeys for customers, the starting point would be to identify the different personas that exist within a company's customer base and develop use cases around those personas.
- *Analysis of the* **customer life cycle.** Broadly, a customer's life cycle can be broken down into five principal parts: (1) awareness of a need, (2) decision to buy or contract with an enterprise to meet that need, (3) use of the product or service bought, (4) support for the product and the ongoing relationship, and (5) managing potential churn and customer retention.
- *High-level customer interviews.* Customer interviews should allow us to identify a more granular breakdown of these five life-cycle steps and also will allow an enterprise to develop a better understanding of what the customer goes through, even before first interacting with the company. For example, how, where, and in what context did the customer become aware of a certain need? Was the customer talking to a friend? Did the customer have a promotion or a salary raise? Is the customer going through a change in life stage? What were the customer's general perceptions about the company's offering before starting to interact with the company? Did those perceptions change after the customer started interacting with the company or after buying a product or service? These customer interviews should be set up with a small sample of customers from each of the preidentified customer groups.
- *Voice of customer (VOC).* There are several VOC tools available to help companies understand the actual details of what different customers go through at different stages of the life cycle when interacting with the enterprise.
- *Voice of employee (VOE).* Detailed interviews of employees, emphasizing various business process owners, will allow the enterprise to link the customer's perspective with the company's own internal processes. Gaps between the two indicate potential improvement opportunities.
- *Analysis of high-level information flows.* It is important to identify **critical data elements (CDEs)** that facilitate decision making and process execution. During employee interviews with process owners, information should be compiled about which CDEs are captured or missing, updated consistently or out of date, disseminated effectively or stored in silos, utilized to generate customer insight or stored but not effectively used.

(continued)

(*Continued*)

- *Touch-point analysis.* Understanding customer behavior and issues at each touch point is critical. This includes visiting physical locations to observe the different customer interactions and analyzing queue and CRM data in those physical locations. It also covers analyzing customer behaviors across all channels including the call center, Web site, and app. Furthermore, understanding the transition of customers between the different channels and ensuring the consistency across those channels is what would enable a true omnichannel experience.

The above constitute different inputs to better understand, for each interaction, the *benefits*, *efforts*, and *frictions* from the customer's perspective and determine their root causes. [*Author's note:* See Chapter 13 for a more detailed section on **customer journey mapping.**]

Customer Dialogue: A Unique and Valuable Asset

Interaction with a customer, whether it is facilitated by electronic technologies or not, requires the customer to participate actively. Interaction also has a direct impact on the customer, whose awareness of the interaction is an indispensable part of the process. Since interaction is visible to customers, interacting customers gain an impression of an enterprise interested in their feedback. It is a vital part of the customer experience with the brand or the enterprise. The overarching objective on the part of the enterprise should be to establish a dialogue with each customer that will generate customer insight—insight the enterprise can turn into a valuable business asset, because no other enterprise will be able to generate that insight without first engaging the customer in a similar dialogue.

This is one of the key benefits of the Learning Relationship we've been discussing, and it is based on the fact that different customers want and need different things. This means we also should expect different customers to prefer different *interaction methods.* One customer prefers e-mail to phone; another likes a combination of e-mail and regular mail; still another only visits social networking sites, such as Twitter. The level of personalization that the Web affords to a customer also should be available in more traditional "customer-facing" venues. Retail sales executives in the store, for instance, should have access to the same knowledge base of customer information and previous interactions and transactions with the enterprise as a **customer service representative (CSR)** at corporate headquarters, **customer interaction centers,** or **customer contact**

centers. Enterprises must be able to identify which channels each of their customers prefers and then decide how they will support seamless interactions. Those enterprises that fail to provide these interaction capabilities can lose sales and compromise relationships.[14]

> The goal is not to understand a *market* through a *sample* but to understand each *individual* in the population through *dialogue*.

The goal for the customer-strategy enterprise is not just to understand a *market* through a *sample* but also to understand each *individual* in the population through *dialogue*. The dialogue information that is of most interest to the enterprise falls into two general categories:

1. *Customer needs.* The best method for discovering what a customer wants is to interact with him directly. Each time he buys, the enterprise discovers more and more about how he likes to shop and what he prefers to buy. Interactions are important not only because the customer is investing in the relationship with the enterprise, but also because the enterprise learns substantive information about the customer that a competitor may not know. Interaction gives the enterprise valuable information about a customer that a competitor cannot act on.

2. *Potential value.* With every customer interaction, customers help the enterprise estimate more accurately their **trajectory** and their **actual value** to the enterprise. Getting a handle on a customer's potential value, however, is often problematic. Through dialogue, a customer might reveal more specific plans or intentions regarding how much money she will spend with the enterprise or how long she will use its products and services. Insight into a customer's potential value could include, among other things, advance word of an upcoming project or pending purchase; information with respect to the competitors a customer also deals with; or referrals to other customers that could be profitably solicited by the enterprise. This type of information is not usually available from a customer's buying history or transactional records and can be obtained only through direct interaction and dialogue with the customer.

---

[14] Daniela Yu and John H. Fleming, "How Customers Interact with Their Banks," *Gallup Business Journal*, May 7, 2013, available at http://www.gallup.com/businessjournal/162107/customers-interact-banks.aspx, accessed February 7, 2016; and Patricia Warrington, "Multi-Channel Retailing and Customer Satisfaction: Implications for e-CRM," *International Journal of E-Business Research* 3, no. 2 (April–June 2007): 57–70.

Customizing Online Communication

Tom Spitale
Principal, Impact Planning Group

"Nice product. Bad price. Let me go check the competition's site." Every chief executive in the world has felt the double-edged sword of online commerce. On one hand, the Internet boosts performance as the enterprise interacts with customers, suppliers, or channels at low costs. However, it has lowered the cost of entry for every competitor in the world. The Internet often is seen as the weapon of competitive choice for those only interested in competing on low price.

Executives at one health care insurer found a unique approach for using their Web site to block competition. The standard question in their industry is: How do we retain healthy customers who care very little about the features and benefits of our insurance policies? Your best customer, in this case, may be a 24-year-old man who runs three miles a day—and this dude is not likely to care much about insurance. If you run a health insurance company, you desperately want to hold on to such healthy customers, because the profit you derive from them will enable you to pay medical expenses for other insurance members who fall ill.

Lose enough healthy consumers and your entire company gets sick. A competitor with a lower price—even if it has a lousy offering—is likely to steal healthy customers away.

The executive team at this insurer decided to use its Web site to wrap a new layer of value around its core product of health insurance: customized health-related information. The company realized this was the best way to become relevant to its desired audience of physically fit consumers: Add communications and services that appeal to their healthy lifestyle, and customize the offers so they are relevant. Its Web site was the perfect vehicle, because while the firm couldn't hire an army of customer relationship experts to offer personal communications to members, it could use dynamic content generation online to mass-customize the message.

To understand which services would be most appealing, the company cataloged wide-ranging content, including media publications tangentially related to health, and came up with innovative ideas. Fitness runners and weight lifters got unique information; cosmetics and baseball game information were added to the mix—all "expanding the need set"[a] of healthy consumers who previously didn't care. This approach gave healthy customers reason to remain loyal ("my health insurer understands my preferences and provides personally relevant advice") *and* reduced benefit costs by providing information that helped those with problems get better.

The lesson: Your Web site can block competitors by surrounding your core offering with a layer of personalized information and value. How would any company duplicate this insurer's online communication customization in a different industry? Utilizing needs-based segmentation or portfolio-building in Web site design is key.

Needs-based segmentation (see Chapter 6) recognizes that different sets of customers have different needs. Filtering out content that is not relevant to each segment—and pointing people quickly to the most relevant content to them—is a valuable differentiator in a time-starved world.

This filtering can be done in a sophisticated fashion or very simply. Amazon .com has invested heavily in its Personal Recommendations strategy. In essence, it is creating a one-to-one relationship with each of its customers based on their individual ratings of books, and—wherever customers are willing to write a review—allowing customers to listen in on each other's comments as well as benefit from ratings and usage. Many customers prefer to see comments from other people, even strangers, before they buy a product.

But what about a B2B company with a limited budget? A boutique strategy consulting firm with less than $5 million in annual revenues is using this concept in a much more straightforward, yet profitable, way. This firm recognizes that its customers approach strategic planning in different ways. For example, some companies enjoy rigor and discipline in their planning processes while others prefer to maintain some "entrepreneurial freedom" in their strategic planning.

The consulting company created a "front door" to its Web site that asks visitors to identify themselves based on one of four types of companies, according to their strategic planning profile. These four types of companies are really "needs-based segments" of firms. Once a visitor has chosen a profile, the Web site content is parsed to create a pathway to more relevant content. For example, the more entrepreneurial segment won't see information on creating entire planning processes. Instead, they will be given information on "quick hit," single-topic issues and see case studies about how other entrepreneurial companies are improving their strategic planning within a very fluid culture. The process-oriented segment will see still different content, offering free webinars on how to build strategic planning road maps or downloadable white papers on how to standardize planning presentations. They can read case studies on how process-oriented companies drive standardization throughout their organizations.

This is different from simply setting up different sections of a Web site with different types of offerings. Visit some B2B Web sites; very few, if any, will have a front door that customizes your pathway through the site.

And yet the financial return on site from this kind of interactive content customization is very high. Amazon.com is doing quite well, despite the fact that it doesn't require a purchase in order to provide you with recommendations.

(continued)

> *(Continued)*
>
> And there are other benefits as well. High percentages of new visitors to the Web site of the consulting firm just profiled reach out to the company through live channels to discuss doing business. A typical quote during that first live conversation? "You listen better than your competitors." Do you think it has something to do with customized interactions on the Web site?
>
> ───────────
>
> [a] Read more about the "expanded need set" in Chapter 10.

Because most customers will not sit still for extensive questioning at any given touch point, the successful customer-oriented enterprise will learn to use each interaction, whether initiated by the customer or the firm, to learn one more incremental thing that will help in growing **share of customer (SOC)** (see Chapter 1) with that customer. This is the concept we call **drip irrigation dialogue**. USAA Insurance in San Antonio, Texas, calls it *smart dialogue.* As the basis for intelligent interaction, USAA uses **business rules** within its customer data management effort to a make a customer's immediate history available to its CSRs as soon as a customer calls. The CSRs also see a box on their computer screens that state the next question USAA needs to have answered about a customer in order to serve him better. This is not a question USAA is asking every customer who calls this month; it is the next question for *this customer.*

In many cases, an enterprise will use **Golden Questions** to understand its customers and thus achieve needs and value differentiation quickly and effectively (see Chapters 5 and 6). Golden Questions are designed to reveal important information

> Golden Questions are designed to reveal important information about a customer while requiring the least possible effort from the customer.

about a customer while requiring the least possible effort from the customer. Designing a Golden Question almost always requires a good deal of imagination and creative judgment, but the question's effectiveness is predetermined by statistically correlating the answers with actual customer characteristics or behavior, using predictive modeling. In general, an enterprise should avoid most product-focused questions, except in situations in which the customer is trying to specify a product or service, prior to purchase. Instead, the most productive type of customer interaction is that which reveals information about an individual customer's underlying need or potential value. To better understand how product-focused questions differ from Golden Questions, examine the hypothetical chart in Exhibit 7.1.

ORGANIZATION GOAL	PRODUCT-FOCUSED QUESTIONS	UNDERLYING NEED OR MOTIVATION OF HIGH-GROWTH CUSTOMERS	GOLDEN QUESTION
My company produces premium pet food. I want to get my message to consumers likely to buy a lot of expensive dog food. I am looking for MVCs.	"Did you buy a lot of dog food last year?" "Do you spend more than $20 a week on dog supplies?"	*I'm a customer, and I really love my pet. I'd do almost anything for him.*	"Do you buy your pet a holiday gift?"
My retail chain sells women's clothing, and I want to find out who is likely to shop at my store and spend a lot of money.	"Did you spend more than $1,000 last year on women's clothing?" "Do you shop for clothes at least once a month?"	*I'm a woman, and my personal appearance is very important to me.*	"Is it okay to wear jeans when you go to the movies, or do you prefer something dressier?"
My brokerage firm offers many products. We want to find the existing clients most likely to consolidate their assets with us, to increase total assets under management.	"Do you have more than two investment accounts?" "Do you have more than $500,000 in liquid assets?"	*Retirement is important to me, but I have other interests as well—such as investing for my son's college education and using some "fun money" to play the market.*	"Have you ever used your savings to play a hot stock?"

EXHIBIT 7.1 Development of Golden Questions

Not All Interactions Qualify as "Dialogue"

Many interactions with customers are simply not welcomed by the customer. In fact, a large portion of customer-initiated interactions with businesses occur because something has gone wrong with a product or service, and the customer needs to contact the enterprise to try to get things put right. It can be frustrating in the extreme for a customer to try to navigate through a complex IVR in order to get a problem resolved, only to realize later that the problem was not resolved and they need to contact the company again. Companies need to become one-stop shops when it comes to complaint handling. Only 21 percent of complaining customers say they felt their problems were resolved on the first contact, and that it was not unusual to need four or more contacts to get things resolved.[15] In other words,

---

[15] Marc Grainer, Charles H. Noble, Mary Jo Bitner, and Scott M. Broetzmann, "What Unhappy Customers Want," *MIT Sloan Management Review* (Spring 2014), available at http://sloanreview .mit.edu/article/what-unhappy-customers-want/, accessed January 8, 2016.

things work just fine until they don't, and then the poor customer has to really work hard—without being on the payroll—to get what she should have had just for doing business with a company. One of the best books on managing contact-center interactions with customers is *The Best Service Is No Service: How to Liberate Your Customers from Customer Service, Keep Them Happy, and Control Costs*.[16] Author Bill Price is the former vice president of Global Customer Service at Amazon.com, certainly a sterling example of a highly competent customer-strategy enterprise, and coauthor David Jaffe is a consultant in Australia, focused on helping companies manage their customer experiences. The whole point is that customers hate having to make complaint calls, so doing things right to begin with offers a far better experience for customers than any kind of special treatment from the "customer service" department. In this excerpt from *The Best Service Is No Service*, the authors consider all the ways customers can be simply annoyed at the necessity of contacting the companies they buy from and interacting with them.

When the Best Contact Is No Contact

Bill Price
President, Driva Solutions

David Jaffe
Consulting Director, LimeBridge Australia

Let's consider how often some organizations force us to make contact with them:

- A leading cable TV company requires three contacts for each new connection—why not just one contact?
- Some mobile phone companies handle as many as ten to twelve contacts per subscriber per year, whereas others have only three to four. Why do we need to call mobile providers so often? Shouldn't we just be making calls and paying bills, preferably online?
- A water utility was averaging two contacts for each fault call. The first call should have been enough to fix the problem. The subsequent calls asked, "Why isn't it fixed yet?" or "When are you coming to fix it?"—not good enough.
- A leading self-service bank averaged one contact per customer per year and nearly two for each new customer. Don't we sign up for self-service applications like Internet banking so that we don't have to call? Other banks have half this contact rate, so clearly something is broken.

---

[16] Bill Price and David Jaffe, *The Best Service Is No Service: How to Liberate Your Customers from Customer Service, Keep Them Happy, and Control Costs* (San Francisco: Jossey-Bass, 2008).

- A leading insurance company was averaging more than two contacts per claim. The first contact makes sense, setting the claim in motion, but why were the subsequent contacts needed?
- "Customers reported making an average of 3.5 contacts in an attempt to resolve their most serious customer-service problem in the past year."[a] Why isn't this 1.0 contact or, perish the thought, zero contacts because nothing needs to be resolved in the first place?

We should make it clear that we are not talking about such interactions as placing orders, making payments, or using self-service solutions, such as checking balances, that the customers chose to use. Instead, we are talking about having to call or take the time to write or visit a branch to get something done or to get something fixed. In some industries, these contact rates are much worse: Every contact with a technical support area of an Internet provider or computer manufacturer is a sign that something is broken. Ideally, customers should never need to make these contacts.

Source: Reprinted with permission from Bill Price and David Jaffe, *The Best Service Is No Service: How to Liberate Your Customers from Customer Service, Keep Them Happy, and Control Costs* (San Francisco: Jossey-Bass, 2008), p. 7.

[a] Jane Spencer, "Cases of 'Customer Rage' Mount as Bad Service Prompts Venting," *Wall Street Journal,* September 17, 2003, p. D4.

Tapping into feedback from customers is an immensely powerful tactic for improving a company's sales and marketing success. But customers will share information only with companies they trust not to abuse it. (See Chapter 9 for more on privacy issues.) Here are some ways to earn this trust, encouraging customers to participate more productively, improving both the cost efficiency and the effectiveness of customer interactions:

- *Use a flexible opt-in policy.* Many opt-in policies are all-or-nothing propositions, in which customers must elect either to receive a flood of communications from the firm, or none at all. A flexible opt-in policy will allow customers to indicate their preferences with regard to communication formats, channels, and even timing. To the extent possible, give customers a choice of how much communication to receive from you, or when, or under what conditions.
- *Make an explicit bargain.* Customers have been used to getting news and entertainment for free, in exchange for being exposed to ads or other commercial messages. As customers gain more power to zap commercials, eliminate pop-ups, and avoid unwanted calls, text messages, and e-mail they consider to be spam, marketers who want to talk to customers may need to make an explicit offer, something like this: Click here to receive e-mail offers from us in the future and save 20 percent on this order.

■ *Tread cautiously with targeted Web ads.* Even though targeted online ads are popular with marketers, research has shown that consumers are especially wary of sharing information when targeted Web ads are the result. This doesn't mean don't do it, but it does mean don't pile on. In any case, for behavioral targeting to succeed, an enterprise must have the customer's informed consent.

■ *Make it clear and simple.* Have a clear, readable privacy policy for your customers to review. Procter & Gamble (P&G) provides a splendid example. Instead of posting a lengthy document written in legalese, P&G presents a one-page, easy-to-understand set of highlights outlining the policy, with links to more detailed information. Other companies are catching up. Five years ago, in its online offer to consumers to join the "My Sears Holding Community," the company had a scroll box outlining the privacy policy that was just 10 lines of text but requires you to read 54 boxfuls to get through the whole policy. Buried far into the policy is a provision that lets the firm install software on your computer that "monitors all of the Internet behavior that occurs on the computer."[17] Now, though, the Sears privacy policy is written in pretty clear language and is organized in a more understandable way.[18]

■ *Create a culture based on customer trust.* Emphasize the importance of privacy protection to everyone who handles personally identifiable customer information, from the chief executive officer to contact center workers. Line employees provide the customer experiences that matter, and employees determine whether your privacy policy becomes business practice or just a piece of paper. If your business culture is built around acting in the interest of customers at all times, then it will be second nature at your company to protect customers from irritating or superfluous uses of their personal information—things most consumers will regard as privacy breaches, whether they formally "agreed" to the data use or not.

■ *Remember: You're responsible for your partners, too.* It should go without saying that whatever privacy protection you promise your customers, it has to be something your own sales and channel partners—as well as your suppliers and other vendors—have also agreed to, contractually. Anyone in your "ecosystem" who might handle your own customers' personally identifiable information and feedback will have the capacity to ruin your own reputation. Take care not to let that happen!

If an enterprise wants to conduct dialogues with customers, it must remember that the customers themselves must want to engage in these dialogues. Simply contacting a customer, or having the customer contact the enterprise, does not constitute dialogue, and will likely convey no marketing benefit to the enterprise.

---

[17] Hal Abelson, Ken Leueen, and Harry Lewis, *Blown to Bits: Your Life, Liberty, and Happiness After the Digital Explosion* (Reading, MA: Addison-Wesley, 2008), p. 67.
[18] See Sears's privacy policy at http://searsholdings.com/site/privacy-policy, accessed February 7, 2016.

Contact Centers Take a New Approach to Customer Interactions

Elizabeth Glagowski
Adjunct Professor, Digital Media, Southern Connecticut State University; Editor-in-Chief, Customer Strategist Journal from TeleTech

A Weight Watchers member who is sitting at a restaurant and is unsure what menu item to order can live chat with a certified coach via mobile app any time day or night. Amazon tablet users with questions or tech trouble can click the "Mayday" button to automatically video chat with a live support person who can see their screen and take over the device if necessary. Consumers interested in buying a mobile phone can be routed directly to a sales expert who already knows the types of phones and plans they've searched for on the Web and what city they're in to recommend the most appropriate products and services more quickly.

These are examples of what the modern contact center is all about: immediate, frictionless, value-based interactions.

A company's contact center is a critical customer interaction channel for businesses and consumers. The traditional model has consumers call in with sales and service questions, which are resolved by trained associates over the phone. The model is steeped in efficiency, and as companies grew to serve millions of customers, many contact centers devolved into cost containment operations whose efficiency goals superseded their initial purpose of having quality customer interactions. There are too many poor customer experience examples to count that are the result of companies not meeting user interaction expectations.

That model just won't cut it anymore to meet today's interaction needs of both companies and customers. Now, customers often choose to contact a traditional contact center as a last resort after failing to resolve their issue via the company Web site, mobile app, or physical location. They expect the company to at least be aware of, if not proactively take steps based on, what they did in those other channels before calling the contact center. Progressive businesses understand this and are reframing their contact center operations to address what consumers want, as illustrated by the above examples.

Issues that require a lot of time or effort are reserved for the contact center, while self-service and online options are preferred for simpler or quick interactions. A recent research study of 176 customer experience professionals and 3,515 consumers by TeleTech found that voice is not declining as a channel of choice for issues that are time sensitive or complex.[a] It speaks to the importance of being available everywhere your customers want to add value to the customer relationship.

(continued)

(Continued)

In addition, consumers want a more frictionless experience when they do speak with an associate via the phone. A majority 61 percent of consumers prefer that businesses invest in improving first call resolution as a top priority in the contact center, followed closely by training employees to be empowered and knowledgeable (60 percent), and reducing complexity (transfers, people involved) when solving an issue during an interaction (44 percent).[b]

And the examples above show that the boundaries among interaction channels are blurring. The contact center is no longer a stand-alone silo. The contact center, Web site, mobile apps, and physical channels must all align and integrate as part of a company's overall customer experience strategy, based on the needs of customers.

To compete today, companies must go where their customers are. They must invest in new channels and interactions that customers prefer. And they must observe how and why customers experience the brand now, what they want in the future, and optimize those channels to create a superior experience. The traditional contact center is still important, but it's evolving in new ways to become an even more valuable source of customer relationship strength.

---

[a] "The TeleTech 2015 Customer Experience Benchmark Research Report," 2015. This study conducted by 10EQS on behalf of TeleTech investigated customer experience priorities of businesses and consumers, and found consumers want a simple, frictionless experience whenever they interact with a brand, ahead of technology innovations.
[b] "The TeleTech 2015 Customer Experience Benchmark Research Report," 2015.

Cost Efficiency and Effectiveness of Customer Interaction

Regardless of how automated they are, every interaction with a customer does cost something, if only in terms of the customer's own time and attention, and some interactions cost more than others. The cost of customer interaction can be minimized partly by reducing or eliminating the interactions that the customer does not want. But ranking customers by their value also allows a company to manage the customer interaction process more cost efficiently. A highly valuable customer is more apt to be worth a personal phone call from a manager while a not-so-valuable customer's interaction might be handled more efficiently on the Web site. An enterprise requires a manageable and cost-efficient way to solicit, receive, and process the interactions with its customers. It will need to categorize customer inquiries and responses in some effective way so it can customize its interactions for each customer.

Customer-strategy enterprises concentrate not just on the *efficiency* of the communication channel used for interactions with the customer but also on the *effectiveness* of the customer dialogue itself. Measuring efficiency might include tracking the percent of inbound customer inquiries satisfactorily answered by the enterprise's Web site FAQ section, or monitoring how long customers stay on hold with the customer service department before they disconnect. Measuring effectiveness might include tracking **first-call resolution (FCR)**, or the ratio of complaints handled or problems resolved on the first call. (Consider: Which kinds of measures for a call center—effectiveness or efficiency—will likely lead to better customer experiences and higher trust scores?) Critical to the success of any dialogue, however, is that each successive interaction with the individual customer be seen as part of a seamless, flowing stream of discussion. Whether the conversation yesterday took place via mail, phone, the Web, or any other communication channel, the next conversation with the customer must pick up where the last one left off.

For decades now, technology has been dramatically reducing the expenses required for a business to interact with a wide range of customers. Enterprises can now streamline and automate what was once a highly manual process of customer interaction. Different interactive mechanisms can yield widely different information-exchange capabilities, such as speed trackability, tangibility (the ability to hold it or refer back to it later), and personalization. Interacting regularly with a customer via a Web site is usually highly cost efficient and can be customer driven, yielding a rich amount of information. Postal mail is not as practical for dialogue, because it involves a lengthy cycle time, although it can prove effective for delivering more detailed information to the customer who prefers to keep hard copies. Telephone interaction has the advantages of real-time conversation, but neither phone nor face-to-face interaction facilitates easy tracking of the content of these conversations, and the enterprise trying to employ voice interactions to strengthen its customer relationships must be sure the employees responsible for the interactions are diligently and accurately capturing the key elements of customer dialogues (although scripted phone calls can aid in this effort).

Complaining Customers: Hidden Assets?

Customers generally contact an enterprise of their own volition for only three reasons: to get information, to obtain a product or service, or to make a suggestion or a complaint. Despite the fact that technology should make it easier for customers to contact companies, the Technical Assistance Research Program (TARP) found that customer complaints are declining – not because there are fewer problems but likely because, unfortunately, customers have been trained to expect problems as part of the cost of doing business.[19] TARP discovered that 50 percent of customers with high-value problems would not complain at all, and that number rose to 96 percent for low-value items. Of the B2B customers who have a problem and do not complain, 90 percent will simply take their business somewhere else.[20] But sometimes a complaint can provide an opportunity for real dialogue.

Thus, one way to view a complainer is to see him as a customer with a current "negative" value that can be turned into positive value. In other words, a complainer has extremely high potential value. If the complaint is not resolved, there is a high likelihood that the complaining customer will cease buying, and will probably talk to a number of other people about his dissatisfaction, causing the loss of additional business. But the potential for increased value; for one thing, the customer cares enough to, at least, contact the company to complain. The customer-oriented enterprise, focused on increasing the value of its customer base, will see a customer complaint as an opportunity to convert the customer's immense potential value into actual value, for three reasons:

1. *Complaints are a "relationship adjustment opportunity."* The customer who calls with a complaint enables the enterprise to understand why their relationship is troubled. The enterprise then can determine ways to fix the relationship.
2. *Complaints enable the enterprise to expand its scope of knowledge about the customer.* By hearing a customer's complaint, the enterprise can learn more about the customer's needs and strive to increase the value of the customer.
3. *Complaints provide data points about the enterprise's products and services.* By listening to a customer's complaint, the enterprise can better understand how to modify and correct its generalized offerings, based on the feedback.

To a customer-centered enterprise, complaining customers have a collaborative upside, represented by a high potential value. In fact, they might have the highest potential value: Research from TARP has shown that the most loyal customers are the ones most

> To a customer-centered enterprise, complaining customers have a collaborative upside, represented by a high potential value.

---

[19] John Goodman, *Customer Experience 3.0: High-Profit Strategies in the Age of Techno Service* (New York: American Management Association, 2014); Trevor Lambert, "LEARN from Complaints—A Framework for Handling Grievances Profitably," Linkedin Pulse, November 19, 2014, available at https://www.linkedin.com/pulse/20141119082756-7848549-learn-from-complaints-a-framework-for-handling-grievances-profitably?trk=prof-post&trkSplashRedir=true&forceNoSplash=true, accessed January 8, 2016; and Janelle Barlow and Claus Moller, *A Complaint Is a Gift: Recovering Customer Loyalty When Things Go Wrong,* 2nd ed. (San Francisco: Berrett-Koehler, 2008), p. 74.

[20] Lambert, "LEARN from Complaints—A Framework for Handling Grievances Profitably."

likely to take the time to complain to a company in the first place. It has also found that customers who are satisfied with the solution to a problem often exhibit even greater loyalty than do customers who did not experience a problem at all.[21]

> Customers who are satisfied with the solution to a problem often exhibit even greater loyalty than do customers who did not experience a problem at all.

Because the handling of complaints has so much potential upside, a one-to-one enterprise will not avoid complaints but instead will seek them out. An effort to "discover complaints"—to seek out as many opportunities for customer dialogue as possible—becomes part of dialogue management. **Complaint discovery** contacts typically ask two questions:

1. Is there anything more we can do for you?
2. Is there anything we can do better?

At one European book club, for example, customer service representatives called new members during their first month and asked one simple question: "Is there anything we can do better?" No sales pitch or special promotion has been discussed. The results of this customer satisfaction initiative speak volumes to its effectiveness in retaining customers: nearly an 8 percent increase in sales per member, and 6 percent fewer dropoffs after the first year of membership, among those contacted.

Of course, today many of the "complaints" don't need to be discovered. Now that it's so much easier to tweet a problem, give a low product rating online, or reach a rep easily by chat on computer or mobile, companies are in a position where they can spend less time seeking complaints and more time resolving them.

Here's the point: By complaining, a customer is initiating a dialogue with an enterprise and making himself available for collaboration. The enterprise focused on building customer value will view complaining customers as an asset—a business opportunity—to turn the complainers into loyal customers. That is why enterprises need to make it easy for a customer to complain when he needs to.

---

[21] Marc Grainer, Charles H. Noble, Mary Jo Bitner, and Scott M. Broetzmann, "What Unhappy Customers Want," *MIT Sloan Management Review* (Spring 2014), available at http://sloanreview .mit.edu/article/what-unhappy-customers-want/, accessed February 7, 2016; Goodman, *Customer Experience 3.0: High-Profit Strategies in the Age of Techno Service*; Lambert, "LEARN from Complaints—A Framework for Handling Grievances Profitably"; and Barlow and Moller, *A Complaint Is a Gift*, pp. 104–105.

For their part, most customers see complaint discovery, or having an easy way to get problems solved, as a highly friendly and service-oriented action on the part of a firm. One survey commissioned by an auto dealer discovered that for the vast majority of the 6,500 automobile owners included in the survey, the very act of asking for their opinions made them into happier and more loyal (i.e., more valuable) customers. Customers who received a phone call simply asking about their opinion tended to become more satisfied with the automobile dealer than those who did not receive a call.

Summary

At this point, we've shown with this chapter the importance of customer interaction in the Learning Relationship. The enterprise that creates a sustained dialogue with each customer can learn more about that customer and begin to develop ways to add value that spring from learning about that customer and consequently to creating a product/service bundle that he is most interested in owning or using. And, like drip irrigation, which never overwhelms or parches, a sustained dialogue helps a company get smarter and serves the customer better than sporadic random sample surveys. The customer-based enterprise engages in a collaborative dialogue with each customer in that customer's preferred channel of communication—whether it is the customer interaction center, e-mail, the phone, wireless, the Web, snail mail, or media we haven't thought of yet.

The development of social media, however, has revolutionized a company's capacity to interact with its customers—and its customers' capacity to broadcast their experiences with a company, both good and bad. In the next chapter, we discuss how these different communication channels can help facilitate customer interaction and relationships with customers in general.

Food for Thought

1. TiVo and other digital recording devices collect very specific data about household television viewing. These services make it possible to know which programs are recorded and watched (and when and how many times), which programs are recorded and never watched, and which programs are transferred to another electronic format. The services also know when a particular part of a program is watched more than once (a sports play, or a favorite cartoon, or movie scene, or even a commercial). What are the implications of that knowledge for dialogue? For privacy? For the business collecting the data (i.e., data or a cable company)? How might TiVo or a cable company use this information to increase the value it offers to advertisers and marketers? What would a marketer have to do differently to make the most of this

information? How can DVR companies protect their own customers' privacy? What happens next in this industry as a growing number of consumers cut their cable connections?

2. What problems might occur if an enterprise participates in customer dialogues but its own information and data systems are not integrated well? Do you remember any personal experience in dealing with a company or brand that could not find the right records or information during your interaction with it? How did this make you feel about the company? Did you feel the company was less competent? Less trustworthy?

3. What are some of the explicit bargains companies have made with you in your role as a customer to get some of your time, attention, or information?

4. How does the European book club mentioned in the discussion of complaint discovery actually *know* that it's the calling program that led to 6 percent fewer dropoffs and 8 percent more sales per member? Might it not have been the book selection that year? Or the economy?

5. When you plan to buy a product and want to investigate its benefits and drawbacks, whose advice do you seek? Do you think the advertiser will tell you about the drawbacks, or just the benefits? If you are trying to evaluate the product by researching it online, do you have more confidence in it if the seller makes other customers' reviews available? What if you read a negative comment? Might you still buy the product?

Glossary

Actual value   The net present value of the future financial contributions attributable to a customer, behaving as we expect her to behave—knowing what we know now, and with no different actions on our part.

Addressable   Refers to media that can send and customize messages individually.

Business process reengineering (BPR)   Focuses on reducing the time it takes to complete an interaction or a process and on reducing the cost of completing it. BPR usually involves introducing quality controls to ensure time and cost efficiencies are achieved.

Business rules   The instructions that an enterprise follows in configuring different processes for different customers, allowing the company to mass-customize its interactions with its customers.

Complaint discovery   An outbound interaction with a customer, on the part of a marketer, to elicit honest feedback and uncover any problems with a product or service in the process.

Critical data elements (CDEs)   High-level information flows that facilitate decision making and process execution.

Customer contact center   The functional corporate department or unit charged with the task of receiving, understanding, and dealing with individual customer inquiries and requests, using phone, chat, video, or other communication technologies. Contact centers were formerly known as *call centers* because the only practical way for customers to contact and interact with a company without visiting a store and doing so in person was by phone.

Customer Interaction and Experience Touchmap   A graphical depiction of the interactions a company has with each segment of its customers across each of the available channels. Its purpose is to take an outside-in view of the customer interactions, instead of the traditional inside-out view typically taken in business process reengineering work. Current State Touchmaps depict all the enterprise's current interactions with customers and identify gap areas; Future State Touchmaps depict the desired customer interactions that will be customized based on the needs and values of individual customers.

Customer interaction center   *See* Customer contact center.

Customer journey mapping   A process of diagramming all the steps a customer takes when engaging with a company to buy, use, or service its product or offering. Also called *customer experience journey mapping*.

Customer life cycle   The "trajectory" a customer follows, from the customer's first awareness of a need, to his or her decision to buy or contract with a company to meet that need, to use the product or service, to support it with an ongoing relationship, perhaps recommending it to others, and to end that relationship for whatever reason. The term *customer life cycle* does not refer to the customer's actual lifetime or chronological age but rather to the time during which the product is in some way relevant to the customer.

Customer service   Customer service involves helping a customer gain the full use and advantage of whatever product or service was bought. When something goes wrong with a product, or when a customer has some kind of problem with it, the process of helping the customer overcome this problem is often referred to as *customer care*.

Customer service representative (CSR)   A person who answers or makes calls in a call center (also called a customer interaction center or contact center, since it may include online chat or other interaction methods). Sometimes called a "rep," or representative.

Customer-strategy enterprise   An organization that builds its business model around increasing the value of the customer base. This term applies to companies that may be product oriented, operations focused, or customer intimate.

Customize   Become relevant by doing something for a customer that no competition can do that doesn't have all the information about that customer that you do.

Differentiate   Prioritize by value; understand different needs. Identify, recognize, link, remember.

Digital video recorder (DVR)   A digital recording device (such as TiVo) that uses a hard disk drive to record programming content from cable or other input for use at the time desired by the customer user. Often uses interfaces (such as an on-screen program guide) that are regularly downloaded to the device.

Drip irrigation dialogue   An enterprise's sustained, incremental dialogue that uses each interaction, whether initiated by the customer or by the firm, to learn one more incremental thing that will help in growing share of customer with that customer.

Explicit bargain   One-to-one organizations give something of value to a customer in exchange for that customer's time and attention, and perhaps for information about that customer as well. An example: discounts on prices bought at a store where a customer shows his membership card.

First-call resolution (FCR)   When customer complaints are resolved at their first interaction with a company, whether it is through telephone, e-mail, or any other method of interaction. The measurable benchmark for customer service.

Golden Questions   Questions designed to reveal important information about a customer while requiring the least possible effort from the customer, in order to differentiate customer needs and potential value. The most productive Golden Questions will be customer need based rather than product based.

Identify   Recognize and remember each customer regardless of the channel by or geographic area in which the customer leaves information about himself. Be able to link information about each customer to generate a complete picture of each customer.

IDIC   Stands for Identify-Differentiate-Interact-Customize.

Implicit bargain   Advertisers have in the past bought ads that pay for the cost of producing the media that consumers want—television programming, newspaper copy, magazine stories, music on the radio, and so on. The implied "deal" was that consumers would listen to the ads in exchange for getting the media content free.

Interact   Generate and remember feedback.

Interactive voice response (IVR)   Now a feature at most call centers, IVR software provides instructions for callers to "push '1' to check your current balance, push '2' to transfer funds," and so forth.

Internet of Things (IoT)   A term describing the network of products and other objects that have intelligence or computational capability built into them, along with interconnectedness to the Web, via Wi-Fi, or other technology. As defined by the ITU, a UN agency, the IoT is "a global infrastructure for the information society, enabling advanced services by interconnecting (physical and virtual) things based on existing and evolving interoperable information and communication technologies" (http://www.itu.int/en/ITU-T/gsi/iot/Pages/default.aspx, accessed April 6, 2016).

Mutuality   Refers to the two-way nature of a relationship.

Needs   What a customer needs from an enterprise is, by our definition, synonymous with what she wants, prefers, or would like. In this sense, we do not distinguish a customer's needs from her wants. For that matter, we do not distinguish needs from preferences, wishes, desires, or whims. Each of these terms might imply some nuance of need—perhaps the intensity of the need or the permanence of it—but in each case we are still talking, generically, about the customer's needs.

Nonaddressable   Refers to media that cannot send and/or customize messages individually.

Omnichannel marketing   A marketing buzzword referring to the capability of interacting and transacting with customers in any or all channels, in order to ensure that every interaction takes place in the channel of the customer's own choice.

Share of customer (SOC)   For a customer-focused enterprise, share of customer is a conceptual metric designed to show what proportion of a customer's overall need is being met by the enterprise. It is not the same as "share of wallet," which refers to the specific share of a customer's spending in a particular product or service category. If, for instance, a family owns two cars, and one of them is your car company's brand, then you have a 50 percent share of wallet with this customer, in the car category. But by offering maintenance and repairs, insurance, financing, and perhaps even driver training or trip planning, you can substantially increase your "share of customer."

Social media   Interactive services and Web sites that allow users to create their own content and share their own views for others to consume. Blogs and microblogs (e.g., Twitter) are a form of social media, because users "publish" their opinions or views for everyone. Facebook, LinkedIn, and MySpace are examples of social media that facilitate making contact, interacting with, and following others. YouTube and Flickr are examples of social media that allow users to share creative work with others. Even Wikipedia represents a form of social media, as users collaborate interactively to publish more and more accurate encyclopedia entries.

Trajectory   The path of the customer's financial relationship through time with the enterprise.

CHAPTER 8

Customer Insight, Dialogue, and Social Media

It's a rare person who wants to hear what he doesn't want to hear.

—Dick Cavett

Although the strategy of customer relationships must precede the successful implementation of customer relationship technology, it was the technology that mandated that enterprises map out their path down the road we've been following in the preceding chapters. Customers have always been able to interact with a company, but mainly on the company's terms—through mail, if a customer could get the name of a person to send a letter to; through phone, if a customer could get the right phone number; and maybe through salespeople, if the customer were important enough to warrant a personal sales call and if the salesperson was authorized to provide service to the customer's satisfaction. That was pretty much it. Today, the customer rules. And savvy customers are leveraging social networking tools to get what they want, when they want it, more than ever before. But **social media** also allows new possibilities for dialogue and collaboration between and among customers and enterprises that can benefit both parties. This chapter addresses how a customer-centric company can recognize and reap the positive impact on customer value these technologies potentially provide.

So far we have been talking about interaction and dialogue as if the only thing of importance to a marketer is the dialogue that can take place between an enterprise and a customer. But customers are human beings, and humans prefer conversing with other humans much more than with brands or businesses. Humans are social animals, and the same Internet-based technologies that have made it possible for businesses to interact directly with their customers have also made it possible for humans to interact socially with other humans anywhere on the planet. Moreover, the capabilities inherent in the Internet, via computers, mobile phones, and other devices, make it possible for individual consumers to produce vast quantities of their own content, from blogs and written comments, to pictures, podcasts, and videos. People can now create their own content and then upload it to the network for others to see on a wide array of social platforms, from Facebook and Twitter to Instagram and YouTube. They can choose to make the content available only for select friends or associates, or for a variety of categories of other users, or for everyone.

The "social media revolution" that has occurred as a result of these new technological capabilities may actually dwarf the Industrial Revolution in its ultimate impact on the human race, eventually making possible an entirely new, noneconomic production system based not just on money and exchanges of value, but on social ties, trust, generosity, status, and informal "normative" mores. Complex works and projects, from **open source** software, such as the Linux operating system or the Mozilla family of Web browsers, to detailed and evolving documents such as the user-generated reference work Wikipedia, provide small previews of how this new production system might function and flourish.

But this is a topic for another book. What we are concerned with here is how these rapidly flourishing social ties among people, mediated by a proliferating assortment of software and interactive technologies loosely termed *social media*, are likely to alter an enterprise's ability to interact with its customers and prospects and to create and manage profitable, mutually beneficial relationships with them.

The Dollars and Sense of Social Media

A colleague of ours was angry about the way Orbitz handled a service issue, so she tweeted about it. She also sent a complaint via the company's Web site customer support page. Orbitz responded to her Twitter posts via e-mail and resolved the issue. But in response to our friend's e-mail sent via the "contact us" form on the Web site, the company only sent a generic "we're reviewing your inquiry" e-mail.

This is just one of the many examples of customer interaction via social channels benefiting customers. The question is, does it benefit the company as well? It does,[a] and here are a few examples:

- Portable camera maker GoPro is a natural for user-generated content that spurs customer engagement and saves multimillions on marketing dollars spent. "In place of an art director, acting cast, and team of videographers, GoPro simply hands a wearable camera to an amazing athlete and gets back advertising and marketing gold."[b]

- Barnes & Noble's retail sales of specific books increase when customers discuss those books in its online community.
- User-generated content on Hewlett-Packard's online community site helps improve the company's **search engine optimization (SEO)**. In one case, Hewlett-Packard went from not appearing at all on the first results page of a specific keyword search to dominating that first page.
- *Coffee for Less* realized that top-quality content is one of the best things for SEO. So they made it easy for customers to exchange comments. The company discovered that the language of customer reviews used terminology more like what people used in online search, "which allowed Coffee for Less to pick up more organic keywords."[c]
- Spontaneous customer fan pages had appeared on the Web for Italian food company Barilla's White Mill (Mulino Bianco) products; one cookie had 700,000 fans). Barilla created their own Facebook pages for products, and invited customers to participate in product development by suggesting and voting on product ideas. One fan suggested bringing back the Soldino cookie of her youth. The idea received over 6,000 votes and was selected by the firm. They "reissued" the cookie in a limited-edition run and it was a great success.[d]
- Tibco Software's customer community enables customers to help each other solve technical issues (that's what **crowd service** is). Every time that happens, a customer gets the help he **needs** but the company also saves about $1,000 on a support call. The savings gained more than covers the cost of hosting an online community. "We can show tangible value from our social media strategy," says Ram Menon, executive vice president of worldwide marketing for Tibco.

According to a 1to1 Media study on marketing spending, respondent companies increased their recent spending on reaching customers in new ways:

- Sixty-nine percent increased spending on social media.
- Sixty-eight percent increased spending on e-mail.
- Fifty percent increased spending on search.

The hard-dollar benefits include:

- Increased buzz around a brand, product, or service online. Not only increases awareness but also has the potential to increase sales across channels.
- Improved search results from customer conversations about an organization and its products that happen on a company's online community, blog, customer forum, and the like. Potentially drives more traffic to a company's Web site.

(continued)

(Continued)

- More influence from customer recommendations given on social networks and in online communities than referrals in the offline world. Can lead to more deal closings—in some cases, with less selling required on the part of the company.
- Deeper insight into customers' uncensored preferences, **needs**, and behaviors is invaluable. Potentially leads to improvements in such areas as service delivery, product features, and pricing. Also can lead to better customer experience, increased sales, and greater customer engagement.
- Customers helping other customers online. Crowd service can reduce costs to serve by deflecting calls and e-mails from the contact center, and may result in better service results for customers as well.

Although some executives are still searching for the best way to measure the return on investment of what many call *social CRM*, the bottom-line benefits are clear.[c] That doesn't mean it's easy. Start with the end in mind: Determine your ultimate goal or set of objectives for social media interactions. Then create a strategy to get you there that includes measurable results. As Barnes & Noble, Hewlett-Packard, and Tibco can attest, it's a journey worth taking.

[a] Clara Shih, *The Social Business Imperative: Adapting Your Business Model to the Always-Connected Customer* (New York: Prentice Hall, 2016).

[b] Kevin Bobowski, "How GoPro Is Transforming Advertising as We Know It," *Fast Company*, July 1, 2014, available at http://www.fastcompany.com/3032509/the-future-of-work/how-gopro-is-transforming-advertising-as-we-know-it, accessed February 11, 2016.

[c] Elena Ruchko, "8 Brands Effectively Leveraging User-Generated Content," *TINT* guest blog post, July 28, 2014, available at http://www.tintup.com/blog/8-brands-effectively-leveraging-user-generated-content, accessed February 11, 2016.

[d] Antonella Martini, Silvia Massa, and Stefania Testa, "Customer Co-creation Projects and the Social Media: The Case of Barilla of Italy," *Business Horizons 57*, no. 3 (May–June 2014): 425–434.

[e] Paul Greenberg, *CRM at the Speed of Light: Social CRM Strategies, Tools, and Techniques for Engaging Your Customers,* 4th ed. (New York: McGraw-Hill, 2010).

Source: Excerpted and adapted from Don Peppers and Martha Rogers, Ph.D., "The Dollars and Sense of Social Media," in The Social Customer's e-book, *The Social Contract: Customers, Companies, Communities, and Conversations in the Age of the Collaborative Relationship* (2010), available at http://thesocialcustomer.com/submitform/tscebook030810/?utm source=socap&utm medium=multi&utm campaign=contract ebook&reference=smt socap, accessed September 1, 2010.

Social media can be employed by an enterprise in a number of ways, but we should highlight four that are highly important for an enterprise trying to build stronger customer relationships:

1. Engaging and activating the enterprise's most enthusiastic supporters to "spread the word" about the brand.
2. Empowering customers to defend the enterprise's brand in times of stress, and help it recover from missteps or disasters.
3. Listening in on customer conversations that involve the enterprise and/or its competitors.
4. Enlisting the enterprise's own customers (and, sometimes, other volunteers) to help provide service for other customers

Engaging Enthusiastic Supporters

If a company or brand has some proportion of avid supporters, hobbyists, enthusiasts, or just very loyal fans within its customer base, then using social media to draw these highly enthusiastic customers out and cater to their needs can be a highly rewarding relationship-building strategy. Lego, for instance, the well-known Danish toy manufacturer, certainly has its share of enthusiastic users. The company embraced social media early on and has been reaping the rewards through innovative product ideas and a growing population of enthusiastic customers. One nonprofit, the First Lego League, supports kids' clubs around the globe in forming Lego teams that foster STEM (science, technology, engineering, and mathematics) learning by competing in building robots. Its Web site helps teams connect and share ideas, and spreads news about events.[1] Other online groups have produced insightful product ideas, such as the Lego Ambassadors' Forum, a group of selected Lego fans who communicate regularly with the company on various topics.[2]

Lego Ideas is a Lego co-creation program Web site that lets adult fans submit and everyone view fan-designed Lego sets. There's a contest component; ideas that receive enough votes get reviewed and may be made into products, and originators receive a percentage of the profits. Creators of the Big Bang Theory idea set researched Twitter and Facebook communities related to the TV series to solicit their support for the set in the contest. The genius here is that Lego treats adults and children as one and the same, and participates with customers on YouTube, Instagram, Vine, and Twitter.[3] The best news is that most of the work is done by the customers themselves, which the company gladly helps facilitate.

---

[1] See the First Lego League Web site at http://www.firstlegoleague.org/, accessed January 11, 2016.
[2] See the Lego Ambassador Network Web site at https://lan.lego.com/, accessed January 11, 2016.
[3] Christopher Ratcliff, "Why Is LEGO's Social Media Strategy So Outstanding?" *Econsultancy* blog, June 4, 2014, https://econsultancy.com/blog/64955-why-is-lego-s-social-media-strategy-so-outstanding, accessed February 11, 2016. See also the Lego Ideas Web site, https://ideas.lego.com/howitworks, accessed February 10, 2016.

Zappos, the online shoe store, is another company using social media to reach out and energize avid customers. With an employee culture already centered on "making personal and emotional connections," the company was well positioned from its beginning to lead the way in using social media forums such as Twitter, blogging, and Facebook. Most Zappos employees have Twitter accounts (and its CEO, Tony Hsieh, has tweeted often). It should be no surprise that most people who are even aware of the Zappos brand today initially heard of the firm by **word of mouth**. Employees' tweets at Zappos aren't so much about the company's products as they are about getting to know the people themselves—capitalizing on the commonsense fact that when people feel connected to others as individuals, they are more likely to trust them and want to do business with them. This is not a marketing scheme but transparent and authentic relationship building that clearly benefits both customers and employees.[4]

Cosmetics company Sephora is another example. This enterprise has been able to become even more customer-centric while maintaining a high return on social media by knowing which media outlet is best suited to meet their customers' needs. Sephora uses many channels to connect with customers, each in a different way, using Twitter to respond to individual customer questions, Instagram to post photos of products, and Tumblr for greatest customer engagement. One Tumblr post showed a stunning visual of every lipstick color in a new line photographed on the lips of a popular celebrity.[5] When Sephora sponsored a music festival in Coachella Valley, California, Sephora

> Brand building today is so different than from what it was 50 years ago. Fifty years ago you could get a few marketing people in a small room and decide, "This is what our brand will be," and then spend a lot of money on TV advertising—and that was your brand. If you as a consumer only had your neighbors to talk to, you had to believe what the TV was telling you. Today anyone, whether it is an employee or a customer, if they have a good or bad experience with your company they can blog about it or Twitter about it and it can be seen by millions of people. *It's what they say now that is your brand.*
>
> Tony Hsieh, CEO of Zappos

---

[4] Christopher Ratcliff, "How Zappos Uses Social Media: Twitter, Facebook and Instagram," *Econsultancy* blog, October 1, 2014, https://econsultancy.com/blog/65526-how-zappos-uses-social-media-twitter-facebook-and-instagram, accessed February 11, 2016; Soren Gordhamer and Paul Zelizer, "The New Social Engagement: A Visit to Zappos," *Mashable: The Social Media Guide,* 2009; available at http://mashable.com/2009/04/26/zappos/, accessed February 11, 2016; and Samir Balwani, "Presenting: 10 of the Smartest Big Brands in Social Media," *Mashable: The Social Media Guide,* 2009, available at http://mashable.com/2009/02/06/social-media-smartest-brands/#Btg8UstzcsqX, accessed February 11, 2016.

[5] Lucy Hitz, "4 Things You Didn't Know About Sephora's Cross Channel Social Strategy," *Simply Measured Blog,* August 19, 2014, http://simplymeasured.com/blog/4-things-you-didnt-know-about-sephoras-cross-channel-social-strategy/#sm.109c77t128tdp6w141efwvfw73f, accessed February 11, 2016.

followers received "a slew of insider information and live coverage of the event" on Instagram, Twitter, Facebook, mobile-optimized blog, and Snapchat.[6]

Is it a surprise that companies sponsor events and engage customers on social media when they attend? What is more social than an event?

Empowering Customers to Defend the Brand

On Wednesday, February 14, 2007, just prior to the President's Day holiday weekend, a snow-and-ice storm hit New York City, crippling operations at several airlines. The degree to which it incapacitated JetBlue, however, was of a different order of magnitude altogether. A low-fare new entrant that had previously earned high marks among passengers for efficient service and friendly, capable employees, JetBlue had to cancel more than 1,000 flights over the course of a few days. Angry mobs formed at several of its gates. Passengers were stuck on one plane for a full 10 hours without taking off (and then interviewed about their experience on major network news programs). In the aftermath of the crisis, previously loyal customers publicly bemoaned what an awful company JetBlue had suddenly become, and congresspeople began beating the drum about customers' rights. This nightmare would be enough to make the average CEO want to curl up and hide.

Instead, JetBlue's founder and then-CEO David Neeleman responded quickly and with sincere atonement, hitting every media outlet he could, taking responsibility for the problem, discussing its causes openly and honestly, and issuing apologies not just to all the inconvenienced flyers but to his airline's own crew members as well. He sent apology e-mails to every customer affected and also to the members of the airline's True Blue loyalty program who weren't even flying that weekend. The company posted Neeleman's video apology on its Web site, and the video was soon circulated and posted on YouTube and a variety of other sites, all over the Web.

In addition, the airline announced a Customer Bill of Rights, promising specific compensation payments for delayed and inconvenienced customers in the future, including travel vouchers worth at least $25 for passengers experiencing a ground delay of more than 30 minutes once they arrive at their destination airports (ranging up to full round-trip refund vouchers for arrival ground delays of more than three hours) and vouchers worth at least $100 if ground delays of more than three hours occur on departure. In media interviews, Neeleman said the airline would make its Bill of Rights for customers retroactive and send the appropriate travel vouchers to all passengers already inconvenienced by the previous weekend's operational catastrophe, which he estimated would cost the company $30 million or more, in total. Even after Neeleman's extensive apologies and new policy

---

[6] Brielle Jaekel, "Sephora and Coachella Camp Out on Social Media," *Mobile Marketer*, April 10, 2015, available at http://www.mobilemarketer.com/cms/news/social-networks/20191.html, accessed February 11, 2016.

announcements, however, many customers continued to rail against the airline in a blogosphere thick with customer outrage. Blog sites such as Church of the Customer (now inactive) seethed with resentment at JetBlue for this unmitigated service disaster.

But just when it looked as if no one, anywhere, would step up to JetBlue's defense, someone did. Who? The company's most frequent flyers. These were the folks who, month in and month out, had been treated decently in the past by JetBlue—actually, a good deal more decently than other airlines were treating them. These customers knew that JetBlue's intentions were good, and they trusted in the airline's ability to make it better next time. They believed the company's apology, applauded the remedial steps, and came to the blogs themselves to join the discussion and defend the young airline's reputation. Notice that there's an important trust implication in this story about JetBlue: you can't buy trust equity from customers; you have to earn it every day. When customers lost trust in Jet-Blue, there was nothing beyond their own positive actions JetBlue could do to rebuild it. Only their customers could do that—because of the trust JetBlue had already built with their customers in the past. Building trust now is what will save a company when they make an error in the future—which everybody will, sooner or later.

In their book *Authenticity*,[7] Jim Gilmore and Joe Pine suggest that JetBlue was able to recapture its reputation with its Customer Bill of Rights primarily because such a Bill of Rights fit "authentically" into the character of the JetBlue brand. It was, in fact, exactly the kind of thing you would expect from an airline like JetBlue, which had built its reputation on being fair, open, and honest with customers. Its "authentic" reputation was already one of trustworthiness.

Listening to Customers

Social media are two-way media, and in most cases the interactions and dialogues on social media sites have been initiated and are largely conducted by private individuals, not by company representatives or officials. This means the conversations are objective, frank, and highly informative. They can serve as an excellent resource for understanding what a brand's own customers are thinking about the brand. Yes, "listening" has never been part of most mass marketers' primary skill set, but forward-thinking companies are now realizing what an invaluable resource these social media conversations actually provide. In the next contribution, author and consultant Becky Carroll outlines some of the do's and don'ts of social media listening.

---

[7] James H. Gilmore and B. Joseph Pine II, *Authenticity: What Consumers Really Want* (Boston: Harvard Business School Press, 2007).

The Importance of Listening and Social Media

Becky Carroll
Founder, Customers Rock!; Instructor of Social Media, University of California, San Diego

One of the keys to being successful in the use of social media for marketing is not how we talk to customers; rather, it is how we listen to the ongoing conversations taking place online. Active listening is critical to the creation of the appropriate social media interaction plans. When we skip listening, our customer interactions via social media begin to sound like traditional, one-way broadcast messages; and in this space, such messages will simply be tuned out.

Think of a Cocktail Party

How we interact with customers via social media can be seen as analogous to attending a cocktail party. Upon entering a room, it would be considered rude for you to walk up to a group of people already conversing and start talking about yourself. Unfortunately, however, this is exactly how many firms use social media. If an enterprise sees social media as just another communication channel, it is likely to use the same mass-messaging and marketing "spin" that infuses the company's direct mail campaigns, its Web site, and its advertising. These messages talk *at* people, not *with* people, and are rarely tuned to the needs and concerns of the individual customers being addressed. Definitely rude behavior at a cocktail party, and not appropriate for social media either. Social media is social, and requires *social* activities—conversation, not pronouncements.

If you are a savvy partygoer and you approach a group of people at the cocktail party who are already conversing, you don't say a word. Instead, you spend a few minutes listening to see what's being discussed and to get the proper context. Then, after introducing yourself briefly, you may begin to engage in the conversation by sharing your viewpoint or something relevant and interesting to the other party guests. Or you may enter the discussion by asking a question related to the topic at hand. Either way, you are engaging the other partygoers in a meaningful dialogue. Nontransactional conversations like this are the foundation for using social media to build stronger customer relationships. The familiarity created by a series of social media interactions tends to build better relationships than any series of advertisements could.

How to Listen and What to Listen For

There are two things to listen for in social media: brand and customer. Both are important when determining the optimal methods for interacting with customers

(continued)

(*Continued*)

(inside and outside of social media), but in different ways. And keep in mind that listening, as we describe the process here, doesn't occur just once; it needs to occur continuously, over months and years.

BRAND MONITORING   An enterprise should always listen for social media conversations that mention the firm's brand names or areas of specialization. It should also monitor the social media space for any mentions of executives' names as well as the names of competitors. When monitoring brand social media conversations, these are the questions the enterprise should be trying to answer:

- *Who is talking about the brand?* Do we need to respond? Are they influencers, potential stakeholders, clients, or **most valuable customers?** Who else do they influence? The monitoring effort should track those who start conversations, along with those who add to conversations; over time, it will become apparent that some customers can be enlisted as evangelists, whether they are major influencers, stakeholders, or simply effective conversationalists. (*Note:* A customer's value to the enterprise is certainly related to his or her level of social media influence, so one goal of tracking the people who are conversing about the brand is to have a better idea of who they are and where the most valuable customers are participating.)
- *What are people saying?* Are they praising or condemning? Are they demanding a response? Are they trying to encourage others to act (either negatively or positively)? Understanding how influence takes place will help shape future conversations.
- *Where are they talking?* Are they conversing on the enterprise's own sites or social media properties, or are they having discussions in different forums and communities? Understanding where conversations are occurring will help determine the best places to interact with customers, which often can be in their own "territory."

An enterprise can use many software and subscription tools to listen to the social media conversation or the chatter taking place online. A company should monitor customer conversations through these online tools at least weekly, and possibly daily, tracking the trends on an ongoing basis. It should track the issues that generate most of the chatter and continue to monitor these issues over time. It should also be alert for mentions of key terms and determine quickly whether a response is needed. If someone mentions the brand, or some other relevant term being followed, the enterprise may want to consider leaving a response or comment in the conversation, if appropriate. Quick responses to potentially negative comments can help put out fires and preempt additional inflammatory statements from other frustrated customers.

CUSTOMER MONITORING   Listening for customer insight goes beyond simple observation of what customers are saying via social media sites. Listening pays attention to what customers are saying between the lines, leading to insight about customer behaviors and, ultimately, individual customer needs. This takes place in social media as customers' voice their opinions and insights, along with *unsolicited* feedback (i.e., highly valuable, spontaneous feedback not related to the enterprise's own consumer research). When monitoring customers, here are the questions the enterprise should be trying to answer:

- What are the pain points being highlighted by customers? Are they legitimate concerns? Are they directed toward the company at large, or is something being said about a particular situation or individual? When monitoring these comments, the enterprise should never dismiss customer rants, just because they are emotionally charged. All critical comments—100 percent of them—should be checked out to ensure no underlying issue exists. Even when a customer gets the facts wrong, the perspective or impression still can be valuable. Complaints picked up in social media can also help point out potential unmet customer needs.
- What is the emotion or sentiment being shared, either negative or positive? Uncovering emotions will help reveal how customers feel about the brand, product, or service (or about related and/or competitive brands). Emotions can lead to better understanding of important and influential customer needs.
- What information is being shared about the various customer experience touchpoints? This information can help to supplement customer experience Touchmap details.

Dig into any pain points quickly, efficiently, and without emotion. Once any problems at all are voiced in a social media setting, even if they are relatively minor by nature, they can easily turn into a rant by some other customer (or customers) with a similar experience. As with all human interactions, people engaged in social media interactions easily succumb to the confirmation bias, latching on to every shred of evidence that proves their own view and ignoring conflicting viewpoints. So when a complaint is aired, apologize directly and immediately to the customer for their dissatisfaction, get the **customer service** team involved where appropriate, and learn from the discussion. Social media can alert a company to a potential product or service issue faster than any other channel. This allows the organization to alert contact centers, mobilize resources

(continued)

(Continued)

behind the scenes, and proactively employ social media to alert other customers to a problem in advance.

The insight gained from listening in on social media conversations among customers can easily be used to refine the enterprise's understanding of its customer needs groupings. Some now depend on Command Centers, where businesses listen in and respond to real-time feeds from social media—not only corporations, but also government and nonprofits as well. In fact, a company may find out just as much (or more) about particular needs-based types of customers through their verbatim language on their favorite social media site (be it a consumer-focused or business-focused site) as can be obtained from costly research surveys and interviews. After all, the conversations started by customers in the social media context are likely to be much more genuine than the responses elicited by even the most carefully designed research question-naire. Nevertheless, it's also important for the company to supplement what it learns via social media with additional primary research. Social media is likely to provide great insights, but sometimes it represents only a subset of your customer base.

Now, more than ever, it's critical for customer-centric companies to move beyond organizational silos to listen to their customers across the entire experi-ence, and social media channels offer a superb opportunity for doing this. Social media interactions involving proactive brand and customer listening can serve as a very effective tool for strengthening and deepening a company's customer relationships.

Enlisting Customers to Help Other Customers

The widespread success of open source projects makes it obvious that people have an urge to contribute to benefit others, even when they get no monetary benefit from doing so. They contribute for the satisfaction of accomplishment, for the ful-fillment of creating something, and for the personal pride of authorship that goes with this fulfillment. As it turns out, the urge that people have to create content can be harnessed by an enterprise, if it is careful, and if it provides the right tools and structure. Rather than straightforward self-service, the result is something that has become known as *crowd service.*[8]

According to one *New York Times* article that chronicles the rise of this kind of customer service and describes it in terms of what will help a company help its

---

[8] As far as we can tell, CustomerThink's Bob Thompson was first to use the term *crowd service,* a particularly descriptive and appealing label, analogous to *crowd sourcing.*

customers, the result might be the same as if a company were willing to pay for the service for those customers:

> *Here's the job description: You spend a few hours a day, up to 20 a week, at your computer, supplying answers online to customer questions about technical matters like how to set up an Internet home network or how to program a new high-definition television.*
>
> *Justin McMurry of Keller, Tex., volunteers up to 20 hours a week in Verizon's community forums, helping the company's Internet, TV and phone customers.*
>
> *The pay: $0.*
>
> *A shabby form of exploitation? Not to Justin McMurry, who spends about that amount of time helping customers of Verizon's high-speed fiber optic Internet, television and telephone service, which the company is gradually rolling out across the country.*
>
> *Mr. McMurry is part of an emerging corps of Web-savvy helpers that large corporations, start-up companies, and venture capitalists are betting will transform the field of customer service.*
>
> *Such enthusiasts are known as lead users, or super-users, and their role in contributing innovations to product development and improvement—often selflessly—has been closely researched in recent years. There have been case studies of early skateboarders and mountain bikers and their pioneering tweaks to their gear, for example, and of the programmers who were behind open-source software like the Linux operating system. These unpaid contributors, it seems, are motivated mainly by a payoff in enjoyment and respect among their peers.[9]*

Crowd service is an extremely potent economic force and probably best epitomizes the power that social media interactions have for revolutionizing how businesses will operate in the not-too-distant, even more socially interactive future.[10] Nor is Verizon alone in applying these ideas. Lithium has more than 100 clients for its service, including such name-brand companies as Best Buy, AT&T, Nintendo, and Linksys. Natalie Petouhoff, former analyst with Forrester Research, Inc., has documented how a number of enterprises turn their own customers into ardent, capable workers dispensing customer service to other customers—for no monetary benefit whatsoever. (See Petouhoff's "Crowd Service: Customers Helping Other Customers" later in this chapter.)

---

[9] Steve Lohr, "Customer Service? Ask a Volunteer," *New York Times*, April 25, 2009; available at www .nytimes.com/2009/04/26/business/26unbox.html?r=2&scp=1&sq=Justinpercent20McMurry&st=cse, accessed September 1, 2010.

[10] Verizon's platform for facilitating crowd service is provided by Lithium Technologies, but other software companies offering similar capabilities include Jive Software, HelpStream, and Telligent.

Occasionally—not too often—you may get a question through Amazon.com from a potential buyer of a product you've already bought. It's easy to answer the question, and Amazon has brokered the help in a way that's low cost to participants and helpful to buyers, and likely completely authentic because the answer comes from a buyer and not a sockpuppeteer (see more about sockpuppeting below).

Customers Helping Customers

Why does this work?

In a *BusinessWeek* interview with Frank Eliason, the Comcast employee who initiated his own responsibility for handling customer issues via Twitter, Eliason made it part of his job to help customers with problems they brought to him on Twitter. One day he mentioned on Twitter that he wouldn't be available the next day to help customers. When he returned the following day, he expected to catch up on all the customer complaints he'd missed out on. To his surprise, he found that some of the Comcast customers following him on Twitter had taken it upon themselves to reach out to other customers and ask if they could help. They even used Eliason's trademark "Can I help?" as the first outreach to customers who required assistance.

Eliason said in the article, "That day I understood the effectiveness of what we do." Every company could learn that same lesson. Customers who feel connected to a brand will become advocates, even when the brand is a hated cable company. In this case, customers weren't out promoting the brand to their friends, but they were spreading goodwill by clearing up problems that otherwise would have created animosity toward Comcast.

Did customers in this case help because they were loyal to Comcast or because they were loyal to Eliason? The hope is that they associated him with the brand and had become loyal to both.[11]

Perhaps the explanation behind this can be found in the interesting finding that "givers" are both more and less likely than "takers" to succeed. Some givers are practically pathological in their need to sacrifice family, grades in school, and professional credit and success to help others. But the best givers are considered "otherish"—willing to help others while also taking care of themselves (like the best companies) and these individuals tend to rise fastest in professional settings. As Adam M. Grant, author of *Give and Take: Why Helping Others Drives Our Success,* points out, "If takers are selfish and failed givers are selfless, successful givers are

---

[11] This discussion about Frank Eliason was adapted with permission from Jeremy Nedelka, "Customers Helping Customers," January 22, 2009, 1to1 Media's Think Customers Blog, available at http://www.1to1media.com/weblog/2009/01/customers_helping_customers.html, accessed February 15, 2016; you can find the *BusinessWeek* interview at Rebecca Reisner, "Comcast's Twitter Man," BloombergBusiness, January 13, 2009, available at http://www.businessweek.com/managing/content/jan2009/ca20090113_373506.htm, accessed February 15, 2016.

otherish: they care about benefiting others, but they also have ambitious goals for advancing their own interests."[12]

Crowd Service: Customers Helping Other Customers

Dr. Natalie L. Petouhoff
Vice President and Principal Analyst, Constellation Research; Guest Lecturer, UCLA Digital Marketing and Customer Service

In 2009, Forrester found that 44 percent of U.S. online adults are "persuaders"—those who tell others about products that interest them. They're brand motivated, open to ads, and highly active in social applications.[a] And in those conversations, these persuaders are not just affecting a few people, they are affecting millions, often in the time frame of a nanosecond, through social media vehicles as diverse as Facebook, MySpace, LinkedIn, blogs, third-party community Web sites, and perhaps even your own company's Web site. Using these new technologies, anybody can post information about anything at any time, including views about your own company's products and services. No matter where they choose to converse, engage, or persuade, customers increasingly have a free voice in the affairs of your company. What's disconcerting for many companies is that they can't control this voice. Many are finding it difficult to get used to the fact that their customers, their employees, and their suppliers are talking about them through unregulated social media. But companies do have a choice. They can choose to abstain from this conversation and allow anything to be said about them, without their knowledge or participation. Or they can choose to join the conversation and try to help customers get what they want—including honest opinions and advice, objective service and support, and informed assistance for solving problems they encounter.

One of the most thrilling and interesting developments in how companies have come to rely on social media is in the area of customer service. In the old days, customer service had to answer all customer questions directly. A company's customer service department might do this over the phone, or sometimes via e-mail, and of course contact-center capabilities often now include chat and co-browsing technologies. Naturally, companies *want* their customers not to have to call in at all, and we are all familiar with the concept of "self-service" when it comes to fixing problems—whether they are problems with a credit card account, or a computer printer, or a trip to Spain, or a vacuum cleaner. The customer goes to the company's Web site and expects to find the solution

(continued)

---

[12] Adam M. Grant, *Give and Take: Why Helping Others Drives Our Success* (New York: Viking, 2013), Kindle edition, location 2631–2632.

(Continued)

to the problem in the frequently asked question (FAQ) section or perhaps in a downloadable user's manual. If the problem is one that many other customers frequently encounter, the company might even have chosen to highlight some guidelines right on the site. But today's customer doesn't want to read the whole 100-page manual, they want the one paragraph out of the manual that answers their question. The key is providing advanced knowledge management capabilities, but most companies don't distinguish between the types of search or realize the need to use natural language processing to help identify the context of the question and its resulting answer.

Often companies see self-service as a way to minimize their own service costs and, if it's done right, customers like self-service for the same reason they like automated teller machines (ATMs) more than standing in line at a bank branch during bankers' hours to get cash: because they are in control. But especially for very complicated or technical problems, or for issues that require some degree of personal judgment or experience, self-service often just doesn't work very well, leaving a customer unsatisfied and a service problem unsolved. And then it means that your investments in self-service go up in smoke, because when self-service doesn't work, customers call and are angry and desperate for help. This leaves you wide open to having customers comment about how lousy your service is. Especially if you hide your 1-800 number, and the customer who can't find the answer online is also deterred from calling you.

Today, however, using the tools of social media, a company can solve a customer's complex or difficult problem by harnessing the insight and expertise of thousands, or even millions, of other customers. Rather than self-service, some pundits are calling this "crowd service." This is a transformation in who is solving what. Instead of asking the company to solve a problem with its own product or service, customers are asking other customers to help them solve their problem. At first, this might seem a little risky to many companies. (What if customer 1 gives customer 2 the wrong information? Who is liable?) Inherent in the very idea of crowd service is the notion that the company itself will be giving up some degree of control over its own service processes, but experience to date shows that this is actually much less of a problem than most executives would think.

Myfico.com is a site where consumers who no longer have good credit can register, buy products, and work toward improving their credit. What myfico .com found, though, was that because it was a government-regulated business, its call center agents could not provide answers to customers' many questions. What myfico.com couldn't do was provide advice on what products to buy and what process to follow to improve a customer's credit scores, even though it sold products on its Web site specifically designed to do that. Faced with a dilemma, the customer service folks at myfico.com turned to social media.

What exactly did they do? They created an online community (via a Lithium Technologies platform). What myfico.com did not know was if anyone would join a community to talk about messed-up credit scores. It's generally not the type of thing that you want to admit. So as the brave souls at myfico.com designed their community, they did the single most important thing: They invited super-users (experts in the field of consumer credit) to join the community. As myfico.com launched, it had a nagging doubt about whether anyone would actually step forward to join. It also did the second most important thing one has to do in social media initiatives: It marketed and advertised the community. It sent out e-mails to all those customers who had bought something from myfico.com.

How does this story turn out? With 850,000 unique registered users, myfico.com is one of the most interactive and vibrant communities online. What myfico.com realized was that if it could draw, engage, and keep super-users in its community site, those super-users would answer the questions that agents couldn't. How did they get around the legal aspects? Specific guidelines around community policies.

The third thing myfico.com did right was to deploy a community platform technology that allows customers (users) to rate the answers super-users provided. So when 10,000 people say "Yes, this answer was useful and solved my issue," you can have confidence that the answer has been tested and found to be accurate and helpful. (Of course, the community platform you use also has to be "game" proof, meaning that there are controls that won't allow one or several customers to vote for a solution more than once. This way, a super-user can't game the system to increase their followership or apparent expertise.)

You might be wondering what the business results are with this community, right? What myfico.com found was that sales increased by 61 percent for those in the community! Why? Simply because customers were getting straight answers from people who had used myfico.com and felt they benefited from the company. What better marketing avenue could you ever wish for?

Are other companies' results similar? In many cases, yes. Consider iRobot, for instance. Executives at iRobot, a manufacturer of consumer robot vacuums (e.g., the Roomba) knew that top-notch technical and customer support was critical to the brand's success and revenue growth. But its customer support technologies were not integrated into a seamless customer experience, nor had the company considered employing social media as a part of its customer care efforts. The global technical support director at iRobot led an effort to revamp customer service, incorporating a social media initiative to allow existing iRobot customers to help other customers. The company's management embraced the idea immediately, realizing the power of using social media to improve its

(continued)

(*Continued*)

customer service. And with the actionable voice of the customer data it began collecting, the company transformed not only its service process but the way the whole organization worked together. The results? Customer-focused business decisions by integrated multidisciplinary teams working together to solve customers' issues, develop new products, create fanatical customer experiences, increase customer retention and revenue, and reduce costs for customer service, marketing, and engineering.

What about a company that decides to build its own communities (as opposed to contracting with an outside vendor, such as Lithium Technologies, which helped both myfico.com and iRobot)? Although it's not recommended unless software is one of your core competencies, Intuit has shown it can be done. Intuit began more than 25 years ago with a mission to revolutionize people's lives by solving their important problems. The company wanted to make so profound an impact for each customer that people would not be able to imagine going back to the old ways. The company's flagship products are Quicken, QuickBooks, and TurboTax. In 2007, with the acquisition of Digital Insight, Intuit also began creating the next generation of online banking, and today the company helps banks and credit unions offer easier and simpler online financial services to their customers.

To continue to transform the way people manage their money and their small businesses, Intuit has embraced social technologies and social media. Kira Wampler, Director of Social Media Interactions for Intuit's SmallBusiness United .com, is not a traditional marketer and was quick to realize that rather than using social media simply to push content to its constituents, Intuit needed to tap customers' feedback and incorporate it into the way it handled the service task. When Wampler ventured into the social sphere to monitor and listen to customers, she said what impressed her was the passion with which customers were talking about Intuit's products. But she also found that sometimes this passion did not have a positive sentiment. Rather than simply monitoring for negative comments and then turning them over to someone else for handling, Wampler began responding directly to customers. She apologized. She began by soliciting what Peppers and Rogers call **complaint discovery** and asked, "What would be better if . . . ?" And she didn't stop there; she went back into the company and actually made the changes that customers were looking for. Once she did that, she tweeted the changes or posted them on the e-review sites. As customers realized that there was someone behind the brand who actually cared, jaws began to drop. Intuit was not some big monolithic monster that didn't pay attention. Instead, customers saw the heart that all Intuit employees put into their work.

As a result, in the first few months of Wampler's care, sentiment in the cloud went up by 30 percent. Wampler had proven that even just one brave soul showing she cared made a difference. Over the next five years, Intuit was able to drive better and better online customer sentiment and awareness for its consumer and small business offerings, and increased marketing campaign effectiveness. It also systematically integrated voice-of-the-customer data into its product development process, improving customer support while lowering support costs.

One important key to social media is what I call the 1-9-90 rule, which describes how to visualize the ratio of contributions different participants will make in an online social community. In most communities, about 1 percent of the population post, about 9 percent respond to posts, and 90 percent just read the posts. To return to the cocktail party analogy often used to characterize the dynamics of social media, at a party you have several different types of people in the crowd. There are some who are interested in others and interested in sharing, and aren't shy about doing so. They are driven by a need to contribute. Some other guests, as they come in the door, spot those gregarious folks who have a crowd around them. Although they aren't the type to lead the crowd themselves, they enjoy hanging with the 1 percent who do, and they're good at responding to or riffing off what the crowd leaders are saying. And then there is the rest of the party, and you could think of them as the audience. They come to the party to be entertained, to rub shoulders with and to listen to the 1- and 9-percenters. This is not only the way a party comes together; it's the makeup of a healthy online community as well.

Two things are important to understand about the 1-9-90 dynamic.

1. If you want a vibrant online social community, you have to invite the people who will drive the conversation. So you must ask yourself: have you invited this 1 percent? That is, have you publicized the community in venues where these 1 percenters can be found, and will your community be attractive for them? You may also need a community manager to help others participate in the conversation.

2. Just as important, you must realize that for 90 percent of your community's population, "engagement" might not involve actual "participation." Don't mistake lack of actual conversational input as lack of interest. These people still read, they consider, they think . . . and they *use* the information you have in the community to make decisions, to make recommendations, to solve their own problems, and so forth. I have worked with companies that, when they see just 10 percent of registered users posting or responding, wonder if the effort was really worth it. But you have to remember, if someone comes to a party and just hangs out, never even opening his mouth, he still must be enjoying it in some way. Otherwise, why would he come to the party at all?

Sometimes, of course, when you venture down the social business path, you have to show upper management some results. Good community management

(continued)

(Continued)

software will help you monitor the health of your community and discern what is and is not working, providing reports that include various community metrics, benchmarking, and influencer reporting along with analysis on how to maximize your investment. Lithium's software, for instance, will compare your community's performance to the attributes of other communities, drawn from a data pool with more than a decade's worth of data. In addition to an analysis of your overall community, you can also get a handle on how successfully you are cultivating your super-users. You'll have quarterly community success checkpoints to compare to previous periods, allowing you to measure and refine your community strategy as you accumulate experience.

Using Facebook to Its Fullest

What if you can't afford an online community? Maybe you opt for a Facebook fan page. But if you do this, you need to consider adding a software tool that transforms fan discussions into actionable content that ripples throughout the organization: product development, relationship marketing, brand management, and public relations. Customer interactions, conversations, and relationships are what transform **customer relationship management (CRM)** into social CRM. Companies such as Get Satisfaction and others like it have adapted their successful conversational and peer-to-peer support model specifically for Facebook, allowing brands to engage social customers directly. This kind of software collects and organizes all social knowledge (questions, feedback, concerns, and praise) found inside Facebook into a central platform that can be shared and leveraged across all customer-facing channels to help a company become more customer-centric.[b]

And Then There Is Twitter

Although opinions have varied on whether Twitter has any real use or sustainability, much less as an application for enterprise businesses, as of this writing over 100 companies are actively using this microblogging tool to improve their customer service, and whether Twitter itself persists or is replaced by similar networks, our research shows that customers are turning to Twitter over traditional contact-center channels because they find that:

1. Their complaint via traditional channels has fallen through the cracks.
2. They are not being heard or taken seriously.
3. The digital ecosystem affords Twitter agents more flexibility to be objective and empathetic than agents are allowed to be in more traditional customer service channels.

4. They get immediate resolution to issues that require cross-departmental solutions.
5. They avoid the call center, where customers could feel that they end up with the raw end of the deal.
6. The crowd can participate in solving a customer's issues, providing better answers.

One great example (from 2010) of a company putting Twitter to productive customer service use is Carphone Warehouse (CPW), Europe's leading independent retailer of mobile phones and services, operating more than 2,400 stores in nine countries.[c] CPW observed a range of issues in the content it monitored on Twitter—complaints, such as negative in-store customer experiences, customer service requests, links to posts on third-party sites like ComplaintCommunity .com, and links to complaints on Facebook. Particularly worrying were links to third-party anti-CPW Facebook groups. What CPW wanted was to participate in the crowd, learn from its customers' reported experiences and conversations with other customers, and then use this insight to improve its services and product offerings.

One of the things that CPW learned by using Twitter is that unhappy customers will post comments in their own blog and tweet about it to their followers, including a link to the blog post that goes out to the world, in effect pushing their own blogged complaint out to a much wider audience of other customers and potential customers. Using RSS feeds, CPW began picking up these kinds of tweets and trying to turn them around within an hour. Using the Direct Message function in Twitter, CPW would contact the customer and ask him to e-mail CPW with his contact information and more details about the problem. Not only could CPW resolve a customer's issue directly, they could also detect when a problem tended to occur more frequently, showing up on many posts in the Twitter cloud. Using this crowd-sourced knowledge, it could update missing information on CPW's Web site, alert CPW's channel operations department with respect to the misunderstanding in the CPW store, amend details on the order confirmation e-mail, and notify contact centers and headquarters about which credit/debit cards can be used online and in CPW stores.

CPW found that social media provide a certain immediacy when dealing with customer issues. So the company uses Twitter to deal with first-line customer queries about handset setup, repair queries, stock availability, and delivery issues. When it tweets out an answer, it knows that many others (sometimes hundreds of people) will see it and benefit from it. Every time CPW points a customer in the right direction via Twitter, it educates thousands of others as well. For example, when customers want to know whether a certain town has a CPW store, CPW tweets them a link to the store locator. In one case, a European

(continued)

(Continued)

was on a train in the United States. The customer sent a tweet to CPW asking how to remove a SIM card from his iPhone, and CPW tweeted the customer a solution within minutes. (In the "Twitterverse," geographic boundaries are no longer a barrier to service!)

Customers frequently comment or complain about companies on third-party sites, and CPW uses RSS feeds to carefully monitor many of these sites. At Complaint Community, for instance, a customer posted the message:

> *I have just been into Carphone Warehouse to collect a Bluetooth earpiece for a work colleague. When I arrived at the store, I saw the Motorola Communications set for her model advertised in the shop at £29.99. When they scanned it at the register, the price came up as £59.99. . . . I have looked at the Carphone Warehouse site and still cannot find details on who to contact to rectify my complaint and hope that Complaint Community can help me.*

Within hours, a CPW customer service employee e-mailed the customer directly, to ask if he could help and resolve the situation:

> *Hi. . . . I work for Carphone Warehouse. I am the Online Help Manager for them. Thank you for your open and honest feedback. In the first instance, let me apologise for the experience you have had. I am currently looking into it based on the details you have provided and will be back in touch shortly. If you wish to contact me directly in the meantime, please feel free to do so by e-mail.*

After replying directly to this e-mail, the customer immediately went back to Complaint Community and posted a positive message about the help he had received:

> *I have been contacted by a helpful customer services manager . . . from Carphone Warehouse . . . I must say I am incredibly impressed, as I didn't expect this level of excellent customer service from such a huge organization.*

One thing very important to remember about social media is that once customer complaints are "in the cloud" (i.e., sent out on Twitter or posted on a Web site), they become part of a permanent record. They will always be searchable, so getting customers to update their original complaint will help a company regain positive brand sentiment. In this CPW case and others similar to it, not only will a customer get the help they need, but hundreds of other customers will likely be witness to it.

[a] Josh Bernoff with Cynthia N. Pflaum, Emily Bowen, and Angie Polanco, "Persuasive Consumers Are Socially Connected," Forrester Research, Inc., February 17, 2009, available at http://www.forrester.com.

[b] Get Satisfaction launched March 10, 2010, under the leadership of CEO Wendy Lea. Get Satisfaction provides a "Crowd Service" tab on a brand's fan page, where customers can begin four different types of wall discussions: Ask a Question, Share an Idea, Report a Problem, or Give Praise. When customers post a question, the Get Satisfaction search engine finds similar threads to give consumers instant answers to commonly asked questions. Customers can respond to any thread (i.e., voice a similar problem, suggest a remedy, emerge as an advocate in response to another's complaint, or offer a new twist to a product suggestion). Community members can also make their experience heard by simply clicking "me too." Representatives of the brand can also participate, to offer response and establish themselves as a brand that "listens." By inviting this type of community participation inside of a community platform like Facebook, a company can get real-time market feedback, generate new product and service ideas, and encourage peer-to-peer support and advocacy.

[c] Natalie Petouhoff, "How Carphone Warehouse Uses Twitter and Social Media to Transform Customer Service," Forrester Research, Inc., January 26, 2010, available at http://www.forrester.com.

Dr. Petouhoff's mention of the 1-9-90 rule and of super-users (the 1-percenters) is worth thinking carefully about whenever an enterprise begins to participate in social networks of any kind. Social networks are known to follow a "power law" distribution of influence, rather like the classic 80-20 distribution of customer value known as the Pareto principle (see Chapter 5). Influence within a network—or value within a customer base—is not something that can be arrayed along a more traditional bell-curve distribution. Rather, in networks of customers, employees, constituents, or influencers, we are almost always likely to find that a relatively small number of super-users have a disproportionate influence over the network.

This means that in order to participate in social media with any real success, an enterprise has to recruit to its team super-users themselves. In most corporate social network situations, this should be done by providing the trappings and symbols of status—designations such as "gold" or "platinum" supporter, for instance. Status and recognition of super-users can best be facilitated in an enterprise's social networking platform by allowing readers and responders to rate the contributions of different participants, and then the platform ranks them, for all to see.

It is this noneconomic aspect of social media, characterized by a power-law distribution of influence and importance, that offers the possibility of transforming our entire economic system, over time. In a seminal work on the economics and justice of a more networked information society, *The Wealth of Networks: How Social Production Transforms Markets and Freedom*, Yochai Benkler suggests that two different kinds of rewards have always motivated human behavior: the quest for economic standing and the quest for social standing. According to Benkler:

> *These rewards are understood as instrumental and, in this regard, are highly amenable to economics. Both economic and social aspects represent "standing"— that is, a relational measure expressed in terms of one's capacity to mobilize resources. Some resources can be mobilized by money. Social relations can mobilize others. For a wide range of reasons—institutional, cultural, and possibly technological—some resources are more readily capable of being mobilized by social relations than by money. If you want to get your nephew a job at a law firm in the United States today, a friendly relationship with the firm's hiring partner is more likely to help than passing on an envelope full of cash. If this theory of social capital is correct, then sometimes you should be willing to trade off financial rewards for social capital.*[13]

If Benkler's model is indeed correct, when an enterprise goes to the trouble of creating a social media community of customers serving other customers, social rewards will be much more beneficial to motivate super-users than economic rewards. Economic rewards (from free products to cash payments) may in fact erode the effectiveness of the network entirely.

Klout was founded in 2007, as a way for companies to get a glimpse of the social influence of their customers (and job applicants). Customers with high scores were given perks and samples, but keeping the score up was very difficult, and the scoring process seemed to users to be capricious. More and more people simply opted out, so Klout could not publish their scores, and many others began to feel as though keeping up the score had turned them into hamsters on a treadmill. What finally gave people pause was the claim by Klout that the score indicated relative influence, and scored Justin Bieber as 9 percent more influential than president of the United States Barack Obama.[14]

In 2014, Klout was acquired by Lithium and receded in relevance. The idea of measuring and using influence is still interesting and useful, but the consensus going forward seems to be that it's better to observe, and act on, actual social behavior rather than drive the inauthentic kind.[15]

---

[13] Yochai Benkler, *The Wealth of Networks: How Social Production Transforms Markets and Freedom* (New Haven, CT: Yale University Press, 2006), pp. 95–96.

[14] Seth Stevenson, "What Your Klout Score Really Means," *Wired*, April 24, 2012, available at http://www.wired.com/2012/04/ff_klout/, accessed February 11, 2016.

[15] Jon Nathanson, "How Klout Finally Matters," *Slate*, May 1, 2014, available at http://www .slate.com/articles/business/the_bet/2014/05/klout_is_basically_dead_but_it_finally_matters .html, accessed February 11, 2016.

Age of Transparency

If there is one all-pervasive requirement for social media effectiveness, by people and companies alike, it is the need for honesty, straightforwardness, and transparency. On one level, these values are driven by people themselves, because no one will tolerate deception and dissembling for long in any ordinary social relationship. Trustworthiness is probably the most important element when it comes to social relations among people, and if companies wish to engage in the same kinds of social relations as people do, then trustworthiness will be required of them as well.

It may be shameful to reflect on, but traditional mass marketing does not really require trustworthiness at all. It merely requires believability. Marketing and public relations (PR) messages are carefully crafted to be as appealing as possible, and the "spin" put on a tagline or a press release is an important marketing asset. Inherent in the whole idea of spin is the fact that there is a genuine reality—presumably known to the marketer or the author of the spin—while a separate, created reality is meant to be conveyed by the spin. Because they aren't stupid, and they know that sellers have a vested interest in persuading them to part with their money, customers have learned to maintain a healthy skepticism about advertising claims, in general. Consumer research bears this fact out. One report found that 14 percent of consumers say they trust advertisements while 78 percent trust the opinions of their peers, and more than half trust total strangers whose opinions they find online. There is nothing evil here, and no one can really blame a marketer for wanting to put a brand or a story in the best possible light. The only reason such deception was tolerated in the past, however, was that it was beyond anyone's capacity to detect, and even when the deception was detected, it was beyond anyone's capacity to spread the news. But no longer. Spin is out, transparency is in, and the fact that this higher ethical standard is being applied today by more and more consumers in a wider and wider variety of marketing and selling situations owes much to the social media revolution and to the kind of word-of-mouth recommendations and experience sharing that goes on among consumers now electronically.

As Interactions Multiply, Trust Becomes More Important

Trust has always been touted as important, certainly. But one of the most important implications of a more highly interconnected world is the increased level of trust and trustworthiness we expect from others. The fact is that trust is becoming a more essential attribute of human culture, for several reasons, as people connect with one another more efficiently. First, of course, is the simple fact of transparency. The more interacting we do, the more transparent things will inevitably become. From WikiLeaks and the Arab Spring[16] to a cable TV repairman asleep on your couch[17] or an airline's luggage handlers mistreating bags,[18] people will find things out.

It's important, however, not to confuse transparency with trustworthiness itself. Transparency increases the importance of trust because if something can be transparently exposed to the light of day without causing undue embarrassment then it must be considered inherently trustworthy and ethical. On the other hand, *the reverse is not true.* Keeping a secret might be valid for reasons of discretion, privacy, or competition, and not exposing everything all the time does not necessarily imply unethical or untrustable behavior. Businesses and governments have legitimate reasons for keeping secrets, and often these reasons are even enforced by laws and regulations. If your marketing department, for instance, were to voluntarily release its confidential pricing plans for a new product, tipping off your competitors, your executives could be jailed for collusion.

In September 2006, Wal-Mart set up a blog entitled "Wal-Marting Across America," which featured two intrepid recreational vehicle (RV) owners, known only as Jim and Laura, driving from Wal-Mart to Wal-Mart across the United States, visiting stores to buy

> Transparency increases the cost of hiding the truth. More efficient interactivity exposes truths that used to be inexpensive to hide.

things and interviewing a whole stream of ever-upbeat Wal-Mart employees, and then posting their insights on the blog. Other bloggers, however, suspected that Jim and Laura were fictitious, and not "real" people driving their RV across the country. Soon it was revealed that the two bloggers were actually paid contract writers for Wal-Mart and that they had been hired by Edelman Public Relations, the company's PR firm, to create a series of glowing articles. This ignited a firestorm of protest from others in the blogosphere, and Richard Edelman himself apologized on his own blog for having created the idea.[19]

Enterprises wanting to engage their consumers via social media need to be highly cognizant of the requirement for straightforward transparency in all social

---

[16] Peter Walker, "Amnesty International Hails WikiLeaks and Guardian as Arab Spring 'Catalysts,'" *Guardian* (UK) online, May 13, 2011, available at http://www.theguardian.com/world/2011/may/13/amnesty-international-wikileaks-arab-spring, accessed April 22, 2016.

[17] ComplaintsBoard.com, "Comcast Sleeping," available at https://www.youtube.com/watch?v=viw2TVBygBg, accessed April 22, 2016.

[18] Since Dave Carroll and Sons of Maxwell posted their legendary YouTube video "United Breaks Guitars" in July 2009, which has generated a keynote speaking career and case study materials, a genre of luggage-mishandling videos has cropped up on YouTube. For just one example, see "Mistreating Luggage," available at https://www.youtube.com/watch?v=lzmJr1a-BHU, accessed April 22, 2016.

[19] Pallavi Gogoi, "Wal-Mart vs. the Blogosphere: Fallout from the Retailer's Blog Scandal May End Up Hitting PR Firm Edelman," MSNBC citing *Newsweek* article, October 16, 2006, cited at http://www.msnbc.msn.com/id/15319926/, accessed January 11, 2016.

media communications. If a company creates a blog for communicating with customers and others, it has to pay close attention to the authenticity and sincerity of its postings. Spin and marketing language are just not close enough to transparency for the blogosphere. A blog can be an incredibly powerful and persuasive tool for an enterprise, but only if it is used in a trustworthy and honest way.

In his manual for companies engaging their customers in social media, *The New Influencers*, Paul Gillin argues:

> *The premium on transparency may be the single greatest cultural shift that businesses will face as they engage with social media. The move from messages to conversations will tax many marketers and swamp some. The emerging culture of transparency and openness in social media is a story taking shape, but it's clear that companies that choose to participate will need to speak to their communities in very different ways.*[20]

> The move from messages to conversations will tax many marketers and swamp some.

Wal-Mart eventually came back to the blogosphere with a series of honest, employee-written blogs—conversational postings from real people about real issues, treated personally. Many of the employees who author various blog posts for Wal-Mart will write about their own kids' baseball teams in one posting, and the next day their posting will give the "straight skinny" on the best deals at their particular Wal-Mart store that day. Occasionally, a Wal-Mart blogger will even advise readers what products aren't such good deals. Most companies that have figured out how to infuse their social media activities with honesty, transparency, and authenticity have come at it from the same direction. Several thousand employees at Microsoft, for example, write occasional blog posts about their work, their company's products, and their lives in general. At most companies that have well-respected blogs that attract communities of customers, the blog-writing process itself is only loosely supervised as to content. Rules are applied to ensure quality writing and honest opinions, and to avoid legal issues and other potential dangers, but within these rules, forward-thinking enterprises allow their employees to create their own content.

So what about the opposite of faking your own good reviews? What if a competitor poses as your customer and posts a negative review?

This can be a problem in an online world characterized by anonymous user IDs, where masquerading is practical and easy and registrations can be treated as disposable. Remember the old *New Yorker* cartoon? On the Internet, nobody knows you're a dog.[21]

---

[20] Paul Gillin, *The New Influencers: A Marketer's Guide to the New Social Media* (Sanger, CA: Quill Driver Books, 2007), p. 14. Also see Daniel D. Dennett and Deb Roy, "Our Transparent Future," *Scientific American* 312, no. 3 (March 2015).

[21] This classic "no one knows you're a dog" cartoon first appeared in the *New Yorker* (July 5, 1993, p. 61).

But here's the point of transparency: Any competitor who stoops to this kind of dirty trick is playing a very dangerous game himself. Even if he succeeds for a while in remaining anonymous, sooner or later he is likely to be outed by the same transparency dynamic that operates on everyone else, and technology's advances make this a more and more probable outcome.

For example, Samsung faced a lawsuit in Taiwan and significant fines when the company was accused of hiring students in South Korea to post negative reviews of a competitor's product and positive comments about its own. When the deceit was sniffed out, as it so often is, Taiwan Samsung felt compelled to make a public apology on Facebook, reaffirming its values of honesty and transparency.[22] Posting positive book reviews for a fee has become a lucrative business for many as favorable reviews boost sales for authors. One provider of fraudulent reviews was eventually exposed by an angry customer who posted a negative review of his service, saying he didn't produce the quality of review she felt she deserved for her money. Consequently, Google took ads for the reviewer's services off its site, and Amazon removed his reviews from its data-base.[23] The problem, however, continues to loom large. Bing Liu, a researcher at the University of Illinois–Chicago who is working on a program to detect illegitimate reviews, estimates "one-third of all consumer reviews on the Internet are fake."[24]

A **sockpuppet** is an online anonymous persona employed to hide a person's identity. And sockpuppeting has become a time-honored technique not just for protecting your own privacy but also for getting up to mischief—deceiving others, manipulating opinion, cheating on your spouse or partner, or violating trust in some other way.

Fake reviews and other forms of "opinion spam" are a significant enough threat that sites depending on reviews for their credibility have often put in place complex algorithms designed to filter out fakes. These algorithms are similar to the spam filters that block out inauthentic e-mail messages. Yelp blocks a substantial number of the reviews it receives, but it also allows you to view the blocked reviews. The company won't discuss its algorithm. One Cornell research team publicized the fact that they had developed a new set of algorithms for detecting opinion spam, and

---

[22] BBC, "Samsung Probed in Taiwan over 'Fake Web Reviews,'" BBC News, April 16, 2013, available at http://www.bbc.com/news/technology-22166606, accessed February 11, 2016.
[23] "Book Reviewers for Hire Meet Demand for Online Raves," *New York Times*, August 8, 2012, available at http://www.nytimes.com/2012/08/26/business/book-reviewers-for-hire-meet-a-demand-for-online-raves.html?pagewanted=1&_r=2&partner=rss&emc=rss, accessed February 11, 2016.
[24] "Book Reviewers for Hire Meet Demand for Online Raves." For more on Liu's work, see https://www.cs.uic.edu/~liub/FBS/fake-reviews.html, accessed February 11, 2016.

they were immediately approached by a number of firms, including Hilton Hotels, TripAdvisor, and Amazon.[25]

Amazon's customer review system is considered integral to the success of the company. Amazon has made several moves to protect this asset and its credibility. Amazon's review system averages all the ratings submitted for a product to award it a star rating, one to five stars. Fake reviews, or reviews bought by sellers to boost rating of product and sales, undermine the system. In April 2015, Amazon sued four Web sites that offer review writing and placement services for a fee, and in October 2015, it sued more than 1,114 providers of fake review services.[26]

In June 2015, Amazon rolled out a new review platform that has learning technology. Developed in-house, the new system "will give more weight to newer reviews, reviews from verified Amazon purchasers, and those that more customers vote up as being helpful."[27] The new criteria for sorting reviews will affect the order the reviews appear in and the calculation of the five-star rating. Amazon also solicits reviews of products from verified buyers to boost reliable product assessment. Amazon is believed to have the largest review bank, outranking even big specialist stores in certain categories. And though thought to be by some a rather clunky example of social media, no one argues with the Amazon review system's success for leveraging community feedback.[28]

But something interesting about the e-social revolution is that it is rapidly reducing the usefulness of anonymous comments when it comes to sharing and

---

[25] The Cornell study is "Finding Deceptive Opinion Spam by Any Stretch of the Imagination," by Myle Ott, Yejin Choi, Claire Cardie, and Jeffrey T. Hancock, published in *Proceedings of the 49th Annual Meeting of the Association for Computational Linguistics*, pp. 309–319, Portland, Oregon, June 19–24, 2011. The paper itself can be found at http://aclweb.org/anthology/P/ P11/P11-1032.pdf, accessed February 11, 2016, and is referenced in Streitfeld, "In a Race to Out-Rave, 5-Star Web Reviews Go for $5." See also Ben Kunz's insightful Google+ post "You're Lying," August 20, 2011, https://plus.google.com/113349993076188494279/posts/ Pcew2kqRLUe, accessed February 11, 2016.

[26] BBC, "Amazon Targets 1,114 'Fake Reviewers' in Seattle Lawsuit," BBC.com, October 18, 2015, available at http://www.bbc.com/news/technology-34565631, accessed February 11, 2016; and Jonathan Stempel, "Amazon Sues to Block Alleged Fake Reviews on Its Website," Reuters, April 9, 2015, available at http://www.reuters.com/article/2015/04/10/us-amazon-com-lawsuit-fake-reviews-idUSKBN0N02LP20150410#Fd2151tF1bbSSEQT.97, accessed February 11, 2016.

[27] Ben Fox Rubin, "Amazon Looks to Improve Customer-Reviews System with Machine Learning," Cnet.com, June 19, 2015, available at http://www.cnet.com/news/amazon-updates-customer-reviews-with-new-machine-learning-platform/#, accessed February 11, 2016.

[28] BBC, "Amazon Targets 1,114 'Fake Reviewers' in Seattle Lawsuit"; Stempel, "Amazon Sues to Block Alleged Fake Reviews on Its Website"; Rubin, "Amazon Looks to Improve Customer-Reviews System with Machine Learning"; and Himanshu Sareen, "Why Amazon Is the Most Social, Least Social-Friendly Commerce Platform," *Social Media Today,* September 4, 2013, available at http://www.socialmediatoday.com/content/why-amazon-most-social-least-social-friendly-commerce-platform, accessed February 15, 2016.

evaluating brands, opinions, products, or services. One of Facebook's biggest assets, for instance, is that it's almost impossible to pose as someone else on the service. After all, who's going to "friend" someone they never heard of? And if you do agree to be friended by someone you don't know very well, isn't it because you share some mutual acquaintances, or perhaps a school or business relationship? Chris Kelly, Facebook's onetime head of privacy, maintains that "the friend infrastructure and an identity base ultimately is the key to safety. Trust on the Internet depends on having identity fixed and known."[29]

One of the quickest ways for people to verify the trustworthiness of information or opinion, including product reviews, is to see whether their friends or associates find it trustworthy—if they vouch for it.

So as the importance of trust increases and our e-social connections multiply, you can look for a rising number of services and applications that allow consumers to filter what they pay attention to by tapping the opinions or judgments of their friends and colleagues. More and more, it becomes a part of the "experience" on the way to buying or using a product or service, as well as living the rest of life.

This kind of **social filtering** will soon come to dominate how people evaluate information and opinion for its trustability. Rather than just looking at the opinions of complete strangers when they evaluate a product or service, your customers will very possibly check the opinions of their friends first. Or of the friends of their friends.

So, although many customers have more trust in a five-star review from a stranger they never heard of (and who could easily be a paid shill) than they do of advertising claims, customers will more and more be able to see what their friends, or the friends of their friends, or maybe even *their* friends, have said about some product or service.

Today, of course, we are just scratching the surface of consumer-to-consumer interaction. In 15 or 20 years, Moore's law suggests there will likely be a thousand times as many product and service reviews and a thousand times as much information content, from news articles to blog posts and Twitter trends. And 15 or 20 years after that we'll have a million times as much as today. So service applications that get the jump on helping consumers benefit from social filtering are likely to see a strong competitive advantage within just a few years, because we'll all be relying more and more on our friends' opinions for help. It will be part of a trusted relationship in the long run and part of the customer experience in the short run.

If a company wants to influence social sentiment, but in a trustable way, forget sockpuppeting and instead start by trying to think about what actually motivates an influential blogger or Twitter user—someone whose opinions matter to thousands of followers. Yes, most key influencers would be offended if you offered to compensate them for a favorable post, but they are still human beings, and like all the rest of us, they have ambitions too. They want to be noticed and to increase their own influence. They want to write better, more original and authoritative posts.

---

[29] Chris Kelly is quoted in David Kirkpatrick, *The Facebook Effect: The Inside Story of the Company That Is Connecting the World* (New York: Simon & Schuster, 2011), p. 13.

And there are a number of noneconomic services or benefits you can provide to key social media influencers that will help them achieve some of these ambitions. If you're a student of employee motivation, what we're talking about here is focusing not on "extrinsic" benefits, such as compensation and perks, but on "intrinsic" benefits, such as appreciation, encouragement, camaraderie, and fulfillment.

And before delving into the intrinsic benefits that influencers will find most appealing (see sidebar), a quick word of caution: Be sure you understand your influencers' own perspectives. The overwhelming majority of social influencers do not consider themselves to be experts on any particular business category, company, or brand per se. Rather, they think of themselves as having an authoritative point of view with respect to some particular issue or problem of concern to them and their followers. It might be a business issue or a health issue or a relationship issue. But it's unlikely that they will think of their own central mission in terms of rating or evaluating the products and services offered by you or your competitors. Their central mission is to be of value to their friends and followers—those who depend on their opinion and thinking. Talking favorably or unfavorably about a particular brand or product has to be seen in this context—as a service they are performing for the benefit of their own network of friends.

Influencing the Influencers

The intrinsic benefits social media mavens value most can be categorized in terms of acknowledgment, recognition, information, and access. You can remember these benefits easily if you remember the mnemonic ARIA, as in the solo sung by your favorite opera star.[a]

Acknowledgment: Simply identifying influential bloggers or social media influencers and acknowledging them with your own message will go a long way toward having a positive influence. If you haven't yet assigned people in your organization the task of identifying those tweeters and bloggers with the most credibility and influence in your particular category, then it's time to do so. When you identify someone important, reach out to her, and do it genuinely. Post a comment on her blog, retweet a smart update, e-mail her with a thoughtful (but non-self-serving) suggestion. Acknowledge her existence, and by implication her significance, by letting her know that you know she exists and that you are paying attention.

Recognition: Bloggers, product reviewers, and others who become expert in your business's category want to be recognized as such. Recognition is a key motivator for all of us, but it's even more crucial in the social media world, where monetary compensation is completely inappropriate. So be sure to recognize a key blogger by forwarding the link to his or her Web

(continued)

(Continued)

site on to others. You might even consider mentioning very authoritative bloggers in your own press communications, providing not only recognition to the blogger but additional sources for whatever reporters or other commentators follow your firm. If you have a crowd service system that relies on some knowledgeable customers handling the complicated inquiries of other customers, be sure to recognize the most expert contributors or the most prolific participants with special badges, emblems, or status designations. Everyone wants to be platinum in something.[b]

Information: Information is power. Think about it. More than anything else, *information* is exactly what influential bloggers want to provide their readers, and what Twitterers want to provide their "tweeps" (like "peeps" for "people"). Key influencers want the inside dope, the straight skinny. So when you identify social media influencers in your category, be sure to provide them with all the information you can reasonably manage. Don't provide truly confidential or commercially sensitive information, unless you think it might do more good for you if it were to become widely known (assuming, of course, that it's not illegal or unethical to release it). But even without violating anyone's confidence or divulging the kind of "inside" information that might get a public company in trouble, you can almost certainly provide a key influencer with a more useful perspective and insight about your business or your category, including the problems you face, the threats to your business you are trying to avoid, and the opportunities you see.

Access: Just as useful as providing insightful information is letting an influencer make direct contact with the author of the insight, or the operating person at your business who is most connected to the information. Talk about getting the straight scoop. Probably nothing will pay bigger dividends in terms of social media influence than simply allowing the influencers themselves to have access to some of your own people, your own experts and authorities. Providing this access is, all by itself, a form of acknowledgment and recognition also. Not everyone gets this kind of access, because you can't take the time for everyone. But you should definitely take the time for someone who has an important enough following in social media.

Source: From Don Peppers and Martha Rogers, Ph.D., *Extreme Trust: Turning Proactive Honesty and Flawless Execution into Long-Term Profits* (New York: Portfolio/Penguin, 2016).

[a] Thanks to Zeynep Manco, a consultant in the Istanbul office of Peppers & Rogers Group, for the clever ARIA acronym.

[b] See Taffy Brodesser-Akner, "Influencers: Turning Microcelebrity into a Big Business," *New York Times Magazine*, September 19, 2014, pp. 44–50.

Influencing the influencers, if done right, will help empower customers to share their ideas and thoughts with other customers, to help other customers solve their problems, and to simply participate more in the social world that surrounds every set of commercial transactions. In addition to the benefits a company will realize in terms of being seen as more trustable, this kind of customer-oriented activity is almost certainly going to create better customer experiences and generate additional revenue and business as well. Twenty-year-old eBay, for instance, created customer support forums for its customers so buyers and sellers could exchange tips and suggestions, but it later found that customers who were active users of the support forums were generating 50 percent more revenue for the firm!

As a result of social media, the word gets out, and it can't be stifled. Secrets—particularly dirty, nasty, deceptive secrets—are quickly exposed for what they are. "Word of mouth" spreads faster than ever through social media, as customers share their experiences and impressions with each other. Good products are easier to find by checking out customer reviews, and bad products die quicker deaths, as people communicate with each other more and more prolifically. Sacha Baron Cohen's 2009 movie *Bruno*, for example, was apparently awful, at least in the eyes of those who paid to go see it the night it was released. In an event remarkable for its speed and severity, box office receipts fell 40 percent within 24 hours of the movie's release, as opening-night viewers texted and tweeted it into oblivion, interacting with their friends through what is now a vast social media infrastructure. According to *L.A. Times* film critic John Horn, this rapid a death for a bad movie was unprecedented. "Even if they had a turkey, [studios] used to get two weeks of business before the stink really caught up to the film," according to Horn. "Now they have 12 hours."[30] In 2015, *Ted 2* suffered instantly, whereas *Max,* a hero dog story, and *Jurassic World* prospered so fast that theatres had to reconfigure the number of screens offering the popular films.[31]

> **B**efore customers connected, advertising ruled. Now that customers talk to each other, it's the customer experience that counts.

Most people are familiar with the kinds of product reviews that usually can be obtained online for a variety of purchases. Surprisingly, however, a majority of companies, at least as of this writing, do not host those kinds of reviews on their own Web sites. That is, only

---

[30] NPR (formerly National Public Radio), "Summer at the Movies, and the Livin' Ain't Easy," *All Things Considered,* hosted by Robert Siegel and Madeleine Brand, July 17, 2009; transcript available at www.npr.org/templates/transcript/transcript.php?storyId=106742097, accessed February 11, 2016. Also see Todd Cunningham, "'Ted 2' Struck by Lightning-Fast Negative Social Buzz at Box Office," *The Wrap,* June 28, 2015, http://www.thewrap.com/ted-2-struck-by-lightning-fast-negative-social-buzz-at-box-office/, accessed January 11, 2016.
[31] Cunningham, "'Ted 2' Struck by Lightning-Fast Negative Social Buzz at Box Office."

a small minority of marketers allow their customers to post honest reviews of the products and services that they sell, for the benefit of other customers. Research shows that when an enterprise allows honest reviews on its own Web site, its closing ratios increase—that is, the percentage of shoppers who go ahead and make purchases improves. So it is puzzling that more companies aren't already hosting product reviews. Regardless of whether it's through Google or someone else, the technology is readily available, and the consumer demand for this kind of service may be irresistible, because humans want to talk to other humans. And when they talk about products, they won't be talking about the spin on the tagline or brand promise. They'll be talking about their own customer experience with the product. Before customers connected, advertising ruled. Now that customers talk to each other, it's the customer experience that counts.

Summary

In this chapter, we have outlined how a forward-thinking enterprise can best employ the tools and capabilities of social media to engage with customers. Our goal here has been to discuss the principles, since the technology will continue to change rapidly. Without question, social media has exponentially increased opportunities for companies to interact with their customers and develop Learning Relationships at rates previously impossible. But at the same time, successful marketing today requires a much higher standard of trustworthiness and transparency.

Enterprises, however, cannot simply interact with individual customers and expect them to remain loyal. The Learning Relationship must mature even further. The enterprise needs to address another task in the Identify-Differentiate-Interact-Customize process by *customizing* the relationship with each customer—by modifying how it behaves with her, how it communicates with her, and how it manufactures products or provides services for her. A relationship can't exist without customization; without a change in behavior that results from feedback, the best a company can do is give the appearance of a relationship. But how can customization be done effectively and efficiently? We take a closer look at that issue in Chapter 10, after we consider the privacy issue that inevitably arises when we address customer interaction and data.

Food for Thought

1. You've been appointed as the new chief marketing officer (CMO) for a large packaged-goods company. Your CEO has decided that your company will be the premier "relationship" company in your industry.
   - What could that mean?
   - How will you execute that?

- What will you use as data collection tools?
- What role will interactivity play in your plans?
  What role will e-mail play? Mobile devices? Social networking platforms? Be as specific as you can.
2. Now imagine you work for a large automotive company and answer all the questions in number 1. Are your answers different? Why or why not?
3. Now answer the questions in number 1 for:
   - A natural gas company
   - A retail shoe chain
   - A company that makes pneumatic valves for construction
   - The U.S. Navy
   - Other kinds of organizations (you decide)
4. What do you think about Comcast customers taking Frank Eliason's place for the day? Would you ever help a fellow consumer through Twitter or Amazon or any other Web site? Would you be shocked if a stranger offered to help you?

Glossary

Age of Transparency   The era of human history characterized by increasing levels of transparency in all human affairs, as a result of the pervasive interconnectedness of people, using social media and other ubiquitously available communications technology.

Complaint discovery   An outbound interaction with a customer, on the part of a marketer, to elicit honest feedback and uncover any problems with a product or service in the process.

Crowd service   Customers helping other customers solve problems online.

Customer relationship management (CRM)   As a term, *CRM* can refer either to the activities and processes a company must engage in to manage individual relationships with its customers (as explored extensively in this book), or to the suite of software, data, and analytics tools required to carry out those activities and processes more cost efficiently.

Customer service   Customer service involves helping a customer gain the full use and advantage of whatever product or service was bought. When something goes wrong with a product, or when a customer has some kind of problem with it, the process of helping the customer overcome this problem is often referred to as *customer care.*

Most valuable customers (MVCs)   Customers with high actual values but not a lot of unrealized growth potential. These are the customers who do the most business, yield the highest margins, are most willing to collaborate, and tend to be the most loyal.

Needs   What a customer needs from an enterprise is, by our definition, synonymous with what she wants, prefers, or would like. In this sense, we do not distinguish a customer's needs from her wants. For that matter, we do not distinguish needs from preferences, wishes, desires, or whims. Each of these terms might imply some nuance of need—perhaps the intensity of the need or the permanence of it—but in each case we are still talking, generically, about the customer's needs.

Open source   Products (software, etc.) created by unpaid individuals, usually in collaboration with others online, typically distributed for free.

Search engine optimization (SEO)   The process of affecting the visibility of a Web site or a Web page in a search engine's unpaid results—often referred to as *natural, organic,* or *earned results.* [Wikipedia]

Social filtering   The practice of relying on opinions or judgments of friends and colleagues, particularly when evaluating the reliability of product reviews.

Social media   Interactive services and Web sites that allow users to create their own content and share their own views for others to consume. Blogs and microblogs (e.g., Twitter) are a form of social media, because users "publish" their opinions or views for everyone. Facebook, LinkedIn, and MySpace are examples of social media that facilitate making contact, interacting with, and following others. YouTube and Flickr are examples of social media that allow users to share creative work with others. Even Wikipedia represents a form of social media, as users collaborate interactively to publish more and more accurate encyclopedia entries.

Sockpuppet   An online anonymous persona employed to hide a person's identity.

Word of mouth (WOM)   A customer's willingness to refer a product or service to others. This referral value may be as small as an oral mention to one friend, or a robust announcement on social media, or may be as powerful as going "viral."

CHAPTER 9

Privacy and Customer Feedback

Being good is good business.

—Anita Roddick

Getting customer information is easy. You can buy it from the government, from list brokers, from competitors even. But getting customer information *from* customers is *not* easy, as we've seen in the last two chapters. Yet it's absolutely necessary, because the only real competitive advantage an enterprise can have derives from the information it gathers from a customer, which enables it to do something for him that no one else can. Competitors without a customer's personal information are at a disadvantage. That is the one compelling reason an enterprise must interact with its customers and reward them for revealing their personal information. It is also the main reason why an enterprise should never misuse the information it owns about a customer or violate a customer's trust—because a customer is the most valuable asset the firm has, and the ability to get a customer to share information depends so much on the comfort level a customer has with giving that information to an enterprise.

Interestingly, for the first time since we all became aware of privacy as an issue, enterprises and customers share a common interest: protecting and securing the customer's information. At least that's true of customers who are thinking about the implications of their far-flung data and of enterprises that are building their value through strategies designed to build the value of the customer base.

In this chapter, we first look at some general privacy issues and how they are being addressed. We next examine the distinct issues raised by data held and exchanged online.

Every day, millions of people provide personally identifiable information about themselves to data collection experts. As a result, an average U.S. consumer is buffeted by thousands of marketing messages daily[1]—far too many to hit any consumer's consciousness. (Ask yourself this: How many do *you* remember from yesterday? All the others wasted their money trying to get a message across to you!) Consumers sometimes unknowingly divulge their personal data during commercial transactions, financial arrangements, and survey responses. And the Web has escalated the privacy debate to new heights. Never before has technology enabled companies to acquire information about customers so easily. Watchdog privacy advocates and government regulators are mobilizing against the threat to a consumer's right to privacy.

Consider these points:

- Privacy policies of individual companies vary tremendously, as does compliance with these policies (largely self-generated and self-enforced).
- Privacy preferences vary tremendously among individuals and across nations and cultures.
- Hundreds of new privacy laws have been introduced worldwide in the past 10 years.
- Courts around the world are awarding significant damages to consumers and Internet users over claims of privacy violation.
- New technologies that support data collection, Internet monitoring, online surveillance, data mining, automatic mailing, personal searching, phishing, identity spoofing, and identity theft (now a billion-dollar industry)[2] are rolling out into the electronic marketplace every month.

---

[1] The number now circulating (on the level of urban legend) is 5,000 marketing messages daily. In 2009, Forrester predicted an average of 9,000 marketing messages sent annually to the primary inbox by 2014. Shar VanBoskirk, "U.S. Interactive Marketing Forecast, 2009–2014," Forrester Research, Inc., July 6, 2009, p. 19; available at http://www.forrester.com, accessed September 1, 2010. VanBoskirk also noted, "By 2019, marketing leaders will spend more than $103 billion on search marketing, display advertising, social media marketing, and email marketing." Shar VanBoskirk, "US Digital Marketing Forecast, 2014 to 2019," Forrester Research, Inc., November 4, 2014, available at www.forrester.com, accessed February 7, 2016. See also MarketingCharts staff, "Average Email Subscriber Gets 416 Commercial Messages per Month," MarketingCharts, August 29, 2013, available at http://www.marketingcharts.com/online/average-email-subscriber-gets-416-commercial-messages-per-month-36280/, accessed February 7, 2016.

[2] "Don't Get Taken Guarding Your ID," *Consumer Reports*, January 2013, available at http://www.consumerreports.org/cro/magazine/2013/01/don-t-get-taken-guarding-your-id/index.htm, accessed February 7, 2016; and Gary Garner, "ID Theft Billion-Dollar Industry, Says Federal Trade Commission," *Mississippi Business Journal,* July 21–27, 2008, p. 35.

- Personalized, customized products and services over the Internet—most of which require users to provide more personal information than they have ever given to companies before—are growing.[3]
- When deciding to download smartphone apps, 90 percent of app users report that knowing how their personal information will be used is "very" or "somewhat" important[4]—and many are shocked to discover how much personal data is sent to their smartphone manufacturers without their knowledge.[5]

> In the twenty-first century, we realize that customer data are among the most valuable assets an enterprise can have, because the personal information about a particular customer that no other enterprise has is a unique asset that can provide an insurmountable competitive advantage in dealing with that single customer. For a customer-based enterprise to be successful in this century, it needs to protect that information—to hold it sacred.

And yet, in the twenty-first century, we realize that customer data are among the most valuable assets an enterprise can have, because the personal information about a particular customer that no other enterprise has is a unique asset that can provide an insurmountable competitive advantage in dealing with that single customer. For a customer-based enterprise to be successful in this century, it needs to protect that information—to hold it sacred. Privacy and **personalization** are inextricably interwoven. Customers who feel like they could lose control over their own information are not likely to become willing participants in a dialogue. Privacy should not be taken lightly by the customer-based enterprise.

For the enterprise interested in increasing its share of each customer's business, there has to be a balance between getting enough information from customers to help them do business with the firm while respecting their right to lead a private life. The dilemma for the customer-centric firm is how to remain sensitive to privacy while improving the business to suit each customer's individual **needs.** This is in stark contrast to a product-selling company, which likely views privacy simply as a roadblock on the road to profitability.

---

[3] Frank E. Gillett, "Brief: Data from the Digital Self Is Powering New Competition for Customers," Forrester Research, Inc., August 15, 2014, available at https://www.forrester.com/Brief+Data+From+The+Digital+Self+Is+Powering+New+Competition+For+Customers/fulltext/-/E-RES116624, accessed February 7, 2016; and Charles Jennings and Lori Fena, *The Hundredth Window* (New York: Free Press, 2000).

[4] Monica Anderson, "Key Takeaways on Mobile Apps and Privacy," Pew Research Center, available at http://www.pewresearch.org/fact-tank/2015/11/10/key-takeaways-mobile-apps/, accessed January 11, 2016.

[5] Jeff Rossen, "Is Your Smartphone Tracking Where You Go," *NBC Nightly News*, April 29, 2015, 8:05 PM ET, available at http://www.nbcnews.com/nightly-news/your-phone-snooping-you-n350511, accessed January 11, 2016; and Craig Timberg, "Verizon, AT&T Tracking Their Users with 'Supercookies,'" *Washington Post,* November 3, 2014, available at https://www.washingtonpost.com/business/technology/verizon-atandt-tracking-their-users-with-supercookies/2014/11/03/7bbbf382--6395--11e4-bb14--4cfea1e742d5_story.html, accessed January 11, 2016.

The privacy debate continues as the interactive and interconnected era matures. Despite the ongoing controversy over a person's legal right to privacy, customers find it difficult to quantify the damage they incur when their privacy has been violated. It is difficult to place a monetary value on the abuse of personal information, unlike other crimes, such as a car theft. For that matter, what value is forfeited when someone's credit card number is exposed to a third party who does not use it?

Our society subscribes to two antithetical beliefs simultaneously: that people should have the right to remain inconspicuous to others but that people also have the right to learn the identity of someone else when we need to. For instance, a consumer might want anonymity when shopping, especially online. But the same person might support a system that reveals the identity of computer hackers or those who plant e-viruses. To ponder further, our society requires the display of license plate numbers, for public revelation of each automobile owner. Should we also have "license plates" for Internet users so it would be easy to track them down when they commit an offense, such as identity theft or launching a virus maliciously?

Three events since the beginning of the century have shaped our opinion of privacy, at least in the Western world:

1. The terrorist attacks in the United States on September 11, 2001, called into question the wisdom of ironclad privacy protection and the anonymizing technologies available online.
2. The increased capabilities of **social media** and their surge in popularity, especially among younger consumers (see Chapter 8), have significantly increased the volume and detail of personal information many people make available online.
3. A spate of hacking incidents that have left customers' private data open and vulnerable, such as Sony and Home Depot and spouse-cheater site Ashley Madison, which promised customers that sensitive data would be deleted, but it was eventually stolen and exposed.[6] Hackers may want to steal, socially object, or look under the rug and show everybody what's there.

In 2014, a Gallup poll showed that more Americans worry about being hacked than any other crime—more than being robbed or attacked by a terrorist.[7] Supporting

---

[6] Stephanie Balaouras, Heidi Shey, Enza Iannopollo, and Rick Holland, "Lessons Learned from the World's Biggest Customer Data Breaches and Privacy Incidents, 2015," Forrester Research, Inc., December 2, 2015, available at http://www.forrester.com; Barrett Devlin and Danny Yadron, "Sony, U.S. Agencies Fumbled after Hacking," *Wall Street Journal*, February 23, 2015, p. 1; and Danny Yadron, "Ashley Madison's Stolen Data Is Posted," *Wall Street Journal*, August 20, 2015, B3.

[7] Rebecca Riffkin, "Hacking Tops List of Crimes Americans Worry About Most," Gallup, October 27, 2014, available at http://www.gallup.com/poll/178856/hacking-tops-list-crimes-americans-worry.aspx, accessed January 11, 2016. According to the poll, respondents' number one

that worry is a belief uncovered by a Pew Research Center study: 76 percent of American adults say they are "not too confident" or "not at all confident" that records of their activity maintained by the online advertisers who place ads on the websites they visit will remain private and secure. Roughly two-thirds of respondents say the same thing about social media sites, search engine providers, and online video sites.[8] And according to a *Harvard Business Review* survey, 97 percent of responders are concerned about governments and businesses misusing their data: "80 percent of Germans and 72 percent of Americans are reluctant to share information with businesses because they 'just want to maintain [their] privacy.'"[9]

Ironically, although most Americans do seem to think privacy is fairly important, a lot of U.S. popular culture has been inspired by snooping: So-called reality television programs, such as *Survivor, Keeping Up with the Kardashians,* and *Property Brothers,* have enabled viewers to peer into the private lives of ordinary other people. It has become a cultural norm to be flies on the walls of a stranger's personal conversations when his cell phone rings while riding a bus or a plane. Voyeurism seems to be more in vogue, so long as no one is snooping on *me.*

But the increasing popularity and use of social media has led to what might also be an epidemic of exhibitionism (discussed later in this chapter), at least among the younger generation. One of the authors pointed out to his then-teenage son that the son needed to be careful what he posted about himself online, since, in 20 years, when the son was 37, he may have his dirty laundry come back to haunt him if he gets interviewed for a job. The son said, "Dad, don't you think the guy who interviews me then will have his own dirty laundry?" It's possible that kids who were born after 2000 will simply not get the idea of privacy, since they will have been raised in a world of increasing transparency.[10]

---

worry (with 69 percent of respondents saying they worry frequently about it) was "having the credit card information you have used at stores stolen by computer hackers," and the number two worry (with 62 percent of respondents saying they worry frequently about it) was "having your computer or smartphone hacked and the information stolen by unauthorized users."

[8] Mary Madden and Lee Rainie, "Americans' Attitudes about Privacy, Security, and Surveillance," Pew Research Center, May 20, 2015, available at http://www.pewinternet.org/2015/05/20/americans-attitudes-about-privacy-security-and-surveillance/?beta=true&utm_expid=53098246--2.Lly4CFSVQG2lphsg-KopIg.1&utm_referrer=http%3A%2F%2Fwww.pewresearch.org%2Fkey-data-points%2Fprivacy%2F, accessed January 11, 2016.

[9] Timothy Morey, Theodore "Theo" Forbath, and Allison Schoop, "Customer Data: Designing for Transparency and Trust," *Harvard Business Review,* May 2015, available at https://hbr.org/2015/05/customer-data-designing-for-transparency-and-trust, accessed February 7, 2016.

[10] Taylor Soper, "What Snapchat Teaches Us About the Way Teens Define Privacy," *Geek Wire,* April 25, 2014, available at http://www.geekwire.com/2014/snapchat-privacy/, accessed February 7, 2016; and Pew Research Center, "Teens, Social Media, and Privacy," May 21, 2013, available at http://www.pewinternet.org/files/2013/05/PIP_TeensSocialMediaandPrivacy_PDF.pdf, accessed January 11, 2016.

The Trust Advantage of Robust Data Stewardship

John Rose
Senior Partner and Managing Director, Boston Consulting Group

As companies continue to use consumer data in new and ever increasing ways to create value, data privacy and misuses of personal data are becoming increasingly large issues for consumers and governments are increasingly pursuing regulatory and legislative approaches to protecting them. To the extent to which organizations that collect and use data are addressing these concerns, they are often doing so primarily from a legal and/or policy perspective.

However, this approach is likely to be wholly inadequate. Properly handling the evolving issues of data privacy and data misuse can create significant economic and social value. If a company thrives in this space and forges a reputation as a trusted data steward, it stands to increase its access to consumer data and the enormous potential it presents. There are similarly significant, but negative, consequences to handling these issues poorly in terms of the potential to harm or break a company's faith with its customers—damaging its brand and leading to the loss of revenues and market share in its core businesses.

We believe this is a C-suite management issue that is not getting adequate C-suite attention from most companies and, at BCG, are pursuing a multiyear effort to understand evolving consumer attitudes toward the use of their data and the related issues that companies will need to address. As part of this ongoing effort, we fielded a survey in late 2015 of over 8,000 consumers in the United States, United Kingdom, Germany, France, Spain, and Italy. This survey, following on a similar survey fielded in 2013, yields significant insights into the ways in which consumers view these issues and the steps companies need to take to create and enhance consumer trust.

In our 2013 survey, 83 percent of U.S. consumers agreed that they need to be cautious about sharing personal data online. By the end of 2015 this figure increased to 86 percent and increased for all but one age range surveyed (where the percentage remained flat). While it is unsurprising that Gen-Xers and Baby Boomers strongly agree with this sentiment (89 percent and 92 percent, respectively), the prevailing wisdom is that the Millennial generation does not care about personal privacy in the world of social media and ever increasing connectedness. However, our two surveys have found that this is categorically not the case. Seventy-nine percent of 18- to 24-year-olds and 81 percent of 25- to 34-year-olds agreed with the importance of caution when sharing personal data. Even though this is modestly lower than for older generations, the real insight is that four out of five Millennials believe you need to be cautious about sharing personal information.

While U.S. consumers overwhelmingly agree with the need for caution when sharing their personal data, it is important to note that not all types of data are considered equally private. Our survey asked consumers how private they considered 30 different types of information and found that there was a 59 percentage point difference between the information considered the most private (credit card data which 79 percent of respondents found to be private) and the information considered the least private (satisfaction with a product, which only 20 percent of respondents found to be private). Credit card, financial, tax and health data were among the types of personal information considered the most private, with at least 70 percent of U.S. consumers claiming to find such data types "moderately" or "extremely" private. At the other end of the spectrum, information such as brand preferences and feedback on products were among the data types considered least private. However, the spread between the most and least private types of data is decreasing, and many types of personal information that were considered less private in our 2013 survey, such as a consumer's age, gender, interests, or even name increased in how private consumers consider them in the past two years. Consumers are becoming steadily more aware of how seemingly innocuous data can be combined with additional data to create uncomfortably detailed profiles of their lives.

Access to consumer data is an integral part of today's economy and is a key to success for many companies. Consumers will share their data if they trust the company they are engaging with and so long as they do not think the information will be misused. Exhibit 9.1 highlights the percentage of the consumer

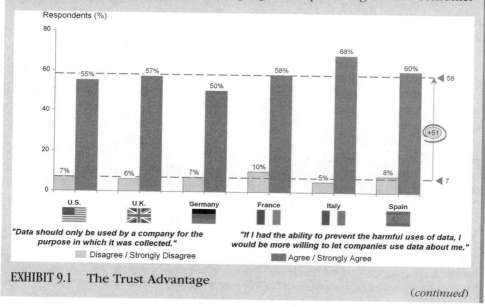

EXHIBIT 9.1   The Trust Advantage

(continued)

(Continued)

populations in the six surveyed countries in 2015 that are willing to let their data be used for purposes other than those it was collected for, as well as those who claim they would be more willing to share their data with companies if they knew they could prevent harmful uses. The spread between these numbers illustrates what we have called the "Trust Advantage." In both 2013 and 2015, the mitigation or prevention of harmful uses is a key way for companies to build trust with customers and increase their access to consumer data. We believe that this advantage will continue to yield dramatically increased access to data for the foreseeable future.

Basic consumer impressions of the trustworthiness of a company are another key indicator for a company's success in accessing and using personal information. The amount a consumer trusts a company has a direct and meaningful impact on how much or how little data they are willing to share. In situations where a consumer fully trusts a company, they are between four and five times more likely to share their data than if they are either unsure of or do not trust a company. These facts illustrate the importance that companies must place on their reputation as data stewards. In 2016, being known as a reliable and trustworthy data steward is coming to be a key element of a company's "brand." See Exhibit 9.2.

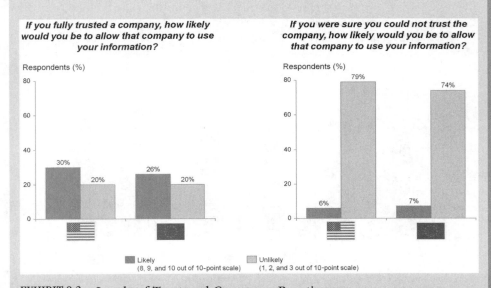

EXHIBIT 9.2   Levels of Trust and Consumer Reactions

Companies across all industries need to be aware of the steadily increasing caution that consumers of all ages are exhibiting when it comes to sharing their personal data and of the differing degrees of privacy with which consumers view different types of personal data. Moreover, in order to gain the trust of customers and reap the rewards and advantages that this trust brings, companies must work to bolster their reputation for trustworthiness, to know their customers' limits when it comes to sharing and using personal data, and to ensure that their customers understand how their data is being used and that it is not being used for harmful purposes.

Most companies today are focused on the issue of protecting data from cyberattacks and other forms of data breaches, but the 2015 survey shows that companies should be even more worried about data misuses. While 60 percent of U.S. and 64 percent of European consumers said they either stopped fully or reduced their use of a company following a data breach, those numbers are greater for perceived data misuse—rising to 76 percent and 78 percent, respectively. These statistics also highlight the fact that while companies often focus on access to data in the context of being able to pursue new uses or create new value, the real danger of unpleasantly surprising customers with unexpected uses of data is the loss of customers, revenue, and market share in a company's core business.

It is important for many companies to change their approach to data collection and usage. Many companies approach data privacy as a legal or policy issue and not an operating or "line" issue. Our contention, supported by the survey data on consumer behavior following perceived data misuse, suggests that the real harm is an economically meaningful backlash to a company's core business. Most perceived misuses of personal data are, in fact, well within the legal, regulatory, and permissioning frameworks of the geographies in which they occur. They are typically also within the bounds the privacy policies of the companies who are perceived of misusing the data. However, the fact that a data use was legally permissible and consistent with a company's **privacy policy** does little to placate a consumer who feels his or her privacy had been violated.

The goal is to understand these issues and the steps that companies should consider taking, and thus we are in the process of developing a methodology that companies can use to assess the potential economic impact of different potential misuses of data as well as a normative data base of best (and worst) practices associated with data stewardship.

Privacy concerns have long existed in traditional shopping methods, not just the Web. Walk into a supermarket or department store and the customer is often asked to hand over a loyalty card in exchange for a purchase coupon. But what if he buys something in a retail store and simply uses a standard bank credit card? In such a case, the store has very little way of tracing the information about that shopping transaction and may have difficulty linking it to a particular customer, unless the customer is having the merchandise delivered. (It should be noted that the credit card company will have a complete record of that transactional information, for that customer, store to store.) Some stores have found a way to gather information from nearly all in-store purchases, regardless of payment type. Its store personnel ask customers for permission to affix a bar code to the back of a customer's own (say, non-Nordstrom) credit card, giving the store the capability to track its customers' purchases made with other credit cards. Starbucks and other merchants that have mobile apps that enable payment from a device can link purchases to personal ID info. Stores are also using beacons/cameras to track customers; if a customer has given her personal information to an app, the store can link behavior/transactions to make a personal profile. Facial recognition technology is so advanced, it could become the de facto ID of the future, and debate has already begun about the privacy issues inherent in in-store cameras scanning faces and **identifying** customers.[11]

Profiling of a customer's personal data is standard protocol in the direct-mail industry and has been for nearly a century. Traditionally, this has meant that catalog retailers and credit card companies have collected names and addresses for their own use and have sold or rented those lists to other direct marketers. Phone a catalog merchant, and the buying process involves divulging an address and phone number. For that matter, call L.L. Bean or many other catalog companies, and the **customer service representative** might even be able to identify the customer before he states his name, thanks to the caller ID technology integrated into the company's call center. **Interactive voice response** systems, when programmed with metadata detailing the kind of calls individual customers have made in the past, can ensure that the **most valuable customers** end up at the top of the queue not only to speak directly with a customer service representative, but with the most experienced.[12] NICE (http://www.nice.com) and other companies now offer voice recognition software that rapidly authenticates caller ID from any phone to save time and reduce fraud.

---

[11] "Starbucks Mobile Apps & Mobile Payment," Starbucks Coffee Company fact sheet, March 2014, available at https://news.starbucks.com/uploads/documents/Fact_Sheet_-_Starbucks_Mobile_Apps_and_Mobile_Payment_-_MAR2014.pdf, accessed February 8, 2016; Stephanie Clifford and Quentin Hardy, "Attention, Shoppers: Store Is Tracking Your Cell," *New York Times,* July 4, 2013, available at http://www.nytimes.com/2013/07/15/business/attention-shopper-stores-are-tracking-your-cell.html?_r=0, accessed February 8, 2016; and Jimmy Rose, "How Facial Recognition Will Change Shopping in Stores," *ExtremeTech,* June 23, 2015, available at http://www.extremetech.com/mobile/208815-how-facial-recognition-will-change-shopping-in-stores, accessed February 8, 2016.

[12] Shauna Geraghty, "5 Benefits of Call Center Software That Allows Teams to Field Calls Based on Value," *Talkdesk* blog, May 6, 2015, available at https://www.talkdesk.com/blog/5-benefits-of-call-center-software-that-allows-teams-to-field-calls-based-on-value/, accessed January 11, 2016; and Patrick Barnard, "Call Center Efficiency through Improved Customer Categorization," TMCnet, December 31, 2009; available at: www.tmcnet.com/channels/call-center-solutions/articles/71846-call-center-efficiency-through-improved-customer-categorization.htm, accessed September 1, 2010. See also the Salesforce Lightning Console at http://www.salesforce.com/service-cloud/features/service-agent-console/, accessed February 6, 2016.

Remembering a customer and his logistical information makes it easier for him to order and also leads him to believe he is important to the enterprise. The Internet offers the greatest opportunity to date for gathering personal customer information, as long as a mutually valuable relationship between provider and consumer is honored. Over time, data collected about Web site visitors empower companies with a keen ability to identify their most valuable customers and deploy relevant marketing campaigns—as long as the information customers enter is true, that is.[13] But, in general, customers themselves are recognizing the convenience of being known by the Web sites they visit: A 2006 Ponemon Institute survey found only 8 percent of people "very frequently" delete **cookies** (down from 14 percent in 2004), and 24 percent "never" delete them. Further clarifying that convenience is outweighing past privacy concerns, 63 percent said marketers should understand their interest before advertising to them, and 55 percent said that Web ads that suit their needs improve or greatly improve their online experience.[14]

However, even questionable security is a deal breaker for most customers. Sixty-three percent of respondents to a National Cyber Security Alliance and Symantec poll did not complete a Web site purchase due to security concerns—with the majority of those choosing not to purchase "simply not sure" about whether the site was secure. As important as convenience may be, more than 75 percent of respondents said they would be just as likely to make a purchase from a Web site if it required additional steps to verify their identity. According to a Forrester report, "About three-fifths of consumers actually look at privacy policies," and "When a company's privacy policy (including its mobile apps) seems confusing or leaky, many consumers will forego completing a transaction with that firm."[15] Clearly, customers want both maximum convenience and maximum (identity) security, creating a very precise tightrope for customer-centered businesses to walk.

> Managing customer relationships in the interactive age requires enterprises to collect information about customers in a "virtuous cycle" in which they can deliver additional value to individual customers.

Enterprises gather information about their customers and create loyalty programs to build lasting relationships. But with increasingly complex product choices, many sophisticated customers enjoy comparing and contrasting products to find the best price and most efficient service—and want

---

[13] Mindi Chahal, "Consumers Are Dirtying Databases with False Details," *Marketing Week*, July 8, 2015, available at https://www.marketingweek.com/2015/07/08/consumers-are-dirtying-databases-with-false-details/, accessed January 11, 2016.

[14] Kelly Shermach, "Growing Acceptance of Cookies," *Sales and Marketing Management* 158, no. 7 (2006): 20. Also see Lee Rainie, Sara Kiesler, Ruogu Kang, and Mary Madden, "Anonymity, Privacy, and Security Online," Pew Research Center, September 5, 2013, available at http://www.pewinternet.org/2013/09/05/anonymity-privacy-and-security-online/, accessed February 6, 2016.

[15] Fatemeh Khatibloo, "Personal Identity and Data Management Success Starts with Customer Understanding," Forrester Research, Inc., March 17, 2015, available at http://www.forrester.com; "Americans' Online Shopping Decisions Affected by Security Concerns, Poll Finds," *PR Newswire* 17 (November 2009), *Academic OneFile*, accessed March 8, 2010.

both the information and the privacy to make a decision on their own terms, without being pressured too soon to make a purchase. The goal, therefore, is for the enterprise to find out as much information *about* a customer and use it *for* that customer to make the buying experience more valuable to that customer in various ways. Managing customer relationships in the interactive age requires enterprises to collect information about customers in a "virtuous cycle" in which they can deliver additional value to individual customers. Once the customer begins receiving personalized attention and customized products, he is motivated to divulge more information about himself.

For instance, another recent Forrester report concluded that many consumers believe sharing personal data through loyalty programs enhances their customer experience with that brand. Consumers surveyed found the following loyalty program **benefits** "important" or "very important":

- Instant discounts—77 percent.
- Reward certificates—69 percent.
- Points, miles, or other loyalty currency—65 percent.
- Printable coupons—64 percent.
- Enhanced customer service—59 percent.
- Mobile coupons and/or rewards—54 percent.
- Ability to earn special status—54 percent.[16]

Although the preponderance of evidence shows that consumers do like the customized offerings and other advantages companies can give them by tracking their data, it is essential to guarantee that the customized benefits provided will not jeopardize their privacy. Customers must know that the company will use that data in a limited way for services agreed on in advance. Without such trust, **customization** is not a benefit. Once earned, trust in an enterprise enhances customer loyalty. But enterprises need to address customer concerns about privacy, to offer guarantees, and stick to them. Those enterprises that gain the customer's trust first often will have the first-mover advantage. (We talk more about privacy pledges later in this chapter.) Most important, Dr. Dimitrios Tsivrikos found trust to be more powerful than rewards for consumers: "The extent to which individuals reported to trust an organization was four times more important than any other factor based on exchange rewards such as receiving specially tailored offers or free products."[17]

---

[16] Emily Collins and Samantha Ngo with Srividya Sridharan, Shar VanBoskirk, Emily Miller, and Matthew Izzi, "The Loyalty Program Participant Profile," Forrester Research, Inc., September 28, 2015, available at http://www.forrester.com, accessed June 16, 2016.

[17] Dr. Dimitrios Tsivrikos, a business and consumer psychologist at University College, is quoted in Aimia, "Aimia Global Loyalty Lens Report," 2015, available at http://aimia.com/content/dam/aimiawebsite/Aimia2015GlobalLoyaltyLensReport/Aimia%202015%20Global%20Loyalty%20Lens%20Report/AIMIA-Loyalty-Lens-Research-Report.pdf, accessed February 7, 2016.

Some believe that a customer might be more trusting of an enterprise and would provide the personal information that can foster a mutually beneficial relationship if the enterprise simply first asks the customer his permission to do so. The relationship in which a customer has agreed to receive personalized messages and customized products forms the basis of *permission marketing,* an idea from author Seth Godin, who points out that "The combined shortage of time and attention is unique in today's **Information Age.** Consumers are now willing to pay handsomely to save time, while marketers are eager to pay bundles to get attention." He compares *interruption marketing,* which is the kind we're all used to, with *permission marketing,* which offers marketers a chance to talk only to the customers who volunteer to get their messages. Godin likens the two kinds of marketing to two ways of getting married:

> *The Interruption Marketer buys an extremely expensive suit. New shoes. Fashionable accessories. Then, working with the best database and marketing strategies, selects the demographically ideal singles bar.*

> *Walking into the singles bar, the Interruption Marketer marches up to the nearest person and proposes marriage. If turned down, the Interruption Marketer repeats the process on every person in the bar.*

> *If the Interruption Marketer comes up empty-handed after spending the entire evening proposing, it is obvious that the blame should be placed on the suit and the shoes. The tailor is fired. The strategy expert who picked the bar is fired. And the Interruption Marketer tries again at a different singles bar.*

> *If this sounds familiar, it should. It's the way most large marketers look at the world. They hire an agency. They build fancy ads. They "research" the ideal place to run the ads. They interrupt people and hope that one in a hundred will go ahead and buy something. Then, when they fail, they fire their agency!*

> *The other way to get married is a lot more fun, a lot more rational, and a lot more successful. It's called dating.*

> *A Permission Marketer goes on a date. If it goes well, the two of them go on another date. And then another. Until, after 10 or 12 dates, both sides can really communicate with each other about their needs and desires. After 20 dates they meet each other's families. Finally, after three or four months of dating, the Permission Marketer proposes marriage.*

> *Permission Marketing is just like dating. It turns strangers into friends and friends into lifetime customers. Many of the rules of dating apply, and so do many of the benefits.*[18]

---

[18] Thanks to Seth Godin for his contribution to this section. See also his classic book *Permission Marketing* (New York: Simon & Schuster, 1999).

Trust, as discussed in Chapter 3, is always critical. Customers are dubious of unfamiliar enterprises that have not been recommended to them. Some customers won't buy anything online until they've seen other customers' reviews and comments, even though those other customers are total strangers.

Although we talk about privacy as if it were a single topic, it is really an umbrella term, and if you ask customers what bothers them about privacy, you will get several answers.

- The most common is a concern about criminal activity—misuse of stolen credit card numbers, usurpation of identity. This concern nearly always comes back to the issue of data security.
- Distinct from the first point is a concern about others knowing things about them they would rather not have "out there" as common knowledge.
- Another issue is the idea that they would rather not be bothered if they don't want to be: spam is driving them crazy (if it comes through their mobile device, they even have to pay for the minutes and the texts!), and marketing calls at dinner are a nuisance.

Meanwhile, if you ask enterprise executives what the term *privacy* means to *them*, and they're honest with you, you may find that *privacy* is a risk of fines on each breached record and a potential minefield for public relations. To the lawyers, it may be about regulation compliance and litigation avoidance. But to those in the organization whose mission is to build the value of the customer base, *privacy* is what customers think it is, and it's also:

- Getting information from customers who are comfortable giving it.
- Using the information to build mutual value with each customer.
- Protecting customer data as a valuable competitive asset (through data security, protective processes, and customer-focused culture).
- Communicating data protection to customers.

Relationships require trust, and privacy is one of its underpinnings.

Moreover, as each organization moves to globalize its operations, its leaders will need to be aware of and comply with the many legal requirements of the nations in which it serves customers, and they will need to respect the individual cultures of these countries. Enterprises will also need to protect the accuracy, transmission, and accessibility of their customer records. In the next few sections, we examine how enterprises protect the precious customer data they collect. We also peer into the many differences between privacy rules in the United States and Europe.

Individual Privacy and Data Protection

Larry A. Ponemon, Ph.D.
Chairman, The Ponemon Institute

Businesses and governments have a responsibility to maintain the security and integrity of personal data that they process. The competitive pressure to profit from data collected about a customer by analyzing it for the purposes of personalization and customization collides with privacy concerns. Advocates believe it can help customers save time and effort and supply them with better targeted offers and improved **customer service.** When users provide personally identifiable information during a transaction, they are looking for assurance that their personal data will not be misused. Although the data can be traced to a computer, most data collected are anonymous. It is when a user provides personally identifiable information by filling out a form or volunteering personal information during a transaction that the concerns of potential abuse grow stronger. Other areas of particular concern include linking personally identifiable profiles with more extensive demographic or credit card information or connecting and reselling information from disparate data sources.

Chief Privacy Officers Protect Customer Privacy—Ours or Theirs?

Some enterprises, recognizing the new importance of the spectrum of privacy issues, particularly if their business faces global trading issues, have created the full-time position of chief privacy officer instead of assigning this responsibility to existing positions, such as the chief information officer or the chief technology officer. Corporate icons such as American Express, Citigroup, Prudential Insurance, and AT&T have hired privacy officers who in many cases report directly to the chairman or the CEO. At the Internet Advertising Bureau's Privacy Forum, Rich LeFurgy, Internet Advertising Bureau chairman and general partner, Walden VC, has explained it this way: "At the center of all business models is consumers. Protecting their PII (personally identifiable information) is the key to the future."

The responsibilities of the chief privacy officers (CPOs) (often undertaken by the chief information officer) include addressing the following:

- How does the company ensure that consumers will be notified about what information is collected?
- How can the company protect personal data from unauthorized use?
- How does a company provide consumers access to their personal information and the ability to change it?
- How does a company have guidelines for the use of personal information?

(continued)

(Continued)

- Does it have a complete data-flow map showing the flow of information?
- What procedures ensure consumers are notified of changes in privacy policies?
- Is notification enough? Or is awareness required?
- What procedures exist to ensure business partners use personal information according to policy?
- Is compliance enough? Or is establishing trust required?
- How often does the company train employees on fair information and privacy practices?

As enterprises continue to globalize their operations, they need to be sensitive to, and in compliance with, the legal requirements and cultural sensitivities of the individuals with whom they do business. In addition, they need to protect adequately the accuracy, integrity, transmission, and accessibility of their electronic records and, in some nations, paper records. Regulatory compliance is not achieved without cost to the organization; and, where regulation exists, it must be complied with. However, beyond reducing the risk of regulatory noncompliance, the benefits of good privacy practice include:

- *Reduction of cost* by eliminating the collection and management of unnecessary information.
- *Reduction of the risks* associated with inaccurate or out-of-date information.
- *Improvement in consumer and employee trust* and confidence in the use and security of personal data.

Ultimately, the business concerns about issues surrounding privacy fall into two categories:

1. *Individual privacy.* On an international level, the United Nations Declaration of Human Rights and the European Convention on Human Rights recognize privacy as a fundamental human right. Many nations have constitutional provisions, legislation, or court decisions that define the individual's right to privacy as the right to be left alone—to be free from unwarranted intrusion.
2. *Data protection.* Businesses and governments have a responsibility to maintain the security and integrity of the data that they process. For businesses, this primarily means information gathered about individual customers and employees that is collected in the course of completing business transactions.

Today, consumer privacy concerns have been heightened by the technological changes surrounding the Internet. Technological improvements also put new pressures on businesses. Online companies that are under intense pressure to differentiate themselves are motivated to enhance value by outfitting their sites with increased personalization, requiring more granular customer data. Consumers express concern that inaccurate information can be used against them or affect them in the future, that personal information will be disclosed to third parties without their knowledge and consent, and that the security that surrounds their data is lacking. Identity theft provides just one example of how real these concerns are.

A comprehensive approach to data protection and privacy compliance identifies and resolves the issues while noncompliance creates unnecessary risks. By identifying the elements of current regulatory and self-regulatory approaches to privacy, it is possible to derive a set of common elements that can serve as a starting point for an organization's global privacy compliance initiatives. Such a framework should include the following key elements.[a]

- *Notice*. The enterprise provides data subjects with clear and prominent notice of who is collecting their personal information, the intended use of the information, and its intended disclosure.
- *Choice*. The enterprise offers data subjects choices as to how their personal identifying information will be used beyond the use for which it was provided; choices would encompass both internal secondary uses such as marketing back to data subjects, and external secondary uses such as disclosing data to other entities.
- *Access*. The company enables data subjects to obtain appropriate access to information that it holds and to correct or amend that information where necessary.
- *Data security*. The enterprise takes reasonable precautions to protect data from loss, misuse, alteration, or destruction and ensure that those to whom data is transferred have adequate privacy protection.
- *Data integrity*. The firm keeps only personal data relevant for the purpose for which it has been gathered, consistent with the elements of notice and choice.
- *Onward transfer*. The firm transfers data only as consistent with the elements of notice, choice, and security.
- *Enforcement*. The company ensures compliance with key privacy elements and provides recourse for individuals, such as complaint and dispute procedures, verification of ongoing compliance, and obligation to remedy problems arising from noncompliance.

---

[a] Wylie Wong, "Sun Switches Gears on Security," *CNET News,* July 25, 2002.

Privacy in Europe Is a Different World

The privacy debate in Europe is just as fierce as in the United States, although the rules about privacy are starkly different in Europe. In the United States, an individual's habits and behavior may be examined by an employer, a retail merchant, and by companies on the Web. This information is then used to target the customer for marketing purposes or is resold to other companies. By contrast, in most European countries, it is illegal to monitor an individual under any of these circumstances and use the information to target the customer. The ground rules for privacy for members of the European Union (EU) are laid down in the **European Union Data Protection Directive,** originally adopted in 1995, which applies to electronic and paper filing systems, including financial services. (The EU's new General Data Protection Regulation was proposed in 2012, due to take full effect in 2017.)[19] The directive required EU member states to amend national legislation to guarantee individuals certain rights to protect their privacy and to control the contents of electronic databases that contain personal information. The data covered by the directive are information about an individual that somehow identifies the individual by name or otherwise. Each European nation's government implements the directive in its own way.

Under the directive, information about consumers must be collected for specific, legitimate purposes and stored in individually identifiable form. Those collecting the data must tell the consumer who ultimately will have access to the information. The rules are stricter for companies that want to use data in direct marketing or to transfer the data for other companies to use in direct marketing. The consumer must be explicitly informed of these plans and given the chance to object. U.S. and European principles on privacy share a key similarity. The Data Protection Directive and U.S. privacy laws attempt to protect human rights. However, both do little to check the growth of government databases or information-collection powers.[20]

Europeans do not allow the sharing of personal information between enterprises; this area is not yet regulated by the U.S. government.[21] In contrast to the United States, where more of a free-market approach is taken to many things,

---

[19] Chris Sherman and Enza Iannopollo, "Q&A: EU Privacy Regulations," Forrester Research, Inc., June 14, 2015, available at http://www.forrester.com.

[20] See Phil Lee, "How Do EU and US Privacy Regimes Compare?" *Field Fisher Privacy and Information Law Blog,* March 5, 2014, http://privacylawblog.fieldfisher.com/2014/how-do-eu-and-us-privacy-regimes-compare, accessed January 11, 2016; and the proposed EU General Data Protection Regulation, January 25, 2012, available at http://ec.europa.eu/justice/data-protection/document/review2012/com_2012_11_en.pdf, accessed February 7, 2016.

[21] European Code of Practice for the Use of Personal Data in Direct Marketing, available at http://www.fedma.org/fileadmin/documents/SelfReg_Codex/FEDMACodeEN.pdf, accessed February 7, 2016; and Jeff Langenderfer and Anthony D. Miyazaki, "Privacy in the Information Economy," *Journal of Consumer Affairs* 43, no. 3 (Fall 2009): 380–390.

including customer privacy protection, the European Privacy Directive prohibits enterprises from transferring electronic records of personal information—including names, addresses, and personal profiles—across borders. It is at least partly intended to reduce trade barriers within the EU by standardizing how various companies treat individual information in different countries. If European nations must follow the same standards about privacy protection, then trade between nations can occur more freely. Personal data on EU citizens may be transferred only to countries outside the 15-nation bloc that are deemed to provide "adequate protection" for the data. But the rising use of social networking sites worldwide is putting the European Privacy Directive to the test. A strict reading implies those who "tag" their friends in Facebook, upload videos to YouTube, or post other personal material to social networking sites without consent are breaking the law.

According to J. Trevor Hughes, president and CEO of the International Association of Privacy Professionals, one of the biggest data privacy challenges is that the industry is not only new but constantly changing. "We don't know all the rules of the road. This is not a mature space. The technologies that drive privacy issues today are emerging technologies. It seems like every six months—every quarter, even—we see a new technology that forces us to think about how we use data in a completely new way."[22]

European Organization for Economic Cooperation and Development Privacy Guidelines

1. Data must be collected using lawful and fair means and, where possible, with the consent of the subject.
2. Data must be accurate, complete, and up to date to ensure quality is adequate for use.
3. Purposes of data usage should be specified prior to collection and should not be subsequently extended.
4. Personal data should not be disclosed without legal cause or the consent of the data subject.
5. Data should be protected by reasonable security safeguards.

(continued)

---

[22] AvePoint, "IAPP President & CEO J. Trevor Hughes on Data Privacy," YouTube video, October 8, 2013, available at https://www.youtube.com/watch?v=3eniaZVpXBc, accessed February 6, 2016; Sarah Spiekermann, Alessandro Acquisti, Rainer Böhme, and Kai-Lung Hui, "The Challenges of Personal Data Markets and Privacy," *Electronic Markets* 25, no. 2 (June 2015): 161–167; and "Regulations Probe 'Tagging,' Consent," International Association of Privacy Professionals Daily Dashboard, March 24, 2010; available at: www.privacyassociation.org/publications/2010-03-24-regulators-probe-tagging-consent/, accessed September 1, 2010.

(Continued)

6. The existence and nature of personal data should be discoverable.
7. Data should be available to the subject to enable the correction of inaccurate information.

Source: Partial list excerpted from "The OECD Privacy Framework," 2013, available at http://www.oecd.org/sti/ieconomy/oecd_privacy_framework.pdf, accessed February 7, 2016.

Stated Goals of the New EU General Data Protection Regulation

1. Protect citizens' privacy and control of data collection and use.
2. Give EU countries a consistent policy to make business among member and nonmember nations fluid.

The rationale of the Data Protection Regulation is to protect privacy, in order to "build trust in online environment," which is good for economic development. Lack of trust "makes consumers hesitate to buy online and adopt new services. This risks slowing down the development of innovative uses of new technologies." The regulation cites reports that Europeans have the perception that there are significant risks to sharing data online. Key new privacy regulation has been added since the inception of the original directive, including the need for explicit consent, which must be given to the enterprise collecting data by "subject." Consent cannot be assumed, and the subject may withdraw consent at any time. Much of the revision has to do with streamlining governance and enforcement, which some see as a loosening of the regulations, although fines for violators will be increased.[23]

Data protection negotiations between the United States and the EU reached a pivotal point in July 2000, when the European Commission declared that the Safe Harbor arrangement put in place by the U.S. government to protect personal data transmitted in the course of Internet commerce must meet EU standards. The Safe Harbor agreement stated that if U.S. enterprises agreed to a certain set of minimal privacy standards when doing business in Europe, they would be free from litigation. It was aimed at heading off the possibility that data transfers to the United States might be blocked following the enactment of the EU's Data Protection Directive. Under Safe Harbor, U.S. companies could voluntarily adhere to a set of data protection principles recognized by the commission as providing adequate protection and thus meeting the requirements of the directive regarding transfer of data out of the EU.

---

[23] Proposed General Data Protection Regulation, January 25, 2012, available in full at http://ec.europa.eu/justice/data-protection/document/review2012/com_2012_11_en.pdf, accessed February 7, 2016.

The Safe Harbor standards, however, were not as rigorous as what Europeans set for themselves. As part of the agreement, the U.S. Federal Trade Commission (FTC) and U.S. judicial system were authorized to impose sanctions on companies that violate data privacy rules. The U.S. Commerce Department kept tabs on self-regulating companies, which had to apply annually for membership in the department's register. Although participation in the U.S. Safe Harbor scheme was optional, its rules were binding on U.S. companies that decided to join, and they were enforced by the FTC.

Although U.S. companies had been transferring data from the EU to the United States under the Safe Harbor framework since 2000, the European Court of Justice, the EU's highest court, struck down the Safe Harbor agreement in 2015, saying that it "was flawed because it allowed American government authorities to gain routine access to Europeans' online information. The court said leaks from Edward J. Snowden, the former contractor for the National Security Agency, made it clear that American intelligence agencies had almost unfettered access to the data, infringing on Europeans' rights to privacy."[24] Furthermore, the European Court noted that Europe's 500 million citizens did not have the right to bring legal cases in the United States if their privacy was infringed on.[25]

The Privacy Directive serves an important purpose within Europe, by synchronizing these various government policies, to make it easier for any company to do business across the continent. However, some U.S. enterprises are criticizing it as little more than a nontariff trade barrier, designed primarily to ensure that any new, pan-European customer service infrastructures are staffed by employees working within the boundaries of the EU itself.

Where it exists, a regulatory approach such as the Privacy Directive may or may not be effective at curbing the abuse of individual consumer privacy. But it could potentially curb Europe's economic growth prospects and threaten consumers' own interests as well. Managing relationships in the interactive age depends on the collection and use of individual customer information. As enterprises become increasingly global, it is vital that this information be accessible to sales, marketing, and customer care professionals worldwide. It is the only way to provide seamless, personal service—based on a unified view of the customer—across borders. Call centers or Web sites in Ireland might serve consumers in the United States or Argentina as well as in France or Italy.

---

[24] Mark Scott, "Data Transfer Pact between U.S. and Europe Is Ruled Invalid," *New York Times*, October 6, 2015, available at http://www.nytimes.com/2015/10/07/technology/european-union-us-data-collection.html?_r=0, accessed February 7, 2016.

[25] Scott, "Data Transfer Pact between U.S. and Europe Is Ruled Invalid"; and Courtney Bowman, "US-EU Safe Harbor Invalidated: What Now?" Proskauer Privacy Law Blog, October 6, 2015, available at http://privacylaw.proskauer.com/2015/10/articles/european-union/us-eu-safe-harbor-invalidated-what-now/, accessed February 7, 2016.

The potential impact of the directive, if enforced as written, is extreme. Sweden's privacy agency told American Airlines in 1999 that it could not transmit information about Swedish passengers to its U.S.-based Sabre system. This, in effect, would have prevented the airline from individualizing its service offering to its Swedish customers. Under the directive, it is even conceivable that a person could be arrested for saving business card data to his laptop and trying to cross the border with it.

Phil Lee, a legal blogger, points out, "While they may go about it in different ways, the EU and United States each share a common goal of protecting individuals' privacy rights. Is either regime perfect? No, but each could sure learn a lot from the other." He offers a comparison, pointing out that both offer protections, but come from a different cultural perspective. In EU privacy is protected as a "fundamental right" under its Charter of Fundamental Rights, which is the equivalent of our Constitution. Europeans have strong feelings about it. While Europe has the broadest privacy protections, the United States also has protection through a combination of narrower, more specific laws, for example, federal rules for specific risk scenarios (such as the Children's Online Privacy Protection Act), sector-specific rules (e.g., Health Insurance Portability and Accountability Act), or state-driven rules (California Online Privacy Protection Act). Ironically, one of the differences is about litigation; while Europeans have broad protection, they do not sue or bring class actions for damages. Instead, they must appeal to regulators. In the United States, industries must be vigilant about privacy policy to avoid litigation.[26]

No matter where in the world it conducts business, the **customer-strategy enterprise** tries to remain sensitive to how privacy rules are enforced and respected. Critical, too, is that the enterprise show to the world that it respects each customer's right to privacy through the publication of and adherence to its own written privacy pledge.

Privacy Pledges Build Enterprise Trust

If the enterprise is to establish a long-term relationship with a customer based on individual information, it will recognize that customer data are its most valuable asset, will secure and protect those data, and will share the policy for that protection in writing with its customers, partners, and vendors in the form of a privacy pledge. That pledge will permeate its own culture and be part of its employees' DNA. The privacy pledge will spell out:

- The kind of information generally needed from customers.
- Any benefits customers will enjoy from the enterprise's use of this individual information.

---

[26] Lee, "How Do EU and US Privacy Regimes Compare?"

- Any events that might precipitate a notification to the customer by the enterprise.
- An individual's options for directing the enterprise not to use or disclose certain kinds of information.
- Specific steps to secure and protect customer information.

Enterprises sometimes jeopardize their relationships with customers by engaging in unethical moves that compromise customer privacy for short-term marketing gain. That's why enforcing a privacy policy is reassuring to many customers. Fortunately, according to a survey done by the Retail Industry Leaders Association and Retail Systems Research, 72 percent of top retailers understand that customers are concerned about privacy and that their personal information must be protected.[27] But being careful with customer data is not enough for the enterprise. Such a company must also get agreements in writing with all its vendors and partners that confirm they too will comply with enterprise privacy standards. A Midwestern bank committed to protecting its customers' information learned that a printing company that produced checks for the bank's customers had been copying the names and addresses of customers, routinely printed in the upper left corner of the checks, and reselling that information to list brokers. These list sellers in turn were selling the information to insurance agencies, garden supply companies, competitive financial services institutions, and others.

As the privacy debate rages, customers are, more and more, aware of whether they are given a chance either to **opt in** (proactively elect to receive future communications from the enterprise) or **opt out** (tacitly choose to receive them by inaction, unless they actively opt out). Consumer groups tend to favor opt-in as a better protection for consumers, whereas industry groups point to very low participation levels and, ironically, fewer targeted messaging efforts, and therefore tend to favor opt-out. Frequently, however, this opt-in or opt-out choice is an all-or-nothing toggle switch. To treat customers in a more one-to-one fashion, best practice today is to offer choices to the customer, with respect not just to the types of information he may choose to receive but also as to the frequency with which he is contacted with this information.

---

[27] "According to RILA Survey: Protecting Customer Data Is a Top Priority for Retailers," *PRNewswire*, March 1, 2010, available at http://www.prnewswire.com, accessed September 1, 2010. Unfortunately, there's still a lot of work to be done. Boston Retail Partners found that only about two-thirds of retailers reported payment security as their top concern for 2015, "Boston Retail Partners POS/Customer Engagement Benchmark Survey 2015," available at https://bostonretailpartners.com/resources/2015-poscustomer-engagement-benchmarking-survey/, accessed February 7, 2016. A Forrester report by Heidi Shey, Enza Iannopollo, and Fatemeh Khatibloo states the following statistics for percentage of company security decision makers that see privacy has a silver lining: "22% in US, 31% in Canada, 45% in India, 34% Brazil, 39% in China, 18% Australia, 28% Germany, 21% UK, 17% France," from "Build a Privacy Organization for Consumer Data Management," Forrester Research, Inc., November 16, 2015, available at http://www.forrester.com.

What greater assets do any company, online or off, have to dangle in front of other companies than the private data of thousands, or even millions, of customers? Do the rules change when a company is bought out or goes bankrupt? What happens to a company's privacy pledge when there no longer is a company? And what guarantee is there that the new owner of your data will honor the same privacy standards as the former owner?

There is a simple, universal solution: The global business community needs to prevent such abuses, and preferably without government intervention. In this **Age of Transparency,** technologies are cropping up to help the process. Software enables online users to control how sites collect, control, use, and share their personal information. With privacy pledges under scrutiny, more enterprises are adopting and publicizing them. Nonetheless, many enterprises still do not state their policies, and others never share user data with third parties.

What constitutes a good privacy protection policy? For starters, it should explain to customers what kinds of information the company needs from them, how the information will be used, and how it will *not* be used. It should also explain the benefits a customer would gain by sharing personal information. Enterprises need to promote their privacy policies beyond the Web site, mobile apps, and corporate promotional collateral, including it in direct-mail pieces, invoices, and other company mailings. A privacy policy will reinforce the foundation on which each customer relationship is built. Trust is an essential part of any Learning Relationship, and a privacy policy helps build that trust.

Building a trusted relationship goes far beyond simply writing a privacy policy and posting it on the Web site. Unless the enterprise is careful as to how it uses sensitive customer information, the opportunity for forming Learning Relationships may disappear. It is important to recognize, however, that some individuals do not want companies to know which Web sites they visit or anything about their personal information. In the headlong rush of enterprises to use the latest databases, data-mining techniques, neural nets, and Internet-based information collection systems, some have neglected or overlooked this important issue. Moreover, a customer's willingness to collaborate with an enterprise by interacting with the firm could be one important measure of the customer's value to the enterprise.

It is important to explain the motives for wanting to create a relationship with a customer. Enterprises need to describe to customers how they will benefit by exchanging personal information with them. Once customers have read the privacy pledge and understand that their personal information will not be sold or shared irresponsibly, they simply want to know how providing their personal data will affect customer service. Beyond the security or convenience of the actual transaction, what assurance does a customer have that his personal information will not be misused or abused? After all, most customers have experienced the irritation of "getting on a list" and, as a consequence, received unsolicited direct mail and outbound telemarketing calls. Ironically, if a customer does not provide information to an enterprise about what he likes to buy, the likelihood is that he will receive more junk spam or direct-mail pieces that promote products and services of little interest to him and his needs. Clearly, this question has yet to be definitively resolved.[28]

These and many other privacy-related questions may never be fully settled. But the customer-based enterprise has to monitor changing privacy issues closely. Intensifying the privacy debate is the way customer information is being collected and used on the Internet. The Web has created a powerful medium to collect and analyze customer data. But how can enterprises afford customers the same privacy protection online as they do in the "real world"? And how sensitive are customers to divulging personal information on the Web?

10 Points to Consider in Developing a Company's Privacy Pledge

Every enterprise that maintains a Web site or collects personal information about its customers needs to establish an explicit privacy protection policy. The enterprise might call it a Privacy Pledge or a Privacy Bill of Rights, but it needs to consider covering these 10 key points:

1. Itemize the kind of information it collects about individual customers.
2. Specify how personal information will be used by the company. If its policy is to use this kind of information only within the company on a need-to-know basis, and not to make it accessible to unauthorized employees at any time, the enterprise needs to explain this policy explicitly.
3. Make whatever commitments it can make with respect to how individual customer information will *never* be used (e.g., personal information is never sold or rented to others or never used to change prices or insurance premiums, etc.).
4. State the benefits an individual customer can expect as a result of its use of his information (faster or preferential service, reduced costs, etc.).
5. List a customer's options for directing the enterprise not to use or disclose certain kinds of information.
6. State how a customer can change or update personal information it has collected. For example, can the consumer access his profile or account information online or modify it?

(continued)

---

[28] Timothy Morey, Theodore "Theo" Forbath, and Allison Schoop, "Customer Data: Designing for Transparency and Trust," *Harvard Business Review,* May 2015, available at https://hbr .org/2015/05/customer-data-designing-for-transparency-and-trust, accessed January 11, 2016; Fatemeh Khatibloo, "Personal Identity and Data Management Success Starts with Customer Understanding," Forrester Research, Inc., March 17, 2015, available at http://www.forrester .com, accessed January 11, 2016; and Amit Poddar, Jill Mosteller, and Pam Scholder Ellen, "Consumers' Rules of Engagement in Online Information Exchanges," *Journal of Consumer Affairs* 43, no. 3 (2009): 419–448.

(*Continued*)

7. Identify events that might precipitate a notification to the customer by the enterprise. If, for instance, a court subpoenas your customer records, will you notify any customers whose information was subpoenaed?
8. Specify the situations in which it accepts or denies liability for damages incurred through the collection and use of customer data, such as through credit card fraud or misuse.
9. Provide specific procedures allowing a customer to order the company to stop collecting data about him, or to purge his information files at the company.
10. Make the pledge readable and easily accessible—easy to find, easy to read, easy to understand. Let the customer people override the legalese. The point is not what the pledge says, but what customers understand about it—brief, concise, clear, fair.

The bottom line is that the information that technology provides about your customers, and the increasingly cost-efficient tools you have to interact directly with customers and to facilitate them interacting with each other, should be used to build more trust. It really won't matter what your formal privacy protection policy is, or how well you comply with whatever antispam regulations are enforced, if you don't see the problem through the right end of the telescope—that is, from the customer's perspective. Fail to take this point of view and you are still going to be undermining your customers' trust.[29]

Submitting Data Online

For many consumers who buy online, the protection of their personal information is a valid concern. To the selling enterprise, however, information is like currency—it enables them to identify customers and customize their offerings based on that information.

By personalizing their products and services for online customers, enterprises stand to enhance their revenue—but only if they disclose how customers' data will be used.[30] Still, online users believe that Web sites should be accountable for

---

[29] "With Big Data Comes Big Responsibility: An Interview with MIT Media Lab's Alex 'Sandy' Pentland," *Harvard Business Review* 92, no. 11 (November 2014): 101–104.

[30] Elizabeth Aguirrea, Dominik Mahra, Dhruv Grewalb, Ko de Ruytera, and Martin Wetzelsa, "Unraveling the Personalization Paradox: The Effect of Information Collection and Trust-Building Strategies on Online Advertisement Effectiveness," *Journal of Retailing* 91, no. 1 (March 2015): 34–49.

explaining to them how their information will be used, as more and more consumers feel out of control regarding their personal information.[31] According to a Pew Internet & American Life survey on cloud computing:

- Ninety percent of users would be "very concerned" if the company storing their data sold it to another company.
- Eighty percent would be "very concerned" if companies used their data for marketing purposes.
- Sixty-eight percent would be "very concerned" if service providers analyzed their information and then displayed ads to them based on their actions.[32]

According to an Ernst and Young study, 70 percent of consumers say they are "never happy" for companies to share their personal data with third parties.[33]

Furthermore, customers are concerned enough that they believe the government should do more to protect their data; only 34 percent believe the government should not get more involved.[34] Web site personalization requires consumers to submit information about themselves, such as their names, zip codes, interests, and even credit card numbers. Consumers personalize the online sites they visit to enhance their online experiences, but many do not want to have their information shared among Web sites without their knowledge.

Beginning with TRUSTe in 1997 it has become important for eCommerce websites to include a **trust seal** that certifies by a third party that the data a customer submits to the site are secured and protected, and thus sensitive information such as credit card numbers and social security numbers is safe. The most trusted seals are Norton, McAfee, TRUSTe, and BBA Accredited. Although customers may not keep

---

[31] Mary Madden, "Privacy and Cybersecurity: Key Findings from Pew Research," January 1, 2015, Pew Research Center, http://www.pewresearch.org/key-data-points/privacy/, accessed January 11, 2016; and Ponemon Institute, "2008 Most Trusted Companies for Privacy: Study of U.S. Consumer Perceptions," December 2008; available at: www.ponemon.org/research-studies-white-papers.

[32] Pew Research Institute, "Use of Cloud Computing Applications and Services," Pew Internet & American Life Project report 2008, available at www.pewinternet.org/Reports/2008/Use- of-Cloud-Computing-Applications-and-Services.aspx?r=1, accessed September 1, 2010.

[33] Ernst and Young, "Big Data Backlash," Ernst and Young, November 12, 2013, available at http://www.ey.com/Publication/vwLUAssets/EY_-_The_Big_Data_Backlash/$FILE/EY-big-data-backlash-report.pdf, accessed February 15, 2016; infographics available at http://www .ey.com/UK/en/Services/Specialty-Services/Big-Data-Backlash#, accessed February 15, 2016.

[34] Madden, "Privacy and Cybersecurity: Key Findings from Pew Research." See also Mary Madden and Lee Rainie, "Americans' Attitudes about Privacy, Security and Surveillance," Pew Research Center, May 20, 2015, available at http://www.pewinternet.org/2015/05/20/americans-attitudes-about-privacy-security-and-surveillance/, accessed February 15, 2016.

up with the newest and best Web trust seals, we check for the reassurance that a reliable third party is watching before we enter our personal data on any Web site.[35]

Personalization online helps customers to access the specific content and products they are looking for while giving the enterprise access to their browsing habits. For many enterprises, the objective of personalization on the Web is to increase customer loyalty through return visits. Privacy advocates claim that the instances of abuse of consumer data are a sign of how Internet marketers are overstepping their boundaries. The marketers, in turn, argue that data gathering is merely a non-threatening way of fine-tuning marketing for the convenience of consumers. A firm will have to accomplish two things to break down the mistrust barrier between the customer and the online merchant:

1. *Offer assurances of confidentiality.* Customers want to know whether their personal data will be sold or used beyond simply information gathering.
2. *Build Learning Relationships based on trust.* Enterprises will need to develop individual, personalized relationships with their customers to promote trust and enhance loyalty.

As privacy protection advocates in Australia, the United States, and Europe continue to fuel the debate that it is wrong for companies to abuse personal information about their customers on the Web, enterprises will need to take a balanced view, not second-guess what their customers "really" want. The customer-strategy enterprise will strive to protect an individual's privacy online but also weigh the real benefits of personalization against its real costs.

The truth is, we leave our electronic fingerprints in the ether because it saves us time, because we like sharing photos and stories with others, and because it would

---

[35] John Rampton, "Importance of a Trust Seal on Your eCommerce Website," *Forbes,* December 16, 2014, available at http://www.forbes.com/sites/johnrampton/2014/12/16/importance-of-a-trust-seal-on-your-ecommerce-website/, accessed February 7, 2016; and Christian Holst, "Which Site Seal Do People Trust Most: 2013 Survey Results?" January 22, 2013, Baymard Institute, available at http://baymard.com/blog/site-seal-trust, accessed February 7, 2016. It's not always easy for the trust brokers to engender trust. The FTC fined TRUSTe for misrepresenting itself as a nonprofit organization on clients' Web sites, and in more than 1,000 cases failing to live up to its claims of annually recertifying its clients who were awarded the seal. TRUSTe agreed to pay $200,000 to settle the case. Thomas Claburn, "TRUSTe Not So Trustworthy," *InformationWeek,* November 17, 2014, available at http://www.informationweek.com/mobile/mobile-business/truste-not-so-trustworthy/d/d-id/1317534, accessed February 7, 2016; Edward Wyatt, "FTC Penalizes TRUSTe, a Web Privacy Certification Company," *New York Times,* November 17, 2014, available at http://www.nytimes.com/2014/11/18/technology/ftc-penalizes-truste-a-web-privacy-certification-company.html?_r=0, accessed February 7, 2016; and Benjamin Edelman, "Adverse Selection in Online 'Trust' Certifications and Search Results," Electronic Commerce Research and Applications, 2010, available at http://www.benedelman.org/publications/advsel-trust-se.pdf, accessed February 7, 2016.

be nearly impossible to function in modern society any other way. Web sites know who you are because whenever you log in, you tell them, and because they leave cookies, and because they have your IP address. What companies need to know is that customers would rather do business with a company they trust to handle this information fairly and safely.[36]

So much changed about the U.S. national attitude toward privacy on September 11, 2001. With the terrorist attacks on New York and Washington, D.C., U.S. national security was threatened as it had never been before. But on a more personal level, citizens felt that their individual safety was in jeopardy. The threat of additional terrorist attacks led to a heightened state of security at many public places, including airports, sporting events, and bridges and tunnels.

Universal ID

One solution offered after September 11, 2001, was the creation of a Universal ID card for each citizen to carry. The card could contain an electronic thumbprint of the cardholder so the person could be easily identified if questioned. This concept is akin to automobile license plates, which automatically expose the owner of the vehicle to the police, who simply need to check the plate number against their database. Would citizens be opposed to carrying a card that revealed personal information to anyone who swipes their cards? What about an embedded radio frequency identification (RFID) chip?

In the immediate aftermath of September 11, the civil rights of private citizens became a public issue. How much could the government encroach on a person's right to privacy in the shadow of terrorism? How much was okay if it made us all safer? What if it only made us *feel* safer? (Have you ever heard airport security referred to as "security theatre"?) Could the government begin to check the backgrounds and personal information of anyone it deemed to be a suspicious terrorist? There's no easy, immediate answer to what is always a best practice in privacy. The capabilities to get and share data about individuals become cheaper and easier daily. Smart cards can carry not only your retinal scan and fingerprints with you everywhere but your entire medical record.[37] And Intellicheck already enables bars to swipe your driver's license to ascertain your legal age (and then, in

---

[36] Hal Abelson, Ken Ledeen, and Harry Lewis, *Blown to Bits: Your Life, Liberty, and Happiness after the Digital Explosion* (Reading, MA: Addison-Wesley Professional, 2008).

[37] Smart Card Alliance, "Frequently Asked Questions"; available at: http://www.smartcardalliance.org/smart-cards-faq/, accessed January 11, 2016.

many states, to also suddenly "know" your Social Security number, gender, weight, address, etc.).

The real commercial questions are these:

■ What do we need to "know" to serve a customer better and make him more valuable to us?
■ What information do we really need to "know" that?
■ Once we get that information, how do we balance distribution at the front lines with the need to protect a customer's privacy?
■ What are the limits in how we will share or distribute data?
■ How will we protect and secure the data?
■ How do we build privacy and trust into our profitability strategies?

Summary

The fluid collaboration between enterprise and customer is ceaseless throughout the life of the relationship. But for the relationship to flourish, customers sometimes will have to reveal personal information about themselves to the enterprise. The enterprise, in turn, will have to promise to keep this private information private. Indeed, privacy—the customer's right to it, and the enterprise's protection of it—has become an important, and controversial, subject of the Information Age.

Food for Thought

1. Who owns a customer's information?
   ■ Who should profit from it?
   ■ How would that work?
2. Is anonymity the best solution to privacy?
3. What is the difference between privacy and data security, and how should that difference affect the way we use customer data?
4. Compare the situation of Big Business versus Big Brother having detailed information about you.

Glossary

Age of Transparency   The era of human history characterized by increasing levels of transparency in all human affairs, as a result of the pervasive interconnectedness of people, using social media and other ubiquitously available communications technology.

Benefits   Advantages that customers get from using the product. Not to be confused with needs, as different customers will get different advantages from the same product.

Cookie   A small text file stored on your local hard drive that contains information that a particular Web site wants to have available during your current session (like your shopping cart), or from one session to the next. Cookies give sites persistent information for tracking and personalization.

Customer service   Customer service involves helping a customer gain the full use and advantage of whatever product or service was bought. When something goes wrong with a product, or when a customer has some kind of problem with it, the process of helping the customer overcome this problem is often referred to as *customer care.*

Customer service representative (CSR)   A person who answers or makes calls in a call center (also called a customer interaction center or contact center, since it may include online chat or other interaction methods).

Customer-strategy enterprise   An organization that builds its business model around increasing the value of the customer base. This term applies to companies that may be product oriented, operations focused, or customer intimate.

Customization   Most often, customization and mass customization refer to the modularized building of an offering to a customer based on that customer's individual feedback, thus serving as the basis of a Learning Relationship. Note the distinction from *personalization,* which generally simply means putting someone's name on the product.

European Union Data Protection Directive   Requires EU member states to amend national legislation to guarantee individuals certain rights to protect their privacy and to control the contents of electronic databases that contain personal information. Information about consumers must be collected for specific, legitimate purposes and stored in individually identifiable form. Those collecting the data must tell the consumer, who will ultimately have access to the information, and companies wanting to use data in direct marketing must explicitly inform consumers of these plans and give them a chance to object.

Identify   Recognize and remember each customer regardless of the channel by or geographic area in which the customer leaves information about himself. Be able to link information about each customer to generate a complete picture of each customer.

Information Age   "A period in human history characterized by the shift from traditional industry that the Industrial Revolution brought through industrialization, to an economy based on information computerization." [Wikipedia]

Interactive voice response   Now a feature at most call centers, IVR software provides instructions for callers to "push '1' to check your current balance, push '2' to transfer funds," and so forth.

Most valuable customers (MVCs)   Customers with high actual values but not a lot of unrealized growth potential. These are the customers who do the most business, yield the highest margins, are most willing to collaborate, and tend to be the most loyal.

Needs   What a customer needs from an enterprise is, by our definition, synonymous with what she wants, prefers, or would like. In this sense, we do not distinguish a customer's needs from her wants. For that matter, we do not distinguish needs from preferences, wishes, desires, or whims. Each of these terms might imply some nuance of need—perhaps the intensity of the need or the permanence of it—but in each case we are still talking, generically, about the customer's needs.

Opt in   When customers proactively elect to receive future communications from an enterprise.

Opt out   When customers proactively elect *not* to receive future communications from an enterprise.

Personalization   Refers to a superficial ability to put a customer's name on something—to insert a name into a message, for example, or to monogram a set of sheets. Note the distinction from *customization,* which means creating an adapted product or service or communication based on the customer's individual feedback.

Privacy policy   A written document detailing how a company will share (or not share) data collected from its customers. Ideally, it should explain to customers, in simple language, what kinds of information the company needs from them, how the information will be used, how it will not be used, and the benefits a customer would gain by sharing personal information.

Social media   Interactive services and Web sites that allow users to create their own content and share their own views for others to consume. Blogs and microblogs (e.g., Twitter) are a form of social media, because users "publish" their opinions or views for everyone. Facebook, LinkedIn, and MySpace are examples of social media that facilitate making contact, interacting with, and following others. YouTube and Flickr are examples of social media that allow users to share creative work with others. Even Wikipedia represents a form of social media, as users collaborate interactively to publish more accurate encyclopedia entries.

Trust seal   A certification by a third party that the data a customer submits to the Web site is secured and protected, and thus sensitive information such as credit card numbers and social security numbers are safe. Examples include Norton, McAfee, TRUSTe, and BBA Accredited.

CHAPTER 10

The Payoff of IDIC: Using Mass Customization to Build Learning Relationships

Accepted wisdom is that, on average, each American household has about 300 branded products—food items, cleaning goods, over-the-counter remedies, grooming products. Yet there are about 30,000 stock-keeping units (SKUs) in the average supermarket, and many more in the big stores. That means that each shopper sifts through 100 times as many products she doesn't want as she does finding the ones she buys. If she's shopping online, she may be offered thousands of options to get to the one she wants. But the truth is that "choice" is not the same as getting things our way. Most of the time, in fact, especially for routine purchases, people don't want more choice. They just want what they want. They want to satisfy their need, and choosing from a large assortment of alternatives is the only way they can accomplish this. **Customization**, however, involves producing a single product, or delivering a single service, to satisfy a single customer's need without requiring the customer to go to the trouble of having to choose from a wide variety of other products or services. This is the payoff of the Learning Relationship—to the customer and to the company. This chapter shows how the customer-based enterprise should use what it learns about each customer to **customize** and/or personalize some aspect of its offering for that customer, in order to increase its share of that customer's business. The whole point is to know more about a customer than the competition does and then to deliver something in a way the competition cannot.

Treating different customers differently could be prohibitively expensive, if every interaction and transaction had to be individually crafted as a tailored offering for a single customer. Fortunately, information technology can be used to improve and streamline the manufacturing and service delivery processes, so that an enterprise can deliver individually different products or services to different individual customers cost efficiently. This technique is called **mass customization.**

For the past 100 years, enterprises have standardized their products and services to take advantage of economies of scale. They have standardized the product and their messages about the product, and they have standardized its distribution. In the process, they have also standardized the customer. Even sophisticated segmentation strategies aggregate customers into groups a marketer

> For the past 100 years, enterprises have standardized their products and services to take advantage of economies of scale. They have standardized the product and their messages about the product, and they have standardized its distribution. In the process, they also have standardized the customer.

defines as being alike, so the communication and the offer made to all customers in a "segment" can be standardized. By contrast, the **customer-strategy enterprise,** spurred by the rising power and declining cost of information processing, interconnectedness, and customization technologies, identifies each of its **most valuable customers (MVCs),** remembers everything it learns about each one, and acts on that learning in all its dealings with that customer.

Mass customization can be defined as the mass production of goods and services in lot sizes of one. Stan Davis, who first coined the term in his groundbreaking book *Future Perfect*, says the term implies delivering "customized goods on a mass basis."[1] The principles of mass customization are not limited to physically produced goods; they can also be applied to the customization of services and communication. For some customers, being treated individually with personalized services and communication may be an even more important dimension than being treated to uniquely tailored products made possible by individualized production.[2]

How Can Customization Be Profitable?

The mechanics of mass customization are simple in theory. A mass customizer does not really *customize* anything at all—at least not from scratch. What a mass customizer actually does is not customization but *configuration.* The mass customizer preproduces dozens, or hundreds, of "modules" for a product and/or its related services, delivery options, payment plans, and the like. Then, based on an individual customer's **needs,** the company puts different modules together to yield thousands, or even millions, of possible product configurations, but a customer will only be

---

[1] Stanley M. Davis, *Future Perfect* (Reading, MA: Addison-Wesley, 1987).
[2] Forrester calls these "individualized experiences": see Tony Costa, "Personalization and the Rise of Individualized Experiences," Forrester Research, Inc., December 9, 2014, available at http://www.forrester.com. Also see Amit Poddar, Jill Mosteller, and Pam Scholder Ellen, "Consumers' Rules of Engagement in Online Information Exchanges," *Journal of Consumer Affairs* 43, no. 3 (2009): 419–448.

offered one or a very few.[3] When an enterprise embraces mass customization and determines how to modularize its offerings, it must thoroughly understand all of the component elements its products or services can be combined with, connected to, reduced from, or built onto. By determining the related products or services it could offer to customers, either by producing them itself or by forming alliances with other firms, the enterprise takes a critical step in the mass customization process (see Exhibit 10.1).

Consider how a credit card company might go about mass-customizing its credit card. Perhaps the company is capable of offering 10 different interest rates, 5 different annual fee schedules, and 4 different physical card designs. Altogether, in other words, the credit card company can make 19 different modules of the product. But these modules fit together to make a total of 10 × 5 × 4, or 200 different credit card configurations. This is the basic principle of mass customization, and it applies to manufacturing in the same way. A window manufacturer, for instance, could offer 5 different sash types, 10 windowpane styles, 3 grades of insulation, and 12 frames. That would be 30 modules that could configure a total of 1,800 different windows, many of which would never be requested but any of which *could* be configured on demand. An important part of this process is the customer interface that makes individual configuration easy for both the customer and the company.

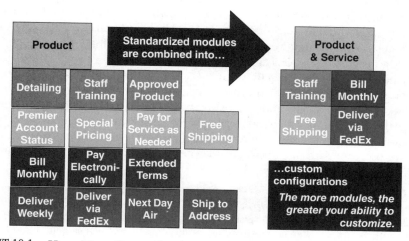

EXHIBIT 10.1   How Mass Customization Works: Example

---

[3] Jordan Reynolds, "Mass Customization: The Modular Model," *IndustryWeek*, June 2, 2014, available at http://www.industryweek.com/innovation/mass-customization-modular-model, accessed February 8, 2016; P. T. Xu, "Integrated Vehicle Configuration System—Connecting the Domains of Mass Customization," *Computers in Industry* 61, no. 1 (January 2010): 44–52; and Don Peppers, Martha Rogers, Ph.D., and Bob Dorf, *The One to One Fieldbook* (New York: Doubleday Broadway Books, 1999).

The biggest obstacle to mass-customizing a manufactured product, as opposed to a delivered service, is simply ensuring that different parts actually work with one another and can be fit together easily. But if a product's components can be put together in a standardized way, or *modularized*, then the process of mass customization actually can reduce a company's all-in costs, when compared to traditional mass production. Using **modularization,** building to order is inherently more efficient than building to forecast, because the enterprise need not take ownership of the parts any earlier than it needs them, and often the final product itself isn't even built—or the parts even ordered—until the product has already been paid for by a customer. Mass customization can significantly reduce speculative manufacturing as well as inventory costs, and these two **benefits** are often enough to more than offset the cost of producing digitally combinable components. Indeed, cost reduction is one of the principal reasons manufacturing companies consider mass-customization technologies in the first place.[4]

Consider NikeID shoes, which has been customizing shoes since 1999, and now capitalizes on sharing sites such as Instagram, where buyers show off their newly configured colors and styles.[5] Original Stitch lets customers configure a shirt from 200 fabrics, 10 button styles, and multiple monogram options. "With more than 176 trillion different possible combinations, each design is as unique as the customer that built it," says founder Jin Koy. Original Stitch has no inventory and no warehouse for shirts, but does help you post your new design on Facebook and Twitter for your friends.[6] Adagio Teas encourages custom blends on their Web site, which incorporates comments and reviews, and social media sharing.[7]

Analogous cost reductions are possible when mass-customizing a delivered service. By giving a customer exactly what she wants—and especially if the enterprise remembers this preference for the next interaction—the entire transaction can be streamlined, made not only more convenient for the customer but more cost efficient for the firm. Some banks, including Wells Fargo, can remember your "usual" transaction, if you have one, at automated teller machines (ATMs). In these banks, when you put your card into an ATM and enter your personal identification number

---

[4] John Fossey, "Mass Customization—The New Manufacturing Paradigm," *Manufacturing Trends and News,* August 11, 2015, available at http://www.mfg-trends.com/2015/08/11/mass-customization-the-new-manufacturing-paradigm/, accessed February 8, 2016.

[5] Mary Lisbeth D'Amico, "Nike Gears Customized Shoe Campaign to Instagram Users," *ClickZ,* April 26, 2013, available at http://www.clickz.com/clickz/news/2264540/nike-gears-customized-shoe-campaign-to-instagram-users, accessed February 8, 2016.

[6] "Original Stitch Launches Mass Customization E-commerce Platform for Designing and Customizing Shirts for Men—In Time for Father's Day," press release, *Business Wire*, May 13, 2014, available at http://venturebeat.com/2014/05/13/original-stitch-launches-mass-customization-e-commerce-platform-for-designing-and-customizing-shirts-for-men-in-time-for-fathers-day/, accessed February 8, 2016.

[7] See Adagio's company Web site at http://www.adagio.com/signature_blend/create_new.html, accessed February 8, 2016.

(PIN), the first menu item will offer you your usual cash withdrawal amount and receipt preference. This means the first question for returning customers will not be "What language do you prefer to use?" or "Do you want to (a) check your balance, (b) withdraw funds, (c) make a deposit, (d) transfer funds between accounts, or (e) other?" but instead will be "Would you like your usual $250.00 cash deducted from your checking account—yes or no?" Remembering a customer's "usual" not only provides faster and more convenient service for him, but it also yields more efficient asset utilization for the bank—that is, the ATM asset will generate more value to the bank when customers use it faster, and from the customers' perspective, the line moves faster.

Demand Chain and Supply Chain

When a firm remembers a customer's specification and uses this memory to deliver a product or service to that specification later (i.e., customization), the customer has a clear incentive to stay loyal. The more complex the product or service is, and the more "customization" that can be embedded in the company's treatment of the customer, the more likely the customer will be to remain loyal, even in the face of pricing pressure. It's partly the convenience factor, and partly simple trust. However, to create such a Learning Relationship, the enterprise must be capable not only of *remembering* the customer's information but also of acting on it. It must be able to integrate its back-end production or service-delivery operations, **supply chain,** with its front-end sales, marketing, or customer service operations, **demand chain.**

For this reason, managing individual customer relationships effectively requires that an enterprise's demand-chain activities be coordinated with, if not integrated into, its supply-chain activities. Good customer relationships on top of a weak supply chain merely provide customers with a clearer view of the mediocrity of a company's underlying logistical capabilities, undermining a customer's trust in the enterprise by calling the company's competence into question.[a] Customer experience management that is not effectively tied to supply chain management (SCM) results in:

- *Underdelivering.* Front-office strategies and processes will increase customer interactions—and customer expectations. If the back office can't deliver on what the front office promises, then "hollow **customer relationship management (CRM)**" will result, and customer satisfaction will decrease. This is a violation of the "competence" element of trust discussed in Chapter 3: Do Things Right.

(continued)

(Continued)

- *Overdelivering.* Customer strategies and processes that don't provide "cost transparency" into SCM information may result in delivering products or services that are unprofitable for the firm. Even while customers may be satisfied that their individual needs are being met, the firm loses money on every transaction, and such overdelivery is clearly not sustainable.
- *Lost share-of-customer opportunities.* Without integration, the supply chain can't capitalize on the information about customer needs that customer insight uncovers in order to form new supplier partnerships that intelligently and profitably increase the scope of a firm's offerings.

Because implementing CRM technologies and adopting customer strategies require supply-chain activities to be coordinated with and integrated into demand-chain activities, it is clear that managing customer relationships should no longer be thought of as a purely "customer-facing" set of business processes. When an enterprise truly succeeds in its customer-specific initiatives, that critical business practice will impact virtually all the firm's processes, with customer-specific insight and action permeating the supply chain, the product development cycle, the financial systems, service delivery, and even the firm's organizational structure.

Once an enterprise truly embraces "building customer value" as a business practice, it will find itself compelled to drive every activity, every process, and every strategy around the customer. Everything that the firm *does*—every action it takes—eventually will revolve around the customer. Moreover, this process integration will extend even beyond the enterprise itself, allowing customers to serve themselves (and each other, using **crowd service**) in increasingly sophisticated and detailed ways and enabling channel members to configure, order, install, and service products according to the individual requirements or preferences of particular customers. Customized treatment of individual customers requires robust yet flexible processes that join demand chain and supply chain together.

---

[a]Ginger Conlon, "Supply Chain and the Customer Experience," *Think Customers: The 1to1 Blog*, January 16, 2009; available at: http://www.1to1media.com/weblog/2009/01/supply_chain_and_the_customer.html, accessed February 8, 2016.

Not All Customization Is Equal

Management adviser Joe Pine literally wrote the (classic) book on mass customization.[8] He and his business partner, James H. Gilmore, have chronicled a business

---

[8] B. Joseph Pine II, *Mass Customization* (Cambridge, MA: Harvard Business Press, 1993).

evolution—from creating standardized value through mass production to creating customer-unique value through mass customization. Pine and Gilmore have hypothesized four distinct approaches to mass customization:

1. ***Adaptive customization*** offers a standard, but customizable, product that is designed so that customers can alter it themselves. One lingerie company makes a slip that a customer can cut off in a finished way to make the slip the length she wants.

2. ***Cosmetic customization*** presents a standard product differently to different customers. Catalog company Lillian Vernon encourages buyers to personalize backpacks and sleeping bags with a child's name.

3. ***Collaborative customization*** conducts a dialogue with individual customers to help them articulate their needs, identify the offering that fulfills those needs, and then make customized products for them. Ross Controls, a Michigan-based manufacturer of pneumatic valves and other air control systems used in heavy industrial processes in such industries as automobile, aluminum, steel, and forestry, learns about its customers' business needs so it can collaborate with them on precisely tailored designs.

4. ***Transparent customization*** provides each customer with a customized product or service without necessarily telling her about the customization itself. This is what the Ritz-Carlton does, when it configures a guest's stay based on the preferences the guest expressed during previous visits to the hotel chain. The guest who gets a hypoallergenic pillow in her room may not even be aware that this is customized service; she may think that her request was such a good one that now all the pillows in all the hotels have been changed to what she wants.[9]

Notice that *adaptive* and *cosmetic* customizers offer customers a better way to get what they want, compared to a mere standardizer; but also notice that these customizers *have no memory* of the **personalization** they do offer, thereby requiring customers to begin the specification process again with the next order. And that next transaction will depend entirely on the customer for its initiation. Therefore, adaptive and cosmetic customization offer no real sustainable competitive advantage against a competitor offering the same thing.

In contrast, notice that *collaborative* and *transparent* customizers maintain a distinct competitive advantage because they *remember* what a customer wants and can therefore better predict what she will want next time—reducing her need to make a choice. In many instances, the company takes a proactive role in offering to the customer what she's most likely to want next. The customer is able to get from a

---

[9] For more on the four types of mass customization, see James H. Gilmore and B. Joseph Pine II, "The Four Faces of Mass Customization," *Harvard Business Review* 75, no. 1 (January–February 1997), available at https://hbr.org/1997/01/the-four-faces-of-mass-customization, accessed June 21, 2016.

collaborative or a transparent customizer something she can't get elsewhere—even from a competitor that offers the exact same thing—unless she goes to the trouble (and risk) of starting all over in a new Learning Relationship.

Gilmore and Pine say that many companies resist mass-customizing their offerings and instead "manage the supply chain" by placing more and more variety into their distribution channels and leaving it to buyers to fend for themselves. Manufacturers maintain large inventories of finished goods, and service providers maintain excess personnel and provisions to meet potential demands. These

> The customer is able to get from a collaborative or a transparent customizer something she can't get elsewhere—even from a competitor that offers the exact same thing—unless she goes to the trouble (and risk) of starting all over in a new Learning Relationship.

practices add costs and complexity to operations. Customers then must sort through numerous alternatives they don't want to find the one that most closely approximates what they do want. In many situations, a majority of buyers never do find an exact match for their own personal tastes; instead, they settle for the one that seems to be the best fit overall, considering both the positives and the negatives. Gilmore and Pine call this **customer sacrifice**—it's also known as the **satisfaction gap**—the difference between what customers want and what they're willing to settle for (see Chapter 1). Producing greater variety in anticipation of potential, yet uncertain, demand often represents a last-ditch attempt to preserve the mass-production mindset in the face of rapidly fragmenting markets, say Gilmore and Pine.[10]

An enterprise focused on building customer value, by contrast, brings information about an individual customer's needs directly into its operations in order to achieve efficient, on-demand production or provisioning. This effectively turns the old supply chain into the back end of a *demand chain*.[11] In this process, the firm diminishes the importance of product price in favor of *relationship value* (see Exhibit 10.2).

EXHIBIT 10.2   Supply Chain versus Demand Chain

Mass Production	Mass Customization
Supply chain management	Demand chain management
Economies of scale	Economies of scope
Make to forecast	Make to order
Speculative shipping costs	Goods presold before shipping
Inventory carrying costs	Just-in-time inventory

---

[10] James H. Gilmore and B. Joseph Pine II, *The Experience Economy* (Cambridge, MA: Harvard Business School Press, 1999); and Pine, *Mass Customization.*

[11] Paul Grefen, *Beyond E-Business: Towards Networked Structures* (New York: Routledge, 2016), p. 85–87; Pankaj M. Madhani, "Demand Chain Management: Enhancing Customer Value Proposition, *European Business Review*, March 10, 2013; and Per Hilletofth, "Demand Chain Management: A Swedish Industrial Case Study," *Industrial Management & Data Systems* 109, no. 9 (2009): 1179–1196.

SPAR is the brand name for a chain of more than 12,000 grocery stores and outlets operating in 40 countries and generating some €32 billion in worldwide sales annually.[12] The company refers to itself as a kind of "soft" franchise operation, because most of its stores carrying its brand name are owned and operated independently. SPAR is the wholesaler for the stores in the chain, providing most—but not all—of the products sold by the member stores. SPAR's customers are the store operators themselves, and the company performs many services for them, in addition to wholesaling. For some storeowners, SPAR does the books and minds the payroll, for instance.

One of SPAR's innovations worth a closer look has been implemented in Austria, a relatively strong market for the firm, where it has a 30 percent share.[13] In 2003, SPAR Austria implemented a system that preconfigures its wholesale deliveries to a store in the same order in which the items are shelved in that store. So as the stock clerk rolls the trolley down the aisle at her store, she can effortlessly find the next items for the store's shelves, simplifying the process and saving considerable time and cost for the storeowner. Importantly, the ease with which SPAR Austria's products can be placed on a store's shelves provides an incentive for the storeowner to rely as much as possible on SPAR rather than going to the trouble of dealing with an additional supplier. Even if for a few items the other supplier might offer a more advantageous price, getting *goods onto shelves* costs less with SPAR.

Of course, each store's configuration is different, so SPAR's preconfiguration requires the firm to maintain an up-to-date record of each store's individual configuration. But it must also act on that information cost efficiently by changing the actual product delivery configuration for each store. Until this program was launched, the configuration of grocery products as they leave SPAR's own warehouses was not something that would have been considered a "customer-facing" activity. Mass-customizing those configurations, however, so as to treat different customers differently is very definitely a customer-facing action and perfectly illustrates how difficult **customer centricity** makes it to draw a line between supply-chain and demand-chain activities. (We are seeing a shift from **supply chain management** to **demand chain management.**) It has allowed SPAR to shift the core of its business from the price-driven "grocery-goods supplier" to a unique collaborative supplier of "goods stocked on your shelves," which has a very different value. More recently, SPAR has assisted stores with the SPAR Express layout that reflects key customer missions such as "enjoy now" or "take home," and SPAR even helps stores train their own employees at SPAR Academy. This is the heart of the payoff of mass customization: Collaboration leads to a new definition of the business a company is in, and this

---

[12] Available at http://www.spar-international.com/sparworldwide/keyfigures.html, accessed January 19, 2016.
[13] "Growing Our Future Together: SPAR International Annual Report 2014," available at http://www.spar-international.com, accessed January 19, 2016.

new **business model** defies **commoditization,** even when somebody else tries to do the same thing the same way.[14]

Mass customizers can adjust to changes in markets and technology easily, as they can rapidly shift their production, creating new products to accommodate changing environments. Fewer customer orders will be lost because mass customization always can, within overall capacity limits, build the products in demand. This contrasts again with mass-production factories, each of which has its own capacity limitations—limitations that usually cannot be offset by excess capacity elsewhere in the company. Distribution based on lower inventory levels at a build-to-order factory can prevent shortages caused in distribution channels. The result is fewer opportunity losses.[15]

Because customized products can be ordered with only the options customers want, customers will not be forced to buy a "bundled" option package to get the one option they really want. Even at a premium price, customers may still save money by avoiding unwanted options.

The mass-customizing enterprise is driven by observing and remembering individual customer requests and by comparing them to what other customers have requested. The success of mass customization as a relationship-building tool stems from the fact that a customer can participate in the actual design and development of her own product. As a result of her own collaborative effort, the customer is much more likely to be satisfied with the overall performance of the product and to find it costly to start over with a competitor, even when that competitor could do the same thing the same way.

Examples of mass customization abound in business today, both in business-to-consumer (B2C) and in business-to-business (B2B) settings. Navistar (previously International Truck & Engine Corp.) has used mass customization to learn more about its customers. It has introduced a custom truck configurator on the company's website, where prospective customers can create hundreds of different designs—providing important information about customers in an industry where the manufacturer has

---

[14] This idea of rethinking the industry and business a company is in was well described by Chan Kim and Renee Mauborgne in their book, *Blue Ocean Strategy: How to Create Uncontested Market Space and Make the Competition Irrelevant* (Boston: Harvard Business School Press, expanded edition, 2015).

[15] Stephen E. Chick, Arnd Huchzermeier, and Serguei Netessine, "Europe's Solution Factories," *Harvard Business Review* 92, no. 4 (April 2014): 111–115; and Anshuk Gandhi, Carmen Magar, and Roger Roberts, "How Technology Can Drive the Next Wave of Mass Customization," McKinsey & Company, February 2014, available at https://www.cob.unt.edu/itds/faculty/becker/BCIS5520/Readings/How_technology_can_drive_the_next_wave_of_mass_customization_2014_02.pdf, accessed February 8, 2016. Also see H. Agbedo, "A Note on Parts Inventory and Mass Customization for a Two-Stage JIT Supply Chain with Zero-One Type of Bills of Materials," *Journal of the Operational Research Society* 60, no. 9 (September 2009): 1286–1291, for more on the realities of material management in the electronics and automobile industries, which have found mass customization most profitable.

little contact with the buyer. Customers still need to buy from the dealer, but now even the dealer can know more about its customers' preferences before they buy: serious Web site inquiries are sent to the dealer closest to the prospective client for direct follow-up.[16] Also, since the mid-1990s, Harley-Davidson has been encouraging bikers to design their own motorcycles using their online Customizer program, where they can create a custom design and take it to a dealer to build it.[17]

Technology Accelerates Mass Customization

No matter how much value an enterprise adds, it is the value a customer adds for herself that makes a product or service worth a higher price. As the demand for personalized and customized products grows, more enterprises are offering build-to-order services to enable customers to configure products to their own needs—and improvements in technology have made it possible. Technology is enabling enterprises to meet their customers' demands through mass production, but in ways that offer people their own choice of products that are personalized and made to measure.[18] The Web, for instance, has become an ideal tool for mass customization, precisely because *anything that can be digitized can be customized*. The Web permits consumers to submit their specifications online directly to the manufacturer or sales executive.

> Anything that can be digitized can be customized.

> It is the value a customer adds for herself that makes a product or service worth a higher price.

Capital One Financial Corp. developed a successful mass-customization model that changed the credit card industry.[19] The company is best known for gathering and analyzing consumer and customer data. Technology enables Capital One to observe and evaluate customer preferences and behavior and to do so dynamically, by **market segment.** The

---

[16] See http://www.internationaltrucks.com/configurator/hx, accessed February 8, 2016; and Kevin Zimmerman, "Rockin' Your Rig," *1to1 Magazine's Weekly Digest,* May 12, 2008, available at www.1to1media.com/view.aspx?DocID=30854, accessed February 10, 2016.

[17] Available at http://www.harley-davidson.com/content/h-d/en_US/home/hd1-customization/build-your-harley.html, accessed February 8, 2016.

[18] Gandhi, Magar, and Roberts, "How Technology Can Drive the Next Wave of Mass Customization."

[19] See https://www.capitalone.com/credit-cards/benefits/personalize/, accessed February 6, 2016. Capital One, of course, mass-customizes products that take the form of digitized information and, in that sense, has an easier challenge than, say, an industrial manufacturer. But the same principles—modularization, closing the feedback loop, improvement through increased service levels at decreased cost to serve, and so forth—apply to both.

company can forecast trends and strategically shift its focus away from commoditized products, such as balance transfer cards, before the market is saturated with offers from competitors. Capital One planned for the obsolescence of balance transfer cards and plotted a course to move the credit card company into mass customization. This strategy enabled the firm to leverage its information resources to identify customers with low-limit, high-fee potential and to send these customers the marketing materials about products that would likely interest them, such as secured cards for people with poor credit. Using a database that contains the histories of all consumer interactions with Capital One enabled the firm to customize its credit card offerings. Capital One's ImageCard also has allowed customers to add a personalized image to their card for free—well worth it, considering that it increases security and is popular enough with customers to increase use per card by 15 to 20 percent.[20]

One technology that has begun to deliver on its promise of affordable customization is **3-D printing**. Created in 1980s by engineer Charles Hall, 3-D printing was typically used for making a plastic or resin prototype of an object that would then be manufactured. 3-D printing takes a digital file of a 3-D object and uses software to print it in layers to form the object. Today materials used in printing include not only plastics, but silver, gold, and other metals, ceramics, wax, even food. And uses are growing. The machines are falling in price, and Staples and Amazon now offer 3-D printing services, and the list of 3-D-printed products generally available includes nuts, bolts, earbuds, eyeglasses, athletic cleats, jewelry, cremation urns, Star Wars figurines, architectural models, and even entire houses.[21] Pop-up stores in shopping malls now offer 3-D selfies, so you can have a tabletop statue of yourself or your pet.

The ultimate in customization may be 3-D printing of biological parts that allow custom-made medical solutions—stents that fit exactly into a person's unique individual valves, titanium plates that are printed to precisely replace damaged bones in faces, and knee implants. Sometimes a 3-D printed model of a patient's body part is

---

[20] "Doing Business the Digital Way: How Capital One Fundamentally Disrupted the Financial Services Industry," Capgemini Consulting, 2014, available at https://www.capgemini.com/resource-file-access/resource/pdf/capital-one-doing-business-the-digital-way_0.pdf, accessed February 8, 2016. According to Serverside Group, customized cards have proven their ability to foster loyalty, reduce churn, and increase card utilization with front-of-wallet placement. Some of the results they tout for their bank and credit union clients include BBVA Compass Bank (54 percent account activation increase), American First Credit Union (68 percent increase in member usage), Newscastle Permanent Building Society (15 percent increase in customer acquisition rate), and BBVA Compass Bank (3 percent increase in customer retention), available at http://thefinancialbrand.com/35074/custom-bank-debit-credit-card-designs/, accessed February 2, 2016. Also see Adam Elgar, "Card Personalization Can Generate 'Top of Wallet' Use in Tough Economy," *CardLine* 9, no. 15 (April 2009): 37.

[21] Jerome Groopman, "Print Thyself," *New Yorker*, November 24, 2014, available at http://www.newyorker.com/magazine/2014/11/24/print-thyself, accessed February 8, 2016.

used by surgeons for practice. The holy grail will be a working organ, printed with live cells.[22] Already 3-D printing has overhauled the American hearing aid industry.[23]

Although a lot of major manufacturing such as cars, planes, and drones, is moving toward 3-D printing to save money, 3-D printing also offers small businesses a way to enter the market affordably. With 3-D printing, inventors and personalizers can produce a new product on demand, bypassing the need for inventory, investors, working through online 3-D communities and marketplaces such as Shapeway.[24] It raises huge questions about legal ownership of parts and other physical objects, but giant machines could be used to produce inexpensive housing (imagine giant Lego blocks!) to reduce homelessness and displacement.[25]

Customizing products and services can yield a competitive advantage if the enterprise deploys the correct design interface and remembers its customers' unique specifications and interactions. By linking an individual customer's interactions with previous knowledge of that customer, and then using that learning to drive the production process, the enterprise takes an integrative approach to competition—one customer at a time.

Customization of Standardized Products and Services

> It's important to realize that even companies that cannot customize a product per se still can customize what they offer to individual customers and thus build Learning Relationships.

When the executives of a company believe they can sell only standardized products, sometimes those executives bemoan their inability to participate fully in the strategic payback of the customer relationship revolution. It's important to realize that even companies that cannot customize a product per se still can customize what they offer to individual customers and thus build loyalty through customer experience, and also build Learning Relationships. A company may, for example, be able to change the product, add features, or combine it with other products. It may be able to sell standardized product, but provide various services that enable a customer to receive personalized attention before and after

---

[22] Groopman, "Print Thyself."

[23] Richard D'Aveni, "The 3-D Printing Revolution," *Harvard Business Review* (May 2015): 40–48; see also EnvisionTEC's company Web site, http://envisiontec.com/3d-printing-industries/hearing-aid/, accessed February 8, 2016.

[24] "Will 3D Printing Change the World?" PBS *OffBook* series, aired March 1, 2013, available at http://video.pbs.org/video/2339671486/, accessed February 8, 2016. See also Shapeways company Web site, http://www.shapeways.com, accessed February 6, 2016.

[25] John Newman, "3D Printed Pre-fab Housing Erected in Shanghai," *RapidReadyTech*, April 7, 2014, available at http://www.rapidreadytech.com/2014/04/3d-printed-pre-fab-housing-erected-in-shanghai/, accessed February 8, 2016.

she buys the product, and make it possible for her collaboration with the firm to benefit her. The company that truly cannot mass-customize its products can look for service and communication opportunities to build in mass customization that makes the customer's investment in the relationship pay off—for both the customer and the company. There are many customization options beyond the physical product itself, and many ways an enterprise can modify how it behaves toward an individual customer, other than customizing a physical product. These include mass customization of:

- Configuration of the product or services surrounding it
- Bundling of multiple products or services
- Packaging
- Delivery and logistics
- Ancillary services (repair, calibration, finance, etc.)
- Training
- Service enhancements
- Invoicing
- Payment terms
- Preauthorization

The key, for any enterprise trying to plan ways to tailor its products and services for individual customers, is to visualize the "product" in its broadest possible sense—not simply as a product but as an object that provides a service, solves a problem, or meets a need. One widely cited *Harvard Business Review* article suggested, for instance, that we should try to think of products as being "hired" by customers to do a "job,"[26] and this is even more true as the **Internet of Things** makes products smarter and smarter and companies can know and remember more and more about each customer who uses the product.[27] This is exactly what we mean when we talk about visualizing the broadest possible definition of the service a product provides, or the problem it solves, for a customer. And this is where a strict adherence to the discipline of differentiating customers by their *needs* will pay off. What a customer needs and what she buys are often two different things. But if an enterprise has a full understanding of the customer's own need, then that enterprise can often devise a customized set of services or products that will meet that need. Meeting the customer's need is the service being performed by the enterprise, and the product itself is the means for delivering that service, or for doing that "job."

---

[26] Clayton M. Christensen, Scott Cook, and Taddy Hall, "Marketing Malpractice: The Cause and the Cure," *Harvard Business Review* 83, no. 12 (December 2005): 74–83.

[27] Michael E. Porter and James E. Heppelmann, "How Smart, Connected Products Are Transforming Companies," *Harvard Business Review* 93, no. 10 (October 2015): 96–114.

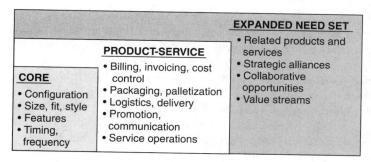

EXHIBIT 10.3   Expanded Need Set

This product-as-service idea can be thought of in terms of three successively complex levels in the set of needs a customer is trying to meet (see Exhibit 10.3):

1. The *core product* itself includes its physical nature, if it is an actual product, or its component services and executional elements, if the core product is actually a service. Customizing the core product could include:
   - Product configuration
   - Features or capabilities
   - Fit and size
   - Color, design, style
   - Timing or frequency
2. The product-service bundle includes the services and features that surround the core product. Customization of the product-service bundle could include:
   - Invoicing, billing, and cost control (i.e., helping the customer manage or control costs)
   - Additional services
   - Packaging and palletization of the products
   - Promotion and marketing communication
   - Help lines and product support
3. The **expanded need set** includes product or service features that could meet related customer needs, enhancing or expanding the customer's original set of needs. Activities undertaken to customize an expanded need set could include:
   - Offering related products or services.
   - Forming strategic alliances with other firms serving the interests of the same customers.
   - Providing the customer with opportunities to collaborate in product or service design.
   - Offering **value streams** of services or benefits following the actual sale of a product or service (more on value streams later in the chapter).

As the definition of the customer's need is broadened and as the need set is expanded, the definition of the product itself will become more complex. With a more complex product, the enterprise can make customization more beneficial. At each successive level of product complexity, the enterprise has another opportunity to remember *something* that later will make a difference to a specific individual customer. Remember, when a customer base is characterized by customers with dramatically different needs, remembering an individual customer's own personal needs or preferences will be highly beneficial to the customer. The more different the customers are in terms of their needs, the more benefit each customer will see in engaging in a Learning Relationship.

Thus, when customers have more uniform needs, as is particularly true of companies selling commodity-like products and services, the customer-strategy enterprise should try to expand the need set. Customers then will be seen as more diverse in the way they individually define their needs. The enterprise should assess which products and services it now offers that can cement the loyalty and improve the margin on its customers, even if the firm's competitors offer the same products and services at the same price, customized in the same way. Simply improving the quality of a product or service, while advantageous in the short term, will not necessarily yield a competitive benefit over the long term. A customer-strategy enterprise instead tries to improve a product's quality by customizing some aspect of it to suit the different needs of an individual customer in order to build a collaborative Learning Relationship with that customer. If the firm is selling a commodity-like product, what it actually customizes might not be the core product but the bundle of services surrounding the product or a configuration of additional products and services designed to meet an expanded definition of the customer's need.

One of the easiest ways for a B2B enterprise to customize its product-service bundle, for example, is to remember how and when *each customer* wants to be invoiced. A credit card company with corporate cards, a phone company, or any other firm that sells a high-transaction product or service to other businesses might consider offering some customers the opportunity to tailor the invoices to weekly totals rather than monthly ones. Or a firm could provide the invoices on a quarterly summary basis, or even offer to allow the customer itself to specify which time periods to invoice at one time. Some banks are already offering some personalization capabilities for formatting of monthly statement options. Enterprises that already offer customized products can benefit by customizing these ancillary services even further.

In addition to the services and operations that naturally accompany a core product, most products and services can easily be associated with a customer's other, related needs. When a customer buys a car from a car dealer, for instance, she will likely need automobile insurance, loan financing, a good mechanic, and, possibly, a carwash subscription. Catering to an expanded need set means providing extra services to meet the customer's broadest possible set of needs.

Some hotels, such as Estelar La Fontana Hotel in Bogotá, Colombia, cater to the international business traveler. If a guest has a trip to Bogotá planned, the hotel will set up her appointments in advance for her. All the guest need do is tell the hotel the names and phone numbers of the people she will meet. The deeper an enterprise can penetrate a particular customer's needs, the more likely that enterprise will be able to cement a Learning Relationship with the customer, earning the customer's loyalty not simply out of gratitude but because it is more convenient for that customer to remain loyal. As long as she is certain her own interests are being protected, the customer will trust the enterprise with a greater and greater share of her business.

Think of this simple example: A grocery store can't "customize" the products in its stores, or even the stores themselves. But starting with Tesco in 1995, even grocery stores can customize their discounts and other offers to the individual needs of each customer. Tesco didn't start by trying to design the largest database it could, but instead focused on designing the smallest store of data that would give it useful information. Using this data, in 2005, roughly 10 million customers each quarter were mailed some four million variations of coupon offers, based on each individual customer's history and profile. At that time, the program generated £100 million of incremental sales annually for the retailer.[28]

Today, a number of retailers offer cards such as Kroger's Plus Card, which delivers highly relevant, personalized coupons through their "Loyal Customer Mailings," also available through a mobile app, which allows customers to sort digital coupons by relevance to them.[29]

Value Streams

Some enterprises believe they have nothing to offer their end-user customers to entice them to want relationships. A firm that produces a single product, infrequently purchased, is in this kind of situation. One strategy for a one-product company would be to create a "stream of value" behind the actual product sale. Here's the choice: Find another customer for the product you sell, and then another and another, to generate more and more transactions; or find a related stream of products and services you could offer in order to get a greater **share of customer** from each of the customers you've already acquired.

> Here's the choice: Find another customer for the product you sell, and then another and another, to generate more and more transactions. Or find a related stream of products and services you could offer in order to get a greater share of customer from each of the customers you've already acquired.

Usually a value stream relies on some type of follow-on service, after the product sale, but it could also be an interaction designed to generate income later from customer referrals. The home builder who, in order to satisfy customers and generate more referrals, calls her customer the week before the one-year warranty expires and offers to inspect the home for any persisting problems

[28] Don Peppers and Martha Rogers, *Return on Customer: A Revolutionary Way to Measure and Strengthen Your Business* (New York: Currency/Doubleday, 2005), pp. 50–52.

[29] Ronald R. Urbach, "Kroger Gets Its Fuel from Customer Rewards," *Madison Ave. Insights,* April 24, 2014, available at http://www.madisonaveinsights.com/2014/04/24/kroger-gets-its-fuel-from-customer-rewards/, accessed February 8, 2016.

is creating a value stream behind the sale of the home. The simple fact is that most people who build a home won't build another any time soon. But having received this kind of service, they will likely tell their friends about their positive experience, and the builder could generate a much higher level of referral service, and existing customers will call when they want to put on an addition.

We could cite other examples. A furniture retailer could create a different kind of value stream behind its infrequently sold products, selling a sofa with a free upholstery cleaning, to be scheduled by the customer one year after the initial purchase. That way, when it comes time to schedule the cleaning appointment, the retailer would be reestablishing contact with the customer, to the customer's own benefit. At that point, the retailer could generate more revenue from the customer in any number of ways—selling a longer-term subscription to furniture cleaning, or selling items of furniture to go with the original purchase, and so forth. A clothing store could offer a dry cleaning or repair service for the clothing it sells. Customers who buy their suits from the store and pay an extra fee could have all of their dry cleaning, pressing, laundering, tailoring, and sewing done for the first two or three years, perhaps.

Note that in each of these hypothetical cases, the enterprise increases the revenue generated from each customer by expanding the needs set, and builds an interactive Learning Relationship at the same time. The value stream approach has been used to encourage warranty card registration, particularly by software vendors whose products are bundled into the original equipment manufacturer's personal computer hardware.

> Value streams eventually lead to supplemental revenue streams for the enterprise. A customer is willing to pay for the ancillary product or service because it is valuable to *her*. But, meanwhile, the enterprise will be strengthening its ongoing relationship by exchanging information with the customer, as the value stream is delivered.

Those who mail in the registration (or who connect to register online) could receive 90 days' free advice and help in putting the software to work. Value streams eventually lead to supplemental revenue streams for the enterprise. A customer is willing to pay for the ancillary product or service because it is valuable to *her*. But, meanwhile, the enterprise will be strengthening its ongoing relationship by exchanging information with the customer, as the value stream is delivered.

Bentley Systems Creates Value Streams

What is the best way for an organization to remain actively involved with each of its customers—even when those customers may be years away from making another purchase? This is a key question for companies in some types of business, and it is a question likely to be faced especially by B2B organizations.

Bentley Systems faced just such a dilemma: It already owned a huge share of its market, so a strategy focused primarily on market development would not deliver the kind of results sought by the company's management. Instead, Bentley turned to a strategy that emphasized account development, launching an entirely new, subscription-based service to meet the needs of its clients.

One of the world's leading providers of software for the architecture, engineering, construction, and operation (AECO) market, Bentley Systems Incorporated had annual revenues topping $600 million. The company's primary products consisted of architectural and engineering design software applications that it sells for a workstation environment. Imagine that the typical Bentley customer buys a three-year software solutions contract worth $1 million, and might take as long as 18 months to close the deal. At any given moment, Bentley might have dozens of such deals in the works, all in various stages of development. Once a deal has been inked, it might be four or five years before the customer is ready for another purchase of similar magnitude. If nothing else, this makes it exceptionally difficult to project revenue very far into the future, as all of next year's revenue has to come from new customer sales or winbacks.

Many B2B organizations don't have a strategy or system in place to take advantage of the quiet intervals between sales. It's not that they're unaware of these intervals. More likely, they've been trained or acculturated to see them as lost time, as dead zones in the purchase cycle. Sometimes these quiet times represent opportunities simply to deploy their customer acquisition resources elsewhere.

Or perhaps they're looking at the problem backward. Most enterprises believe it's important to know the purchase cycles of their customers: If you know the moment when your customer is ready to buy, you will be in a better position to sell your customer something—at that moment.

This type of reasoning works if you're in a business where you get to see your customers relatively often. Some B2C businesses—such as supermarkets, drugstores, and other retailers—can count on seeing their customers at least once or twice a week. But organizations that sell products such as boats, cars, refrigerators, manufacturing tools, real estate property, or high-end business equipment have customers who purchase much less frequently. If you have customers who buy from you only every few years, how can you establish and cultivate customer relationships?

There are two basic ways to address this type of challenge: You could sell or give away a range of additional services related to your product—cleaning, adjusting, calibrating, refilling, repairing it under a warranty's terms, configuring other products and services to go with your product, and so forth; or you could alter your business model to "subscribe" customers to your product, rather than selling it to them. In either case, you're talking about trying to create a value stream to supplement or replace a sales pattern marked by infrequent spurts of purchasing activity, enabling you to maintain and strengthen relationships with your clients over a longer period of time.

(continued)

(*Continued*)

Greg Bentley is the one who spearheaded the company's evolution beyond product sales. His choice was to wrap a wide array of ancillary services and perks into a single, all-encompassing subscription plan called SELECT.

SELECT provides subscribing customers with literally dozens of benefits, such as 24/7/365 technical support, discounts on Bentley products, free platform swaps, and free software upgrades. SELECT customers are allowed concurrent licensing of their Bentley software, which essentially means the licenses are transferable from moment to moment within the company. This benefits the customers by giving them greater flexibility to redeploy expensive software applications among their users. And it benefits Bentley by expanding usage and creating demand for more software products.

The beauty of SELECT is that it functions as both a dependable income stream and a robust customer retention tool. Imagine when a customer signs up for the subscription plan, Bentley can bank on that customer's loyalty. For the duration, Bentley has a window of opportunity to sell more products to a customer who already has declared her allegiance.

The important idea here is that it is not only possible but also essential to create a practical system for bridging the gap between infrequent sales, if you plan to build your business success around customer relationships. SELECT is an example of a system designed to bridge this gap. It helps Bentley stay involved with its customers; it makes it easier for Bentley to cross-sell a variety of its products; and it allows Bentley to focus on growing the firm's share of customers instead of just its share of market.

In the final analysis, the most enduring legacy of SELECT may be how it fundamentally changed the way Bentley Systems measures success and allocates resources for the future. Under the old model, Bentley set annual goals for increasing its sales revenue, and it measured its own performance against these goals. This essentially kept the company locked into a customer acquisition mode, no matter how many innovative programs or initiatives it designed to break free. The launch of SELECT, and its rapid acceptance by customers, liberated Bentley to measure its performance with a refreshingly simple set of metrics tied to customer retention and development.

Bentley has found it advantageous to move "up the food chain" to deliver more comprehensive service packages to its clients. SELECT can be used to provide seamless document management, including filing, archiving, and transmittal to involved third parties. And the right way for Bentley to gain the most leverage out of SELECT is for the company to reorient its thinking about the nature of its customer base to begin with. With SELECT, rather than selling products to customers, Bentley is *subscribing* customers to an ongoing stream of products and services. Running a subscription business is very different from running a product transaction business.

In addition, many of Bentley's customers almost certainly want to develop their own value streams of services to transcend the periodic projects they do for their own clients. SELECT provides Bentley with an ideal opportunity to begin helping them in this task.

SELECT was set up as a program that should be configured in such a way as to allow an architectural firm to go into not just the "project" business of designing and constructing a building, but into the "long-term management" business of taking care of the building, maintaining it, and upgrading it even after it has been built. Because Bentley's program can provide continual, updated documentation of a project's design, it can also help the architectural firm do a lot more than just creative work. A building is a complex system of pipes, wires, ducts, heating and cooling elements, and lighting treatments, not to mention the surrounding landscaping, lawn maintenance, irrigation and gardening care, as well as driveway and parking lot construction and maintenance. The more of this comprehensive system that SELECT can accommodate, the more Bentley's clients will rely on it to drive their own profitability.

When Bentley looks for additional ways to strengthen its relationships with its customers, the company might want to consider services that aren't tied directly to SELECT. It's not hard to imagine Bentley helping its customer firms with the preparation and financing of the bid they render for a project. Or instituting training classes for a client's engineers or architects—not just in the use of Bentley's software, but in the nuances of design. Or hosting Web sites and other IT infrastructure for a client, allowing the client to manage its own far-flung collection of independent architects and engineers more efficiently. See Exhibit 10.4 for a comparison between Bentley's old "product" business model and the new "relationship" business model.

- High market share
- Infrequent sales spikes
- Next year's sales goal: Find new customers to meet sales quotes.

- Broaden product line to meet more client needs over time.
- Focus on end-user needs instead of market development.
- Next year's sales goal: Re-up the SELECT subscribers, sell $500 of product to each licensed seat, get a few new customers.

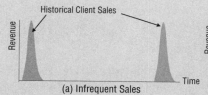

EXHIBIT 10.4   (a) Infrequent Sales versus (b) Continuing Value Streams

Source: Adapted from Don Peppers and Martha Rogers, Ph.D., *One to One B2B* (Currency/Doubleday, 2001). Updated February 15, 2016. Bentley Systems, Inc. company information available at its Web site, https://www.bentley.com/, accessed February 8, 2016.

Mass customization, as we defined the term near the beginning of this chapter, involves creating a product by digitally combining a number of different modules representing premanufactured or preconfigured product and service components. The business processes that result in a product or service being rendered for a customer in a certain way can also be thought of, metaphorically anyway, as "modules" of the enterprise's overall behavior toward a customer. The instructions that an enterprise follows in configuring different processes for different customers are **business rules** that allow the company to ensure that its own behavior is delivered in what amounts to a mass-customized way—that is, tailored, as a matter of routine, to each situation. As Bruce Kasanoff explains in the next section, monitoring how the business rules operate at an enterprise is an important task, especially for any customer-strategy enterprise.

A Quick Primer on Business Rules

Bruce Kasanoff
Business writer and consultant

Business rules are the instructions that tell software—or people—how to operate. They are a reusable set of instructions that enable an organization to operate in a consistent yet flexible way. Ronald Ross, cofounder of the consulting firm Business Rule Solutions, LLC, says, "Business rules are literally the encoded knowledge of your business operations." "Upgrade platinum flyers to first class before gold flyers" is a business rule. So is "Most valuable customers are those who order at least $1,500 of merchandise in a year."

"Personalization is the killer app for business rules," says Ross. He argues that because business rules drive most of the leading personalization and e-commerce applications, companies now have a compelling reason to invest the time and effort in documenting the way they want to do business.

Instructions That Live Outside of Programming Languages

Business rules are not new; what is new is that increasingly many rules are being created and changed via interfaces accessible to nontechnical business managers. Rules used to live deep within programming that was difficult and time consuming to change. The resulting inflexibility of systems resulted in equally inflexible companies. By "externalizing" some business rules, enterprises are seeking to be more adaptable and efficient as they get closer to their customers, to deliver customized service.

Not every rule should be accessible to business managers, who lack the technical training—or the inclination—to manage systems reliably and securely, but more and more are accessible to nontechnical managers as the technology makes it possible.

Dealing with inflexible companies can be maddening for customers. Take a bank, for example, that requires a loan application for every customer, regardless of the customer's net assets or history with the bank. You can almost hear the assistant manager saying, "The system won't let me process your application without a completed application." She's right; that requirement is probably buried deep within the bank's programming, where it would take years to change.

The business rules approach makes it possible for such requirements to be contained in a far more accessible location. Thus, the bank could create a rule that would accommodate special circumstances. The rule might say: "If the customer has a clean credit report, the loan is secured, and the customer agrees to keep at least 20 percent of the loan's value in cash in her account, then waive the application requirement."

Transferring Knowledge from Your Head

It is difficult to transfer the knowledge of each employee—and of the organization as a whole—into a set of effective rules, and the very fact that it is so difficult is one reason business rules are so valuable. Think about the best salesperson you have ever met. Now imagine being able to capture what makes him so talented and imbue an automated system with those qualities. That is one promise of business rules, but the challenge is to translate his approach into a manageable number of repeatable principles. In this example, you might start with rules such as these:

- Listen to the customer's needs before you present any products, services, or offers.
- Present offers specific to the customer's stated needs before you show other special offers.
- Show the blue items first, because this customer has shown a preference for blue, then yellow, then gray.

Stew Leonard's is a Connecticut-based "dairy store" that is world-renowned for staying close to its customers and generating immense sales. In a largely nonautomated setting, the store has captured its principles in a set of rules that produce extraordinary service and a highly effective merchandising system.

One of those rules is that if an item is not properly marked for price, the customer gets it for free. I experienced this firsthand while buying an eight-pound

(continued)

(Continued)

piece of filet mignon for a holiday celebration. When a price didn't come up on the register, the cashier gave it to me for free. I began to protest—the meat was worth at least $50—but she explained that because the company did so much volume, it was cheaper to give the meat away than to hold up the checkout line. And, besides, Stew Leonard's has "The customer is always right" carved in stone at the front of the store.

New Rules, New Skills

It is not hard to create a simple business rule, such as "Send a thank-you e-mail to every customer who places an order." It is difficult, however, to create and manage a full complement of rules; yet this is exactly what is required when the goal is to treat different customers differently. As rules multiply, the odds increase that they will cancel each other out or cause unexpected results. This is especially problematic when multiple business units target the same customers. What if 10 units create rules that specify what happens when a new prospect visits the firm's Web site? Does the prospect get 10 different offers, all seemingly oblivious to each other, or does one take precedence?[a]

One of the first challenges is to develop rules for interacting with individual customers. Although customization has become much more pervasive, many still lack a full understanding of the customers. Until the rise of the Web, any firm that sold through a distribution channel had long been disconnected from its end users. Even enterprises that deal directly with customers have often engaged in monologues ("Buy this; it works") rather than true dialogues ("What works for you?").

The solution is customer portfolio management—putting one person or team in charge of making a customer or group of customers more valuable to the firm and then giving the customer manager exclusive access and final authority to each customer as well as ultimate responsibility for the value of the customer. (You'll read more about this in Chapter 13.)

Who "Owns" the Customer Relationship?

In a typical company, Product Manager A wants the Web site to send an offer for his product to every new site visitor. But Product Manager B wants to send an offer for her product. No one can document the correct processes, because no one agrees on them. Thus, the increasing use of business rules to drive the automation of customer interactions will accelerate the pressure on enterprises to shift from product management to customer management organizational structures.

If one division "owns" a certain group of customers, then it is clear who is responsible for managing the rules that apply to those individuals. The process of creating and managing rules highlights the limitations of product management structures. These organizations were logical when the toughest challenge an enterprise faced was creating and selling high-quality products. But, today, the toughest challenge is managing relationships, often in real time. If divisions are competing internally, they make decisions that aren't in the customer's interest.

Part of the problem is that large enterprises are, well, large. So business rules need to be created using a common vocabulary. Ron Ross explains: "You must be able to trace who is using what terms in what context; you need to be able to trace the impact across the business environment." While business rules can theoretically be created using everyday language, each term must be used with more precision and consistency than we use in normal conversation.

Another issue in large businesses is traceability: being able to follow the impact of certain rules across the entire business environment. "You need to know what task each rule relates to," says Ross, "and you also want to be able to trace rules to the parties that have a stake in a particular rule. When it comes time to change the rule, you must know whom to call." This is a good application for the **Customer Interaction and Experience Touchmap** described in Chapter 7.

What to Expect

The more you study the use of business rules to drive personalization, the more obvious it becomes that the approach has tremendous potential but is still in its infancy. While there are no tried-and-true best practices, it is possible to offer some conclusions about what will likely work best.

Minimize the number of enterprise-wide rules. Only about 2 to 3 percent of all business rules are "core rules" that impact the entire enterprise and specify qualities that give the firm its identity and differentiating qualities, Ross says. These rules usually existed long before the advent of automated systems. Here is an example that used to apply at Domino's Pizza: All pizzas are delivered within 30 minutes or the pizza is free. This rule drove the company and its marketing messages, but it eventually was changed after communities began to question whether the pressure on drivers to deliver so quickly was resulting in serious traffic accidents. Note that rules such as this need to include two portions: the rule itself and what happens if the rule is violated.

(continued)

Use the simplest approach possible. The more complex an approach, the more likely it is to fail. The question to ask is: What are the simplest changes that will have the most powerful positive impacts on customer relationships? One practice to consider is that all databases containing customer information have at least one field with a common, firm-wide format, enabling the firm to link individual customer data from one unit to the next when necessary. Sometimes this approach can be simpler than building a data warehouse or requiring all business units to conform to more restrictive data conventions.

Combine business rules with other approaches. Matching business rules with specialized data mining, domain-specific algorithms, and other applications will generate better results. Ontologies provide a consistent, logical model for accommodating multiple data sources and goals. Done right, they provide a flexible system for understanding and managing interactions with individual customers.

Maintain a separate rule base. A rule base is essentially a database for rules. By separating business logic from specific applications, rules can be shared by numerous applications. This approach speeds development and increases flexibility. As the number of rules grows, it becomes increasingly important to be able to test in advance what impact the addition of new rules will have. This task is easier when all the rules are stored in a common location and format.

---

[a]*Authors' note about the difference between personalization and customization:* Many companies and writers in this field use these terms interchangeably, and that's probably okay. But generally, when there is a distinction, it's usually as given in the glossary. Perhaps it's helpful to think of personalization as Pine and Gilmore's "adaptive" and "cosmetic" customization, whereas what we refer to as customization is more along the lines of "collaborative" and "transparent" customization. Think of it this way: Personalization is what happens when a company puts the customer's name at the top of a letter that is otherwise the same for everyone in the customer segment, whereas customization in the same application would mean that a company has put the customer's name at the top of the letter, and has adapted the content throughout the rest of the letter to the individual customer who received it.

Culture Rules

Mass customization makes a lot of intuitive sense, but aren't there still some situations that won't be covered by an enterprise's business rules? What happens when a customer presents some problem or need for which there is no valid, preconfigured set of solutions that can be rendered in a cost-efficient way?

An enterprise can automate the contact report a sales rep has to file, but no computer can look into a client's eye and judge whether to push for the sale or ask another question first. And no enterprise can write a business rule that requires employees to delight customers. The employees themselves have to want to do that. An enterprise's secret sauce is its *culture*—the unwritten rules and unspoken traditions that define how employees actually approach their jobs. This is what guides employees when there is no policy—no applicable business rules. Culture is what employees do when no one's looking.

> Culture is what employees do when no one's looking.

Abraham Lincoln was once asked the secret of General Ulysses S. Grant's success during a particularly difficult Civil War campaign. Always ready with an anecdote, Lincoln told the reporter it reminded him of a story about the great "automaton" chess player that had astonished Europeans nearly a century before. Popularly known as the Mechanical Turk, it had been constructed to resemble a mechanical man, dressed in a costume like a Turk, seated behind a wooden cabinet, and apparently capable of playing chess. It had defeated many human players, but after one celebrated competitor suffered two embarrassing defeats at the hands of the machine, he angrily wrenched off the cabinetry to peer inside and then rose up to exclaim, "Hey! There's a person in there!" That, said Lincoln, was the secret of Grant's success.

It is also the final, underlying secret of any business enterprise's success when it comes to satisfying customers and ensuring they continue to create value. There has to be a person in there somewhere. No matter how well the business rules are architected, and no matter how many "modules" of product or service delivery are available to drive the mass-customization effort, human judgment always will have to be accommodated in the enterprise's customer-facing processes. It's impossible to serve customers well without it, and generally the more important decisions are the ones that require the most judgment and innovation. For a customer, the most vital problem or difficult issue often involves some type of crisis situation—a situation that is likely to be unusual or at least one that hasn't already been anticipated by the enterprise. This means that almost by definition, any issue of utmost importance to a customer is likely to be something that falls through the cracks if an enterprise is operating entirely by predocumented processes and procedures. The enterprise won't be able to specify it in advance. There has to be a person in there, capable of making the right judgment call.

As a result, nowhere does an enterprise's corporate culture play a more important role than in dealing with customers, because doing this often requires conceptual-age, nonroutine skills such as empathy, creativity, and sensitivity.[30] Many companies try to

---

[30] Daniel H. Pink, *A Whole New Mind* (New York: Riverhead, 2005). See also Maxie Schmidt-Subramanian, "How to Measure Emotion in Customer Experience," Forrester Research, Inc., November 13, 2015, available at http://www.forrester.com.

cut costs by outsourcing and automating their more routine customer service tasks. Most find out the hard way that it's a big mistake to outsource judgment calls. Nor is it the best idea to hardwire all a company's policies and processes entirely into "the system," leaving no room for flexible responses to unanticipated situations.[31]

A few years ago, American Express redesigned its customer service. The company "removed call center scripts, traditional behavior-based quality monitoring metrics, and limits on average handling time. Instead of focusing on traditional productivity measures largely aimed at controlling call center costs, [the company] made it a key success measure to earn the enthusiastic recommendations of card members. The American Express team's framework substitutes guidelines for hard limits, judgment for scripts, and coaching for monitoring." Service expenses actually went down because employees "devised and shared" solutions to common problems.[32]

Not long ago a friend of ours went online to book family trips on two different airlines for successive weekends. The first trip was on a well-established carrier with a great service reputation, but it is heavily unionized and often hemmed in by its own bureaucracy. It was a complicated itinerary involving coordinating with some other people, so our friend first booked her family's outbound trip, then did some more calling to make sure the return flight was coordinated with others before booking it too. But guess what? When she booked the return flight, she realized that a round trip would cost less than either of the one-way trips just purchased. So she called the reservations office directly now, having been defeated by the online experience, and—you guessed it—"No, sorry, no can do." Basically, she was told, she had bought the tickets online and a deal was a deal, that's that. Then the agent even said something to the effect that "Yes, I know it's unfair, but I am powerless to make the change; the system just won't let me."

Fast-forward to the following weekend, and our friend was on the way to a different weekend destination with her family, this time on a new entrant carrier, one of the price competitors. You book your seat, and it's a great low price but absolutely nonrefundable. The family ran into a traffic snarl and arrived at the airport way too late for the flight. Our friend found herself thinking that this was going to be a very expensive weekend for not going anywhere at all. But when the family got to the counter, an agent said something like "Sorry you missed your flight, but why don't you just take a room at the airport hotel tonight and I'll put you all on the 7 a.m. flight tomorrow morning? Tell you what, I'm also going to waive the $50 rebooking fee, and I'll call your destination hotel, see if they can resell your rooms for tonight, maybe save you some money."

---

[31] Chris DeRose and Noel Tichy, "Here's How to Actually Empower Customer Service Employees," *Harvard Business Review*, July 1, 2013, available at https://hbr.org/2013/07/heres-how-to-actually-empower-customer/, accessed February 8, 2016; and Rob Markey, "Earn Customer Loyalty without Losing Your Shirt," *Harvard Business Review*, July 17, 2012, https://hbr.org/2012/07/earn-customer-loyalty-without, accessed February 8, 2016.
[32] Markey, "Earn Customer Loyalty without Losing Your Shirt."

Here are two different companies with two different ways to handle exceptional customer service situations. Although it's important to do a competent job using efficient processes, good service cannot spring solely from processes or rules or systems. The important process for winning customer loyalty is *customization*, which has been the subject of this chapter. We need to remember that mass customization is simply a process for customizing more cost efficiently. However, it is in the exception to the rules, the unusual and problematic situation, the **moment of truth**, that a company has to rely on individual people to make wise decisions. If an enterprise has the wrong employee culture, for whatever reason, good systems and processes actually might magnify this problem. Instead, particularly in the service sector, the enterprise wants frontline employees who are not only *empowered* to make decisions and take action (as the first airline's employee was not) but also *motivated* to make those decisions in a way that is in the long-term interest of the firm (i.e., in a way that customers feel they have been treated fairly).[33]

The payoff for enterprises that engage in customization is twofold. In most cases, by employing automation and business rules to mass-customize its products or the delivery of its services, the enterprise actually can reduce its unit production costs, on an all-in basis, essentially because it will only make those goods that customers will have already bought. More important, however, customization will enable the enterprise to engage in a *collaborative* Learning Relationship with each customer.

Summary

Instead of expecting a customer to use what *she* knows about a company to figure out what she should buy, the customer-focused enterprise uses what *it* knows about the customer to figure out what she genuinely needs. In the process, such an enterprise increases the number of transactions it gets from a customer, makes it progressively easier for that customer to come back to that enterprise for purchases and service, and likely increases the profit per transaction.

Our story of managing customer experiences and relationships in the interactive era now takes a turning point. We have laid the foundation of relationship theory and provided a comprehensive examination of each of the four tasks of the IDIC methodology: Identify-Differentiate-Interact-Customize. We have shown the importance of Learning Relationships and the sensitive issues related to privacy protection. We have peeked at the technical tools that help to accelerate the relationship management process and reinforced how technology does not, and should not, manage customer relationships alone.

---

[33] Excerpted and adapted from Don Peppers and Martha Rogers, Ph.D., *Rules to Break and Laws to Follow: How Your Business Can Beat the Crisis of Short-Termism* (Hoboken, NJ: John Wiley & Sons, 2008), pp. 113–115.

With Part III (beginning with Chapter 11), we begin to look at what it means to manage the customer relationship process. We discuss the challenges an enterprise faces in measuring and maintaining a customer-based initiative and look at the quantifiable metrics associated with managing customer experiences and Return on Customer. We delve into the science of customer analytics as a method to predict each customer's behavior and anticipate his needs so he will be treated the way he wants and remain a customer. Finally, we show how transforming into an enterprise that grows through building customer value requires a number of different infrastructure changes that will need to be addressed by managers who fully understand and support the underlying concepts we have been discussing so far—and so much more that we have yet to discuss.

Food for Thought

1. How will Lego practice mass customization? To think about mass customization for Legos, consider:
   - Who are the customer types for Lego? (Think retailers, B2B.) Who are the MVCs? The **most growable customers (MGCs)? The below zeros (BZs)?** (See Chapter 5.)
   - What are customers buying when they buy Legos? (It's not "toy building bricks.")
   - If customers buy packages of Legos to resell, what else do they need? What is their expanded need set?
   - What is the opportunity to lock customers into a Learning Relationship and build share of customer for Lego?
   - Is there any opportunity, ever, at all, for Lego to build Learning Relationships with any end user? How and why?
2. If customization is such a good idea, why don't we see more of it in the marketplace right this minute?
3. Name half a dozen examples of mass customization or expanded needs sets in the enterprises where you do business.
4. Imagine the 3-D photography tied to 3-D color printing that allows the creation of individualized tabletop sculptures of customers themselves, their children, and their pets. Although the product has immediate commercial promise, the real question is how a company as well as a customer could benefit from having this data stored about individuals. What are some ancillary applications?

Glossary

3-D printing   Through the use of a printer and precise computer programming, the ability to "print" 3-D figures made of plastic or food or other substances.

Adaptive customization   Offering a standard but customizable product that is designed so that customers can alter it themselves.

Below zero (BZ)   The below-zero customer will, no matter what strategy or effort is applied toward him, always cost the company and its best customers more than he contributes.

Benefits   Advantages that customers get from using the product. Not to be confused with needs, as different customers will get different advantages from the same product.

Business model   How a company builds economic value.

Business rules   The instructions that an enterprise follows in configuring different processes for different customers, allowing the company to mass-customize its interactions with its customers.

Collaborative customization   Conducting a dialogue with individual customers to help them articulate their needs, identifying the offering that fulfills those needs, and then making customized products for them.

Commoditization   The steady erosion in unique selling propositions and unduplicated product features that comes about inevitably, as competitors seek to improve their offerings and end up imitating the more successful features and benefits.

Cosmetic customization   Presenting a standard product differently to different customers.

Crowd service   Customers helping other customers solve problems online.

Customer centricity   A "specific approach to doing business that focuses on the customer. Customer/client-centric businesses ensure that the customer is at the center of a business philosophy, operations, or ideas. These businesses believe that their customers/clients are the only reason they exist and use every means at their disposal to keep the customer/client happy and satisfied."[34] At the core of customer centricity is the understanding that customer profitability is at least as important as product profitability.

Customer Interaction and Experience Touchmap   A graphical depiction of the interactions a company has with each segment of its customers across each of the available channels. Its purpose is to take an outside-in view of the customer interactions, instead of the traditional inside-out view typically taken in business process reengineering work. Current State Touchmaps depict all the enterprise's current interactions with customers and identify gap areas; Future State Touchmaps depict the desired customer interactions that will be customized based on the needs and values of individual customers.

Customer relationship management (CRM)   As a term, *CRM* can refer either to the activities and processes a company must engage in to manage individual relationships with its customers (as explored extensively in this textbook), or to the suite of software, data, and analytics tools required to carry out those activities and processes more cost efficiently.

---

[34] "Client Centric," Investopedia, available at http://www.investopedia.com/terms/c/client-centric.asp, accessed February 15, 2016.

Customer sacrifice   *See* Satisfaction gap.

Customer-strategy enterprise   An organization that builds its business model around increasing the value of the customer base. This term applies to companies that may be product oriented, operations focused, or customer intimate.

Customization   Most often, customization and mass customization refer to the modularized building of an offering to a customer based on that customer's individual feedback, thus serving as the basis of a Learning Relationship. Note the distinction from *personalization,* which generally simply means putting someone's name on the product.

Customize   Become relevant by doing something for a customer that no competition can do that doesn't have all the information about that customer that you do.

Demand chain   As contrasted with the supply chain, "demand chain" refers to the chain of demand from customers, through retailers, distributors, and other intermediaries, all the way back to the manufacturer.

Demand chain management   According to Pankaj M. Madhani, demand chain management reduces or if possible eliminates "buffers of inventory in the supply chain and at the same time deliver what the customer demands." It's distinct from supply chain management in that it includes the view of the customer as an integral part of the chain, and focuses "on real-time flow of demand-related information from . . . end-users to . . . suppliers." Its goal is "to coordinate the demand creation and the demand fulfillment processes to gain competitive advantage by differentiating not only the products but also the delivery process, as well as to exploit synergies between marketing and SCM."[35]

Expanded need set   The capability of a company to think of a product it sells as a suite of product plus service plus communication as well as the next product and service the need for the original product implies. The sale of a faucet implies the need for the installation of that faucet, and maybe an entire bathroom upgrade and strong nesting instinct.

Internet of Things (IoT)   A term describing the network of products and other objects that have intelligence or computational capability built into them, along with interconnectedness to the Web, via Wi-Fi or other technology. As defined by the ITU, a UN agency, the IoT is "a global infrastructure for the information society, enabling advanced services by interconnecting (physical and virtual) things based on existing and evolving interoperable information and communication technologies."[36]

---

[35] Pankaj M. Madhani, "Demand Chain Management: Enhancing Customer Value Proposition," *European Business Review*, March 10, 2013, available at http://www.europeanbusinessreview .com/?p=1945, accessed April 22, 2016.

[36] Available at http://www.itu.int/en/ITU-T/gsi/iot/Pages/default.aspx, accessed April 6, 2016.

Market segment   A group of customers who share a common attribute. Product benefits are targeted to the market segments thought most likely to desire the benefit.

Mass customization   *See* Customization.

Modularization   Configuring a product's components to put them together in a standardized way, in order to facilitate the process of mass customization and reduce company costs.

Moment of truth   Interactions with a customer that have a disproportionate impact on the customer's emotional connection, and are therefore more likely to drive significant behaviors.

Most growable customers (MGCs)   Customers with high unrealized potential values. These are the customers who have the most growth potential: growth that can be realized through cross-selling, through keeping customers for a longer period, or perhaps by changing their behavior and getting them to operate in a way that costs the enterprise less money.

Most valuable customers (MVCs)   Customers with high actual values but not a lot of unrealized growth potential. These are the customers who do the most business, yield the highest margins, are most willing to collaborate, and tend to be the most loyal.

Needs   What a customer needs from an enterprise is, by our definition, synonymous with what she wants, prefers, or would like. In this sense, we do not distinguish a customer's needs from her wants. For that matter, we do not distinguish needs from preferences, wishes, desires, or whims. Each of these terms might imply some nuance of need—perhaps the intensity of the need or the permanence of it—but in each case we are still talking, generically, about the customer's needs.

Personalization   Refers to a superficial ability to put a customer's name on something—to insert a name into a message, for example, or to monogram a set of sheets. Note the distinction from *customization,* which means creating an adapted product or service or communication based on the customer's individual feedback.

Satisfaction gap   The difference between what customers want and what they're willing to settle for.

Share of customer (SOC)   For a customer-focused enterprise, share of customer is a conceptual metric designed to show what proportion of a customer's overall need is being met by the enterprise. It is not the same as "share of wallet," which refers to the specific share of a customer's spending in a particular product or service category. If, for instance, a family owns two cars, and one of them is your car company's brand, then you have a 50 percent share of wallet with this customer, in the car category. But by offering maintenance and repairs, insurance, financing, and perhaps even driver training or trip planning, you can substantially increase your "share of customer."

Supply chain   A company's back-end production or service-delivery operations.

Supply chain management   "The management of the flow of goods and services. It includes the movement and storage of raw materials, work-in-process inventory, and finished goods from point of origin to point of consumption." [Wikipedia]

Transparent customization   Providing each customer with a customized product or service without necessarily telling him about the customization itself.

Value stream   A compilation of related products and services a company could offer to an existing customer in order to get a greater share of customer from each customer already acquired.

PART III

Measuring and Managing to Build Customer Value

Customer relationships cannot be installed; they must be adopted. And building customer value requires process, organization, technology, and culture management. It's a shift in strategy after 100 years dominated by mass marketing. The management of customer experiences as a way to get a greater share of each customer's business and to build the value of the customer base is a journey, not a destination.

CHAPTER 11

Optimizing around the Customer: Measuring the Success of Customer-Based Initiatives and the Customer-Centric Organization

We've long felt that the only value of stock forecasters is to make fortune tellers look good. Even now, Charlie [Munger] and I continue to believe that short-term market forecasts are poison and should be kept locked up in a safe place, away from children and also from grown-ups who behave in the market like children.

—Warren Buffett

Traditional marketing measures such as response rates, cost per thousand (CPM), gross ratings points (GRP), and awareness levels help a company understand how successful a campaign has been or how successful or efficient a particular message is, on average, in reaching a target market. But when using interactive technologies and dealing with customers one at a time, the key task most marketers face is how to optimize the enterprise's behavior around individual customers rather than products. Optimizing the enterprise around a customer is the problem confronted whenever a firm is trying to decide how to design a Web site, how to define objectives and scripts for a contact center, or how to frame the selling strategy for a face-to-face meeting with a customer. The question being asked in these situations isn't, "What's the best overall message for this particular product, when talking to everyone?" but "What's the best message for this particular customer, during this particular interaction?" As we learned in the chapters on Identify-Differentiate-Interact-Customize (Chapters 3–10), the customer-centric competitor hopes that by optimizing the enterprise's behavior around a particular customer during a particular interaction or event, the firm will be able to maximize the value created by that customer, including not just the short-term, current-period value created by immediate product sales or costs generated, but also the long-term value created by changes in the customer's predisposition toward the brand.

Customers create long-term value because they have memories.[1] Each customer's decision whether to buy from a business today will be based at least partly on his memory of any past experience he's had with the firm, or perhaps on his impressions of it based on his friend's past experience. The important thing is that every time a customer has an experience with any business, his intention or likelihood of buying from that business in the future is liable to change. Nice experience? Likely to buy more later. Might even talk about the brand with a friend or online. Bad experience? Likely not to buy much in the future. Also might criticize the brand to a friend or to a bunch of people online.

Although this is not a textbook on accounting or economics, nevertheless it's important to remember that the actual economic value of any business enterprise can be measured in terms of the discounted net present value of the future stream of cash flow that the enterprise is expected to generate. So when a customer's likelihood of buying in the future changes, or when her likelihood of sharing her experience with a friend changes, the company's likely future cash flow also changes—which means that the company's actual economic value goes up or down as a result of the customer's changing frame of mind. This is the long-term component of the value that customers create.

For the overwhelming majority of companies, this kind of value creation (or, sometimes, value destruction) is not captured in the financial statements. Note, however, that the customer experience driving an increase or decrease in the enterprise's value occurs in the present. Although the firm may not realize the cash effect for days or weeks or months, the value itself is created or destroyed today, with the customer's current experience. Moreover, this is happening whether marketers at the enterprise think about it or not and whether they try to measure it or not. Even though the financial systems of most firms don't recognize the long-term value constantly being created or destroyed by the individual current experiences of their customers, the financial metric that we introduced in Chapter 5, customer **lifetime value (LTV)**, is specifically designed to capture it. To reprise the concept, a customer's LTV is defined as the net present value of the future stream of cash flow attributable to that customer. It therefore directly represents the long-term financial benefit of a customer's continuing patronage. When the customer becomes more predisposed to buy from the enterprise, her LTV will increase. When the customer

---

[1] This chapter is based in large part on Peppers and Rogers's books *Rules to Break and Laws to Follow: How Your Business Can Beat the Crisis of Short-Termism* (Hoboken, NJ: John Wiley & Sons, 2008) and *Return on Customer: Creating Maximum Value from Your Scarcest Resource* (New York: Currency/Doubleday, 2005), updated for 2016.

becomes less enamored with the enterprise's brand, her LTV will decrease. As a result, the increases and decreases in a customer's LTV can be thought of as the direct, dollars-and-cents quantifications of the long-term value created or destroyed in particular customer interactions.[2]

However, there is a certain tension between encouraging customers to create value in the short term (through immediate sales) and encouraging them to create value in the long term (through changes in the customer's predisposition). Focusing on either task can undermine the other. If a firm markets too aggressively in order to build up current sales, it will almost certainly damage a customer's long-term value—maybe by cannibalizing sales it would have made in the future anyway, or perhaps by irritating the customer into not wanting to receive further communications or not even wanting to do more business. But by the same token, if a company smothers a customer in great service in order to maximize the future business he does with the firm—well, great service isn't free either, and the funds required today to provide this service reduce whatever short-term value the customer might create. Therefore, companies have to strike a balance, because they need to create both short- and long-term value.

Unfortunately, for most businesses, the temptation to maximize the short term is nearly irresistible. Publicly held companies may have the excuse of investor pressures, but even nonpublic companies will succumb to the short-term temptation if they allow themselves to forget about the way customers really create value. An endemic problem among businesses is the fact that the traditional measures of financial success drive short-term thinking and actions, and these measures just do not account for all the ways customers actually can create shareholder value. Reconciling the conflict between current profit and long-term value is one of the most serious difficulties facing business today. Failing to take a properly balanced approach not only penalizes good management practices but also undermines corporate ethics by encouraging managers to "steal" from the future to fund the present. Often companies end up destroying value unintentionally—or worse, they know they are destroying value but feel they have no real choice about it. At the extreme, a firm might even resort to overpromising or tricking customers out of their

---

[2] V. Kumar has been one of the leaders in the work on measuring the profitability of customers and calculating lifetime value. See V. Kumar, *Profitable Customer Engagement: Concept, Metrics, and Strategies* (New Delhi: Sage, 2013) for chapters on Customer Lifetime Value, Customer Referral Value, Customer Influence Value, Customer Knowledge Value, and how to integrate all of them. Also see V. Kumar and Werner Reinartz, "Customer Analytics Part I" and "Customer Analytics Part II" in *Customer Relationship Management: Concept, Strategy, and Tools*, 89–141 (Heidelberg: Springer, 2012); and Morten Holm, V. Kumar, and Carsten Rohde, "Measuring Customer Profitability in Complex Environments: An Interdisciplinary Contingency Framework," *Journal of the Academy of Marketing Science* 40, no. 3 (May 2012): 387–401. Finally, see V. Kumar and Anita Pansari, "Aggregate and Individual Level Customer Lifetime Value," in *Handbook of Research on Customer Equity in Marketing,* eds. V. Kumar and Denish Shah, 44–75 (Cheltenham, UK: Elgar, 2015).

money, in order to maximize short-term profit. Of course, doing this almost certainly hampers future sales and destroys long-term value by eroding the trust that customers have in the firm.

Balancing between such extremes in order to maximize overall value creation is not a new or revolutionary idea. As early as 1996, in an innovative and forward-thinking *Harvard Business Review* article, Bob Blattberg and John Deighton suggested that a firm should apply "the **customer equity** test" to balance marketing expenditures between customer acquisition and customer retention efforts. They even proposed a mathematical model for fitting exponential curves to find the optimum levels of acquisition and retention spending, based on executives' answers to some level-setting questions.[3] And the very concept of "brand equity," which was a widely used metaphor during the heyday of mass advertising, was based on the idea that a brand's value could be built up over time, with appropriate messaging, and that this store of value could become a genuine asset for driving competitive success.[4]

A 2003 white paper from Peter Mathias and Noel Capon of Columbia Business School considers the implications of managing customers for three "quite different outcomes: maximizing revenue in the near term, maximizing profitability in the short to intermediate term, and optimizing the asset value of customer relationships—customer relationship capital—over the long term."[5] The paper suggests that salespeople traditionally have been held accountable for short-term revenues, but as more organizations have come to emphasize key account management over the last decade, the metric of success has shifted perceptibly from customer revenue to customer profitability. To be successful in the future, say the authors, a firm will have to "take the long view" and "maximize the net present value **(NPV)** of future profit streams from these customers."

Of course, even when executives understand the value of long-term planning, many say pressure from boards and shareholders forces them to act for short-term gains. According to a 2013 McKinsey survey of executives:

- "63% of respondents said the pressure to generate strong short-term results had increased over the previous five years.
- 79% felt especially pressured to demonstrate strong financial performance over a period of just two years or less.
- 44% said they use a time horizon of less than three years in setting strategy.

---

[3] Robert C. Blattberg and John Deighton, "Manage Marketing by the Customer Equity Test," *Harvard Business Review* 74, no. 4 (July–August 1996): 136–144.

[4] Roland T. Rust, Valarie A. Zeithaml, and Katherine N. Lemon, *Driving Customer Equity: How Customer Lifetime Value Is Reshaping Corporate Strategy* (New York: Free Press, 2000).

[5] Peter F. Mathias and Noel Capon, "Managing Strategic Customer Relationships as Assets: Developing Customer Relationship Capital," *Velocity,* Strategic Account Management Association 5 (Q1, 2003): 45–49.

- 73% said they *should* use a time horizon of more than three years.
- 86% declared that using a longer time horizon to make business decisions would positively affect corporate performance in a number of ways, including strengthening financial returns and increasing innovation."[6]

And let's say executives get the go-ahead from their board—there's still the question of how to measure intangible assets like customer equity over the long term.[7] Charles Tilley notes, "Eighty percent of the market value of companies now lies in intangible assets. Yet many accounting practices and processes do not reflect this shift."[8] So, much of what passes for long-term strategic planning ends up focusing on metrics like cost assessment rather than revenue flow, because they're a lot easier to predict and manipulate. Companies can't control customers, but they can control costs! But as Roger L. Martin points out, although focusing on ways to influence customers can seem risky and unpredictable, it's crucial, because "over the longer term, all revenue is controlled by the customer."[9]

Determining the appropriate measurements to be used in quantifying the results of a company's marketing efforts has always been a particularly elusive task, and to many it seems to have been made doubly difficult by the complexity of customer-specific marketing initiatives that new interactive technologies make possible. The very culture at many firms is intertwined with more traditional measures of success—or what we might call *legacy metrics*: quarterly product sales; cost of goods sold; number of new customers acquired; earnings before interest, taxes, depreciation, and amortization (EBITDA); return on investment (ROI); return on equity (ROE)—the tried and true. It shouldn't be surprising that companies often find it challenging to supplement such legacy metrics with updated measurements designed around capturing the values that individual customers create, one customer at a time.

It is precisely because customers create both long- and short-term value that the customer-centric competitor will be well served to think of individual customers as being similar to financial assets—assets that are generating some cash flow now and are likely to continue generating cash flow for some time into the future. Each customer, in other words, represents a bundle of likely future cash flows—costs and revenues tied to that particular customer's most likely future behavior.

---

[6] Dominic Barton and Mark Wiseman, "Focusing Capital on the Long Term," *Harvard Business Review* 92, no. 1/2 (January/February 2014): 44–51.

[7] Thorsten Wiesel and Bernd Skiera, "Customer Equity Reporting," in *Handbook of Research on Customer Equity Marketing*, eds. V. Kumar and Denish Shah (Cheltenham, UK: Elgar, 2015): 466–482.

[8] Charles Tilley, "Reporting for the 21st Century," in *Perspectives on the Long Term*, eds. Dominic Barton and Mark Wiseman, pp. 84–89.

[9] Roger L. Martin, "The Big Lie of Strategic Planning," *Harvard Business Review*, January–February 2014, available at https://hbr.org/2014/01/the-big-lie-of-strategic-planning, accessed June 21, 2016.

The asset value of a customer is the customer's LTV. Consumer marketing firms with databases of transactional and other customer records can use statistical modeling techniques to forecast their customers' future behaviors and then calculate the LTVs represented by those behaviors. This is not an exact science, however, and no matter how sophisticated the computer modeling becomes, it will never be completely accurate, for the simple reason that predicting the future never can be completely accurate. (Of course, the accepted calculations of the "tried and true" have limitations in accuracy too. See Chapter 5.) However, many would argue that using predictive models to forecast future customer behavior is not substantively different from, and not inherently any less accurate than, using similar statistical models to forecast future economic variables, such as the supply and market demand for a particular product or service. In any case, the basic principle that a customer's asset value should be thought of in terms of the future cash flows he represents is very useful, especially when we consider how this asset value goes up and down on a daily basis with the customer's current experience.

The problem is that while LTV is a known and accepted concept in marketing circles, few marketers and even fewer finance people fully appreciate its real implications. Customers have memories and free will, so (unless we're talking about the utilities monopoly) the treatment they receive from an enterprise today has a significant impact on the value they can be expected to yield for that enterprise not only today but also in the future. If a customer can be thought of as a financial asset, then changes in the value of this asset—changes in the customer's LTV—are important. When a customer's opinion of a firm improves or deteriorates, based on her experience with the firm today, her LTV goes up or down, and the amount of this increase or decrease in LTV is real economic value that has been created or destroyed as a result of the customer's experience in the present. In this light, changes in the LTV of a customer are every bit as important, financially, as the current-period sales or costs attributable to that customer and captured on financial statements.

Consider this analogy: Suppose a business has some physical asset, perhaps a warehouse full of spare parts. Then suddenly the asset is rendered worthless by a disaster. Suppose a hurricane wipes out the warehouse, and the firm isn't insured for the loss. If that were to happen, generally accepted accounting principles (GAAP) would require the firm to write down the value of that asset, and this quarter's income would be reduced by the amount of the write-down. Now think again about the customer's asset value. Suppose, instead of a hurricane wiping out a warehouse full of spare parts, there is instead some kind of **customer service** snafu, with the result that a very valuable customer becomes angry and upset with the firm. Because of this, his LTV plummets to zero (or even below zero, because he might communicate his bad feelings about the firm to his friends!). Didn't the company's value decrease when that happened? Surely, its future cash flow will decline if that customer's opinion is not turned around again, right? Of course, the accounting treatment for this kind of "customer" event is quite different from that prescribed for the destruction of a physical asset carried on the balance sheet—but for now, we won't focus on the accounting issues but on the simple reality of the economic loss to a company represented by an unresolved customer complaint.

The fact that a customer's asset value (or LTV) will increase or decrease with his current experience, because he'll remember that experience later, means that a customer-centric enterprise has to account for the value it is creating from customers in a different way from the way a product-centric enterprise accounts for the value created by its products. Products don't have memories, while customers do. Note that how a company treats parts and supplies today will not affect the future cost of these supplies, or the profit to be earned from the products created with them. But how a company treats customers today will definitely affect the future profits likely to be generated by those customers.

Today's accounting courses don't often acknowledge customers as significant financial assets. But in the nonaccounting real world, customers are the only genuine value-creating assets any business has. As we said in Chapter 1, the only reason a business exists at all is to create and serve customers. Customers create, on the most basic level, virtually 100 percent of any enterprise's value. Customers define a business as a business. And it ought to be clear to the most casual observer that a customer's experience with a company, its products, or its brands has an economic impact that goes beyond the current financial period. Any company that spends advertising money to improve its brand image is explicitly acknowledging this fact. Such a firm is investing money based on the assumption that customer intentions have a financial value. If it can affect those future intentions today, then it hopes to see the cash effect tomorrow.

When it comes to understanding how Learning Relationships based on trust create financial value for a business, there are basically two approaches to the issue: a simple, philosophical approach and a quantitative, analytical approach. Both start with customers, for one simple reason: By definition, all the revenue you will ever generate will come from the customers you have now and the ones you will have in the future. (*Take note:* Brands, products, patents, logos, sales regions, and marketing campaigns do not pay money to a firm; only customers do.) The simple approach is to state your company's value proposition as a straightforward quid pro quo:

1. You want each customer to create the most possible value for your business.
2. On the whole, a customer is likely to create the most value *for* you at about the point he gets the most value *from* you.
3. The customer gets the most value from you when he can *trust* you to act in his own interest.

Some companies—especially those that have grown up in the interactive age—have so internalized this view of the customer as a value-producing financial asset that it affects their whole philosophy of business. Amazon's Jeff Bezos says his firm would rather spend on free shipping, lower prices, and service enhancements than on advertising. "If you do build a great experience, customers will tell each other about that," he says.

In fact, Bezos clarifies that "if you're long-term oriented, customer interests and shareholder interests are aligned. In the short term, that's not always correct." In fact, he says he cares about shareholders and that's why he cares about Amazon's long-term share price.

He has pointed out that a long list of initiatives such as Kindle, Amazon Web Services, and Amazon Prime—all of which have paid off in the long run but ran as a loss in the short term—would never have been started if the financial results at Amazon had always had only a two- or three-year horizon.[10]

Customer Equity

Products, brands, stores, bank branches, patents, information technology systems, marketing promotions and campaigns—even the best employees—do not pay money to any organization. Only customers—by definition—generate revenue. And if customers are the only genuine source of value creation for a business, then all the customers an enterprise has must be responsible for creating 100 percent of that enterprise's shareholder value. This is the basic idea behind the concept of *customer equity.* If we sum all the LTVs of an enterprise's current and future customers, then we have calculated the actual economic value of that enterprise as a going concern.[11] Thus, if all of a company's cash flows come from its customers, then the sum of all current and future customers' LTVs is the same thing as the economic value of

---

[10] "Jeff Bezos on Leading for the Long-Term at Amazon," HBR IdeaCast, ed. and interviewer Adi Ignatius, *Harvard Business Review,* January 3, 2013, available at https://hbr.org/2013/01/jeff-bezos-on-leading-for-the.html, accessed February 12, 2016.

In the interview, Bezos said: "I do not follow the stock on a daily basis, and I don't think there's any information in it. Benjamin Graham said, 'In the short term, the stock market is a voting machine. In the long term, it's a weighing machine.' And we try to build a company that wants to be weighed and not voted upon. . . .When things get complicated, we simplify by saying what's best for the customer? And then we take it as an article of faith if we do that, it'll work out in the long term. So we can never prove that. In fact, sometimes we've done price elasticity studies, and the answer is always we should raise prices. And we don't do that because we believe—and again, we have to take this as an article of faith—we believe by keeping our prices very, very low, we earn trust with customers over time, and that that actually does maximize free cash flow over the long term."

[11] However, the way in which a firm adds lifetime values together to get the customer equity of a group of customers will depend on the actual LTV calculation being used. If a firm uses a "fully allocated" cash flow figure, incorporating all fixed and variable operating costs, then LTVs can simply be arithmetically summed to get customer equity. Often, however, it can be more useful to use marginal contribution when calculating LTV, in which case unallocated costs would have to be added back in to customer equity, as individual LTVs are rolled up into larger and larger groups of customers. This may sound like a complex accounting problem, but the truth is it's just ensuring that costs and revenues are neither omitted nor double-counted when summing customer LTVs to derive customer equity.

the firm (i.e., the **NPV** of the firm's future cash flows). Take away a profit-generating customer, and the value of a firm declines. Improve the cash flow expected from a customer, and the firm's value increases.

> One of the hazards of short-term thinking is that even a firm with current high profitability may find that it is not "banking" enough customer equity to sustain its future financial success.

The term *customer equity* can describe the effectiveness of customer strategies and implementation because it is primarily determined by the total value of the enterprise's customer relationships. For a customer-centric competitor, a company's customer equity can be thought of as the principal corporate asset being tended. One of the hazards of short-term thinking (i.e., of marketing efforts designed to produce current-period sales without much attention being paid to customer LTV) is that even a firm with current high profitability may find that it is not "banking" enough customer equity to sustain its future financial success.

Not long ago Dell got into financial trouble, as its earnings failed to keep up with expectations. For years, thanks to its groundbreaking direct-to-consumer **business model**, the company had been the only major personal computer manufacturer making any money, with profit margins a full 10 points higher than most of its rivals. But according to *BusinessWeek,* "Rather than use that cushion to develop fresh capabilities, Dell gave its admirers on Wall Street and the media what they want: the highest possible [short-term] earnings."[12] The result was that Dell failed to maintain its profitability and in 2007, the original chief executive officer (CEO), Michael Dell, had to be brought back to take over again and try to restore the company to its former luster. Then, within just a few months, the company announced it would have to restate four years of earnings results because "unidentified senior executives and other employees manipulated company accounts to hit quarterly performance goals."[13] The company bought back its own stock and went private again in order to have the luxury to focus on customers and innovation for the long term.[14]

Some companies—such as JC Penney—have tried to improve their stock value by trying on new, short-term strategies but didn't first test what customers wanted—with disastrous results.[15]

---

[12] Nanette Byrnes and Peter Burrows, "Where Dell Went Wrong: In a Too-Common Mistake, It Clung Narrowly to Its Founding Strategy Instead of Developing Future Sources of Growth," *BusinessWeek,* February 19, 2007, pp. 62–63.

[13] Byrnes and Burrows, "Where Dell Went Wrong."

[14] Michael Dell, "Going Private Is Paying Off for Dell," *Wall Street Journal,* November 24, 2014, available at http://www.wsj.com/articles/michael-dell-going-private-is-paying-off-for-dell-1416872851, accessed February 11, 2016.

[15] Jim Aisner, "What Went Wrong for JC Penney?" *Harvard Business School Working Knowledge,* August 21, 2013 http://hbswk.hbs.edu/item/what-went-wrong-at-j-c-penney, accessed February 11, 2016; Joann S. Lublin and Dana Mattioli, "Penney CEO Out, Old Boss Back In," *Wall Street Journal,* April 8, 2013, available at http://www.wsj.com/articles/SB10001424127887324504704 578411031708241800, accessed February 11, 2016; Associated Press, "Penney's Stock Plummets after Another Bad Quarter," *Observer-Reporter,* November 13, 2013, available at http://www

Comcast, whose notorious customer service resulted in a recent ACSI rating as second-lowest-ranking company for customer service, began to make noises in 2014 of a merger with Time Warner, which had ACSI's lowest ranking. The merger was later abandoned. Customers gave their lowest marks for major customer service touch points: call centers and Web sites. Customers often feel they have no options even though they are terribly unhappy.

In one example of poor customer service that went viral, customer Ryan Block started recording a call with Comcast after his wife handed him the phone following her request that the service be disconnected, very upset by the call center rep repeating questions she had already answered. It's clear from the recording that the rep would only stop badgering Mr. and Mrs. Block when he got the answer "Okay, we won't disconnect the service." Comcast apologized, but the recording had "struck a chord with hundreds of thousands of listeners; many commented saying they're hoping Google Fiber enters the market in more cities so consumers have better Internet options."[16]

One analyst wrote, "Comcast has done well for shareholders. Over the past five years, shares rose from roughly $16 to $53. However, knowing that a significant portion of their earnings may depend on providing poor customer service in order to prevent customers from buying their own equipment bothers me." He said *he would not recommend the stock* [italics ours], since customers are unhappy enough to be looking for alternatives, leaving Comcast vulnerable to any competition that emerges.[17]

.observer-reporter.com/apps/pbcs.dll/article?AID=/20121113/NEWS08/121119748, accessed February 11, 2016; Chris Crum, "Will J.C. Penney's Social Media Strategy Help It Win Back Customers?" *WebPro News,* May 5, 2013, available at http://www.webpronews.com/heres-jc-penneys-apology-video-asking-customers-to-come-back-2013--05/, accessed February 11, 2016; Maria Halkias, "Ullman Steps Down, Again, as Penney CEO," *Dallas News,* July 31, 2015, available at http://www.dallasnews.com/business/retail/20150731-parting-gifts.ece, accessed February 11, 2016; and "J.C. Penney Co. Inc.," MarketWatch, http://www.marketwatch.com/investing/stock/jcp, May 2015 and January 7, 2016.

[16] ASCI, "Telecommunications and Information 2014," Press release, May 20, 2014, available at https://www.theacsi.org/news-and-resources/press-releases/press-2014/press-release-telecommunications-and-information-2014, accessed February 11, 2016; "Statement from FCC Chairman Tom Wheeler on the Comcast-Time Warner Cable Merger," Press release, FCC, April 24, 2015, available at https://apps.fcc.gov/edocs_public/attachmatch/DOC-333175A1.pdf, accessed February 11, 2016; and Elise Hu, "Comcast Embarrassed by the Service Call Making Internet Rounds," NPR, July 15, 2014, http://www.npr.org/sections/alltechconsidered/2014/07/15/331681041/comcast-embarrassed-by-the-service-call-making-internet-rounds, accessed February 11, 2016.

[17] Ken Kam, "Comcast: Can Bad Customer Service Be Good Business?" *Forbes,* February 3, 2015, http://www.forbes.com/sites/kenkam/2015/02/03/comcast-can-bad-customer-service-be-good-business/, accessed February 11, 2016.

Short-term gain, long-term loss.

Dell certainly wasn't the first business to suffer because it tried to maximize quarterly earnings and profit, and Comcast won't be the last. U.S. automakers succumbed to a similar problem when they failed to plan for how newly available Japanese imports might alter consumers' tastes in cars. Consumer electronics manufacturers in the United States made the same mistake with respect to their Pacific Rim competitors. Retailers that ignored the significance of Wal-Mart's new business model have yet to catch up. Most semiconductor manufacturers failed to embrace very large-scale integration (VLSI) chip technology when it replaced transistors, and their business was taken over by new entrants like Intel and Hitachi. In industry after industry, companies focused exclusively on current sales and profit falter primarily because they are focused exclusively on current sales and profit.

> In industry after industry, companies focused exclusively on current sales and profit falter primarily *because* they are focused exclusively on current sales and profit.

Many executives recognize that their company's obsession with short-term results is fundamentally destructive but feel powerless to do anything about it. Others feel equally strongly that if they just focus relentlessly on immediate sales and profit, then the long term will be okay. But this is a false assumption, because the investment community's obsession with short-term performance is irrational and destructive. Just before the recession of 2008, William Donaldson, former chairman of the Securities and Exchange Commission (SEC), commented, "With all the attention paid to quarterly performance, managers are taking their eyes off of long-term strategic goals."[18] And we don't have to look any further than the financial meltdown and Great Recession of 2008–2009 to see the consequences of rampant, unchecked short-termism.

And yet, since then, SEC Commissioner Daniel M. Gallagher has bemoaned the same issue, blaming the demands of individual and institutional investors.[19] But not all investors think short-termism is a good investment; Larry Fink, chairman and CEO of BlackRock, the world's largest money manager, believes corporate leaders have a greater duty to "the company and its long-term owners" than to "every investor or trader who owns their companies' shares at any moment in time," and promises support to companies whose corporate leaders follow this model.[20]

Customer-centric firms, because they deal more carefully with the issue of customer value creation, are naturally more oriented to balancing long- and short-term goals. Indeed, the very idea of using a customer-centric program to improve, say,

---

[18] Joseph McCafferty, "The Long View," *CFO,* May 1, 2007, pp. 48–52.

[19] Daniel M. Gallagher, "Activism, Short-Termism, and the SEC: Remarks at the 21st Annual Stanford Directors' College," June 23, 2015, available at http://www.sec.gov/news/speech/activism-short-termism-and-the-sec.html, accessed February 12, 2016.

[20] Larry Fink, Letter, reposted on *Business Insider,* April 14, 2015, http://www.businessinsider.com/larry-fink-letter-to-ceos-2015--4, accessed February 12, 2016.

customer satisfaction and loyalty is based entirely on generating future profits as a result of providing good service currently.

The difficulty comes in convincing the board that long-term investment in customers and customer engagement is a good idea for shareholders. The average tenure of a chief customer officer (CCO) is only about 30 months, and most CCOs who outlast that tenure report it took them three-to-five years before they could "clearly demonstrate the significant value that they had offered to the company." In the first year they typically spend a lot of time putting out customer fires, then they begin to focus on key customers and what they want out of the relationship with the company and how to address customer **needs** and balance them with requirements of the business. According to Blake Morgan, the director of the Chief Customer Officer Council, the time frame when thinking of how to measure and build customer equity is years, not quarters.[21]

An article in *Fortune* magazine[22] pointed out that many customer-centric firms concentrate on raising their "returns on specific customer segment" and that this results in a "rerating" of a company's profits/earnings ratio, as Wall Street "decides that the company can sustain [its] profit growth for years into the future."

In 2014, CVS Pharmacy announced that it would no longer sell cigarettes or tobacco products in any of its 7,600 nationwide stores. The second largest U.S. pharmacy estimated it stood to lose $2 billion annually from the loss of tobacco sales, but CEO Larry Merlo, a 58-year-old former pharmacist, said, "Cigarettes have no place in an environment where health care is being delivered. This is the right decision at the right time as we evolve from a drugstore into a health-care company." The move clearly required CVS to rethink the balance of short-term profits and long-term value of the company.[23]

Knowing that removing cigarettes does not necessarily mean people will quit smoking, CVS also launched a "uniquely personalized" smoking cessation program that involves all its stores, its 900 MinuteClinics, and its "leading administrator of drug prescription benefit coverage." CVS has also made online resources available and is partnering with the American Cancer Society and service providers in local communities.

---

[21] Blake Morgan, "What Does a Chief Customer Officer Actually Do?" *Forbes,* September 21, 2015, podcast interview with Curtis Bingham, Founder and Director, Chief Customer Officer Council, available at http://www.forbes.com/sites/blakemorgan/2015/09/21/drivingcustomer engagementpodcast/#1a81b0417629, accessed February 12, 2016.

[22] Larry Selden and Geoffrey Colvin, "Five Rules for Finding the Next Dell," *Fortune,* July 12, 2004, p. 102.

[23] Timothy W. Martin and Mike Esterl, "CVS to Stop Selling Cigarettes," *Wall Street Journal,* February 5, 2014, available at http://www.wsj.com/articles/SB1000142405270230485110457 9363520905849600, accessed February 12, 2016; and R. P. Siegel, "CVS Sets Example by Taking the High Road on Tobacco Sales," *Triple Pundit,* May 13, 2015, http://www.triplepundit .com/special/disrupting-short-termism/cvs-sets-example-by-taking-the-high-road-on-tobacco-sales/, accessed February 12, 2016.

From its launch on Sept. 3, 2014, through December 2014, CVS pharmacists counseled more than 67,000 patients filling a first prescription for a smoking cessation drug or prescription nicotine replacement therapy (NRT), and consulted with thousands more smokers seeking advice about over-the-counter NRT products. . . . Purchases of over-the-counter NRT products that assist smokers trying to quit increased by 21 percent in that timeframe compared to the previous four months. And, customers picked up 2.3 million tobacco cessation brochures at CVS/pharmacy and thousands of "Last Pack" encouragement toolkits, reaching millions of additional smokers with education, information and support.[24]

A year later, CVS Health conducted a study into the effects of its decision to stop selling tobacco after one year. In states where CVS/pharmacy has greater than 15 percent market share, there was a 1 percent decrease statewide in cigarette pack sales over the 8 months since CVS removed tobacco from its stores, amounting to 95 million fewer packs. There was a 4 percent increase in the sale of nicotine patches in the month following the removal.[25] Key to this discussion was the reaction by analysts and investors. ISI Group analyst Ross Muken wrote in a note to investors:

The ultimate economic impact on CVS/Caremark will not be known for some time but financial analysts have been supportive of the change. We believe the move will be viewed as a positive long-term decision by CVS/Caremark, despite the near-term profit drag, as it paves the way for increased credibility with both healthcare consumers and payers.

A classic customer equity success story is that of Verizon Wireless, the mobile phone company. During the four-year period from the end of 2001 through the end of 2005, this firm, which was at the time a joint venture between Verizon and Vodafone, dramatically increased its customer equity. According to publicly reported figures, the company earned $21 billion in operating income in those four years while growing its customer base from 29.4 million handsets in use to 51.3 million. This kind of acquisition story is the kind that makes headlines and was touted as a great reason to invest in Verizon. But during the same period, Verizon Wireless quietly reduced its monthly customer **churn rate** on postpaid retail (contract) customers from 2.6 percent to 1.1 percent.

---

[24] Siegel, "CVS Sets Example by Taking the High Road on Tobacco Sales"; see also CVS Web site, cessation hub: http://www.cvs.com/quit-smoking/index.html. The Web site offers support for quitters with ask a pharmacist and visit MinuteClinic options, a survey to determine level of dependence, success stories, info on nicotine replacement, tips, and more.

[25] "We Quit Tobacco, Here's What Happened Next," *CVS Health,* September 2015, http://www.cvshealth.com/research-and-insights/cvs-health-research-institute/we-quit-tobacco-heres-what-happened-next, accessed February 12, 2016.

A back-of-the-envelope calculation[26] would show that partly because of the reduced customer **turnover** rate, Verizon Wireless's customer equity grew by around $20 billion during this period. In other words, Verizon Wireless actually created nearly twice as much shareholder value as was reflected in its income statements during these four years. About half of this increase in customer equity was attributable to the new customers acquired; the other half came from the increased average LTV of all its customers due to the dramatic reduction in customer churn during the period. Consider that the reduction in turnover would have required Verizon to take steps that made it easier to stay a customer—better service, proactive reminders, hassle-free solutions to problems such as a lost phone—all capabilities that could be seen as distracting from the acquisition mission.

Significantly, Verizon Wireless relied on some highly sophisticated **predictive analytics** to anticipate and reduce customer churn. The truth is, Verizon Wireless's four-year surge in value creation was probably a one-time event for the company because the more customer churn has been reduced, the harder and costlier it becomes to reduce it further. But other wireless firms throughout the world face opportunities every bit as rich as this, and for the most part they have failed to take advantage of them. In fact, if anything, there is strong evidence that many mobile telecom companies are running in the opposite direction, chipping away at their customer equity as they compete fiercely to acquire new customers at any cost— even when it means acquiring customers with lower and lower LTVs at higher and higher acquisition costs.

In Chapter 3, we described what a trustable telecom company would look like, and asked the key question: If customers understood what a "trustable" company was like, would they be willing to pay more, and how much?

Additional research indicates health care insurance customers would be willing to pay an average of $25 more a month to do business with a company they trust.[27] A survey involving more than 2,400 respondents, all U.S. residents and customers at one of the five major U.S. mobile operators—AT&T, Sprint, T-Mobile, U.S. Cellular, or Verizon[28]—began by asking respondents how much they thought their mobile services provider could be trusted. The results found very significant differences on a variety of issues that add up to a great deal of money for a business. Most significantly, *participants said they would be willing to pay about $11 more per month, on average, for a mobile carrier consistently demonstrating a higher level of trustability.*

---

[26] Peppers and Rogers, *Rules to Break and Laws to Follow*, p. 263.

[27] For more on the value of trust in health care, see "Measuring the Value of Trust in Healthcare," www.peppersandrogersgroup.com, accessed April 2016. Peppers & Rogers Group's 2012 Customer Trust in Healthcare study examines the role trust plays in the relationship between health insurers and consumers, and how that trust connects to financial strength.

[28] Thanks to Tom Lacki for his additional insights about the research on trustability and mobile carriers.

Let's do the math: If you run a telecom company and your customers would be willing to pay you an additional $11 per month, 12 months a year, then for every 10 million customers your company has, you are face-to-face with a potential revenue increment of more than $1.3 billion. Three of the major players have about 70 million customers, so for each of them, increased customer equity due to higher levels of trustability could be worth nearly nine billion dollars. Only a fraction of this would be needed to accomplish most of the trustable actions listed in Chapter 3. The rest would drop to the company's bottom line, improving customer experiences and loyalty in the long term.[29]

So how do we decide how much you can really afford to spend *today* in order to create a better experience for the customer, to build the current and future value of your relationship with her, based on her expected future change in behavior? Trustability is a question we have to answer with two ways. The first approach to the question of how trustability creates financial value is a philosophical approach, an inevitable response to technology-driven interconnectivity and the transparency it creates. But the second is a quantitative, analytical approach, and that helps more in our strategic planning and our rewards and reporting. Here's how to think about it:

Every business executive knows that customers are financial assets.

> Each customer is like a tiny bundle of future cash flow with a memory.

And, as is the case with any other financial asset, every customer has a certain value, based on the cash flow he can be expected to produce for the business over his lifetime.

The usual term for this customer asset value is *lifetime value* (LTV). And while no one can ever know with certainty how much cash flow any particular customer will generate in the future, increasingly sophisticated analytical tools do allow businesses today to model their current customers' likely future behaviors statistically, based on what previous customers have done—that is, similar customers in similar situations. It will never be completely accurate, of course, because no matter how good the analysis is, predicting the future is impossible. But as data become richer and analytical tools become more capable, this kind of modeling has become more and more practical for a variety of businesses.

In a nutshell, two different kinds of current-period business success are on every company's menu, and it's critical to know the recipe for both:

Good current profitability, while generating more customer trust and customer equity (have your cake and eat it too); or

Good current profitability, while eroding customer trust and customer equity (use your cake up so there's nothing left).[30]

---

[29] Our understanding of the difficulties of operating a mobile carrier in a more trustable way came from an interview we did with Peppers & Rogers Group consultants responsible for this client, Ozan Bayulgen and Zeynep Manco, Peppers & Rogers Group Istanbul office, August 2011.
[30] See our discussion of these issues in Don Peppers and Martha Rogers, Ph.D., *Extreme Trust: Turning Proactive Honesty and Flawless Execution into Long-Term Profits* (New York: Portfolio/Penguin, 2016), and *Rules to Break and Laws to Follow* (John Wiley & Sons, 2008), pp. 80–84.

But when we examine it closely, building the value of customers through trustability and improved customer experiences is in fact financially attractive for a business even though in many situations it may cost money up front in the form of forgone profits or newly incurred expenses, as many business improvements do. If current-period earnings were the only criterion by which Amazon ever evaluated its financial performance, it would never do anything so "stupid" or "irrational" as refusing to make a profit from a willing (if forgetful) customer, by reminding you that you previously bought something most people only buy once. But the fact is that when Amazon warns you before you forgetfully buy something you probably don't want, the company gains something far more financially valuable than the profit they could have made off of your forgetfulness. In addition to the increased likelihood that you'll recommend Amazon to friends and colleagues, they'll be solidifying your loyalty and continued patronage (after all, you'll now want to buy all your books from Amazon so they can prevent you from accidental repeat purchases, right?).

The clue to understanding why trusted customer relationships can be financially attractive to a firm is recognizing that many of its economic benefits don't come immediately but over time, as returning customers buy more and as a company's solid reputation continues to generate more new business. Quantifying these benefits—including the value of increased customer loyalty, referrals, and additional sales—requires a robust customer analytics capability, as well as a financial perspective that fairly balances short- and long-term results.

Today's most successful firms focus on the long-term value of their customers, and the importance of maintaining their trust and confidence, despite the fact that sometimes the actual economic value can be difficult to quantify. In his portrait of one such forward-thinking firm, *Googled: The End of the World as We Know It*, Ken Auletta tells the story of how its founders approached their IPO (initial public offering):

> *Google's two 31-year-old founders were driving the company with a clarity of purpose that would be stunning if they were twice their age. Their core mantra, which was echoed again and again in their IPO letter, was that "we believe that our user focus is the foundation of our success to date. We also believe that this focus is critical for the creation of long-term value. We do not intend to compromise our user focus for short-term economic gain."*[31]

---

[31] The facts about how Google operates were found in Ken Auletta, *Googled: The End of the World as We Know It* (New York: Penguin Press, 2009), p. 111. Please note: The point we're making here is generally true, but ads are ranked according to an AdRank, which is a complex formula that also includes relevance to search keywords and other ads in the list. It's not purely based on user clicks but is primarily so. Confirmed from Google's Investor Relations page, available at http://investor.google.com/corporate/faq.html, accessed September 22, 2011. Regarding ads and how they're ranked, see http://adwords.google.com/support/aw/bin/answer.py?hl=en&answer=6111.

In *The Facebook Effect: The Inside Story of the Company That Is Connecting the World*, author David Kirkpatrick repeatedly makes reference to the fact that the company's founder is not consumed with making money in the present but with creating lasting value:

> *They all knew Zuckerberg only approved projects that fit into his long-range plan for Facebook. "Mark is very focused on the long run," says one participant in the meetings. "He doesn't want to waste resources on anything unless it contributes to the long run. . . ." While Zuckerberg had been forced by circumstances to accept advertising, he did so only so he could pay the bills. Whenever anyone asked about his priorities, he was unequivocal—growth and continued improvement in the customer experience were more important than monetization.*[32]

> It is the customer relationship that links long-term consequences with short-term actions.

To forward-thinking online companies like Google and Facebook (not to mention Amazon, Apple, Zappos, and other successes), *it is the customer relationship that links long-term consequences with short-term actions.* These companies are following a course of action that is intuitively obvious to them even if it might be difficult to quantify mathematically. Don't forget: Jeff Bezos was monomaniacally focused on Amazon.com's ultimate success even though the company lost money for 28 consecutive quarters after it was formed.[33]

What Is the Value Today of a Customer You Don't Yet Have?

If customer equity includes the value not just of current customers but also of prospective customers, then prospects must have some value to a firm. A current customer has a lifetime value, but how can a prospective customer have a LTV, even though a firm isn't doing any business with him and may in fact never do business with him?

As strange as it may sound, the fact is that an enterprise's prospect does have an LTV for the enterprise today—even if it doesn't really know whether a genuine customer relationship will ever materialize. As long as there is some probability that the prospect will become a customer, then the prospect has an expected value to the firm today.

(continued)

---

[32] The quote about Facebook came from David Kirkpatrick, *The Facebook Effect: The Inside Story of the Company That Is Connecting the World* (New York: Simon & Schuster, 2011), p. 258.

[33] Launched in 1994, Amazon.com posted its first quarterly profit on December 31, 2001. "Amazon Posts First Profit," *Communications Today* 8, no. 16 (January 24, 2002): 1.

(*Continued*)

Very simply put, the LTV of a prospective customer is equal to her LTV if she were to become a customer, multiplied by her *likelihood* of becoming a customer.

To take one highly simplified example of customer equity calculation, suppose we expect a 4 percent conversion rate from our whole prospect pool each year. If we have, say, a 20 percent market share and we lose 16 percent of current customers each year, then a 4 percent annual acquisition rate from noncustomers exactly offsets that attrition rate (20 percent × 16 percent = 80 percent × 4 percent). In other words, our hypothetical business is in a steady state, neither growing nor shrinking, but simply acquiring new customers at a rate that exactly replaces defecting ones.

Now let's suppose new customers added from our prospect pool have an average LTV of $100 when they come into the franchise (after accounting for the attrition rate once they become customers), and we'll use a discount rate of 20 percent when valuing future cash flows.

Thus, 4 percent of our prospects will come in next year, and when they do come in, each will have an LTV of $100. Using a 20 percent discount rate means that this year's discounted value of each of those LTVs that are added next year is only $80 (80 percent × $100). The following year's crop of converted prospects have a discounted LTV this year of $64 (80 percent × 80 percent × $100), and so forth. Each individual prospect's current value today is a probability-weighted calculation, based on the fact that there is a 4 percent likelihood the prospect will come into the franchise in any given year.[a]

Year 1 $100 × 80% × 4% = $3.20
Year 2 $100 × 64% × 4% = $2.56   (20% net reduction)
Year 3 $100 × 51.2% × 4% = $2.05   (20% net reduction)
Year 4   etc.

Now, to calculate the total current value of a prospective customer (i.e., the NPV of the probabilistic cash flows each year), we must add together all these probability-weighted LTVs for all future years. These numbers ($3.20, $2.56, $2.05, etc.) comprise an infinite series. Ordinary high school math (See? *We knew* it would come in handy!) shows that the sum of this series can be calculated in this way:

Average LTV per prospect $3.20 ÷ 20% = $16.00

In this example, if our total market consists of 1 million customers and prospects, then our total customer equity is approximately $33 million, because we have 200,000 current customers (20 percent market share) times $100 LTV each ($20 million), and we also have 800,000 prospective customers, each with a $16 LTV ($12.8 million).

Note that because prospects have probability-weighted LTVs, we can generate a higher **Return on Customer (ROC)** (see "Return on Customer" section later in this chapter) not just by targeting our customer acquisition campaigns at higher-LTV prospects, but also by taking actions to increase the *likelihood* of particular prospects becoming customers. If our business-to-business (B2B) firm conducts a free seminar for prospective customers, for instance, the prospects who elect to attend have almost certainly increased their likelihood of becoming customers. If our consumer-marketing firm offers free samples to prospective customers, the ones who respond to the offer are more likely to become customers, as are the smartphone users who download our app. Because we need to know whether it makes sense to run a seminar for prospects or to give samples away, we must consider the current value of these customers we don't yet have. Increasing the value of prospective customers is a legitimate and time-honored business activity.

But what about when a prospect becomes a customer? In our example, a customer has an LTV of $100, so when we convert a prospect to a customer, doesn't that mean we've increased our customer equity by $100?

No. If the prospect was already worth $16 to us, then the net increase in value to our firm in making that prospect into a customer was only $84. Think of it in terms of a new customer being activated at a $100 LTV, at the same time that a prospect is being "deactivated" with a $16 LTV. Another way to think about it is that the prospect had a probability-weighted LTV, and the probability changed. When he became a customer, the probability of his becoming a customer increased to 100 percent from what it used to be, which was 16 percent (16 percent is the weighted average of a 4 percent annual probability, discounted at 20 percent per year, forever).

Technically, each prospective customer has an "actual value" to our firm of $16, and an additional "**unrealized potential value**" of $84. We could easily think of a prospective customer as a customer with a great deal of growth potential—a customer with whom we so far have a 0 percent **share of customer**. So our mission, as a business, is to realize some of that potential, by changing the customer's otherwise expected future behavior.

---

[a] *Purists note:* The exact calculation would adjust the 4 percent probability down slightly each year, because the probability of a prospect becoming a customer in Year 2 is 4 percent times the 96 percent probability that he didn't already become a customer in Year 1, and so on.

Customer Loyalty and Customer Equity

The CVS and Verizon Wireless discussions clearly illustrate the fact that customer loyalty is likely to play a large part in any enterprise's effort to maximize the value its customers create. Executives frequently cite the problem of improving customer loyalty as one of the key reasons for embarking on a customer-centric initiative to begin with. This is because for many businesses, even small increases in average customer loyalty can have quite significant effects on their financial results in the long term. But because customer loyalty doesn't create nearly so much short-term value as it does long-term value, the most useful way to analyze the impact of an improvement in customer loyalty is usually to examine its impact on a firm's underlying customer equity.

This was exactly the approach taken by Sunil Gupta and Donald Lehmann.[34] In an important classic study, Gupta and his colleagues examined the financial reports of five different publicly held companies—Ameritrade, Amazon, Capital One, eBay, and E*TRADE—in order to try to estimate each company's customer equity. Then they calculated the impact on each firm's customer equity of changes in different marketing variables, including the average cost of new customer acquisition, the average profit margin, and the average customer retention rate, or loyalty.

What they found was quite remarkable, as shown in Exhibit 11.1, which compares four of the five companies:

- If the cost of new customer acquisition is reduced by 10 percent, customer equity values of these firms will increase by between about 0.5 and 1.5 percent.
- If product margins are raised by 10 percent, the customer equity levels of the firms will go up by roughly the same 10 percent.
- But if customer loyalty is increased 10 percent, then the customer equity levels of the firms improve by roughly 30 percent.

EXHIBIT 11.1   **Effect of Increasing Customer Value on Acquisition Cost, Margin, and Retention**

	Customer Equity ($b)	Percent Increase in Customer Value for a 10 Percent Improvement in		
	Base Case	Acquisition Cost	Margin	Retention
Amazon	2.54	0.51%	10.51%	28.34%
Ameritrade	1.45	1.19%	11.19%	30.18%
eBay	2.11	1.42%	11.42%	30.80%
E*TRADE	1.89	1.11%	11.11%	29.96%

Source: Sunil Gupta and Donald Lehmann, *Managing Customers as Investments: The Strategic Value of Customers in the Long Run* (Philadelphia: Wharton School Publishing, 2005).

[34] Sunil Gupta and Donald Lehmann, *Managing Customers as Investments: The Strategic Value of Customers in the Long Run* (Philadelphia: Wharton School Publishing, 2005).

A 10 percent boost in customer loyalty for these companies, in other words, increases their overall value, as companies, by about 30 percent! Traditionally, everyone talked about the importance of acquisition, but retention is how you build the value of the company. Because it costs more to get a new customer than to keep one, and because retention improves customer equity by three times as much as acquisition, then it's important to measure retention in order to drive a greater focus on customer experience and relationships. In other words, measure what matters.

Gupta and his colleagues had to use publicly
reported financial data, and they limited themselves to
analyzing five companies with fairly straightforward and
easily modeled business structures. Each of the firms
sells directly to end-user customers, for instance, so there were no complicated channel or distributor relationships to consider, and each has a high concentration of repeat customers who do business frequently. But the implications of this study still should be applicable to more complex businesses with more complicated business models.

In any business, customer retention may or may not be the most appropriate variable to try to evaluate. Customer values can change in many ways. Customer attrition or retention is like an on-off switch, but in most categories, customers should be thought of more in terms of volume dials. Increasing the amount of business your customer does, or at least avoiding a reduction in the business she does, could be a much more useful objective in many cases. A survey of the behaviors of more than 1,000 U.S. households across a variety of industries concludes that while reducing defection definitely represents an opportunity for most businesses, there is far more financial leverage in simply increasing the amount of business done by customers, or avoiding *reductions* in the volume of business done.[35]

Jill Avery at Harvard details four mistakes companies commonly make about acquisition, retention, and churn. Companies:

1. Don't measure the real cost of churn because of the natural time lapse between failing the customer and the churn, which is often six to eight months later.
2. Don't look at churn as a behavior on the part of the customer that is a response to behavior on the part of the company, but unfortunately look at churn as a number.
3. Think there is a magic number for churn: Buy different numbers acceptable for different business models.

---

[35] Scott Neslin, Sunil Gupta, Wagner Kamakura, Junxiang Lu, and Charlotte Mason, "Defection Detection: Improving Predictive Accuracy of Customer Churn Models," *Journal of Marketing Research* 43, no. 2 (May 2006): 204–211. This project was funded by the Teradata CRM Center at Duke University. For the survey of U.S. households, see Stephanie Coyles and Timothy C. Gokey, "Customer Retention Is Not Enough," *Journal of Consumer Marketing* 22, no. 2/3 (2013): 101–105.

4. Don't realize that churn is really an acquisition problem. If a company determines which customers will be the most valuable and the most likely to engage, churn will go down because the company has brought in and kept customers to whom your company has the most value and who have the most value to your company.[36]

Customer loyalty itself is not always easy to define. If a consumer who considers himself loyal to a particular retail brand of gasoline is to stop at a different brand's filling station because it is more convenient at a given time, has he become less loyal than he was? When a business that buys all its office furniture from a particular contractor decides to put the next set of furniture purchases out to bid, is that "defection"?

Most companies end up creating a practical definition of retention for their customers that includes two features.[37] Unless the customer has a single, subscriber-like relationship with a company and clearly "leaves," retention is rarely considered an all-or-nothing variable. Thus, at an initial level, retention tends to be defined progressively—from "downgrading" behavior, to "inactive" status, to "no longer a customer." For some firms, a downgrading pattern itself is an indicator of increased risk of loss. A cable customer with premium channels and many pay-per-views each month may downgrade to just basic cable, or even to local broadcast only, until he completely defects to streaming.

At a second level, any definition of retention must also recognize the multiple relationships that a customer may have with a firm in terms of products that span business units. Customers who terminate a relationship in one area—paying off a home mortgage with a bank, for instance—may or may not retain a strong and active relationship in other areas, such as retail banking, investments, and credit. And marketers can't come to grips with this phenomenon at all unless they take an enterprise-wide view of each customer, across all business units and channels.

Although any lost customer is a real loss, understanding the nature of the loss will help to manage the costs of trying to reactivate customers or even to win them back. At the base level, it's important to distinguish between customer attrition and customer defection. Attrition almost always results from a circumstance outside the direct control of a business—an elite business traveler retires, an office supplies

---

[36] Amy Gallo's interview with Jill Avery, "The Value of Keeping the Right Customers," *Harvard Business Review,* October 29, 2014, available at https://hbr.org/2014/10/the-value-of-keeping-the-right-customers/, accessed February 12, 2016. See also Timothy L. Keiningham, Lerzan Aksoy, Alexander Buoye, and Bruce Cooil, "Customer Loyalty Isn't Enough. Grow Your Share of Wallet," *Harvard Business Review* 89, no. 10 (October 2011): 29–31, for introduction to the Wallet Allocation Rule.

[37] Thanks to Dr. Linda Vytlacil, formerly at Carlson Marketing Group and now Vice President of Global Customer Insights & Analytics at Walmart, for this discussion of how to think about customer retention, attrition, and defection.

buyer declares bankruptcy, a retail customer moves to another territory. Defection, by contrast, is a customer loss that might have been mitigated, because the customer is clearly choosing to move part or all of her business to the competition (e.g., a landline customer choosing to drop her service in order to go "only mobile" or to go to voice over Internet protocol [VoIP]). By distinguishing defection from attrition, we can isolate the drivers of each behavior and invest where we are likely to earn the highest Return on Customer.[38]

There is also the question of tenure. In any population of customers, those most likely to defect will be the first to do so. Thus, the longer any particular group of customers has remained "in the franchise," the less likely any of them are to defect in any given time period. Stated another way, the average annual retention rate among any population of customers will tend to increase with time.[39] When we talk in general about "improving retention," we have to be quite careful, because the least loyal customers are always the newest ones. The easiest way for almost any enterprise to improve its *average* retention rate would simply be to stop acquiring new customers altogether! Again, resolving this problem requires a metric that can balance immediate profits and costs against the long-term value being created or destroyed.

In the final analysis, regardless of whatever behavior change a company can effect in its customer base—whether it is an increase in purchasing or a reduced likelihood of attrition—all of the financial results are captured in the LTV and customer equity numbers. The only question is how accurately the LTV equations have been constructed and modeled.

Forecasting customers' future behaviors and estimating the financial impact will never be simple, but with the customer analytics and statistical tools now available, it's not exactly rocket science anymore either. Some straightforward factors contribute to increases or decreases in an enterprise's customer equity:

- Acquire more customers.
- Acquire customers who are more valuable to begin with (i.e., acquire customers likely to have higher LTVs).
- Increase profit per customer.
- Reduce servicing costs per customer.
- Sell customers additional products or services.
- Reduce the rate of customer attrition.
- Increase the propensity of customers to refer other customers.

---

[38] We often hear about "replacing" a customer who has defected. But this idea has a fallacy. A company can never truly replace a customer it wanted to keep. If it acquires another customer, it could have had two.

[39] You'll find a more thorough discussion of customer "vintages" in Don Peppers and Martha Rogers, Ph.D., *Enterprise 1to1: Tools for Competing in the Interactive Age* (New York: Currency/Doubleday, 1997), pp. 365–366.

- Add social and influence value—willingness to rate products and services, participation in social media, etc.[40]
- Improve willingness to recommend **(Net Promoter Score [NPS])**.[41]

Many of these factors can be measured currently, even though their primary effect is to alter how customers buy in the future. These are some of the **leading indicators** of LTV change, and we will return to this topic later in this chapter.

But first, we need to answer a bigger question. If customer-centric companies concentrate on maximizing the value that their customers create, and these customers create value both in the long and the short term, is there a single, overall metric that would help an enterprise gauge the efficiency with which its customers are creating value?

Return on Customer

When companies engage in untrustable behavior, we find a nearly manic obsession with short-term financial results and almost total disregard for longer-term financial implications. Short-termism generates many dysfunctional and even self-destructive business practices, as profit-oriented companies dismiss the long-term consequences of their actions in order to generate current-period profits—profits that feed the bonus pool, pump up the stock price, and meet analysts' expectations. Short-termism is characterized by unadulterated self-interest and directly conflicts with trustability, but it is still easily the most pervasive and destructive business problem on the planet today.[42]

In one survey of 401 chief financial officers (CFOs) of large, publicly traded companies in the United States, for example, 78 percent of them confessed that they would be willing to give up actual "economic value" for their firms if that was necessary in order to hit the quarterly numbers.[43]

---

[40] Bruce D. Weinberg and Paul D. Berger, "Connected Lifetime Value: The Impact of Social Media," *Journal of Direct, Data and Digital Marketing Practice* 12 (2011): 328–344.

[41] Net Promoter Score (NPS), developed by Satmetrix Systems, Inc., Bain & Co., and Fred Reichheld, is a popular measure of the difference between customer satisfaction and dissatisfaction based on a customer's willingness to recommend a product, company, or brand.

[42] You can also learn a lot from "Prepaid Cards: Second-Tier Bank Account Substitutes," a Consumers Union report by staff attorney Michelle Jun, September 2010, available at http://www.defendyourdollars.org/Prepaid%20WP.pdf, accessed June 14, 2011.

[43] We found fascinating the CFO survey that found 78 percent of executives would sacrifice "economic value" to make this quarter's numbers: Emery P. Dalesio, "Executives Sacrifice Shareholder Value to Please Street," Associated Press State & Local Wire, February 9, 2004. "Three-quarters of business executives admit they massage earnings reports to meet or beat Wall Street expectations and would sacrifice shareholder value to keep earnings on a smooth upward slope, according to a survey released Monday. The study of 401 senior financial executives by researchers at Duke University and the University of Washington found that 55 percent would delay starting a project to avoid missing an earnings target. Four out of five executives said they would defer maintenance and research spending to meet earnings targets. The preference for smooth earnings growth instead of even slight variations is so strong that 78 percent of the surveyed executives would give up economic value in exchange, the study said."

Short-termism like this emphasizes the "selfish" aspect of free-market competition, without allowing room for the empathetic, nonselfish side of every person's nature. Elinor Ostrom, the first woman to win the Nobel Prize in Economics, has suggested that "when we assume people are basically selfish, we design economic systems that reward selfish people."[44] Obviously, there's no longer any question that a free-market system is much more efficient and fair than any state-controlled system could ever be, but the "greed is good" philosophy that animates so many is testimony to the fact that it offers its biggest rewards to the most selfish people.

The truth is, however, that short-termism only reigns supreme at most businesses because *the financial metrics we apply to business are not economically true measures of success.*[45] They never have been, and they haven't substantially changed since being introduced at the beginning of the Industrial Age. The way most businesses "do the numbers" to document their financial performance focuses entirely on the past—that is, on the most recent financial period. Most companies' financial reports to shareholders include absolutely no consideration of the way the most recent performance has either helped or harmed a firm's prospects for generating future profits, leaving this detail to the stock market analysts and others to figure out. Yes, a good business will track customer satisfaction or maybe even NPS or customer lifetime values.[46] Ultimately, though, these figures *should* have more effect on how earnings are calculated. Unfortunately, today earnings from the most recent financial period are the Supreme Performance Metric, the key performance indicator (KPI) to beat all other KPIs.[47]

Managers sometimes take comfort in the sophistication and precision of their short-term financial metrics, ignoring the long-term effects simply because they can't be as precisely defined. But this is like the classic joke about the man who lost his car keys late one night and is now looking for them near a street corner, even though he lost them half a block away, closer to where his car was parked. When a police officer asked the obvious question—Why?—the man glanced up at the street lamp illuminating the corner and said, "Because the light's better here."

---

[44] Elinor Ostrom quoted in Clay Shirky, *Cognitive Surplus* (New York: Penguin Press, 2010), p. 111.
[45] Most companies report and reward based on historic numbers and leave prediction and projection to others. Steven Pinker suggests that our *understanding* of time is severely limited, psychologically, and that this is evident purely from the structure of language itself. After all, when time is expressed grammatically in most languages, there are only three real tenses: the here and now, the future unto eternity, and the history of the universe before now. Moreover, he says, because the human experience of time is entirely subjective, "it speeds up or slows down depending on how demanding, varied, and pleasant an interval is." Steven Pinker, *The Stuff of Thought: Language as a Window into Human Nature* (New York: Viking, 2007), p. 190.
[46] Orkun Oguz, "Finding Your Place on the Customer Measurement Grid," *Strategy Speaks* blog post, July 20, 2011, available at http://www.peppersandrogersgroup.com/blog/2011/07/customer-strategist-orkun-oguz-8.html, accessed February 12, 2016.
[47] If you want to extend your examination of how KPIs are often used, see Gretchen Morgenson and Joshua Rosner, *Reckless Endangerment: How Outsized Ambition, Greed, and Corruption Led to Economic Armageddon* (New York: Henry Holt/Times Books, 2011), for an outstanding narrative of the entire mortgage mess that led to the recession of 2008.

The simple fact about business metrics: If you aren't measuring the right things to begin with, you're not going to get better results by measuring them more accurately.

> When your headlights aren't on, the best rearview mirror available isn't likely to improve your driving.

Nowhere was this no-headlights philosophy more in evidence than during the run-up to the 2008 Great Financial Crisis, a global disaster brought about by rampant, overconfident short-termism. Short-term metrics and incentives, when they are applied to businesses based on current-period financials, almost inevitably end up promoting the interests of commission seekers, bonus-earning senior managers, and short-term investors. Usually, this is directly counter to the legitimate interests of a company's shareholders, not to mention its customers, employees, partners, and other stakeholders.

So how do we measure better in order to make the most of the customers we have, and will have—the customers who are, by definition, a company's only source of revenue? *If it is in a company's own economic self-interest to be trustable,* then how should that company measure and report its value if it is building customer equity through trusted Learning Relationships and the better customer experiences that result? And what if a company's short-term actions increase current numbers but decrease future value at the same time? Companies cannot simply ignore the reputational damage they would do to themselves if they were to resort to spamming or rampant telemarketing, and as interactivity accelerates, and trustworthiness becomes even more important, it won't just be spamming that damages a reputation.[48] Untrustworthy activities will cause genuine economic harm to a business, and its cost is likely to dwarf whatever short-term profits a business might have been able to generate. Because while economics may not be everything, when it comes to operating a profit-making company with a payroll to meet and shareholders to satisfy, it's *almost* everything. It's extremely important to realize, therefore, that while acting in a customer's interest will sometimes require a company to incur a short-term cost, it will nearly always be economically beneficial for the firm in the long run. So how can we calculate how much a firm can invest in building customer value to support short-term profits and increased long-term value?

It has never been possible to succeed for long with a business that offered substandard product quality or uncompetitive pricing. A business might generate extra profits for a brief period by cutting back on quality or raising prices above the norm, but as customers acquire the information needed to compare one company's

---

[48] There's a lot of information out there about spam. See, for instance, http://www.barracudacentral .org/index.cgi?p=spam, which calculates spam percentages daily, or http://www.spam-o-meter.com/stats, which calculates spam percentage over time. On October 18, 2011, this site calculated the percentage of spam worldwide as 89.9 percent, measured over the previous three years.

offerings with others, it is inevitable that lower-quality, higher-price companies will lose out to higher-quality, lower-price competitors.[49]

To begin with, a company has to consider that customers, even if numerous, are finite in number. A company can make more products, but cannot manufacture more customers. And if customers are a scarce productive resource—imposing a constraint on a company's growth—then it would make sense for executives to track how efficiently they use this scarce productive resource to create value. When an enterprise wants to track the efficiency with which it deploys capital to create more value, it uses some metric such as return on investment. Return on Customer[SM] (ROC[SM])[50] is a metric directly analogous to ROI (and thus usually is pronounced are-oh-see) and specifically designed to track how well an enterprise is using customers to create value.[51] (For an example of how a company can use up customer value, see the section "Using Up Customers" in Chapter 14.) ROC can provide a company with financial bifocals—a single lens through which it can see its earnings from customers clearly, whether these earnings are up close and immediate or in the more distant long term.

To understand the ROC metric, start with a simple analogy. Imagine that last year you bought a stock for $100, and during the year you received a dividend payment of $5, while the stock price climbed to $110 by the end of the year. Your total ROI for the year would have been 15 percent. You put up $100 initially, and the total new value created amounted to 15 percent of that initial investment. If, however, the stock price had fallen $10 during the year, from $100 down to $90, then your total ROI would have been a negative 5 percent, and even though you received a $5 dividend, you would have suffered a net loss overall.

Now apply that thinking to customers. Suppose you begin the year with a customer who has an estimated LTV of $100, and during the year you make a profit from the customer of $5. By the end of the year, let's suppose your predictive modeling calculation shows that the customer's LTV has increased to $110. In that case, your ROC for the year would be 15 percent. But this measurement of the economic performance of a particular customer will capture not just the sales you generate from the customer during the year but also the change, if any, in the customer's value to your business—LTV, that is, or the value of his likely future purchases, recommendations to friends, and so forth, as modeled in your customer database.

To understand why ROC is important, go back to the stock purchase for a minute, and imagine that the only information you have is how much the dividend is. You can't see whether the value of the underlying stock is increasing or not. In

---

[49] Whitney MacMillan, chairman emeritus of Cargill, makes the case for the critical value of building social capital within your company and offers a proven formula for how to do it. See Whitney MacMillan, "The Power of Social Capital," *Harvard Management Update* 11, no. 6 (June 2006): 1–4.

[50] Return on Customer[SM] and ROC[SM] are registered service marks of Peppers & Rogers Group.

[51] Don Peppers and Martha Rogers, "Return on Customer: A Core Metric of Value Creation," *Customer Strategist* 2, no. 1 (March 2010): 30–39.

that case, even though the actual value of the stock will be going up and down all the time, you really can't say how well your investment is doing. So far as you're concerned, as long as the dividend continues or increases, you seem to be doing just fine, but the truth is that without also knowing how the underlying stock price is changing, it's impossible to say whether you're really creating value or not. If you had a stockbroker who wouldn't tell you, you'd fire that stockbroker.

The fact is that many companies are content to measure, carefully and sometimes with maniacal precision, their current sales from customers, without ever noticing, or measuring, or demanding to know how much the customer equity lying underneath the current numbers has gone up or down. But because customers are a scarce resource for businesses, when a company doesn't try to measure how much of that resource is being used up to create its current numbers, it is getting an incomplete picture of its financial performance.

Return on Customer = Total Shareholder Return

Total Shareholder Return (TSR) is a precisely defined investment term, and refers to the overall return a shareholder earns from owning a company's stock over some period of time.[a] According to one financial authority:

Total Shareholder Return represents the change in capital value of a listed/quoted company over a period (typically one year or longer), plus dividends, expressed as a plus or minus percentage of the opening value.[b]

This definition is based on what a shareholder's actual cash flow would be if he were to buy the stock at the beginning of the period and sell it at the end. The shareholder gets cash dividends during the period, and by the end of the period there may also have been some up-or-down change in the capital value of the stock itself. In a perfect world (economically speaking, that is), a publicly traded firm's market-driven "capital value" would equal its discounted cash flow (DCF) value, corrected for the effects of its capital structure. But of course there's no way to prove or disprove this because no one really knows what any company's discounted cash flow is going to be in the future. Nevertheless, it's widely accepted that the market price of a public company's stock at any point in time should generally reflect the marginal investor's best guess as to the company's discounted future cash flow.

To understand the "ROC = TSR" argument, start with the premise that all revenue and costs created by any company's business operation[c] must come from its customers at some point, directly or indirectly. If the discounted cash flow value of an operating business is created entirely by customers, then its discounted cash flow is composed of a whole lot of individual LTVs. All the firm's current and future customer LTVs added together (i.e., its customer equity) will therefore equal its total discounted cash flow. As a result:

Return on Customer (ROC) equals a company's current-period cash flow, plus the change in its discounted cash flow value during the period, expressed as a percentage of its beginning discounted cash flow value.

In other words, ROC is simply a different route to prospective TSR—a method that breaks the economic value of a business into smaller and smaller customer-specific units, all the way down to specific, individual customers. ROC calculations don't rely on changes in share price, but if a firm's shares are publicly traded then stock price can still provide an important additional reference point for validating the firm's total customer equity.

A final note about shareholder return: The formal definition of TSR may refer only to publicly traded companies, but all companies have "shareholders." Whether shareholder return is calculated in order to flesh out an SEC filing or just to decide how much everybody gets paid this year, and whether shareholder meetings take place on the 68th floor, or at the investment company's office, or around the kitchen table, shareholder return is the most fundamental metric of value creation for any kind of business.

Both shareholder return and ROC apply to every company that needs a bookkeeper.

Source: Adapted from Don Peppers and Martha Rogers, Ph.D., *Return on Customer: Creating Maximum Value from Your Scarcest Resource* (New York: Currency/Doubleday, 2005), pp. 15–16.

[a] When we talk about "shareholder return," we're really talking about the rate at which an enterprise is creating value for its owners.

[b] The definition of TSR came from Value-Based Management.net, at www.valuebased management.net/methods tsr.html, accessed January 19, 2016.

[c] In considering a firm's "business operation," we are purposely disregarding capital structure and thinking only of the firm's actual business as a business.

A firm can calculate ROC for a particular customer, if it has reliable information about that customer's LTV, change in LTV, and profit for the period, or it can calculate ROC for a particular group or segment of customers, as well. If the firm calculates its ROC with respect to its total customer equity, the result will be mathematically the same as its TSR during the period (see "Return on Customer = Total Shareholder Return," above). Remember that a firm's customer equity is virtually the same thing as the value the firm has as an operating business.

Therefore, ROC equals TSR.

Return on Customer = Total Shareholder Return

Suppose we try to estimate ROC and use it to begin tunneling a path through the mountain of a company's financial performance while at the same time the company's accountants try to estimate the firm's TSR (based on its discounted cash flow value as a going concern), and begin tunneling toward us from the opposite side of the mountain. The mathematics suggest that we should meet at roughly the same place in the middle. And because of the ROC = TSR connection, a company can be truly happy with its ROC only if it exceeds its cost of capital, because only then is the firm actually creating value, overall, for its shareholders. (Obviously, if an investment doesn't earn a return greater than a firm's cost of capital, the firm is better off not making the investment at all. Whenever a firm creates net new shareholder value, this is because its total shareholder return has exceeded its cost of capital by at least a tiny margin for some period of time.)

Therefore, when a firm's ROC for some marketing initiative is less than its cost of capital, whether it is calculating ROC for the whole company or for some smaller subset of customers and prospects, it would be better off not undertaking the initiative. No value is created for a business when TSR is lower than the cost of capital, and because ROC = TSR, no value is created for a firm when ROC is less than the cost of capital either. Even though a firm may be showing a current-period profit from some set of customers, if its ROC for those customers is less than its cost of capital, then it isn't benefiting its shareholders, because not enough customer equity is being generated.

Many companies that show little growth or hard-fought, tepid earnings are actually not creating net new shareholder value at all but simply harvesting the customer LTVs they already have "in the bank." If an enterprise wants to grow and continue to grow, it has to ensure that every sales, service, and marketing initiative will yield an ROC greater than its cost of capital. That way, even as it is realizing earnings in the current period, it will also be building enough new customer equity to support future earnings.

Analyzing a company's ROC at the enterprise level can help clarify its financial prospects in ways that traditional financial statements aren't likely to reveal. To help you visualize this, Exhibit 11.2 shows an array of five different hypothetical

EXHIBIT 11.2 Are You Creating, Harvesting, or Destroying Value?[a]

	Company 1	Company 2	Company 3	Company 4	Company 5
Customer equity at beginning of year	$1,000	$1,000	$1,000	$1,000	$1,000
Customer equity at end of year	$1,200	$1,200	$1,020	$950	$900
Change in customer equity during the year	$200	$200	$20	(−$50)	(−$100)
Profit during the year	$50	(−$50)	$30	$50	$50
Total customer value created	$250	$150	$50	$0	(−$50)
Return on Customer	25%	15%	5%	0%	(−5%)
	Value Creators		**Value Harvesters**		**Value Destroyer**

[a] We are indebted to the insights of Taylor Duersch and other members of Carlson Marketing's Decision Sciences team, now a part of Groupe Aeroplan, for helping us to clarify the role that customer equity plays in future earnings. Taylor Duersch is now Vice President of Global Customer Analytics and Research at Wal-Mart.

companies divided into three categories, depending on whether each company is creating value, destroying it, or merely harvesting it.

Companies 1 and 2 in this exhibit are **value creators**. For these two companies, the combination of short- and long-term value created by their customers is occurring at a rate that is almost certainly higher than their cost of capital. In each case they are ending their year with higher customer equity than they started with, so they can expect to grow their earnings in future years as well. Although it's clear each company is creating net new value for its shareholders, in Company 2's case, this net new value is being created despite the fact that the firm's current profits are actually negative.

Companies 3 and 4, however, are what we would call **value harvesters**. They are simply treading the financial water by harvesting customer profits that already have been "put in the bank" in the form of customer equity. Their ROC is not negative, but it is clearly below their cost of capital. Although each is earning a current profit, neither one is replenishing its customer equity enough, so it's unlikely that either of these companies will be able to achieve much growth in future years. They may continue to report lukewarm, increasingly difficult profits for the time being, but sooner or later, their customer equity will no longer be sufficient to sustain a profit at all. Technically, they may not be destroying shareholder value yet, but if these firms were people, they would be living off their savings.

As a **value destroyer**, Company 5 is in the worst situation of all, with ROC below zero. True, the company has scraped out a profit this year, but this profit was achieved only by stealing even more from the future. One can imagine a car manufacturer offering the deepest-ever discounts in order to prop up the fourth quarter's numbers, in the process saddling itself with a saturated market and customers trained to wait for more discounts, creating a much more difficult problem when it comes to making next year's numbers. Company 5 is on the skids, whether this is revealed in its current financial statements or not. It may be reporting a profit to shareholders. But shareholders who dig deeper will see that this firm doesn't have the operating and financial strength necessary to sustain this level of earnings for long. What this firm is really doing is "eating itself" and reporting the meal as a profit.

From the figures in Exhibit 11.2, it should be clear what kind of company represents the best value for an investor, although to a large extent savvy investors will have already discounted each firm's stock price to reflect its growth prospects. Nevertheless, if a firm succeeds in converting itself from one class to another—say, from value harvester to value creator—this will likely have a major impact on its economic value as an operating business. As investors uncover this information, the firm's stock will almost certainly be revalued in a significant way.

The Verizon Wireless situation we discussed earlier in this chapter resembles Company 1's situation in the exhibit. The firm produced good earnings while simultaneously accumulating even more customer equity. We calculated Verizon Wireless's ROC in each of those four years, and it averaged a whopping 68 percent annually. Stated differently, each year during the period we analyzed, Verizon

Wireless created enough total new value to equal about two-thirds of its value as an operating company at the beginning of that year.

Yes, such a high ROC for four years running represents a remarkable spurt of value creation, but the way to think about it is that each year Verizon Wireless was revaluing its entire customer base, steadily improving the overall value of its business. Its success in customer retention was building up the company's customer equity account to a level that could support even higher earnings.

Estimates for Verizon's competitors during the same period revealed ROC measures ranging from only 19 percent to below zero. Even if all of the companies, including Verizon, offered investors about the same *current* returns, which company would you rather invest in? Or work for? Or acquire? Or be the customer of?

Tracking customer LTV allows a firm to calculate ROC in a variety of situations, sometimes in order to decide what the best course of action is and sometimes simply to avoid self-defeating business decisions that generate unanticipated (or unmeasured) costs. At many firms, for example, customer acquisition programs are evaluated simply on the basis of the quantity of new customers acquired rather than on their quality (i.e., their expected LTVs and growth potential). Profit optimization programs often look at cost savings without considering customer retention issues. And retention programs designed to reduce churn might do so by maintaining marginally profitable customers or even unprofitable ones.

These are, in fact, the self-defeating criteria by which many telecom companies evaluate their own actions. Because they don't track changes in customer LTVs, they have no real understanding of the overall value they are creating or not creating with their everyday tactical decisions. For the most part, many telecommunications firms seem to have an indiscriminate hunger simply to win any new customers they can and to avoid losing their current ones, no matter what the LTV economics are in either situation. These firms are making decisions designed to maximize their current-period earnings, and it's possible that they actually are doing so. The problem, however, is that this undermines their companies' long-term viability. They actually may be destroying more value than they are creating.

According to one group of industry experts,[52] many if not most telecom firms have seen the average LTV within their customer bases decline quite significantly in recent years:

> *Some [telecom companies], for example, have tried to reduce churn by offering discount plans and other incentives—but ended up retaining customers they would have been better off losing and making formerly marginal customers unprofitable. Others have tried to contain the surge in unpaid bills by tightening credit limits on new applicants but are now turning away many customers who would have been profitable.*

---

[52] Adam Braff, William J. Passmore, and Michael Simpson, "Going the Distance with Telecom Customers," *McKinsey Quarterly* 4 (2003): 83–93.

In essence, according to this authority, here's one example of a whole industry full of companies that are strip-mining their base of customers and prospects in order to feed their current-period results. As they continue with these policies, it becomes harder and harder to pump up the current period, while at the same time the customer environment is becoming increasingly polluted with uneconomic offers and unprofitable programs. It is anyone's guess as to whether telecom firms are actually *willing* to sacrifice the future in their increasingly desperate effort to prop up the present, or they simply are *unaware* of what they are really doing, because they don't have the right customer-centric metrics in place.

Measuring, Analyzing, and Utilizing Return on Customer

ROC is a decision support tool for executives and can be used to evaluate total enterprise efficiency in creating and sustaining customer equity while generating short-term returns.

Combining the foundational analytical models of customer equity, churn, and lifetime value, we calculate ROC, and the result incorporates not just the return generated by a customer in the current period but also any positive or negative changes in the customer's LTV during the period. Thus, the most intriguing quality of the ROC metric is that it balances the effect of short-term results with long-term ones. At the enterprise level:

$$ROC = \frac{P^{(t)} + \left(CE^{(t)} - CE^{(t-1)} \right)}{CE^{(t-1)}}$$

where:

$P^{(t)}$ = company cash flow in period t

$CE^{(t)}$ = customer equity in period t

Type of Data to Be Used in Analytical Models

ROC analysis requires a good understanding of customer behavior and hence requires good handling of customer data. Maturity of internal data collection and storage processes along with a data-sharing organizational culture are critical in establishing the basis for proper ROC study and consistency of results. Some of the critical customer information we would like to have access to include: demographic customer information, customer revenue, customer transactions, customer channel usage, customer complaints, claims, customer life stage, sophisticated cost allocation methodologies, and so forth.

(continued)

(Continued)

Calculating ROC (Bottom-to-Top Approach)

Calculating ROC requires models addressing acquisition, retention, and growth for calculating parameters and quantifying relations that enable LTV and customer equity estimations.

The ROC calculation has two major steps:

1. Measure the marketing activities and analyze their effect on customer acquisition, retention, and growth, which all form the basis for analyzing the value of a particular customer or customer group.
2. Estimate customer LTV and total equity of all customers at a certain time point.

Analytical studies, such as customer segmentation, profiling, churn modeling, propensity modeling, response modeling, and cost analysis, will provide the behavioral traits of one customer at a certain time, based on what we know now:

$$\theta^{(t)} = \left\{ \theta_1^{(t)}, \theta_2^{(t)}, \ldots, \theta_r^{(t)} \right\}$$

where:

θ_1: Probability to repeat purchase
θ_2: Likelihood to churn
θ_2: Probability to respond to an offer
θ_3: Probability to increase revenue
θ_4: Potential growth
θ_5: Lifestyle/Life stage phase
θ_6: Acquisition cost
θ_7: Price/Margin

Although the technological advances in recent years and increasing speed of computing tools make the statistical modeling effort relatively easier, most of the work still involves ensuring that the right attributes are collected accurately, reflecting relevant customer behaviors and appropriate values within the model. Making these decisions often involves a great deal of judgment and sometimes creativity as well.

Customers' behaviors drive their values, so customer value is a function of whatever behavioral traits we can measure and estimate:

$$\hat{\pi}_k^{(t)} = f^{(t)}\left(\theta^{(t)}\right)$$
$$\hat{\pi}_k^{(t)} = \left\{ \hat{\pi}_k^{(t+1)}, \hat{\pi}_k^{(t+2)}, \ldots \right\}$$

Note: Occasionally, we may need to use proxies to track these behavioral traits when we don't have sufficient and reliable data.

Customer LTV is the sum of these value points over the entire length of the customer's relationship with the enterprise (or some other acceptable time frame within that business or industry), discounted back to time *t*.

$$CLV_k^{(t)} = \sum_{s=t+1}^{n} \hat{\pi}_k^s d^s$$

Note: Use of discount rate can change the valuation, and desired discount rate depends on company's actual assessment of cost of capital (i.e., preference of future cash versus current cash).

Customer equity at a certain time *t* is the sum of all a firm's customers' LTV:

$$CE^{(t)} = \sum_k CLV_k^{(t)}$$

Finally, ROC is the sum of the short-term value in time *t* and change in customer equity from *t* − 1 to *t* divided by total customer equity of the firm at time *t* − 1:

$$ROC = \frac{P^{(t)} + (CE^{(t)} - CE^{(t-1)})}{CE^{(t-1)}}$$

$$P^{(t)} = \sum_k \pi_k^{(t)}$$

Conceptually, if we consider that total customer equity is equal to total value that a company can generate from its customers over its lifetime (or over some foreseeable, appropriately long term), then customer equity can be assumed to be roughly equal to total enterprise value. And if we assume that the company is an investment that can be sold or reinvested in each period, ROC can be approximated to the sum of:

(ROI) Return generated by total enterprise in the short term = $P^{(t)}/CE^{(t-1)}$

and

Change in underlying enterprise value = $\dfrac{(CE^{(t)} - CE^{(t-1)})}{CE^{(t-1)}}$

To make ROC a part of daily decision making, results of the models should be converted into customer actions and dashboards. Using analytical models and data-mining/reporting tools, multiple dashboards and a combination or intersection of multiple actions can be designed to best serve customers included in that particular study.

(continued)

(Continued)

The power of ROC in balancing these two occasionally conflicting actions makes this metric helpful for evaluating a company's performance and making the right executive decisions. At the enterprise level, under strong pressure by Wall Street to hit short-term targets, ROC can give an approximation for how company valuation changes over time while still incorporating the effect of short-term results. ROC gives the ability to measure, quantify, and communicate the impact of these investments on customer equity and allows executives and analysts to speak the same language. Additionally, the bottom-up approach that we utilize in calculating ROC gives enough flexibility for dissecting data in multiple dimensions and therefore provides the ability to look at the ROC performance of divisions, business units, customer segments, or marketing programs. With ROC embedded in the performance management process, executives can encourage department-level decisions based not only on short-term profit but also on long-term customer equity.

Constantly updating the ROC model and feeding results back to it enables the evaluation of alternative investments in light of ROC and running multiple scenario analyses. For example, an information technology investment requiring $2 million and resulting in $2.7 million in short-term cost savings would be very attractive to any executive. But wouldn't this project be prioritized higher if we could calculate that the investment would also help build 30 percent of customer equity over the next 24 months?

At the most granular level, ROC can be linked to a particular customer for in-depth insight, making it a great tool for customer service departments in the form of real-time customer dashboards. In these dashboards, agents can observe ROC at the customer level: in churn scores, the current microsegment the customer is assigned to, next-best product offers, claim resolution priorities, rules, actions, and so forth. Equipped with these real-time monitors, customer service agents can diligently treat different customers differently, satisfying the most critical requirement for improving customer equity and thus ROC.

Equally, sales organizations can use ROC to track customer-level or group-level performance of sales account executives. Using dynamically updated customer dashboards visible to these executives and their managers, planning, target setting, and incentive management activities can incorporate ROC into the equation. In doing so, companies can maintain sufficient pressure on their sales organizations to deliver results in the short term while sustaining customer equity, customer trust, and the long-term viability of the company. For example, a sales division of an insurance company can be penalized or rewarded based not only on how many new policies it brings in during the current period but on how the overall **customer portfolio** value changes within the same period.[53]

---

[53] Thanks to Onder Oguzhan, former analytics subject matter expert at Peppers & Rogers Group, for his contributions to this section.

Leading Indicators of LTV Change

Once a firm is practiced enough in analyzing LTVs to begin monitoring how changes in LTV are caused, it can begin to apply the ROC metric to manage its marketing initiatives and its overall business more productively, focusing on the most important factors in improving its customers' LTVs. If customer loyalty is the dominant factor in an enterprise's customer equity calculation, then improving customer loyalty will be key to success. If profit on value-added service is the dominant variable, then services should be emphasized. Making the right business decision will depend on the current performance of a firm's LTV parameters and on the effort required to influence the improvement of these parameters. Improving on a metric where performance is already high is generally more difficult (and costly) than focusing on an area with more room for improvement. Once Verizon Wireless had reduced its monthly churn from 2.6 percent to 1.1 percent, for instance, it will not be possible to duplicate that reduction, and the firm likely will have to find other ways to increase its customer equity if it wants to sustain such a high ROC.

ROC requires an enterprise to predict future customer behavior changes using currently available information. In essence, a company's analytics program must identify and track the leading indicators of LTV changes. The question is, what data are available today to forecast up or down movements in a customer's LTV?

The predictive modeling process involves two basic steps.

The first step involves devising an equation for LTV that includes whatever transactional records or other data are available on customers' actual past spending (and other measurable behaviors, such as visits to the Web site or social media platforms, trackable referrals, complaints, etc.). It's best if there are several years' worth of transactions, but often a company will have to make some assumptions based on business judgment or sampling. Such records might include, for instance, each customer's purchases every year, the margin on those purchases, and the number of years the customer has done business with the firm. Essentially, the company is using the computer to go back through historical customer records and make the actual calculations of LTV for as many individual customers as possible.

The second step is to identify the most predictive currently available variables with respect to the LTVs calculated in the first step. If we start by calculating LTVs for individual customers using historical records, we then comb back through all the information we have about those individual customers in order to pick out correlations and relationships with their individual LTVs. The data to be used should include purchase transactions to the extent possible but might also include complaint and service records, demographic (B2C) or firmographic (B2B) information, needs-based research, or even information on customer attitudes—essentially, any information at all that can be obtained in a customer-specific form, with respect to the customers whose LTVs already are calculated.

In the end, the objective is to generate a second equation for LTV, but this will be an equation that uses currently available data to predict an individual customer's LTV rather than using transaction data to calculate it retrospectively, as is the case for RFM (recency, frequency, and monetary value), which often is used by database marketers. One large consumer service business devised a predictive model for LTV based on 10 years of customer transaction records. The company first ran a statistical analysis to see what independent variables most affected a customer's likelihood of returning, because likelihood of returning seemed to be the most important single factor in determining LTV. Using the findings from this analysis, the company created an equation for predicting the future revenue from each customer. This formula was not limited to transactional records but included "outside" variables as well, such as the general level of consumer confidence in the economy at large. Each customer's future contribution was estimated by applying historical margin to his or her predicted future revenue.[54] As one of their executives explained:

> For a very high level summary of the LTV calculation, we ran a regression to see what independent variables affect a [customer's] likelihood of returning. We then used the coefficients of the successful variables to create a formula for predicting future revenue for each [customer]. At least one of these was external—something like consumer confidence. Finally we applied the historical contribution of each [customer] to get to future contribution. Our LTV calculation contains only future expected contribution. We applied the formula to historical customer data to get LTV from previous years.

Determining drivers of LTV

In the end, in addition to **demographic data**, the company's LTV model used such variables as the first type of service purchased, the average rate paid, and how recently the last service was purchased.

The variables driving any firm's LTV model can be thought of as the leading indicators of LTV change. The model won't ever be perfect, because predictions never are. There always will be problems having to do with the availability of data, analytical issues, and other obstacles. But reliability will improve with experience, as a firm learns to collect, monitor, and weight the information more and more accurately. The leading indicators of LTV change fall into four general categories:[55]

1. *Lifetime value drivers*. These are the elements of the LTV equation itself—the actual components that determine how much value the customer creates for the company, over time.[56]

---

[54] The information from the large consumer service business is proprietary but was documented for us in an e-mail from a colleague sent to the authors, including the executive statement we've been allowed to share.

[55] See footnote 3 in Chapter 5 for a more complete review of customer lifetime valuation.

[56] While LTV has a lot to do with purchasing behavior and intent, as well as other facts about customers, the influence a customer has over the preferences and purchases of others becomes more and more important in this mix. See Bruce D. Weinberg and Paul D. Berger, "Connected Lifetime Value: The Impact of Social Media," *Journal of Direct, Data and Digital Marketing Practice* 12 (2011): 328–344.

2. *Lifestyle changes.* When a customer takes a new job, or gets pregnant, or retires, or gets married or divorced—when his or her lifestyle or personal situation undergoes a substantial change, the LTV may also be affected.

3. *Behavioral cues.* The number of contacts initiated, the services or products contracted, the number of complaints or comments submitted, and payments made or not made are all examples of behavioral cues.

4. *Customer attitudes.* These include such things as satisfaction level, willingness to recommend your company or products, and likelihood of buying from you again. A customer's attitudes have a strong influence on his or her future behavior.

Lifetime Value Drivers

Academicians as well as businesses are paying more and more attention to the issue of customer loyalty, LTVs, and customer equity.[57] But loyalty isn't the only thing that goes into an LTV model. Cross-selling rate, share of customer, and even influence on other customers can legitimately be considered to be economic drivers of a customer LTV model, with different degrees of importance, based on the business model at issue.

With today's emphasis on social networks and customer **word of mouth** (see the discussion in Chapter 8), the degree to which any one customer might serve as a reference for an enterprise's brand with other customers is increasingly important, and another example of an LTV driver. One academic study published in *Harvard Business Review* examined the value of word-of-mouth referrals generated by customers for both a financial services firm and a telecommunications firm.[58] What the

---

[57] We've already discussed the elements of a lifetime value equation in great detail, but there is an increasing level of academic interest in this issue. Some of this discussion and research has been driven by an effort to explain the Internet stock bubble at the turn of the new century. For example, one study of business-to-consumer Internet companies found that a Web site's reach and "stickiness" (i.e., visitor retention) were closely correlated with genuine market value, as evidenced by the fact that those dot-com firms whose Web sites had relatively less reach and stickiness tended to lose a great deal more of their value when the bubble burst. Elizabeth Demers and Baruch Lev, "A Rude Awakening: Internet Shakeout in 2000," *Review of Accounting Studies* 6 (2001): 331–359. See also Weinberg and Berger, "Connected Lifetime Value: The Impact of Social Media," for the effect on LTV that social and online influence of a customer has over the preferences and purchases of others.

[58] For an insightful look into how online and face-to-face word of mouth (WOM) relate, see Ed Keller and Brad Fay, *The Face to Face Book: Why Real Relationships Rule in a Digital Marketplace* (New York: Free Press, 2012). See Ya You, Gautham G. Vadakkepatt, and Amit M. Joshi, "A Meta-Analysis of Electronic Word-of-Mouth Elasticity," *Journal of Marketing* 79 (March 2015): 19–39; Sinan Aral, "What Would Ashton Do—and Does It Matter?" *Harvard Business Review* 91, no. 5 (May 2013): 25–27; V. Kumar and Rohan Mirchandani, "Increasing the ROI of Social Media Marketing," *MIT Sloan Management Review* 54 (Fall 2012): 55–61; and V. Kumar, J. Andrew Petersen, and Robert P. Leone, "How Valuable Is Word of Mouth?" *Harvard Business Review* 85, no. 10 (October 2007): 139–146.

study's authors found was that typically less than half the customers who report that they plan to refer a customer to a firm actually do so, and after that, only a small fraction of customers who are referred to a business actually become profitable customers in their own right. Therefore, the study's authors contend, it is vital to understand the dynamics of customer word of mouth as a part of calculating LTV, because while referrals can be highly valuable, they are not so easy to track and measure. (This is the same study that compared customer spending value with customer referral value, and we discussed that aspect of it in Chapter 5.)

Lifestyle Changes

Demographic information and vital statistics can be useful tools to help model a customer's LTV. A big advantage of using these kinds of data is that often they can be obtained from third-party databases, independent of a company's own transactional and other records. Because these data are available independently, often a firm can use demographic and other data to predict the LTVs of *prospective* customers with whom it may have had little or no past contact, by comparing them demographically to similar current customers. (However, many databases don't contain an individual customer's demographic information; instead, they use a combination of census data and overlaid projections based on address or zip code.)

A lot of demographic information won't change much in the short term and won't be much help in predicting LTV changes. Unless it's a touchy subject, age is predictable based on birth year. But a lot of demographic information will change over time. The race of the children I adopt may cause me to rethink my own racial identity, and it's more common now even for gender to change. And, of course, it's not unlikely that a firm often has to revise incorrectly keyed data entries for these kinds of items).[59] The demographic information that will certainly change, however, is the kind of data we generally associate with a person's lifestyle or personal situation. Categorizing customers by their lifestyles is one of the most frequently found elements of any customer management program. It's logical to think that a customer's LTV will change with his or her age, albeit gradually. But more sudden changes in a person's lifestyle are even more important, such as professional or career moves, household address changes, and changes in marital status, children added to the household, education level, or health.

For some businesses, lifestyle changes are extremely important indicators of LTV. Getting married, moving, or getting divorced, for instance, precipitates all sorts of buying activity, from appliances to cars. It's important for a business to have some

---

[59] "The Effect of Dirty Data on Business: The Biggest Data Quality Challenges," white paper, Experian, 2013, available at https://www.edq.com/globalassets/whitepapers/the-biggest-data-quality-challenges-ebook.pdf, accessed February 12, 2016; and Verne Kopytoff, "Big Data's Dirty Problem," *Fortune,* June 30, 2014, available at http://fortune.com/2014/06/30/big-data-dirty-problem/, accessed February 12, 2016.

mechanism to learn about customers' lifestyle changes, whether through an online profile update or perhaps special offers for special occasions.

Business customers, too, go through stages and "lifestyle changes." When a business becomes less profitable or more profitable, its buying behavior likely will change. When a privately held business goes public, or when a company acquires another firm, its behavior will change. Pharmaceutical companies, for example, watch for changes in the professional lifestyles of the physicians who write prescriptions, such as taking on new partners or employees, adopting new medical practices, relocating offices, or acquiring new medical technologies. Similar changes occur within clinics and hospitals. Technology firms watch for lifestyle changes among companies that are heavy technology users, including changes in the size or makeup of a firm's internal information technology staff, and increased (or decreased) interest in outsourcing or offshoring.

Behavioral Cues

Suppose a business has a satisfied consumer customer spending $100 a month, with an estimated LTV of $10,000. Now suppose this customer calls in to complain about a faulty product or an episode of bad service. The call center rep handles the complaint professionally. As a result, the customer not only remains satisfied but actually writes a complimentary letter to the firm and tweets to friends and followers. It is highly likely that this customer's LTV will have increased dramatically with that transaction. The transaction created actual value for the company right then, even though the firm hadn't yet collected any cash as a result of the customer's increased propensity to buy or to recommend it to friends. In point of fact, the firm actually might have incurred a current-period cost to satisfy the complaint.

But that kind of transaction is a very big and obvious behavioral cue. There are many other such cues, not always as big and obvious, but just as predictive. In a business like telecom, or financial services, or retail, an abundance of behavioral cues exists within the billions of data points in many companies' customer transaction databases. A credit card customer begins to use her card less (or more). A mobile phone user signs up for a different plan. A customer buys a second product upgrade in just two months. A frequent business traveler begins flying in fully paid first-class seats or changes her address away from the airline's hub city. Behavioral cues apply equally well to B2B firms selling to corporate clients. Such firms may detect an increase in the number or quality of the people at the customer company who are involved in the business, or an early contract renewal, or a reduction in the service agreements in force at a customer's business site. Perhaps one client agrees to a more comprehensive service contract while another puts part of the business out for bid.

Behavioral cues have always been important to high-volume financial services businesses, primarily as an aid to managing credit risk. A credit card firm is likely to review its database of cardholder transactions closely in order to spot any anomalies that might indicate either that a card has been stolen or that a cardholder is getting into debt over his head. You might remember a call from your credit card company when you first used it in another country, or when you bought that larger-than-usual piece of jewelry, or when you ordered some expensive products online. Typically, the card company will call the cardholder just to verify that he or she is really the one engaging in these unprecedented activities and to reassure itself that the card is still actually in the holder's possession and hasn't been lost or stolen.

Behavioral cues are not hard to identify, and some of them can be easily understood at first glance:

- When a husband and wife each carry a credit card using the same account, the couple is much less vulnerable to competitive offers from other cards than either would have been as an individual cardholder.
- When a new customer buys a car on the recommendation of a friend, he is more likely to be satisfied for a longer period, and to consume additional branded services from the automobile company, such as financing and warranty extensions.

Obviously, a business should track transactions involving purchase and consideration, but it should also remember that not all interactions involve purchases. In addition to purchasing events, an enterprise should keep track of Web pages visited, sales calls received, surveys completed, and call center inquiries, for instance. It's not necessarily the wisest policy to pester customers themselves for data, but it's always smart to capture whatever interactions and transactions occur naturally during the course of business. The more transactional data points a firm has with respect to its customers, the more opportunity it will have for using the data to deduce the future behavior of particular customers or groups of customers within its customer and prospect base.

Remember the large consumer service business we mentioned earlier? The company's LTV model was useful as far as it went, but executives lamented that it would have been far more useful had the company been able to access additional records. They would have liked to account for each customer's supplementary spending, because this is a key element of the company's profit. But their systems couldn't make the connection. The company also sent out a regular satisfaction survey to recent customers, and although it used the results to improve its overall service, these data might have proven even more useful in predicting individual LTVs—not to mention improving a particular customer's value by meeting the needs she indicated in the satisfaction survey, perhaps generating additional business as a result.

At one of Canada's largest banks, customer portfolio managers are evaluated and rewarded in a way that mandates their continued interest in building short-term revenue as well as long-term customer equity. If you were the portfolio manager for a group of customers (who likely don't know of your existence), you'd be the gatekeeper for communications from the bank to each of those customers. It would be your job to figure out how to eliminate roadblocks to doing more business with each of those customers, and—by taking the customers' point of view based on analysis and insight—to maximize the value created by each of those customers. You wouldn't allow the mortgage people, say, to send everybody in your portfolio a mass mailing, but rather would insist that messages be sent only to those who'd find it relevant. At the end of the quarter, you would be rewarded based on two measurements:

1. How much profit did the bank make on your portfolio of customers this quarter?
2. As of this quarter, what is the three-year projected value of the customers in your portfolio?

This two-part compensation model guarantees that you will not be tempted to do anything that will make money in the short term but jeopardize long-term customer equity—no hidden fees, no service cuts valued by customers, nothing that will cut the long-term number. Unless both numbers are good, you still won't get a bonus.

Customer Attitudes

Other leading indicators of lifetime value change come not from observable customer behaviors but from attitudes—moods and points of view that can be accurately assessed only via surveys or fielded market research. Attitudes are important, however, because they influence behavior, so to the extent a firm tracks such attitudes, it should be able to make informed judgments about changes in its customer equity.[60] Although it's certainly not a linear relationship, in general, a customer who is highly satisfied with a firm's product or service is more likely to remain loyal to that firm, more likely to refer other customers to it, and more likely to buy additional products

---

[60] Customer attitudes, like other "soft" (nonfinancial) measures, were once the epicenter of a controversy. On one side were those who believed that customer attitudes, brand value, employee turnover, and other nonfinancial measures would prove to be clear predictors of future performance, and on the other side were those who maintained that a lot of what we believe, such as "customer satisfaction adds value" and "reduced employee turnover reduces costs," is simply folklore. See Allan Hansen, "Nonfinancial Performance Measures, Externalities, and Target Setting: A Comparative Case Study of Resolutions through Planning," *Management Accounting Research* 21, no. 1 (March 2010): 17–39; and Robert Bruce, "Non Financial Measures Just Don't Add Up," *Financial Times*, March 29, 2004, p. 10. But more recent studies tend to support the predictive value of "attitude" or "attitudinal loyalty." See Rich Karlgaard, *The Soft Edge: Where Great Companies Find Lasting Success* (San Francisco: Jossey-Bass, 2014); Vincent O'Connell and Don O'Sullivan, "The Influence of Lead Indicator Strength on the Use of Nonfinancial Measures in Performance Management: Evidence from CEO Compensation Schemes," *Strategic Management Journal* 35, no. 6 (June 2014): 826–844; and Donna M. Booker, Dan L. Heitger, and Thomas D. Schultz, "The Effect of Causal Knowledge on Individuals' Perceptions of Nonfinancial Performance Measures in Profit Prediction," *Advances in Accounting* 27, no. 1 (June 2011): 90–98.

or services from it than is a customer who is not highly satisfied.[61] At its core, Fred Reichheld's Net Promoter Score, discussed in Chapter 5, is based on the idea that a customer's willingness to recommend a product to a friend or colleague is directly correlated with the customer's own satisfaction with the product and with the future sales the product will generate from that customer. Some authorities have achieved moderate success in correlating customer satisfaction levels with market value.[62] Just as important, any decrease in customer satisfaction or willingness to recommend the company would almost certainly indicate a decline in a company's value.

The degree to which a firm is perceived to pay attention to its customers also affects customer attitudes and willingness to do business with it in the future. One classic study, jointly led by Roper Starch Worldwide and Peppers & Rogers Group, showed that among bank customers who rated their banks as providing good customer service, an ability to treat a customer as a distinct individual (such as providing a personal contact, sending only relevant messages, and anticipating the customer's needs) made a significant difference in that customer's future intentions. Twenty-six percent of those who rated their banks high on customer service but low on such "relationship capabilities" stated that they were likely to switch away at least one product in the next year. By contrast, among those who rated their banks high on customer service *and* relationship capabilities, just 1 percent stated any intention to switch products.[63] This astounding contrast is a strong

---

[61] But measuring customer satisfaction is not as straightforward as it might sound. Although we know "customer satisfaction" has ardent supporters for lots of good reasons, in our minds, the greatest criterion for its value as a metric is whether it is a good predictor of future customer value. The same is true for the Net Promoter Score.

[62] See "CFI Group: Research Links Customer Satisfaction to Stock Returns," *Business Wire*, July 5, 2012, http://www.businesswire.com/news/home/20120705005269/en/CFI-Group-Research-Links-Customer-Satisfaction-Stock, accessed February 12, 2016; Vladimir Ivanov, Kissan Joseph, and M. Babajide Wintoki, "Disentangling the Market Value of Customer Satisfaction: Evidence from Market Reaction to the Unanticipated Component of ACSI Announcements," *International Journal of Research in Marketing* 30, no. 2 (June 2013): 168–178; Xueming Luo, Ran Zhang, Weining Zhang, and Jaakko Aspara, "Do Institutional Investors Pay Attention to Customer Satisfaction and Why?" *Journal of the Academy of Marketing Science* 42, no. 2 (March 2014): 119–136; and Christopher Ittner and David Larcker, "Are Non-Financial Measures Leading Indicators of Financial Performance? An Analysis of Customer Satisfaction," *Journal of Accounting Research* 36 (1998): 1–36. Also see Ellen Garbarino and Mark S. Johnson, "The Different Roles of Satisfaction, Trust and Commitment in Customer Relationships," *Journal of Marketing* 63 (April 1999): 70–87. These researchers found that for low-relational customers, satisfaction is a better predictor of future behavior, but for high-relational customers, trust and commitment are more important.

[63] For more about the Roper Starch and Peppers & Rogers Group study, see "Customer Relationship Management in Financial Services: A National Perspective," Roper Starch Worldwide, CNO-385, September 2000. For an in-depth description of the research, see Jonathan Brookner and Julien Beresford, "One to One in Retail Financial Services: New Strategies for Creating Value Through Customer Relationships," Peppers & Rogers Group and LOMA (Life Office Management Association, Inc.), 2001.

endorsement for a customer relationship's benefits in retaining customers, at least when it comes to retail banking, and we've seen similar findings in the telecommunications industry.[64]

The key to ensuring that customer attitudes serve as a useful tool in tracking real-time LTV changes is to identify the correlations between a customer's current attitude—or change in attitude—and his or her actual behavior in the future (observable behaviors such as new purchases, repurchase, referrals, complaints and interactions, service calls, etc.). Measuring a customer's *change* in attitude would be particularly helpful for businesses that don't have the advantage of a sizable volume of customer transactions.

Stats and the Single Customer

To maximize ROC, an enterprise has to gain some practice in using LTV as a tool and in tracking changes in LTV over time. It can never be known exactly how much an investment in acquisition will yield, or how to measure retention precisely over an extended period, or how much additional business actually will be stimulated by a particular offer. Yet from empirical observations an analyst eventually will be able to deduce how LTV is likely to be influenced by various drivers and by the attitudes of customers. The big challenge will be to fashion the company's strategies not just to maximize this quarter's sales or "new customers added" but rather to maximize the rate at which the enterprise is creating overall economic value, in the long term as well as the short term.

Of course, statistical analysis has its limits. In a group of a million consumers, a statistical model can predict aggregate behavior, such as a likely response rate or attrition rate, with reasonable accuracy. Such models can detect behavior patterns that tend to indicate some future actions, such as defection, providing the manager with an ability to intervene. They can also be used as benchmarks.

---

[64] Jeffrey Prince and Shane Greenstein determined that switching a bundle would keep 40 percent of customers from switching phone/cable/Internet service, "Does Service Bundling Reduce Churn?" *Journal of Economics & Management Strategy* 23, no. 4 (Winter 2014): 839–875. Also see Alex Turnbull, "How One SaaS Startup Reduced Churn 71% Using 'Red Flag' Metrics," *Kissmetrics* blog, posted December 2013, https://blog.kissmetrics.com/using-red-flag-metrics/, accessed February 12, 2016; Emma K. Macdonald, Hugh N. Wilson, and Umut Konus, "Better Customer Insight—in Real Time," *Harvard Business Review* 90, no. 9 (September 2012): 102–108; and Michael Henrich and Martin Weiss, "Bundling Wins: The Case for Cable and Mobile Integration," white paper, Solon Strategy, July 2011, available at http://www.solonstrategy.com/uploads/tx_soloncm003/Solon_White_Paper_Telecoms_-_Bundling_Wins_01.pdf, accessed February 12, 2016. In another article, David Myron notes that "bundling two services usually reduces customer churn by 25 percent. Bundling a third product reduces it by an additional 13 percent, and a fourth product reduces churn by an additional 6 percent." "Telecoms Focus on Services, Not Price, to Reduce Churn," *Customer Relationship Management* (May 2004).

But reduce the size of the overall group being analyzed, and the stability of these statistical calculations begins to break down. At the level of the individual customer, even the most sophisticated statistical models are subject to a great deal of randomness and noise.

However, once a company does drill all the way down to the level of an individual customer, it can make direct, one-to-one contact, and this kind of interaction will always trump statistical models. If a firm has really good, up-to-date, reliable data about an individual customer, and if those data are based on direct interaction with the customer, then it should be able to predict the customer's behavior much more precisely than it could if the customer were simply one customer within some statistical cluster. For this reason, direct interaction with customers will provide an enterprise with the most useful and reliable leading indicators of those customers' future behavior.

For a company serving just a few hundred B2B customers, statistical models are rarely as useful as the objective judgments of the sales and account managers closest to the customers. These judgments, too, are just educated forecasts, but they can be made more reliable and accurate by adhering to a standardized set of criteria. Has a contract been proposed? Is there a standing purchase order? Do we provide the back-end maintenance as well as product installation? Is the relationship characterized by partnership and collaboration? Can this customer refer other customers to us? Have they done so in the past? Judgments made on the basis of such objective but nonquantitative criteria are critical to making educated decisions about customer LTVs. They help get a firm as close as possible, as objectively as possible, to understanding the actual values of individual customers.

Maximize Long-Term Value and Hit Short-Term Targets

The latest dashboard report on the CEO's desk at Bank ABC in Europe is brilliant. It says performance of his bank has been nothing short of stellar in the latest period. The bank is a large one in its market, and has not been scarred very badly by the financial sector troubles plaguing many smaller banks. Moreover, an aggressive strategy involving both branch expansion and advertising to attract the customers of some of the banks perceived as riskier has apparently paid off handsomely, with deposits and net income both up 15 percent for the period. Market share, in terms of assets under management, is up 2 percent over all. Board members are happy, shareholders are happy, the executive team is happy. And why shouldn't they all be happy? The bank's financial performance this period was stellar, as indicated on its most recent income statement (see Exhibit 11.3).

EXHIBIT 11.3   Income Statement of Bank ABC

Bank ABC Financials	Bank ABC	
	Last Period	This Period
Checking deposits	€170,000	€195,500
Savings deposits	€350,000	€402,500
Total deposit volume	€520,000	€598,000
Market selling rate	6.50%	6.50%
Earnings on total deposits	€33,800	€38,870
Interest paid, checking	0.50%	0.50%
Funding cost, checking	€850	€978
Interest paid, savings	4.50%	4.50%
Funding cost, savings	€15,750	€18,113
Total funding cost	€16,600	€19,090
Gross profit on deposits	€17,200	€19,780
Gross expenses	€15,288	€17,582
Net profit for bank	€1,913	€2,198
Year over year growth		**15%**

As festivities continue, however, an insidious truth is lurking beneath the surface. ABC is actually destroying shareholder value and nobody is aware of it. Its financial results emphasize product lines, and while product lines can all be profitable, it is not products that create value. By definition, customers create all value, and the first task for Bank ABC in interpreting its own financial statement should have been to try to understand its financial results in terms of which customers accounted for which parts of it. A relatively simple and inexpensive market survey at the bank would have revealed three principal types of retail customer, at the end of the current period:

- *"Loyalists," who have always done business with Bank ABC,*
- *"Shoppers," who shop around fairly regularly, and*
- *"New Acquisitions," brought in with the advertising, who have chosen to flee to Bank ABC in the wake of the financial crisis.*

Profile details of each group are shown in Exhibit 11.4.

Survey data such as this would have allowed Bank ABC executives to better allocate costs among these three different groups of customers, and also to calculate average lifetime values, as well as each type of customer's expected length of tenure at the bank (that is, the average duration of each type of customer's patronage at Bank ABC). But even before considering the potentially

(continued)

(Continued)

EXHIBIT 11.4   Three Types of Customer at Bank ABC

Loyalists	Shoppers	New Acquisitions
Total number: 12 million	Total number: 7 million	Total number: 1.5 million
Average age: 45	Average age: 35	Average age: 55
Bank ABC is their only bank in deposits. They may be working with other banks in other products.	They work with multiple banks and are frequently exploring alternatives, shopping for the best deals.	They work with multiple banks.
They go to branches often. Use of alternative channels is relatively low.	They are heavy users of Internet banking.	Very few of them use alternative channels.
Their price sensitivity is low.	Switching from bank to bank is easy, even for individual products, because they rely so heavily on the Internet.	They are likely to switch to smaller banks offering higher rates, once the financial crisis abates.
Loyal customers, they do not indicate any churn intentions.	Many of these customers are always hunting for the best rates.	Their main reason for coming to Bank ABC is its financial soundness, in the wake of the financial crisis.
Average churn rate: 5% p.a.	**Average churn rate: 20% p.a.**	**Average churn rate: 20% p.a.**

serious implications of significantly higher churn rates among two types of customers, the current-period income statement for the bank could have been broken into three distinct parts based on these three customer groups. Loyalists and New Acquisitions, for instance, are responsible for a disproportionate share of branch expenses because they use branches much more frequently. And advertising costs should be allocated mostly to the "New Acquisitions" group. A revised financial statement of the bank's results, this time with revenues and costs allocated more appropriately to the three customer groups that make up the bank's customer base, is shown in Exhibit 11.5.

It should be obvious now that the acquisition campaign has not actually been quite as successful as had been assumed. It turns out that New Acquisitions, as customers, are not very profitable, consuming an inordinate amount of call center and branch expense. Compared to Shoppers, who are several times more numerous than New Acquisitions, yet have the same total level of checking and savings deposits and yield the same total gross profit as a group,

EXHIBIT 11.5   Bank ABC's Income by Customer Group

Allocated Financials (000)	Loyalists	Shoppers	New Acquisitions
Number of customers (000)	12,000	7,000	1,500
Checking deposits	€127,500	€34,000	€34,000
Savings deposits	€262,500	€70,000	€70,000
Total deposit volume	€390,000	€104,000	€104,000
Deposits per customer	€32,500	€14,857	€69,333
Gross profit on deposits	€12,900	€3,440	€3,440
Allocated expenses:			
Branch expenses	€7,222	€1,317	€2,545
Call center expenses	€1,734	€885	€574
Retention concessions	€-	€46	€46
Advertising	€160	€129	€2,400
Other	€342	€91	€91
Total allocated expenses	€9,458	€2,468	€5,656
Net allocated profit	**€3,442**	**€972**	**€(2,216)**
Profit per customer	€286.83	€138.86	€(1,477.33)
Profit per cust w/o advert	€300.17	€157.29	€122.67

the expenses required to handle New Acquisitions are much higher. Even after eliminating the cost of advertising (on the assumption that once customers have been acquired, the job of mass advertising has been done), the bank's expenses required for handling all the New Acquisitions are still about a third higher than for handling all the Shoppers, and on a per-customer basis the difference is acute. The per-customer profit figures are also revealing. It's lucky for the bank that Loyalists, at this juncture anyway, are the most numerous customers, because profit per Loyalist is by far the highest, whether advertising is counted or not.

There is, however, an even more important issue to be raised with respect to Bank ABC's financial condition, and this has to do with whether it is paying enough attention to its long-term prospects, and the quality of its customer equity. A short-term focus can easily undermine the long-term value of a bank. This should not be a surprising revelation, in the wake of the financial industry crisis of 2008–2009. Numerous pundits and gurus have discussed the perils of focusing on short-term results. Nevertheless, stock exchanges around the world are ruthlessly critical of banks failing to hit end-of-year targets. Being a bank executive is a thorny task these days: On the one hand, countless newspaper articles are lambasting your focus on end-of-period results and deprecating the recklessness of your peers in managing their risks. On the other hand, analysts

(continued)

(*Continued*)

continue to judge bank performance by the numbers in the quarterly financial reports. Everybody acknowledges a need to strike a balance between short-term and long-term results, but nobody can agree on how to do it.

It is important for every bank to understand that its customer activities create value both in the short term, by delivering current-period profits (or losses), and in the long term, by creating (or destroying) customer equity. Return on Customer[SM] is a straightforward performance metric combining these two objectives. But regardless of whether this metric is formally calculated, the most important issue for a bank is to monitor the lifetime values of its customers over time, and the most direct and useful way to do this is simply to drill down on its business by individual customer, or by customer segment.

Exhibit 11.6 is a sobering set of numbers that uses the churn rates of these various customer groups, along with their profitability-per-customer numbers (after advertising expense has been removed), to derive average customer lifetime values for the three different types of customers. In addition, some possible strategies for improving each group's profitability, over time, are evaluated, in order to see how much leverage there might be for the bank to improve LTV. Shoppers and New Acquisitions each are expected to churn at a rate of about 20 percent per year, which means their average tenure will only be about 3 years, compared to about 13 years for Loyalists. In other words, the number of Loyalists the bank starts with in Year 1 will be cut by 50 percent around year 13, while Shoppers and New Acquisitions will both be half gone in just 3 years (hardly seems worth the effort, right?). To derive customer lifetime values, we simply assumed that each customer would go on earning the same profit, year after year, provided that they remained a customer. Then we reduced this profit each year by the customer's churn rate (to account for the likelihood that this profit would no longer be coming in at all), and we applied a rather generous financial discount rate for net present value calculations of 10 percent. (A discount rate as high as 20 percent would be applicable to many businesses, but this is a large bank with little actual financial risk.)

EXHIBIT 11.6 Customer Lifetime Value of Different Groups for Bank ABC

Per-Customer LTV	Loyalists	Shoppers	New Acquisitions
Churn rate	5%	20%	20%
Half-life of expected customer tenure	13 years	3 years	3 years
Avg Customer 20-year LTV, w/o advertising	€1,980	€561	€437
Value of increasing cross-selling by 10%	€325	€87	€87
Value of reducing churn by 5%	N/A	€105	€82

What Exhibit 11.6 shows is that the Loyalists, per customer, have four to five times more long-term value (customer LTV) than either of the other types of customers. Moreover, even if a marketing effort to improve cross-selling by 10 percent is successful, this effort will still increase customer LTVs by less than 20 percent each.

Perhaps of more immediate interest to the bank would be the fact that in the New Acquisitions group, the loss *per customer* in the current period is over €1,400, because of the heavy one-time advertising burden, so there is just no way at all that the firm can ever pay itself back for that average loss, given these customers' tepid lifetime values. In other words, the customer-acquisition campaign might have succeeded in adding customers, but because of the extremely short duration of these customers' tenures, and the consequently low lifetime values they exhibit, it was still a dismal failure as a marketing campaign. In the end it chewed up a not-inconsequential amount of Bank ABC's shareholder value.

The executive team was very happy about the acquisition of this new group of customers, but they should have been feeling exactly the opposite. They should have been using the available information to question their decision to spend so much for so little actual economic benefit. Had Bank ABC's executives been fully aware of their bank's financial situation, doubtless their end-of-year party would not have been so cheerful.

The Bank ABC story makes it clear where priorities of the bank should be. So why do companies have such a hard time following the right path? The insurmountable barrier is the target-setting mechanism followed by most, if not all, banks. They invariably set their targets in terms of products: Sell this many credit cards, extend that many new mortgage loans, book that many new deposits into current accounts, and so forth. By focusing only on the profitability of products, campaigns, or channels, they fail to recognize how different customers may have different effects on financial results. And because they didn't look very carefully at their customers, they missed the fact that some of these customers would be doing very little (if anything) to benefit the bank within just a few years.

Trying to change completely the way targets are set is likely to be a quixotic attempt for many banks. When everybody in the stock market is holding his breath to see end-of-year growth on deposit volumes, it can be challenging to convince executives to evaluate these traditionally important figures in the context of the equally important ideas of customer equity and Return on Customer. If Bank ABC were to organize its thinking, its data, and its analysis on a customer-by-customer basis, consider the steps they might take in the next planning and budgeting cycle:

1. *Investigate customer growth opportunities:*
   a. *Look for product volume asymmetries in the Loyalist group, that is, high deposit volume with low credit card volume.*

(*continued*)

(Continued)

    b. Identify cross-sell opportunities by data mining effort. In other words, find products for customers in a way that benefits those customers.

    c. Uncover primary motivators for the Loyalist group to accept cross-sell offers in different product categories by a market survey. In other words, **differentiate most valuable customers** *by needs and behaviors, and communicate with those customers accordingly.*

    d. Use needs and behavior differentiation strategies to design relevant offers and messaging for customers, in a timely way—in order to identify possible value propositions and customer growth strategies.

    e. Test value propositions and strategies.

    f. Calculate expected ROC in each case, considering the likelihood of acceptance of cross-sell offers, cost of extending these offers, and resulting changes in cash flow from customers in this group.

2. Investigate retention priorities:

    a. Investigate what might be needed to entice Shoppers to remain with the bank, perhaps with a survey and some qualitative research.

    b. Calculate the cost of retention offers needed to address their issues.

    c. Identify the value proposition alternatives as well as retention strategies.

    d. Calculate expected churn rate decrease for each value proposition and strategy alternative.

    e. Test value propositions and strategies.

    f. Estimate expected ROC in each case considering possible reduction in churn rate, cost of reducing churn by meeting the needs of this group, and resulting change in cash flow streams from customers in this group.

3. Act on acquisition priorities:

    a. Survey customers who do not currently do business with the bank.

    b. Identify conditions to churn to this bank and expected customer lifetime values if they can be acquired.

    c. Calculate cost of meeting their conditions, that is, cost of acquisition.

    d. Identify different value propositions and strategies that will cater to different customer groups who do not currently work with the bank.

    e. Test value propositions and strategies.

    f. Calculate expected Return on Customer in each case, considering cost of acquisition and cash flow streams expected from acquired customers.

    g. Emphasize a cessation in acquisition of high-cost, low-profitability customers.

4. Finalize plans and budget by optimizing acquisition, retention, and growth around ROC:

    a. Trade off growth/retention/acquisition priorities based on Return on Customer values expected from different value propositions and strategies.

> **b.** *Set priorities and allocate budget by selecting value propositions and strat-egies that will yield highest Return on Customer. This will define exactly what the bank will be doing in growth/retention/acquisition.*
>
> **c.** *Finalize product-based targets and budget by considering:*
>
> **i.** *Cross-sell targets to Loyalists and associated expense budget.*
>
> **ii.** *Impact of reduced churn rate of Shoppers on product targets and asso-ciated retention budget.*
>
> **iii.** *Product volume to be brought in by New Acquisitions and associated acquisition budget.*
>
> Bank ABC will not necessarily meet all conditions demanded by all three groups. The process described above not only sets priorities for the bank in terms of how much to spend for growth/retention/acquisition, but it also helps to define how to spend the money by identifying the value propositions and strategies that need to be adopted. We should also remember that every group is likely to have subgroups and sub-subgroups. A bank with millions of retail customers should not settle for just three basic customer "types." But at Bank ABC, if they don't even analyze their business with a very few, basic groups of different kinds of customers, they will probably never be able to manage their business effectively. And, when the end comes, they are likely to be completely unaware. They might even have been celebrating just the previous year!
>
> ---
>
> Special thanks to Yücel Ersöz for his work on these subjects and this adaptation of his article, "Maximize Long-Term Value and Hit Short-Term Targets," *Customer Strategist* 2, no. 1 (March 2010): 40–44. Formerly a partner at Peppers & Rogers Group, Middle East, Yücel Ersöz is director of organizational development and HR systems at Turkcell.

Summary

The metrics associated with managing customer relationships can provide invalu-able insight into the profitability potential of the enterprise's customer base and the viability of the enterprise's new customer-strategy business processes. The cus-tomer-centric enterprise does, however, have to concern itself with other measure-ments and analyzing other pieces of information that are more specific to growing the overall value of each customer. Treating different customers differently can entail a detailed analysis of each customer to determine how the enterprise can alter his **trajectory** with the enterprise. Often this analysis can help turn customer infor-mation into knowledge the enterprise can use to help customers meet their needs.

The triggers, or predictors, of individual customer action and opportunity usu-ally cannot be seen without detailed analysis. This is the increasingly complex and far-from-intuitive science of *customer-based analytics* and *customer experi-ence analytics*, and having this discipline well represented on an enterprise-wide cross-functional team is critical. Sophisticated statistical models powered by technology can uncover some remarkable and highly predictive patterns. The ability to "mine data" is so valuable that its precise manifestations can be proprietary within certain companies. In the next chapter, we uncover some of these scientific applications of analytics within the customer-strategy enterprise.

Food for Thought

1. Let's imagine you are the customer portfolio manager of a wireless phone company. How should you be evaluated at the end of the quarter? Straight sales from your customers? Net sales (sales minus cost to serve)? Customer satisfaction? Would it make sense for you to be evaluated on a combination of how much your company made from your customers this quarter and also—as of this quarter—what the two-year projected value of your customer base is? Five-year projected value? Why?
2. If a company rewards employees based on a combination of current and future values of customers, how might that change decision making?
3. Should the value of customers a company doesn't yet have be calculated and taken into account in the present quarter? Why or why not?
4. How is retention different from share of customer (SOC) as a measure and how would it be used differently? Why are both important?

Glossary

Business model   How a company builds economic value.

Churn rate   The rate at which customers leave and enter the franchise. High churn indicates a simultaneously high number of defecting customers and high number of new customers. Usually a symptom of low customer loyalty. Also called *customer churn* or *turnover.*

Customer equity   The sum of all the lifetime values (LTVs) of an enterprise's current and future customers, or the total value of the enterprise's customer relationships. A customer-centric company would view customer equity as its principal corporate asset.

Customer portfolio   A group of similar customers. The customer-focused enterprise will design different treatments for different portfolios of customers.

Customer service   "Customer service" involves helping a customer gain the full use and advantage of whatever product or service was bought. When something goes wrong with a product, or when a customer has some kind of problem with it, the process of helping the customer overcome this problem is often referred to as "customer care."

Demographic data   Directly supplied data that include age, income, education level, marital status, household composition, gender, home ownership, and so on.

Differentiate   Prioritize by value; understand different needs. Identify, recognize, link, remember.

Leading indicators   The variables driving any firm's LTV model, which tend to fall into four general categories: LTV drivers, lifestyle changes, behavioral cues, and customer attitudes.

Legacy metrics   Metrics based on running a business before technology made it possible to treat different customers differently. Such metrics would include things such as quarterly product sales, cost of goods sold, number of new customers acquired, and financial metrics such as EBITDA (earnings before interest, taxes, depreciation, and amortization), ROI (return on investment), and TSR (total shareholder return). Also refers to any measurements a company has traditionally used.

Lifetime value (LTV)   The net present value of the future stream of cash flow attributable to that customer. LTV directly represents the long-term financial benefit of a customer's continuing patronage.

Lifetime value drivers   The elements of the LTV equation—the actual components that determine how much value the customer creates for the company over time.

Most valuable customers (MVCs)   Customers with high actual values but not a lot of unrealized growth potential. These are the customers who do the most business, yield the highest margins, are most willing to collaborate, and tend to be the most loyal.

Needs   What a customer needs from an enterprise is, by our definition, synonymous with what she wants, prefers, or would like. In this sense, we do not distinguish a customer's needs from her wants. For that matter, we do not distinguish needs from preferences, wishes, desires, or whims. Each of these terms might imply some nuance of need—perhaps the intensity of the need or the permanence of it—but in each case we are still talking, generically, about the customer's needs.

Net Promoter Score (NPS)   A compact metric owned by Satmetrix and designed initially by Bain's Fred Reichheld to quantify the strength of a company's word-of-mouth reputation among existing customers, and widely used as a proxy for customer satisfaction. See www.satmetrix.com.

NPV   Net present value.

Predictive analytics   A wide class of statistical analysis tools designed to help businesses sift through customer records and other data in order to model the likely future behaviors of other, similar customers.

Return on Customer (ROC)   A metric directly analogous to return on investment (ROI), specifically designed to track how well an enterprise is using customers to create value. ROC equals a company's current-period cash flow (from customers) plus the change in customer equity during the period, divided by the customer equity at the beginning of the period. ROC is pronounced are-oh-see.

Share of customer (SOC)   For a customer-focused enterprise, share-of-customer is a conceptual metric designed to show what proportion of a customer's overall need is being met by the enterprise. It is not the same as "share of wallet," which refers to the specific share of a customer's spending in a particular product or service category. If, for instance, a family owns two cars, and one of them is your car company's brand, then you have a 50 percent share of wallet with this customer, in the car category. But by offering maintenance and repairs, insurance, financing, and perhaps even driver training or trip planning, you can substantially increase your "share of customer."

Total Shareholder Return (TSR)   Represents the change in capital value of a listed/quoted company over a period (typically one year or longer), plus dividends, expressed as a plus-or-minus percentage of the opening value.

Trajectory   The path of the customer's financial relationship through time with the enterprise.

Turnover   Also known as *churn rate* or *customer churn*. The rate at which a company loses some customers and acquires others in their place.

Unrealized potential value   The difference between a customer's potential value and a customer's actual value (i.e., the customer's lifetime value).

Value creators   Companies with increasing customer equity over time. The combination of short- and long-term value created by their customers occurs at a rate that is higher than their cost of capital.

Value destroyers   Companies with ROC below zero, regardless of current profitability.

Value harvesters   Companies whose ROC is below their cost of capital (but not yet negative), so that they are using up customer profits that have already been "put in the bank" in the form of customer equity. These companies may earn a current profit, but because they are not replenishing their customer equity enough, their future growth potential is limited.

Word of mouth (WOM)   A customer's willingness to refer a product or service to others. This referral value may be as small as an oral mention to one friend, or a robust announcement on social media, or may be as powerful as going "viral."

CHAPTER 12

Using Customer Analytics to Build the Success of the Customer-Strategy Enterprise

Progress might have been all right once but it has gone on too long.

—Ogden Nash

To the customer-centric enterprise, data about individual customers are like gold nuggets that, if collected and used effectively, can increase the value of the customer base significantly. **Data mining** is a frequently used term for the process of extracting useful nuggets of information from a vast database of customer information; but as the relationship revolution has taken hold, the data-mining process itself has also undergone an important transformation. In the pre-interactive age, data-mining techniques were used to uncover information about the types of customers to whom particular offers should be made, answering the question: Who is the next most likely customer to buy this product? Today, the question asked by companies engaged in managing ongoing, interactive relationships with individual customers is: What is the next most likely product that this particular customer will want to buy? As we have seen throughout this book, rather than optimizing around each product, the customer-strategy enterprise needs to optimize around the customer.

In truth, both product optimization and customer optimization have roles to play in any competitive enterprise's efforts to get, keep, and grow customers. But in the interactive age, much more so than in the past, individual customer information drives the central engine of competition. Without reliable insights into the value and needs of individual customers, the customer-based enterprise will be completely rudderless.

(continued)

(Continued)

In this chapter, we look at **customer analytics**—the way we think of data mining now—and learn about the fundamental issues facing customer-strategy companies when they are working with and using large amounts of customer data.

Experts define the term *data mining* largely in terms of its usefulness in uncovering hidden trends or yielding previously unknown insights about the nature of a firm's customers. SAS Institute defines data mining as "the process of finding anomalies, patterns, and correlations within large data sets to predict outcomes."[1] Michael J. A. Berry and Gordon S. Linoff, who have written several books on the subject, define data mining as "the process of exploration and analysis, by automatic or semiautomatic means, of large quantities of data in order to discover meaningful patterns and rules," and, for the customer-centric company, founded on the belief "that business actions should be based on learning, that informed decisions are better than uninformed decisions, and that measuring results is beneficial to the business."[2] And Jill Dyché, partner and cofounder of Baseline Consulting, says data mining is "a type of advanced analysis used to determine certain patterns within data . . . most often associated with predictive analysis based on historical detail, and the generation of models for further analysis and query."[3]

Rather than limit ourselves to the term *data mining*, however, we prefer the term *customer analytics*. Although data mining and customer analytics are not really different things, the analogy to mining itself implies a batch process, with the enterprise searching out nuggets of information and then putting them to use. The reality, however, in the interactive age, is that businesses need to have continuously developing, real-time insights into the nature of their individual customers, not only so that the right marketing campaign can be created and launched, but also so the customer can be given the appropriate offer in real time **(real-time analytics)**, while she is on the phone, reading a newspaper online, shopping at the Web site, or standing at the checkout counter.

Customer analytics, therefore, offers the missing link to understanding customers:

> Customer analytics enables the enterprise to classify, estimate, predict, cluster, and more accurately describe data about customers, using mathematical models and algorithms that ultimately simplify how it views its customer base and how it behaves toward individual customers.

[1] Available at http://www.sas.com/en_us/insights/analytics/data-mining.html, accessed February 15, 2016.
[2] Michael J. A. Berry and Gordon S. Linoff, *Mastering Data Mining* (New York: John Wiley & Sons, 2000); Berry and Linoff, *Data Mining Techniques for Marketing, Sales, and Customer Relationship Management* (Indianapolis: John Wiley & Sons, 2004), p. 3.
[3] Jill Dyché and Evan Levy, *Customer Data Integration: Reaching a Single Version of the Truth* (Hoboken, NJ: John Wiley & Sons, 2006), p. 275. See also Jill Dyché, *e-Data: Turning Data into Information with Data Warehousing* (Reading, MA: Addison-Wesley, 2000).

prediction.[4] Prediction helps enterprises use the value of customer information to optimize each interaction with each customer. Today, leading companies integrate the most relevant elements of their customer-analytics algorithms into their actual touch point applications. If a customer behaves a certain way, then the mathematical algorithm can analyze that behavior and instantly access the most relevant offer for that customer, taking into account everything the enterprise knows or is able to predict about each customer, in real time. Customer analytics enables the enterprise to classify, estimate, predict, cluster, and more accurately describe data about customers, using mathematical models and algorithms that ultimately simplify how it views its customer base and how it behaves toward individual customers.

The dilemma facing many companies that amass huge customer databases today is simply how to make sense of the data. Analytical software has become a critical component of the customer-strategy enterprise, and the data scientists who can operate such software are in great demand. The mathematical data models that analytical software can produce are inherently simplifications of the "real world"—they represent how customers have behaved before and will likely behave again. They enable a company to view correlations within large sets of customer data and within and among various parts of its business. By analyzing historic information and applying it to current customer data, these mathematical models and algorithms can predict future events, with varying degrees of accuracy, based not just on the amount of data collected but also on the power of the analysis applied to the data. Using customer analytics, an enterprise can sometimes predict whether a customer will buy a certain product or will defect to a competitor.

Verizon Wireless Uses Analytics to Predict and Reduce Churn

As you may remember from the previous chapter, Verizon Wireless, a joint venture between Verizon and Vodafone, dramatically increased its **customer equity** during the four-year period from the end of 2001 through the end of 2005 (see Chapter 11). It accomplished this feat with a mix of excellent customer acquisition tactics and superb retention improvement—dramatically reducing the monthly churn rate on retail contract customers from 2.6 percent to 1.1 percent.

And how did Verizon actually accomplish this dramatic surge in value creation? Through a sophisticated use of customer analytics. First, Verizon developed a "predictive churn model" (PCM) to identify as far in advance as possible

(continued)

---

[4] Deborah L. Vence, "Astute Analytics," *Marketing News* 41, no. 20 (December 2007): 34; and Robert Nisbet, John Elder, and Gary Miner, *Handbook of Statistical Analysis and Data Mining Applications* (Salt Lake City, UT: Academic Press, 2009).

(Continued)

those particular customers who might be about to leave the franchise soon. The models also matched these likely churners with specific, relevant, and timely offers—different offers being more or less relevant for different types of customers, with different calling patterns, demographics, and other characteristics. In addition, Verizon generated a "predictive takers model" (PTM)—that is, a model of the types of customers most likely to *accept* its offer and remain in the franchise. By combining its use of PCM with PTM, Verizon was able to cull the relatively large number of customers who were identified as having a high propensity to leave into a much smaller group of customers who would be more likely to accept Verizon's offer and remain loyal.

Simultaneously, analytics helped predict the right kind of plan for other subscribers, based on each customer's individual call usage pattern. Many customers who were not on the optimum plan were then contacted and offered a more relevant plan; retention went up within this larger, already more loyal population as well.

Importantly, one of the factors Verizon's management credits for making this analytics program a success is the fact that the effort was fashioned by a multidisciplinary team, with representatives from several different, non–information technology (IT) departments.

Business benefits accruing to Verizon Wireless from its use of customer analytics include not just the very significant long-term revenue increase due to more loyal customers but immediately reduced marketing costs as well. For instance, the company's direct-mail budget for "churner mailing" was reduced by 60 percent because of the highly targeted nature of its analytics-driven marketing campaigns.

Sources: Don Peppers and Martha Rogers, Ph.D., *Rules to Break and Laws to Follow: How Your Business Can Beat the Crisis of Short-Termism* (Hoboken, NJ: John Wiley & Sons, 2008), p. 84; and Christophe Giraud-Carrier, "Success Stories in Data/Text Mining," Brigham Young University, available at https://facwiki.cs.byu.edu/DML/index.php/, accessed September 1, 2010.

Companies produce large amounts of data through a wide array of customer-related business processes, including order entry, billing, reservations, complaint handling, product specification, Web interactions, and sales calls. The data often are fed into a data warehouse, where much of it lies hidden in "data tombs," forgotten about for years. Often, even when a firm has the customer analytics resources necessary to unleash the value of its data, it soon discovers that much of its information is "dirty" (expired, irrelevant, nonsequential, or nonsensible) and needs to be "cleaned" (eliminated, updated, correlated, and refined). As customer analytics tools and technology become more affordable and easier to use, however, enterprises are starting to feel competitive pressure to improve their capabilities in this area.[5] The various activities involved in readying customer data for analysis, and the **analysis process** itself, include:

- *Classification,* or assigning instances to a group, then using the data to learn the pattern of traits that identify the group to which each instance belongs.
- *Estimation,* for determining a value for some unknown continuous variable, such as credit card balance or income.
- *Regression,* which uses existing values to forecast what continuous values are likely to be.
- *Prediction,* or using historical data to build a model to forecast future behavior.
- *Clustering,* which maps customers within the database into groups based on their similarities. (See more about clustering in the following section.)

CRM in the Cloud

As open source computing and **social media** have both evolved, newer and more robust tools for managing customer relationships have become available. First-generation, enterprise **customer relationship management (CRM)** systems brimmed with functionality but were often costly and time consuming to implement, and sometimes difficult to update and maintain as well. Second-generation solutions improved cost of ownership by moving to a hosted software-as-a-service (SaaS) delivery model—without sacrificing features—but this still kept companies locked into proprietary platforms. Now, as social and open source computing technology becomes more capable, businesses can manage more and more of the CRM task "in the cloud," so to speak. This can reduce the complexity and costs of maintaining robust customer relationships while increasing their ability to mine customer insights that lead to competitive advantage.

(continued)

---

[5] See Hugh J. Watson, "Bridging the IT/Business Culture Chasm," *Business Intelligence Journal* 14, no. 1 (2009): 4–7; Matthew Shanahan, "Moving Target: Understanding Customer Demand," *Information Today* 27, no. 2 (February 2010): 21; Detlev Zwick and Janice Denegri Knott, "Manufacturing Customers: The Database as New Means of Production," *Journal of Consumer Culture* 9 (2009): 221–248; Hugh J. Watson, Dale L. Goodhue, and Barbara H. Wixom, "The Benefits of Data Warehousing: Why Some Organizations Realize Exceptional Payoffs," *Information and Management* 39 (2002): 491–502; and Hugh J. Watson, David A. Annino, Barbara Wixom, K. Liddell Avery, and Mathew Rutherford, "Current Practices in Data Warehousing," *Information Systems Management* (Winter 2001): 47–55.

(Continued)

Customer Management Evolves, and So Do the Tools

The art of managing customer relationships has evolved dramatically over the past 20 years, thanks in large part to the fragmentation of media and, more recently, the shift in control from company to customer. The traditional sales and marketing funnel, in which prospects are led from awareness to consideration to purchase in an orderly, linear fashion, has been scrambled beyond recognition. It's no longer a big bureaucracy talking to peons who can't talk back. Companies are no longer in charge. They're influential participants, but participants nevertheless.

This level playing field has been groomed primarily by social media, which has democratized the creation and sharing of information. Social media has made trust-based relationships more important. There are two elements of that relationship: Customers have to believe companies have their interests at heart, and companies have to be competent enough to execute and fulfill the obligation.

As the traditional vendor/customer relationship has evolved, so has the technology to support the relationship. This evolution of CRM software can be tracked through three main stages:

1. *Enterprise CRM.* Popularized during the 1990s, enterprise applications for CRM were based on client/server computing and represented a quantum leap in functionality over simple spreadsheet and contact-management applications. Unfortunately, the complexity of these applications also made them costly to implement and maintain. In some instances, adoption rates lagged because end users were forced to adapt to processes dictated more by software design than by business needs. The sometimes rigid requirements for data entry and workflow resulted in slow buy-in among users, particularly the marketing and sales people who stood to benefit the most from the use of the tools. (In one widely publicized survey, some 80 percent of salespeople reported that their own firm's CRM solution didn't work.) Although this resistance to process change was a significant barrier to many CRM implementations, the perceived benefits of improving customer account management—from increased satisfaction and loyalty, to more cross-selling opportunities—made CRM systems a must-have for many large organizations.

2. *SaaS CRM.* CRM vendors began taking their first steps into the cloud in the early 2000s, offering hosted, SaaS solutions that took the implementation burden off the shoulders of the corporate IT group—and brought the benefits of robust CRM to small and medium-size businesses. These offerings were more scalable than their predecessors, allowing companies to add seats or functionality as needed (hence the term *on demand*). IT overhead was reduced, since hosting was outsourced to the software provider. (The Gartner Group estimates that businesses have seen project savings between

25 and 40 percent after deploying CRM applications through SaaS and that 30 percent of new **customer service** and support application investments will be through the SaaS model by 2012.)[a] Maintenance improved as well, with vendor updates more seamlessly integrated into the subscription-based offerings. Although the deployment model improved significantly, however, the development model retained many of the characteristics of CRM enterprise solutions. SaaS solutions were still largely proprietary and entirely controlled by the vendor, resulting in limited customization capabilities on the front end and limited integration possibilities on the back end. Nevertheless, SaaS represented a significant step forward in the evolution of customer management and is part of a broader movement that shows no signs of slowing down. SaaS solutions accounted for 18 percent of the overall CRM market in 2008—with that revenue percentage reaching 33 percent in some CRM subsegments, according to Gartner.

3. *CRM in the cloud.* This step in CRM's technological evolution is slowly coming into focus. By combining SaaS with the commercial open source development model, an "open cloud" CRM solution can be created that proponents say reduces investment risk significantly. Portable across platforms and partners, interoperable with other open source data and applications, and more customizable by end users, an open cloud CRM solution also allows customers themselves to participate in the environment rather than simply serving as targets or leads. In effect, this turns the focus of CRM away from the "M"—management—and more toward the "R"—relationship. Twitter, blogs, wikis, YouTube, and RSS feeds all become tools in the CRM toolbox. But here's a key point: IT no longer owns the toolbox. See Exhibit 12.1.[b]

One could argue that "CRM in the cloud" is not even CRM anymore. It's a self-service model in which the customers themselves are taking over.

Cloud computing has the potential to provide key customer insights. Access to a broader set of data residing in cloud environments, including social networks, gives companies more insight into how best to reach customers at any point in the customer life cycle, from awareness, to consideration, to repurchase. This will enable rapid redeployment of sales and marketing resources to activities that have the most impact.

A company can't change customer behavior if its customer managers don't know anything about what the customer needs or is doing with the product. Overwhelmingly, companies organize their data around who their most valuable customers are. That's looking at it from the wrong end. In best practices, companies organize the data around customer needs as well as customer values.

This is where the open cloud can have a significant impact, because it enables companies to track more than just transactions. There's a seemingly

(continued)

(Continued)

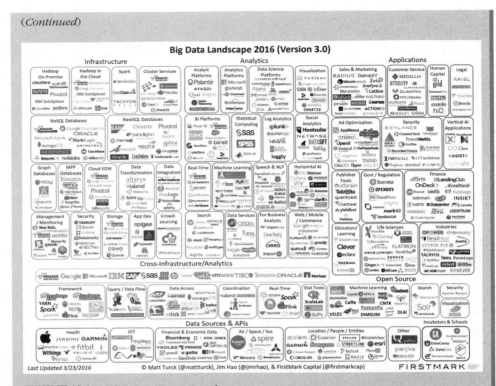

EXHIBIT 12.1   The Big Data Landscape
Source: The Conference Board, Inc., © 2016

endless cache of unstructured data wafting around the Web, and the companies that can capture it, analyze it, and act on it are the ones that will carve out competitive advantage.

The goal is to see the situation faced by each customer through that customer's own eyes. The open cloud may provide an important lens to bring that view into focus.

Source: Adapted from Peppers & Rogers Group and Sugar CRM white paper, "Getting Social: The Open Road to 'CRM 3.0,'" 2009, available at www.1to1media.com/view .aspx?docid=31736, accessed September 1, 2010.

[a] "Gartner Says that 30 Percent of New Customer Service and Support Application Investments Will Be through the SaaS Model by 2012" (November 2008), available at www.gartner.com/it/page.jsp?id=808112, accessed September 1, 2010.

[b] Thanks to Mark Turck, Partner at FirstMark Capital, for his ideas and the use of this graphic.

Customer analytics is especially useful for consumer marketing companies that collect transactional data through call centers, Web sites, or electronic points of sale. Banks, credit card companies, telecommunications firms, retailers, and even airlines adopted customer analytics as a vital part of their business operations earlier than other companies. These kinds of companies tend to generate large volumes of customer-specific information in the natural course of operating their businesses, often resulting in vast data warehouses, containing terabytes of data.

Royal Bank of Canada has been focused on customer relationships in its retail banking business for well over a decade and a half now and became a "best practice" case study in this area years ago. One of the secrets of the bank's success is the fact that it constantly monitors the behavioral cues in its customer database in order to optimize current income results against likely changes in lifetime value for individual customers. It has a great deal of data, but it must also do the right analysis in order to spot the cues. For instance, until recently the bank's "Behavioural Based Modeling" system calculated the effects its various products and services had on customer lifetime values by using customer-specific revenues, but using the average (i.e., non-customer-specific) cost-to-serve figure. The problem is that banking customers don't all cost the same to serve. Different customers incur different costs. One customer might prefer dealing with the bank online, for instance, while another might prefer the more expensive teller window. Customers will generate different levels of credit risk, processing charges, and other expenses. After upgrading its software, Royal Bank of Canada began tracking customer-specific costs as well as revenues. The result was that the accuracy of its lifetime value figures improved immensely, with more than 75 percent of its consumer customers moving two or more deciles in rank as a result.

In evaluating its actions for different customers, Royal Bank of Canada optimizes "overall efficiencies," a term the bank uses to include both current income and life-time value (LTV) changes in the calculation. One example of a policy change based on maximizing overall efficiencies has to do with "courtesy overdraft limits." This product is now provided for the vast majority of consumer customers rather than just its heavy-hitters. Each customer's overdraft limit is set based on that particular customer's overall relationship with the bank. Anyone who has been a customer for at least 90 days, has a low-risk credit score, and has made at least one deposit in the last month will have some level of overdraft protection. Not only does this enhance each customer's experience with the bank, but it actually increases the bank's efficiency during the check-clearing process, reducing the number of write-offs and allowing account managers to focus on sales activities. (It also reduces the number and cost of contact center calls handling irate customers who want their overdraft fees reversed.)

Overall, since initiating the program, the bank has increased the profitability of its average client by 13 percent and increased the number of high-value clients by 20 percent.[6]

---

[6] Don Peppers and Martha Rogers, Ph.D., *Return on Customer: Creating Maximum Value from Your Scarcest Resource* (New York: Currency/Doubleday, 2005), p. 97.

Customer analytics contributes to better sales productivity and lower marketing costs in many different ways:

- By making it possible to send more relevant information and offers, analytics helps to improve shopper-to-buyer conversion rates.
- Instead of offering one product to many customers, analytics makes it possible to offer specific and more targeted cross-sell and up-sell opportunities, which can result in measurably increased sales.
- By taking steps to keep customers longer, analytics can help increase customer lifetime value, profitability, and Return on Customer.
- Companies use analytics to improve operational effectiveness through smarter, more relevant (and therefore, usually, faster and less costly) customer service.
- Analytics can be used to reduce the interaction time and effort, making information exchange or transactions easier, faster and, therefore, more likely.
- Analytics improves the customer's perception of the level of service as a result of relevant messaging during an interaction.
- Analytics makes improved service levels for best customers possible.[7]

For example, Coach, the global designer and retailer of accessories and gifts, has successfully used insight gleaned from customer analytics to deliver exceptional **customer experiences** with maximum cost effectiveness. Because the Coach mission statement is "treating customers as guests in their own home," the customer's in-store experience is key. Predictive analytics have allowed Coach not only to predict how many sales it will generate and identify its top 1 to 2 percent of customers but to predict when those customers will most likely come into the store. Coach incorporates weather forecasts and traffic patterns into its data analysis, ensuring that its staff will be ready when the best customers are most likely to visit rather than needlessly allocating staff resources when they're not.[8]

Those who use customer analytics, therefore, are trying to create an unobstructed view of the customer, allowing the enterprise, essentially, to see things from the customer's own perspective. By delving into a customer's history, analytical programs can help the enterprise customize the way it serves or manufactures a product for a customer to suit that customer's individual needs. In essence, customer analytics helps the enterprise to transform its customer data into critical

---

[7] William M. Saubert, "Using Customer Analytics to Improve Customer Retention," *Bank Accounting & Finance* 22, no. 3 (April–May 2009): 33–38; Brendan B. Read, "Why Performance Analytics Is Important," *Customer Interaction Solutions* 27, no. 2 (July 2008): 24–25; and Kevin Cavanaugh, "Achieving Intelligent Interactions with Analytical CRM," *DM Review* 11, no. 5 (May 2001): 44–47.

[8] "How Coach Uses Data to Live Up to Its Brand," *1to1 Case Study: Customer Initiatives in Action*; available at: www.1to1media.com/downloads/Casestudy_Coach101507.pdf, accessed May 6, 2010.

business decisions about individual customers. Customer analytics software can reveal hidden trends about a customer and compare her behavior to other customers' behavior.[9] In addition, customer analytics can play an important role in customer acquisition, by helping the enterprise decide how to handle different prospects differently and by predicting which ones are more likely to become the most valuable customers.[10]

In 2001, Tesco, the U.K. retailer with the highly successful Clubcard frequent-shopper program, bought a 53 percent stake in Dunn Humby, its data-mining partner. In 2006, it raised its stake to 84 percent. Tesco knows that its customer data are its most valuable asset. Dunn Humby and Tesco became partners in 1995, when Tesco was launching its Clubcard initiative, and since then the firm has helped Tesco evaluate and act on what it learns from its Clubcard customers, managing massive data sets and enabling Tesco to increase the value of its customer base.[11]

Tesco and other astute customer-strategy enterprises have learned that customer data have a dollar value associated with them, and the more accurate the information, the better the enterprise can compete. Customer analytics can provide *metadata*—information about information—spotting characteristics and trends that enhance customer retention and profitability. Furthermore, customer analytics can be a technique for examining the profitability of specific products that individual customers purchase. As the late Fred Newell pointed out in *Loyalty.com*, analytics helps profile customers so that characteristics of loyal customers can be identified to predict which prospects will become new customers. Data mining can manage customer relationships by determining characteristics of customers who have left for a competitor so that the enterprise can act to retain customers who are at risk of leaving. Moreover, analytics helps an enterprise learn the mix of products to which a group of customers is attracted so it can learn what the customers value. "With this knowledge," Newell writes, "we can mine the customer file for similar customers to offer suggestions they are likely to value. Without data and its being analyzed to develop information and knowledge about the way things are happening in the real world, all we have are opinions. Every expert we have talked to gives the same answer: 'Data mining is knowledge discovery.'"[12] Customer analytics is not a technology—it is a *business process*.

---

[9] Matthew Shanahan, "Moving Target: Understanding Customer Demand," *Information Today* 27, no. 2 (February 2010): 21; and Angela Karr, "Analytics: The Next Wave of CRM," *Customer Interface* 14, no. 5 (May 2001): 44.

[10] Saubert, "Using Customer Analytics to Improve Customer Retention"; and Thomas J. Siragusa, "Implementing Data Mining for Better CRM," *Customer Interaction Solutions* 19, no. 11 (May 2001): 38.

[11] Elizabeth Rigby, "Eyes in the Till," *Financial Times* (London), November 11, 2006, p. 16; and Martha Rogers, Ph.D., "It's Aces High for Tesco and Dunn Humby," *Inside 1to1,* August 6, 2001; available at: www.1to1media.com/view.aspx?DocID=18843, accessed September 1, 2010.

[12] Frederick Newell, *Loyalty.com* (New York: McGraw-Hill Professional Book Group, 2000).

The next level of analytics might be applying financial characteristics to the data analysis, in order to yield a more accurate view of the actual economic consequences of particular customer actions. For instance, an enterprise might know that a promotion should go to customers fitting a certain profile, but it probably will have more difficulty

> Customer analytics is not a technology—it is a *business process*.

correlating the cost of the promotion with its likely outcome, at least on a customer-specific basis. In the next epoch of customer analytics, the mathematical algorithms will look across a range of promotions and associated costs to determine which tactics will generate the most profit, ideally taking into consideration the current return as well as the long-term effect on equity simultaneously. Ultimately, customer analytics will generate a revolution in how marketing decisions are made, driving companies increasingly toward solutions based on highly detailed marketing simulations.

In the end, however, the reason for analyzing all of these data is simply to develop a deeper relationship with each customer, in an effort to increase the overall value of the customer base, or as some would say, "optimize" the enterprise's customer relationships.

In the next section, Dr. James Goodnight, the founder and CEO of SAS Institute, explains how customer intelligence works in this era of data-driven relationships to customers.

Customer Intelligence in the Era of Data-Driven Marketing

Jim Goodnight
Founder and CEO, SAS Institute

With a growing variety of channels, today's marketing ecosystem is more complex than ever before. Customers are more savvy and demanding, and frequently switch among the many channels available to them. Meanwhile, marketing budgets are plummeting, competition is expanding, and decisions have to be made not only faster, but also smarter. Simply put, it's no longer possible for marketers to manage on gut instinct alone. Given this new environment, most in the industry are struggling to answer three questions:

- How can I better know my customers?
- How do I keep them engaged and loyal to my brand?
- How do I balance my budgets to keep both customers and management happy?

These questions are deceptive in their apparent simplicity, so it's worth exploring each of them in turn.

How Can I Better Know My Customers?

One of today's biggest marketing challenges is the proliferation of channels. That doesn't just mean Web, mobile, and brick-and-mortar stores. Buyers can be found everywhere from print media to social media, broadcasting to podcasting. What many regard as one channel—mobile—is actually several channels at once. And this creates real problems for customers. Say you want to calculate an insurance rate. Few things are more annoying than entering your details and requirements online, only to call that same bank and find that the person on the other end of the line has none of the information you took the time to enter. And yet, frustrating scenarios just like that continue to play out daily, damaging customer relationships and eroding profits.

Not being recognized across channels can be a deal-breaker for many customers. That's because digital has completely revolutionized buying behavior. Consumers are permanently connected, and they expect to be treated as unique. In the vast sea of messages and offers consumers receive each day, they have only time and patience for content that is personalized and relevant. Social media has empowered the consumer to expect nothing less.

The good news, though, is that with all that bouncing from channel to channel, consumers leave many data traces, and all that data add up to become big data. By analyzing these big data traces (structured and unstructured, residing within the company walls and without), marketers can get to know their customers with an unprecedented level of detail.

What Should I Tell Customers to Keep Them Engaged and Loyal to My Brand?

Marketing experts know they need to send the right message at the right moment to the right customer through the most effective channel, and the profession has come a long way in its ability to do just that. As a result, marketing has evolved from being intrusive, with brands delivering monologues, to being convenient, with event-driven messages achieving relevance, but not necessarily timeliness. Data-driven marketing offers the potential to create marketing that is not just convenient, but also context-appropriate, allowing brands to respond to a **moment of truth** at exactly the right time.

Marketing is at its most effective when it is answering immediate needs. For instance, a telco company can offer a data renewal opportunity to a traveling customer who wants to use his phone to find a nice restaurant, but is up against his data limit. An office supply company can contact a consumer because the printer ink she loyally purchases each month is due to be refreshed soon. Most companies have not yet reached this stage. In a subsequent section, we'll discuss the marketing spectrum and its common stages of evolution.

(continued)

(Continued)

How Do I Balance My Budgets to Keep Both Customers and Management Happy?

This last question is perhaps the most difficult to answer. Peter Drucker once said that "The aim of marketing is to know and understand the customer so well that the product or service fits him perfectly. . . and sells itself." True as that may be, the flaw in this statement is that it ignores the interests of the company. Obviously, it is essential to keep a customer happy, and to get that customer to buy a product or service. But just as crucial is making sure that marketing efforts align with the company's overall strategy to maximize their efficiency and profitability. Suppose that a retailer has two campaigns personalized for Jane in one week: one with a margin of $30 that is to be sent on Tuesday and one with a margin of $155 that would go out on Thursday. Since the company's contact policy says that a customer cannot be contacted more than once a week, many would just let the first one go out, and delete the second. But clearly the optimal choice for the company would be the second. Smart analytics make sure that organizations remain customer-centric while, at the same time, picking the choices that are the best for the organization. Surprisingly few marketing organizations are equipped to do this.

How Marketing Can Solve Its Three Biggest Challenges

Solving the three challenges we've just discussed will require two evolutions in marketing, one human and one technological. On the human side of things, marketers need to evolve from "Mad Men" to "Math Men," and on the technology side, marketers need a centralized marketing analytics platform.

From Mad Men to Math Men

Marketing experts are notoriously intuitive and creative. They have to be, because marketing campaigns that do not surprise or delight will not capture or sustain customers' attention. While experience can be a guide to which campaigns are likely to work, today's data deluge creates an enormity of valuable information to process, and savvy marketers should never leave that kind of value on the table.

The best marketing professionals are those who understand the power of data and have enough analytical understanding to know what they can accomplish with it. This does not mean that marketers need to be statisticians or fully fledged data scientists, but they should be comfortable in using approachable analytics, which can be easily applied and interpreted by business laypeople. With data as a resource, relying on a gut feeling no longer suffices.

Centralized Marketing Analytics

A common mistake in digital marketing is expecting that a single big data analytics solution is going to suddenly transform the company into a customer-centric virtuoso. That's magical thinking. If software is to deliver what it promises, it must be part of an ecosystem: integrated into the overall IT architecture and following a strategic, evolutionary plan.

When it comes to customer analytics, organizations need to have a clear direction in mind and execute that digital strategy systematically and deliberately. . . especially when there is a large gap between the status quo and the ideal situation.

A data-driven marketing platform is a network of interconnected analytics that delivers insights that can be turned into the most valuable actions, based on a set of intelligent business rules. Advanced big data analytics allow managers to extract actionable insights from their treasure trove of customer data, creating a 360-degree customer view.

But the insights themselves are not enough. They must be turned into customer-centric marketing and sales actions, with real-time campaigns being the most evolved step. Last but not least, companies should adopt house rules to define priorities, constraints, customer preferences, channel restrictions, budgets, and contact permissions. Such rules act as balancers, addressing the needs of the customer while finding the course of action that will benefit the company the most.

A Road Map to Analytics and Data-Driven Marketing

Obviously, not every organization will be at the same stage in its marketing evolution. See Exhibit 12.2. If we consider marketing maturity along a spectrum, one end of the scale is **mass marketing**. A surprisingly large number of companies are still operating in that phase of evolution. These are the organizations that mainly rely on "above the line" communication via mass media: television and radio advertising, print, and Internet. In this very traditional form of marketing, the messages are not tailored and are primarily outbound. Since this approach often lacks relevance, it can be highly ineffective in terms of value for money.

A bit more evolved are the organizations that target marketing campaigns on the basis of broad **customer segments**, which can be rule-based or analytically driven. Rule-based segmentation focuses on broad, predefined sociodemographic characteristics. It's true that single mothers age 35 to 40 with a net income of $5,000 a month can share some of the same preferences. Yet to realize the limits of this approach, you only need to think of the behavioral differences

(continued)

(Continued)

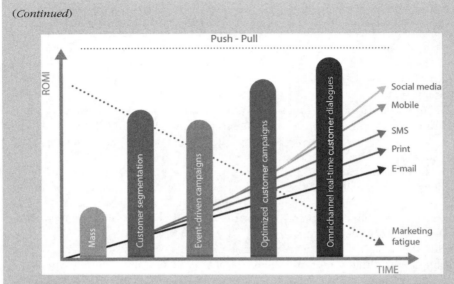

EXHIBIT 12.2   Impact of Analytics on Data-Driven Marketing Campaigns

between you and your best friend, even though both of you probably reside in the same segment. By contrast, when segmentation is analytics-based, the insights delivered will be a lot more valuable. If Joan, for instance, bought product A from a Web site and other customers who are very similar to her bought product A as well as product B, then chances are that Joan will be receptive to product B as well.

Companies that are even more advanced base their campaigns on specific triggers, like a complaint to a call center or a customer moving house. This type of approach is called **event-driven marketing**. From there, we move to **optimized customer campaigns**, which consider the customer's propensity to buy, and how that relates to the margin of a product. Optimized campaigns maintain the smartest balance between **customer centricity** and the company's objectives by taking into consideration budget and contact policy constraints.

At the end of the spectrum, **omnichannel real-time customer dialogues** provide genuine contextual marketing, which enables marketing professionals to deliver the right message in the right channel at the right time, taking into account both contact policies and company objectives. This idea of customer-focused marketing designed to optimize customer value (to and from the customer) was introduced by Don Peppers and Martha Rogers, Ph.D., in their many books on building stronger relationships and better customer experiences, knowing your customer well enough to have a natural and relevant dialogue that moves beyond "campaigns," with the ultimate goal of optimizing the value of each customer and prospect, thanks to improved data collection and analytical capabilities.

The further an organization moves along this data-driven maturity line, the lower the marketing fatigue of the customer and the bigger the return on marketing investment. With this evolution, companies also tend to move from a push to a pull marketing strategy, as inbound marketing is more effective with empowered, oversolicited customers.

But it doesn't stop with relevant messages and efficient campaigns; companies must continually analyze and reevaluate their actions to optimize them for full effect. Closing this marketing loop is one of the most difficult challenges for organizations to overcome. Let's take a moment to consider a case study from an organization that's using analytics to evolve its marketing efforts.

Case Study: The Orlando Magic

Professional sports teams in smaller markets often struggle to build a big enough revenue base to compete against their larger market rivals. By using analytics, the Orlando Magic rises above its position in the 20th-largest market to be among the top revenue earners in the NBA.

The Magic accomplish this feat by studying the resale ticket market to price tickets better, to predict season ticket holders at risk of defection (and lure them back), and to analyze concession and product merchandise sales to make sure the organization has what the fans want every time they enter the arena. The club has even used analytics to help coaches put together the best lineup.

"Our biggest challenge is to customize the fan experience, and analytics help us manage all that in a robust way," says Alex Martins, CEO of the Orlando Magic. Having been with the Magic since the beginning (working his way up from PR director to president to CEO), Martins knows the value that analytics adds. Under Martins's leadership, the season-ticket base has grown as large as 14,200, and the corporate sales department has seen tremendous growth.

Like all professional sports teams, the Magic are constantly looking for new strategies that will keep the seats filled at each of the 41 yearly home games. "Generating new revenue streams in this day of escalating player salaries and escalating expenses is important," says Anthony Perez, Vice President of Business Strategy. But with the advent of a robust online secondary market for tickets, reaching the industry benchmark of 90 percent renewal of season tickets has become more difficult.

(continued)

(Continued)

In the case of season ticket holders, the team uses historical purchasing data and renewal patterns to build decision tree models that place subscribers into three categories: most likely to renew, least likely to renew, and fence sitters. The fence sitters then get the customer service department's attention come renewal time.

The results speak for themselves. "In the first year, we saw ticket revenue increase around 50 percent. Over the last three years—for that period, we've seen it grow maybe 75 percent. It's had a huge impact," said Perez.

"We adopted an analytics approach years ago, and we're seeing it transform our entire organization," says Martins. "Analytics helps us understand customers better, helps in business planning (ticket pricing, etc.), and provides game-to-game and year-to-year data on demand by game and even by seat."

Summary: Why a Data-Driven Marketing Process Matters

Clearly, then, data-driven marketing has many advantages. Among the most striking:

- Improved customer satisfaction and loyalty
- Increased profitability through cross-sell and up-sell
- Reduced cost-to-serve and higher ROI

Improved Customer Experience

Smart marketing analytics help companies identify complex moments of truth for every customer based on their behavior. The more an offer provides what the customer expects, the greater the level of satisfaction. Better recognizing the needs of customers across all channels also drives a reputation for great service, which increases the value of the brand.

Reduced Cost-to-Serve and Better ROI

From among all the communications that are planned for a single customer, smart analytics select the ones with the highest probability score and those that are likely to be the most profitable. Marketing analytics help measure what works and what does not, and where you ought to put your budget to drive maximum results. This enables you to stop spending money on consumers who do not actually matter to your company or your strategy, freeing up resources for those channels that have the highest success rate.

Increased Cross-Sell and Up-Sell

Using analytics, organizations can score which products are a good up-sell and cross-sell without annoying customers with aggressive and irrelevant messaging, resulting in a higher average spend.

Customers demand far more than superior e-commerce, or even an omnichannel "presence." They expect an authentic, individualized experience that matters to them. They are using multiple channels, making snap decisions, and can change their mind in a moment.

Aligning with this new reality is necessary for business survival. To survive—let alone thrive—customer centricity must be ingrained in a company's operating model. It involves understanding customers more fully; engaging customers in ways that matter to them, and delivering brand promises faster and more efficiently than the competition. This means companies must adopt bold approaches—fusing data analytics, operational processes, and emotive brand experiences—to prompt tailored, timely customer interactions that deepen brand advocacy, and thus loyalty. The race will be won by the companies that know the most about their customers and who quickly apply that knowledge to keep them and grow them.

Here's an example of a company that uses customer insight to increase profitability.

Boosting Profits by Up-Selling in Firebrand Real Estate Developers

Firebrand Real Estate Developers (FRED)[a] is a residential real estate development company specializing in the development of a broad range of properties from mass housing to ultra-luxurious residences.

FRED's business model includes:

- *Land acquisition.* FRED either purchases the land or makes a revenue-sharing agreement where the landowner gets a percentage of revenues generated in return for the land.
- *Project development.* Sales and design teams of FRED define the main features of the development (i.e., size and types of units, amenities, construction quality) and provide a design brief to the architect who completes the design.
- *Presales and construction.* FRED begins selling the units as construction begins. Buyers of units have a variety of financing options. They can either

(continued)

(Continued)

get mortgage loans from a variety of banks or use facilities provided by the financing arm of FRED.

- *Options selection.* About halfway through the construction period, FRED invites buyers to select finishing materials and optional features they would like to see in their future home.
- *Delivery.* FRED delivers the units within the time frame defined in the contract made with the buyer when presales take place. If the buyer has not completed installment payments, the title deed is granted with liens in favor of whoever provided financing to the buyer—either the bank or FRED's financing arm.
- *Completion of sales.* Units that have not been sold at the end of the construction period become the property of FRED (and landowner, if a revenue-sharing agreement had been made) to be sold later or rented. At this stage, prices are usually higher than in presales period.

Groundbreaking to delivery of units typically takes 24 to 30 months. Most buyers choose payment plans that take 10 to 30 years to complete all installments. Therefore, in many cases, title deeds are granted with liens. Approximately 85 percent of all buyers use mortgage loans provided by banks, whereas the remaining prefer loans offered by FRED's financing arm. FRED typically selects two to three banks as financing partners on its projects to provide a seamless financing process for its customers. FRED also negotiates on behalf of prospective buyers the fees and commissions—the hidden costs of mortgage loans—to be charged by banks to mortgage loan users.

If a bank loan is used, FRED gets the full payment at presale. From then on, the buyer makes installment payments directly to the bank. If the purchase is financed by FRED, the customer makes installment payments to FRED. In this case, the customer can refinance later on with a bank loan and fully pay her debt to FRED.

The Challenge

There are several important considerations in FRED's business model:

- The higher the percentage of units sold during the presales period, the better. Preselling units means financing the construction with buyers' money.
- Competition between developers for the very little vacant land that remains in the city is stiff. Like all its competitors, FRED makes most of its profit by selling options.
- FRED can sell only predefined packages of options. Otherwise, the complexity of construction outweighs the benefits of selling options.

- To make a higher profit margin on options packages, FRED must:
  - Not have too many different types of packages, which will confuse the buyer and make decision making much harder.
  - Provide packages that fit a broad range of tastes.
  - Foresee how many of which package will be sold to negotiate better prices with suppliers.

Obviously, customer intelligence is a key component of FRED's business model: It will be able to make a handsome profit only if it can foresee which customers of which project will be interested in what types of packages.

What do options packages look like? Typically, options packages are produced by variations of the most critical unit components. These components are what makes a unit attractive to the buyer's eye. As one might expect, invisible features, such as concrete quality, roof insulation, and so on, hardly make a difference. What makes the difference are the finishes. Therefore, options packages typically include variations of:

- Flooring material and quality in living room and bedrooms.
- Tile design, quality, and size in bathrooms and kitchen.
- Design and quality of kitchen cabinets and materials used in countertops.
- White goods and home electronics that are provided in the unit.
- Materials used in custom-built, walk-in cabinets.

Almost an infinite number of variations are conceivable, but, as noted, only a limited number of predefined packages can be offered. Usually the number of packages is limited to three to four. It is a major challenge for FRED to define just the right packages so that every buyer will want to purchase one. Each unit sold without an options package is a failure for FRED because it makes almost no profit and a failure for the buyer because he will have to deal with lots of decisions and finish work after receiving the unit, which is a process almost no homebuyer looks forward to.

The Solution

To solve the business problem, FRED turned to customer intelligence. To be able to define the options packages for a broad range of projects it was developing, the company started with reviewing what it already knew about customers. Profiling home buyers started with identifying the dimensions of a customer profile for this specific market.

(continued)

(*Continued*)

FRED determined that any home buyer in the market could be profiled by these dimensions:

- *Purchase reasons.* Surveys indicated that each buyer falls into one of these categories:
  - Investing in a property
  - Moving to a larger home
  - Buying a first home
- *Payment plans.* Based on payment data in previous projects, FRED determined that these dimensions defined payment preferences of buyers.
  - Down payment percentage
  - Payback period length
  - Interest rate mechanism preferred
- *Sociodemographics.* Surveys conducted by FRED indicated that out of the many different dimensions that can be used to define the sociodemographic profile of a customer, the dimensions that mattered were:
  - Marital status
  - Age of parents
  - Age of children
  - Income level
- *Unit price and size.* Based on options packages preferred in previous projects, FRED determined that the price and size of the apartment purchased were also important in forecasting buyer behavior. Specifically, these dimensions were important:
  - Size of the apartment
  - Per-square-meter price of the apartment

Using these profiling dimensions, data from previous projects, and data obtained from market surveys, FRED segmented its customers. The result of the study indicated five distinct customer types (see Exhibit 12.3).

- The next challenge for FRED was to match options package preferences with segments. Data from previous projects would be used to this end. Nevertheless, because each development project is unique, FRED needed a way of standardizing the options package properties to be able to compare one project with another. Understanding customer behavior, particularly as it relates to options package decisions, helped solve the puzzle. By studying survey data FRED figured out that other than investors, all segments purchased the most expensive home for which they could afford to pay monthly installments within their payment terms.

EXHIBIT 12.3   Customer Segments in the Market Where FRED Competes

	Investors	Young Families—Medium Income	Young Families—High Income	Young Families—Low Income	Space Seekers	Luxury Seekers
Purchase Reason						
(Investing in a property, moving to a larger apartment, and/or buying a first home)	Investing in a property	Buying a first home	Moving to a larger apartment Buying a first home	Buying a first home	Moving to a larger apartment Buying a first home	Moving to a larger apartment Buying a first home
Payment Plans						
Down payment percentage	10%–15%	20%–30%	20%–50%	10%–15%	20%–30%	20%–30%
Payback period length	20–30 years	5–10 years	5–10 years	20–30 years	5–10 years	5–10 years
Interest rate mechanism preferred	Variable rate	Fixed rate	Fixed rate	Fixed rate	Fixed rate	Fixed rate
Sociodemographics						
Marital status	Mixed	Married	Married	Married	Married	Mixed
Age of parents	45+	30–45	30–45	30–45	45+	45+
Age of kids	Late teens and +	None or early years	None or early years	None or early years	Late teens and +	Mixed
Income level	US$ 250,000 and +	US$ 125,000–250,000	US$ 250,000 and +	US$ 50,000–125,000	US$ 125,000–250,000	US$ 500,000 and +
Unit Price and Size						
Unit price of apartment	US$ 1,000–1,500	US$ 2,500–3,500	US$ 3,000–5,000	US$ 1,000–1,500	US$ 1,500–2,500	US$ 5,000 and +
Size of the apartment	50–90 sqm	80–110 sqm	120–250 sqm	80–110 sqm	120–250 sqm	200 sqm and +

- When it came to options packages, these segments were thrifty. Total price of the package was viewed in complete isolation from the price paid for the apartment.
- Although investors calculated the percentage of their total cost represented by options package, for other segments, cost of options package was correlated with income rather than price of the apartment.

(continued)

(Continued)

Applying the Solution in the Next Project

Once all pieces of the puzzle fell into place, FRED was ready to apply the customer intelligence generated on a project. The first test run was on a $270 million residential development project, the largest FRED had ever undertaken. Target yield, or the discount rate that equalized discounted cash flow of the project to zero, was 15 percent. FRED achieved 17 percent, despite cost overruns and a more sluggish than expected market with a slower sales rate, thanks to the margin contribution of options packages.

How did FRED succeed in transforming customer intelligence into dollars and improved return on investment? By sticking with the basics.

As outlined in Exhibit 12.4, the project primarily targeted three customer segments: young families of medium and high income, and space seekers. The old real estate maxim of "location, location, location" applied in this case to eliminate luxury seekers, since the location of this project was not a place where they would seek to reside.

EXHIBIT 12.4   Unit Distribution and Revenue Expectations in FRED's New Project

Type of Units	Size of Units (sqm)	Number of Units	Sellable Area (sqm)	Average Unit Price (US$/sqm)	Average Price per Unit (US$)	Expected Revenue (US$)
1 BR + 1 LR	60	240	14,400	3,000	180,000	43,200,000
2 BR + 1 LR	90	240	21,600	2,700	243,000	58,320,000
3 BR + 1 LR	110	160	17,600	2,500	275,000	44,000,000
4 BR + 1 LR	140	160	22,400	2,400	336,000	53,760,000
5 BR + 1 LR	170	120	20,400	2,300	391,000	46,920,000
5 BR + 2 LR	230	50	11,500	2,300	529,000	26,450,000

TOTAL: 970 units
         272,650,000 in revenues
BR: Bedroom
LR: Living room

At this time, FRED had an idea as to what kinds of options packages could be suitable for this unit mix and pricing, but management could be sure only after seeing the profile of buyers. Actualized sales figures are provided in Exhibit 12.5.

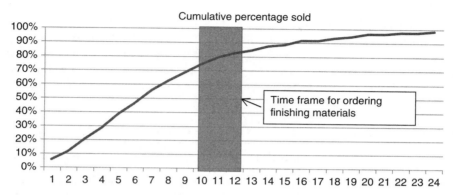

EXHIBIT 12.5   **Cumulative Percentage Units Sold by Month in FRED's New Project**

Options packages had to be designed, suggested to buyers, and ordering of finishing materials completed by the twelfth month to finish the project on time. Based on the profile of buyers, FRED had to design the right combinations of options packages, try to sell every buyer an options package, and forecast what prospective buyers of unsold units could demand ahead of time so as to be able to order just the right amount of materials.

Figuring that two months should be enough to complete sales of options packages, FRED designed the packages by the end of the tenth month, when 70 percent of the units had been sold. By looking at the buyer profile until that time and matching it with customer preferences data, FRED was able to design the packages in a very short amount of time. FRED designed four types of packages, summarized in Exhibit 12.6.

EXHIBIT 12.6   **Options Packages FRED Offered to Customers**

Type of Unit	Size of Unit (sqm)	Average Price of Unit (US$)	Price of Options Package (US$)			
			Package 1: Home Basics	Package 2: Standard	Package 3: Deluxe	Package 4: Imperial
1 BR + 1 LR	60	180,000	7,500	9,000		
2 BR + 1 LR	90	243,000	10,500	13,200		
3 BR + 1 LR	110	275,000	12,600	15,900	17,400	22,500
4 BR + 1 LR	140	336,000	15,900	19,200	21,300	27,900
5 BR + 1 LR	170	391,000	18,600	22,500	25,200	32,100
5 BR + 2 LR	230	529,000	24,300	28,200	30,600	40,500

(continued)

(*Continued*)

When options packages were offered to customers, distribution of sales across segments (summarized in Exhibit 12.7) helped FRED forecast with more accuracy total options revenues by the end of the project. Based on buyer behavior in past projects, FRED was able to produce an options package purchase probabilities outline (see Exhibit 12.8) to forecast total options package revenues.

EXHIBIT 12.7   FRED's New Project Units Sales by Month 10

	Distribution of Sales Across Segments at End of Month 10					
	1 BR + 1 LR	2 BR + 1 LR	3 BR + 1 LR	4 BR + 1 LR	5 BR + 1 LR	5 BR + 2 LR
Investors	86%	66%	19%			
Young Families—Medium Income	14%	34%	72%		9%	
Young Families—High Income				25%	25%	57%
Young Families—Low Income						
Space Seekers			8%	75%	66%	43%
TOTAL	100%	100%	100%	100%	100%	100%

EXHIBIT 12.8   Options Package Purchase Probabilities in FRED's New Project

	Expected Options Package Sales					
	1 BR + 1 LR	2 BR + 1 LR	3 BR + 1 LR	4 BR + 1 LR	5 BR + 1 LR	5 BR + 2 LR
Package 1: Home Basics	64%	57%	35%	0%	3%	0%
Package 2: Standard	23%	27%	34%	22%	24%	26%
Package 3: Deluxe	1%	3%	10%	32%	31%	36%
Package 4: Imperial	0%	0%	3%	26%	23%	21%
TOTAL	89%	87%	82%	81%	81%	83%

By month 10, FRED expected a total options revenue of $12.7 million. In reality, it exceeded this target by roughly 12 percent. By the end of month 24, when 99 percent of units had been sold, FRED generated an options revenue of $14.3 million.

Conclusion

FRED was able to increase its revenues from the project by 4.7 percent by selling options packages. More important, because of the much higher profitability of options packages, net project profit increased by 11 percent. In doing this, FRED created value not only for its own shareholders but also for its customers. By providing options packages that closely fit customer needs, FRED was able to relieve the customers' burden of selecting and completing the finishing work themselves. Surveys reveal that completion of finishing work after delivery of apartments is the least favorable part of buying a new home for the majority of buyers. Just as important, this is the most common source of problems between contractors and tenants during the move-in period. Without customer analytics, FRED would have been unlikely to create the same value for both its shareholders and its customers and still be able to complete the project on time with top-quality finishing work.

Thanks to Yücel Ersöz, former partner at Peppers & Rogers Group, for his contributions to this section.

---

[a] Not the company's real name.

Here's another example that illustrates how data mining can be elevated to insight and prediction of customer behavior.

Looking for the Right Time to Sell a Mortgage Loan

In emerging markets, the sources of revenue are changing. Lower interest rates, the diminishing crowding-out effect of government debt in the race for funds, and enhanced consumer confidence are encouraging savers to become borrowers. As a result, retail bankers are finding out that they have to look for ways to make money by finding products for their customers such as loans in the form of mortgages, credit cards, auto loans, and the like. This business model has a completely different set of requirements from that of the old days, when retail banking was all about collecting money from savers and selling it to debt-laden government. Instead, retail bankers must be at the right place at the right time to sell the next loan to the consumer.

Best Savings Bank (BSB)[a] embraced this challenge by changing the way it looks at customer data. Instead of a black-box approach in data mining to determine prospective customers for mortgage loans, the bank started with the

(continued)

(Continued)

basics of consumer behavior in the market where it was competing. In other words, instead of finding customers for products, it looked at how it could find products for customers.

Exhibits 12.9 and 12.10 provide the basic characteristics of consumer groups who would qualify for a mortgage loan.

Surveys indicate that different consumer segments opt for different payback periods on their mortgage loans. Although segments A and B prefer short-term (5- to 10-year) payback periods, segments B and C prefer medium-term (10- to 20-year) periods, and segments D and E usually prefer long-term (20- to 30-year) periods. Exhibit 12.11 shows home prices these different segments can afford.

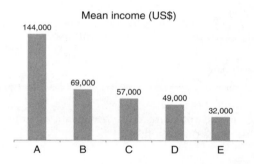

EXHIBIT 12.9   Consumer Segments by Average Income

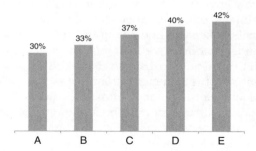

EXHIBIT 12.10   Percentage of Disposable Income Used for Mortgage Payments across Segments

EXHIBIT 12.11   Maximum Home Price per Customer Segment

Income Level	Mean Income ($)	Maximum Monthly Payment	Maximum Price That Can Be Afforded			
			5-Year Loan	10-Year Loan	20-Year Loan	30-Year Loan
A	144,000	3,600	202,298	313,652	408,687	437,103
B	69,000	1,898	106,628	165,321	215,412	230,390
C	57,000	1,758	98,761	153,123	199,519	213,391
D	49,000	1,633	91,783	142,305	185,423	198,315
E	32,000	1,120	62,937	97,581	127,147	135,988

The Challenge

Although BSB had extensive customer data, bank executives believed that pitching the mortgage loan offer to customers at just the right time (i.e., when the customer is actually thinking of buying a new home) would prove to be a difficult task. They decided to identify the pieces of data that would tell them when different types of customers would likely consider buying a new home.

In the market where BSB operates, home buyers are required to make a down payment that equals 20 percent of the value of the home with their own funds. Banks are allowed to fund only up to 80 percent of the home value to cushion against a fall in prices. Because the bank knew which income group would go for which kind of housing, the first task was to figure out a reasonable estimate of household income, a figure that was not readily available in the bank's data systems.

To estimate this figure, the customer analytics team combined the data available in the systems and to survey results in a smart way. The amount of savings customers had in BSB and their credit card charges with BSB cards were readily available. What was missing was an estimate of total savings and total credit card expenses in all banks—in other words, the customer's **share of customer** (or share of wallet). These data came from market research surveys. Next, the analytics team needed to link these clues with monthly income estimates. Market research surveys indicated that 70 percent of all expenditures of segments under consideration took place by credit card charges. By adding the average rate at which these segments increased their deposits—a proxy for their monthly savings rate—the team was able to produce the income estimates provided in Exhibit 12.12, which illustrates results for five sample customers.

(continued)

(Continued)

EXHIBIT 12.12   Annual Income Estimates for Five Sample Customers Computed by Analytics Team (All Currency Figures in USD [$])

Customer	Savings Account Balance	Savings Flow Rate per Month	Monthly Credit Card Charge	Bsb Share of Customer for Credit Card Expenses	Bsb Share of Customer for Savings	Customer's Estimated Annual Income
X	12,425	1,100	1,237	50%	100%	55,611
Y	27,325	1,750	2,249	75%	100%	72,406
Z	23,345	1,000	4,362	100%	100%	86,777
T	27,896	2,450	6,747	100%	100%	145,063
U	43,233	3,750	8,765	100%	100%	195,257

In Exhibit 12.12, the savings flow rate is the average monthly increase of deposits of the customer in the bank and share of savings and share of credit card expenses are the estimated share of wallet of BSB in these product categories.

It was obvious to the customer analytics team that customers like X, Y, Z, T, and U were saving for a specific purpose. Market research revealed that in the long term, customers with demographic profiles and savings amounts similar to these actually were saving to buy a new home or for their children's college education. Typically these customers were age 35 to 45, had $15,000 to $40,000 in savings accounts, and saved at a rate of $1,000 to $4,000 per month. This information helped the team pinpoint the target group.

Finally, by making use of the public information and previous mortgage loan records, the customer analytics team was able to identify which customers would be eligible to consider buying a new home, provided that their current rate of savings continued at this pace. Exhibit 12.13 summarizes the results.

EXHIBIT 12.13   Optimum Timing for Offering a Mortgage Product to Selected Customers

	Values in USD($)				
Customer	Estimated Annual Income	Expected Home Value	Required Down Payment	Estimated Savings	Months to Eligibility
X	55,611	225,073	45,015	12,425	30
Y	72,406	226,045	45,209	27,325	10
Z	86,777	239,413	47,883	23,345	25
T	145,063	259,879	51,976	27,896	10
U	195,257	349,802	69,960	43,233	7

This insight not only provided a way to retain customers but also helped BSB manage customers with a much longer horizon in mind. In the market where BSB operates, significant customer churn takes place as savers withdraw all their savings from a bank and finance their new home with a different bank that was at the right place at the right time. It is much harder to get the customer back once he has been lost as a result of this churn.

As a result of this initiative, BSB has been able to reduce customer churn to other banks with mortgage products by 25 percent and improved its sales conversion rate in mortgage offers by 33 percent.

Conclusion

As banks in emerging markets learn to adapt to the changing landscape in retail banking, customer analytics techniques similar to the one discussed here will guide them in charting unknown territories. Banks that are intent on deriving customer insight and acting on it to survive this challenge will find doing so much simpler than they may have expected. Complicated data analyses usually are not required to extract customer value if one knows where to look.

Thanks to Yücel Ersöz, former partner at Peppers & Rogers Group, for his contributions to this section.

---

[a] Not the company's real name.

Summary

Big data and data in the cloud have opened up deeper and wider analytical capabilities to companies whose goal is to build stronger relationships with and better experiences for customers. But one thing is clear: No matter how powerful the algorithms, they are only as good as the data we have about customers, and our intelligence about how to use them.

But note: In a speech given by Claudia Perlich, Chief Data Scientist at Distillery and Adjunct Professor at NYU, in January 2016, she made the point that in studies of Internet activity, there may be a map of the United States that shows "mountains" where the most people are active online generally (or with a particular social Web site or looking for certain topics). So the pile of users in the big cities can be quite tall. But all these maps have a default spot; if the location of the user is unknown through GPS or other means, that person's location defaults to the center of the specified area (state, city, country, etc.). In the United States, therefore, the most populous region for online activity in the entire country is a Kansas cornfield. The point is, we have to be careful about what we think we know.

We have now covered two critical parts of customer-based enterprise "measurement": We have examined some of the ways an enterprise can measure the success of its customer value–building initiatives, and we have explored how advanced customer analytics can help predict how a customer will behave in a relationship, how a firm can positively influence that relationship behavior, and how much it's worth to the enterprise to do so. Analytics affect the "customer" issues for the company, but understanding how value is created for today and tomorrow affects decisions for the chief financial officer; the chief information officer; human resources recruiting, training, evaluation, and compensation; product development; the chief executive review and board decisions; appraisal of merger-and-acquisition opportunities; and even public reporting of competitive advantage.

If we can measure it, we can manage it. That's why the next chapters are about how to manage an organization to build the value of the customer base. Making the transition

> If we can measure it, we can manage it.

to a customer-strategy enterprise requires a careful examination of the way the company is structured and a rethinking of many business processes. Chapter 13 focuses on two key themes: What does a relationship-building enterprise, based strategically on growing customer equity, look like? What are the organizational and transitional requirements to become a customer-based enterprise? Next we take a closer look.

Food for Thought

1. From the customer's perspective, which is better: to buy through one channel or through several channels? The obvious answer is to have multiple channels available—order from the Web, make returns at the store, check on delivery by phone—and have all of those contact points able to pick up where the last one left off. But is there any advantage—to the customer—of using only one channel? Why does research show that customers who use more than one channel are more likely to be more valuable to a firm than those who use only one?

2. Often, the challenge in using predictive models boils down to a misunderstanding of the nature of cause and effect. Although statistical analysis might reveal that two observable events tend to happen at similar times, it does not necessarily mean that one event "causes" the other. What is more important: to understand *what* will happen next or *why* it will happen?

3. Customer analytics can be used for improving retention rates. How?

Glossary

Analysis process Includes classification, estimation, regression, prediction, and clustering.

Customer analytics Enables the enterprise to classify, estimate, predict, cluster, and more accurately describe data about customers, using mathematical models and algorithms that ultimately simplify how it views its customer base and how it behaves toward individual customers.

Customer centricity A "specific approach to doing business that focuses on the customer. Customer/client centric businesses ensure that the customer is at the center of a business philosophy, operations or ideas. These businesses believe that their customers/clients are the only reason they exist and use every means at their disposal to keep the customer/client happy and satisfied."[13] At the core of customer centricity is the understanding that customer profitability is at least as important as product profitability.

Customer equity The sum of all the lifetime values (LTVs) of an enterprise's current and future customers, or the total value of the enterprise's customer relationships. A customer-centric company would view customer equity as its principal corporate asset. Also see definition of *customer equity* in Chapter 1.

Customer experience The totality of a customer's individual interactions with a brand, over time.

Customer relationship management (CRM) As a term, *CRM* can refer either to the activities and processes a company must engage in to manage individual relationships with its customers (as explored extensively in this textbook), or to the suite of software, data, and analytics tools required to carry out those activities and processes more cost efficiently.

Customer segment A group of customers who are suited for the same or similar marketing initiatives because of particular qualities or characteristics they have in common.

Customer service Customer service involves helping a customer gain the full use and advantage of whatever product or service was bought. When something goes wrong with a product, or when a customer has some kind of problem with it, the process of helping the customer overcome this problem is often referred to as *customer care.*

Data mining The process of exploration and analysis of large quantities of data in order to discover meaningful patterns and rules.

Event-driven marketing Marketing campaigns and initiatives characterized by offers or communications that are "triggered" by preidentified events.

---

[13] "Client Centric," Investopedia, available at http://www.investopedia.com/terms/c/client-centric.asp, accessed February 15, 2016.

Mass marketing   An attempt to appeal to an entire market with one basic marketing strategy utilizing mass distribution and mass media.

Moment of truth (MoT)   Interactions with a customer that have a disproportionate impact on the customer's emotional connection, and are therefore more likely to drive significant behaviors.

Omnichannel real-time customer dialogue   The "conversation" that happens in real time with a customer, across any and all channels, enabling marketing professionals to deliver the right message in the right channel at the right time to each customer, taking into account both contact policies and company objectives.

Optimized customer campaigns   Marketing campaigns that take into account each different customer's propensity to buy, and how it relates to profit, based on a product's margin. Optimized campaigns maintain the smartest balance between customer centricity and the company's objectives by taking into consideration not just customer likelihoods, but budget and contact policy constraints as well.

Real-time analytics   Instant updates to the customer database that allow services in multiple geographies, communication channels, or product lines to respond to customer needs without waiting for customary weekly or overnight updates.

Share of customer   For a customer-focused enterprise, share of customer is a conceptual metric designed to show what proportion of a customer's overall need is being met by the enterprise. It is not the same as "share of wallet," which refers to the specific share of a customer's spending in a particular product or service category. If, for instance, a family owns two cars, and one of them is your car company's brand, then you have a 50 percent share of wallet with this customer, in the car category. But by offering maintenance and repairs, insurance, financing, and perhaps even driver training or trip planning, you can substantially increase your "share of customer."

Social media   Interactive services and Web sites that allow users to create their own content and share their own views for others to consume. Blogs and microblogs (e.g., Twitter) are a form of social media, because users "publish" their opinions or views for everyone. Facebook, LinkedIn, and MySpace are examples of social media that facilitate making contact, interacting with, and following others. YouTube and Flickr are examples of social media that allow users to share creative work with others. Even Wikipedia represents a form of social media, as users collaborate interactively to publish more and more accurate encyclopedia entries.

CHAPTER 13

Organizing and Managing the Profitable Customer-Strategy Enterprise, Part 1

Work is of two kinds: first, altering the position of matter at or near the earth's surface relative to other matter; second, telling other people to do so.

—Bertrand Russell

Throughout this book, we have described the **customer-strategy enterprise** by defining the principles of creating a customer-strategy business. In this and the next chapter, we will focus on how a firm establishes itself as an enterprise focused on building the **value of the customer base** and how it can make the transition from product management to managing for **customer equity.** What does a customer-value-building enterprise look like? How does a company develop the organization, skills, and capabilities needed to execute customer-oriented programs? How does the enterprise create the culture that supports these principles? How will it integrate the pieces of the organization that have traditionally been managed as separate silos (or "chimneys" or "smokestacks")? To begin our discussion, this chapter examines how the customer-strategy enterprise is different from the traditional organization.

If we can measure it, we can manage it. Now that we have become better at the metrics of customer valuation and equity, can we hold someone responsible for increasing the value of customers and keeping them longer? Most companies have brand managers, product managers, store managers, plant managers, finance managers, **customer interaction center** managers, Web masters, regional sales managers, branch managers, and/or merchandise managers. These days, even beyond the obvious high-end personal and business services, more and more companies have customer **relationship managers**. Now that technology drives a dimension of competition based on keeping and growing customers, the questions to ask are:

- Who will be responsible for the enterprise's relationship with each customer? For keeping and growing each customer? For building the short-term revenues and long-term equity and value of each customer?
- What authority will that **customer manager** need to have in order to change how the enterprise treats "her" customers, individually?
- How will she use tools and technology to create better experiences for her customers?
- What will she have to do?
- By what criteria and metrics will success be measured, reported, and used for compensation?

In this chapter, we ask the questions: How will executives at the enterprise develop management skills to increase the value of the customer base? How will our information about customers—and our goal to build the value of the customer base—inform every business decision we make all day, every day?

We have shown that in the customer-strategy enterprise, the goal is to maximize the value of the customer base by retaining profitable customers and growing them into bigger customers; by eliminating unprofitable customers or converting them into profitable relationships; and by acquiring new customers selectively, based on their likelihood of developing into high-value customers. The overriding strategy for achieving this set of objectives is to develop Learning Relationships, built on trust, with individual customers, in the process customizing the mix of products, prices, services, and/or communications for each individual customer, wherever practical.

It should be apparent that the new enterprise must be organized around its customers rather than just its products. Success requires that the entire organization reengineer its processes to focus on the customer.[1] In this chapter, we examine the basics of management at a customer-strategy enterprise. Our goal is to understand the capabilities necessary to create and manage a successful customer-strategy company. We draw a picture of what the organizational chart looks like and explain how to make the transition, overcome obstacles, and build momentum. We also have a look at the role of employees in the customer-strategy enterprise.

Before any of that, though, let's look at what it means to manage **customer experiences**—what they are and how to make them better.

---

[1] Sheryl Pattek, "Reboot Your Organization for Modern Marketing," Forrester Research Inc., December 5, 2014, available at http://www.forrester.com; and Brendan Witcher, "One Customer, One Organization, One P&L," Forrester Research, Inc., November 17, 2015, available at http://www.forrester.com.

Customer Experience: What, Why, and How

Alan Pennington
Customer experience expert and author; senior executive advisor and coach; Chairman, SpectrumCX

The term *customer experience* has become more and more popular over the past 20 years. As customers have interconnected themselves and acquired more and more power in their relationships with companies, companies have asked themselves more and more, "What is it like to be our customer, and what *should* it be like?" Closing that gap might be called **customer experience management.**

Let's think for a few minutes about what customer experience is and is not. How does "customer experience" relate to building customer relationships as well as **customer value management?** Why is "customer experience" more important now than ever, discussed at higher and higher levels in an organization? And what are the fundamental principles and steps that companies will follow to improve the experiences their customers have, and the profitability of the company as a result?

At its most basic a customer experience is an outcome of the activities of a company—it can be physical or virtual and is often a combination of both. Think about online shopping, which is carried out on the Internet, but the delivery of your product happens in the physical world.

While it is true that the customer experience has been talked about for a long time it has only recently begun to be seen as a key component of business strategy and a discipline that needs expertise to manage. What are the differences between **customer centricity,** user experience, **customer service**, and customer experience? How is customer experience different?

Customer Centricity

According to Investopedia, *customer centricity* is a "specific approach to doing business that focuses on the customer. Customer/client centric businesses ensure that the customer is at the center of a business philosophy, operations or ideas. These businesses believe that their customers/clients are the only reason they exist and use every means at their disposal to keep the customer/client happy and satisfied."[a]

If we accept this definition, it means that the customer agenda will be at the center of company thinking and dominant in the company, driving both strategic choices and day-to-day actions.

(continued)

(Continued)

User Experience

Because it has been adopted by the digital community to describe how they map and design interfaces and try to ensure that the online experience is as effective as possible, *user experience* is a term usually associated with systems testing and user acceptance. Typically, it is focused on a moment in time or a specific activity such as making an online purchase. Generally, "user experience" work does not embrace the wider experience (for example: How did I come to be on the Web site? What was the physical delivery experience? How did that map against my expectations?).

Customer Service

Investopedia defines *customer service* as "the process of ensuring customer satisfaction with a product or service. Often, customer service takes place while performing a transaction for a customer, such as making a sale or returning an item. Customer service can take the form of an in-person interaction, a phone call, self-service payment systems, or by other means."[b]

Customer service is seen in isolation and specifically related to an interaction, usually involving a human component but not always, since, technically, dispensing cash from an ATM is providing customer service.

Customer Experience

Customer experience has a much wider definition. It is about the end-to-end experience that customers have over their lifetime engagement with a company, product, or service. It includes all channels and both the physical and virtual components of those experiences, for example, from the chair you sit in to how an agent made you feel during a particular transaction.

It is about the consistent delivery of the brand-driven customer promise and resulting customer expectations through the physical experience. It is about taking an outside-in view of the experience of interacting with a company, product, or service.

Why Has Customer Experience Emerged as a Strategic Driver?

The financial crisis of 2008–2010 forced companies to reassess how to manage their businesses moving forward and one of the levers that emerged as critical was the customer experience. The rush to cut costs was a onetime opportunity and there were unintended consequences, as senior executives did not understand the impact on the customer experience and therefore the effect on loyalty.

Add to this the fact that product and price have continued to converge and we as customers are becoming more empowered and aware, and the ability to create real competitive differentiation through the "experience" is now seen as one of the few sustainable strategies. Consider the way that car product quality has converged, with Skoda moving from being the laughingstock of Europe in terms of quality and design to European Car of the Year.

We have also seen the problem in the early stages of the growth of customer experience that was an inability to show a positive connection between inadequate investments in customer experience and the bottom line of the company being rapidly eroded, supported through empirical evidence.

What Is the Financial Case for Customer Experience?

It has taken many years to build sufficient evidence to make the case for the return on investment on customer experience to be able to convince boardroom skeptics. But the evidence to support the link between commercial bottom line and stock market success and the delivery of a superior customer experience continues to grow every year. The latest round of studies has reinforced this view, showing that where the customer experience is rated highly, the stock performance is similarly high, and vice versa.

Studies in both the United Kingdom and the United States reinforce this correlation; what is significant is that both studies below now have trends over many years that are consistent. First, in the following chart, we see that the U.K. "Customer Experience Top 100" achieved double the five-year revenue growth of the FTSE 100.

Customer Experience Excellence Top 100 Growth by Sector Compared to FTSE 100 from 2012 to 2015

	FTSE 100	CEE Top 100
Financial Services	+5.4%	+14.2%
Travel & Hotels	+3.7%	+5.1%
Non-Grocery Retail	+6.5%	+15.8%
Grocery Retail	+0.2%	+5.7%

Source: KPMG-Nunwood CEEC 2015 U.K. Analysis.

Second, in Exhibit 13.1, we see that U.S. customer experience leaders from 2007 to 2012 significantly outperformed the S&P 500.

(continued)

(Continued)

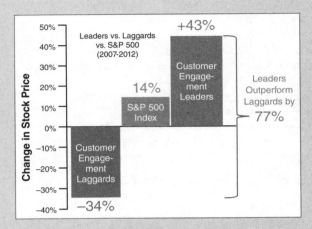

EXHIBIT 13.1   U.S. Customer Experience Leaders vs. Laggards vs. S&P 500, 2007–2012
Source: Watermark Consulting.

At a more local company level we can now track improvements, both quantitative and qualitative, that impact both sides of the balance sheet that are directly trackable to customer experience delivery. For example:

- Reducing the cost of failure—where that is defined as the cost to the company of resolving customer issues that relate to the failure to deliver the customer promise.
- Tracking the conversion rate improvements for new customers following an experience redesign.
- Reducing staff churn and associated hiring and training costs.
- Tracking levels of retention following experience-based interventions.

To further make the commercial case, consider how much a company invests in marketing to create a customer expectation and how much the resulting cost would be to then underdeliver at the point of contact.

Advertising that sometimes misleads the customer was something that a few years ago was an acceptable practice, but today the customer is much more informed and demanding. Take the example of a bank account that is designed to attract new current account customers—the marketing tactic is to load the account with additional benefits from online banking, a loyalty program, cell phone insurance, and perhaps access to airline lounges. This may seem to be an attractive proposition until customers try to access the benefits and find that they have to do significant work across multiple channels just to register. The company is actually making it hard to access the benefits to minimize sign-ups, perhaps remembering that every time a lounge is accessed that is a cost to the company so perhaps the effort to minimize use is deliberate, or perhaps customers may suspect as much.

Customer relationships are built on trust and indeed the very value of some products and services is based on trust—for example, we trust that an insurance company will pay out should we ever need to make a claim on a policy. At an emotional level we form bonds of trust and these are either confirmed or eroded based on our actual experience measured against our expectation. Imagine if the ATM you prefer to use to withdraw your cash worked only 50 percent of the time. Truth is, we expect 100 percent service level from ATMs. Anything less makes us subconsciously suspicious of whether the bank can be trusted with our money.

Understanding the Experience from a Customer Perspective

All companies have an internal view of their experience even if it is not described as "customer experience." Every company of any scale will use the development and management of process maps that detail how and what activity is delivered. Many companies have whole departments looking to streamline and drive efficiency from those processes—**business process reengineering (BPR)** teams. There are established methodologies to undertake this BPR work, from Six Sigma to Kaizen, and all of the tools are typically engineering-based and designed to look for process inefficiencies in an industrial environment.

In the absence of alternative approaches these have been applied to the critical processes that determine "how" an experience is delivered.

Approaches such as these that rely on quantitative measures as the prime indicator of success can be seen as a blunt instrument when it comes to customer experience. For example, if call centers are managed based on minimizing the duration of a call (and thus keeping the cost of each call low), companies often lose sight of the qualitative components that are critical to delivery of the customer experience. Here it is about attention to detail; for example, ending a positive call with the question, "Is there anything else I can help you with today?" can appear as an opportunity to cut two seconds from every call duration—as technically this is not about the core call answering. Gross that figure over tens of thousands of calls and you have a seemingly clear financial reason to "cut the two seconds." What this analysis misses is both the opportunity to end a call with a positive experiential signoff and the opportunity to resolve another customer issue contemporaneously within the same call, even at the risk of extending its duration. Which is more important—the length of the call or the value of the customer to the company (which depends on its opposite)?

(continued)

(*Continued*)

The Customer Experience Toolkit

In parallel with the growth of customer experience awareness, we have seen a range of tools, software, and management approaches being developed that enable companies to engage with their experience in a structured and logical way. These tools are now approaching maturity, having been tested over hundreds of engagements across markets.

These tools and techniques are available to integrate the internal process management that is an inside-out view with a customer driven outside-in view. The challenge is to align the outside in with the inside out so, which comes first? Companies tend to have the inside-out view already and it is used to manage investments and underpins the measurement framework. What is needed is to provide the outside-in view so that the processes can be tested to see if they are delivering against that requirement.

The tools include experience maturity assessments, **customer journey mapping**, customer experience measurement, and customer experience design and redesign. The tools are supported by a growing number of external consultancy teams and now emerging specialist training and development companies focused on equipping companies to grow their own talent.

The Key Question

The question to answer is not "how do we become a customer-centric company?" It is "how can we elevate the customer component of our business strategy and decision making to a position of parity or more with the other established components, including sales, commercial, price, product, and technology?"

To achieve this would have a significant impact. It represents an achievable business goal. It importantly avoids alienating wide swaths of the management who are not engaged with the customer and see such a focus as either not relevant to their goals or even as a threat to their power and authority.

How to Start a Customer Experience Push

The approach requires a company to have some basic building blocks in place to successfully engage in a coordinated engagement with the customer agenda that is most likely to succeed. This simple set of 10 questions gives the company a chance to understand its state of readiness to engage:

- What is the current customer experience promise/proposition?
- What do customers need to receive from the company in experiential terms?
- How well does the company deliver on the customer experience promise today?

- Is it clear to everyone in the company what experience we want to deliver to our customers?
- Do we have an outside-in end-to-end life cycle or customer experience journey map of "what it's like to be our customer"?
- What customer measures exist today?
- What is the hierarchy of the current measurement framework?
- Which customer interactions are the most important for the company's customers?
- What does our company do really well in terms of the current customer experience?
- What does our company do really badly today in terms of our customer experience? What could the company just do better?

A failure to be able to answer positively, with a high degree of honesty in terms of the response, any or all of these questions suggests that some foundational work is required to give the company the best opportunity to succeed.

Let's assume for a moment that a company has none of this available, has a virtual blank sheet of paper, and now needs to examine the key foundational steps that the company can take to begin to make progress with a customer experience agenda. A company needs to have access to some basic components from which it can formulate a plan to deliver and measure customer experience–driven change:

- A customer experience articulation
- A set of customer experience challenges
- A customer journey map
- A customer experience measurement framework

Customer Experience Articulation

This is a short sentence that captures the essence of the actual experience that the company intends to deliver. This is intended to be used on a regular basis and not to be words on a wall that are never translated into action. It is key that the articulation is derived from the preexisting work and is seen as an evolution and articulation of the "how" that can be delivered.

For example, a financial services business with the following mission statement—

> *"Our mission is to provide our insureds with superb coverage and claims handling through careful and diligent underwriting of risks and business-friendly solutions"*

(continued)

(Continued)

—could have the following as an experience articulation:

"We insist that our customers have an experience that is human, meets or exceeds their expectation, and makes the complex simple."

The use of the word *insist* is important, as it drives a very positive and proactive message. The words are designed to translate the Mission into a deliverable proposition and to guide the "how." *This articulation is now the "North Star" that guides future thinking in terms of customer experience.*

Customer Experience Challenges

This then is taken a step further by deriving the customer experience challenges, which act as *the touchstones* for all staff to use to answer the question: "Are we doing the right thing? Are we making the right choices?"

In this case, the customer experience challenges could be:

- Make the complex simple
- Human
- Easy to do business with
- Fix problems fast

If we consider a business situation where these challenges can be applied, it could be as simple as reviewing a policy document and applying the first three challenges (not every challenge will apply in every situation). By doing this, changes can be made to language, content, channel of communication, call center scripts, and many more areas.

Customer Journey Mapping

The next stage is to map each interaction that a customer has and what it feels like to be a customer from the customer perspective. Customer journey mapping is a structured way to understand your customers' wants, **needs,** and expectations *at each stage* of their interaction with you, from initial awareness to departure and perhaps return.

Customer journey mapping (CJM) is a tool for visualizing how customers interact with an organization across multiple channels and touch points at each stage of the customer life cycle (or part of it). It provides a factual basis for change, a map of the interactions that take place and the emotions created at each touch point.

Put simply, a customer journey map is an "outside-in" view and is captured purely from the perspective of a customer. For example, when thinking about buying a new car, you may well read magazines and reviews and often talk to people who will provide their own recommendation. This is all captured in a customer journey map, as it is a map of what we actually do as customers. CJMs will typically have a series of life-cycle stages (for example, "Welcome, Service, Renew") and each is then supported by a set of interactions that the customers have either directly with the company or with third parties.

See more on customer journey mapping later in this chapter.

Highlighting the Critical Interactions

The individual interaction that we have with companies is often the make or break of that commercial relationship; however, not all interactions are equal in terms of their ability to drive behaviors.

Next, companies need to be able to prioritize early focus. This is done by defining and focusing on the interactions that have a disproportionate impact on the customer's emotional connection with the company and therefore those that will drive behaviors that translate into action. These are often referred to as **moments of truth (MoTs)** and pain points. Often, the two converge.

In the majority of cases, even in the virtual world the key interactions involve an element of human interaction or are identified as interaction in which the customer has an elevated emotional interest in the outcome. So an ATM transaction is unlikely to be an early priority, but an online loan application or a customer's first visit to a new gym is an example of heightened emotional engagement and the opportunity to either meet or exceed expectations and so create negative or positive memories.

Designing Customer Experience Improvements

Having prioritized key areas and identified that there are experience improvement opportunities, the challenge is to redesign those experiences from an outside-in perspective, then to connect the resulting solution to the inside-out processes highlighting the required changes, and deploying and measuring customer outcomes.

The experience design approach uses the experience challenges as the touchstones using a cross-functional team to reimagine the experiences from a customer needs perspective. It is important to ignore what might be seen as internal barriers at this stage to fully explore the possibilities.

Attention to the finer details of an interaction is also important—for example, if a customer is applying for a new bank account and the process will take

(continued)

(Continued)

30 to 45 minutes, what is the chair that they sit in going to be like? How will you keep them engaged while the bank staff input data? Experience design is about all of the senses and the mind actually responds to nonverbal stimulus as well as verbal—consider why major high-end hotels have a signature scent that you notice when you first enter the hotel. It is designed to evoke positive memories and recall positive experiences—for the business traveler, even the sense of having arrived home.

The outputs of any redesign should consist of a range of opportunities to improve but the majority should be small scale, implementable quickly, requiring little or no cost increases, and indeed potentially reducing the cost to serve while improving the experience.

A Customer Experience Measurement Framework

How should we measure the customer experience improvements?

There is a range of measures that have been developed that are commonly used metrics in the customer experience field. These include Net Promoter Score, Customer Effort, Customer Satisfaction, and others.

No single measure gives a company the level of insight into the customer experience; instead, a small basket of measures is required, sometimes referred to as a *customer dashboard*. It is then not about actually having the measures but how the company uses the measures to drive actions to improve.

The key is to focus on *customer outcomes, not company outcomes*—if we do the former, then the latter will follow as a matter of course, and correlations can be run later, with the goal of building predictive analytics.

Most companies have more metrics than they can sensibly manage already, so adding measures can be a difficult and time-consuming job.

The smart companies in the world of customer experience recognize that they need to reimagine existing measures and convert them to customer outcome based. The other advantage is that you can quickly create customer relevance at a localized level in the organization without the need to introduce something new.

Flexibility in the set of measures that a company monitors can also be important because it may be that, in experiential terms, different measures have a higher degree of customer or business relevance.

To pull this together, let's use the example of an educational publishing company.

The business has an annual peak of business when it needs to ship a new set of textbooks to schools.

At different points in the year the senior management team needs to track different customer measures. These are not new measures and are currently seen as operational measures. If we map out the key internal processes during the year, we have a series of critical events that have a knock-on effect because if any part of the chain fails to meet time and quality targets, the next step will be impacted and in the end, customers will not have the product they need to teach pupils. These include:

1. Editors commissioning the textbooks.
2. Authors writing the books.
3. Production producing the books.
4. Warehouse distributing the books.
5. Finance invoicing correctly for the books.

The board needs to see the operational measures associated with each of these as the customer experience metrics for that month or perhaps quarter and rotate their attention over the year. The metrics can include both quantitative and qualitative components to ensure the company understands "how customers feel" about the products and the service.

You will note that even finance comes under the microscope as a deliverer of the customer experience. A poor experience with invoicing may cause the customer to seek another supplier in subsequent years. A wide range of business functions has to operate effectively in order for the ultimate customer experience—the delivery of textbooks successfully over that short period in any year.

Customer Experience Is the Result of Technological Change and Interconnectedness

Customers talk to each other more than they ever could before. As a result, what they say about us matters, and what they say will be the direct result of their experiences with us. The discipline of customer experience is emerging as a key component of business strategy in companies around the world and across sectors. It is relevant in consumer-to-consumer (C2C), business-to-business (B2B), and business-to-business-to-consumer (B2B2C), and it could be argued that it is more important today in a B2B context, as one significant multimillion-dollar contract win could depend on the experiential difference offered by competing vendors where their core product and price are equal.

The financial case for the return on investment in customer experience continues to be made at both the business profit-and-loss and the stock performance levels for shareholders.

The skills required to both understand the customer experience and how to influence it are still in their nascent stage in terms of the numbers of professionals in the space but the tools and software have matured to a large degree.

(continued)

(*Continued*)

The next few years will see real growth in customer experience professionals and we will see an adaptation of the organization design to incorporate customer experience in the same way that marketing, sales, and commercial are today. The increasing number of chief customer officers (CCOs) and senior vice presidents (SVPs)/VPs Customer Experience underlines this.

In practical terms, companies need to see the customer agenda as an ongoing, and significant, part of their business strategy—not as a stand-alone or sole driver. The way to develop the customer agenda is to first understand where you are today, then create a road map to where you need to be based on your mission, vision, and customer proposition. Then through hundreds and then cumulatively thousands of tiny changes that individually are easy, cheap, and quick to deliver across the company but that add up to significant change, evolve both the experience and the company culture over time.

Source: Adapted from Alan Pennington, *The Customer Experience Book* (Upper Saddle River, NJ: FT Press, 2016).

[a] "Client Centric," Investopedia, available at http://www.investopedia.com/terms/c/client-centric.asp, accessed February 15, 2016.
[b] "Customer Service," Investopedia, available at http://www.investopedia.com/terms/c/customer-service.asp, accessed February 15, 2016.

Now let's take a look at what some of the experts say about how to fix experiences—by fixing service.

How Do We Fix Service?

Bill Price
President, Driva Solutions

David Jaffe
Consulting Director, LimeBridge Australia

Let's look at the issues that have prevented significant improvements in service. Here we identify seven reasons that service isn't getting better and seven responses, the Best Service Principles:

Principle 1: Eliminate Dumb Contacts

Customer demand for service equals the volume of requests that customers make of companies when they need help, are confused, or have to change something. In most companies, demand is a given; lots of time and effort go into forecasting demand based on past demand, measured in 30-minute increments across a range of contact channels. Then companies work hard at matching their resources to this demand: putting people on the right shifts at the right time, finding partners if needed, and so forth. These companies are so busy trying to manage the demand and their "service supply" that few, if any, question why the demand is there in the first place. For example, how many companies report that they have made themselves easier to deal with by reducing the demand for contact? How many boards of directors monitor their rate of contact as well as the speed and cost? Very few companies think this way (although Amazon comes close by proclaiming year-by-year reductions in contacts per order). There is an unfortunate obsession with how quickly phones and e-mails are answered. The standard across most service operations is to report and track how quickly things were done, not how well they were done or how often, or why they needed to be done at all.

This issue of demand for contact is fundamental to our thinking. If companies want to rethink service radically, they need to rethink the need for service. Our book is titled *The Best Service Is No Service* because too many service interactions aren't necessary; they reflect, instead, as we've begun to show, the dumb things that companies have done to their customers: processes that customers don't understand, bewildering statements, incorrect letters, badly applied fees and charges, or services not working as the customer expects. Fundamental changes in service require companies to question what has driven the demand for service.

Principle 2: Create Engaging Self-Service

How often have you given up on a Web site or gotten lost in one? Have you ever listened to a set of toll-free menus and been overwhelmed by the choices, and tried desperately to find the option that lets you talk to an operator? How often have you filled out an application form online and then been told that you don't meet the criteria for an online application? How often have you searched for an online service and found that it is no longer available? How often have you been flummoxed by the operating manual for a new electronic device or for your new car? These are just some of the examples of the dumb things that organizations do or don't do in self-service.

When self-service works well, customers love it. Companies like Amazon .com and firstdirect.com couldn't have grown the way they have if customers didn't like well-designed self-service. ATMs took off because they were much more convenient than queuing in a branch. Internet banking is so convenient that it has increased the volume of transactions and inquiries that customers perform.

(continued)

(Continued)

Why do so many companies get it wrong? Our perspective is that they understand neither the need for self-service nor how to create self-service solutions that their customers will embrace.

Principle 3: Be Proactive

The reason why companies have to invest so much time trying to predict demand and then supplying appropriate resources is that the modus operandi is one of reactive service: If the customer calls, the company is there to deal with it. But in many cases the company knows that there is a problem yet still waits for the customer to contact the company to fix it.

Take product recalls, for example. Recently, a leading company that had no idea which of its customers had the affected product needed to wait for customers to try to figure it out and then call the company, sometimes in panic mode.

Principle 4: Make It Really Easy to Contact Your Company

Do you ever get the impression that some companies would rather not hear from you? Have you ever been on a Web site and searched in vain for a phone number to call? Have you ever found that companies expect you to get service only when they want to give it to you? If any of these situations seems familiar, it's another example of a company making itself hard to contact.

Principle 5: Own the Actions across the Company

A bizarre myth has grown up in many companies that the head of customer service is responsible for customer service. Although we recognize that someone needs to be held accountable and be dedicated to service, we do not believe that the service operations can fix service without the help of all the other company departments and, increasingly, outside partners in the **supply chain** or in other functions. Although the head of service does need to forecast the demand for service, and handle those contacts well, many other areas of a business cause the customer contacts that drive the demand—for example, billing, IT, marketing, credit, and finance. IT and process and product areas can also influence how well the customer service area can service the demand. The norm is for the head of customer service to be held accountable for the standard and methods of service. Our perspective is that responsibility for service must be spread across the whole organization.

Principle 6: Listen and Act

Some companies have millions of contacts per year with their customers, yet they still spend considerable money and time researching their customers. In fact, head-office functions such as marketing, product design, and IT have gotten further and further from frontline delivery; the information gap has increased between the head office's understanding of the customer and the behaviors and wants of customers as expressed at the front line. The interactions that companies have with customers today offer an amazing amount of insight about customers, the company's products and services, and even competitors—if companies can tap into what their customers are telling them. Unfortunately, most companies have not even thought to "listen" to their customers in this way when these interactions occur.

This disconnect is illustrated by the gap between the perceptions of CEOs and those of customers in general. . . . In one study by Accenture, over 70 percent of CEOs believed that their companies provide "above average" customer care, but nearly 60 percent of these companies' customers stated that they are somewhat or extremely upset with their most recent customer service experience.

Unfortunately, CEOs and board members are cosseted—they often fly first class, have "personal" or "relationship" bankers, get queued faster, and rarely set foot in a branch or pay their own bills. Because they have become disconnected with what their own customers experience, they will have to listen even harder.

Managers in larger companies who control market and customer research or set the budget for service rarely, if ever, spend time with the frontline staff who are dealing directly with customers. In small businesses this isn't the case—an owner who runs a restaurant or cafe doesn't need to conduct research into what his customers like or dislike. He hears it directly from customers: If customers are asking for cake or health food or gluten-free products or soy milk, the restaurant owner can respond quickly, or quickly be out of business. It's too bad that many companies have forgotten how to listen in this way.

Principle 7: Deliver Great Service Experiences

Companies have created large centralized contact centers or service functions, separated service from sales or production, added lots of new technology, deluged themselves with meaningless or misleading metrics, and built walls around the customer service functions. They have then become stuck delivering service experiences that have forgotten the customer; stuck obsessing about speed, not quality; and stuck thinking that faster is more efficient. It is hardly a surprise that many customer experiences disappoint customers.

(continued)

(Continued)

Companies Are Stuck with Service Experiences That Have Forgotten Who the Customer Is

Customers are often expected to navigate the organization and repeat account information and what happened ad nauseam, from agent to agent. The processes simply haven't been designed from the customers' perspective, and it shows. For example, customers are justifiably miffed when companies (still!!) ask them to repeat their credit card number, frequent flyer account number, or order identification number after just having done so in an **interactive voice response (IVR)** or with another agent or, as is increasingly the case, after doing so online. "Don't you know me?!?" they might say. Then companies add in complexity for customers, such as by asking them to repeat data the company already knows or to provide information to comply with a procedure that someone in the legal department dreamed up. These are just two illustrations of experiences that haven't been designed with the customer in mind.

Source: Adapted from Bill Price and David Jaffe, *The Best Service Is No Service: How to Liberate Your Customers from Customer Service, Keep Them Happy, and Control Costs* (San Francisco: Jossey-Bass, 2008), pp. 8–19.

Improving Customer Service at an Online Financial Services Firm

In one instance, an online financial services firm was reengineering the customer interaction center to implement many of the principles we've been discussing. The firm separated its customer base into four groups based on key customer characteristics (assets and use of the services). Once it identified its customer groups, it was easy for the firm to identify the knowledge, skills, and abilities that were required to support them. The firm implemented routing technology to redirect customer calls based on the customer grouping and the skill set of the available representatives. The firm created automated **business rules** that could utilize the best available personnel to handle the needs of each individual customer in the call queue. Prior to this change, any customer could be routed to any customer service representative (CSR). It was not unusual, for example, to have a **most valuable customer (MVC)** routed to a newly hired and ill-informed rep or a rep who lacked the required skills to execute particular transactions. This required a customer hanging up and (if the firm was lucky) calling again; or perhaps the customer would be transferred to another CSR. The changes resolved these problems. A key benefit for the rep was the ability to work through a learning curve—she was directed to the types of calls that she could handle, and this significantly decreased stress levels, which reduced all the company costs related to turnover.

When you *do* need customer service, high-quality customer service is one of the beneficial outcomes of adopting customer strategies. Enterprises must keep in mind the cost of *not* providing sufficient service, thereby risking the loss of customers, the cost of lost long-term customer equity, and the expensive task of acquiring new customers. General wisdom places the estimate for customer defections due to a poor sales or service interaction between the customer and the enterprise at about 70 percent. It isn't necessary for a company to make formal **Return on Customer (ROC)** calculations to understand that the short-term losses in revenue and long-term customer equity cost to shareholders of poor service far outweigh the current perceived "savings" of reducing service quality.

Moreover, an enterprise must balance the cost of providing customer service with the needs and desires of the customer in such a way that the customer will find sufficient value in the enterprise to remain a customer. At a minimum, certain standards of accuracy, timeliness, and convenience must be in place to placate most customers. The right technology and processes must first be deployed, followed by the training and adoption of service practices by customer-facing representatives.

But what is the "right amount" of customer service? What do customers actually need and want? Are we doing the same expensive things for everybody when our most valuable customers would be even happier with less expensive service (think mobile or online banking versus service counter at the bank branch)? Taking different customer needs into consideration, what is the least expensive amount for the enterprise to spend on service that works for the customer? Which channel do customers want to use? Can they be easily moved to one that costs less—especially customers with low **actual value** and **potential value**? And should different levels of service be offered to different kinds of customers? Might customer service mean different things to different customers? When is self-service appropriate? Certainly these and other questions should be addressed if an enterprise is to find the balance of service that serves both the customer and the budget. Some companies still look at customer service as a cost center, but others see it as building customer equity, and opportunity. The difference is palpable in the resulting customer experience. Art Schoeller describes the general problem: Enterprises "constantly seeking to offload more expensive agent-assisted interactions to self-service" for cost savings may seem to dovetail with consumers increasingly seeking and relying on self-service with digital devices, but "many organizations provide a disappointing customer experience, with 57 percent of U.S. online consumers reporting they have had unsatisfactory service interactions in the past 12 months."[2] The solution is finding the right balance for the customer and matching service and mode to the consumer need at the moment.

Schoeller continues: "While consumers hop channels to research products and services, there usually is a moment of truth when an informed agent can make the

---

[2] Art Schoeller, "Connect the Dots between Customer Self-Service and Contact Centers," Forrester Research, Inc., February 24, 2014, available at http://www.forrester.com.

right offer and close the sale. Companies that capture consumer interaction data from web and mobile self-service touch points can more effectively match the right agents with prospects."

In another example, United Airlines developed a mobile app designed around the stress points of travel day. Flight updates, rebookings, food options, and self-check-in were all set up to give customers a sense of control when they most need reassurance. In mid-2012, 1.5 million passengers had downloaded the app. Nine months later, usage levels reached 6 million. By June 2014, users totaled 10 million. It's obvious that this is self-service that has been of value to customers, but as significantly, the app also led to major cost savings to the company as staffing at United counters fell by half.[3]

Is "good" customer service in the eyes of the beholder? Some criteria an enterprise could consider from the customer's perspective include:

- Saving time or money
- Accuracy of a transaction
- Speed of service
- Ease of doing business
- Providing better (not just more) information
- Recording and remembering relevant data
- Convenience
- Allowing a choice of ways to do business
- Treating customers as individuals
- Acknowledging and remembering the relationship
- Fixing problems quickly
- Thanking the customer

Not all of these elements are equally important to all customers. Any one of these criteria could be a deal breaker to one customer and of no consequence to another. Adding or upgrading customer services uniformly for everyone is an expensive way to raise the bar. Better to know what's important to an individual customer and then to make sure that customer gets the services most important to him.

Adding or upgrading customer services uniformly for everyone is an expensive way to raise the bar. Better to know what's important to an individual customer and then to make sure that customer gets the services most important to him.

Many enterprises have learned that the integration of the contact center with all other communication vehicles may be the first step toward successful completion of the customer's mission. For example, live online customer service, text-based chat, and Web callbacks are some of the vehicles that can elevate good, basic customer

---

[3] Julie A. Ask, "United Airlines Drives Self-Service," Forrester Research, Inc., June 16, 2014, available at http://www.forrester.com.

service to excellent and highly satisfactory service, the latter of which translates into customer retention, growth, loyalty, and profitability.

In the next section, Chris Zane, named a Customer Champion by 1to1 Media, explains how his whole business focuses on customer experiences and service.

Customers, Customer Service, and the Customer Experience

Christopher J. Zane
President, Zane's Cycles

Zane's Cycles is a bicycle retailer similar to the one just down the street from you. So why would you be interested in Zane's Cycles and my style of doing business? Everyone believes their own organization offers great customer service, but how can you know for sure that your customers won't get the "It's-not-my-problem" attitude I recently experienced with the staff at the lost baggage department of a major airline? I can say with authority that I can.

I founded Zane's Cycles in October 1981 as a junior in high school at the age of 16. I was working at a bike store in summer 1981, and the owner decided to liquidate the inventory because of high operating costs (the prime interest rate at the time was 21 percent). This gave me the opportunity to purchase an operating business for the cost of the inventory. I first had to convince my parents that it was time for me to operate a storefront business. I figured I could persuade them because I also had been running Foxon Bike Shop, a bike repair business, from our garage since I was 12. Let me tell you, this took a lot of convincing. After agreeing to personally pay back a $23,000 loan with interest to my grandfather, regardless of the success or failure of the business, my parents endorsed my desire to become a small business retailer. First year's sales—a respectable $56,000. This year's sales—an even more respectable $17.5 million.

As I'm sure you can imagine, this growth was not without its bumps in the road or, better stated, those huge, teeth-rattling, "am-I-going-to-come-out-alive?" potholes that suddenly appear from underneath a truck traveling in front of you on the highway. These experiences, however, have made Zane's Cycles a unique and successful retail environment. Zane's Cycles is more than a bicycle store, and I want to share the concepts that helped build the environment my customers enjoy. Please keep in mind that not every business needs to implement these specific programs, but the idea is to create something new, different, and exciting for your customers and staff.

I would much rather spend my day among customers and staff who are laughing and genuinely having a good time than addressing issues from customers feeling they have been mistreated or are unappreciated for their patronage. This is why there is constant communication with the staff about embracing a

(continued)

(Continued)

customer experience culture. The following are a few quotes that are constantly reinforced and are top-of-mind throughout the Zane's organization:

- Customer service starts when the customer experience fails.
- The only difference between us and our competition is the experience we deliver.
- We want our customers to have more fun here than at Disney World.
- And finally, from my friend Len Berry's book, *Discovering the Soul of Service*, great service not only improves business, it improves the quality of life.

In order to build and sustain a culture that lives up to these simple ideas, the employee responsible for delivering the experience needs not only to be passionate but also to be empowered to deliver the dream—constantly.

Probably the most important tool in the customer experience toolbox is understanding the customer **lifetime value (LTV)**. It's easy to deliver on the promise of a unique and enjoyable experience when the customer you're working with is buying a bike for a few thousand dollars, but when you are trying to juggle five customers and the sixth needs help getting a bike out of her car for a free service adjustment and it's raining—well, that's when knowing the customer LTV provides the discipline to maintain the focus to ensure a unique experience. At Zane's Cycles, starting with the first bike at age three and ending with your last bike, usually the retirement present to yourself, our customer LTV is $12,500. Simply, the customer with the free service today is as valuable as today's few-thousand-dollar bike purchaser over a 60-year relationship.

Customer service starts when the customer experience fails. If you, as a customer, are greeted by a friendly and upbeat employee at the start of your search for a product or service, and throughout your interaction with the business continually experience a positive and honest exchange regardless of the staff member with whom you're engaged, the need for resolution diminishes and your loyalty strengthens.

The only difference between us and our competition is the experience we deliver. When it comes to products or services, the true difference between similar offerings is hard to determine. Bikes are bikes, televisions are televisions, oil changes are oil changes, and dry cleaning is dry cleaning, and usually the prices are very similar as well, since everyone has the same cost of doing business. We choose to support one business over another because this one helps me load the bike in the car, or explains why I should select a smaller screen because of the size of the room, or there is a cover over the seat and steering wheel so my interior doesn't get soiled, or the collar tabs are in the short pocket. The experience determines decision.

We want our customers to have more fun here than at Disney World. The Magic Kingdom is exactly that: expensive, crowded, hot, loud, but it's still a magical place because what's most important is that the people there want us to have a good time. Every interaction exceeds our expectations, and the constant innovation of the experience is the foundation on which they were created. Being constantly focused and driven to create a positive and fun experience for our customers that exceeds their expectations will make us better then Disney because we're not expensive, crowded, hot, or loud.

Great service not only improves business, it improves the quality of life. In an environment where delivering great service to the customer is the single focus, many things happen: Satisfied, happy customers are nice to the employees; happy, intrinsically satisfied employees are nice to each other; happy teams are successful, justifying higher pay and benefits; families of well-paid employees are happy; and our quality of life has improved. If we're going to spend 2,000 hours a year doing anything, why not spend it in a fun environment with people we enjoy?

Obviously, none of this is possible if your team is composed of people who don't have the personality to deliver the experience. I have built my team with genuinely nice people and then provide the tools and training to guarantee their success. Once there is an understanding of the customer LTV, and employees embrace the attitude associated with the principles above, it's time to empower them to deliver a unique experience in a way that is consistent with their unique personality. Let the fun begin!

At many firms, the "customer service" function is thought of as a cost of doing business rather than as an integral part of the products or services actually being sold to customers. It is easy to spot an enterprise with this attitude. This is the company that hides its toll-free number on the Web site and that has an impenetrable interactive voice response (IVR) system (see Chapter 7).

Increasingly, customer transactions are moving to an e-commerce model, and transactions normally handled with a phone call are now being done electronically, via the Web site. In many customer service areas, this has changed the mix of calls that are handled by the customer service rep. "Easy" transaction (order-taking) calls are now being replaced with more difficult customer situation calls (complaints, inquiries, billing and invoicing questions, etc.). This can increase the level of stress experienced by the customer service reps.

Traditional measures for customer interaction centers have focused on "talk time" and "one and done" measures. (See a more complete discussion about the customer interaction center in Chapter 7.) As we dig deeper into customer metrics, we start measuring average talk time for valuable customers versus customers who call into the customer interaction center frequently and yet do not generate enough revenue to warrant high levels of service. We begin to understand which customers are buying a wide range of products and services offered by an enterprise and which customers should be but aren't. Many customer interaction center managers are left to fight a battle to increase talk time for the customers who warrant more attention, but they lack the analytics and resulting insights ("the facts") to be able to justify that decision. This is where partnering with the customer manager is key: the justification for these measures should be in the customer strategies.

The fact is, however, that a customer-strategy company often can keep its costs down by centering on customer needs. Calls are more often resolved in one session and in less total time. Customer service reps do not "chase down" information or transfer customers from department to department. Voice response unit options are reordered to present the most likely option desired by *that* customer as soon as the customer is identified. This process can significantly decrease phone costs for an enterprise maintaining a toll-free phone line. And it requires that people within the enterprise start thinking like customers, or taking the customer's point of view during key interactions (such as a sales call or customer care call), and combine this point of view with the **customer strategy** and business rules that have been identified for this customer. Change often demands new skill sets. As the enterprise begins to define specific roles and responsibilities (or job descriptions) for various customer care representatives, it also will need to develop training and development plans and recruitment and staffing plans. These descriptions include competencies and behaviors that will be required of all employees—things like customer empathy— and skills associated with different roles. Employees might determine how they "touch" the customer directly or indirectly by supporting another department.

An often-neglected step in this process is planning around the way customer care representatives are supported, measured, and compensated to reinforce the new behaviors, which should incorporate the customer-centered metrics described earlier. Unfortunately, the reporting capabilities in many enterprises are not up to the task, and some great customer-oriented efforts have gone awry because this last step was not implemented. Employees often want to "do the right thing" but are not supported or measured adequately or correctly. More important, many companies equate **customer relationship management** with "customer service," when in fact customer service—important as it is—*is not* the same as relationships, customer experience management, or customer equity building. The heart of a Learning Relationship is a memory of a customer's expressed needs so that this customer can be treated in a way that works for him without his having to be asked again, and so a dialogue can pick up right where it left off. Customer service, in contrast, is often more like *random acts of kindness* masquerading as customer relationship management.

Relationship Governance

One of the biggest single difficulties in making the transition to an enterprise that pays attention to its relationships with individual customers and creating better experiences for them is the issue of **relationship governance.** By that we mean: Who will be "in charge" at the enterprise when it comes to making different decisions for different customers? Optimizing around each customer, rather than optimizing around each product or channel, requires decision making related to customer-specific criteria, across all different channels and product lines. When Customer A is on the Web site or on the phone, the enterprise wants to ensure that the very best, most profitable offer is presented *for that customer.* The firm's call center shouldn't try to compete with its own stores to try to get the customer to buy from them, nor should the product manager for Product 1 compete with the product manager for Product 2 and try to win the customer for one product line or another. What the customer-centric enterprise wants is to deliver whatever offer for this customer is likely to create the most value, overall, for the company and the customer without regard to any other organizational or department goals or incentives that might have been established at the firm. This, in a nutshell, is the problem of *relationship governance.* The challenge most companies face when they make a serious commitment to managing customer relationships becomes obvious once the firm pulls out its current organizational charts, which usually are set up to manage brands, products, channels, and programs. Most companies have organized themselves in such a way as to ensure that they can achieve their objectives in terms of product sales or brand awareness across the entire population of customers they serve.

But in the age of interactivity, managing customer relationships individually will require an enterprise to treat different customers differently within that customer population. Inherent in this idea is the notion that different customers will be subject to different objectives and strategies and that the enterprise will undertake different actions with respect to different customers. So we ask again: With respect to any particular customer, who will be put in charge, and held accountable, within the enterprise, to make sure this actually happens? And when that person is put in charge of an individual customer relationship, what levers will he control in order to execute the strategy being applied to "his" customer? How will his performance be measured and evaluated by the enterprise, for the current period as well as the long term? (Recall the Canadian bank example we cited in Chapter 11, a company where **customer portfolio** managers are measured in the current quarter for the current revenue by the bank of the customers in their portfolios and for the three-year projected value, as of today, of that same group of customers.)

This is the problem of relationship governance. It's one thing for us to maintain, safe between the covers of this book, that in the **interactive age** a company should manage its dialogues and relationships with different customers differently, making sure to analyze the values and needs of various individual customers, adapting its behavior for each one to what is appropriate for that particular customer. It's another thing to carry this out within a corporate organization when, at least for many companies at present, no one is actually in charge of making it happen. In the first chapter of this book, we showed the orthogonal relationship of **customer orientation** and product orientation: finding customers for products or products for customers. We can extend this customer orientation thinking in the way it's shown in Exhibit 13.2.

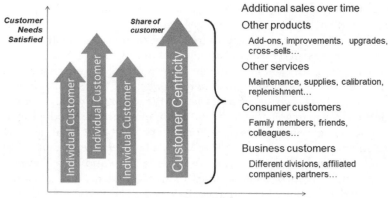

EXHIBIT 13.2   Share of Customer = Share of Need

The customer-oriented company will focus on one customer at a time and try to find the next right offer, service, and/or product for that customer. And another one and another one, winning a greater and greater share of each customer's business by generating top-notch customer experiences and building Learning Relationships. But how is a company structured to accomplish this mission?

Exhibit 13.3 is an oversimplified example of a "typical" old Industrial Age organization chart. In such an organization, each product or brand is the direct-line responsibility of one individual within the organization. In this way, the enterprise can hold particular managers and organizations responsible for achieving various objectives related to product and brand sales. The brand or product manager is, in fact, the "protector" of the brand or product, watching out to make sure that it does well and that sales goals or awareness goals are achieved. The manager controls advertising and promotion levers to ensure that the best and most persuasive message will be conveyed to the right segments and niches of customers or potential customers. This is all in keeping with the most basic goal of an old-fashioned Industrial Age company: *to sell more products to whoever will buy them.*

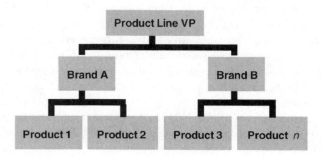

EXHIBIT 13.3   Product Management Organization

The most basic goal of the customer-strategy enterprise, however, is to increase the long-term value of its customer base, by applying different objectives and strategies to different customers. Yes, in the process it's practically certain that more products will be sold in the short term. But in order for the primary task to be accomplished, someone within the organization has to be put in charge of making decisions and carrying out actions with respect to each individual customer, even if that task is completely automated.

In Exhibit 13.4, a different organization chart is drawn for the customer-value-building company, one that emphasizes *customer management* rather than product management. In an enterprise organized for customer management, ideally every customer will be the direct-line responsibility of a single customer manager (even though the customer may not be aware that the manager is in charge, as he works in the background to determine the enterprise's most appropriate strategy for that customer and then to make sure it is carried out). Because there are likely many more customers than there are management employees, it is only logical that a customer manager should be made responsible for a whole group of customers. We refer to such a group as a *customer portfolio*, avoiding for the present the phrase **customer segment**, in order to clarify the concept.

A customer portfolio is made up of unduplicated, unique (and identified) customers. No customer will ever be placed into more than one portfolio at a time, because it is the portfolio manager who will be in charge of the enterprise's relationship with the customers in her portfolio and the resulting value of that relationship.

If we allow a customer to inhabit two different portfolios, then we are just creating another relationship governance problem—which portfolio manager will actually call the shots when it comes to the enterprise's strategies for *that* customer? How will we calculate that customer's value accurately? And who gets credit or blame if the customer's value rises or falls?

A customer manager's primary objective is to maximize the long-term value of his own customer portfolio (i.e., to keep and grow the customers in his portfolio),

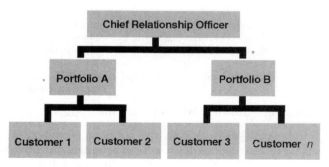

EXHIBIT 13.4   Customer Management Organization

and the enterprise should reward him based on a set of metrics that indicate the degree to which he has accomplished his mission. In the ideal state, the enterprise's entire customer base might be parsed into several different portfolios, each of which is overseen by the customer manager, like a subdivided business that creates value in the long term and the short term as of today. (See Exhibit 13.5.)

Clearly, if we plan to hold a customer manager accountable for growing the value of a portfolio of customers, then we'll also have to give her some authority to take actions with respect to the customers in the portfolio. The levers that a customer manager ought to be able to pull, in order to encourage her customers to attain a higher and higher long-term value to the enterprise, should include, literally, every type of action or communication that the enterprise is capable of rendering on an individual-customer basis. In communication, this would mean that the customer manager would control the enterprise's **addressable** forms of communication and interaction: direct mail as well as interactions at the call center, on the Web site, ads displayed on the customer's screen when he's visiting another Web site, on his mobile device, and even (to the extent possible) in face-to-face encounters at the store or the cash register. In effect, the customer manager would be responsible for overseeing the enterprise's continuing dialogue with a customer. In terms of the actual product or service offering, ideally the customer manager would be responsible for setting the pricing for her customers, extending any discounts or collecting premiums, and so forth. The customer manager should own the offer,[4] and the communication of the offer, with respect to the customers in the manager's portfolio.

Not Campaign Management . . .   Customer Portfolio Management

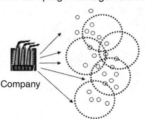
Company

	Not Campaign Management	Customer Portfolio Management
• Customers Targeted	• Anybody who will buy, including BZs	• MVCs and MGCs
• Objective	• Launch positive ROI campaigns	• Maximize lifetime value of customer portfolio
• Customer Reaction	• Block interactions	• Invite interactions
• Acceptance Rate:	• 2–5%	• 30–70%
• Nature:	• Transaction: Buy something now	• Relationship: Buy more vs. buy now

EXHIBIT 13.5   Managing Customer Portfolios for the Long Term

---

[4] The phrase "owns the relationship" disturbs some people; after all, a relationship can't be "owned." Within the context of this book, "owning" a relationship means "is accountable for," in the sense of "owns up to."

> The customer manager should own the offer, and the communication of the offer, with respect to the customers in the manager's portfolio.

The enterprise will still be creating and marketing various programs and products, but the customer manager will be the "traffic cop," with respect to his own portfolio of customers. He will allow some offers to go through as conceived, he will adapt other offers to meet the needs of his own customers, and he will likely block some offers altogether, choosing not to expose his own customers to them.

In a high-end business or personal services firm, such as a private bank, the role of customer manager is played by the firm's relationship manager for each client. The relationship manager owns the relationship and is free to set the policies and communications for her own individual clients, within the boundaries set by the enterprise. The enterprise holds her accountable for keeping the client satisfied, loyal, and profitable. The company probably does not formally estimate an individual client's actual LTV, in strict financial terms; more than likely it has a fairly formal process for ranking these clients by their long-term value or importance to the firm. A relationship manager who manages to dramatically improve the value of her client's relationship to the enterprise will be rewarded.

However, most businesses have many more customers than a private bank, or a law firm, or an advertising agency. For most businesses, it would simply be uneconomic for a relationship manager to pay individual, personal attention to a single customer relationship, to the exclusion of all other responsibilities. Realistically, then, the way most of the addressable communications will be rendered to individual customers, at the vast majority of companies, will be through the application of business rules. Just as business rules are used to mass-customize a product or a service (see Chapter 10), they can be applied to mass-customize the offer extended to different customers as well as the communication of that offer. Thus, one of the customer manager's primary jobs will be to oversee the business rules that govern the enterprise's mass-customized relationship with the individual customers in his own portfolio.

In addition to customer relationship managers, the one-to-one enterprise will need **capabilities managers** as well (see Exhibit 13.6).[5] Their role is to deliver the capabilities of the enterprise to the customer managers, in essence figuring out whether the firm should build, buy, or partner to render any new products or services that customers might require. We could think of capabilities managers as being something like product managers at large. The products and capabilities they bring to bear, on behalf of the enterprise, actually will not necessarily be marketed to customers but very likely instead to the customer managers in charge of the enterprise's relationships with customers.

None of this is to say that companies can afford to forget about product quality, or innovation, or efficient production and cost reduction. These tasks will be just as important as they always have been, for the simple reason that few customers

---

[5] From B. Joseph Pine II, *Mass Customization* (Cambridge, MA: Harvard Business School Press, 1993).

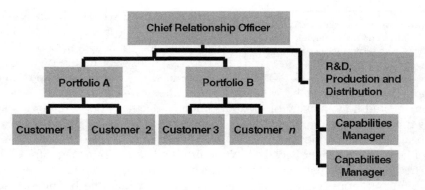

EXHIBIT 13.6   Product Managers Become Capabilities Managers

would choose to continue relationships involving subpar products or service. How-ever, as we've already discussed, product and service quality by themselves do not necessarily lead to competitive success, because no matter how stellar a company's service is, nothing can stop a competitor from also offering great service—or a great, breakthrough product, or a low price. In the final analysis, the most important single benefit of engaging a customer in an ongoing relationship is that the rich context of a Learning Relationship creates an impregnable competitive barrier, with respect to that customer, making it literally impossible for a competitor to duplicate the customer experience the customer is now receiving.

In order to track whether the effect of what we're doing for customers is or is not working, more and more companies are engaged in customer experience jour-ney mapping. The journey mapping tracks what it's like to be our customer now, visualizes what it should be like, and sets up the plan to close the gap. Valerie Peck, cofounder and CEO of SuiteCX, a journey mapping tool, tells us what mapping is and does, and how to do it.[6]

Understanding Customer Experience through Customer Journey Mapping

Valerie Peck
Cofounder, SuiteCX; Founder, East Bay Group Consulting

Understanding customer experience (CX) is a critical necessity for companies that want their fingers on the pulse of the only real group that counts—the

---

[6] Full disclosure: One of the textbook's authors (Rogers) serves on the board of SuiteCX.

customers, who are those paying for products or services. When done well, it can and should involve every aspect of the company—its strategy, tactics, investments, hiring approaches, products, and services, and how it creates and lives its brand promise. Companies who excel at CX are more profitable and enjoy significant competitive advantage.

Competitive Advantage and Profitability

Customer experience maturity correlates to financial results. Seventy-seven percent of companies with above average customer experience maturity levels reported that their financial results in 2014 were better than their competitors, compared with only 55 percent of those with below average customer experience maturity.[a] Also, from 2007 to 2015, customer experience leaders consistently outperformed the market (see Exhibit 13.1).

Every company delivers a customer experience, whether it's deliberate or not. It is part of a three-legged stool: (1) product/service packages, (2) relationship (trust), and (3) CX. Many companies have outstanding products/services packages—they are priced right, positioned properly, and target a specific segment of consumers/businesses—the whole "package." A prospect or repurchaser also has to have at least a sufficient degree of trust that the company they are working with is going to meet or exceed their need and expectations. Succinctly said, they will "do the right thing" and they "do things right" (see Peppers and Rogers, *Extreme Trust,* 2016). Finally, there is the component of the customers and their experience. If there is significant friction in the buying process or in the ongoing use of that product/service package, then customers or prospects will "vote with their feet" and go elsewhere, or worse, become a negative influence on others who are considering that product/service.

Executives estimate that their potential revenue loss for not offering a positive, consistent, and brand-relevant customer experience is 20 percent of their annual revenue. (That would be $400 million for a $2 billion firm.) And even worse, once lost, 27 percent of customers are lost forever.[b] Other typical reactions to a poor CX or low trust include:

- Blocked phone numbers (80 percent).
- Closed accounts (84 percent).
- Unsubscribing from e-mail lists (84 percent).

(continued)

(Continued)

- Deleted apps because of push notifications (82 percent).
- Unfollowing brands on social channels (86 percent).[c]

It's no wonder that 72 percent of executives polled in a recent Forrester survey say that improving the experience of their customer is likely to be their organization's top priority, and that 63 percent say that addressing rising customer expectations is their top business priority over the next 12 months.[d] Also, according to the Temkin Group, the percentage of large organizations in Temkin's top three customer experience maturity levels has increased from 23 percent in 2014 to 32 percent in 2015.[e]

As we discuss CX here, we are defining it the same way Wikipedia does: the experience with a company at every "touch point" with a customer. In other words, this discussion is about what a company can do to make the customer's experience better—not necessarily every possible thing that could happen to a customer, including the kinds of things outside the control of the company. It's about the experience that is intended for a customer at an individual and personal level more than the general experience received. Customer experience is therefore more about *their* "experience" and not generalized to the customer's world.

But understanding customer experience should go beyond the aggregate of the company-controlled aggregate of CX. This is about the actual—real—customer journey solely from the perspective of the customer. Some call it *outside-in*. In some cases, especially at the start of the customer's journey, the company has no idea that they are even being considered! This journey includes stages and activities that often do not involve the company/provider.

The next step is figuring out how a company will deliver great customer experiences. First and foremost, it requires deep self-awareness—awareness of what it is as a company, of its purpose, values, strengths, and weaknesses. Customer journey mapping is a tool some companies use that helps put the puzzle together.

Customer journey mapping (CJM) is a powerful tool for envisioning, designing, and visualizing a holistic experience from the customers' point of view. It helps a company understand the customers' journey from their initial need for a company's product or service, to the way they research the competition, how they select a company, the purchasing process, using the product or service, and repurchasing or churning out.

In fact, according to the Aberdeen Group, companies that adopt customer journey mapping programs outperform others in a variety of ways[f]:

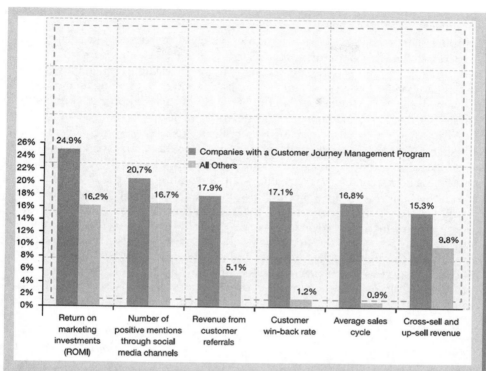

Source: Aberdeen Group, "The CMO Dilemma: Bridging the Gap between Love and Money," May 2015.

The goal is to help a company document its customers' journey (using sales and marketing materials, data, survey results, etc.) to create journey maps based on compelling rational and emotional evidence. To create a great CX, a company must first understand the customer's experience. Journey mapping allows for collaboration and sharing, and getting everyone at the company on the same page to form the basis of a longer-term strategic plan to build customer value.

Objectives of Using CJM

The main objective of all customer maps is to visualize the touch points/interaction points between a customer and a company, company asset, brand, or

(continued)

(Continued)

product. The secondary objectives range widely, from describing a customer experience, journey, or moment of truth to analyzing a customer path from point "a" to purchase. CJM is a tool that, along with standard strategic planning, helps a company better understand and engage its customers by viewing their interactions with the company across the full life cycle of their experience, preferably broken further down by definable customer segments.

CJM may not seem like a mission-critical exercise to some, but in fact, after conducting hundreds of these projects over the years, we can confirm there has not been one instance where a company has not found immediate revenue enhancement or cost-savings opportunities simply by conducting a simple CJM workshop. One global automotive company saved hundreds of thousands of dollars and improved customer satisfaction rates when the journey mapping effort revealed that six separate surveys were going out to new car buyers within the first two weeks of buying the car. By discovering and fixing this issue, the company mitigated customer frustration by consolidating surveys and sharing results internally instead of asking customers for the same answers over and over. Communications and satisfaction improved almost immediately and costs dropped. Not surprisingly, response rates increased.

Journey mapping and the resulting road maps that result from them have been instrumental in many ways, and we find that there are both tangible and intangible benefits from mapping:

Tangible

- Documentation of each interaction point.
- Clear presentation of what's working, what's not, and why not.
- Strategic insights.
- Actionable tactics.
- Collaborative planning process.

Intangible

- Engagement of key stakeholders across divisions and business units.
- Improved absorption of information.
- Forum for breaking down silos.
- Rationalization of company, employee, and customer needs.
- Emotional buy-in through visual storytelling.

What Is a Journey?

It generally starts when a customer identifies that they need or want something. In the information-rich world we live in, we find that customers, both B2C and

B2B, interact first with other customers, research trusted information sources, access third-party reports, look at surveys and rating/rankings, and poll their "social peers" before they ever reach out to a company. In some cases, 70 percent of their decision-making process is completed before they even go to a store, land on a product page, or download a mobile app.[g]

Once they engage with a "finalist," they move forward to engage with that company and ultimately either make a purchase or abandon the journey—to go to a competitor or just do nothing.

Once that customer has converted—that is, purchased a product or service— the next phase begins the relationship, which is the actual use of that product/ services. This is a time with ups and downs, inquiry, and issues as well as benefits and rewards. Ideally, they repurchase. In many cases customers "churn" or go to competitors or cease use of a product without the company ever being aware. Finally, when enough goes right from the customer's viewpoint, she may refer someone to the product or company. That full cycle is often called a life cycle or journey. This drawing presents a typical journey flow:

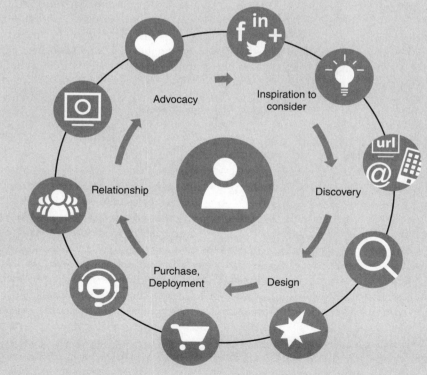

Source: East Bay Group, 2016.

(continued)

(Continued)

From the company's perspective, "life cycles" tend to be continuous and linear, whereas actual customer journeys may not be. Customers tend to approach decisions in a way that may be quite convoluted. It often includes influencers, competitors, and lots of online/offline interactions. This example is a customer's decision-making process in planning a trip:

Using CJM, a company can create the basis for actionable, repeatable documentation of each customer group as they interact with the company from start to finish.

What Is Not Customer Journey Mapping?

Many people mistake journey mapping for an inside-out view of their *interactions to* a customer, not taking into account that the customer is actually doing many things invisible to the company or not actually seeing that outbound lob that a company is pushing out. Many companies also focus on their e-mail or Web sites—the easiest place to track a customer. That results in seeing a digital clickstream that shows the company where its customers move around its mobile or digital properties. Unless that's the company's only way of interacting with its customers and vice versa, then it only sees a portion of the big picture.

CJM is also not looking at your database using analytics around aggregate performance or response metrics. Remember, we are feeling beings who can think, and mapping will need to evaluate emotional elements as well as rational.

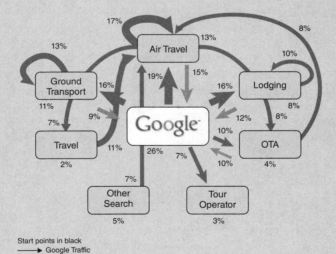

Start points in black
⟶ Google Traffic

Base: Purchasers in the travel market.
Note: Arrows represent proportion of users who go from one site type to another in the purchase session.
(Audience movement under 7% not stated.)

Source: East Bay Group, 2016.

Finally, it's not the equivalent of any single-dimension measure, such as Net Promoter Score or a social sentiment measure such as "likes." Both of these elements serve a purpose, but they tend to measure only those willing to take the time to give a company a score and don't usually measure what or why, which are critical components a decision maker needs to know to create a journey that is frictionless, simple, and effective.

How is CJM different from process work? Many companies have spent significant time, money, and training on programs such as business process optimization (BPO) and Six Sigma as well as process-driven quality. All of these have "flows"—starting and ending points, annotation, and data. Many have cascading levels of information, similar to what you might see in a journey map. The most important difference is that a customer journey map begins at the customer's starting point, motivations, and desired outcomes rather than the company's. It allows for the inclusions of customer emotions and tells a story. It tends to be "art meets science"; it can visualize a broad range of insights, benchmarks, and data. Although it can incorporate a strict set of rules (as does, say, Six Sigma), it usually doesn't and tends to require insight from the mappers based on research. Finally, it embraces emotion and feeling with a laser focus on what customers are doing, thinking, and feeling while they interact with the company. In many ways, it is the difference between a customer-centric company and a product-centric company.

Customer Experience (CX) versus User Experience (UX)

CX design looks at the entire experience and requires a great deal of business skills. A customer is any person getting in contact with the brand whether or not they may at some point use one or several products provided by the brand. The customer's interactions with the brand are varied and a customer may become a user of several different products or services at some point across her journey. Here is a typical customer journey—buying a TV:

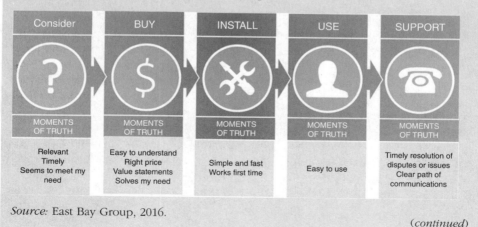

Source: East Bay Group, 2016.

(continued)

(Continued)

UX is part of CX, so each product needs to be user friendly. In UX, a user involves a product that should be used. The activities and experience surrounding this are basically limited to that product, even if that "product" is an app, a Web site, a service, or a physical object.

Here is an example of UX, driven by CX:

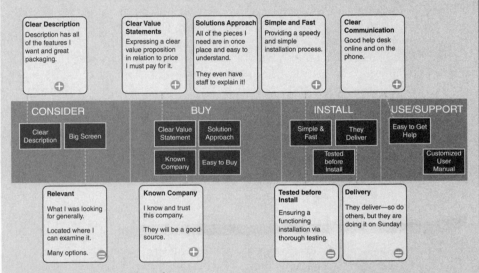

Source: East Bay Group, 2016.

The customer experience as a whole is, of course, influenced by the quality of the UX at each point, but CX is especially interested in the entire customer journey from start to finish, with multiple products or channels used in that journey, including video, wav files, and content from interaction channels and other sources.

What Makes a Good Map?

The best maps provide:

- A visualization of customer interactions through many filters (emotional/rational) organized by the customer's perspective.
- A living document that evolves with the constantly changing organization it supports.

- A harmonized reflection of the voice of the customer as well as the voice of the institution (VOI) and the voice of the employee (VOE).
- Art meets science with a dash of chemistry.
- A level of detail that makes sense for the purpose.

Types of Maps

Customer journey maps tend to vary widely. The map designs tend to fall into one of three categories. Some of the more common ones you might find when searching online:

- *Customer stories*. Generally heavily focused on emotional and behavioral elements. These tend to be highly stylized and often are presented in video format.
- *Campaign marketing or touch maps*. Focused on the outbound interactions associated with a communications strategy or tactical optimized campaign using e-mail, direct mail, or mass media. These tend to look more like process flows with if/then and flow chart–like elements.
- *360-degree experience maps*. Visualizations based on a comprehensive set of rational and emotional data pulling from customer transactions, campaign performance data, survey scores such as Net Promoter Score (NPS), behavioral data, social sentiment, digital tracking and focus groups, and ethnographic or audience user research. These can pull from the visuals above.

Creating Maps

Every map has a number of building blocks that provide a step-by-step guide to creating a map. Though there are many approaches to mapping, the majority eventually use all of these building blocks to create usable, actionable outputs.

Project plans provide the steps in an organized way, and we find that most mapping projects follow the general flow of understanding the as-is or current state and then visualize the to-be or future state. All of the elements collected to support these states then can be analyzed and put into findings, recommendations, and insights that enable a company to, when prioritized, create an actionable road map for improvement. Though this project approach seems to have a start and finish—good for time boxing and ensuring that results are obtained—the overall process of mapping should not be "one and done" but

(continued)

(*Continued*)

continuous depending on the pace of change in the company and the importance of that change.

The following is a typical project plan for a holistic mapping project:

Source: East Bay Group, 2016.

Key Steps and Standard Building Blocks in Mapping

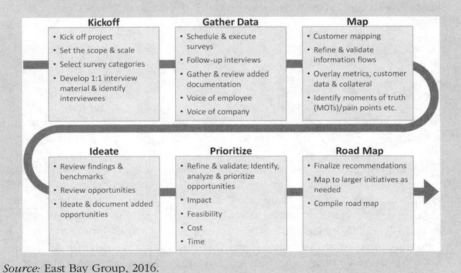

Source: East Bay Group, 2016.

There are six key steps in mapping though there may be many different inputs and outputs or approaches. The first step always focuses on the scope of the project. Having a purpose such as identifying pain points or friction in the buying process or looking for opportunities to improve on retention or customer engagement are good examples of focused objectives.

Once you have zeroed in on the focus area, you can choose to gather the relevant data. Research such as 1to1 interviews, the incorporation of surveys and voice of the customer (VOC) and voice of the employee (VOE) brings color to the maps from an emotional viewpoint. Then rational data such as existing performance, behavioral, transactional data, social sentiment, audience user research, metrics such as Net Promoter Score, and so on, can be used for quantitative purposes

The mapping process can start by identifying each touch or interaction first, sometimes called an inventory. This is where you need to understand the inbound, outbound, and interactive touches that your company is engaging in as well as those happening outside your walls. We find that arraying them in a grid first with the life cycle on top and departments or channels down the side provides a first look that helps you collect the relevant information and prepares you for other views. This is where you can augment the touches with key insights that reflect moments of truth (where a decision is made), pain points, barriers, high points, low points, and all sorts of other designations to help fill out the picture. Once you have fleshed out the inventory with all of the elements you have on hand, you may find gaps that need to be filled. Most companies have plenty to work with right from the start.

Once the mapping process has an inventory, the team can use it in different means—storytelling, processes, front-stage/backstage views—to see where the gaps or friction points are. Think about putting yourself directly into the customers' shoes and mapping their experience versus what the company expects them to do or thinks they should do. A different picture quickly surfaces in many cases. Trying a bit of mystery shopping also informs the story, especially if your shoppers play the part of each of the company's customer personas.

After the stories and touches, combined with other inputs such as VOC/VOE and VOI (the current state for operations, people, process, technology, and channel capabilities), mapping can start documenting what is being revealed, and you may want to ideate on this, possibly by using a workshop to identify what's working and what is not.

(continued)

(Continued)

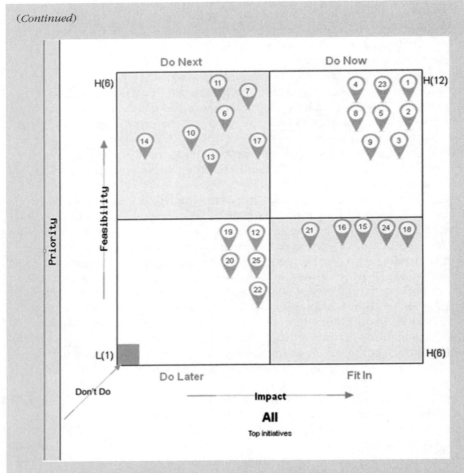

Source: East Bay Group, 2016.

You'll want to note your successes as well as your areas requiring improvement. They will go a long way to helping drive change in a positive manner.

Findings then need to be organized so that impacts and recommendations can be developed, bucketed into logical groupings, and then prioritized based on impact (CX and revenue) and feasibility (cost/level of effort).

Finally, taking the prioritized list and applying a time frame creates a road map to work from:

CJM Outcomes

The outcomes of mapping are varied. Most at least provide insights into the company that help to bring a reality forward that it's not what *a company* has designed

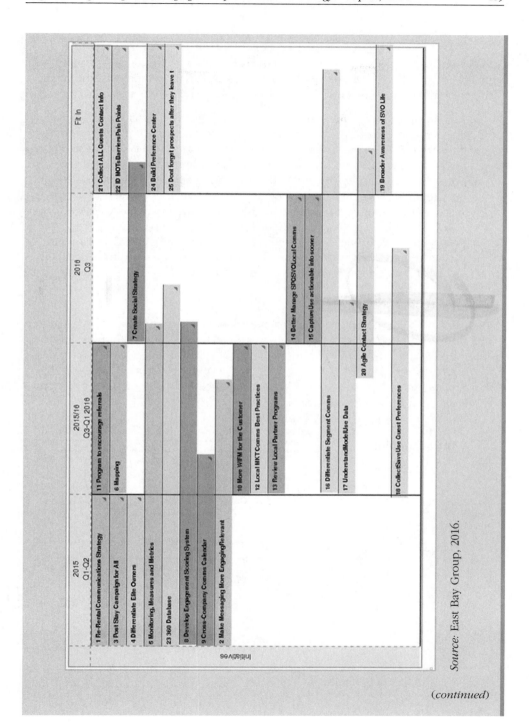

Source: East Bay Group, 2016.

(continued)

(*Continued*)

and wants to sell but what *the customer* wants to buy. In addition, it exposes where to spend resources to ensure that the company is competitive and has its finger on the customers' pulse. Some of the more tactical outputs tend to be:

- *Low-hanging fruit.* Quick fixes or opportunities that don't require a lot of time or resources to provide revenue or customer engagement/retention.
- *Performance metrics/dashboard recommendations.* What key pivot points really make a difference versus sometimes too inwardly facing metrics.
- *Input into standard operating procedures (SOP) document.* How you should be interacting, over what channel, and with what messaging and cadence. This ties to communication and precision campaign plans as well.
- *Road map initiative charters.* Next steps for bigger projects.
- *Post-project planning for continuous improvement.* Mapping will be revisited at frequent intervals to ensure that there is progress and to reveal other areas requiring improvement or offering opportunity.

Benefits of Personas in CJM

Personas help the company relate to the customer and understand what they are thinking/doing/feeling. They can more easily pull in emotional cues and help a company understand differences in behaviors. The graphic "Millennials vs. Boomers" on page 493 is an example of how two different personas buy insurance—the Millennial, who is highly digital, and the Boomer, who is more interested in a face-to-face interaction.

Examples of a persona or segment description:

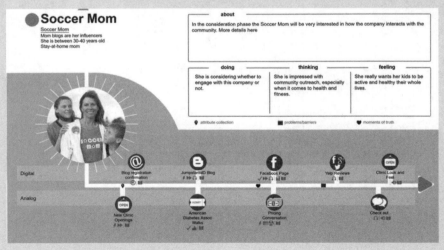

Source: East Bay Group, 2016.

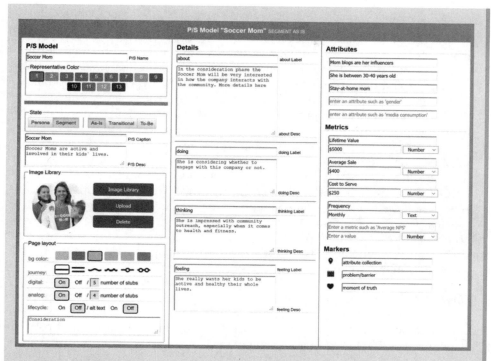

Source: East Bay Group, 2016.

Display personas at every touch point and highlight the touches that most matter to each persona.

Show personas as they change over time from current state through transitional stages to the future state.

If the objective is to transform experience stories into campaigns for execution, statistical segments are highly useful to target and engage with differentiation.

Additional Considerations

GOVERNANCE—WHO SHOULD OWN MAPPING? The answer includes not only heads of customer-facing departments, such as marketing, customer service, e-commerce, and direct sales, but also other departments, such as finance, human resources, and even purchasing, legal, and back-office teams. We have found that the broader the cast for a project that is transformational, the more likely it is to succeed. These people may not think that they are needed, but if a company sends statements or bills, hires customer-facing staff, or sends out required regulatory documentation, then all of these departments are indeed customer-facing, too.

(continued)

(Continued)

HOW OFTEN DOES A COMPANY NEED TO MAP? ISN'T ONCE ENOUGH?   Customer journey mapping is not a one-and-done exercise. Customers change, the company changes, and so does the customers' experience. While a moment-in-time view can help a company understand the current state today, it's also important to look to the future. What is the experience customers should have? What are the major opportunities for improvement? What are the major milestones that need to be completed along the way? Journey mapping becomes an ongoing effort, starting with the current state and revisiting the work on a regular basis in order to show progress. It can and should be used to drive strategy through execution in areas such as customer service, new product development, CX transformation, and communications and campaign design. Further, mapping can be applied to a number of areas. It should be an ongoing exercise pulling in continuous learning from the firm's VOC/VOE efforts. Other uses for mapping include competitive research, new product development, improving the hiring process, and supporting ongoing Six Sigma work (since many changes recommended there ultimately affect the customer base).

DIFFERENT APPROACHES TO MAPPING   There are many approaches to mapping once the basic building blocks are organized, depending on the industry type and approaches to mapping. This drawing depicts the influencers and path to experience design based on company personality:

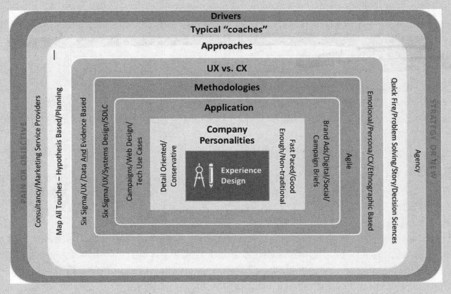

Source: East Bay Group, 2016.

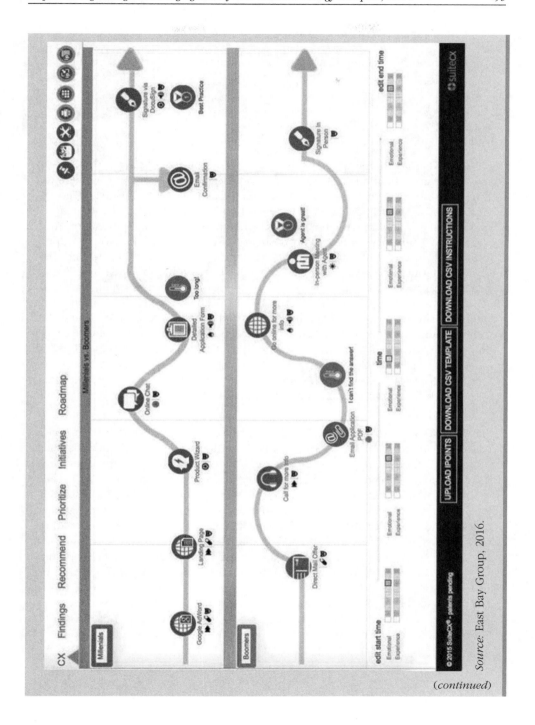

Source: East Bay Group, 2016.

(continued)

(Continued)

There are three general categories of companies:

- Detail first
- Emotion first
- Blended

DETAIL FIRST   Detail-oriented, data-rich companies tend to have a bottom-up approach, documenting each touch first and then mapping them by segment and life-cycle phase. They tend to have Six Sigma "DNA" and oversight/governance teams. Their approach leans toward collecting *all* of their interactions, fleshing them out with data, emotional elements, pain points, moments of truth, and so on. Then they map storylines or processes to determine gaps or opportunities. Most have clear questions they are asking—hypothesis based—and they want clear outcomes. Map formats generally start with X/Y grids and evolve quickly to process-looking stories. Telco, financial companies other than mid-sized banks, insurance, manufacturing (B2B), and high tech tend to fall into this category. Though not universal, this group tends to lean more on consultancies to help them develop/deliver mapping projects. Detail-first teams often get too far down in the weeds and stray to data only and digital clickstream tracking and must guard against making journey maps into processes. Detail-first teams also tend to adopt tools more quickly and have experience to create relevant maps and drive to continuous improvement.

BRAND DRIVEN OR MORE "EMOTIONAL"   Others, however, take a top-down approach based on emotional, social, or brand-driven elements. Consumer products, pharmaceutical companies, and start-ups tend to fall into this group. They tend toward using their creative or digital agency for inspiration and execution. Their brand promise–driven stories drive their marketing efforts and tend to use high-level aspirational personas versus data-derived segments. They want to visualize quickly and then identify areas of interest. The stories lead to ideas/innovation; they get distracted easily and sometimes start focusing just as much on product/packaging as experience as their market research teams are focused on optimizing mass marketing and inside-out options. They often have to back up and pull in data to move forward. Outcomes are not as clearly articulated; this is due often to the type of interactions they are familiar with (mass versus 1to1). This group does well starting with agile workshops using sticky notes and ideation. They want fast answers.

BLENDED   The last group is more balanced. Either they have higher CX maturity or they have experienced guides who help them see the relative advantages of a particular approach for the objective or use case at hand. Banks often fall into this category, as they have a wealth of data and customer insight at their fingertips and are often highly brand driven. The blended approach can be agile or structured, based on hypotheses or based on real customer data. As noted, this group tends to work with specialist/boutique firms experienced in CX. They are the most likely to embed CX into their culture, use it as a metric and tool for transformation, and broadly utilize the techniques to find promise or correct pain points.

Ultimately, the journey mapping effort, to be successful, must result in a sufficient balance between rational and emotional elements, in order to provide the depth of knowledge required to yield an actionable road map of initiatives for improvement. Without that balance, executing on a 360-degree experience is very difficult, if not impossible.

Case Study: JumpStartMD

Challenge: JumpStartMD (JSMD), a medically supervised weight loss and lifestyle improvement company with clinics throughout the San Francisco Bay Area, was experiencing growing pains as it expanded across the diverse San Francisco Bay Area. After a rapid growth spurt, revenues started leveling off and in some areas declining. Referrals—the lifeblood of the company—were also declining.

To find the most pressing pain points quickly, the company pulled together a team of experts and approached the task by collecting JSMD's aggregate patient data (visits, time in program, program success or dropoff, lifetime value [LTV], etc.). Data enhancement and statistical segmentation helped the mapping team understand their customers more fully. The data revealed that their two most valuable segments dropped out at regular intervals: Segment 1 (Road Warrior Women [RWW]) when they traveled and Segment 2 (Entertaining Couples) when they entertained.

Then, mapping showed *why*: They weren't receiving the specific tips/techniques they needed at the moment they needed them. For example, RWW got to Week 5 with some success, but when they traveled they had no tips to help them deal with hotel/restaurant meals and they had no tangible incentive to keep on the straight and narrow. The same was true for the Entertaining Couples when they hosted friends and relatives.

(continued)

(*Continued*)

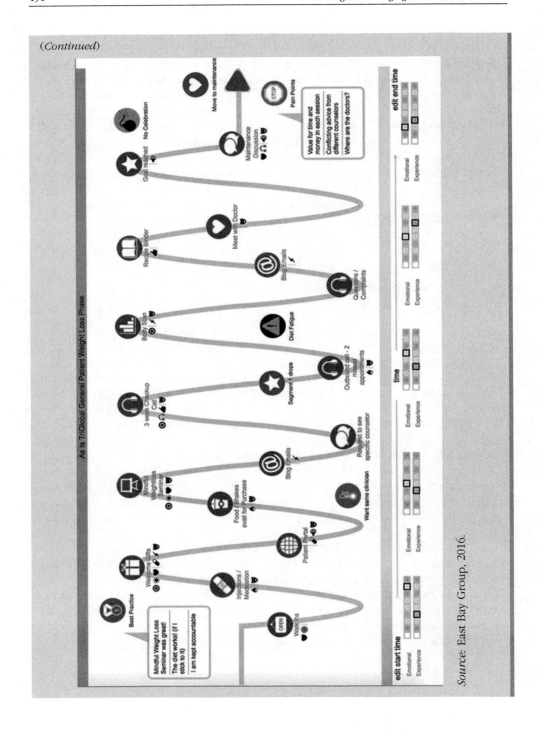

Source: East Bay Group, 2016.

Using a focused voice of the customer and voice of the employee survey to understand how they were doing in the critical "weight loss phase," where typically the mapping revealed the highest dropoff of patients, JSMD drilled down to identify possible solutions. Journey mapping, tied with VOC, which revealed that customers loved the tangible proof of a body scan, and VOE, which indicated that these groups had a weakness for good wine, led directly to some findings.

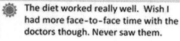
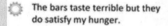
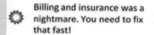
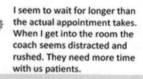
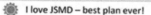

The diet worked really well. Wish I had more face-to-face time with the doctors though. Never saw them.

The bars taste terrible but they do satisfy my hunger.

Billing and insurance was a nightmare. You need to fix that fast!

I seem to wait for longer than the actual appointment takes. When I get into the room the coach seems distracted and rushed. They need more time with us patients.

I love JSMD – best plan ever!

It was really difficult to stay on this diet as I entertain and love wine.

Love my coach. She has great tips to help me stay on the plan.

VOC Inputs
Voice of Customer Dialog

Source: East Bay Group, 2016.

It turned out that although JSMD's sales team used Salesforce.com to manage their sales process and appointments, once they converted from prospects to customers, the company had no customer experience management (CEM) system or operational programs to keep patients engaged. Further, since the clinic staff was time constrained due to strict process flow and efficiency metrics, they didn't have time to connect with their patients to overcome these gaps. Every team was on its own, doing the best they could but not comparing their insights or supporting each other. This resulted in CX challenges; especially at the point patients were facing their own challenges such as diet fatigue.

Solution: Based on CJM findings that compared as-is mapping with ideal state, JSMD focused on transforming the cultural, operational, and technical silos of sales, marketing, and clinic operations to work together to change their customers' experience. The as-is state mapping showed what was happening visually, and the team immediately saw that they needed to provide better incentives (body scans), ensure the front desk made appointments at the critical weeks, and provide more tips/techniques based on the knowledge they had of their customers' personas. The resulting ideal state (to-be) CJM provided a road map to create new processes that resulted in much improved CX.

(continued)

(*Continued*)

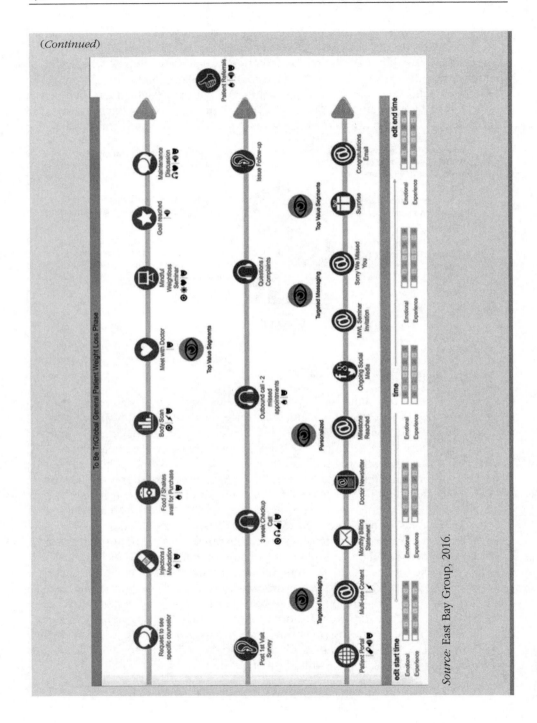

Source: East Bay Group, 2016.

The company needed a customer-centric data and marketing automation solution to better track, engage, and interact appropriately with current patients. They also needed a customer database to collect all of the information in Salesforce.com, their financial ledger, and their patient management system in one place to provide metrics and insights. They needed to be able to connect with their patients wherever they were and to help give them incentives to stay on the program.

Result: The company realized an immediate improvement of revenue due to decreased patient drop-off. Survey results showed improvement in comments around the patient experience, and patient referrals were on the rise. They put together a strengths, weaknesses, opportunities, and threats (SWOT) team, expanded their mapping to incorporate each life-cycle phase, and are using it as part of their strategic planning and tactical improvements. They have also developed sales and marketing training based on their segmentation and 1to1 marketing concepts. Finally, they implemented a marketing automation tool to help manage the new comprehensive contact strategy across life-cycle stages to engage and reward their patients across each step of their journey.

Sign-up today for our Healthy Holiday Eating Workshop | View in Browser

JumpstartMD

Lifestyle Workshop - Healthy Holiday Eating

The holidays are crazy and finding time for yourself is tough. Trying to focus on losing weight during the holidays is especially challenging. Make yourself a priority, and set aside 90 minutes to join us in our Healthy Holiday Eating workshop.

We will teach you how to navigate this hectic time of year with a resolute strategy.

- Explore the circumstances that can make the holiday season difficult and stressful, particularly while developing healthy new habits.
- Learn strategies to carve out the time and space you need to maintain focus on your weight loss and health goals.
- Create a proactive "holiday resolution" and personal game plan to help you stay true to your goals.

Register Today. These workshops fill up quickly.

Locations and Dates:

Source: East Bay Group, 2016.

(continued)

(Continued)

Case Study: Xanterra

At Xanterra, a large hospitality conglomerate specializing in action/adventure trips, the goal was to drive revenue using a new segmentation and marketing platform needed to understand the guest journey. Marketing was challenged with pulling emotional and rational information together. By developing journey maps for top brands and properties, the company was able to identify strengths and weaknesses for each property across the customer life cycle, and used the resulting mapping as the basis for following-year go-to-marketing strategy, creating life-cycle marketing using a new CRM database and toolkit.

What changed: "Once we were able to see (for the first time) the visualization of the voice of our customer from the end to end customer journey, we began a multiphased effort. It started by addressing what we called 'low-hanging fruit opportunities.'" Xanterra then began to develop much more robust customer communications strategies for each of their brands. This consisted of persona- and behavioral-based e-mail and targeted social communications where several of their brands have seen e-mail campaign performance improvements in the triple digits. The results took their average performing campaign to a higher-performing campaign with more relevant offers through creative and messaging by segment. They went from an average revenue increase of $0.08 per e-mail to $0.73 per e-mail, or an improvement of 839 percent. Annual revenue has increased 1 percent on $500 million based on Xanterra marketing team metrics.

Pitfalls and Barriers

Many companies struggle to get value out of their journey maps because they omit essential content, lack a clear purpose, and have poor design. At a minimum, journey maps need to include essential information—such as the target customers and their desired goal or outcome—as well as detailed information that describes what customers are doing, thinking, and feeling along the way. In addition, high-quality journey maps include key findings such as pain points or high-importance interactions. Together, these key components form the core of the journey map, enabling employees and partners to see how well the company's experiences satisfy the customer's needs and expectations. Some of the barriers to success in mapping are typical. A few are described here.

PITFALL Mapping only outbound touches you know about. This is really a map of company-originated communications or marketing campaign plan. Generally, it does not address the whole customer experience. It omits initiation points as well as feedback loops.

SOLUTION A customer journey map begins from the customers' starting point, and it presents empathy, motivations, and desired outcomes rather than the company's expected ROI/RFM. A company must map and annotate all interactions to get a full picture.

BARRIER   Siloed organizations. Companies struggle with CX because it requires sharing information across the enterprise. It also requires getting agreement not only on what needs to be done but also on who will do it. Being successful at CX requires a deep understanding of customer needs and values, as well as all the internal people, processes, and technologies that impact the customer experience. Many department heads don't have the cross-functional technology and organizational skills to understand what needs to be done, let alone how to get the leadership on board to plan and execute.

SOLUTION   Be as deep and wide as possible in identifying every interaction and the root causes of interactions; legal, compliance, hiring, and the like often have immense impact without really being "in the loop."

BARRIER   Lack of clear metrics. Company metrics tend to be focused on individual department performance, not on meeting cross-departmental goals. Achieving margins and reducing costs tend to be the most significant priorities. Customer experience gets put on the back burner as goals such as risk avoidance, project completion time, and technology stifle innovation and reward the status quo.

SOLUTION   Create CX-centric metrics to monitor progress. Focus on business outcomes rather than task completion. Revisit the customer journey periodically to measure success against the original baseline. Ensure having clear metrics that ladder up to corporate dashboards so that executives clearly see the trends and impact of CJM.

PITFALL   No common definition of best customer experience. Marketing, sales, and service are not aligned on who is the best customer and what a good experience looks like. If each area continues to operate independently and by their own definitions, customers will feel a disjointed experience at every point of engagement. Creating a seamless experience for the customer requires common organizational understanding, data sharing, and shared goals for improvement.

SOLUTION   Ensure that all training, communications, and change management share common definitions and terminology.

PITFALL   No clear view of actionable outcomes. Interesting collections of facts that are not actionable, especially if there is not a clear understanding of how they connect with each other or with the customer.

SOLUTION   Focus on actionable insights and the initial objectives.

PITFALL   Mapping processes rather than journeys. This approach tends to provides lots of data but no real insight into the emotions of the employees or customers, limiting actionable insights.

(continued)

(Continued)

SOLUTION   Ensure the map tells a compelling story that creates empathy for what the customer goes through. Be sure to add emotional inputs, social, ethnographic research, and VOC/VOE.

---

[a] Temkin Group, "The State of Customer Experience Management, 2015," available at http://temkingroup.com/research-reports/the-state-of-customer-experience-management-2015/, accessed June 24, 2016.
[b] Oracle, "Global Insights on Succeeding in the Customer Experience Era," February 2013, available at http://www.oracle.com/us/global-cx-study-2240276.pdf, accessed June 24, 2016.
[c] Martin Hayward, "The Four Futures: The Digital Loyalty Survey," Aimia, 2013, available at https://www.aimia.com/content/dam/aimiawebsite/CaseStudiesWhitepapersResearch/english/Aimia_Whitepaper_FourFutures_DigitalLoyaltySurvey.pdf, accessed June 24, 2016.
[d] Sheryl Pattek and Nigel Fenwick, "A Customer-Obsessed Operating Model Demands a Close Partnership with Your CIO," Forrester Research, Inc., April 12, 2016, available at www.forrester.com.
[e] "Customer Experience Management Is Improving as Leaders Earn Stronger Financial Results, According to New Temkin Group Research," *PR Newswire*, May 12, 2015, available at http://www.prnewswire.com/news-releases/customer-experience-management-is-improving-as-leaders-earn-stronger-financial-results-according-to-new-temkin-group-research-300081381.html, accessed June 28, 2016.
[f] "Adaptive Journey Mapping Is the Path Forward," 1to1 Media In Action Series (2016), p. 4, available at http://go.1to1media.com/mapping?SourceIA0416=splash, accessed June 24, 2016.
[g] Jason Hekl, "B-to-B Buyer's Survey Findings," Sirius Decisions, Cisco training presentation, 2015.

One of the most important questions executives can ask is whether better customer experiences and relationships will pay off for a company. In a seminal study, Jeff Gilleland and his colleagues asked that question. Essentially, they compared how far along on the customer-orientation journey companies were, and compared the performance levels of companies at high and low levels. Here's what they discovered.

Customer Experience Capabilities and Competencies Compared to Financial Performance

Jeff Gilleland
Vice President of Marketing, Sales, and Service Solutions, GENPACT

Most marketers acknowledge that today's big challenge is managing the customer's experience across products, touch points, and channels, and over each customer's life cycle. This goes beyond the kind of *customer relationship management* (CRM) that focuses too much on a single product or channel transaction—the short term. Alternatively, *customer experience management* (CEM) requires designing an experience for each customer based on knowledge of that customer, delivering it across products and channels, and measuring individual outcomes that enable improvement of future interactions. Simply stated, CEM is about creating learning relationships—and setting up those relationships to build customer equity and shareholder value—over the *long term.*

But companies are in different places on their journey toward CEM and creating learning relationships, What capabilities do companies have in place to manage the customer's experience across products and channels? What benefits accrue for companies with the most mature capabilities?

The research done as part of the Customer Experience Maturity Monitor (CEMM),[a] a research project jointly conducted by SAS Institute and Peppers & Rogers Group, has shown that a company must have more than the desire to manage the customer experience; it must have enterprise capabilities that leverage customer *insight* to better manage individual customer interactions and continuously *improve* results. Importantly, for these capabilities to work, the company must have a *customer orientation*—a culture that focuses on the customer and builds trust.

Research Dimensions

The research measured organizational capabilities and competencies in four categories: customer orientation, customer insight, customer interaction, and improvement (see Exhibit 13.7). In total, respondents rated their companies on 58 individual variables; key learning highlights are discussed in the following section.

One of the golden rules of marketing has always been "Know your customer." Historically, doing this required deep knowledge about a **market segment.** It included understanding the unmet needs and wants of a particular target market, including demographics, attitudes, consumption patterns, media habits, lifestyle, and other dimensions that enabled you to define a homogenous group. And then you tailored the 4 *Ps* of marketing based on your knowledge about this market segment. This approach to "target marketing" worked pretty well for decades. It enabled marketers to develop products, value propositions, advertising creative, and media buys that were well targeted to a particular market. But in today's world of CEM, how does this approach stack up?

(continued)

(Continued)

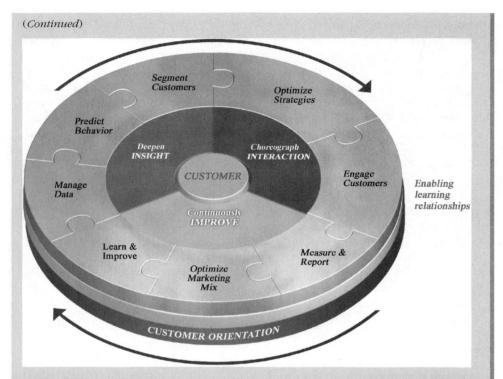

EXHIBIT 13.7   CEMM Measured Customer Orientation and 3-I Capabilities

A Critical Gap: 62 Percent versus 29 Percent

For success, CEM requires a company to learn *continuously* from individual customers and to demonstrate, to each customer, that it is listening to them. One of the big CEMM findings around customer improvement (à la learning from customers) was this gap: A total of 62 percent of respondents agreed with this statement: "My company treats customers differently, based on an understanding of the needs of each one individually." However, only 29 percent rated their capabilities as *good* or *excellent* in response to this statement: "Customer profiles are continuously updated to reflect all customer activity (purchases, returns, etc.) as well as outbound (campaigns) and inbound contact (channel visits, call center, Web, stores/branches, etc.)."

Customer Orientation

Although capabilities to manage the customer experience lag, a customer orientation is emerging. In the CEMM survey, 75 percent agreed that their company motivates employees to treat customers fairly. And 66 percent agreed that their company takes the customer's point of view when making business decisions. Also encouraging, 69 percent agreed that their company considers the impact that business decisions have on the future value of its customers.

Customer Experience Maturity Equals Competitive Advantage

So where are companies in their customer experience maturity? Composite scores were created for each company based on how it rated its capabilities across 58 variables—which placed each company on a maturity continuum from 1 to 5. As you can see from Exhibit 13.8, 74 percent of companies scored at Levels 2 and 3.

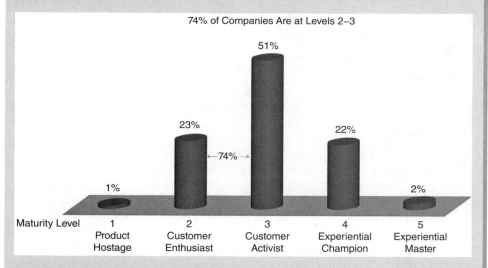

EXHIBIT 13.8   Customer Experience Maturity Continuum

Companies were also asked to rate their overall competitiveness: *worse than, same as, or better than their key competitors*. By comparing the maturity of capabilities with relative competitiveness, the research could determine the value of improving CEM capabilities.

The research findings revealed a direct link between the maturity of a company's customer experience management capabilities and its relative competitiveness. For companies that have progressed to the highest levels of maturity (Levels 4 to 5), the advantage is twofold to threefold (see Exhibit 13.9).

(*continued*)

(Continued)

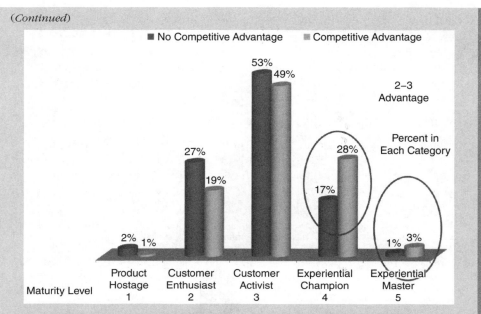

EXHIBIT 13.9   Competitive Advantage Accrues with CEM Maturity

CEMM Summary

Many companies have made great progress in their journey toward managing the customer's experience for competitive advantage. They are building enterprise technologies that not only manage customer relationships across products and channels but also learn from individual customers. These companies are evolving their **business models** *from* using insight just for better target marketing to using insight to provide perceptible value to customers through a richer experience.

Customers are rewarding these companies not only with their loyalty but also with their advocacy. And in our new world of social media, customer advocacy can be a powerful force.

---

[a] *Customer Experience Maturity Monitor* (CEMM): A global research study initiated in 2008–09 by SAS Institute and Peppers & Rogers Group. The initial research included responses from 434 companies. The first phase of the research involved in-depth interviews with over 50 companies focusing on the activities and programs they engage in to ensure a positive experience for their customers. This information was combined with surveys among 384 companies worldwide, which audited their customer experience practices and customer orientation philosophies. The results of this project serve as the benchmark data for the CEMM and provide the foundation for the analysis of ongoing research among companies in different countries and industries as well as in individual companies wishing to understand their customer experience maturity levels. "SAS" and all other SAS Institute, Inc. products or service names are registered trademarks of SAS Institute, Inc.

Summary

Now that we've described the larger-scale processes needed to transition from a product-centric to a customer-centric enterprise, we need to get specific: What needs to be done throughout the organization to make this transition? Part 2 of our discussion of managing the customer-centric enterprise in Chapter 14 covers just that.

Food for Thought

1. Choose an organization and draw its organizational chart. How would that chart have to change in order to facilitate customer management and to make sure people are empowered, evaluated, measured, and compensated for building the value of the customer base? Consider these questions:
   a. If a customer's value is measured across more than one division, is one person placed in charge of that customer relationship?
   b. Should the enterprise establish a key account-selling system?
   c. Should the enterprise underwrite a more comprehensive information system, standardizing customer data across each division?
   d. Should the sales force be better automated? Who should set the strategy for how a sales rep interacts with a particular customer?
   e. Is it possible for the various Web sites and call centers operated by the company to work together better?
   f. Should the company package more services with the products it sells, and if so, how should those services be delivered?[7]
2. For the same organization, consider the current culture, and describe it. Would that have to change for the organization to manage the relationship with and value of one customer at a time? If so, how?
3. At the same organization, assume the company rank-orders customers by value and places the most valuable customers behind a picket fence for 1to1 treatment. What happens to customers and to customer portfolio managers behind that picket fence?
4. In an organization, who should "own" the customer relationship? What does that mean?
5. What are the best ways to compensate and reward customer managers?

---

[7] Don Peppers, Martha Rogers, Ph.D., and Bob Dorf, *The One to One Fieldbook* (New York: Doubleday Books, 1999).

Glossary

Actual value   The net present value of the future financial contributions attributable to a customer, behaving as we expect her to behave—knowing what we know now, and with no different actions on our part.

Addressable   Refers to media that can send and customize messages individually.

Business model   How a company builds economic value.

Business process reengineering (BPR)   Focuses on reducing the time it takes to complete an interaction or a process and on reducing the cost of completing it. BPR usually involves introducing quality controls to ensure time and cost efficiencies are achieved.

Business rules   The instructions that an enterprise follows in configuring different processes for different customers, allowing the company to mass-customize its interactions with its customers.

Capabilities manager   The person at an enterprise charged with delivering the capabilities of the enterprise to the customer managers, in essence figuring out whether the firm should build, buy, or partner to render any new products or services that customers might require. Customer managers "represent" their own customers' interests within an enterprise, while capabilities managers have the authority and responsibility for meeting the demands placed on the enterprise by the customer managers.

Customer centricity   A "specific approach to doing business that focuses on the customer. Customer/client centric businesses ensure that the customer is at the center of a business philosophy, operations or ideas. These businesses believe that their customers/clients are the only reason they exist and use every means at their disposal to keep the customer/client happy and satisfied."[8] At the core of customer centricity is the understanding that customer profitability is at least as important as product profitability.

Customer equity (CE)   The sum of all the lifetime values (LTVs) of an enterprise's current and future customers, or the total value of the enterprise's customer relationships. A customer-centric company would view customer equity as its principal corporate asset. See also the definition of *customer equity* in Chapter 1.

Customer experience   The totality of a customer's individual interactions with a brand, over time.

Customer experience management (CEM)   The integrated process of designing an experience for each customer based on knowledge of that customer, delivering it across products and channels, and measuring individual outcomes that enable improvement of future interactions. The goal of CEM is to create Learning

---

[8] "Client Centric," Investopedia, available at http://www.investopedia.com/terms/c/client-centric .asp, accessed February 15, 2016.

Relationships with customers, thereby building customer equity and shareholder value over the long term.

Customer interaction center   Where all calls are handled, regardless of type, for a certain customer segment or customer portfolio.

Customer journey mapping   A process of diagramming all the steps a customer takes when engaging with a company to buy, use, or service its product or offering. Also called *customer experience journey mapping*.

Customer manager   A customer manager is the person at an enterprise who is "in charge" of particular customer relationships. The customer manager's objective is to increase the value of the customers in his or her charge, and the authority required to do this should include responsibility for every type of individually specific action or communication that the enterprise is capable of rendering to the customer. In communication, this would mean that the customer manager would control the enterprise's addressable forms of communication and interaction, with respect to his or her specific customers.

Customer orientation   An attitude or mind-set that attempts to take the customer's perspective when making business decisions or implementing policies.

Customer portfolio   A grouping of customers based on value and understood by the needs they have in common as well as the needs they have individually expressed by their interactions and transactions through various touch points over time. In contrast to grouping customers by *segments*, where customers are treated as look-alikes within the segment (meaning that segment marketing is really mass marketing, only smaller), the customer-strategy enterprise will work to manage portfolios of individual customers.

Customer relationship management (CRM)   As a term, *CRM* can refer either to the activities and processes a company must engage in to manage individual relationships with its customers (as explored extensively in this textbook), or to the suite of software, data, and analytics tools required to carry out those activities and processes more cost efficiently.

Customer segment   A group of customers who are suited for the same or similar marketing initiatives because of particular qualities or characteristics they have in common.

Customer service   Customer service involves helping a customer gain the full use and advantage of whatever product or service was bought. When something goes wrong with a product, or when a customer has some kind of problem with it, the process of helping the customer overcome this problem is often referred to as *customer care*.

Customer strategy   An organization's plan for managing its customer experiences and relationships effectively in order to remain competitive. At its heart, customer strategy is increasing the value of the company by increasing the value of the customer base.

Customer-strategy enterprise   An organization that builds its business model around increasing the value of the customer base. This term applies to companies that may be product oriented, operations focused, or customer intimate.

Customer value management   Managing a business's strategies and tactics (including sales, marketing, production, and distribution) in a manner designed to increase the value of its customer base.

Interactive age   The current period in business and technological history, characterized by a dominance of interactive media rather than the one-way mass media more typical from 1910 to 1995. Also refers to a growing trend for businesses to encourage feedback from individual customers rather than relying solely on one-way messages directed at customers, and to participate with their customers in social networking. (Also called interactive era.)

Interactive voice response (IVR)   Now a feature at most call centers, IVR software provides instructions for callers to "push '1' to check your current balance, push '2' to transfer funds," and so forth.

Lifetime value (LTV)   Synonymous with "actual value." The net present value of the future financial contributions attributable to a customer, behaving as we expect her to behave—knowing what we know now, and with no different actions on our part.

Market segment   A group of customers who share a common attribute. Product benefits are targeted to the market segments thought most likely to desire the benefit.

Moment of truth (MoT)   Interactions with a customer that have a disproportionate impact on the customer's emotional connection, and are therefore more likely to drive significant behaviors.

Most valuable customers (MVCs)   Customers with high actual values but not a lot of unrealized growth potential. These are the customers who do the most business, yield the highest margins, are most willing to collaborate, and tend to be the most loyal.

Needs   What a customer needs from an enterprise is, by our definition, synonymous with what she wants, prefers, or would like. In this sense, we do not distinguish a customer's needs from her wants. For that matter, we do not distinguish needs from preferences, wishes, desires, or whims. Each of these terms might imply some nuance of need—perhaps the intensity of the need or the permanence of it—but in each case we are still talking, generically, about the customer's needs.

Potential value   The net present value of the future financial contributions that could be attributed to a customer, if through conscious action we succeed in changing the customer's behavior.

Relationship governance   Defines who in the enterprise will be in charge when making different decisions for different customers, with the goal of optimizing around each customer rather than each product or channel.

Relationship manager   *See* customer manager.

Return on Customer (ROC)   A metric directly analogous to return on investment (ROI), specifically designed to track how well an enterprise is using customers to create value. ROC equals a company's current-period cash flow (from customers) plus the change in customer equity during the period, divided by the customer equity at the beginning of the period. ROC is pronounced are-oh-see.

Supply chain   A company's back-end production or service-delivery operations.

Value of the customer base   *See* Customer equity.

CHAPTER 14

Organizing and Managing the Profitable Customer-Strategy Enterprise, Part 2

Transitioning from Traditional Business to Customer Centricity

The human mind treats a new idea the way the body treats a strange protein; it rejects it.

—P. B. Medawar

More and more, companies have made big progress toward thinking about customer experiences, growing customer value deliberately, and managing for trusted customer relationships. Many new companies, such as Amazon.com, were born and raised this way. But thousands of companies that appeared way back in the twentieth century, or who have been managed by people who did, are still oriented around products, marketing campaigns, and sales regions, and are looking for the least disruptive way possible to deal with big customer databases, **social media,** and other new technologies.

It should go without saying that an existing enterprise based on traditional structures and management will not simply be able to paste a customer-management organizational structure atop its existing organization. Moreover, the change, in terms of success metrics, management roles and responsibilities, and the required capabilities of the enterprise, is profound. In truth, the transition never actually ends, because there will always be additional steps the enterprise can take to improve its relationships with its customers. So if a company is starting as a well-oiled product-marketing organization, taking the first tentative steps toward customer management requires a good deal of planning. In this chapter, we address the evolutionary reality of organizational change as well as practical guidelines for each department during the transition.

During the transition to a customer-centric model, enterprises frequently underestimate the degree to which all facets of the business—beyond "marketing" and other customer-facing parts of the company—will be affected by the changes and the ongoing efforts that will be required to achieve full business benefits. The organizational and cultural transition to customer management can sometimes represent a genuine *revolution* for the enterprise, but it is more likely to be successful when it can be treated as an *evolution* within the organization.

Becoming a Customer-Strategy Organization

Marijo Puleo, Ph.D.
Managing Partner, Make Change Positive

You walk into the headquarters of a corporation a few minutes early for a job interview. In doing research about this company on Google and LinkedIn and Wikipedia, you kept coming across articles that talked about the values of this company and its strong performance. As you walk into the lobby, you expect to see artwork and pictures of company products as you saw in the other offices of the companies you interviewed with. Instead, you see a beautiful and elegant sign that says, "We make a difference in the lives of our customers and our employees." You look around and see 15 pictures of customers and employees, and you immediately connect with them—who they are, what they want in life, and how they live. A few are using the company's products in the photos, but most are not. It is as if a moment of each of their everyday lives was captured for this tribute.

You start to approach the receptionist, who has made eye contact and is smiling broadly. Instead, a well-dressed woman standing next to the desk calls your name. You look surprised and say, "Yes, that's me." She says, "Great! We have been expecting you. I'm Linda from human resources, and the team is waiting upstairs." As you walk through the halls, the customer tribute continues. You see framed photos and letters from customers. You quickly glance at the photos of families and see words like *delight, surprised, broken, taken care of, recommend you, know me,* and *made a difference.* You also see charts titled "Customer Scorecards" and "Employee Scorecards" filled with bars and lines, generally all pointing in an upward direction. You notice that the marketing, sales, and **customer service** teams are located together, and many people are talking in the hallways, with a few groups reviewing the charts.

As you walk by a meeting room, it looks like some information technology people are discussing a project. You overhear one person say, "Let's review the customer requirements." What did he say? Not the department timetable, not the product specifications, but the *customer* requirements. You finally arrive at the conference room, where four (you hope future) team members and the hiring manager are waiting. They all smile, introduce themselves, and shake your hand, letting you know whom you will be meeting with throughout the day. The manager asks you how your trip into the office was and if you need anything to make you feel more comfortable. You get the sense already that they are genuinely interested in you being at your best. You are almost embarrassed at how warm and inviting this whole experience is, and it makes you even more motivated to work here. Already you can feel that customers and employees are important to everything they do here.

Sound far-fetched? Some companies do operate in this way and perform well across all levels of measurement.[a] Increasingly, organizations are becoming more and more complex, and it is easy to lose the voice of the customer and the employee in the daily mix of e-mails, meetings, and tasks. There are more requirements, more communication channels, more technologies, and customers are becoming more complex to understand and serve. How do these companies do this? Every human being wants to be understood and to connect meaningfully with others. This can happen in an ad hoc way, but it is a purposeful activity to consistently deepen relationships with customers and connect with employees.

To increase **customer equity**, an organization needs to pay careful attention to aligning its vision, values, culture, resources, organizational priorities, and measurements. This alignment begins with three critical elements: (1) a compelling vision, (2) defined by leadership that (3) defines and shapes a customer-centric culture. If all three are firmly in place, the rest of the alignment (resources, projects, organization alignment, etc.) can cascade from there. Richard Barrett states:

> *The leader and the leadership team choose the values of the organization and actively live them. They reinforce the values by constantly referring to them and make them part of every organizational system and process. They sustain a high performing culture by regularly mapping the culture and the individual performance of every executive and manager.[b]*

(continued)

(Continued)

Once the alignment around vision, leadership, and culture is under way, the enterprise needs to adopt an infrastructure that can support all of the business-related processes and functions that characterize a customer-focused model. Large financial investments can be made in information technology, employee training and hiring, communication systems, and other areas related to the transformation, but purchasing and installing tools and technologies will be pointless without adapting the enterprise and its employees to using them properly and enthusiastically. The majority of customer-strategy "failures" didn't crash and burn because of software integration problems or inadequate employee software training. Most customer efforts fail because the company never learns to manage the enterprise in light of new company capabilities or to align those resources, priorities, and capabilities with **customer relationship management (CRM).**

To complete the transition, international organization design expert Jay Galbraith outlines changes that need to be made to become truly customer-centric. The degree to which an organization can incorporate these elements determines the degree of **customer centricity,** according to Galbraith.

- *Strategy.* The overall commitment to develop solutions that will solve the customer's need and focus on the most profitable, loyal customers or portfolios.
- *Structure.* The organizational concept that incorporates customer segments, customer teams, and customer profit-and-loss (P&L).
- *People.* Includes several elements:
  - *Personnel approach.* The power base resides with the people who know the most about the customer and are rewarded accordingly.
  - *Mental model.* Rather than thinking "How many uses for this product?" (divergent thinking), convergent thinking asks: "What combination of products is best for this customer?"
  - *Sales bias.* The bias should be on the side of the buyer in the transaction; the company should advocate for the customer.
  - *Culture.* Company culture should be a relationship culture, which searches for more customer needs to satisfy.
- *Process.* The information flow incorporates customer relationship management and solution development.
- *Rewards.* The measures that influence motivation, including customer satisfaction, **share of customer, lifetime value**, and customer equity.[c]

Once an enterprise commits to adopting a customer-centric model, it needs to rethink the product-centric customs and processes it has relied on for years.

Traditionally, enterprises develop their technologies, support, and infrastructure to manufacture products or services and deliver those products or services to the customer in the most cost-efficient way. In turn, the technology and information captured in the systems drive business processes that influence employee behavior and how these employees **interact** with customers.

This may not appear too much of a change—just put the customer in the middle instead of products. Most enterprises, in fact, will say that this shift is not a big departure from the way they've always done business, because they have already designed their products or services for particular customer segments. However, in those companies, the internal processes and metrics are designed to increase share of market around defined customer segments. For example, metrics around cost of delivery, cost to manufacture, commissions, and so forth abound in a typical enterprise. Many enterprises understand the cost to process and pay an invoice, but they do not understand the value of a customer beyond a total revenue measure. Some enterprises have a "sense" of which customers are valuable, but they lack the facts and figures of customer value differentiation to justify a particular level of service and continue to engage in product-centric business and culture.

It is difficult for employees in an enterprise to make this transition because truly adopting a customer-focused strategy can challenge many of their deeply held values and beliefs about how business is done and how success is defined. One of the most challenging aspects of this new strategy is the amount of coordination and trust that needs to be developed between departments and functions. Managing customer relationships can be an unorthodox way of doing business for them, and it requires many unique skills, such as negotiation and understanding a broader view of the enterprise. Furthermore, the treatment of employees sets the tone for how customers are treated. Employees who cannot develop consensus internally are challenged to deliver to customers.

Frequently, the enterprise also must encourage its customers to change how they operate, a critical step often ignored in the overall process. Everything begins and ends with the customer. The customer-centric enterprise depends on customer participation, even when customers are unaware of their involvement. Ranjay Gulati describes a situation at a big-box electronics store, where the customer teams were watching video surveillance footage of customers leaving the store without making a purchase. An operations team would ask, "How many customers left without buying anything?" But the customer-centric question to ask is, "*Why* didn't these customers buy anything? What did they come in looking for and did not find?"

The answer was found by thinking in the customers' shoes. The data had already shown that women purchase 55 percent of consumer electronics and

(continued)

(Continued)

influence about 75 percent of purchases. Many current and potential customers were busy mothers who were looking for solutions. The salespeople loved to talk about the technical aspects of products (e.g., the number of pixels and memory capacity of a camera). The conversation works well for someone who is interested in the technical details and latest features. However, the busy mom wasn't interested in technical specifications; she wanted a camera that made it easy to take pretty good digital pictures of her kids and e-mail them to family members.

The store chain realized that its stores were geared to appeal to male consumers and were turning off female customers. It worked with merchandising, store layout, and salespeople to reengineer a new store format and train employees to be more consultative and aware of customer needs. It empowered employees to make proposals to test changes in policies, procedures, layouts, and merchandising.

If the store had not cascaded the change and alignment throughout the entire system, it could have created a system of competing commitments and generated a degree of dysfunction and entropy. Despite a few pockets of internal resistance, the firm was able to implement the solution through most of the organization, and the company is committed to completing the rollout of the new store format. It is, in essence, continuing to refine and continuously improve the elements mentioned earlier. Results show that stores with the customer-centric operations with customer segment treatments used were performing 9 percentage points better than the traditional product-centric operations, according to Gulati.[d]

In a truly customer-centric organization, customer input defines how employees will interact with customers, in turn creating processes, developing new roles, and effecting change in the basic "how" of new product and service creation. Change in the entire organization and the voice of the customer are present in every department and division, and tangibly present all throughout the business.

---

[a] Scott Lochridge and Jennifer Rozenzweig, *Enlightenment Incorporated: Creating Companies Our Kids Would Be Proud to Work For* (Dragonfly Organization Resource Group, 2009).
[b] Richard Barrett, *Building a Values-Driven Organization: A Whole System Approach to Cultural Transformation* (Burlington, MA: Elsevier, 2006), p. 85.
[c] Jay R. Galbraith, *Designing the Customer Centric Organization: A Guide to Strategy, Structure, and Process* (San Francisco: Jossey-Bass, 2005), pp. 15–21.
[d] Ranjay Gulati, *Reorganize for Resilience: Putting Customers at the Center of Your Business* (Boston: Harvard Business Press, 2009), pp. 19–31.

The organizational and cultural transition to customer management represents a genuine revolution for the enterprise, but it is more likely to be successful when it can be treated as an evolution within the organization.

Here, we discuss three ways to speed this evolution process, any or all of which can be adopted by an enterprise:

1. Pilot projects and incremental change.
2. **Picket fence** strategy.
3. Segment management and portfolio management.

Pilot Projects and Incremental Change

Most companies launch their customer initiatives in a series of pilot projects. There are so many things to do, if a customer-specific perspective is to be adopted, that usually it is a relatively simpler process for a company to "cut and paste" various self-contained customer initiatives into the enterprise's current method of operating. The objective, over the longer term, is to accumulate a large number of small improvements.

It is not necessary to resolve the customer-governance problem throughout the organization in order to launch a pilot project or to make an incremental change. Instead, the IDIC (Identify-Differentiate-Interact-Customize—see Chapters 3 to 10) implementation process itself is an ideal vehicle for conceiving and executing incremental changes. A small change might involve, for instance, obtaining, linking, and cataloging more customer identities, using a sweep of existing databases containing customer information. Or it could involve setting up a prioritized service level for customers now identified as having higher long-term value to the enterprise, or higher growth potential. Many incremental change initiatives are also likely to involve streamlining the customer interaction processes, so as to cut duplicative efforts or to resolve conflicting communications.

Particularly for large and complex organizations, often the most direct and immediate route to a broad transition for the overall enterprise is to implement a series of incremental changes, one small step at a time. Hewlett-Packard (HP), for instance, was a customer pioneer, and began trying to wean its corporate culture away from the simple worship of products in the 1990s, launching an effort to create a better balance for the enterprise, in which both customer growth and product excellence would be prized.

According to Lane Michel, at that time a marketing manager at HP (later a partner at Peppers & Rogers Group, and now VeraHeart), staying focused on incremental gains helped HP win acceptance for its overall program. "We try to avoid boiling the ocean," says Michel. "Then again, it's important to show immediate results. Those early successes earn you the right to take bigger steps."[1]

---

[1] Don Peppers, Martha Rogers, Ph.D., and Bob Dorf, *The One to One Fieldbook: The Complete Toolkit for Implementing a 1to1 Marketing Program* (New York: Currency/Doubleday, 1997). Updated 2016.

One example of such an incremental step was the customer-interaction program engineered by the Barcelona Division of HP's Consumer Products Group, which produced, among other things, the DesignJet high-end printer. In order to make it possible to have a continuing dialogue with its customers, the division developed a Web site, HP DesignJet Online, to serve as a user-friendly channel for interactive customer communication. The password-protected site offered self-diagnostic tools to DesignJet customers as well as a quarterly newsletter, a user feedback section, new product notifications, and an upgrade program. The division counted on the site to increase market share, reinforce customer loyalty, and provide a steady stream of timely market knowledge.[2] Many other companies have set up similar programs to interact with users.

Another incremental but important step taken by HP was the development of a central and global electronic customer registration system, along with a master set of questions and a master customer database to store the information. The initiative was born from ideas and feedback generated across several of the company's groups and geographies. The new system replaced paper registration, which had proved a poor method for collecting usable customer data.

Over time, baby steps like these added up to great strides. By 1999, HP had roughly 100 such incremental initiatives under way at various locations around the world, which it called "one-to-one campfires." Each was being tracked and monitored centrally, with information made available throughout the HP enterprise on the firm's intranet at a special relationship marketing section. Nearly every one of these initiatives, also, could be categorized easily in terms of which aspect of the IDIC implementation process it represented. Some of these early initiatives blossomed into major programs causing the reformulation of product designs, operational retooling, customer interactions, and management roles accountable for returns on investments made.

Keeping the process going required champions and leaders of change. At HP, these leaders initially had titles such as relationship marketing manager, customer advocacy manager, and installed base loyalty manager.[3] Over time, vice presidents and marketing managers across HP took leadership of the company's drive into customer experience, measurable results, and segment-wide changes.

A large number of incremental changes can add up to big change. In addition, an incremental change project itself could serve as a pilot for rolling out a particular idea or strategy across an entire division or enterprise. Pilot projects are a common method many companies use to make the kinds of changes required in the transition to a **customer-strategy enterprise**. But a pilot project differs, slightly anyway, from other forms of incremental change. A pilot project is, in essence, a feasibility study. It usually represents a test bed for trying out a new policy or strategy that, if successful, will be rolled out in a broader application. Therefore, the success metrics

---

[2] Peppers, Rogers, and Dorf, *The One to One Fieldbook*, updated 2016.
[3] Peppers, Rogers, and Dorf, *The One to One Fieldbook*, updated 2016.

of the individual pilot project will have less to do with the actual profitability or business success of the pilot itself and more to do with an assessment of whether the idea represented by the pilot project would be beneficial if it were rolled out to the broader organization. And pilots have a built-in advantage when it comes to metrics. Because, by their nature, they usually involve only a selected portion of the enterprise, it is easier to measure the pilot's performance against a "control group"— meaning, in essence, the rest of the enterprise, doing business as usual.

Incremental change projects are rarely undertaken to resolve the problem of **relationship governance** for the enterprise. One of the key benefits, in fact, of concentrating on the IDIC process implementation methodology is the fact that significant progress can still be made without having to come to grips with this very thorny problem. At some point, however, any enterprise that wants to begin engaging customers in actual relationships, individually, will have to deal with the issue of relationship governance, and there are at least two methods for dealing with it on an incremental or transitional basis.

Picket Fence Strategy

The right way to transform a company gradually into a customer management organization is not to do it product by product or division by division but customer by customer. And one way to begin such a transition is by placing just a few customers "under management," then adding a few more, and a few more (see Exhibits 14.1 and 14.2). In order to make this type of transition successful, it must be recognized that the enterprise will be operating under different rules with respect to the customers under management than it will be with respect to all other customers. In essence, the customers under management will be fenced off and treated differently from the remainder of the customer base. As the transition progresses, the number

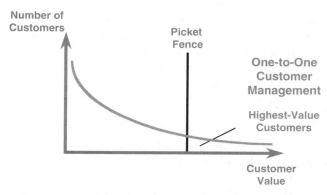

EXHIBIT 14.1   Set Up a Picket Fence

■ Link individual data over time.

■ Calculate individual share of customer and lifetime value.

■ Establish and maintain dialogue—get them off the mailing lists.

■ Mass-customize to meet individually expressed needs.

■ Allocate resources to this customer relative to this customer's value.

■ Find products for customers.

One-to-One Picket Fence

EXHIBIT 14.2   How to Treat Customers behind the Picket Fence

of customers behind this "picket fence" will increase. As the portion of the customer base behind the picket fence continues to grow larger, the enterprise will be effecting a gradual transition to a customer management organization.

If an enterprise has ranked its customers by value, it can prioritize its transition in such a way as to place the more valuable customers behind the picket fence first. When customers go under management, the implication is that a **customer manager** in the enterprise will be setting objectives and strategies for each of them individually. The objective and strategy set for any particular customer should reflect the entire enterprise's relationship with that customer. For this reason, at least with respect to the customers behind the picket fence, the customer managers must have not only an integrated view of the enterprise's offering to and interactions with those customers, but they also must have authority to make policy and implement programs, on behalf of the enterprise, for everything from levels of service to inclusion in online pop-up advertising.

The picket fence transition strategy is especially compelling for companies that already **identify** their customers individually, during the natural course of their business, and **differentiate** them by value. This would include banks and financial services firms, telecommunications companies, personal services businesses, some retailers, and most business-to-business (B2B) companies with internal sales organizations. The highest-value customers at many companies like these are already being singled out for attention. If a retailer, for instance, has identified any customers who merit special treatment, it is likely they are the store's very high-volume, repeat spenders; the "special treatment" might include assigning personal shoppers or **relationship managers** to watch over the individual interests of such customers. Because the picket fence strategy is already in place at such a firm, the enterprise's goal should be to extend the idea and automate it, by codifying the **business rules** that are being applied and ensuring that proper metrics are in place.

Remember that the customer manager should own the business rules for determining all of the communications that her customers receive. This means that the enterprise's general online offers, mobile messaging, or direct-mail pieces would not go to customers behind the picket fence without the initiation or approval of the customer manager responsible for them. For each customer behind the picket fence, there should be a particular objective and a strategy for achieving that objective, set by the customer manager. In fact, the customer manager will herself be rewarded and compensated based on her ability to meet the objectives set for each of her customers, one customer at a time. Over time, as technology makes it better and more cost-efficient to process customer information, and the enterprise gains more knowledge and confidence in the process, it can expand the picket fence and put more customers behind it.

Although the transition involves expanding the area behind the picket fence (i.e., placing more and more customers under management), the enterprise most likely will never actually place all of its customers behind the fence. Some customers, for instance, may not be willing to participate in a relationship of any kind, or to exchange information. Moreover, no matter how cost efficiently the enterprise has automated the process, there will always be customers who are not financially worth engaging in relationships.

Segment Management

Another way to begin the transition to a customer management organization is with segment managers. The picket fence transition is a customer-specific process that places an increasing number of individual customers under management; the segment management transition is a *function*-specific process that gives segment managers an increasing number of roles and capabilities with respect to their segments.

Remember that we chose the term *portfolio* rather than segment with deliberation, when we introduced the concept of customer management. The primary reason for this choice was to convey the thought that, in a **customer portfolio,** the customers themselves are uniquely identified and unduplicated: No customer would be in more than one portfolio at a time. And just as you manage each stock in your stock portfolio individually, you would manage each customer in your customer portfolio individually.

But even if an enterprise has not identified its customers uniquely, it still can differentiate them approximately, using survey-based consumer research and other tools. Even though the enterprise might not be able to classify any specific customer into a particular segment with certainty, the segments themselves represent different types of customers who have **needs** and values that are different from the customers populating other segments.

Segment management is particularly appropriate for the types of businesses that have greater difficulty identifying and tracking customers individually. The picket fence transition works best for companies that either identify customers in the natural course of their business or can easily do so, whereas the segment manager transition works for all other companies. A consumer packaged-goods company, for instance, might have a highly developed customer management organization already in place to ensure that its relationships with its retailer customers are managed profitably, but the company is unlikely to have the identities of more than a microscopic fraction of its consumer-customers—even those who interact with the company's brands through Facebook or other online media. Such a firm might establish an organization of consumer segment managers who are responsible for shaping the firm's advertising and promotion efforts with respect to particular segments of consumers, across a variety of different products and brands.

A *segment management* organization, therefore, can be thought of as a transition state somewhere between product management and customer management. The most critical missing ingredient in a segment management operation is likely to be the capability to identify individual customers and track their interactions with—and individual values to—the enterprise over time. Until the enterprise is able to add this capability, it will not be able to move from segment management to true **customer portfolio management.** But even in the absence of customer-specific capabilities, a segment management organization still can be a useful tool for an enterprise to begin treating different customers differently and for creating the value proposition for the relationships that eventually could come.

Customer Portfolio Management

At the heart of the customer management idea is the concept of placing customer managers in charge of *portfolios* of separate and individually identifiable customers who have been differentiated by their value to the enterprise and grouped by their needs. It is these customer managers who are charged with managing customer profitability. This is the core structure of the customer management organization, one in which each individual customer's value and retention is the direct responsibility of one individual in the enterprise. Managers may each be in charge of a large number of customers or portfolios, but the responsibility for any single customer is assigned to one customer manager (or, in a B2B setting, often to a customer management team). That manager is responsible for building the enterprise's share of customer (SOC) for each of the customers in his portfolio and for increasing each customer's lifetime value (LTV) and **potential value** to the enterprise (see Chapter 5).

The responsibility for customer management may spring from the marketing department, or sales management, or product development, or even, occasionally, from the database and analytics department, where the customer data are housed. Wherever in the organization customer management resides, however, it must have a clear voice in the enterprise and have enough power to make decisions and influence other areas of the enterprise. One difficulty for this group is that the enterprise might try to hold it accountable for increasing the value of customers but fail to give it the authority to take the appropriate actions with respect to those customers. In the customer-value-building enterprise, the customer strategies should become the unifying theme for the organization; other areas of the enterprise should be made to understand how their own departmental goals relate to the customer strategies developed by the customer management group, and these other departments should be held accountable for executing the strategies ultimately designed to increase customer equity.

Transition across the Enterprise

> Many organizations learn the hard way that customer portfolio management cannot be installed; it must be *adopted*.

Many companies believe that the biggest hurdle to becoming a successful customer-strategy enterprise is choosing and installing the right software, or setting up Big Data or the idea of managing and analyzing a dizzying flood of customer data. This unfortunate outlook has led to poor results on customer initiatives. Many organizations learn the hard way that customer relationships cannot be installed; they must be *adopted*. The biggest hurdles to successful customer management have little to do with technology. The greatest obstacles are a firm's traditional organization, culture, processes, metrics, and methods of compensation. The transition needed will affect not just the whole enterprise but each of its parts as well. Let's take a look at the changes that the enterprise will face.

Transition Process for the Sales Department

The sales force plays a critical role in the customer-strategy enterprise. As the "eyes and ears" of the organization, salespeople often interact with the customer at the customer's place of business. It is during these visits that salespeople develop an information-rich **customer's point of view**. Using **sales force automation (SFA)** software, sales reps now can easily share customer learning with their firms.

Some of the sales force is focused on driving transactions for lower-volume customers, and the skill sets of these salespeople are well suited for these activities. Other salespeople have different skills, working with customers across all levels of the customer organization and focusing on maximizing share of customer. Once considered the "lone wolf" of the organization, these salespeople effectively divide their time among sales calls, analysis of customer information, and participation in internal customer-strategy development. Regardless of position, however, salespeople understand how to develop customer insights and to provide customer information to the enterprise in an actionable way. Some information is entered into the SFA tool, and other information is shared during customer review meetings or via communications with the research and development department, customer service, or other departments.

The transition to a customer-strategy enterprise will be easy for some salespeople, whereas it will challenge the skill sets of some of the top sales performers. These principles will make a great deal of sense for salespeople who have already been practicing visionary selling, consultative selling, or strategic selling, or using the trusted advisor approach[4] and they probably will embrace these ideals readily. But the salesperson who relies, for example, on retailer business customers to "buy forward" in order to make quarterly product sales quotas may find the transition more difficult. Applying customer management principles requires taking a long-term view of the customer, a view that may conflict directly with the short-term focus that prevails in many sales organizations.

The sales team can help confirm that those selected as **most valuable customers (MVCs)**[5] are indeed the best customers. The sales team can also find **most growable customers (MGCs)** who have been missed. It will be important for the organization to provide the sales team with information across other touch points in the organization, such as the Web and the customer service center. Real-time information is required to coordinate all interactions with a customer, and feeding in this information can be a significant change for many salespeople. The trade-off is that the enterprise can handle a lot of the most tedious record keeping and servicing very efficiently, freeing up the salesperson for real relationship building and customer growth.

One of the most significant changes for a recently automated sales force is that the daily life of salespeople will wind up onscreen for all to see. In addition, fewer salespeople will have greater responsibility,[6] putting pressure on all sales personnel to conform and adopt new policies and procedures. During this transition period,

---

[4] David Maister, Charles H. Green, and Robert Galford, *The Trusted Advisor* (New York: Touchstone, 2000); Charles H. Green, *Trust-Based Selling* (New York: McGraw-Hill, 2006); and Charles H. Green and Andrea P. Howe, *The Trusted Advisor Fieldbook: A Comprehensive Toolkit for Leading with Trust* (Hoboken, NJ: John Wiley & Sons, 2011).

[5] See Chapter 5, "Differentiating Customers: Some Customers Are Worth More Than Others," for more about MVCs and other customer value categories. Differentiating customers according to their value (and their needs) represents a core component of the IDIC process: Identify, Differentiate, Interact, and Customize. Ultimately, there are five primary customer-value categories: most valuable customers (MVCs), most growable customers (MGCs), low-maintenance customers, super-growth customers, and below-zero customers.

[6] Michael Ahearne, Douglas E. Hughes, and Niels Schillewaert, "Why Sales Reps Should Welcome Information Technology: Measuring the Impact of CRM-Based IT on Sales Effectiveness," *International Journal of Research in Marketing* 24, no. 4 (December 2007): 336–349; and Richard Lee, *The Customer Relationship Management Survival Guide* (St. Paul, MN: HYM Press, 2000).

therefore, it is important to negotiate some key agreements when implementing new policies and programs:

- *Prioritize key information that is needed about customers.* Salespeople should not be spending their time typing. They should be interacting with customers and learning more about customer needs.
- *Address ways that salespeople can save time and earn higher commissions.*
- *Integrate customer information wherever possible.* Some salespeople spend significant amounts of time typing the same information into applications that have different purposes (order entry system, billing system, forecasting reports, etc.).
- *Negotiate which information is for enterprise use and which information is "for their eyes only."* It is important for the salesperson to remember key customer information, such as family member names, spouse's birthday, and so on, to create a personal bond; but this may be interesting to others in the enterprise only if someone has to substitute for the sales rep in a personal meeting. Today, salespeople have greater demands for input, including data, customer information, financial statistics, and customer insights that drive decisions. As a result, salespeople need a wider range of skills, and have greater pressure and responsibility. The switch "from product to solutions selling and integrating services has led salespeople to become the drivers of processes that link the customer's problems and needs with internal configuration and resource base."[7]

MULTIDIVISION CUSTOMERS   Knowledge-based selling traditionally has occurred in business-to-business (B2B) scenarios but has not always been applied across divisions of a company. One reason a customer-centered approach to doing business is so compelling is precisely that it enables an enterprise to leverage a single customer relationship into a variety of additional profit streams, cross-selling many different products and services to a customer in a coordinated way. The sales function plays a critical role in this relationship but is not alone in executing it.

Customer-strategy enterprises rarely isolate their customer initiatives within a single division. In a multidivisional enterprise, the divisions sell to overlapping customer bases, doing business with a single customer in several different divisions. Enterprise-wide cross-selling is not possible if the pilot project is limited to a single division and if the division databases are not integrated to facilitate a one-customer view.

In many cases, a B2B enterprise that set out to transform itself into a more customer-oriented firm ended up restructuring the sales force entirely, in order to ensure that the sales of different products to the same customers would be better coordinated, and appear more rational to the customer.

---

[7] Javier Marcos-Cuevas and Lynette Ryals, "The Changing Role of Salespeople and Consequences for Required Capabilities: A Review and Empirical Exploration," *The Sustainable Global Market Place: Proceedings of the 2011 Academy of Marketing Science Annual Conference* (2011): 311–314.

Using Up Customers

We know a multiline insurance company in the United States we'll call Company X. It sells auto, property, life, and health insurance through a network of its own agents, each having the authority to sell any of the company's products. Some of these products generate more profit than others. Life insurance, as one example, tends to sell at a higher margin and is less subject to fraud, when compared to auto insurance. To protect agent profitability and maintain order within the distribution channel, Company X doesn't allow any of its own agents to solicit clients from any of its other agents. So once an agent lands a new customer, no other agent from that company can ask that customer for additional business.

The problem is that for a variety of reasons—background, predisposition, expertise—some agents simply don't sell all of Company X's insurance products with equal enthusiasm and effectiveness. Consider an agent who has a fine track record for recruiting new auto insurance customers but then rarely, if ever, elects to sell any other line of insurance product to them. She has found that she can build herself a bigger book of business, faster, simply by concentrating on acquiring more and more auto insurance customers, a task she is exceedingly good at, rather than spending time and energy learning how to sell property or life insurance, or some other product, to her existing customers. Of course, every new customer she recruits won't be buying any other type of insurance from Company X, because no other agent is allowed to solicit, while the agent herself is unlikely to suggest other products.

In effect, Company X is "using up" a whole customer whenever it sells an auto policy through this agent. If there were an unlimited supply of new or prospective customers, this wouldn't be a problem, but the supply is not unlimited. Even putting aside the fact that a single-product customer has a greater proclivity to wander away to a competitor, the real issue here is that every time the company gets a customer and does not get the most possible value from that customer, the company loses a real monetary opportunity. And it cannot simply make this opportunity up by finding more customers.[a]

With the right metrics and a thorough analysis, Company X might discover that the value this agent leaves on the table with each new customer recruited is more than the value generated by each auto policy she sells. If that were the case, then this particular agent is not creating value for the company at all but destroying it. That's right: Company X may actually be destroying value every time this particular agent recruits a new customer. There a several solutions to this problem. One is to use available software, such as Agency Revolution, to make sure all leads have been followed through, and that additional offers are appropriately made to customers, either through teaming current salespeople or by virtually connecting customers with the right salespeople. In either case, the rewards will be for increasing the value of a customer rather than closing a product sale.[b]

Company X's business has been based on the belief that as long as its sales and marketing effort is effective, it can always acquire more customers from somewhere. But this is a false assumption. Instead, to make the right decisions as a business, you must always take into consideration the population of customers and prospective customers truly available to you. After considering the whole population of customers and prospects, your job is to employ that population to create the most possible value for your firm.[c]

Because customers are scarcer than other resources, using up customers is more costly than using up other resources.

If you let this thought sink in for a minute, you'll realize that it requires you to adopt a different perspective on your business, and this perspective will lead you to make different decisions. Evaluating your **business model,** or your company's various sales and marketing and other activities, from the standpoint of return on investment or payback ratio or some other financial metric, is important, but it's even more important to evaluate every action you take based on how many customers you have to use up to achieve the financial results you want. (See a more complete discussion of **Return on Customer** and customers as a scarce asset in Chapter 11.)

Source: Adapted from Don Peppers and Martha Rogers, Ph.D., *Rules to Break and Laws to Follow: How Your Business Can Beat the Crisis of Short-Termism* (Hoboken, NJ: John Wiley & Sons, 2008), pp. 43–45. Updated 2016.

[a] Sometimes companies use up customers with technology. Jill Dyché, author of several excellent books on customer data coordination and management, explains how CDI (customer data integration) would help distinguish between John Smith (the very valuable customer) and John Smith Jr. (the deadbeat) so we don't turn down the former for a high-profit loan. Getting the process right is as important as getting the philosophy and the compensation right.

[b] Henrik Naujoks, Bodo von Huelsen, Gunther Schwarz, and Stephen Phillips, "For Insurance Companies, the Day of Digital Reckoning," Bain & Company, March 18, 2013, http://www.bain.com/publications/articles/for-insurance-companies-the-day-of-digital-reckoning.aspx, accessed February 12, 2016.

[c] See Naujoks, von Huelsen, Schwarz, and Phillips, "For Insurance Companies, the Day of Digital Reckoning," for a summary of how insurance companies are generally behind in digital adoption, and could benefit both in customer relationship capabilities and data collection by updating web pages, setting up decision trees, etc. In many cases, this could even help the sales agents find the next right products for existing customers.

COMPENSATING THE SALES FORCE   Sales force compensation is often one of the most important drivers of change, partly because the salesperson's salary and bonus usually depend on product sales results. One challenge facing the enterprise is deciding how to compensate salespeople and others for encouraging and ensuring customer loyalty and growing the long-term value of a customer, even when there may be no short-term product sale involved. The fact is that many salespeople are compensated in ways that make them indifferent to customer loyalty. In some cases, new-customer incentive programs actually *benefit* the salespeople when **customer churn** increases, enabling them to resell a product or service to a relatively educated customer. If customer loyalty and profitability are the objectives, then the enterprise needs to explore compensation systems that reward sales reps on the basis of each individual customer's long-term profitability (or LTV). There are at least two ways an enterprise can accomplish this:

1. *Value-based commissions derived from customer, rather than product, profitability.* The enterprise identifies certain types of customers who tend to be worth more than others and pays a higher up-front commission for acquiring or selling to this preferred type of customer. It considers lower commissions for "price" buyers or returning former customers as well as other variable commission plans that emphasize acquisition and retention of customers whose value is greatest to the enterprise overall, not just to the salesperson.
2. *Retention commissions.* The enterprise pays a lower commission on the acquisition of a customer. Instead, it links compensation to the profitability of a customer over time. For example, instead of paying a $1,000 commission just for landing a customer, the company pays $600 for a new account and $400 per year for every year the customer continues to do business with the enterprise.

Transition Process for Marketing

The marketing group is responsible for traditional marketing activities, including creating brand image and awareness, communicating with the customer, utilizing the Internet and other old and new channels, and, often, creating communications within the enterprise (e.g., an intranet, company newsletters, and project communications).

In the customer-strategy enterprise, the marketing department will perform these traditional roles for customers who remain outside of the picket fence. It also may help to prepare communication messages or even business rules for customer managers who are building relationships for customers under management. In addition to deploying the traditional instruments of marketing, such as advertising and promotion, a number of other functions for the marketing department to perform are unique to a customer-specific approach, including:

- Customer analytics (see Chapters 12 and 13), a specialized skill set that involves building customer databases, modeling customer LTV, gathering and analyzing data, and programming. The customer analytics group also may be responsible for tracking and reporting the internal metrics needed to measure the effectiveness of customer programs.
- Establishment of test cells and control groups.

- Campaign development and management, including dialogue planning.
- Offer specification, designed to appeal especially to higher-value customers and prospects.
- Customer management, as a line-management function, which has been described previously.
- Insight into short-term profitability and long-term customer equity and **Total Shareholder Return (TSR)**.

Transition Process for Customer Service

A service organization (or "**customer care**,") might be the appliance repair personnel, the hotel staff, operators answering the 800-telephone number, representatives monitoring Web site chat and social media for customer questions or complaints, or the delivery crew. Every product that's manufactured and sold has a service organization associated with it in some way, whether customers obtain the product directly from the enterprise or through a channel organization. In the customer-strategy enterprise, the service organization has access to more customer information than in other traditional enterprises, and uses this information to deliver a valuable experience or to collect information (or both). For example, in a customer-strategy enterprise, the delivery driver might be asked to survey a customer's warehouse informally and take note of the number of competitors' cartons that are stacked within view of the delivery door. This information can help an enterprise begin to understand its share of customer.

Ironically, as pressures mount for enterprises to cut costs and improve efficiency, the customer service area may be squeezed in the process. In the customer-strategy enterprise, the customer service area plays a key role in executing customer strategies, including collecting, analyzing, and utilizing data while servicing the customer. Customer calls are routed based on value and need, and the most appropriate **customer service representative** is assigned the call based on the skills of the rep. During the call, customer-defined business rules are applied to maximize the impact of the interaction with the customer, and the reps have been trained in how to interact most effectively with various customers. Also, the individual needs, talent, and experience of the reps are considered in the routing decisions. Reps are encouraged to enhance the skills needed to serve each customer efficiently and effectively. As customer needs change, the skills of the reps also must evolve.

Transformation from Product Centricity to Customer Centricity

Moving from product to customer centricity requires both a company-wide transformation of mind-set and the establishment of organization, process, information, and technology requirements. Challenges arise mainly during the

(continued)

(Continued)

integration and company-wide implementation of customer-centric strategies. Research indicates that 99 percent of marketers express that having a single, fully integrated corporate view of each customer across the enterprise—which we see as the basis of customer centricity—is important to their business. Yet only 24 percent think their organization has achieved full integration.[a] But some companies—such as JetBlue Airways, Southwest Airlines, and Capital One—are noted for having built cultures, processes, and data systems so focused on customers that they are benchmarked by organizations around the world.

One company that has successfully implemented customer centricity is a multinational telecommunications and mobile network provider. In the late 2000s, the company was no longer the single operator in its primary region and faced competition from the second Fixed Network Operator Licensee as well as from three other mobile operators. With the saturation of the fixed-line market, decreasing revenues from traditional income sources due to increased competition, and much-criticized service quality that created significant churn risks, the telecommunications company realized the need for a comprehensive customer-centricity strategy that would protect its subscriber base while ensuring acquisition for the next-generation offerings it wanted to launch.

The company defined and began the implementation of a complete customer-centric transformation.[b] As a first step, the current state of customer centricity in the company was assessed within the IDIC framework, to understand the company's capability of identifying, differentiating, interacting, and communicating with customers or customer groups. Customer insight development via data analysis and segmentation followed the assessment. At this point, the customer population was assigned to customer segments based on their value, needs, and behaviors, and integrated segments were developed. For example, "cream" was a segment within residential customers who had extensive social networks and frequent calls. Their needs were more in the area of business communication and high-speed Internet usage. Some of the other segments included "mobi," which was made up of medium-value customers with high national mobile usage; "bytes," who had high data needs; and the "move up" segment, made up of currently low-value customers with untapped potential.

Next, the company developed capabilities to lead the change via "Customer Governance and Organizational Adaptation." It wanted to move from product management to segment management in its organization to ensure that customer-specific strategies were centrally developed and executed in a coordinated way across the organization. However, it also recognized that it would not be possible to make this switch all at once for all customers. As a result, the company prioritized its segments and started segment management with the most critical segments (particularly regarding industry competition) in its portfolio. Although the company started segment management implementation with high-value segments, its execution plan made sure that customer-centricity principles were implemented for all customer segments along the **customer life cycle**, resulting in overall service quality improvement. End-to-end customer ownership was defined, and execution took place throughout all channels and customer touch points, including the field technicians, contact center, marketing, and sales. Customer portfolio management for mass and business markets was launched, which enabled the company to capture synergies across products and channels, providing one voice to the customer in communication planning and centralized ownership to ensure coordination of customer experience across channels. Understanding the needs of the customers and providing differentiated treatment to all segments was critical in providing the company with a competitive advantage.

Execution included training for employees, reporting and monitoring structures, and the alignment of incentives with the new model's priorities. "Deploying agent-level customer satisfaction measurement" to all customer-facing employees effectively helped incorporate the customer's voice into measuring customer satisfaction at an operational level. Key reporting and tracking metrics and a customer-centricity dashboard were utilized to track portfolio and segment performance and link them to employee performance.

A "Customer Centricity Program Management Office" was established and led the change throughout the whole transformation with project managers and task forces. One of the challenges, which was resistance due to role and responsibility changes, was overcome by timely and frequent communication in the form of workshops and interviews.

---

[a] "The 2015 Digital Marketer," Experian, 2015, available at http://experian.co.uk/assets/marketing-services/reports/report-digital-marketer-report-2015.pdf, accessed January 21, 2016.
[b] Based on a client engagement conducted by Peppers & Rogers Group. Name of client disguised for purposes of privacy. Thanks to Pelin Turunc, former consultant to Peppers & Rogers Group, Europe, for her contributions to this section.

Transition Process for Other Key Enterprise Areas

Finance, research and development (R&D), information technology/information services (IT/IS), and human resources (HR) also need to make the transition to a customer-strategy organization, but these changes are not as readily apparent as those required by the marketing, sales, and customer service organizations. All four areas are directly responsible for *capabilities building*—or how well the organization is able to adapt and change to the new processes. For now, let's look at how the transition affects these other areas of the enterprise in more detail.

Finance

As the organization moves to customer centricity, the finance function takes on new roles within the enterprise, and these are required to help implement a smooth transition:

- Accounting systems should be set up to measure customer profitability and LTV easily, and the enterprise will need the support of the financial area to help define these metrics.
- Having measured customer value and the rate of customer value, the company will be able to use these measures to determine Return on Customer (ROC), which will support TSR. These measures will also provide a stronger level of accountability from the marketers than basic return on marketing investment (ROMI) or return on marketing resources (RMR) or marketing resources management (MRM).
- Having defined and learned to report these metrics, the finance leadership will work with line and staff managers and HR to develop appropriate customer-based compensation and reward systems for employees whose responsibility is to build customer equity and manage customer relationships and retention.

Building a strong customer-centric organization requires financial support to implement new programs and technology, and it requires accounting and management support to ensure costs and results are properly tracked and understood. The finance department will play a critical role in developing and evaluating the business case for implementing customer-centric initiatives.

One of the most important transitions at a customer-centric enterprise has to do with how the firm tracks, understands, and deals with the very concept of value creation. The customer-centric firm is one that understands that it is customers who create all value. But, as we learned in Chapter 11, customers create both short-term value, when they buy things and incur costs today, and they create long-term value, when they change (today) their likelihood of buying in the future—that is, when their lifetime values go up or down. In earlier chapters we also introduced the concept of "customer equity," which represents the sum total of all the lifetime values of a firm's current and future customers, and we showed that because this number actually should be the same as a firm's "enterprise value," the ROC metric, at the enterprise level, could be shown to equal a firm's "Total Shareholder Return." At the enterprise level, the mathematical equations for both these quantities are identified.

So one very important role for the finance department at a customer-centric enterprise is to embrace the idea that the firm's customer equity is an important intangible asset, somewhat like capital. Through the budgeting and planning process, a finance department already monitors the enterprise's financial capital in order to avoid destroying value unintentionally (or using it up too fast). The same kind of discipline should be applied to monitoring the firm's customer equity. Unlike financial capital, however, with the right actions, a firm's customer equity actually can be replenished and increased, even as it is employed to generate current cash flow from customers.

If a finance department could track ROC at the enterprise level, it could help the firm avoid eroding its value as a business over time. Any firm that doesn't track ROC might easily adopt programs that lead to unintended value destruction—programs that may generate better current-period profits at the expense of "using up" even more value from the customer base.

Because customers can be thought of as a productive asset for a business, and customer equity is similar to capital, the ROC metric can be compared to another financial metric already familiar to many large enterprise financial managers, Economic Value Added. "EVA™," as it is known, is a measure used to account for the cost of the capital required by a business, in order to give companies a more accurate picture of the value they actually create with their operations. Two businesses with identical cash flows are not identically valuable, if one firm requires more capital than the other to produce those cash flows.[8] Even if a firm measures its success in terms of return on assets, its financial results still can be deceiving unless it factors in its cost of capital. According to one EVA proponent, IBM's corporate return on assets was over 11 percent when it was at its most profitable, but at the same time it faced a realistic cost of capital of nearly 13 percent. So even though it seemed "profitable," one could argue that IBM was not actually creating value for its shareholders. A company may be unaware that it is diluting its financial capital unless it tracks EVA. In the same way, a customer-centric enterprise may be unaware it is diluting its customer equity unless it tracks its overall ROC.

Thus, the finance department's role in transitioning to customer centricity is absolutely critical. The department's basic function at any company is to track and understand how the company creates value for its shareholders and then to report the information to those who need to know—including internal managers and the shareholders themselves. To compare the likely economic impact of alternative actions, a company must always know how much capital each action will require, but it should also know how much customer equity will be consumed.

Research and Development

Research and development is another key area in many customer-strategy enterprises. R&D is responsible for creating innovative customer solutions and, therefore, works closely with marketing or sales (as it has done traditionally in the past). However, in the customer-strategy enterprise, it is the depth and quality of customer information that makes the difference. The customer manager group works within its own department to understand common customer needs, and these common

---

[8] Economic Value Added® and EVA® are registered trademarks of Stern Stewart & Co.

needs drive some of the R&D group's work. For some customers, there are needs driving the R&D efforts that will not be seen by other customers for a long time because the most valuable or most growable customers are intimately involved in the R&D work. This work will give these customers a competitive advantage in the marketplace. For example, an MGC (most growable customer) might be a service organization working with a technology supplier to create a wireless network for the sales force and service workers that will enable them to react to their customer needs instantaneously. This capability to respond dynamically will have a competitive advantage, and this capability is at the heart of innovation, both in the arena of product development as well as business modeling and customer relationships.

Information Technology/Information Services

Often, there is a centralized technology function (information technology, or IT) within large enterprises that is responsible for the technology infrastructure (networks, mainframes, routers, etc.). There may be groups (information services, or IS) that are dedicated to functions within the company and that work with the departments to implement applications that help conduct business (HR applications that manage payroll and employee records, other applications that run the order-entry system, logistics and planning, **customer interaction center** systems, etc.). Both of these functions are directly responsible for enabling the execution of customer strategies.[9]

Sometimes IT/IS organizations go awry when they sponsor the CRM projects. Sometimes IT specialists overestimate their own skills in business strategy, but more often than not, the IT/IS organization runs the project management office (PMO) of the CRM project. This can work when IT/IS actually understands the importance of aligning technology implementation with the business strategy. If the IT organization, data builders, and analytics arenas cannot align the technology implementation and the business strategy, the customer management effort and the entire PMO should be governed by the business end of the

> If the IT organization cannot align the technology implementation and the business strategy, the customer management effort and the entire PMO should be governed by the business end of the enterprise.

---

[9] Phil Murphy, "Customer-Centric Application Rationalization," Forrester Research, Inc., February 25, 2015, available at www.forrester.com; "Customer-centric IT: Enterprise IT Trends and Investment 2013," Ernst and Young, 2015, available at http://www.ey.com/Publication/vwLUAssets/Customer-centric_IT/$FILE/CIO_KLUB_report_2013_low_resolution.pdf, accessed February 12, 2016; R. J. B. Jean, R. R. Sinkovics, and D. Kim, "Information Technology and Organizational Performance within International Business to Business Relationships: A Review and an Integrated Conceptual Framework," *International Marketing Review* 25, no. 5 (2008): 563–583; and Barbara Wixom and Hugh J. Watson, "An Empirical Investigation of the Factors Affecting Data Warehousing Success," *MIS Quarterly* 25, no. 1 (March 2001): 17–41.

enterprise. That said, business units often lack the project management skills to implement large-scale projects—and this expertise is often in the IT/IS area.

Human Resources

The customer-strategy enterprise requires knowledge workers—people who will recognize and act on relevant customer information, as well as people who will make or break rules as needed. As we mentioned in Chapter 3, customer experience depends on trust. It used to be pretty easy to set up a rulebook for customer experience, but no longer. Creating great customer experiences means being able to not only break a rule, but respond to something that has no rule. Customers already know this—if they call a company and the first person can't solve their problem, they'll simply hang up and call back until they find someone who can.

So human resources now means recruiting and training people who can think on their feet and thus create a great customer experience. You need smart people working in a strong culture who do exactly what you would have done when nobody's looking, as they respond to real-time tweets.

HR can directly influence the shift toward becoming a customer-strategy company in several ways:

- *Redefining the organization.* By taking an active part in defining the new roles and responsibilities, the HR function can map out the transition plans for many key areas of the enterprise. Part of doing this requires that HR help the business define the changes and understand how employees will be affected by those changes.
- *Evaluating whether the company has the capability to change as required by the newly developed customer strategies.* Some important limiting factors may arise such as the qualifications of the labor pool available and local salary expectations.
- *During the transition plan, addressing all of the key recruiting, training, and ongoing support issues.* Is there adequate funding to help employees migrate to these new responsibilities? Often these are "line items" in a project plan but are not incorporated into annual training and development budgets or plans.
- *Creating career path opportunities that did not exist before.* The responsibilities of customer interaction center reps or salespeople can grow over time as their skill sets can mature. For the more senior-level executives, a well-rounded employee who has worked directly with customers will become more valued in a customer-value-building organization. Customer-focused thinking will affect recruiting, too.
- *Demanding and rewarding customer-value-building successes.* The HR leaders of a customer-centric company will hold employees accountable not just for activity but for results measured in current net revenue from customers as well as current measures of long-term equity built by customers.

■ *Actively trying to manage and develop the corporate culture.* Technology now enables the lowliest employee to leap tall corporate hierarchies with a single click, subverting the power of organization charts and structured personnel policies. This means that corporate culture is even more important when it comes to determining a company's ultimate success. And a corporate culture that will give a customer-centric enterprise the best chance to succeed will be one that is centered on earning and keeping customer trust.

This last point, regarding corporate culture, is worth spending some time on, because it is so critical to success. Importantly, as businesses continue to streamline, automate, and outsource, corporate culture is becoming more important than ever before. A number of factors are at work here, including the increased complexity of modern organizations, greater sophistication of the workforce, globalization, and communications technologies that are accelerating the pace of routine business processes.

We should always remember the fact that, as far as an enterprise's customers are concerned, the ordinary, low-level customer-contact employee they meet at the store, talk to on the phone, or interact with during a service transaction of any kind—that employee is the company. And corporate culture is the most potent tool available for ensuring that everyone at the enterprise is pulling in the same direction.

Culture is an elusive yet critical part of any company's nature. Everyone talks about it, but no one can really put a finger on it. You could think of a company's culture as something like the DNA of its business operation. It consists of the shared beliefs and values of managers and employees, usually passed on informally from one to another. A company's culture consists of the mostly unwritten rules and unspoken understandings about "the way we do things around here." Culture is what guides employees when there is no policy. *Culture is what employees do when no one's looking.*

> Culture is what guides employees when there is no policy. *Culture is what employees do when no one's looking.*

As a company matures, shared values and beliefs harden into business practices and processes, until workers and managers find it increasingly difficult to describe their own cultures or to separate cultural issues from organizational structure and process issues. At some organizations, managers take a proactive role in guiding or shaping their own corporate cultures, trying to ensure that the informal beliefs and values of employees and managers support the organization's broader mission. The Toyota Way, Wal-Mart's Four Basic Beliefs, IKEA's aversion to bureaucracy, and the egalitarian HP Way have all contributed importantly to the long-term success of those firms, and managers at each of these companies actively encourage an employee culture based on these value statements.

But regardless of whether a company overtly tries to manage it or not, every organization has a culture. Difficult or conflicting cultures tend to be the biggest factors accounting for why mergers and strategic alliances fail, why change management efforts don't gain traction at a firm, and why major corporate strategy initiatives fizzle. And culture is also one of the biggest single impediments to most customer-centric transitions. In fact, a culture with bad karma will impede virtually every effort a firm could make toward better and more integrated customer-facing processes.

This is because culture is propagated the old-fashioned way—by imitation, that marvelously important survival tool. A new employee comes onboard and "learns the ropes" by finding out just how things are done around here. When she encounters a new situation, she'll ask someone who's been around for a while. Successful behaviors are those that are rewarded by the organization, so how an enterprise provides recognition and incentives is important, but just as important is how the employees already working within the firm tend to socialize the values, processes, and rules when it comes to teaching newbies how to fit in.

The culture at an enterprise will reflect how it measures success, how it rewards people, what tasks it considers to be important, what processes it follows to accomplish those tasks, how quickly and effectively it makes decisions, and who approves decisions. The culture will reflect how friendly or competitive employees are with each other, how trusting they are, how much disagreement is tolerated, how much consensus is required, what privileges go with rank, what information is available to whom, what customers or suppliers are the most valued, and what actions are considered out of bounds. Although any enterprise can write down the values it aspires to and post those values on the wall, if the values are to become part of the real culture, then all the company's systems, metrics, processes, rewards, and HR policies must be aligned with them, too.[10]

In terms of ensuring success for a customer-centric transition, the HR department needs to take a proactive approach to the enterprise's corporate culture, dealing directly with the many values and issues that lie beneath the surface of the firm's organization chart. Employees view many HR functions unfavorably: HR "polices" the rules and procedures, or it is viewed as a purely administrative function. The transition to customer management can serve as an opportunity for HR to address proactively the many issues that arise in the transition, because the changes are wide and deep. Directly or indirectly, though, they all echo back to the basic relationship issue of trust: Do things right, and do the right thing, proactively.

---

[10] See Lindsay McGregor and Neel Doshi, "How Company Culture Shapes Employee Motivation," *Harvard Business Review*, November 25, 2015, available at https://hbr.org/2015/11/how-company-culture-shapes-employee-motivation, accessed January 21 and February 12, 2016; also see Don Peppers and Martha Rogers, Ph.D., *Rules to Break and Laws to Follow: How Your Business Can Beat the Crisis of Short-Termism* (Hoboken, NJ: John Wiley & Sons, 2008), pp. 98–101.

Managing Employees in the Customer-Strategy Enterprise

The road to becoming a customer-value-building enterprise is fraught with speed bumps. We have shown so far how the transition requires a new organizational infrastructure—one that is populated by customer managers and capabilities managers who fully support the migration from day one. The enterprise moving to a customer-strategy business model will likely require new capabilities for relating to customers individually. It will need to assess where the gaps lie in its established capabilities so it can improve its focus on customers, not just products, and build profitable, long-term customer relationships.

Organizations used to be simpler to manage, because most tasks were routine, most problems could be anticipated, and desired outcomes could be spelled out in official policy. An employee's job was to follow the policy. But with the advent of new information and communications technologies, more and more of these routine tasks have been automated or outsourced, and the resulting organizations are slimmer and more efficiently competitive. What remains at most firms, and will continue to characterize them, are the functions and roles that cannot be automated or outsourced. These are the kinds of jobs that require employees to make decisions that cannot be foreseen or mapped out and therefore aren't spelled out in the standard operating processes. These jobs require nonroutine decision making. Many of them involve high-concept roles and other functions that simply can't be covered by a rule book.

At a bank in Australia, one contact center manager was very determined to create an environment that created good experiences for thousands of customers who reached the contact center every day. Although many of the issues, problems, and queries raised by customers could be handled by training and established protocol, there were inevitably many callers and online customers who presented new issues. Rather than frustrate the customer by making her wait while the rep went to find a "supervisor," the contact center manager encouraged reps to figure out what would be good for the customer and fair to the company, and if that rep could get another rep to agree the idea was sound, the original rep could help the customer promptly and effectively. Later the incident could be incorporated into future training, if it seemed to predict a trend, but even in the moment, it saved executive time and created a better customer experience.[11]

In *A Whole New Mind*, author Dan Pink persuasively describes this new, postautomation, postoutsourcing "Conceptual Age." It may once have been true that information workers would inherit the world, but today's information workers can live in Ireland or China, and even doctors and lawyers are finding their jobs increasingly threatened by computers and online substitutes. Indian technology schools turn out some 350,000 new engineers a year, and most of them are willing to work for $15,000 annual salaries. So what type of work can't be outsourced or automated? Pink says

---

[11] Story told to the authors in 2015.

the type of work that will characterize successful executives in the future (at least in the United States and other advanced Western economies) is work that involves creativity and sensitivity and requires skills in design, entertainment, storytelling, and empathy. This idea makes sense. Consider lawyers, for instance: Legal research and paperwork can be outsourced to Ireland or India, but cases have to be argued to juries in the courtroom, in person. Or doctors: X-rays can be evaluated remotely and diagnoses rendered, but bedside manner has to happen, well, bedside.[12]

This trend is already showing up in employment figures. According to one prediction, about half of total employment in the United States is in the high-risk category of being at least partly automatable in the next decade or so. Even in the seemingly human fields of diagnosing illness and fraud detection, for example, estimates suggest "that sophisticated algorithms could eventually substitute for approximately 140 million full-time knowledge workers worldwide."[13] In another view, **supply chain**, production and transactional jobs, which recently made up about 60 percent of the workforce, are being automated rapidly, while the other 40 percent of jobs, involving nonroutine decision making, have grown two and a half times faster in recent years and pay 55 percent to 70 percent more than routine jobs.[14] There are limits; certain manual labor require human dexterity that is not likely to be replaced with robots very soon—such as dentists, cooks, and gardeners. The nonroutine jobs require workers to deal with ambiguous situations and difficult issues—problems that often have no direct precedent or at least no "correct" solution—in creative areas, and in arenas requiring interpersonal contact; machines are not good at "motivating, nurturing, caring, and comforting people." So entrepreneurs, kindergarten teachers, salespeople, CEOs, and nurses have job security for the foreseeable future.[15]

A company can automate the contact report a sales rep has to file, but it can't get a computer to look into a client's eye and judge whether to push for the sale right away or ask another question first. Jobs like this require judgment, creativity, and initiative on the part of the employee. As a result, according to one study, many companies are turning their attention to "making their most talented, highly

---

[12] Daniel H. Pink, *A Whole New Mind: Why Right-Brainers Will Rule the Future* (New York: Riverhead, 2005), pp. 36–37.

[13] Carl Benedikt Frey and Michael A. Osborne, "The Future of Employment: How Susceptible Are Jobs to Computerization," September 17, 2013, p. 19, http://www.oxfordmartin.ox.ac.uk/downloads/academic/The_Future_of_Employment.pdf, accessed February 12, 2016.

[14] Frey and Osborne, "The Future of Employment: How Susceptible Are Jobs to Computerization"; and Bradford C. Johnson, James M. Manyika, and Lareina A. Yee, "The Next Revolution in Interactions," *McKinsey Quarterly*, no. 4 (2005): 21.

[15] Erik Brynjolfsson as quoted in Nick Heath, "AI Is Destroying More Jobs Than It Creates and How We Can Stop It," *TechRepublic,* August 18, 2014, http://www.techrepublic.com/article/ai-is-destroying-more-jobs-than-it-creates-what-it-means-and-how-we-can-stop-it/, accessed February 12, 2016.

paid workers more productive," because this is the surest way to gain competitive advantage.[16]

Companies have spent the last several decades economizing, streamlining, and automating their more routine, core processes, but the cost and efficiency advantages they secured from these activities were short-lived, as the benefits of automation quickly permeated whole industries and their competitors became equally efficient. Efficiency, cost cutting, running lean and mean—these are just the greens fees required to remain in the game. By contrast, when a company gains an advantage by making its nonroutine decision-making employees more productive and effective, that company is building a competitive advantage, described by three authors writing in the *McKinsey Quarterly* as likely being:

> *more enduring, for their rivals will find these improvements much harder to copy. This kind of work is undertaken, for example, by managers, salespeople, and customer service reps, whose tasks are anything but routine. Such employees interact with other employees, customers, and suppliers and make complex decisions based on knowledge, judgment, experience, and instinct.*[17]

If an enterprise can figure out how to manage these "conceptual age" employees better, in other words, it will have an advantage that is hard for a competitor to see or imitate. Good managers will "grapple with the tricky business of redefining processes and roles."[18] The secret, however, is not technology and process, because it just can't be spelled out like that. If it could be documented in advance and defined as a process, then it could be automated, right?

Just as the customer-strategy enterprise strives to keep and grow its customers, so too must it seek to keep and grow its best employees. The truly customer-centric organization will be better able to do this, however, because of its very corporate mission. If the firm's mission is encapsulated by earning the trust of customers, always acting in the interest of customers, this philosophy itself can provide the underpinnings for a culture of trust to permeate the entire organization. If employees are taught that every problem at the firm needs to be tackled from the standpoint of respecting the interests of the customer involved, then it is only a very short step to suggest that employee problems should be addressed from the standpoint of respecting the interests of the employee.

---

[16] Johnson, Manyika, and Yee, "The Next Revolution in Interactions," 21; and Michael Chui, James Manyika, and Mehdi Miremadi, "Four Fundamentals of Workplace Automation," *McKinsey Quarterly* (November 2015), available at http://www.mckinsey.com/insights/business_technology/four_fundamentals_of_workplace_automation, accessed February 12, 2016.

[17] Johnson, Manyika, and Yee, "The Next Revolution in Interactions," 21.

[18] Chui, Manyika, and Miremadi, "Four Fundamentals of Workplace Automation."

Jonathan Hornby, visionary and performance management expert at SAS Institute, cites an example of a bank in which Department A believed Department B was a drain on resources (and this attitude was likely a drain on company culture). Their manager used a tool created by Joel Barker called the Implications Wheel®, where employees were prompted to specify the first-order, second-order, and third-order implications of a certain action—in this case, eliminating Department B. By the time both departments completed this exercise, Department A realized that their potential customers came directly from Department B, and they changed their position of their own accord. Strategic managers will come up with similar creative ways to encourage trust and transparency between employees as well as with customers.[19]

Mike Volpe, CMO of Hubspot, described a moment when the company had doubled and he realized he was becoming a bottleneck to his team by requiring his approval on everything they did. He also began town hall meetings called "Ask Mike Anything," and feedback showed that trust and happiness improved as he trusted his staff more, and they could query him openly in a way that helped them trust him more.[20]

Trustworthiness is not an elastic concept. It doesn't stretch. No one ever has just "some" integrity.[21] You either have integrity or you don't. You are either trustworthy or you are not trustworthy. And if earning the trust of customers is the central mission at a company—the primary way it creates value through first-rate experiences, and grows—then it is highly likely that this business will also enjoy the trust of its employees, since research confirms that employees' trust in and helpfulness to each other is the primary indicator of the success of work teams and achieving objectives.[22] And earning and keeping the trust of employees may be the single most critical step to having a productive and value-creating organization.

---

[19] Jonathan Hornby, *Radical Action for Radical Times: Expert Advice for Creating Business Opportunity in Good or Bad Economic Times* (Cary, NC: SAS Institute, Inc., 2009), 10–13.

[20] Carolyn O'Hara, "Proven Ways to Earn Your Employees' Trust," *Harvard Business Review,* June 27, 2014, https://hbr.org/2014/06/proven-ways-to-earn-your-employees-trust/, accessed February 12, 2016.

[21] We are indebted to Lt. Gen. (Ret.) J. W. Kelly, who made comments about the inelasticity of integrity in his commitment dinner speech to USAFA Class of 2007, August 9, 2005, USAFA, Colorado Springs, as reported in the *Association of Graduates Magazine.* Also see Sarah Brown, Daniel Gray, Jolian McHardy, and Karl Taylor, "Employee Trust and Workplace Performance," *Journal of Economic Behavior & Organization* 116 (August, 2015): 362–378; and Jessica Rohman, "Why Workplace Culture Is Key to Business Success," *Great Place to Work* blog, January 19, 2014, http://www.greatplacetowork.com/events-and-insights/blogs-and-news/2430-you-cant-legislate-a-smile#sthash.YDq7qElu.dpbs, accessed February 12, 2016.

[22] Adam Grant, "Givers Take All: The Hidden Dimension of Corporate Cultures," *McKinsey Quarterly* (April 2013), available at http://www.mckinsey.com/insights/organization/givers_take_all_the_hidden_dimension_of_corporate_culture, accessed February 12, 2016.

Never forget, also, that employees are not only networked with each other, they're networked with the rest of the known universe. The same interactive technologies that empower customers to share their experiences electronically with other customers also empower the employees at any firm to share their own experiences with the employees at other firms. The old "command and control" philosophies of management—philosophies that might have worked reasonably well throughout most of the twentieth century, are no longer very effective. It's been over a decade since Doug Monahan, founder and chairman of tech marketing firm Sunset Direct, sent this charming message to employees:

> *I expect my computers to be used for work only. Should you receive a personal call, keep it short. Should you receive a personal email, I expect the email either not answered, or a brief note telling whoever is sending you emails at work to stop immediately. Should I go through the machines, which I assure you, I will be doing, and I find anything to the contrary, you will be terminated immediately. For those who think I am kidding, and do not get with this program, I promise you that by Christmas Eve 8:00 you will be gone.*[23]

Not surprisingly, it's difficult for a company such as Sunset Direct to trust employees. And for good reason. In such a setting, it's nearly impossible for anyone to feel good about anybody; and, whatever culture develops, it certainly won't be based on trust. Soon after this ominous threat was issued, however, and in direct violation of the edict, a Sunset Direct employee used one of the company's computers to post Monahan's message on InternalMemos.com, where it has now become a legend. Doug Monahan has realized immortality on the Web, as Scrooge.

Contrast that with the leaders at the companies that have made the lists of "The 100 Best Companies to Work For" and "100 Best Companies for Working Mothers." Carlson Companies has been on both lists. Marilyn Carlson Nelson was at the helm of Carlson, Inc., as its chief executive officer from 1998 to 2008. Here are her views about it.

The Everyday Leader

Marilyn Carlson Nelson

A favorite quote of mine is "We are defined by what we tolerate." Leaders who forget this truism do so at the risk of their organization. Like the ever-observant child, the organization always knows when behavior is being allowed that is

---

[23] Adam Horowitz, "101 Dumbest Moments in Business," *Business 2.0* (January/February 2004): 81.

inconsistent with its purported values. And, ultimately, it will undermine all the good that you might do.

The only sustainable way to develop trust is for leaders to model it. It cannot be imposed. It must be inspired, rewarded, and recognized in as many settings as possible, up and down the organization.

In my book, *How We Lead Matters*, I set out to write about the leadership moments I have experienced or witnessed in others during my career. Soon into the project, I realized that leadership moments don't just happen on the top floor, they also happen on the shop floor; they happen at the board table and the kitchen table. Leadership choices are being made every day by each one of us.

The complexity of the choices made by those in charge that resulted in the Great Recession of 2009 will no doubt engage scholars for a long time to come. One conclusion, however, is immediately evident: Leadership at the top of these failed institutions can be rightly blamed for irresponsible and gluttonous behavior. But there were many others throughout these organizations who tolerated the practices—who had an opportunity to make leadership decisions on a daily basis, but who instead became complicit in their silence.

The truth is for all of us, regardless of title or position. Our legacy of leadership will not be written some distant day in a moment of great triumph; it is being written with each passing day.

The Long View

It's been said that the mark of a true leader is thinking well beyond his or her years—that is, establishing a leadership culture in an organization that becomes the organization's hallmark.

When we heard the news at Carlson headquarters that the World Trade Center towers had been hit on September 11, 2001, we called immediately for a phone bridge to communicate with our employees in more than 150 countries. Our instructions were simple: Take care of each other. Take care of our customers. Take care of our competitors' customers. Take care of your communities.

Finally, we told them that if we lost communication, we were authorizing them to act according to Carlson's credo: "Whatever you do, do with integrity. Wherever you go, go as a leader. Whomever you serve, serve with caring. And never, ever give up."

I think back to an article written for *Fortune* magazine by the business author Jim Collins, who has made a career of studying companies that last and thrive across decades. . . . Speaking to his methodology, he noted that he deliberately excluded some currently prominent names from the list: Microsoft's Bill Gates, GE's Jack Welch, and others like them. His rationale: Leaders cannot be truly judged until 10 years have passed after their tenure.

(continued)

(Continued)

Only then can a leader's impact be known. Did the company or organization stay the course? Did it produce other leaders who were just as successful?

When we think about the world's great leaders, did their impact not become better understood decades later? Only time made clear who was truly great.

Rather than expend all their energies on the short term, leaders who aspire to greatness beyond their time might well be advised to approach the world with this curiosity: What will generations say about them "years beyond their ken"?

Source: Adapted from Marilyn Carlson Nelson with Deborah Cundy, *How We Lead Matters: Reflections on a Life of Leadership* (New York: McGraw-Hill, 2008), pp. 49, 61. Updated 2016. Marilyn Carlson Nelson is the retired chairman of Carlson, Inc., a global travel and hospitality company that includes such brands as Radisson and Regent Hotels, Country Inns & Suites, T.G.I. Friday's restaurants, and Carlson Wagonlit Travel.

We have a spent a good deal of time thinking about how to evolve from traditional product-centric companies to customer-centric companies. But in the final analysis, it is almost certain to be the new companies and the start-ups that employ these tactics to overturn the old way. They have less invested in the current paradigm, and less to lose by destroying it. They will realize from Day One that customers account for all revenue, that building stronger relationships with customers and generating better experiences for those customers is the path to success, and they will deliberately build cultures of trust based on doing things right and doing the right thing, proactively. Gradually, they will use trustability to transform our entire economic system, in the same way that interactivity itself has so dramatically transformed our lives already. They will deploy honesty as a brutally efficient competitive weapon against the old guard.

As standards for trustability continue to rise, the companies, brands, and organizations shown to lack trustability will be punished more and more severely. But the sting of the transparency disinfectant will be greatest when the wounds are new. Very soon, for competitive reasons, all businesses, old and new, will begin to respond to the increase in demand for trustability by taking actions that are more worthy of trust from the beginning—that is, actions that are more transparently honest, less self-interested, more competently executed, less controlling, and more responsive to others' inputs. More proactively trustworthy. Trustable.

Summary

We have been reinforcing the idea that a customer-based initiative is not an off-the-shelf solution but rather a business strategy that will imbue an enterprise with an ever-improving capability to know and respond to its customers' individual needs.

Executed through a cyclical process, customer-strategy principles can provide an enterprise with a powerful source of competitive advantage. But doing so requires organizational commitment, careful planning, and, ultimately, a well-orchestrated array of people, culture, processes, metrics, and technology. Successful implementation comes only with an understanding of the nature of this comprehensive business model.

Customer-centric companies depend on listening to the voice of the customer, managing customer data, and using that data to build better customer relationships through better customer experiences. This happens throughout the organization—not just in marketing, sales, customer care, and customer experience, but also in finance, technology, research and development, and human resources. By definition, all revenue comes from customers, and therefore, ultimately, every employee has a role to play in increasing that customer revenue for this quarter and in the future.

Food for Thought

1. Choose an organization and draw its organizational chart. How would that chart have to change in order to facilitate customer management and to make sure people are evaluated, measured, and compensated for building the **value of the customer base**? Consider these questions:
   a. If a customer's value is measured across more than one division, is one person placed in charge of that customer relationship?
   b. Should the enterprise establish a key account-selling system?
   c. Should the enterprise underwrite a more comprehensive information system, standardizing customer data across each division?
   d. Should the sales force be better automated? Who should set the strategy for how a sales rep interacts with a particular customer?
   e. Is it possible for the various Web sites and call centers operated by the company to work together better?
   f. Should the company package more services with the products it sells, and if so, how should those services be delivered?[24]
2. For the same organization, consider the current culture. Can you describe it? Would that have to change for the organization to manage the relationship with and value of one customer at a time? If so, how?
3. At the same organization, assume the company rank-orders customers by value and places the MVCs behind a picket fence. What happens to customers and to customer portfolio managers behind that picket fence?

---

[24] Peppers, Rogers, and Dorf, *The One to One Fieldbook.*

4. In an organization, who should "own" the customer relationship? What does that mean?

Note: Because this topic spans two chapters, we have included the Food for Thought questions twice for ease of use.

Glossary

Business model   How a company builds economic value.

Business rules   The instructions that an enterprise follows in configuring different processes for different customers, allowing the company to mass-customize its interactions with its customers.

Customer care   *See* Customer service.

Customer centricity   A "specific approach to doing business that focuses on the customer. Customer/client centric businesses ensure that the customer is at the center of a business philosophy, operations or ideas. These businesses believe that their customers/clients are the only reason they exist and use every means at their disposal to keep the customer/client happy and satisfied."[25] At the core of customer centricity is the understanding that customer profitability is at least as important as product profitability.

Customer churn   The rate at which customers leave and enter the franchise. High churn indicates a simultaneously high number of defecting customers and high number of new customers. Usually a symptom of low customer loyalty. Also called *churn rate* or *turnover*.

Customer equity (CE)   The sum of all the lifetime values (LTVs) of an enterprise's current and future customers, or the total value of the enterprise's customer relationships. A customer-centric company would view customer equity as its principal corporate asset. Below the enterprise level, "customer equity" can also be measured as it applies to individual segments or groups of customers.

Customer interaction center   Where all calls are handled, regardless of type, for a certain customer segment or customer portfolio.

Customer life cycle   The "trajectory" a customer follows, from the customer's first awareness of a need, to his or her decision to buy or contract with a company to meet that need, to use the product or service, to support it with an ongoing relationship, perhaps recommending it to others, and to end that relationship for whatever reason. The term *customer life cycle* does not refer to the customer's actual lifetime

---

[25] "Client Centric," Investopedia, available at http://www.investopedia.com/terms/c/client-centric.asp, accessed February 15, 2016.

or chronological age but rather to the time during which the product is in some way relevant to the customer.

Customer manager   A customer manager is the person at an enterprise who is "in charge" of particular customer relationships. The customer manager's objective is to increase the value of the customers in his or her charge, and the authority required to do this should include responsibility for every type of individually specific action or communication that the enterprise is capable of rendering to the customer. In communication, this would mean that the customer manager would control the enterprise's addressable forms of communication and interaction, with respect to his or her specific customers.

Customer portfolio   A group of similar customers. The customer-focused enterprise will design different treatments for different portfolios of customers.

Customer portfolio management   The deliberate management of a portfolio of customers to optimize the value of each customer portfolio to the firm. By utilizing the feedback from each customer, a portfolio manager analyzes the differing values and needs of each customer and sets up the best treatment for each customer to realize the largest return on each relationship, often in an automated way using business rules.

Customer relationship management (CRM)   As a term, *CRM* can refer either to the activities and processes a company must engage in to manage individual relationships with its customers (as explored extensively in this textbook), or to the suite of software, data, and analytics tools required to carry out those activities and processes more cost efficiently.

Customer service   Customer service involves helping a customer gain the full use and advantage of whatever product or service was bought. When something goes wrong with a product, or when a customer has some kind of problem with it, the process of helping the customer overcome this problem is often referred to as *customer care.*

Customer service representative (CSR)   A person who answers or makes calls in a call center (also called a customer interaction center or contact center, since it may include online chat or other interaction methods).

Customer's point of view   Thinking the way the customer thinks, within the context of daily business processes as well as customer interactions. Customer advocacy is the set of actions that results from taking the customer's point of view, or treating the customer the way you would want to be treated, if you were the customer.

Customer-strategy enterprise   An organization that builds its business model around increasing the value of the customer base. This term applies to companies that may be product oriented, operations focused, or customer intimate.

Differentiate   Prioritize by value; understand different needs. Identify, recognize, link, remember.

Identify   Recognize and remember each customer regardless of the channel by or geographic area in which the customer leaves information about himself. Be able to link information about each customer to generate a complete picture of each customer.

Interact   Generate and remember feedback.

Lifetime value (LTV)   Synonymous with "actual value." The net present value of the future financial contributions attributable to a customer, behaving as we expect her to behave—knowing what we know now, and with no different actions on our part.

Most growable customers (MGCs)   Customers with high unrealized potential values. These are the customers who have the most growth potential: growth that can be realized through cross-selling, through keeping customers for a longer period, or perhaps by changing their behavior and getting them to operate in a way that costs the enterprise less money.

Most valuable customers (MVCs)   Customers with high actual values but not a lot of unrealized growth potential. These are the customers who do the most business, yield the highest margins, are most willing to collaborate, and tend to be the most loyal.

Needs   What a customer needs from an enterprise is, by our definition, synonymous with what she wants, prefers, or would like. In this sense, we do not distinguish a customer's needs from her wants. For that matter, we do not distinguish needs from preferences, wishes, desires, or whims. Each of these terms might imply some nuance of need—perhaps the intensity of the need or the permanence of it—but in each case we are still talking, generically, about the customer's needs.

Picket fence   An imaginary boundary around customers selected for management. Customers outside the picket fence likely will be treated as customers have always been treated, using mass marketing and traditional customer care; each customer behind the picket fence, however, will be the management responsibility of a customer portfolio manager, whose primary responsibility will be to keep and grow each of the customers assigned to her.

Potential value   The net present value of the future financial contributions that *could* be attributed to a customer, if through conscious action we succeed in changing the customer's behavior.

Relationship governance   Defines who in the enterprise will be in charge when making different decisions for different customers, with the goal of optimizing around each customer rather than each product or channel.

Relationship manager   *See* Customer manager

Return on Customer (ROC)   A metric directly analogous to return on investment (ROI), specifically designed to track how well an enterprise is using customers to create value. ROC equals a company's current-period cash flow (from customers) plus the change in customer equity during the period, divided by the customer equity at the beginning of the period. ROC is pronounced are-oh-see.

Sales force automation (SFA)   Connecting the sales force to headquarters and to each other through computer portability, contact management, ordering software, and other mechanisms.

Share of customer (SOC)   For a customer-focused enterprise, share-of-customer is a conceptual metric designed to show what proportion of a customer's overall need is being met by the enterprise. It is not the same as "share of wallet," which refers to the specific share of a customer's spending in a particular product or service category. If, for instance, a family owns two cars, and one of them is your car company's brand, then you have a 50 percent share of wallet with this customer, in the car category. But by offering maintenance and repairs, insurance, financing, and perhaps even driver training or trip planning, you can substantially increase your "share of customer."

Social media   Interactive services and Web sites that allow users to create their own content and share their own views for others to consume. Blogs and micro-blogs (e.g., Twitter) are a form of social media, because users "publish" their opinions or views for everyone. Facebook, LinkedIn, and MySpace are examples of social media that facilitate making contact, interacting with, and following others. YouTube and Flickr are examples of social media that allow users to share creative work with others. Even Wikipedia represents a form of social media, as users collaborate interactively to publish more and more accurate encyclopedia entries.

Supply chain   A company's back-end production or service-delivery operations.

Total Shareholder Return (TSR)   Represents the change in capital value of a listed/ quoted company over a period (typically one year or longer), plus dividends, expressed as a plus-or-minus percentage of the opening value.

Value of the customer base   *See* Customer equity.

CHAPTER 15

Futureproofing the Customer-Centric Organization

It is better to know some questions than to know all the answers.

—James Thurber

As long as this book is, it could easily have been longer. We are learning more every day about how to grow the value of the customer base, how to interact with customers more effectively, and how to integrate a customer-centric view of the business into an enterprise's daily operations as well as its long-term strategic planning. In this last chapter, as we close our discussion of managing customer relationships in the interactive age, we need to address one more topic: Where do we go from here? Given the difficulties of transitioning to a customer-centric philosophy of doing business that any enterprise will encounter, what are the traits and behaviors that will be needed by a company's future leaders, including its marketing, sales, and service executives? What guiding principles can help a company deal with the as-yet-unforeseen technological innovations and business process changes likely to continue disrupting the economic environment throughout your own upcoming business career? If we've learned anything from clients, research, and academia in the past 10 years, it's this: Building customer value and becoming more customer oriented is not a destination, it's a journey. And it's very, very difficult to do well. But the payoff can be huge. More and more, the question is not how much it will cost to become a customer-strategy enterprise but how much will it cost *not* to. We can't fit everything we know today about building customer value, or about how to become a customer-strategy enterprise, or build trusted Learning Relationships, into this book, because—as we said at the outset of this book—we are learning more every day. Moreover, within months or even weeks of this revised edition

(continued)

> (*Continued*)
>
> going to press, we're certain there will be still more technological innovations in interaction, customization, social media, and peer-to-peer production that we haven't addressed. What we've tried to do so far in this text is to establish a basic foundation for understanding what customer management is, how it helps an organization, and how companies benefit from it.

A lot of "real" leadership is needed. As we've stated repeatedly, whether we call this customer-strategy journey CRM or one-to-one or demand-chain management, it can be a real challenge. Everybody claims to know what it is. Every consulting company and ad agency offers expensive advice about it. Every boss thinks she understands how to go about this.

> Building customer value and becoming more customer oriented is not a destination, it's a journey.

Leadership Behavior of Customer Relationship Managers

When a firm undertakes a customer-focused effort, a great deal of integration is required in all aspects of the enterprise. The management team has to buy in at the very top; and, if it does, we should expect certain types of activity and behavior at the leadership level. The leaders of any customer-strategy enterprise will accumulate expertise about managing customer relationships and will be cheerleaders for this business model. They will highlight it in company meetings and in business gatherings; they will openly share their expertise in and around the organization; in sum, they will be authorities on the relationship management business model.

In a leadership role, a manager must be capable of sponsoring a customer-focused project and in some cases sheltering the people involved in the pilot project. One of the easiest ways to make progress in the journey toward customer centricity is to engage in a series of increasingly comprehensive pilot projects. But a pilot project does not necessarily make money on its own. Most small pilot projects, in fact, never even have the possibility of making money. They are proofs of concept for larger projects that will be rolled out only if they make sense on the smaller level. The pilot project might be an operational test of a customer-strategy program, or a test of the value-building effectiveness of the program, or a test of the accuracy of a metric or predictive model.

Because the participants in a pilot project are exposed in the business financially—that is, they don't have enough profit underlying their activity to justify their existence—they are supported only by the learning they will gain from the pilot project. It is up to the leader, therefore, to shelter them from any economic downturn that might affect the enterprise from keeping them onboard. Ideally, a pilot project needs to be funded at the beginning, then given some running room—often one or two years—before any future decisions can be made.

> The customer's relationship with an enterprise will be based on the customer's view of the business, not any particular product or division's view of the customer.

A leader will measure her own success and the success of her people differently, establishing new types of metrics for the enterprise's activities and accomplishments. But she will also create a new set of rewards structures. We know from previous chapters that one of the central goals of managing customer relationships is to improve the value of the customer base, over time—that is, to conserve and increase the enterprise's customer equity. This value is nothing more than the sum total of lifetime values (LTVs) of all customers; but the problem is that LTV is a future number based on future behaviors of a customer. It's a number that has to be predicted or foretold, and it is impossible to measure exactly. Thus, a leader has to figure out what the leading indicators are of this future customer value that can be measured, and determine how a firm can tie organizational performance and compensation to those metrics this quarter.

A leader should be willing and able to cross boundaries to generate enterprise-wide results. One thing we know about customer-specific initiatives is that, precisely because they are customer specific, they are neither division specific nor product specific. The customer's relationship with an enterprise will be based on the customer's view of the business, not any particular product or division's view of the customer. It is a relationship that might go across several different divisions and encompass the purchasing of several different products and services. The organization of the enterprise is almost certainly along product and service lines, and that means those divisional structures will have to be crossed to serve a customer across several different divisions. Taking a share-of-customer approach to a business inherently means crossing boundaries. The leader is constantly on the lookout for ways to expand the scope of her customer relationships beyond her own product or division and to reach out and encompass aspects of that relationship that go beyond her particular domain. Crossing boundaries is one of the main reasons to engage the senior leaders at a customer-strategy enterprise, and their involvement is critical because they can cross boundaries more easily and more effectively.

Good leaders will insist on having direct contact with customers. They will attend the focus groups, do phone interviews, listen in at the customer interaction center, and have meetings with business executives at the customer organization. Leaders *want* to be directly connected to customers in as much detail as possible. Leaders *want* to have a realistic picture of what it is like to be a customer of their enterprise. Seeing their enterprise from the customer's point of view is one of the key tasks of making this kind of transition successfully.

For all the practical advice about crossing boundaries, supporting pilot projects, and coming face-to-face with customers, however, the fact is that on this never-ending journey toward customer centricity, every future manager should keep two all-important navigational tools in mind for guidance in difficult situations. As executives struggle to apply the principles in this book to new problems and unanticipated technologies in their own roles at work, they should think of these two navigational tools as lighthouse beacons, shining through a dense fog of unforeseeable economic disruptions and ever more rapid technological change:

1. Strive always to maintain and increase the trust of customers.
2. Innovate, innovate, innovate.

Maintain and Increase the Trust of Customers

Customer trust may just be the next "big thing" in business competition, and the rise of the Internet has given us all a taste of its genuine benefits. Essentially, rising levels of trust have the effect of reducing the heat and friction generated by economic activity, so businesses can focus more on genuinely value creating processes and less on paperwork or administrative and security tasks. This is a critical idea. Technology and rising levels of trust go hand in hand. Trust of others is all the more important in a more networked and interconnected world. But a more interconnected world will tend to produce higher levels of trust as well.

Throughout history, the capacity for human beings to trust others has expanded, and been expanded by, commerce and trade. In his book *The Wisdom of Crowds*, James Surowiecki argues that the spread of Quaker philosophy hastened the rise of a flourishing trade in England and America in the 1700s and 1800s. The Society of Friends places a strong emphasis on integrity and honesty, which are core tenets of their religious beliefs. Quakers subscribe to a "Testimony of Integrity" based on the belief that people should live their lives so as to be:

> *true to God, true to oneself, and true to others. . . . Friends [Quakers] do not believe that one should trick others by making statements that are technically true but misleading.*

Quakers prospered as traders largely because they were able to trust each other. Among other innovations, they introduced practices such as public-stated pricing to improve the transparency of their dealings. Over time, the Anglo-American economy as a whole became more transparent and trustworthy, as non-Quakers preferred to trade with an expanding population of Quaker traders in order to be sure they got a fair deal.[1]

It is clearer today than ever before that fairness and honesty are more likely to characterize developed societies with market economies and free commerce. We

---

[1] James Surowiecki, *The Wisdom of Crowds* (New York: Doubleday, 2004). To see the complete Quaker "Testimony of Integrity," see http://en.wikipedia.org/wiki/Testimony of Integrity.

might associate capitalism with selfishness and greed ("Greed is good," to quote Gordon Gekko, the hero of the 1987 movie *Wall Street*, played by Michael Douglas), but the actual truth is that the success of capitalism owes much more to the fact that our society considers trust and fairness to be important social norms. Trust makes it possible for you to eat prepared food right up until the printed expiration date without fearing sickness, or to shake hands with a fellow businessman to cement a deal even before it is written down in precise legal terms.

Capitalism and free markets have increased the importance of trust and fairness, but the new technologies that free markets rely on have contributed even further to this importance. As the frictional cost of moving goods and information from one locale to another has declined, the sheer volume and rapidity of interpersonal communication have skyrocketed, so that the importance of a merchant's "reputation" is greater than ever before. Three hundred years ago, perhaps, if someone were ripped off by an unscrupulous merchant who didn't live in his own community, he might have told a few friends. But they may not even have been able to recognize and avoid the devious merchant in the future, and in any case this would be as far as the news was likely to travel. In those days, gross generalizations with respect to class or tribe were the most common methods used to enforce fairness. If a merchant from Greece scammed someone in the community with barrels of bad olives, then the whole town would simply shun dealing with Greek merchants in the future. Sounds harsh now, but it worked for townspeople at the time.

Before the rise of electronic communications technologies, the best defense against unfair dealing was simply to do business only with family members or relatives, personal friends, or neighbors and town residents. As commerce developed and communication became easier, however, people began sharing evaluations of the businesses they dealt with and warning others of unscrupulous vendors. Organizations such as the Better Business Bureau came into existence not just to protect customers from being ripped off but also to protect honest merchants from being tarred by the actions of the unscrupulous.

Reputations Go Online

These days, computer technology and inexpensive connectivity allow a merchant's reputation, for better or worse, to be shared much more rapidly and widely, in much richer detail than ever before. Any number of detailed, up-to-date evaluations of a seller's reputation can usually be found posted on various online review sites. People today can easily get the skinny on merchants they've never dealt with before, without even personally knowing anyone who has ever dealt with them. Amazon .com's book reviews and eBay's ratings of individual sellers are both good examples of business practices that empower consumers themselves to maintain the quality of the business offerings—in effect "co-creating" the product information necessary to inform other consumers prior to making purchase decisions. There are dozens of well-known Web sites where the reputations of different kinds of businesses and products can be updated or modified as consumers experience them, and then freely viewed by other consumers. Hotel reputations for service, convenience, and pricing can be probed on TripAdvisor.com, for example, and home-improvement or repair contractor reputations for competence and reliability can be found on Angie's List. At most of these kinds of sites, other customers have posted their reviews of various products, and the more capable review sites allow a consumer to search not just by product category but by reviewer type—that is, to find reviews that are done by people whose past reviews have been rated the most helpful by other consumers, or even by reviewers who have similar tastes as the consumer. "Rating the raters" is an increasingly important mechanism for ensuring a robust and generally accurate review site, and over time we should expect review sites to become even more sophisticated and accurate in their assessments of businesses.

Largely because of cost-efficient interactive technologies, untrustworthiness is now something few businesses can keep secret. Any company that is unscrupulously exploitative of its customers will be quickly and efficiently outed, and its business will suffer. So it's more and more financially risky to take short-term advantage of a customer, even in situations where it might seem easy to get away with. Once. But then a scorching exposé could easily go online where it could be downloaded by others, for years, and perhaps forever.

> You can't un-Google yourself.
> —Linda Kaplan Thaler, CEO,
> Kaplan Thaler Group

One of the very first online word-of-mouth episodes, in fact, is known as the "Yours Is a Very Bad Hotel" case. It seems that late one night in November 2001, two businessmen were due to check into a hotel in Houston, but when they arrived all the rooms were already taken. Apparently, the hotel's night clerk was so surly and dismissive that these businessmen took the effort to create a hilarious 17-slide presentation about the incident, titling it "Yours Is a Very Bad Hotel" and e-mailing it to the hotel company. Now, years later, you can still find this presentation being passed around on the Web. Bloggers proudly point to the fact that they were officially warned by the hotel's parent company to take its brand name off their Web site,[2] but it is, of course, way, way too late for that. If you want to see this example of "permanent" word of mouth for yourself, just go online and search for the phrase "Yours is a very bad hotel" and count the entries. That should tell you just how successful any company can be at cleaning up the customer's milk once it has been electronically spilled. One advertising executive's succinct advice: "You can't un-Google yourself."[3]

---

[2] See www.craphound.com/misc/doubletree.htm for an example of an attempt by Doubletree's parent company to contain the problem. Of course, it's still easy to get a copy of the PowerPoint deck, and this kind of heavyhanded effort just makes Doubletree look even worse. The original disaster could be construed to be the responsibility of poor local customer service at one unit. But this threat is from corporate headquarters. We should all take a lesson.

[3] Linda Kaplan Thaler, quoted in "What's Next?" *Fortune,* February 5, 2007, p. 28.

As we've discussed before, the demand for more and more trustability in business is being facilitated by the increasing use of social media, coupled with the dramatic expansion of peer-produced products and services. Social media interactions and collaborative, open-source developments of software and other information resources are governed by an ethos that is separate and distinct from the ethos governing more traditional, production-for-money economics. Although there is no formal code of conduct, and certainly no regulatory framework proscribing any particular types of activities or messaging in the arena of social interaction and production, there is nevertheless a very strong and fairly cohesive set of expectations as to what behaviors are acceptable, and the "crowd" is more than capable of enforcing these standards. The result is that peer-produced, community-owned products are thriving, in ways no one would have predicted a decade ago.

Overall, the increasing importance of community-owned products and services (software, encyclopedias, product reviews, etc.), coupled with the friend-to-friend ethos and rate-the-rater self-policing mechanisms of social media Web sites, has dramatically escalated the role of plain and simple *trustability* in commercial interactions. The more people begin participating in social media, the more they come to expect trustworthy behavior from the businesses they interact with. And more people are participating every day.

> Treat the customer the way you'd want to be treated if you were the customer.

In short, there is probably no more forward-thinking business strategy to be found than constantly seeking to act in the interests of customers. It would be hard to find any single bit of advice for today's business manager that is simpler, more straightforward, or more important in terms of the benefits provided to the enterprise. So one of the beacons any executive today should steer toward is the beacon of trust. No matter how confused the business situation, no matter how unsettled the industry, and no matter how volatile the technological landscape, one sure "safe harbor" for any business will almost certainly be that of earning and keeping the trust of its customers. Remember the mantra at USAA Insurance, established under the leadership of Brigadier-General Robert McDermott: "Treat the customer the way you'd want to be treated if you were the customer."

Reciprocity in Action

The world's largest credit union, with $44 billion in assets and 3.6 million members, Navy Federal Credit Union in Vienna, Virginia, announced in April 2011 a contingency plan for supporting its members in case of a possible government shutdown. Their major initiatives included covering the April 15 payroll for active military members who have direct deposit of their pay at Navy Federal,

(continued)

(Continued)

expedited approvals for lines of credit, and 0 percent fee balance transfer for credit cards. Members who were concerned about loan payments were invited to call or visit a branch. Navy Federal president and CEO Cutler Dawson said, "For over seventy-five years, Navy Federal has been there to serve its members' financial needs. If a government shutdown does occur, we want [our members] to know that their credit union has programs in place to help them in this time of uncertainty."

Will their members—or their children—ever bank anywhere else?[a]

As we first examined in Chapter 3, trustability—a higher level of trust than mere trustworthiness—consists of three elements:

Do things right.
Do the right thing.
Be proactive.

---

[a] Navy Federal Credit Union, "Navy Federal to Cover Direct Deposit for Active Duty Military Members: Credit Union Announces Contingency Plans Ahead of Possible Government Shutdown," September 24, 2013, available at https://www.navyfederal.org/pdf/press-releases/2013/government_130924.pdf, accessed February 12, 2016.

JetBlue Builds Trust into Its DNA

When people ask a very frequent flyer, "How was your trip?" the best answer we can give is "Fine. I won't remember it tomorrow." But JetBlue handles things differently. They were founded based on the idea of "bringing humanity back to air travel," according to Nancy Elder, Vice President, JetBlue Airlines.[a] "There are 18,000 crew members who ask themselves every day "what would I want in this situation?" such as a flight delay or cancellation. So ground crew and onboard personnel help families with small children proactively find a place for the kids to sleep, and proactively refund money or miles when things don't go just right. Recruitment and training and a culture that is not about a "program" but is all about asking "what can we do to help?" provides the support for this kind of on-the-spot experience:

- A passenger at JFK near New York really wanted her latte at Starbucks, but to make her flight, she had to hurry to the gate, and skip the longish line at the coffee shop. Once she arrived at the gate at the far end of the concourse, she discovered the plane was delayed a few minutes and she could have gotten her coffee and still made the flight. Darn! She tweeted about it—just another one of the little stings of modern travel. The tweet made its way back to the JetBlue personnel at JFK. Obviously, they can't do this every time, but that day they were able to get the Starbucks coffee and bring it to the passenger as she boarded the plane!

■ JetBlue, sensitive to nut allergies among passengers, does not serve peanuts. But a popular vendor at the New Orleans airport does. The mother of a child with a peanut allergy, noticing at the gate that quite a few passengers had bought peanuts from the vendor, asked for help. Ground personnel were able to reseat several passengers to create a buffer between the child and the passengers enjoying their treats.

But JetBlue's trustability goes beyond personal interaction, and is actually an integral part of the company's approach to doing business. When two police officers were killed in New York, JetBlue's leadership, asking "how can we help?" offered any police officer anywhere in the country a free round-trip ticket to attend the memorial service. After all, they reasoned, we have the planes to do it, and we can help. Nearly 5,000 officers took them up on their offer. JetBlue did not announce this move—it was not for public relations. The news got out, but JetBlue tried to keep a low profile on it. Maybe it's because the founders are still wandering around the company, influencing the culture. Maybe it's because every two weeks, the CEO shows up at training programs at the Lodge facility in Orlando in order to meet every new employee. Maybe it's because the leadership at the company cares more about the long-term value of the company, rather than what the short-term stock analysts will say about the company's deep customer care, pet-friendly approach, and helpful attitude—and an analogous devotion to the company's great employees.

Nancy described one of the many times the empathy that JetBlue shows its customers paid off. (Remember, there is no such thing as one-way reciprocity.) She was the designated "supervisor" at a counter in the airport and was trying to help a customer who just could not be satisfied with any of the offers Nancy made, and was frankly complaining very loudly about it. Not one but two passers-by came up to speak to Nancy during the sensitive moment. Both said something akin to "I just love JetBlue." These customers were supporting her, taking sides with the airline they knew would look out for *them*.

---

[a] Phone interview with Nancy Elder, vice president of JetBlue Airlines, January 13, 2016.

Most businesses today consider themselves to be trustworthy, and by yesterday's standards they are. They post their prices accurately, they try to maintain the quality and reliability of their products, and they generally do what they say they're going to do. But that's as far as most businesses go, and by tomorrow's standards it won't be nearly good enough.

The fact is that far too many businesses still generate substantial profits by fooling customers, or by taking advantage of customer mistakes or lack of knowledge, or simply by not telling customers what they need to know to make an informed decision. They don't break any laws, and they don't do anything overtly dishonest. Nevertheless, a lot of traditional, widely accepted, and perfectly legal business practices just can't be trusted by customers, and will soon become extinct, driven to dust by rising levels of transparency, increasing consumer demand for fair treatment,[4] and competitive pressure. A business can continue to try to keep things out of its customers' sight, but technology now makes it more than likely that customers will still find out, one way or another. Some things that companies, governments, and other organizations never meant for people to know, they *will* know. Any business that fails to prepare for this new reality will soon be competed out of business by rivals who figure out how to do a better job of earning the trust of their customers.

What's the difference between Navy Federal Credit Union and the other financial services companies we all know about? Or between JetBlue and some of the other airlines? Many of those other companies, with names familiar to customers around the world, are not bad companies. On the contrary: Their officers are ethical. Their legal departments make sure they don't break any laws. They issue privacy policies and policy statements of all kinds, and then for the most part they do exactly what they say they're going to do. And yet none of us—not even the executives of these well-run institutions—can tell us how they plan to compete against companies that customer love so much they don't consider doing business anywhere else. *What is the difference?*

Being *trustworthy* is certainly better than being untrustworthy, but soon even *trustworthiness* won't be sufficient. Instead, companies will have to be *trustable*.

Trustability is a higher standard than mere trustworthiness.

Rather than simply working to maintain honest prices and reasonable service, in the near future companies will have to go out of their way to protect each customer's interest *proactively*, taking extra steps when necessary to ensure that a customer doesn't make a mistake, or overlook some benefit or service, or fail to do or not do something that would have been better for the customer. Compare traditional "trustworthiness" and strategic "trustability":

---

[4] There have been too many good-to-excellent articles written on trust. But one you should see is by our colleague Bruce Kasanoff, "No More Secrets: How Technology Is Making Honesty the Only Policy," Digital Trends, August 20, 2012, http://www.digitaltrends.com/computing/no-more-secrets-how-technology-is-making-honesty-the-only-policy/, accessed February 12, 2016.

EXHIBIT 15.1   Traditional "Trustworthiness" versus Strategic "Trustability"

A Trustworthy Company		A Highly Trustable Company
1	Carefully follows the rule of law and trains people on its ethics policy to ensure compliance	→	Follows the Golden Rule toward customers and builds a corporate culture around that principle
2	Does what's best for the customer whenever possible, balanced against the company's needs	→	Designs its business to ensure that what's best for the customer is financially better for the firm, overall
3	Fulfills all its promises to customers and does what it says it will do, efficiently	→	Follows through on the spirit of what it promises by proactively looking out for customer interests
4	Manages and coordinates all brand messaging to ensure a compelling and consistent story	→	Recognizes that what people say about the brand is far more important than what the company says
5	Uses a loyalty program, churn reduction, and/or win-back initiative to retain customers longer	→	Seeks to ensure that customers want to remain loyal because they trust the firm to act in their interest
6	Focuses on quarterly profits as the most important, comprehensive, and measurable KPI	→	Uses customer analytics to balance current profits against changes in actual shareholder value

Although most of today's successful companies implement many if not all of the policies and actions on the left side of Exhibit 15.1—that is, trustworthy policies— the vast majority of companies' actions would still *not* be considered *trustable*, and only a very few companies have implemented the policies found on the right side of Exhibit 15.1. Trustworthy, yes, but *highly* trustable? No. A company might be scrupulous in its ethics, completely honest in its brand messaging, and highly involved in tracking its customer satisfaction, but will it be *proactively* watching out for its customers' interests? If it wants to succeed in the Age of Transparency, yes. Because we will all be more and more interconnected—never less—we will live in an increasingly transparent world, and trustability is the only competitive response a company can have.

> *What would a trustable [your company's name here] look like?*
> *How will you compete against companies that balance making a profit with building long-term business value?*[5]

---

[5] An important issue beyond the scope of this book is the idea of companies "doing right for the community." We believe a company that is proactively caring for customers will also treat its own associates well, will genuinely care about the environment (and not just slap on a "green" initiative), and will be a good citizen of the towns and countries where the company makes money. See C. B. Bhattacharya and Sankar Sen, "Doing Better at Doing Good: When,

Innovate, Innovate, Innovate

The second safe harbor beacon on these troubled business seas is innovation—not just in developing new and shinier products, but in constantly rethinking the very business model and how we make money from customers.[6]

In his marvelous book *The Origin of Wealth*, Eric Beinhocker gives a sweeping, comprehensive review of how the thinking in economics has changed over the last two centuries, and he makes a compelling case for the idea that economic progress and development should be seen as a process of evolution. This is quite different from traditional, classical economics, which is based on perfect markets and all-knowing, perfectly rational investors. Traditional economics thinking is based on the constant equilibrium of supply and demand. But Beinhocker's argument is that, in just the last couple of decades, there has been a tectonic shift in thinking, as economists have increasingly glommed on to the fact that "equilibrium" is not a realistic way to describe how the economy works.[7]

In reality, the economy is never in a state of equilibrium. Economic activity is driven by change—by a constant flow of new products and services created by self-interested but not entirely rational people seeking a profit. As new products and services are produced, old ones fail and disappear. New companies come into existence constantly, replacing old ones that sink into business oblivion.

Increasingly, economists are coming to think of the economy as a different kind of evolutionary system. Under this theory, it is progress, creativity, and innovation that are the real drivers propelling economic activity. People create new things and devise new technologies in order to make a profit by meeting some need. The innovations that make the most profit are the most "fit" for survival, so they are likely to have a larger impact on overall progress as the economy continues to evolve into higher and higher technological states.

Changing technology and constant innovation make it extremely difficult for companies to survive and prosper over any substantial period of time. One comprehensive study examined thousands of firms in 40 industries over a 25-year period in order to understand how long the most profitable ones could maintain their superior economic performances—which the researchers defined in terms of a statistically

---

Why, and How Consumers Respond to Corporate Social Initiatives," *California Management Review* 47, no. 1 (Fall 2004), and John Mackey and Raj Sisodia's *Conscious Capitalism* (Boston: Harvard Business Review Press, 2014). The point is this: A trustable company will work toward doing the right thing in all its decisions and will balance the needs of the company with the needs of constituents throughout its operation. The reverse, however, is not necessarily true; there are companies that have some good environmental or charitable initiatives originated in the public relations departments that don't necessarily play fair with customers as an intrinsic business strategy.

[6] The following section is adapted from Don Peppers and Martha Rogers, Ph.D., *Rules to Break and Laws to Follow: How Your Business Can Beat the Crisis of Short-Termism* (Hoboken, NJ: John Wiley & Sons, 2008), Chapters 10 and 11.

[7] Eric D. Beinhocker, *The Origin of Wealth* (Boston: McKinsey & Company, 2006).

significant difference relative to their peers. The study revealed that the periods during which any single company can consistently maintain above-average results are decreasing, regardless of industry, size of firm, or geography. Using a series of rolling 5-year periods for their analysis, the researchers found that just 5 percent of companies are able to string together 10 or more years of superior performance, and less than a half percent of their sample (only 32 firms out of the 6,772 analyzed) performed above their peers for 20 years or more.[8]

The truly outstanding performers in this study were those able to string together a series of short-term competitive advantages rather than maintaining a long-term advantage. You can gain a short-term advantage with a differentiated product or service, but to survive the evolutionary process you need the ability to respond to change and string a number of these advantages together. In Beinhocker's words, the truly successful firms are those that "rise into the top ranks of performance, get knocked down, but, like a tough boxer, get back up to fight and win again."[9] This is certainly how Apple could be portrayed. And 3M. And GE. But note carefully: If this evolutionary view of economic progress is correct, then there really is no such thing as a "sustainable" competitive advantage for a business. Instead, success in business, as in the natural world, comes to those "most responsive to change."

This is not Lake Wobegon, where all the children are above average. Here on Earth half of all businesses are below average, and because of the increasing pace of change, it takes less time than ever to slip below the line.

Economist Paul Romer suggests that one way to understand the role that innovation and new ideas play in an economy is to think of an idea as a kind of product. In contrast to a physical product, however, every newly created idea-product becomes virtually free for anyone to use (not just its creator). Even when patents are plentiful and well written, this is still true. Consider the flurry of accessories businesses that support iPhones and all the non-eBay employees getting rich from eBay—all without violating a single patent but using someone else's very good idea. Because every new idea has the potential to lead to additional ideas, the more there are, the faster they come. This means the business of creating ideas is subject to increasing returns to scale, in sharp contrast to the diminishing returns that characterize traditional economics.[10]

However, while the possibility of increasing returns might lead us to conclude that creating a new idea should be a very profitable activity, we can't forget that if anyone can use a new idea, then it may be difficult for us to make much money

---

[8] The short-lived success period of companies is mentioned in Robert R. Wiggins and Timothy Ruefli, "Hypercompetitive Performance: Are the Best of Times Getting Shorter?" Paper presented at the Academy of Management annual meeting, March 31, 2001, cited in Michael J. Mauboussin, *More Than You Know: Finding Financial Wisdom in Unconventional Places* (New York: Columbia Business School Publishing, 2006), pp. 120–121. Also see Beinhocker's *Origin of Wealth*, pp. 331–332.

[9] Beinhocker quoted from his *Origin of Wealth,* p. 333.

[10] See Paul Romer, "The Growth of Growth Theory," *Economist,* May 18, 2006.

from it ourselves, even after going to all the trouble and expense of having come up with it; that is, profits can be generated only during the time periods that lie between when a new idea is devised and when it is duplicated by competition. And as the pace of change and innovation continues to accelerate, these time periods are getting shorter and shorter.

But here's the real point: Instead of counting on making money from every new idea, a successful enterprise in the future must be able to *produce more new ideas*, constantly. Innovation, creativity, and adaptability are traits that are more important than ever, precisely because they're more common than ever. A business's most successful competitors have these traits. Business conditions change with every new innovation, and you will survive as a business only if you can adapt (i.e., innovate). Although technology has always marched steadily forward, the pace of this march seems to have accelerated in recent years to such an extent that the actual character of business competition has undergone a qualitative shift.

Note carefully, however, that innovation's role is to help *customers* create value. Innovation, by itself, has no value. It can even be destructive. There is already a great deal of hype surrounding innovation, but to create real value for a business, innovation has to involve more than just coming up with cool new ideas for their own sake. That's the kind of "innovation" that brings to market a remote device for home theater systems that can't be decoded without a geek license. Innovation that isn't wanted or valued by customers is just self-indulgence, and many of the most "innovative" technology companies in the world are guilty of it.

To overcome the hype and to focus on *profitable* innovation, we have to keep the customer's future behavior firmly fixed in our minds. We have to constantly be aware of what it is actually like to be that customer; and we have to be willing to act in the customer's interest, even when it sometimes means giving up short-term value for the enterprise itself. But if the whole organization isn't already tuned to the customer's wavelength, this just isn't likely to happen.

Economist Romer suggests that if a government wants to promote economic growth, then it should create what he calls a "climate of innovation." It could do this by, for instance, improving education, subsidizing research, bringing in new ideas from other societies and geographies,[11] and enforcing legal protections for intellectual property rights (interestingly, Yochai Benkler would disagree with Romer's last point, arguing that patent protections today actually inhibit more innovation than they encourage).

Trying to create a climate of innovation is good advice for a business as well. For a business to grow, or even just to survive, it must be able to adapt to change and innovate. So how can an enterprise get better at coming up with new ideas and innovations and then putting them into production or operation? How can it turn employees into more flexible, adaptable, and creative people? And how will you architect your own firm, if your goal is to be adaptable, inventive, and responsive to change?

---

[11] Romer, "The Growth of Growth Theory."

Apple, long regarded as one of the world's most trusted brands, also has a reputation for creativity, consistently ranking first in polls of the world's most innovative companies, even with an occasional disappointing product launch. According to one assessment, four factors have driven Apple's inventiveness:

1. It relies on "network innovation," regularly involving outsiders in its creative process, from technical partners to customers and others, rather than simply locking engineers away in the research and development (R&D) department.
2. It is ruthless about designing new products around customer needs with as much simplicity as possible.
3. It understands that customers don't know what they don't know; that is, breakthrough innovations will often fly in the face of what "the market" is saying. The iPod, for instance, was originally ridiculed when it was launched in 2001.
4. Apple has learned that one secret for constant innovation is to "fail wisely." The iPhone rose from the ashes of the company's original music phone, designed with Motorola. The Macintosh sprang from the original Lisa computer, which failed.[12]

Failing wisely. That's an important clue for setting up a climate of innovation, because every new idea has a high probability of failure, but without making the attempt, the small proportion of successes will never be discovered, either. As hockey superstar Wayne Gretzky once said, "I never made a shot I didn't take." James Dyson, the British vacuum cleaner magnate, claims he built 5,127 prototypes of his revolutionary new vacuum before one of his designs made him a billionaire. The Wright brothers tested some 200 different wing designs and crashed seven of them before successfully lifting off at Kitty Hawk. And WD-40 is called "WD-40" because the first 39 "water displacement" formulas tested by the Rocket Chemical Company in 1953 failed.[13]

To keep the company's chief financial officer from going apoplectic at the thought of supporting a froth of "creative destruction" and intrapreneurship, we should probably classify business failures into two different categories:

1. *Fiasco failures* are the result of stupid mistakes, lack of homework, laziness, misguided decisions, or incompetence, but
2. *Wise failures* are the result of well-executed smart ideas, based on carefully considered risks.

---

[12] "Lessons from Apple: What Other Companies Can Learn from California's Master of Innovation," *Economist* (editorial), June 7, 2007.

[13] For failures that led to success, see http://www.wd40company.com/about/history/, accessed February 12, 2016. Also see Jena McGregor, William C. Symonds, Dean Foust, Diane Brady, and Moira Herbst, "How Failure Breeds Success," *BusinessWeek,* July 10, 2006.

One of the obvious first steps, to encourage innovation, is to staff the company with more creative people, either by hiring more creative people in the first place or by teaching people to be more creative, if that's even possible. The problem is that no one really knows what creativity is or how it happens. Don't let anyone tell you otherwise. Just think about it: If we could define creativity and map out exactly how it occurs, it wouldn't really be "creative," would it? Nevertheless, anyone who thinks or writes much on the subject will agree that one secret to creativity seems to be crossing boundaries, cross-pollinating or combining different concepts, and taking new perspectives on old issues. A creative idea is usually the result of a single human brain making a connection between two previously unrelated concepts and having some blinding insight as a result—often an insight that appears to have nothing at all to do with the original concept. Or maybe it isn't a blinding insight but just a glimmer of understanding, or even a suspicion of something sort of interesting. This is certainly one reason why Romer says the rate of innovation and change is accelerating in the world—because the more new ideas there are, the more combining and cross-pollinating can take place.[14]

In Walter Isaacson's richly documented biography of Albert Einstein, he catalogs a number of factors behind the man's extraordinary creativity, including that he was naturally rebellious and anti-authoritarian; that he was well read not just in physics but in philosophy, psychology, and other disciplines (he borrowed the term *relativity* itself from the budding field of psychoanalysis); and that he drew constant analogies between physics concepts previously thought to be unrelated (acceleration and gravity, for instance). To top it off, of course, Einstein was also a German Jew during the Nazi era—claimed by his home country as a celebrity but shunned by it at the same time.[15]

By most accounts, highly creative people tend to be intelligent and intellectually curious as well as flexible and open to new information. But they are also prone to be intense, motivated, mentally restless, anti-authoritarian, unorthodox, and often (as in Einstein's case) a bit rebellious. For business, a productively creative person must also be extremely goal oriented, able to recognize and define problems clearly, and capable of putting information together in many different ways to reach solutions.

---

[14] It goes without saying that the more innovative you are, the more you will have to deal with change. See Ranjay Gulati and James B. Oldroyd, "The Quest for Customer Focus," *Harvard Business Review,* Reprint R0504F (April 2005): "Getting close to customers is not so much a problem the IT or marketing department needs to solve as a journey that the whole organization needs to make." The article identifies four stages of customer focus: Communal Coordination (collate information), Serial Coordination (get insight from customers' past behavior), Symbiotic Coordination (understand likely future behavior), and Integral Coordination (real-time response to customer's needs), citing Continental Airlines, Royal Bank of Canada, Harrah's, and SBC.

[15] Was Einstein creative because he was a "German Jew" in an era when that was an oxymoron? See Walter Isaacson, *Einstein: His Life and Universe* (New York: Simon & Schuster, 2007).

Regardless of how creative the individual employees are, no enterprise can simply command people to "innovate." It doesn't work that way. All a firm can do is create an environment in which innovation is encouraged to flourish—a climate of innovation. To facilitate this, an enterprise may decide to organize somewhat differently, and it should encourage creativity and experimentation with its policies, in addition to hiring people who are more likely to be original thinkers in the first place. But in the end, no firm's creativity can be commanded. It must spring up from the culture.

Uh-oh. There's that word again. But hey, guess what? *The same corporate culture that will help a company earn the trust of its customers will also help it remain adaptive, resilient, and innovative.*

The Importance of Corporate Culture

Harvard Business School professor Clayton Christensen (of "disruptive innovation" fame) suggests that any company's ability to innovate and adapt depends on how it defines its capabilities, and that a company defines these capabilities differently as it goes through its life cycle. For a young firm, the *resources* it has available—things like people, technologies, expertise, or cash—represent its capabilities. During a company's growth phase, these capabilities begin to morph into well-defined and understood *processes*—including processes for product development, manufacturing, budgeting, and so forth. Then, when a company matures into a larger firm, its capabilities will be defined by its *values*—including things like the limitations it places on its own business, the margins it needs before considering an investment, and its corporate culture. According to Christensen, the reason younger companies are more flexible, adaptable, and inherently innovative is that "resources" are simply more adaptable to change than are "processes" or "values," which, by their very nature, are designed to turn repetitive activities into more efficient and predictable routines, and to minimize variation.[16]

In Christensen's hierarchy, it is clear that he regards a company's values and culture as the most hardened of capabilities, and we certainly agree with that. Nothing is quite so difficult to change as a company's culture, and once "the way we do things around here" becomes "the way we've always done things around here," a company already has one foot in the grave. Christensen's argument also implies that a company simply cannot become large without losing its innovativeness.

However, what if the culture that hardens into a company as it becomes mature is a culture that celebrates change, creativity, and innovation applied to the business? What if the repetitive activities and routines that a firm's culture enshrines have to do with a constant exploration for innovations and improvements? Some

---

[16] For a complete overview of Clayton Christensen's "Disruptive Innovation" theory, see http://www.12manage.com/methods_christensen_disruptive_innovation.html, accessed February 12, 2016.

established, mature companies really do seem to have cultures that allow them to innovate and adapt more effectively, even while adhering to efficient business practices. Apple is not the only large firm with a track record of constant invention. GE, Disney, 3M, Google, and Toyota also come to mind.

Nevertheless, regardless of these successes, there does seem to be an inherent conflict between the process of constantly innovating new ideas and the process of operating an efficient, clockwork-like production organization. An interesting psychological study of professional football players once revealed some telltale differences between defensive and offensive players, by examining their lockers. Apparently, offensive players' lockers were found to be neater and more orderly than those of defensive players, as a rule. Now, there may be many reasons for this, but the most obvious inference is probably right: Offensive players succeed by following well-crafted plans, executed flawlessly. Timing, position, and order are everything to them. Defensive players, in contrast, get ahead by wreaking havoc with others' plans. They are simply more at home with disorder, chaos, and unpredictability.

A similar dichotomy seems to plague business when it comes to managing both execution and creativity. Efficient execution requires order, routine, and invariability. But creativity and innovation involve disorder, randomness, experimentation, and failure. Not many companies have resolved this inherent conflict successfully, although there are a few, just as there are a few pro ball players who can star on either side of the line. As the pace of change continues to accelerate, however, it will be increasingly important to navigate frequently between the close-ordered drill of efficient production and the chaotic experimentation of innovation.

A business enterprise is an organization made up of individual employees and managers who interact with each other and, while pursuing their own individual objectives, produce a collective outcome. Academics call this a "complex adaptive system." Beehives are complex adaptive systems, too, as are economies, social networks, governments, and even weather patterns and galaxies. The behavior that emerges from a complex adaptive system is often different from what you'd expect if you observe the actions of any single member of the system. You could watch a honeybee's actions all day, for instance, and still not be able to predict the shape, texture, or social structure of the hive.

Every year a business makes a profit or incurs a loss, and it builds or destroys customer equity. These events are the collective results of the individual actions of all the employees who make up the company. Like honeybees, the employees are each pursuing their own objectives, but the overall outcome of all the employees working together is the short- and long-term value that the firm creates for its shareholders. And this outcome itself becomes additional feedback driving future employee behavior.

Sometimes the behavior that emerges from a system can appear irrational or counterproductive. For example, if managers and employees can get ahead by achieving immediate, short-term results in their own particular areas, then the firm's overall behavior may be characterized by a lack of coordination among various silos of the organization, coupled with frequent abuses of customers, perhaps in direct violation of the company's written mission statement to "act in the customer's interest at all times." Even though no single manager thinks she is undermining the trust customers have in the firm, the overall behavior of the company might still have that effect.

The success of a complex system—beehives and businesses included—depends on its being able to strike the right balance between exploiting known food sources and exploring for additional sources. Honeybees are great exploiters, doing complex dances for the other bees that direct them to any new food source. But in addition to exploiting known food sources, bees are constantly exploring for new food, even when they already have more than they need. And they are excellent at it. Scientists have shown that bees will find virtually any viable new food source within about two kilometers of their hive with great efficiency, regardless of the nectar resources already available.

The analogy with business is clear. When a business is exploiting its known sources of income, it is living in the short term. Long-term success requires exploration as well as innovation. But one of the biggest problems with most businesses is that they just don't do as good a job as honeybees do when it comes to constantly exploring for additional income sources. The way businesses are organized, financially measured, and rewarded simply makes most of them better at exploiting than exploring.

Not giving enough priority or attention to the "exploration" side of the business is the biggest strategic mistake most companies make. Dell had a marvelously large food source in the form of its novel business model: direct to consumer computer sales, generating revenue even before incurring inventory costs. For years, Dell was the only major personal computer manufacturer making any money, with profit margins 10 points higher than its rivals. In Chapter 11, we talked about how Dell focused on the short term at the expense of the long term. In some ways, we can think of this as Dell's focus on exploitation at the expense of exploration. For Dell, as with most other firms, the tension between exploration and exploitation is complicated by two factors: (1) the ruthlessly short-term dynamic introduced by the expectations of the world's financial markets and (2) the fact that the financial metrics used by most companies are plainly inadequate when it comes to tracking the daily up-and-down changes in the long-term value of a business (i.e., its customer equity).

Suppose, in an experiment, we could alter the DNA of a hive of bees, genetically programming them to focus exclusively on exploitation rather than exploration. Then we put that hive of bees down in the middle of a large field of flowers. What would happen? Over the short term the hive would grow much more rapidly than the surrounding hives, because every available bee would be put to the task of exploiting the field. But what happens next? Once the field is fully exploited, the growth in nectar supplies would tail off, and soon the hive would have to fire its

CEO, get in a new management team, and try to move the whole operation into a different field somewhere.

To balance exploitation and exploration, an enterprise must be willing to devote resources to both activities. Google maintains its innovative edge by encouraging employees to dedicate one day per week to exploring innovative or creative initiatives of their own choosing. Think about it: that's an investment equivalent to 20 percent of the company's overall personnel budget. Emerson Electric has a strategic investment program that allocates as much as $20 million a year as seed capital for employees' various unproven but potentially lucrative concepts.[17] Traditionally, 3M's researchers have been encouraged to spend 15 percent of their time on unstructured projects of their own choosing.

No matter how we define it—exploitation versus exploration, production versus innovation, or selling more today versus selling more tomorrow—it ought to be clear that a business will always experience some tension between short-term profit and long-term value creation. And we've already talked extensively about how important it is for a customer-centric company to balance short-term results and long-term value, optimizing the blend of current sales and changes in customer equity.

But besides the conflict between short-term and long-term measurement of value creation, there is another conflict as well—one that has been identified in a wide variety of both popular and academic business books.[18] This is the conflict that arises when managers must choose how much to concentrate on operating a business for the present versus innovating for the future. Operating a business as flawlessly and efficiently as possible requires setting up fixed routines and repeatable processes while innovation requires you to encourage the nonroutine. To operate efficiently, a manager must eliminate variances, but innovation thrives on variances, at least insofar as they lead to more creative thinking.

This conflict has been sharpened immensely by the radical improvements in information technology (IT) we've seen over the last few decades. These technologies have fueled a global rush of efficiency-improvement and cost-reduction initiatives, as processes are more easily automated, routines are codified, and the everyday frictions of ordinary commerce melt away. The result is that while companies were always better at exploiting than exploring, technology has now made them even *better* at exploiting.

Exacerbating this problem is the fact that while efficiency-improvement programs, such as Total Quality Management, ISO 9000, or Six Sigma, can significantly improve a company's operational execution and streamline its cost structure, they also may tend to limit a company's ability to think outside the box, reducing or eliminating altogether the chance a firm will be able to bring to market a truly breakthrough idea. According to Vijay Govindarajan of Dartmouth, "The more you

---

[17] Emerson Electric: Jeffrey Rothfeder, "The CEO's Role in Innovation: Can a Leader Personally Drive New Ideas? Yes," *Chief Executive* (November 2005).

[18] Eric Beinhocker summarizes some of the leading thinking on this subject in his article "The Adaptable Corporation," *McKinsey Quarterly* no. 2 (2006): 76–87.

hardwire a company on total quality management, [the more] it is going to hurt breakthrough innovation. . . . The mind-set that is needed, the capabilities that are needed, the metrics that are needed, the whole culture that is needed for discontinuous innovation, are fundamentally different."[19] The problem, according to one IT industry analyst, is that innovative ideas can easily meet a roadblock when up against a "long-running, moderately successful Six Sigma quality effort led by fanatics."[20]

Thus, as more and more companies have used technology to streamline and accelerate their operations, they have become either less capable or less willing to consider game-changing innovations, which means the innovations most firms do come up with today tend to be more incremental and short-term in nature. These types of innovations involve less risk and are more likely to return a profit in the short term, of course, but they also have much less upside. The truth is, tiny or incremental improvements in a product barely qualify as real "innovation," but that seems to be the type of innovation preferred more and more.

One academic study, for instance, found that the proportion of truly new-to-the-world innovations under consideration has declined precipitously in recent years, shrinking from 20 percent of all innovations in 1990 to just 11.5 percent in 2004.[21] Another study, focused specifically on the types of patents issued in the paint and photography industry over a 20-year period, showed that after a company completed a quality improvement initiative, the proportion of patents based on prior work (i.e., incremental innovation rather than breakthrough innovation) went up dramatically.[22] Still another study found that 85 to 90 percent of the innovation projects in a typical company's pipeline today represent purely incremental improvements rather than creative breakthroughs.[23]

Is it possible to be both efficient and innovative, both disciplined and creative? Can the *order* of execution coexist with the *chaos* of creation? This problem has always plagued businesses but has been brought into sharp relief by new technologies, which can automate and streamline operations in ways that were just

---

[19] Govindarajan was quoted in Brian Hindo, "At 3M, a Struggle between Efficiency and Creativity," *BusinessWeek,* Bloomberg Business, June 10, 2007, available at http://www.bloomberg .com/bw/stories/2007-06-10/at-3m-a-struggle-between-efficiency-and-creativity, accessed February 12, 2016.

[20] The analyst was quoted by John Parkinson, "The Conflict between Six Sigma and Innovation," *CIO Insight,* July 23, 2007, available at http://www.cioinsight.com/article2/0,1540,2159181,00 .asp, accessed February 12, 2016.

[21] "New to the world" stats from Robert G. Cooper, "Your NPD Portfolio May Be Harmful to Your Business Health," *PDMA Visions* 2004 (January 2005), cited in George S. Day, "Closing the Gap: Balancing Big I and Small i Innovation," paper, Wharton School (July 2002).

[22] M. J. Benner and M. L. Tushman, "Process Management and Technological Innovation: A Longitudinal Study of the Photography and Paint Industries," *Administrative Science Quarterly* 47 (2002): 676–706, cited in Brian Hindo, "At 3M, a Struggle between Efficiency and Creativity," *BusinessWeek*, Bloomberg Business, June 10, 2007, available at http://www .bloomberg.com/bw/stories/2007-06-10-at-3m-a-struggle-between-efficiency-and-creativity, accessed February 12, 2016.

[23] Incremental versus breakthrough study: Day, "Closing the Gap," p. 2.

not possible before. There's hardly a management book written in the last several decades that doesn't make at least a passing reference to this problem, whether it's *Creative Destruction*,[24] suggesting that there is a tension between operating and innovating, or *In Search of Excellence*,[25] advocating that businesses need to be both "tight" and "loose," or *Winning Through Innovation*,[26] arguing that a company must be "ambidextrous" to be successful both as an operator and an innovator.

But probably the single best overall description of the organizational traits more likely to succeed both in operating their current business and in innovating for the future can be found in Jim Collins and Jerry Porras's classic 1994 best seller, *Built to Last*.[27] Collins and Porras identified a number of companies that have been consistently more successful than others in their competitive set not just for a few years but for decades. Then they directly compared the philosophies, policies, and characteristics of these long-lasting companies with other, not-so-successful firms, in order to uncover the secrets of long-term corporate success. What they found was an incredibly resilient ability to hold on to a core set of values while simultaneously tinkering, exploring, and experimenting with new ideas.

Above all, companies that prosper over the long term will almost inevitably have an extremely strong *corporate culture*. At most of the durably successful companies Collins and Porras studied, including Hewlett-Packard, Wal-Mart, Nordstrom, General Electric, Walt Disney, Johnson & Johnson, 3M, and Marriott, among others, the culture is something almost tangible. It is a quality that infuses the employees at these companies with a sense of purpose, a mission that goes well beyond simply making a profit or building shareholder value. The cultures at these long-lasting companies are "almost cult-like"—so strong that a new employee either fits in well or is "rejected like a virus."

While respecting their core ideologies, long-lasting companies constantly experiment with new ideas and innovations, failing frequently but keeping what works. W. Johnson, founder of Johnson & Johnson, famously claimed that "failure is our most important product." Motorola's founder Paul Galvin encouraged dissent, disagreement, and discussion at the company, in order to give individuals "the latitude to show what they could do largely on their own."

Experimentation, trial and error, and accidental innovation play a big role at most of the built-to-last companies studied by Collins and Porras. And this pattern

---

[24] Richard Foster and Sarah Kaplan, *Creative Destruction: Why Companies That Are Built to Last Underperform the Market—and How to Successfully Transform Them* (New York: Doubleday, 2001).

[25] Thomas J. Peters and Robert H. Waterman Jr., (no comma after Waterman, please) *In Search of Excellence: Lessons from America's Best-Run Companies* (New York: Warner Books, 1982).

[26] Michael L. Tushman and Charles A. O'Reilly III, *Winning Through Innovation: A Practical Guide to Leading Organizational Change and Renewal* (Boston: Harvard Business School Publishing, 2002).

[27] Examples and quotes in this section are from Jim Collins and Jerry Porras, *Built to Last* (New York: HarperCollins Publishers, 1994), pp. 37–38, 43, 55, 71, 147, 162.

of random-but-successful innovations is the unmistakable hallmark of a growth process based on an evolutionary model. "If we mapped 3M's portfolio of business units on a strategic planning matrix, we could easily see why the company is so successful ("Look at all those cash cows and strategic stars!"), but the matrix would utterly fail to capture *how* this portfolio came to be in the first place." In other words, 3M's innovative success is yet another example of how a network of innovations grows over time. Its current set of businesses and products was not carefully planned in advance and then developed in an orderly way. Rather, 3M (and most other long-lasting, constantly innovative companies) arrived at its present state as the result of constant tinkering and experimentation, with the best, most desirable innovations claiming more and more of the firm's resources over time.

> A climate of innovation starts with a culture of trust.

One final thought about innovation: The corporate culture that is most likely to stimulate and encourage innovative ideas is one that tolerates dissent and celebrates respectful disagreement. This is a culture in which employees *trust* each other, and they trust management. People in an innovative organization won't always agree, nor should they, but they must disagree respectfully. Handling disagreement in a respectful way holds a lot of implications for the type of workplace that best facilitates a climate of innovation. It means the boss shouldn't just squash conversation by issuing edicts. It means setting up a "zing-free" workplace, where it's not okay to make snide comments about coworkers, either in their presence or behind their backs. It means assuming that people who work together deserve explanation and clarity about what's going on behind the scenes. It means rewarding people who work with others and serve as catalysts for group action, and not just the lone rangers who succeed because they trounce everyone else. It means no one at the company pulls the rug out from under people. What it means, in other words, is that a climate of innovation creates better customer experience, which builds customer equity. And it starts with a culture of trust.

Summary

It's clear from the experiences of traditional companies trying to make the change from the Industrial Age to the Information Age, and from new companies run by people born and raised in the Industrial Age (that's everybody above grade school), that using information as the heart of competitive advantage is *hard*. Many companies have gone awry. Some firms aren't trying. But payoff is happening, for the companies that redefine their core business opportunity as growing the value of the customer base. We learn more about how to do it every day. And the field is growing into one that offers new career opportunities to those who become fluent in a decision-making approach that puts growing the value of the customer base ahead of other tactics.

There's a lot of work to do. Every company on the planet that succeeds in the next two decades will do so because of its ability to concentrate on getting, keeping, and growing the best customers in its industry.

Food for Thought

1. Imagine you have been assigned to change a currently product-oriented company to a customer-oriented firm. Select one. What is the first thing you do? What is your road map for the next two years? The next five?

2. Name two or three different industries. For each, consider completely different business models that are sustainably successful and that would be based on more collaborative and trust-building ways of creating value. Compare the principles of a merely "trustworthy" company with those of a company that can be designated as having high "trustability." How will the higher standard of Extreme Trust be applied?

Name Index

Term Index

.